MATH SCIENCE AND

FOR YOUNG CHILDREN

DEDICATION

This book is dedicated to:
the memory of a dear friend
ADA DAWSON STEPHENS
—R. Charlesworth

and

the memory of
my loving husband
EUGENE F. LIND
—K. Lind

MATH AND SCIENCE

FOR YOUNG CHILDREN
FOURTH EDITION

Rosalind Charlesworth
Weber State University

Karen K. Lind
University of Louisville

with Contributions by
Pam Fleege
University of South Florida

THOMSON
DELMAR LEARNING™

Australia Canada Mexico Singapore Spain United Kingdom United States

THOMSON

—————✳—————™

DELMAR LEARNING

Math and Science for Young Children, Fourth Edition
Rosalind Charlesworth and Karen K. Lind

Executive Director:
Susan L. Simpfenderfer

Executive Production Manager:
Wendy A. Troeger

Executive Marketing Manager:
Donna J. Lewis

Acquisitions Editor:
Erin O'Connor

Production Editor:
J.P. Henkel

Channel Manager:
Nigar Hale

Senior Development Editor:
Melissa Riveglia

Technology Project Manager:
Joe Saba

Cover Design:
TDB, Inc.

Editorial Assistant:
Ivy Ip

Library of Congress Cataloging-in-Publication Data
Charlesworth, Rosalind.
  Math and science for young children / Rosalind Charlesworth, Karen K.
Lind.-- 4th ed.
    p. cm.
Includes bibliographical references and index.
  ISBN 0-7668-3227-9
  1. Mathematics—Study and teaching (Primary) 2. Science—Study and teaching (Primary) I. Lind, Karen. II. Title.
  QA135.6 .C48 2002
  372.7'044--dc21
                              2002019307

NOTICE TO THE READER

Publisher does not warrant or guarantee any of the products described herein or perform any independent analysis in connection with any of the product information contained herein. Publisher does not assume, and expressly disclaims, any obligation to obtain and include information other than that provided to it by the manufacturer.

The reader is expressly warned to consider and adopt all safety precautions that might be indicated by the activities herein and to avoid all potential hazards. By following the instructions contained herein, the reader willingly assumes all risks in connection with such instructions.

The Publisher makes no representation or warranties of any kind, including but not limited to, the warranties of fitness for particular purpose or merchantability, nor are any such representations implied with respect to the material set forth herein, and the publisher takes no responsibility with respect to such material. The publisher shall not be liable for any special, consequential, or exemplary damages resulting, in whole or part, from the readers' use of, or reliance upon, this material.

Contents

Preface

Math and Science for Young Children, Fourth Edition, is designed to be used by students in training and teachers in service in early childhood education. To the student, it introduces the excitement and extensiveness of math and science experiences in programs for young children. For teachers in the field, it presents an organized, sequential approach to creating a developmentally appropriate math and science curriculum for preschool and primary school children. Further, it is designed in line with the guidelines and standards of the major professional organizations: NAEYC, NCTM, NSTA, AAAS, and NRC.

Activities are presented in a developmental sequence designed to support young children's construction of the concepts and skills essential to a basic understanding of mathematics and science. A developmentally appropriate approach to assessment is stressed in order to have an individualized program in which each child is presented at each level with tasks that can be accomplished successfully before moving on to the next level.

A further emphasis is placed on three types of learning: naturalistic, informal, and structured. Much learning can take place through the child's natural exploratory activities if the environment is designed to promote such activity. The adult can reinforce and enrich this naturalistic learning by careful introduction of information and structured experiences.

The test-driven practices currently reemerging produce a widespread use of inappropriate instructional practices with young children. Mathematics for preschoolers has been taught as "pre-math," apparently under the assumption that math learning begins only with addition and subtraction in the primary grades. It also has been taught in both preschool and primary school as rote memory material using abstract paper and pencil activities. This revision emphasizes the recognition by NCTM of the inclusion of the pre-K level in the revised mathematics principles and standards (NCTM, 2000). Science, on the other hand, has been largely ignored with the excuse that teaching the basics precluded allowing time for science. This text is designed to counteract these developments and to bring to the attention of early childhood educators the interrelatedness of math and science and the necessity of providing young children with opportunities to explore concretely these domains of early concept learning. Further integration is stressed with language arts, social studies, art, and music with the goal of providing a totally integrated program.

New Features

Some specific features of the fourth edition include:

◆ Updated to fit NCTM 2000 principles and standards for mathematics.
◆ Assessments and activities for mathematics have been revised to be compatible with NCTM 2000.
◆ Includes the National Science Content Standards for grades kindergarten through four.
◆ References and Further Reading and Resources have been separated and updated.
◆ Naturalistic and informal levels have been inserted in structured task examples.
◆ Examples of World Wide Web resources are included in the units.
◆ The unit on Earth and Space Science and the Environment has been split into two units.
◆ Children's book lists have been updated.
◆ Key terms have been added to each unit.

Ancillaries

Instructor's Manual

The instructor's manual provides suggestions for course organization, introductory activities, multiple choice questions, and answers to Unit Reviews.

Computerized Test Bank

The computerized test bank is comprised of true/false, multiple-choice, short-answer, and completion questions for each chapter. Instructors can use the computerized test bank software to create sample quizzes for students. Refer to the CTB User's Guide for more information on how to create and post quizzes to your school's Internet or Intranet server.

References

NCTM (2000). *Principles and standards for school mathematics*. Preston, VA: National Council of Teachers of Mathematics.

The authors and Delmar Learning make every effort to ensure that all Internet resources are accurate at the time of printing. However, due to the fluid, time-sensitive nature of the Internet, we cannot guarantee that all URLs and Web site addresses will remain current for the duration of this edition.

Acknowledgments

The authors wish to express their appreciation to the following individuals and Early Childhood and Development Centers:

◆ Dee Radeloff, for her collaboration in the writing of *Experiences in Math for Young Children*, which served as the starting point for this book.

◆ Dr. Mark Malone of the University of Colorado at Colorado Springs, who contributed to the planning of this text. Dr. Malone also demonstrated great patience while introducing Dr. Charlesworth to the mysteries of word processing on a personal computer.

◆ Artist Bonita S. Carter, for the care and accuracy taken in her original art.

◆ Kate Charlesworth, for her tolerance of her mother's writing endeavors.

◆ Gaile Clement, for sharing her knowledge and expertise in the area of portfolio assessment with Dr. Charlesworth.

◆ The 30 East Baton Rouge Parish, Louisiana, K–3 teachers who participated in a six-week summer Mathematics/Child Development in-service workshop and to the other workshop faculty, Thelamese Porter, Robert Perlis, and Colonel Johnson, all of whom provided enrichment to Dr. Charlesworth's view of mathematics for young children.

◆ Eugene F. Lind, and Paul and Marian Kalbfleisch, for their encouragement during the writing process.

◆ The following teachers, who provided a place for observation and/or cooperated with our efforts to obtain photographs:

Lois Rector, Kathy Tonore, Lynn Morrison, and Nancy Crom (LSU Laboratory Elementary School), Joan Benedict (LSU Laboratory Preschool), Nancy Miller, and Candy Jones (East Baton Rouge Parish Public Schools) and 30 East Baton Rouge Parish School System K–3 teachers and their students; Krista Robinson (Greatho Shryock), Maureen Awbrey (Anchorage Schools), Elizabeth Beam (Zachary Taylor), and Dr. Anna Smythe (Cochran, Jefferson County Public Schools).

◆ Anchorage Schools computer teacher Sharon Campbell and Rutherford Elementary computer teacher Phyllis E. Ferrell who provided recommendations for using computers with young children.

- University of Louisville graduate students Shawnita Adams, Kate Clavijo, Phyllis E. Ferrell, and Stephanie Gray, who provided assistance in researching and compiling information.
- Phyllis Marcuccio, Editor of *Science and Children* and Director of Publications for the National Science Teachers Association, for generously facilitating the use of articles appearing in *Science and Children* and other NSTA publications.
- The staff of Delmar Learning for their patience and understanding throughout this project.
- The following reviewers, who provided many valuable ideas:

Kathy Head, MA
Lorain County Community College
Elyria, Ohio

Linda Lowman, MEd
San Antonio College
San Antonio, Texas

Leanna Manna, MA
Villa Maria College
Buffalo, New York

Lisa Starnes, EdD
The University of Texas at Tyler
Tyler, Texas

Paula Packer, EdD
Lock Haven University
Lock Haven, Pennsylvania

About the Authors

Rosalind Charlesworth is professor and department chair in the Department of Child and Family Studies at Weber State University in Ogden, Utah. She also works with the faculty of the Department of Teacher Education to develop continuity from preprimary to primary school in the program for students in the early childhood education licensure program.

Karen K. Lind is a professor in the Department of Early and Middle Childhood Education at the University of Louisville, Kentucky, where she is the recipient of the 1993 Distinguished Teaching Professor award from the university. Dr. Lind is the National Science Teachers Association (NSTA) Teacher Education Director and is Chair of the Science Teacher Education Committee. Dr. Lind's career in education has included teaching young children of differing socioeconomic backgrounds in a variety of settings. Dr. Lind has recently returned from the National Science Foundation where she was a program director in the Teacher Enhancement and Instructional Materials Development programs. Dr. Lind is a member of the Board of Examiners for the National Council for Accreditation of Teacher Education (NCATE) and is a member of the NCATE New Professional Teacher Standards drafting committee. Dr. Lind is past president of the Council for Elementary Science International (CESI). She is the early childhood column editor of *Science and Children*, a publication of the National Science Teachers Association (NSTA), and a member of the NSTA Preschool-Elementary Committee. Her research publications and inservice programs focus on integrating science into preschool and primary classroom settings.

Dr. Charlesworth's career in early childhood education has included experiences with both typical and atypical young children in laboratory schools, public schools, and day care and through research in social and cognitive development and behavior. She is also known for her contributions to research on early childhood teachers' beliefs and practices. She also taught courses in early education and child development at other universities before joining the faculty at Weber State University. In 1995 she was named the Outstanding Graduate of the University of Toledo College of Education and Allied Professions. In 1999, she was the corecipient of the NAECTE/Allyn & Bacon Outstanding Early Childhood Teacher Education award. She is the author of the popular Delmar text *Understanding Child Development,* has published many articles in professional journals, and gives presentations regularly at major professional meetings. Dr. Charlesworth has provided service to the field through active involvement in professional organizations. She has been a member of the NAEYC Early Childhood Teacher Education Panel, a consulting editor for *Early Childhood Research Quarterly,* and a member of the NAECTE (National Association of Early Childhood Teacher Educators) Public Policy and Long-Range Planning Committees. She served two terms on the NAECTE board as regional representative and one as vice-president for membership. She was twice elected treasurer of the Early Childhood/Child Development Special Interest Group of the American Educational Research Association (AERA), is past president of the Louisiana Early Childhood Association, and was a member of the Editorial Board of the Southern Early Childhood Association journal *Dimensions.* She is currently on the editorial board of the *Early Childhood Education Journal.*

Concept Development in Mathematics and Science

UNIT 1
How Concepts Develop

OBJECTIVES

After reading this unit, you should be able to:

- Define concept development.
- Identify the concepts children are developing.
- Describe the commonalities between math and science.
- Explain the purpose of the principles for school mathematics.
- Understand the importance of the professional standards for mathematics and science.
- Label examples of Piaget's developmental stages of thought.
- Compare Piaget's and Vygotsky's theories of mental development.
- Identify conserving and nonconserving behavior, and state why conservation is an important developmental task.
- Explain how young children acquire knowledge.

Early childhood is a period when children actively engage in acquiring fundamental concepts and learning fundamental process skills. Concepts are the building blocks of knowledge; they allow people to organize and categorize information. Concepts can be applied to the solution of new problems that are met in everyday experience. As we watch children in their everyday activities, we can observe concepts being constructed and used. For example

- One-to-one correspondence: Passing apples, one to each child at the table; putting pegs in peg-board holes; putting a car in each garage built from blocks

- Counting: Counting the pennies from the penny bank, the number of straws needed for the children at the table, the number of rocks in the rock collection
- Classifying: Placing square shapes in one pile and round shapes in another; putting cars in one garage and trucks in another
- Measuring: Pouring sand, water, rice, or other materials from one container to another

As you proceed through this text, you will see that young children begin to construct many concepts during the preprimary period (the years before children enter first grade). They also develop the processes that enable them to apply their newly acquired concepts and to enlarge current concepts and develop new ones.

During the preprimary period children learn and begin to apply concepts basic to both mathematics and science. As children enter the primary period (grades one through three), they apply these early basic concepts when exploring more abstract inquiries in science and to help them understand more complex concepts in mathematics such as addition, subtraction, multiplication, division, and the use of standard units of measurement.

As young children grow and develop physically, socially, and mentally, their concepts grow and develop as well. Development refers to changes that take place due to growth and experience. It follows an individual timetable for each child. Development is a series or sequence of steps that each child reaches one at a time. Different children of the same age may be weeks, months, or even a year or two apart in reaching certain stages and still be within the normal range of development. This text examines concept development in math and science from birth through the primary grades. For an overview of this development sequence, see Figure 1–1.

Concept growth and development begins in infancy. Babies explore the world with their senses. They look, touch, smell, hear, and taste. Children are born curious. They want to know all about their environment. Babies begin to learn ideas of size, weight, shape, time, and space. As they look about, they sense their relative smallness. They grasp things and find that some fit their tiny hands and others do not. Infants learn about weight when items of the same size cannot always be lifted. They learn about shape. Some things stay where they put them, while others roll away. They learn time sequence. When they wake up, they feel wet and hungry. They cry. The caretaker comes. They are changed and then fed. Next they play, get tired, and go to bed to sleep. As infants begin to move, they develop spatial sense. They are placed in a crib, in a playpen,

	Concepts and Skills: Beginning Points for Understanding			
Period	**Section II** **Fundamental**	**Section III** **Applied**	**Section IV** **Higher Level**	**Section V** **Primary**
Sensorimotor (Birth to age 2)	Observation Problem solving One-to-one correspondence Number Shape Spatial sense			

Preoperational (2 to 7 years)	Sets and classifying
	Comparing
	Counting
	Parts and wholes
	Language
		Ordering, seriation, patterning
		Informal measurement:
		  Weight
		  Length
		  Temperature
		  Volume
		  Time
		  Sequence
			Number symbols
			Sets and symbols	

Transitional (5 to 7 years)		Graphing	Concrete addition and subtraction	
Concrete operations (7 to 11 years)				Whole number operations Fractions Number facts Place value Geometry Measurement with standard units

FIGURE 1–1   The development of math and science concepts and process skills.

or on the floor in the center of the living room. As babies first look and then move, they discover space. Some spaces are big. Some spaces are small.

As children learn to crawl, to stand, and to walk, they are free to discover more on their own and learn to think for themselves. They hold and examine more things. They go over, under, and in large objects and discover their size relative to them. Toddlers sort things. They put them in piles—of the same color, the same size, the same shape, or with the same use. Young children pour sand and water into containers of different sizes. They pile blocks into tall structures and see them fall and become small parts again. They buy food at a play store and pay with play money. As children cook imaginary food, they measure imaginary flour, salt, and milk. They set the table in their play kitchen, putting one of everything at each place just as is done at home. The free exploring and experimentation of the first two years are the opportunity for the development of muscle coordination and the senses of taste, smell, sight, and hearing. Children need these skills as a basis for future learning.

As young children leave toddlerhood and enter the preschool and kindergarten levels of the preprimary period, exploration continues to be the first step in dealing with new situations; at this time, however, they also begin to apply basic concepts to collecting and organizing data to answer a question. Collecting data requires skills in observation, counting, recording, and organizing. For example, for a science investigation, kindergartners might be interested in the process of plant growth. Supplied with lima bean seeds, wet paper towels, and glass jars, the children place the seeds in the jars where they are held against the sides with wet paper towels. Each day they add water as needed and observe what is happening to the seeds. They dictate their observations to their teacher, who records them on a chart. Each child also plants some beans in dirt in a small container such as a paper or plastic cup. The teacher supplies each child with a chart for his or her bean garden. The children check off each day on their charts until they see a sprout (Figure 1–2). Then they count how many days it took for a sprout to appear; they compare this number with those of the other class members, as well as with the time it takes for the seeds in the glass jars to sprout. The children have used the concepts of number and count-

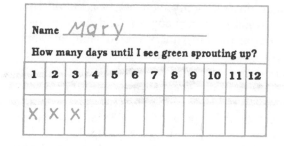

FIGURE 1–2 Mary records each day that passes until her bean seed sprouts.

ing, one-to-one correspondence, time, and comparison of the number of items in two groups. Primary children might attack the same problem but can operate more independently and record more information, use standard measuring tools (i.e., rulers), and do background reading on their own.

Commonalities in Math and Science in Early Childhood

The same fundamental concepts, developed in early childhood, underlie a young child's understanding of math and science. Much of our understanding of how and when this development takes place comes from research based on Jean Piaget's and Lev Vygotsky's theories of concept development. These theories are briefly described in the next part of the unit. First, the commonalities that tie math and science together are examined.

Math and science are interrelated; fundamental mathematics concepts such as comparing, classifying, and measuring are simply called process skills when applied to science problems. (See Unit 5 for a more in-depth explanation.) That is, fundamental math concepts are needed to solve problems in science. The other science process skills (observing, communicating, inferring, hypothesizing, and defining and controlling variables) are equally important for solving problems in both science and mathematics. For example, consider the principle of the ramp, a basic concept in physics. Suppose a two-foot-wide plywood board is leaned against a large block so that it becomes a ramp.

The children are given a number of balls of different sizes and weights to roll down the ramp. Once they have the idea of the game through free exploration, the teacher might insert some questions such as, "What do you think would happen if two balls started to roll at exactly the same time from the top of the ramp?" or, "What would happen if you changed the height of the ramp or had two ramps of different heights? Of different lengths?" The students could guess, explore what happens, using ramps of varying steepness and length and balls of various types, observe what happens, communicate their observations, and describe commonalities and differences. They might observe differences in speed and distance traveled contingent on the size or weight of the ball, the height and length of the ramp, or other variables. In this example, children could use math concepts of speed, distance, height, length, and counting (how many blocks are propping each ramp?) while engaged in scientific observation. For another example, suppose the teacher brings several pieces of fruit to class: one red apple, one green apple, two oranges, two grapefruit, and two bananas. The children examine the fruit to discover as much about it as possible. They observe size, shape, color, texture, taste, and composition (juicy or dry, segmented or whole, seeds, and so on). Observations may be recorded using counting and classification skills (How many of each fruit type? Of each color? How many are spheres? How many are juicy? and so on). The fruit can be weighed and measured, prepared for eating, and divided equally among the students.

As with these two examples, it will be seen throughout the text that math and science concepts and skills can be acquired as children engage in traditional early childhood activities such as playing with blocks, water, sand, and manipulative materials, as well as during dramatic play, cooking, and outdoor activities.

Principles and Standards for School Mathematics and Science

In 1987, the National Association for the Education of Young Children (NAEYC) published *Developmentally Appropriate Practice in Early Childhood Programs Serving Children from Birth through Age Eight*

as a guide for early childhood instruction. In 1997 a revised set of guidelines was published (Bredekamp & Copple, 1997) by NAEYC. In 1989 the National Council of Teachers of Mathematics (NCTM) published standards for kindergarten through grade 12 mathematics curriculum, evaluation, and teaching. This publication was followed by two others, *Professional Standards for Teaching Mathematics* (1991) and *Assessment Standards for School Mathematics* (1995). In 2000, based on an evaluation and review of the previous standards' publications, NCTM published *Principles and Standards for School Mathematics*. A major change in the age and grade category levels is the inclusion of preschool. The first level is now prekindergarten through grade two. It is important that preschoolers are now recognized as having knowledge and capabilities in mathematics. However, it is important to keep in mind that, just as is true of older children, not all preschoolers will enter school with equivalent knowledge and capabilities. It is important to recognize that preschoolers have an informal knowledge of mathematics that can be built on and reinforced. During the preschool years young children's natural curiosity and eagerness to learn can be capitalized on to develop a joy and excitement in learning and applying mathematics concepts and skills. As in the previous standards, the recommendations in the current publication are based on the belief that "students learn important mathematical skills and processes with understanding" (NCTM, 2000, p. ix). That is, children do not just memorize but have a true knowledge of concepts and processes. Understanding is not present when children learn mathematics as isolated skills and procedures. Understanding develops through interaction with materials, peers, and supportive adults in settings where students have opportunities to construct their own relationships when they first meet a new topic. Exactly how this takes place will be explained further in the text.

Principles of School Mathematics

The Principles of School Mathematics are statements reflecting basic rules that guide high-quality mathematics education. There are six principles that describe the overarching themes of mathematics instruction (NCTM, 2000, p. 11).

Equity: high expectations and strong support for all students

Curriculum: more than a collection of activities; must be coherent, focused on important mathematics, and well articulated across the grades

Teaching: effective mathematics teaching requires understanding of what students know and need to learn and then challenging and supporting them to learn it well

Learning: students must learn mathematics with understanding, actively building new knowledge from experience and prior knowledge

Assessment: assessment should support the learning of important mathematics and furnish useful information to both teachers and students

Technology: technology is essential in teaching and learning mathematics; it influences the mathematics that is taught and enhances student learning. (Note the suggested list of software for children in the activities section of each unit, the example Web sites for teachers in each unit,

and the list of software resources and the Web site list in Appendix B.)

These principles should be used as a guide to instruction in all subjects, not just mathematics.

Standards for School Mathematics

Standards provide guidance as to what children should know and be able to do at different ages and stages. Ten standards are described for prekindergarten through grade 12, with examples of the expectations outlined for each standard (Figure 1–3). The first five standards are content goals for operations, algebra, geometry, measurement, and data analysis and probability. The next five standards include the processes of problem solving, reasoning and proof, communication, connections, and representation. These two sets of standards are linked together as the process standards are applied to learning the content. The standards and principles are integrated into the units that follow.

Number and operations standard	
Instructional programs from prekindergarten through grade 12 should enable all students to—	**Expectations for grades pre-K–2** *In prekindergarten through grade 2 all students should—*
Understand numbers, ways of representing numbers, relationships among numbers, and number systems	• count with understanding and recognize "how many" in sets of objects • use multiple models to develop initial understandings of place value and the base-ten number system • develop understanding of the relative position and magnitude of whole numbers and of ordinal and cardinal numbers and their connections • develop a sense of whole numbers and represent and use them in flexible ways, including relating, composing, and decomposing numbers • connect number words and numerals to the quantities they represent, using various physical models and representations • understand and represent commonly used fractions, such as ¼, ⅓, and ½

FIGURE 1–3 Expectations for prekindergarten through second grade. From "Standards for Grades Pre-K–2," *Principles and Standards for School Mathematics* (pp. 392, 394, 396, 398, 400) by the National Council of Teachers of Mathematics, 2000, Reston, VA: Author. Reprinted with permission.

Understand meanings of operations and how they relate to one another	• understand various meanings of addition and subtraction of whole numbers and the relationship between the two operations • understand the effects of adding and subtracting whole numbers • understand situations that entail multiplication and division, such as equal groupings of objects and sharing equally
Compute fluently and make reasonable estimates	• develop and use strategies for whole-number computations, with a focus on addition and subtraction • develop fluency with basic number combinations for addition and subtraction • use a variety of methods and tools to compute, including objects, mental computation, estimation, paper and pencil, and calculators

Patterns, functions, and algebra standard

Instructional programs from prekindergarten through grade 12 should enable all students to—	**Expectations for grades pre-K–2** *In prekindergarten through grade 2 all students should—*
Understand patterns, relations, and functions	• sort, classify, and order objects by size, number, and other properties • recognize, describe, and extend patterns such as sequences of sounds and shapes or simple numeric patterns and translate from one representation to another • analyze how both repeating and growing patterns are generated
Represent and analyze mathematical situations and structures using algebraic symbols	• illustrate general principles and properties of operations, such as commutativity, using specific numbers • use concrete, pictorial, and verbal representations to develop an understanding of invented and conventional symbolic notations
Use mathematical models to represent and understand quantitative relationships	• model situations that involve the addition and subtraction of whole numbers, using objects, pictures, and symbols
Analyze change in various contexts	• describe qualitative change, such as a student's growing taller; describe quantitative change, such as a student's growing two inches in one year

FIGURE 1–3   *continued*

Geometry standard

Instructional programs from prekindergarten through grade 12 should enable all students to—	**Expectations for grades pre-K–2** *In prekindergarten through grade 2 all students should—*
Analyze characteristics and properties of two- and three-dimensional geometric shapes and develop mathematical arguments about geometric relationships	• recognize, name, build, draw, compare, and sort two- and three-dimensional shapes • describe attributes and parts of two- and three-dimensional shapes • investigate and predict the results of putting together and taking apart two- and three-dimensional shapes
Specify locations and describe spatial relationships using coordinate geometry and other representational systems	• describe, name, and interpret relative positions in space and apply ideas about relative position • describe, name, and interpret direction and distance in navigating space and apply ideas about direction and distance • find and name locations with simple relationships such as "near to" and in coordinate systems such as maps
Apply transformations and use symmetry to analyze mathematical situations	• recognize and apply slides, flips, and turns • recognize and create shapes that have symmetry
Use visualization, spatial reasoning, and geometric modeling to solve problems	• create mental images of geometric shapes using spatial memory and spatial visualization • recognize and represent shapes from different perspectives • relate ideas in geometry to ideas in number and measurement • recognize geometric shapes and structures in the environment and specify their location

Measurement standard

Instructional programs from prekindergarten through grade 12 should enable all students to—	**Expectations for grades pre-K–2** *In prekindergarten through grade 2 all students should—*
Understand measurable attributes of objects and the units, systems, and processes of measurement	• recognize the attributes of length, volume, weight, area, and time • compare and order objects according to these attributes • understand how to measure using nonstandard and standard units • select an appropriate unit and tool for the attribute being measured
Apply appropriate techniques, tools, and formulas to determine measurements	• measure with multiple copies of units of the same size, such as paper clips laid end to end • use repetition of a single unit to measure something larger than the unit, for instance, measuring the length of a room with a single meterstick • use tools to measure • develop common referents for measures to make comparisons and estimates

FIGURE 1–3 *continued*

Data analysis and probability standard

Instructional programs from prekindergarten through grade 12 should enable all students to—	**Expectations for grades pre-K–2** *In prekindergarten through grade 2 all students should—*
Formulate questions that can be addressed with data and collect, organize, and display relevant data to answer them	• pose questions and gather data about themselves and their surroundings • sort and classify objects according to their attributes and organize data about the objects • represent data using concrete objects, pictures, and graphs
Select and use appropriate statistical methods to analyze data	• describe parts of the data and the set of data as a whole to determine what the data show
Develop and evaluate inferences and predictions that are based on data	• discuss events related to students' experiences as likely or unlikely
Understand and apply basic concepts of probability	

Problem solving standard

Instructional programs from prekindergarten through grade 12 should enable all students to—	• Build new mathematical knowledge through problem solving • Solve problems that arise in mathematics and in other contexts • Apply and adapt a variety of appropriate strategies to solve problems • Monitor and reflect on the process of mathematical problem solving

Reasoning and proof standard

Instructional programs from prekindergarten through grade 12 should enable all students to—	• Recognize reasoning and proof as fundamental aspects of mathematics • Make and investigate mathematical conjectures • Develop and evaluate mathematical arguments and proofs • Select and use various types of reasoning and methods of proof

Connections standard

Instructional programs from prekindergarten through grade 12 should enable all students to—	• Recognize and use connections among mathematical ideas • Understand how mathematical ideas interconnect and build on one another to produce a coherent whole • Recognize and apply mathematics in contexts outside of mathematics

FIGURE 1–3   *continued*

Communication standard

Instructional programs from prekindergarten through grade 12 should enable all students to—

- Organize and consolidate their mathematical thinking through communication
- Communicate their mathematical thinking coherently and clearly to peers, teachers, and others
- Analyze and evaluate the mathematical thinking and strategies of others
- Use the language of mathematics to express mathematical ideas precisely

Representation standard

Instructional programs from prekindergarten through grade 12 should enable all students to—

- Create and use representations to organize, record, and communicate mathematical ideas
- Select, apply, and translate among mathematical representations to solve problems
- Use representations to model and interpret physical, social, and mathematical phenomena

FIGURE 1–3   *continued*

In 1996 the National Research Council (NRC) published the *National Science Education Standards*, which present a vision of a scientifically literate populace. They outline what a student should know and be able to do to be scientifically literate at different grade levels.

A national consensus is evolving around what constitutes effective science education. This consensus is reflected in two major national reform efforts in science education that affect teaching and learning for young children: the NRC's *National Science Education Standards* (1996) and the American Association for the Advancement of Science's (AAAS) Project 2061 (1989), which has produced *Science for All Americans* (1989) and *Benchmarks for Science Literacy* (1993). With regard to philosophy, intent, and expectations, these two efforts share a commitment to the essentials of good science teaching and have many commonalities, especially regarding how children learn and what science content students should know and be able to understand within grade ranges and levels of difficulty. Although they take different approaches, both the AAAS and NRC efforts align

with the NAEYC (1997) guidelines for developmentally appropriate practice and the NCTM (2000) standards for the teaching of mathematics.

The national science reform documents are based on the idea that active, hands-on conceptual learning that leads to understanding, along with the acquisition of basic skills, provides meaningful and relevant learning experiences. The reform documents also emphasize and reinforce Oakes's (1990) observation that all students, especially underrepresented groups, need to learn scientific skills such as observation and analysis that have been embedded in a "less-is-more" curriculum that starts when children are very young.

The *National Science Education Standards* (1996) were coordinated by the National Academy of Science's National Research Council (NRC) and were developed with the major professional organizations in science and individuals with expertise germane to the process to produce the standards. The document presents and discusses the standards, which provide qualitative criteria to be used by educators and others making decisions and judgments in six major components: (1) Science Teaching Standards, (2) Standards for the Professional Development of Teachers, (3) Assessment in Science Education, (4) Science Content Standards, (5) Science Education Program Standards, and (6) Science Education System Standards.

The *National Science Education Standards* are directed to all who have interests, concerns, or investments in improving science education and ultimately achieving higher levels of scientific literacy for all students. The standards intend to provide support for the integrity of science in science programs by presenting and discussing criteria for the improvement of science education.

The AAAS initiative, Project 2061, constitutes a long-term plan to strengthen student literacy in science, mathematics, and technology. Using a "less-is-more" approach to teaching, the first Project 2061 report recommends that educators use six major themes that occur again and again in science to weave together the science curriculum: models, scale evolution, patterns of change, stability, and systems and interactions. Although aspects of all or many of these themes can be found in most teaching units, *models and scale, patterns of change,* and *systems and interactions* are the themes considered most appropriate for younger children.

The second AAAS Project 2061 report, *Benchmarks for Science Literacy,* categorizes the science knowledge students need to know at all grade levels. The report is not in itself a science curriculum, but it is a useful resource for people developing curriculum.

The NAEYC guidelines for mathematics and science (Bredekamp & Copple, 1997; Bredekamp, 1987) state that mathematics begins with exploration of materials such as building blocks, sand, and water for three-year-olds and extends on to cooking, observation of environmental changes, working with tools, classifying objects with a purpose, and exploring animals, plants, machines, and so on for four- and five-year-olds. For five- through eight-year-old children, exploration, discovery, and problem solving are appropriate. Mathematics and science are integrated with other content areas such as social studies, the arts, music, language arts, and so on. These current standards for mathematics and science curriculum and instruction take a constructivist view based on the theories of Jean Piaget and Lev Vygotsky as described next.

Piagetian Periods of Concept Development and Thought

Jean Piaget contributed enormously to understanding the development of children's thought. Piaget identified four periods of cognitive, or mental, growth and development. Early childhood educators are concerned with the first two periods and the first half of the third.

The first period identified by Piaget, called the sensorimotor period (from birth to about age two), is described in the first part of the unit. It is the time when children begin to learn about the world. They use all their sensory abilities—touch, taste, sight, hearing, smell, and muscular. They also use growing motor abilities—to grasp, to crawl, to stand, and, eventually, to walk. Children in this first period are explorers and need opportunities to use their sensory and motor abilities to learn basic skills and concepts. Through these activities the young child *assimilates* (takes into the mind and comprehends) a great deal of information. By the end of this period, children have developed the concept of object permanence. That is, they realize that objects exist even when they are out of sight. They also develop the ability of object recognition. They learn to identify objects using the information they have acquired about features such as color, shape, and size. As children near the end of the sensorimotor period, they reach a stage where they can engage in representational thought; that is, instead of acting impetuously, they can think through a solution before attacking a problem. They also enter into a time of rapid language development.

The second period, called the preoperational period, extends from about ages two to seven. During this period children begin to develop concepts that are more like those of adults, but these are still incomplete in relation to what they will be like at maturity. These concepts are often referred to as preconcepts. During the early part of the preoperational period, language continues to undergo rapid growth, and speech is used increasingly to express concept knowledge. Children begin to use concept terms such as *big and small* (size), *light and heavy* (weight), *square and round* (shape), *late and early* (time), *long and short* (length), and so on. This ability to use language is one of the symbolic behaviors that emerges during this period.

Children also use symbolic behavior in their representational play, where they may use sand to represent food; a stick to represent a spoon; or another child to represent father, mother, or baby. Play is a major arena in which children develop an understanding of symbolic functions that underlie the later understanding of abstract symbols such as numerals, letters, and written words.

An important characteristic of preoperational children is **centration**. When materials are changed in form or arrangement in space, children may see them as changed in amount as well. This is because preoperational children tend to *center* on the most obvious aspects of what is seen. For instance, if the same amount of liquid is put in both a tall, thin glass and a short, fat glass, preoperational children say there is more in the tall glass "because it is taller." If clay is changed in shape from a ball to a snake, they say there is less clay "because it is thinner." If a pile of coins is placed close together, preoperational children say there are fewer coins than they would say if the coins were spread out. When the physical arrangement of material is changed, preoperational children seem to be unable to hold the original picture of its shape in mind. They lack **reversibility**; that is, they cannot reverse the process of change mentally. The ability to hold or save the original picture in the mind and reverse physical change mentally is referred to as **conservation**. The inability to conserve is a critical characteristic of preoperational children. During the preoperational period, children work with the precursors of conservation such as counting, one-to-one correspondence, shape, space, and comparing. They also work on **seriation** (putting items in a logical sequence, such as fat to thin or dark to light) and **classification** (putting things in logical groups according to some common criteria such as color, shape, size, use, and so on).

During the third period, called **concrete operations** (usually from ages seven to 11), children are becoming *conservers*. That is, they are becoming more and more skilled at retaining the original picture in mind and making a mental reversal when appearances are changed. The time between ages five and seven is one of transition to concrete operations. Each child's thought processes are changing at their own rate. During this time of transition, therefore, a normal expectation is that some children are already conservers and others are not. This is a critical consideration for kindergarten and primary teachers because the ability to conserve number (the pennies problem) is a good indication that children are ready to deal with **abstract symbolic activities**. That is, they will be able to mentally manipulate groups that are presented by number symbols with a real understanding of what mathematical operations mean. Section II of this text covers the basic concepts that children have to understand and integrate in order to conserve. (See Figure 1–4 for examples of conservation problems.)

Piaget's final period is called **formal operations** (ages 11 through adulthood). During this period, children can learn to use the scientific method independently; that is, they learn to solve problems in a logical and systematic manner. They begin to understand abstract concepts and to attack abstract problems. They can imagine solutions before trying them out. For example, suppose a person who has reached the formal operations level is given samples of several colorless liquids and is told that some combination of these liquids will result in a yellow liquid. A person at the formal operations level would plan out how to systematically test to find the solution; a person still at the concrete operational level might start combining without considering all the parameters of the problem, such as labeling each liquid, keeping a record of which combinations have been tried, and so on. Note that this period may be reached as early as age 11; however, it may not be reached at all by many adults.

Piaget's View of How Children Acquire Knowledge

According to Piaget's view, children acquire knowledge by constructing it through their interaction with the environment. Children do not wait to be instructed to do this; they are continually trying to make sense out of everything they encounter. Piaget divides knowledge into three areas.

◆ **Physical knowledge** is the type that includes learning about objects in the environment and their characteristics (color, weight, size, texture,

Original	Physical Change	Question	Nonconserving Answer	Conserving Answer
Same amount of drink 	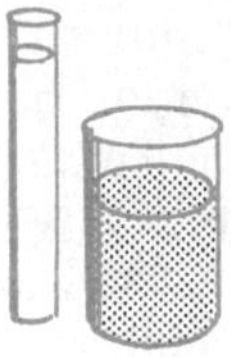	Is there still the same amount of drink?	No, there is more in the tall glass.	Yes, you just put the drink in different size glasses.
Same amount of clay 		Is there still the same amount of clay?	No, there is more clay in the snake because it is longer.	Yes, you just rolled it out into a different shape.
Same amount of pennies 	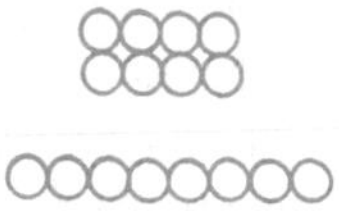	Are there still the same number of pennies?	No, there are more in the bottom row because it is longer.	Yes, you just moved the pennies closer together (points to top row).

FIGURE 1–4   Physical changes in conservation tasks.

and other features that can be determined through observation and are physically within the object).

◆ **Logico-mathematical knowledge** is the type that includes relationships each individual constructs (such as same and different, more and less, number, classification, and so on) to make sense out of the world and to organize information.

◆ **Social** (or conventional) **knowledge** is the type that is created by people (such as rules for behavior in various social situations).

Physical and logico-mathematical knowledge depend on each other and are learned simultaneously. That is, as the physical characteristics of objects are learned, logico-mathematical categories are constructed to organize information. For example, in the popular story *Goldilocks and the Three Bears*, papa bear is big, mama bear is middle sized, and baby bear is the smallest (seriation), but all three (number) are bears because they are covered with fur and have a certain body shape with a certain combination of features common only to bears (classification).

Constance Kamii, a student of Piaget's, has actively translated Piaget's theory into practical applications for the instruction of young children. Kamii emphasizes that according to Piaget, **autonomy** (independence) is the aim of education. Intellectual autonomy develops in an atmosphere where children feel secure in their relationships with adults; where they have an opportunity to share their ideas with other children; and where they are encouraged to be alert and curious, come up with interesting ideas, problems and questions, use initiative in finding the answers to problems, have confidence in their abilities to figure out things for themselves, and speak their minds with confidence. Young children need to be presented with problems to be solved through games and other activities that challenge their minds. They must work with concrete materials and real problems such as the examples provided earlier in the unit.

Vygotsky's View of How Children Learn and Develop

Like Piaget, Lev Vygotsky was also a cognitive development theorist. He was a contemporary of Piaget's, but Vygotsky died at the age of 38 before his work was fully completed. Vygotsky contributed a view of cognitive development that recognized both developmental and environmental forces. Vygotsky believed that just as people developed tools such as knives, spears, shovels, tractors, and the like to aid them in the mastery of the environment, they also developed mental tools. People developed ways of cooperating and communicating and new capacities to plan and to think ahead. These mental tools helped people to master their own behavior. These mental tools Vygotsky referred to as signs. He believed that *speech* was the most important sign system because it freed us from distractions and allowed us to work on problems in our minds. Speech both enables the child to interact socially and facilitates thinking. In Vygotsky's view, *writing and numbering* were also important sign systems.

While Piaget looked at development as if it came mainly from the child alone, from the child's inner maturation, and spontaneous discoveries, Vygotsky believed this was true only until about the age of two. At that point, culture and the cultural signs were necessary to expand thought. He believed that the internal and external forces interacted to produce new thoughts and an expanded menu of signs. Thus, Vygotsky put more emphasis than Piaget on the role of the adult or more mature peer as an influence on children's mental development.

While Piaget placed an emphasis on children as intellectual explorers making their own discoveries and *constructing* knowledge independently, Vygotsky developed the concept of the zone of proximal development (ZPD). The ZPD is the area between where the child is now operating independently in mental development and where she might go with assistance from an adult or more mature child. Cultural knowledge is arrived at with the assistance or scaffolding provided by more mature learners. According to Vygotsky, good teaching involved presenting material that was a little ahead of development. Children might not fully understand it at first, but they would under-stand in time, with appropriate scaffolding. Instruction did not put pressure on development; instruction supported it as it moved ahead. Concepts constructed independently and spontaneously by children laid the foundation for the more scientific concepts that were part of the culture. Teachers must identify each student's ZPD and provide developmentally appropriate instruction. Teachers will know when they have hit upon the right zone because children will respond with enthusiasm, curiosity, and active involvement.

Piagetian constructivists tend to be concerned about the tradition of pressuring children and not allowing them freedom to construct knowledge independently. Vygotskian constructivists are concerned with children being challenged to reach their full potential. Today many educators find that a combination of Piaget's and Vygotsky's views provides a foundation for instruction that follows the child's interests and enthusiasms while at the same time providing an intellectual challenge. The learning cycle view provides such a framework.

The Learning Cycle

The authors of the Science Curriculum Improvement Study (SCIS) materials designed a Piagetian-based learning cycle approach based on the assumption expressed by Albert Einstein and other scientists that "science is a quest for knowledge" (Renner & Marek, 1988). The scientists believed that if science was to be taught, students must interact with materials, collect data, and make some order out of that data. The order that students make out of that data is either a conceptual invention or it leads to a conceptual invention.

The learning cycle is viewed as a way to take students on a *quest for knowledge* that leads to the construction of knowledge. It is used both as a curriculum development procedure and a teaching strategy. Developers must organize student activities around phases, and teachers must modify their role and strategies during the progressive phases. The phases of the learning cycle are sometimes assigned different labels and are sometimes split into segments. However, the essential thrust of each of the phases remains: exploration, concept development, and concept application (Barman, 1989; Renner & Marek, 1988).

During the *exploration phase*, the teacher remains in the background, observing and occasionally inserting a comment or question (see Unit 2 on naturalistic and informal learning). The students actively manipulate materials and interact with each other. The teacher's knowledge of child development guides the selection of materials and how they are placed in the environment so that they provide a developmentally appropriate setting in which young children can explore and construct concepts.

For example, in the exploration phase of a lesson about shapes, students examine a variety of wooden or cardboard objects (squares, rectangles, circles) and make observations about the objects. The teachers may ask them to describe how they are similar and how they are different.

During the *concept introduction phase*, the teacher provides direct instruction; this begins with a discussion of the information the students have discovered. The teacher helps the children record their information. During this phase the teacher clarifies and adds to what the children have found out for themselves by using explanations, print materials, films, guest speakers, and other available resources (see Unit 2 on structured learning experiences). For example, in this phase of the lesson, the children exploring shapes may take the shapes and classify them in groups (squares, rectangles, and circles).

The third phase of the cycle, the *application phase*, provides children with the opportunity to integrate and organize new ideas with old ideas and relate them to yet other ideas. The teacher or the children themselves suggest a new problem to which the information learned in the first two phases can be applied. In the lesson about shape, the teacher might introduce differently shaped household objects and wooden blocks. The children are asked to classify these items as squares, rectangles, and circles. Again, the children are actively involved in concrete activities and exploration.

The three major phases of the learning cycle can be applied to the ramp-and-ball example described earlier in this unit. During the first phase, the ramp and the balls are available to be examined. The teacher inserts some suggestions and questions as the children work with the materials. In the second phase, the teacher communicates with the children regarding what they have observed. The teacher might also provide explanations, label the items being used, and otherwise assist the children in organizing their information; at

this point books and/or films about simple machines could be provided. For the third phase, the teacher poses a new problem and challenges the children to apply their concept of the ramp and how it works to the new problem. For example, some toy vehicles might be provided to use with the ramp(s).

Charles Barman (1989) describes three types of learning cycle lessons in his paper, *An Expanded View of the Learning Cycle: New Ideas about an Effective Teaching Strategy*. The lessons vary according to the way data are collected by students and the type of reasoning the students engage in. Most young children will be involved in descriptive lessons, in which they mainly observe, interact, and describe their observations. Although young children may begin to generate guesses regarding the reasons for what they observed, serious hypothesis generation requires concrete operational thinking (*empirical-inductive lesson*). In the third type of lesson, students observe, generate hypotheses, and design experiments to test their hypotheses (*hypothetical-deductive lesson*). This type of lesson requires formal operational thought. However, this does not mean that preoperational and concrete operational children should be discouraged from generating ideas on how to find out if their guesses will prove to be true—quite the contrary. They need to be encouraged to take the risk. Often they will come up with a variable solution, even though they may not yet have reached the level of mental maturation necessary to understand the underlying physical or logico-mathematical reasons.

Adapting the Learning Cycle to Early Childhood

Bredekamp and Rosegrant (1992) have adapted the learning cycle to early childhood education (Figure 1–5). The learning cycle for young chil encompasses four repeating processes

◆ **Awareness:** a broad people, events, or conc experience
◆ **Exploration:** the con meaning through sens objects, people, events, or

CYCLE OF LEARNING AND TEACHING

	WHAT CHILDREN DO	WHAT TEACHERS DO
Awareness	Experience	Create the environment
	Acquire an interest	Provide opportunities by introducing new objects, events, people
	Recognize broad parameters	Invite interest by posing problem or question
	Attend	Respond to child's interest or shared experience
	Perceive	Show interest, enthusiasm
Exploration	Observe	Facilitate
	Explore materials	Support and enhance exploration
	Collect information	Provide opportunities for active exploration
	Discover	Extend play
	Create	Describe child's activity
	Figure out components	Ask open-ended questions—"What else could you do?"
	Construct own understanding	Respect child's thinking and rule systems
	Apply own rules	Allow for constructive error
	Create personal meaning	
	Represent own meaning	
Inquiry	Examine	Help children refine understanding
	Investigate	Guide children, focus attention
	Propose explanations	Ask more focused questions—"What else works like this?" "What happens if ___ ?"
	Focus	
	Compare own thinking with that of others	Provide information when requested—"How do you spell ___ ?"
	Generalize	Help children make connections
	Relate to prior learning	
	Adjust to conventional rule systems	
Utilization	Use the learning in many ways; learning becomes functional	Create vehicles for application in real world
	Represent learning in various ways	Help children apply learning to new situations
	Apply learning to new situations	Provide meaningful situations in which to use learning
	Formulate new hypotheses and repeat cycle	

FIGURE 1–5 Cycle of learning and teaching. From *Reaching Potentials: Appropriate Curriculum and Assessment for Young Children* (Vol. 1, p. 33), by S. Bredekamp and T. Rosegrant (Eds.), 1992, Washington, DC: National Association for the Education of Young Children. Reprinted with permission.

◆ **Inquiry:** learners compare their constructions with those of the culture, commonalities are recognized, generalizations are made that are more like those of adults

Utilization: at this point in the cycle, learners ͻ apply and use their understandings in new ΄gs and situations

Each time a new situation is encountered, learning begins with awareness and moves on through the other levels. The cycle also relates to development. For example, infants and toddlers will be at the awareness level, gradually moving into exploration. Three-, four-, and five-year-olds may move up to inquiry, whereas six-, seven-, and eight-year-olds can move through all four levels when meeting new situations or concepts. Bredekamp and Rosegrant (1992) provide an example in the area of measurement.

- ◆ Three- and four-year-olds are aware of and explore comparative sizes.
- ◆ Four-, five-, and six-year-olds explore with non-standard units, such as how many of their own feet wide is the rug.
- ◆ Seven- and eight-year-olds begin to understand standard units of measurement and use rulers, thermometers, and other standard measuring tools.

Bredekamp and Rosegrant (1992) caution that the cycle is not hierarchical; that is, utilization is not necessarily more valued than awareness or exploration. Young children may be aware of concepts that they cannot fully utilize in the technical sense. For example, they may be aware that rain falls from the sky without yet understanding the technicalities of the water cycle. Using the learning cycle as a framework for curriculum and instruction has an important aspect: The cycle reminds us that children may not have had experiences that provide for awareness and exploration. To be truly individually appropriate in planning, we need to provide for these experiences in school.

The learning cycle fits nicely with the theories of Piaget and Vygotsky. For both, learning begins with awareness and exploration. Both value inquiry and application. The format for each concept provided in the text is from naturalistic to informal to structured learning experiences. These experiences are consistent with providing opportunities for children to move through the learning cycle as they meet new objects, people, events, or concepts.

Traditional vs. Reform Instruction

A current thrust in mathematics and science instruction is the reform of classroom instruction, changing from the traditional drill and practice memorization approach to adoption of the constructivist approach. A great deal of tension exists between the traditional and reform approaches. *Telling* has been the traditional method of ensuring that student learning takes place. When a teacher's role changes to that of guide and facilitator, the teacher may feel a lack of control. Current research demonstrates that students in reform classrooms learn as well or better than those in traditional classrooms. In this text we have tried to achieve a balance between the traditional and the reform by providing a guide to ensuring students have the opportunity to explore and construct their own knowledge while at the same time providing examples of developmentally appropriate direct instruction.

The Organization of the Text

This text is divided into seven sections. The sequence is both integrative and developmental. Section I is an integrative section that sets the stage for instruction. Development, acquisition, and promotion of math and science concepts are described. A plan for assessing developmental levels is provided. Finally, the basic concepts of science and their application are described.

Sections II, III, and IV encompass the developmental mathematics and science program for sensorimotor- and preoperational-level children. Section II describes the fundamental concepts basic to both math and science along with suggestions for instruction and materials. Section III focuses on applying these fundamental concepts, attitudes, and skills at a more advanced level. Section IV deals with higher-level concepts and activities.

Sections V and VI encompass the acquisition of concepts and skills for children at the concrete operations level. At this point, the two subject areas conventionally become more discrete in terms of instruction. However, they should continue to be integrated because science explorations can enrich children's math skills and concepts through concrete applications, whereas mathematics is used to organize and interpret data collected through observation.

Section VII provides suggestions of materials and resources and descriptions of math and science in action in the classroom and in the home. Finally, the appendixes include concept assessment tasks, lists of children's books that contain math and science concepts, and care requirements for animals.

As Figure 1–1 illustrates, concepts are not acquired in a series of quick, short-term lessons; development begins in infancy and continues throughout early childhood and, of course, beyond. As you read each unit, keep referring back to Figure 1–1; it can help you relate each section to periods of development.

Summary

Concept development begins in infancy and grows through four periods throughout a lifetime. The exploratory activities of the infant and toddler during the sensorimotor period are the basis of later success. As they use their senses and muscles, children learn about the world. During the preoperational period, concepts grow rapidly, and children develop the basic concepts and skills of science and mathematics, moving toward intellectual autonomy through independent activity, which serves as a vehicle for the construction of knowledge. Sometime between ages five and seven, children enter the concrete operations period and learn to apply abstract ideas and activities to concrete knowledge of the physical and mathematical world. The learning cycle lesson is described as an example of a developmentally inspired teaching strategy. Both mathematics and science instruction should be guided by the principles and standards developed by the major professional organizations in each content area. The text presents the major concepts, skills, processes, and attitudes fundamental to mathematics and science for young children as they should be guided through these principles and standards.

KEY TERMS

concepts	preoperational period	social knowledge
preprimary	preconcepts	autonomy
primary	symbolic behaviors	signs
development	centration	zone of proximal development
senses	reversibility	scaffolding
process skills	conservation	learning cycle
understanding	seriation	descriptive lessons
principles	classification	awareness
standards	concrete operations	exploration
sensorimotor period	abstract symbolic activities	inquiry
object permanence	formal operations	utilization
object recognition	physical knowledge	
representational thought	logico-mathematical knowledge	

SUGGESTED ACTIVITIES

1. Using the descriptions in the unit, prepare a list of behaviors that would indicate that a young child at each of Piaget's first three periods of development is engaged in behavior exemplifying the acquisition of math and science concepts. Using your list, observe four young children at home or at school. One child should be six to 18 months old, one 18 months to two and one-half years old, one age three to five, and one age six to seven. Record everything each child does that is on your list. Note any similarities and differences observed among the four children.

2. Interview three mothers of children ages two to eight. Using your list from Activity 1 as a guide, ask them which of the activities each of their children do. Ask them if they realize that these activities are basic to the construction of math and science concepts, and note their responses. Did you find that these mothers appreciated the value of children's play activities in math and science concept development?

3. Observe science and/or math instruction in a pre-kindergarten, kindergarten, or primary classroom. Describe the teacher's approach to instruction, and compare the approach with Vygotsky's guidelines.

4. Interview two or three young children. Present the conservation of number problem illustrated in Figure 1–4 (see Appendix A for detailed instructions). Audio tape or videotape their responses. Listen to the tape, and describe what you learn. Describe the similarities and differences in the children's responses.

5. Look carefully at the standards and expectations outlined in Figure 1–3. Decide which expectations would most likely be appropriate for preschool-, kindergarten-, and primary-level students. Discuss your selections with a small group in class. Each group should appoint a scribe to list your selections and the reasons for your selections and report the group decisions to the class.

6. You should begin to record on 5½″ × 8″ file cards each math and science activity that you learn about. Buy a package of cards, some dividers, and a file box. Label your dividers with the titles of Units 8 through 40. Figure 1–6 illustrates how your file should look.

FIGURE 1–6 Start a math/science activity file now so you can keep it up to date.

REVIEW

A. Define the term *concept development*.

B. Describe the commonalities between math and science.

C. Explain the importance of Piaget's and Vygotsky's theories of cognitive development.

D. Decide which of the following describes a child in the sensorimotor (SM), preoperational (P), or concrete operational (CO) Piagetian stages.

   1. Mary watches as her teacher makes two balls of clay of the same size. The teacher then rolls one ball into a snake shape and asks, "Mary, do both balls still have the same amount, or does one ball have more clay?" Mary laughs, "They are still the same amount. You just rolled that one out into a snake."

   2. Michael shakes his rattle and then puts it in his mouth and tries to suck on it.

   3. John's mother shows him two groups of pennies. One group is spread out, and one group is stacked up. Each group contains 10 pennies. "Which bunch of pennies would you like to have, John?" John looks carefully and then says, "I'll take these because there are more," as he picks up the pennies that are spread out.

E. In review question D, which child, Mary or John, is a conserver? How do you know? Why is it important to know that a child is or is not a conserver?

F. Explain how young children acquire knowledge. Include the place of the learning cycle in knowledge acquisition. Provide examples from your observations.

G. Explain the purpose and value of having principles and standards for mathematics and science instruction.

REFERENCES

American Association for the Advancement of Science. (1989). *Science for all Americans: A Project 2061 report on literacy goals in science, mathematics and technology*. Washington, DC: Author.

American Association for the Advancement of Science. (1994). *Benchmarks in science literacy*. Washington, DC: Author.

Barman, C. R. (1989). *An expanded view of the learning cycle: New ideas about an effective teaching strategy* (Council of Elementary Science International Monograph No. 4). Indianapolis, IN: Indiana University.

Bredekamp, S. (Ed.). (1987). *Developmentally appropriate practice in early childhood programs serving children from birth through age eight*. Washington, DC: National Association for the Education of Young Children.

Bredekamp, S., & Copple, C. (Eds.). (1997). *Developmentally appropriate practice in early childhood programs* (Rev. ed.). Washington, DC: National Association for the Education of Young Children.

Bredekamp, S., & Rosegrant, T. (1992). *Reaching potentials: Appropriate curriculum and assessment for young children* (Vol. 1). Washington, DC: National Association for the Education of Young Children.

National Council of Teachers of Mathematics. (2000). *Principles and standards for school mathematics*. Reston, VA: Author.

National Council of Teachers of Mathematics. (1989). *Curriculum and evaluation standards for school mathematics*. Reston, VA: Author.

National Council of Teachers of Mathematics. (1991). *Professional standards for teaching mathematics*. Reston, VA: Author.

National Council of Teachers of Mathematics. (1995). *Assessment standards for school mathematics*. Reston, VA: Author.

National Research Council. (1996). *National science education standards*. Washington, DC: National Academy Press.

National Science Teachers Association. (1994). An NSTA position statement: Elementary school science. In *NSTA handbook*. Washington, DC: National Science Teachers Association.

Oakes, J. (1995). *Lost talent: The under participation of women, minorities, and disabled persons in science*. Santa Monica, CA: The Rand Corporation.

Renner, R. W., & Marek, E. A. (1988). *The learning cycle and elementary school science teaching*. Portsmouth, NH: Heinemann Educational Books, Inc.

Sachse, T. P. (1993). Curriculum assumptions: Underlying the current reforms in science education. In J. Walter (Ed.), *ASCD curriculum handbook* (pp. 5.83–5.90). Alexandria, VA: Association of Supervision and Curriculum Development.

FURTHER READING AND RESOURCES

Adams, L. A. (2000). Helping children learn mathematics through multiple intelligences and standards for school mathematics. *Childhood Education, 77,* 86–92

Baroody, A. J. (2000). Research in review. Does mathematics instruction for three- to five-year-olds really make sense? *Young Children, 55,* 61–67.

Berk, L. E., & Winsler, A. (1995). *Scaffolding children's learning: Vygotsky and early childhood education*. Washington, DC: National Association for the Education of Young Children.

Charlesworth, R. (1997). Mathematics in the developmentally appropriate integrated curriculum. In C. H. Hart, D. C. Burts, & R. Charlesworth (Eds.), *Integrated curriculum and developmentally appropriate practice: Birth through age 8*. Albany, NY: SUNY Press, 51–73.

Charlesworth, R. (2000). *Understanding child development* (5th ed.). Clifton Park, NY: Delmar Learning.

Children as mathematicians. (2000). *Teaching Children Mathematics, 6* (Focus issue).

Clements, D. H. (2001). Mathematics in the preschool. *Teaching Children Mathematics, 7,* 270–275.

Clements, D. H., & Sarama, J. (2000). The earliest geometry. *Teaching Children Mathematics, 7,* 82–86.

Cobb, P. (1994). Constructivism in mathematics and science education. *Educational Researcher, 23*(7), 4.

Clements, D. H., & Sarama, J. (2000). Standards for preschoolers. *Teaching Children Mathmatics, 7,* 38–41.

Cobb, P. (1994). What is in the mind? Constructivist and sociocultural perspectives on mathematical development. *Educational Researcher, 23*(7), 13–20.

Copley, J. V. (2000). *The young child and mathematics.* Washington, DC: National Association for the Education of Young Children.

Copley, J. V. (Ed.). (1999). *Mathematics in the early years.* Washington, DC: National Association for the Education of Young Children.

Coulter, B. (2000). What's it like where you live? Meeting the standards through technology-enhanced inquiry. *Science and Children, 37*(4), 36–50.

Demers, C. (2000). Analyzing the standards. *Science and Children, 37*(4), 22–25.

Driver, R., Asoko, H., Leach, J., Mortimer, E., & Scott, P. (1994). Constructing scientific knowledge in the classroom. *Educational Researcher, 23*(7), 5–12.

Falkner, K. P, Levi, L., & Carpenter, T. P. (1999). Children's understanding of equality: A foundation for algebra. *Teaching Children Mathematics, 6,* 232–236.

Fennema, E., Carpenter, T. P., Franke, M. L., Levi, L., Jacobs, V. R., & Empson, S. B. (1996). A longitudinal study of learning to use children's thinking in mathematics instruction. *Journal for Research in Mathematics Education, 27,* 403–434.

Geary, D. C. (1994). *Children's mathematical development.* Washington, DC: American Psychological Association.

Gelman, S. (1999). Concept development in preschool children. In American Association for the Advancement of Science, *Dialogue on early childhood science, mathematics, and technology education* (pp. 50–61). New York: Author.

Ginsburg, H. P., Inoue, N., & Seo, K. (1999). Young children doing mathematics. In J. V. Copley (Ed.), *Mathematics in the early years* (pp. 88–91). Washington, DC: National Association for the Education of Young Children and Reston, VA: National Council of Teachers of Mathematics.

Hiebert, J., & Carpenter, T. P. (1992). Learning and teaching with understanding. In D. A. Grouws (Ed.), *Handbook of research on mathematics teaching and learning* (pp. 65–97). New York: Macmillan.

Inhelder, B., & Piaget, J. (1969). *The early growth of logic in the child.* New York: Norton.

Kamii, C. K., & Housman, L. B. (1999). *Young children reinvent arithmetic: Implications of Piaget's theory* (2nd ed). New York: Teachers College.

Karplus, R., & Thier, H. D. (1967). *A new look at elementary school science—Science curriculum improvement study.* Chicago: Rand McNally.

Kline, K. (2000). Early childhood teachers discuss the *Standards. Teaching Children Mathematics, 6,* 568–571.

Lawson, A. E., & Renner, J. W. (1975). Piagetian theory and biology teaching. *American Biology Teacher, 37*(6), 336–343.

Lind, K. K. (1997). Science in the developmentally appropriate integrated curriculum. In C. H. Hart, D. C. Burts, & R. Charlesworth (Eds.), *Integrated curriculum and developmentally appropriate practice: Birth through age 8* (pp. 75–102). Albany, NY: SUNY Press.

Mokros, J., Russell, S. J., & Economopoulos, K. (1995). *Beyond arithmetic: Changing mathematics in the elementary classroom.* Palo Alto, CA: Dale Seymour.

Piaget, J. (1965). *The child's conception of number.* New York: Norton.

Price, J. (1996). Building bridges of mathematical understanding for all children. *Teaching Children Mathematics, 3,* 48–51.

Richardson, K. (2000, October). Mathematics standards for pre-kindergarten through grade 2. *ERIC Digest* [EDO-PS-00-11].

Smith, J. P., III. (1996). Efficacy and teaching mathematics by telling: A challenge for reform. *Journal for Research in Mathematics Education, 27,* 387–402.

UNIT 2
How Concepts Are Acquired

OBJECTIVES

After reading this unit, you should be able to:

◆ List and define the three types of learning experiences described in the unit.

◆ Recognize examples of each of the three types of learning experiences.

◆ State possible responses to specific opportunities for the child to learn concepts.

◆ Be aware of variations in individual and cultural learning styles and the need for curriculum integration.

◆ Know that children learn through interaction with peers as well as adults.

◆ Recognize the value of technology for young children's math and science learning.

Children learn with understanding when the learning takes place in meaningful and familiar situations. As children explore their familiar environments, they encounter experiences through which they actively construct knowledge and discover new relationships. The adult's role is to build upon this knowledge and support children as they move to higher levels of understanding. These initial child-controlled learning experiences can be characterized as **naturalistic learning**. Two other types of experiences are those characterized as **informal learning** and those that are **structured learning**.

Naturalistic experiences are those in which the child controls choice and action; *informal* is where the child chooses the activity and action, but at some point there is adult intervention; and *structured* is where the adult chooses the experience for the child and gives some direction to the child's action (Figure 2–1). Naturalistic experiences relate closely to the Piagetian view, and the informal and structured relate to the Vygotskian view.

Referring back to the learning cycle as described in Unit 1, it can be seen that these three types of experiences fit into the cycle. The learning cycle is basically a way to structure lessons so that all three ways of learning are experienced. Naturalistic experiences are encouraged at the awareness and the exploration levels. Informal experiences are added at the exploration,

TYPES OF ACTIVITY	INTERACTION EMPHASIZED
Naturalistic	Child / Environment
Informal	Child / Environment / Adult
Structured	Adult / Child / Environment

FIGURE 2–1 Concepts are learned through three types of activity.

inquiry, and utilization levels. Structured experiences are more likely to appear at the inquiry and utilization levels.

In providing settings for learning and types of instruction, keep in mind that there are variations in learning styles among groups of children and among different cultural and ethnic groups. Some of these types of variations will be described later in the unit.

Naturalistic Experiences

Naturalistic experiences are those initiated spontaneously by children as they go about their daily activities. These experiences are the major mode of learning for children during the sensorimotor period. Naturalistic experiences can also be a valuable mode of learning for older children.

The adult's role is to provide an interesting and rich environment. That is, there should be many things for the child to look at, touch, taste, smell, and hear. The adult should observe the child's activity and note how it is progressing and then respond with a glance, a nod, a smile, a verbal description of the child's actions or elaboration of the child's comments, or a word of praise to encourage the child. The child needs to know when he is doing the appropriate thing.

Some examples of naturalistic experiences are as follows:

- Kurt hands Dad two pennies saying, "Here's your two dollars!"
- Tamara takes a spoon from the drawer—"This is big." Mom says, "Yes, that is a big spoon."
- Roger is eating orange segments. "I got three." (Holds up three fingers.)

- Nancy says, "Big girls are up to here," as she stands straight and points to her chin.
- Cindy (age four) sits on the rug sorting colored rings into plastic cups.
- Tanya and Tim (both age four) are having a tea party. Tim says, "The tea is hot."
- Sam (age five) is painting. He makes a dab of yellow. Then he dabs some blue on top. "Hey! I've got green now."
- Trang Fung (age six) is cutting her clay into many small pieces. Then she squashes it together into one big piece.
- Sara (age six) is restless during the after-lunch rest period. As she sits quietly with her head on her desk, her eyes rove around the room. Each day she notices the clock. One day she realizes that when Mrs. Red Fox says, "One-fifteen, time to get up," that the short hand is always on the one and the long hand is always on the three. After that she knows how to watch the clock for the end of rest time.
- Theresa (age seven) is drawing with markers. They are in a container that has a hole to hold each one. Theresa notices that there is one extra hole. "There must be a lost marker," she comments.
- Vanessa (age eight) is experimenting with cup measures and containers. She notices that each cup measure holds the same amount even though each is a different shape. She also notices that you cannot always predict how many cups of liquid a container holds just by looking at it. The shape can fool you.

Informal Learning Experiences

Informal learning experiences are initiated by the adult as the child is engaged in a naturalistic experience. These experiences are not preplanned for a specific time. They occur when the adult's experience and/or intuition indicates it is time to scaffold. This might happen for various reasons—for example, the child might need help or is on the right track in solving a problem but needs a cue or encouragement. It might also happen because the adult has in mind some concepts that should be reinforced and takes advantage of a **teachable moment**. Informal learning experiences occur when an opportunity for instruction presents itself by chance. Some examples follow:

◆ "I'm six years old," says three-year-old Kate while holding up three fingers. Dad says, "Let's count those fingers. One, two, three fingers. How old are you?"

◆ Bob (age four) is setting the table. He gets frustrated because he does not seem to have enough cups. "Let's check," says his teacher. "There is one placemat for each chair. Let's see if there is one cup on each mat." They move around the table checking. They come to a mat with two cups. "Two cups," says Bob. "Hurrah!" says his teacher.

◆ With arms outstretched at various distances, Tim (age four) asks, "Is this big? Is this big?" Mr. Brown says, "What do you think? What *is* 'this' big?" Tim looks at the distance between his hands with his arms stretched to the fullest. "This is a big person." He puts his hands about 18 inches apart. "This is a baby." He places his thumb and index finger about half of an inch apart. "This is a blackberry." Mr. Brown watches with a big smile on his face.

◆ Juanita (age four) has a bag of cookies. Mrs. Ramirez asks, "Do you have enough for everyone?" Juanita replies, "I don't know." Mrs. R. asks, "How can you find out?" Juanita says, "I don't know." Mrs. R. suggests, "How about if we count the cookies?"

◆ Kindergartners George and Sam are playing with some small rubber figures called Stackrobats.® George links some together horizontally, while Sam joins his vertically. The boys are competing to see who can make the longest line. When George's line reaches across the diameter of the table, he encounters a problem. Miss Jones suggests that he might be able to figure out another way to link the figures together. He looks at Sam's line of figures and then at his. He realizes that if he links his figures vertically he can continue with the competition.

◆ Dean, a first grader, runs into Mrs. Red Fox's classroom on a spring day after a heavy rainstorm. He says, "Mrs. Red Fox! I have a whole bunch of worms." Mrs. Red Fox asks Dean where he found the worms and why there are so many out this morning. She suggests he put the worms on the science table where everyone can see them. Dean follows through and places a sign next to the can: "Wrms fnd by Dean."

◆ Second grader Liu Pei is working with blocks. She shows her teacher, Mr. Wang, that she has made three stacks of four blocks. She asks, "When I have three stacks of four, is that like when my big brother says 'three times four'?" "Yes," responds Mr. Wang. "When you have three stacks of four, that is three times four." Liu Pei has discovered some initial ideas about multiplication.

◆ Third grader Jason notices that each time he feeds Fuzzy the hamster, Fuzzy runs to the food pan before Jason opens the cage. He tells his teacher, who uses the opportunity to discuss *anticipatory responses*, why they develop, and their significance in training animals. He asks Jason to consider why this might happen so consistently and to think about other times he has noticed this type of response in other animals or humans. Several other children join the discussion. They decide to keep individual records of any anticipatory responses they observe for a week, compare observations, and note trends.

Structured Learning Experiences

Structured experiences are preplanned lessons or activities. They can be done with individuals or small or large groups at a special time or an opportune time. They may follow the learning cycle sequence or be more focused direct instruction. The following are examples of some of these structured activities:

◆ With an individual at a specific time with a specific focus. Cindy is four years old. Her teacher decides that she needs some practice counting. She says, "Cindy, I have some blocks here for you to count. How many are in this pile?"

◆ A learning cycle example. Mrs. Red Fox sets up a new activity center in her room. There is a large tub filled with balls of several different sizes, colors, and textures. The children all have had some experience with balls and are aware of them in the environment. Mrs. Red Fox points out the tub of balls to the students and tells them that they can *explore* the balls, looking at what is the same and different. She provides paper and markers that can be used to record what they learn. Each day the students gather for group reports about their daily activities. Those who have explored the balls report on their findings and share what they have recorded. Mrs. Red Fox asks questions and encourages the students to insert comments and questions. Finally, they discuss other things they might try to find out about the balls and other investigations they might make relative to the balls.

◆ With an individual at an opportune time with a specific focus. Mrs. Flores knows that Tanya needs help with the concept of shape. Tanya is looking for a game to play. Mrs. Flores says, "Try this shape-matching game, Tanya. There are squares, circles, and triangles on the big card. You find the little cards with the shapes that match."

◆ With a group at an opportune time. Mrs. Raymond has been working with the children on the concepts of light and heavy. They ask her to bring out some planks to make ramps for the packing boxes and the sawhorses. She brings out the planks and explains to the group, "These are the heavy planks. These are the light planks. Which are stronger? Where should they go?"

◆ With a large group at a specific time. The students have had an opportunity to explore a collection of bones that they have brought from home. Ms. Hebert realizes classification is an important concept that should be applied throughout the primary grades. It is extremely important in organizing science data. Ms. Hebert puts out three large sheets of construction paper and has the students explore the different ways bones can be classified (such as chicken, turkey, duck, cow, pig, deer) or placed in subcategories (such as grouping chicken bones into wings, backs, legs, and so on).

Note that throughout the examples in this unit the adults ask a variety of questions and provide different types of directions for using the materials. It is extremely important to ask many different types of questions. Questions vary as to whether they are *divergent* or *convergent*, and they vary as to how difficult they are. **Divergent questions and directions** do not have one right answer but provide an opportunity for creativity, guessing, and experimenting. Questions that begin "Tell me about _____," "What do you think _____?," "What have you found out _____?," "What can we do with _____?," "Can you find a way to _____?," "What would happen if _____?," "Why do you think _____?," and directions such as "You can examine these _____" or "You may play with these _____" are divergent.

Convergent questions and directions ask for a specific response or activity. There is a specific piece of information called for, such as "How many _____?," "Tell me the names of the parts of a plant," "Find a ball smaller than this one," and so on. Adults often ask only convergent questions and give convergent directions. Remember that children need time to construct their ideas. Divergent questions and directions encourage them to think and act for themselves. Convergent questions and directions can provide the adult with specific information regarding what the child knows, but too many of these questions tend to make the child think that there might be only one right answer to all problems. This can squelch creativity and the willingness to guess and experiment.

By varying the difficulty of the questions asked, the teacher can reach children of different ability levels For example, in the office supply store center, pencils are 2¢ and paper is 1¢ per sheet. An easy question might be, "If you buy one pencil and two sheets of paper how many pennies will you need?" A harder question would be, "If you have 10¢, how many pencils and how much paper could you buy?"

Learning Styles

In planning learning experiences for children, it is essential to consider individual and culturally determined styles of learning. Learning styles may relate to modalities such as auditory, visual, kinesthetic, or multisensory preferences. They also may relate to strengths in particular areas such as those identified by Howard Gardner in his theory of **multiple intelligences** (Gardner, 1999). Gardner originally identified seven intelligences: *Linguistic*, *Logical-Mathematical*, *Bodily-Kinesthetic*, *Interpersonal*, *Intrapersonal*, *Musical*, and *Spatial*. More recently he added two additional intelligences: *naturalist* and *existential*. Gardner conceptualizes these nine intelligences as combined biological and psychological potentials to process information that can be used in a culture to solve problems or create products that are valuable to the culture. It is important to provide children with opportunities to solve problems using their strongest modalities and areas of intelligence. Too often, conventional learning experiences focus on the linguistic (language) and Logical-Mathematical intelligences and ignore the other areas. Children who may have strength in learning through active movement and concrete activities (bodily kinesthetic learners) or those who learn best through interacting with peers (interpersonal learners) or one of the other modalities may lose out on being able to develop concepts and skills to the fullest. Incorporating peer tutoring and opportunities to do group projects expands on the opportunities for success.

The variety of learning styles can be reached by integrating the various areas of the curriculum rather than teaching each area such as mathematics, science, social studies, language arts, visual arts, musical arts, movement, and so on as separate topics. More and more attention has been paid to integrated approaches to instruction (see Unit 22). In this text we focus on mathematics and science as the major focus with other content areas integrated. However, any one of the content areas can be the hub at different times with different purposes. The section on Further Reading and Resources includes some resources for curriculum integration. Integration is frequently pictured in a weblike structure similar to that constructed by spiders (Figure 2–2). The focus or theme of study is placed in the center, and the other content areas and/or major concepts are attached by the radials.

In planning and instruction, it is important to consider not only diversity in modality-related learning styles but also diversity in race, ethnicity, social class, gender, and out-of-school experiences. Whereas reform mathematics appears to have positive effects on achievement, research has not looked closely at how reform mathematics affects different groups. The reform classroom itself is a culture different from the traditional classroom. The reform movement is progressing from a linear, formal view of the teacher passing out knowledge to passive students to a setting where mathematics is constructed, discussed, and questioned by active students. The reform mathematics and science classroom is an active, productive culture.

Many fundamental concepts in mathematics and science are learned before the child enters school. For example, mathematics learned outside of school is referred to as **ethnomathematics** (Nunes, 1992). This type of mathematics is embedded in the out-of-school cultural activities whose primary purpose is not mathematics but to accomplish a culturally relevant task. Examples would be activities such as counting out equal shares, setting the table, calculating a recipe, exchanging money, or measuring one's height or weight. Each culture has its own way of doing these tasks. The problem teachers face is how to capitalize on what children learn outside of school considering that some of these tasks may apply mathematics differently than it is used in the classroom. Teachers must learn about the everyday lives of their students and how mathematics concepts may be applied on a day-to-day basis. To connect out-of-school to in-school experiences, mathematics and science in school should be introduced by providing students with problems based on everyday experiences. Teachers can then observe as students construct solutions based on their out-of-school life experiences. Once students have developed their own strategies, the conventional strategies or algorithms and formulas can be introduced as an alternative means of problem solution.

Teachers need to be responsive to the diverse cultural values and experiences of their students in order to identify each individual's ZPD and build from where the children are operating independently to where their capabilities can take them with appropriate scaffolding. Multicultural education is not a topic to be presented one week or one month and then forgotten. It should permeate the whole curriculum.

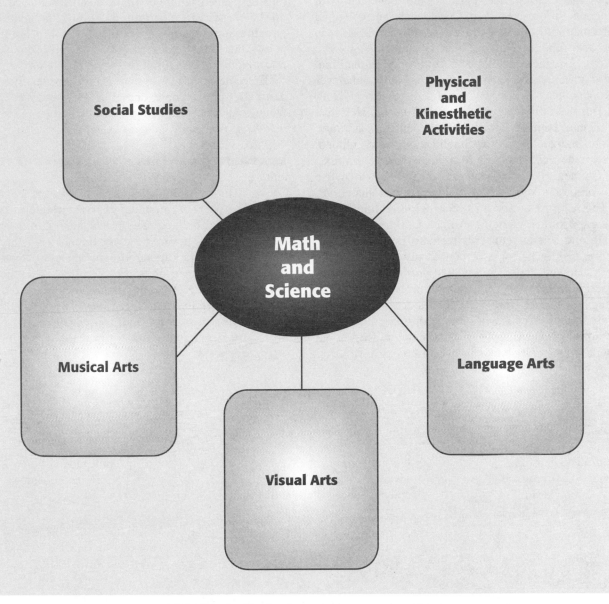

FIGURE 2–2 The basic content area web pattern.

Technology

Technology is providing us with an ever-increasing array of learning tools. For example, kindergarten teacher Addie Gaines developed her own classroom Web site. The site provided a look into her classroom, a list of her favorite places on the Net, and descriptions of some of the projects her students had done using the Net. Her kindergartners became adept at using the links Miss Addie provides for them. They could surf the Web for information as they moved into new integrated projects. They communicated with other classrooms, took virtual field trips, and collected information. Projects that focused on math or science included Quaint Quilts, Great Groundhogs, I Love Ladybugs, Mice Are Nice, Space: Exploring the Final Frontier, Spiders: No Arachnophobia Here!, Whatever the Weather, and the Wonderful Watermelon Unit.

Besides collecting information from the Net children can enjoy a variety of educational software. More and more preschools and elementary schools are including computers in the classrooms. Douglas H. Clements is a major researcher on the effective use of computers with young children (Clements, 1999, 2001). Computer activities can help children bridge the gap from concrete to abstract. Children can learn math and science concepts from software that presents a task, asks for a response, and provides feedback. However, software should go beyond drill and practice and provide for the children's creativity. Creating new shapes from other shapes or using turtles to draw shapes provides children with opportunities for exploration and discovery. Computers also provide social opportunities because children enjoy working together. One or more computers can serve as centers in the classroom. As children explore, the adult can provide suggestions or ask questions. Most importantly, the adult can observe and learn something about how children think and solve problems.

Calculators also can provide a tool for learning. In Unit 27 some simple activities are described that young children can explore with calculators.

Summary

Three types of learning experiences have been described and defined. The teacher and parent learn through practice how to make the best use of naturalistic, informal, and structured experiences so that the child has a balance of free exploration and specific planned activities. When planning activities the children's learning styles and areas of strength should be considered. Technology, both computers and calculators, provides valuable tools for learning math and science concepts.

KEY TERMS

naturalistic learning
informal learning
structured learning

teachable moment
divergent questions and directions
convergent questions and directions

multiple intelligences
ethnomathematics

SUGGESTED ACTIVITIES

1. Observe a prekindergarten, kindergarten, and primary classroom. Keep a record of concept learning experiences that are naturalistic, informal, and structured. Compare the differences in the numbers of each type of experience observed in each of the classrooms.
2. During your observations, also note any times you think opportunities for naturalistic or informal learning experiences were missed.
3. Note whether or not the various types of diversity (learning styles, ethnic, gender, and so on) appear to be considered in the instructional program.
4. Visit a teacher developed Web site. Write up a report describing the ways students use the Internet and contribute to the site.
5. Douglas Clements (1999) describes the software listed on the following page. See if you can find a classroom that has any of these items available and observe children using it. Write a description of the children's thinking and problem solving you observe.

◆ Shapes (Dale Seymour Publications, Fairfield, NJ)

◆ Turtle Geometry program (LCSI, Montreal, Canada)

◆ LEGO-Logo (Lego Dacta, Enfield, CT)

◆ Millie's Math House (Edmark Corp, Redmond, WA)

◆ Kid Pix 2 (The Learning Co. Division of Mattel., Inc., 1999)

REVIEW

A. Write a description of each of the three types of learning experiences described in this unit.

B. Decide if each of the following examples is naturalistic, informal, or structured:

1. "Mother, I'll cut this apple in two parts so you can have some." "Yes, then I can have half of the apple."

2. Nineteen-month-old John is lining up small blocks and placing a toy person on each one.

3. A teacher and six children are sitting at a table. Each child has a pile of Unifix Cubes.® "Make a train with the pattern A-B-A-B."

4. "I think I gave everyone two cookies," says Zang He. "Show me how you can check to be sure," says Mr. Brown.

5. Four children are pouring sand in the sandbox. They have a variety of containers of assorted sizes and shapes. "I need a bigger cup, please," says one child to another.

6. The children are learning about recycling. "Everyone sort your trash collection into a pile of things that can be used again and a pile of things that will have to be discarded."

7. Trang Fung brings her pet mouse to school. Each child observes the mouse and asks Trang Fung questions about its habits. Several children draw pictures and write stories about the mouse.

8. Mrs. Red Fox introduces her class to LOGO through structured floor games. The children take turns pretending to be a turtle and try to follow commands given by the teacher and the other students.

C. Read each of the following situations and explain how you would react:

1. George and Dina are setting the table in the home living center. They are placing one complete place setting in front of each chair.

2. Samantha says, "I have more crayons than you do, Hillary." "No, you don't." "Yes, I do!"

3. The children in Mr. Wang's class are discussing the show they must put on for the students in the spring. Some children want to do a show with singing and dancing; others do not. Brent suggests that they vote. The others agree. Derrick and Theresa count the votes. They agree that there are 17 in favor of a musical show and 10 against.

D. Explain why it is important to consider individual and cultural learning styles when planning instruction for young children.

E. Decide which of the following statements are true about technology.

1. Computers and calculators are not appropriate tools for young children to use.

2. Kindergartners can learn to use the Internet to gain information.

3. The value of computers as learning tools depends on the developmental appropriateness and quality of the software selected.

4. Drill and practice computer software is the most appropriate for young children.

REFERENCES

Clements, D. H. (1999). The effective use of computers with young children. In J. V. Copely (Ed.), *Mathematics in the early years* (pp. 119–128). Washington, DC: National Association for the Education of Young Children and Reston, VA: National Council of Teachers of Mathematics.

Clements, D. H. (2001). Mathematics in the preschool. *Teaching Children Mathematics, 7*(5), 270–275.

Gardner, H. (1999). *Intelligence reframed.* New York: Basic Books.

Nunes, T. (1992). Ethnomathematics and everyday cognition. In D. A. Grouws (Ed.), *Handbook of research on mathematics teaching and learning* (pp. 557–574). New York: Macmillan.

FURTHER READING AND RESOURCES

Adams, T. L. (2000/2001). Helping children learn mathematics through multiple intelligences and standards for school mathematics. *Childhood Education, 77*(2), 86–92.

Artzt, A. F., & Newman, C. M. (1990). *How to use cooperative learning in the mathematics classroom.* Reston, VA: National Council of Teachers of Mathematics.

Baratta-Lorton, M. (1976). *Math their way.* Menlo Park, CA: Addison-Wesley.

Baroody, A. J. (2000). Does mathematics instruction for three- to five-year-olds really make sense? *Young Children, 55*(4), 61–67.

Carpenter, T. P., Fennema, E., Franke, M. L., Levi, L., & Empson, S. B. (1999). *Children's mathematics: Cognitively Guided Instruction.* Portsmouth, NH: Heinemann.

Charlesworth, R. (1997). Mathematics in the developmentally appropriate integrated curriculum. In C. H. Hart, D. C. Burts, & R. Charlesworth (Eds.), *Integrated curriculum and developmentally appropriate practice: Birth through age 8.* Albany, NY: SUNY Press.

Charlesworth, R. (2000). *Understanding child development* (5th ed.). Clifton Park, NY: Delmar Learning.

Copely, J. V. (Ed.). (1999). *Mathematics in the early years.* Washington, DC: National Association for the Education of Young Children and Reston, VA: National Council of Teachers of Mathematics.

Focus issue: Mathematics and culture. (2001). *Teaching Children Mathematics, 7*(6).

Forman, G. E., & Kuschner, D. S. (1983). *The child's construction of knowledge.* Washington, DC: National Association for the Education of Young Children.

Ginsburg, H. P., Inoue, N., & Seo, K. (1999). Young children doing mathematics. In J. V. Copely (Ed.), *Mathematics in the early years* (pp. 88–91). Washington, DC: National Association for the Education of Young Children and Reston, VA: National Council of Teachers of Mathematics.

Helm, J. H., & Katz, L. G. (2001). *Young investigators: The project approach in the early years.* New York: Teachers College.

Isbell, R. (1995). *The complete learning center book.* Beltsville, MD: Gryphon House, Inc.

Jones, E., & Nimmo, J. (1994). *Emergent curriculum.* Washington, DC: National Association for the Education of Young Children.

Kamii, C. (with Housman, L. B.). (2000). *Young children reinvent arithmetic: Implications of Piaget's theory* (2nd ed.). New York: Teachers College.

Kamii, C., & DeVries, R. (1978). *Physical knowledge in preschool education.* Englewood Cliffs, NJ: Prentice-Hall.

Krogh, S. L. (1995). *The integrated early childhood curriculum* (2nd ed.). New York: McGraw-Hill.

Lind, K. K. (1997). Science in the developmentally appropriate integrated curriculum. In C. H. Hart, D. C. Burts, & R. Charlesworth (Eds.), *Integrated curriculum and developmentally appropriate practice: Birth through age 8.* Albany, NY: SUNY Press.

Martens, M. L. (1999). Productive questions: Tools for supporting constructivist learning. *Science and Children, 36*(8), 24–27, 53.

Mokros, J., Russell, S. J., & Economopoulos, K. (1995). *Beyond arithmetic: Changing mathematics in the elementary classroom.* Palo Alto, CA: Dale Seymour.

Richardson, K. (1999). *Developing number concepts: Planning guide.* Parsippany, NJ: Dale Seymour.

Secada, W. G. (1992). Race, ethnicity, social class, language and achievement in mathematics. In D. A. Grouws (Ed.), *Handbook of research on mathematics teaching and learning* (pp. 623–660). New York: Macmillan.

Stein, M., McNair, S., & Butcher, J. (2001). Drawing on student understanding: Using illustrations to invoke deeper thinking about animals. *Science & Children*, *38*(4), 18–22.

Sumrall, W. J., & Sumrall, C. A. (1994). Process skills used effectively. *Science and Children, 32*(3), 41–42.

Wakefield, A. P. (1998). *Early childhood number games: Teachers reinvent math instruction.* Boston: Allyn & Bacon.

UNIT 3

Promoting Young Children's Concept Development through Problem Solving

OBJECTIVES

After reading this unit, you should be able to:

- List and describe the six steps in instruction suggested in this unit.
- Identify examples of each of the six steps in instruction.
- Describe the advantages of using the six steps in instruction.
- Evaluate a teacher's instructional approach relative to the six steps.
- Recognize routine and nonroutine problems.
- Explain the term heuristic and its significance for mathematics problem solving.
- List the five NCTM process standards.
- Understand the value of estimation techniques.
- Implement developmentally appropriate problem-solving assessment and instruction.

The focus of instruction in science and mathematics should be **problem solving** and **inquiry**. Not only should teacher-developed problems and investigations be worked on, but child-generated problems and investigations also should be important elements in instruction. A problem-solving/inquiry focus empha-sizes children working independently and in groups, while the teacher serves as a facilitator and a guide. For the program to succeed, the teacher must know the students well so that she can support them in reaching their full capacities within the zone of proximal devel-opment. This unit outlines the basic instructional pro-

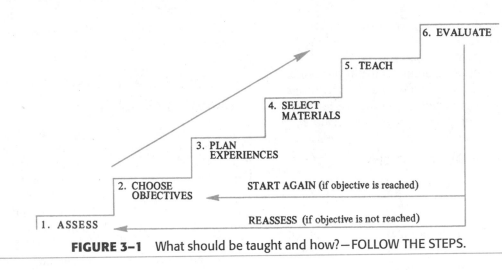

FIGURE 3–1   What should be taught and how?—FOLLOW THE STEPS.

cess and then describes the problem-solving inquiry approach to instruction as it applies to mathematics. In later units, science investigations serve as examples of problem solving and inquiry in science.

The steps involved in planning concept experiences are the same as those used for any subject area. Six questions must be answered (Figure 3–1).

- Where is the child now? **Assess**
- What should she learn next? **Choose objectives**
- What should the child do to accomplish these objectives? **Plan experiences**
- Which materials should be used to carry through the plan? **Select materials**
- Do the plan and the materials fit? **Teach** (do the planned experiences with the child)
- Has the child learned what was taught (reached objectives)? **Evaluate**

Assessing

Each child should be individually *assessed*. Two methods for this are used most frequently. Children can be interviewed individually using specific tasks, and they can be observed during their regular activities. The purpose of assessment is to find out what children know and what they can do before instruction is planned. The topic of assessment is covered in detail in Unit 4.

Specific Task Assessment

The following are examples of some specific tasks that can be given to a child.

- Present the child with a pile of 10 counters (buttons, coins, poker chips, or other small things) and say, "Count these for me."
- Show the child two groups of chips: a group of three and a group of six. Ask, "Which group has more chips?"
- Show the child five cardboard dolls, each one a half inch taller than the next. Say: "Which is the tallest?" "Which is the smallest?" "Line them up from the smallest to the tallest."
- Provide a six-year-old with an assortment of toy cars. Say: "Pretend you have a used car business. A customer wants to buy all your red cars and all your blue cars. Figure out how many of each he would be buying and how many he would be buying altogether. See how many ways you can solve this problem using the toy cars. You may also want to draw a picture or write about what you did."
- Provide a seven-year-old with a container of counting chips, at least 100. Say: "The zoo has a collection of 17 birds. They buy 12 more birds. Five birds get out of the aviary and fly away.

How many birds do they have now? You can use the counters to figure it out. Then draw a picture and even write about what you did."

◆ Place a pile of 30 counting chips in front of an eight-year-old. Say: "Find out how many different sets of two, three, five, and six you can make from this pile of chips." Record your findings.

Assessment by Observation

The following are examples of observations that can be made as children play and/or work.

◆ Does the one-year-old show an interest in experimenting by pouring things in and out of containers of different sizes?
◆ Does the two-year-old spend time sorting objects and lining them up in rows?
◆ Does the three-year-old show an interest in understanding size, age, and time by asking how big he is, how old he is, and "when will _____" questions?
◆ Does the four-year-old set the table correctly? Does he ask for help to write numerals, and does he use them in his play activities?
◆ Can the five-year-old divide a bag of candy so that each of his friends receives an equal share?
◆ If there are five children and three chairs, can a six-year-old figure out how many more chairs are needed so everyone will have one?
◆ If a seven-year-old is supposed to feed the hamster two tablespoons of pellets each day, can she decide how much food should be left for the weekend?
◆ Four eight-year-olds are making booklets. Each booklet requires four pieces of paper. Can the children figure out how many pieces of paper will be needed to make the four booklets?

Through observation the teacher can find out if the child can apply concepts to real life problems and activities. By keeping a record of these observations, the teacher builds up a more complete picture of the child's strengths and weaknesses. The current trend is to collect samples of student work, photographs, audio tapes, and videotapes and construct a portfolio that represents student accomplishments over time. Assessment will be discussed in more detail in Unit 4.

Choosing Objectives

Once the child's level of knowledge is identified, *objectives can be selected*. That is, a decision can be made as to what the child should be able to learn next. For instance, look at the first task example in the previous section. Suppose a five-year-old child counts 50 objects correctly. The objective for this child would be different from the one for another five-year-old who can count only seven objects accurately. The first child does not need any special help with object counting. A child who counts objects at this level at age five can probably figure out how to go beyond 50 alone. The second child might need some help and specific activities with counting objects beyond groups of seven.

Suppose a teacher observes that a two-year-old spends very little time sorting objects and lining them up in rows. The teacher knows that this is an important activity for a child of this age, one most two-year-olds engage in naturally without any special instruction. The objective selected might be that the child would choose to spend five minutes each day sorting and organizing objects. Once the objective is selected, the teacher then decides how to go about helping the child reach it.

Planning Experiences

Remember that young children construct concepts through naturalistic activities as they explore the environment. As they grow and develop, they feel the need to organize and understand the world around them. Children have a need to label their experiences and the things they observe. They notice how older children and adults count, use color words, label time, and so on. An instinctive knowledge of math and science concepts develops before an abstract understanding. When planning, it is important for adults to keep the following in mind.

◆ Naturalistic experiences should be emphasized until the child is into the preoperational period.

◆ Informal instruction is introduced during the sensorimotor period and increases in frequency during the preoperational period.

◆ Structured experiences are used sparingly during the sensorimotor and early preoperational periods and are brief and sharply focused.

◆ Follow the learning cycle format.

Abstract experiences can be introduced gradually during the preoperational and transitional periods and increased in frequency as the child reaches concrete exploratory operations, but they should always be preceded by concrete experiences. Keep these factors in mind when planning for young children. These points are covered in detail in the section on selecting materials. In any case, the major focus for instructional planning is the promotion of individual and group problem solving and inquiry.

Planning involves deciding the best way for each child to accomplish the selected objectives. Will naturalistic, informal, and/or structural experiences be best? Will the child acquire the concept best on her own? With a group of children? One to one with an adult? In a small group directed by an adult? Once these questions have been answered, the materials can be chosen. Sections II, III, IV, V, and VI tell how to plan these experiences for the concepts and skills that are acquired during the early years.

Selecting Materials

Three things must be considered when selecting science and math materials. First, there are some general characteristics of good materials. They should be sturdy, well made, and constructed so that they are safe for children to use independently. They should also be useful for more than one kind of activity and for teaching more than one concept.

Second, the materials must be designed for acquisition of the selected concepts. That is, they must fit the objective(s).

Third, the materials must fit the children's levels of development, that is, they must be developmentally appropriate. As stated, acquiring a concept begins with concrete experiences with real things. For each concept included in the curriculum, materials should

be sequenced from concrete to abstract and from three-dimensional (real objects), to two-dimensional (cutouts), to pictorial, to paper and pencil. Too often, however, the first steps are skipped and children are immersed in paper and pencil activities without the prerequisite concrete experiences and before they have developed the perceptual and motor skills necessary to handle a writing implement with ease. Five steps to be followed from concrete materials to paper and pencil are described as follows. Note that step one is the first and last step during the sensorimotor period; during the preoperational period, the children move from step one to step five; and during the transition and concrete operations periods, they move into step five.

◆ Step 1. Real objects are used for this first step. Children are given time to explore and manipulate many types of objects such as blocks, chips, stones, and sticks and materials such as sand, water, mud, clay, and Play-Doh.® Whether instruction is naturalistic, informal, or structured, concrete materials are used.

◆ Step 2. Real objects are used along with pictorial representations. For example, blocks can be matched with printed or drawn patterns. When cooking, each implement to be used (measuring spoons and cups, bowls, mixing spoons, and so on) can be depicted on a pictorial sequenced recipe chart. Children can draw pictures each day showing the height of their bean sprouts.

◆ Step 3. Cutouts, which can be motorically manipulated, are introduced. For example, cardboard cutouts of different sizes, colors, and shapes can be sorted. Cutout dogs can be matched with cutout doghouses. Cutout human body parts can be put together to make a whole body. Although the materials have moved into two dimensions, they can still be manipulated. Through manipulation of the materials the child can try a variety of solutions to the problem by trial and error and engage in self-correction.

◆ Step 4. Pictures are next. Commercially available pictorial materials, teacher-created or magazine pictures, and cut-up workbook pages can be used to make card games as well as sequencing, sorting, and matching activities. For example, pictures of people in various occupations might be matched with pictures of their equipment. Pictures of a person at different ages can be sequenced from baby to old age. Groups of objects drawn on a card can be counted and matched with the appropriate numeral.

Stop Here If the Children Have Not Yet Reached the Transition Stage

◆ Step 5. At this level, paper and pencil activities are introduced. When the teacher observes that the children understand the concept with materials at the first four levels, this level is introduced. If the materials are available, children usually start experimenting when they feel ready. Now they can draw and write about mathematics.

An example of sequencing materials using the five steps follows. Suppose one of the objectives for children in kindergarten is to compare differences in dimensions. One of the dimensions to be compared is length. Materials can be sequenced as follows:

◆ Step 1. Real objects. Children explore the properties of Unifix Cubes® and Cuisinaire Rods.® They fit Unifix Cubes® together into groups of various lengths. They compare the lengths of the Cuisinaire Rods.® They do measurement activities such as comparing how many Unifix Cubes® fit across the short side of the table versus the long side of the table.

◆ Step 2. Real objects with pictures. The Unifix Cubes® are used to construct rows that match pictured patterns of various lengths. Sticks are used to measure pictured distances from one place to another.

◆ Step 3. Cutouts. Unifix® and Cuisinaire® cutouts are used to make rows of various lengths. Cutouts of snakes, fences, and so on are compared.

◆ Step 4. Pictures. Cards with pictures of pencils of different lengths are sorted and matched. A picture is searched for the long and the short path, the dog with long ears, the dog with short ears, the long hose, the short hose, and so on.

Stop Here If the Children Have Not Yet Reached the Transition Stage

◆ Step 5. Paper and pencil activities are introduced. For example, students might draw long and short things.

At the early steps, children might be able to make comparisons of materials with real objects and even with cutouts and picture cards, but they might fail if given just paper and pencil activities. In this case it would be falsely assumed that they do not understand the concept when, in fact, it is the materials that are inappropriate. Calculators and computers can be used at every step.

The chart in Figure 3–2 depicts the relationship between the cognitive developmental periods—naturalistic, informal, and structured ways of acquiring concepts—and the five levels of materials. Each unit of this text has examples of various types of materials. Section VII contains lists and descriptions of many that are excellent.

Teaching

Once the decision has been made as to what the child should be able to learn next and in what context the concept acquisition will take place, the next step is teaching. *Teaching* occurs when the planned experiences using the selected materials are put into operation. If the first four steps have been performed with care, the experience should go smoothly. The children will be interested and will learn from the activities because they match their level of development and style of learning. They might even acquire a new concept or skill or extend and expand one already learned.

The time involved in the teaching step might be a few minutes or several weeks, months, or even years, depending on the particular concept being acquired and the age and ability of the child. For instance, time sequence is initially learned through naturalistic activity. From infancy, children learn that there is a sequence in their daily routine: sleeping; waking up wet and hungry; crying; being picked up, cleaned, fed, and played with; and sleeping again. In preschool, they learn a daily routine such as coming in,

PERIODS OF DEVELOPMENT	HOW CONCEPTS ARE ACQUIRED		
	Naturalistic	Informal	Structured
Sensorimotor	Real objects Objects and pictures Pictures	Real objects Objects and pictures Pictures	
Preoperational	Real objects Objects and pictures Cutouts Pictures	Real objects Objects and pictures Cutouts Pictures Calculators and computers	Real objects Objects and pictures Cutouts Pictures Calculators and computers
Transitional	Real objects Objects and pictures Cutouts Pictures	Real objects Objects and pictures Cutouts Pictures Paper and pencil Calculators and computers	Real objects Objects and pictures Cutouts Pictures Calculators and computers
Concrete Operations	Real objects Objects and pictures Cutouts Pictures	Real objects Objects and pictures Cutouts Pictures Paper and pencil Calculators and computers	Real objects Objects and pictures Cutouts Pictures Paper and pencil Calculators and computers

FIGURE 3–2 Two dimensions of early childhood concept instruction with levels of materials used.

greeting the teacher, hanging up coats, eating break-fast, playing indoors, having a group activity time, snacking, playing outdoors, having a quiet activity, lunch, playing outdoors, napping, having a small group activity time, and going home. Time words are acquired informally as children hear terms such as *yesterday*, *today*, *tomorrow*, *o'clock*, *next*, *after*, and so on. In kindergarten, special events and times are noted on a calendar. Children learn to name the days of the week and months of the year and to sequence the numerals for each of the days. In first grade, they might be given a blank calendar page to fill in the name of the month, the days of the week, and the number for each day. Acquiring the concept of time is a very complex experience and involves many pre-requisite concepts that build over many years. Some children will learn at a fast rate, others at a slow pace. One child might learn that there are seven days in a week the first time this idea is introduced; another child might take all year to acquire this information. Some children need a great deal of structured repetition; others learn from naturalistic and informal expe-

riences. Teaching developmentally involves flexible and individualized instruction.

Even with careful planning and preparation, an activity might not work well the first time. When this happens, analyze the situation by asking the following questions.

- Was the child interested?
- Was the task too easy or too hard?
- Did the child understand what he was asked to do?
- Were the materials right for the task?
- Were they interesting?
- Is further assessment needed?
- Was the teacher enthusiastic?
- Was it just a "bad" day for the child?

You might try the activity again using the same method and the same materials or with a change in the method and/or materials. In some cases, the child might have to be reassessed to be sure the activity is appropriate for her developmental level.

Evaluating

The sixth step is *evaluation*. What has the child learned? What does he know and what can he do after the concept experiences have been presented? The assessment questions are asked again. If the child has reached the objective, a new one can be chosen. The steps of planning, choosing materials, teaching, and evaluating are repeated. If the child has not reached the objective, the same activities can be continued or a new method may be tried. For example, a teacher wants a five-year-old to count out the correct number of objects for each of the number symbols from zero to 10. She tries many kinds of objects for the child to count and many kinds of containers in which to place the things he counts, but the child is just not interested. Finally she gives him small banks made from baby food jars and real pennies. The child finds these materials are exciting and goes on to learn the task quickly and with enthusiasm.

Evaluation may be done using formal, structured questions and tasks and specific observations as will be presented in Unit 4. Informal questions and observations of naturalistic experiences can be used for evaluation also. For example, when a child sets the table in the wrong way, it can be seen without formal questioning that he has not learned from instruction. He needs some help. Maybe organizing and placing a whole table setting is more than he can do now. Can he place one item at each place? Does he need to go back to working with a smaller number (such as a table for two or three)? Does he need to work with simpler materials that have more structure (such as pegs in a pegboard)? To look at these more specific skills, the teacher would then return to the assessment step. At this point she would assess not only the child but also the types of experiences and materials she has been using. Sometimes assessment leads the teacher to the right objective, but the experience and/or materials chosen are not (as in the example given) the ones that fit the child.

Frequent and careful evaluation helps both teacher and child avoid frustration. An adult must never take it for granted that any one plan or any one material is the best choice for a specific child. The adult must keep checking to be sure the child is learning what the experience was planned to teach him.

Problem Solving and the Process Standards

In Unit 1 the process standards for school mathematics were outlined (NCTM, 2000). These five standards include problem solving, reasoning and proof, communication, connections, and representation. *Problem solving* involves application of the other four standards. Although preoperational children's *reasoning* is different from older children's and adults', it is logical from their point of view. Pattern recognition and classification skills provide the focus for much of young children's reasoning. Adults need to encourage children to make guesses and explain their reasoning. Language is a critical element in mathematics (see Unit 15). Children can explain how they approach problem solving by *communication* with language. Even the youngest students can talk about mathematics and as they become older write and draw about it. The important *connections* for young mathematicians are those made between informal mathematics and the formal mathematics of the school curriculum. The transition can be made through the use of concrete objects and through connecting to everyday activities such as table setting, finding out out how many children are present in the class, or recognizing that when they surround a parachute they are making a circle. Young children use several kinds of *representations* to explain their ideas: oral language, written language using invented and conventional symbols, physical gestures, and drawings.

Skinner (1990, p. 1) provides the following definition of a problem: "A problem is a question which engages someone in searching for a solution." This means a problem is some question that is important to the student and thus gets her attention and enthusiasm focused on the search for a solution. Problem solving is not a special topic but should be a major focus for every concept and skill in the mathematics and science programs. Problem solving becomes a type of lesson where the teacher sets up a situation for children to learn through inquiry.

Problems should relate to and include the children's own experiences. From birth onward, children want to learn and naturally seek out problems to solve. Problem solving in school should build on the informal methods learned out of school. Problem solving through the prekindergarten years focuses on naturalistic and informal learning, which promotes exploration and discovery. In kindergarten and primary, a more structured approach can be instituted. Every new topic should be introduced with a problem designed to afford children the opportunity to construct their own problem-solving strategies. For an overall look at implementing a problem-solving approach for kindergarten and primary students, read Skinner's book, *What's Your Problem?* (1990). Also refer to the resources listed at the end of the unit.

Overview of Problem Solving in Mathematics

Problem solving is a major focus in the mathematics program today. As students enter the transition into concrete operations, they can engage in more structured problem-solving activities. These activities promote children's abilities to develop their own problems and translate them into a symbolic format (writing and/or drawing). This sequence begins with the teacher providing problems and then gradually pulling back as students develop their own problems.

There are two major types of problems: **routine** and **nonroutine**. Consider the following descriptions of students working on problems.

◆ Brent and the other children in his class have been given the following problem by their teacher, Mr. Wang: "Derrick has 10 pennies. John has 16 pennies. How many pennies do they have together?" Brent notes the key words "How many altogether?" and decides that this is an addition problem. He adds 10 + 16 and finds the answer: 26 pennies.

◆ Mr. Wang has also given them the following problem to solve: Juanita and Lai want to buy a candy bar that costs 35¢. Juanita has 15 pennies and Lai has 16 pennies. Altogether do they have enough pennies to buy the candy bar? Brent's attention is caught by the word "altogether," and again he adds 15 + 16. He puts down the answer: 31 pennies.

◆ Brent has five sheets of 8½″ × 11″ construction paper. He needs to provide paper for himself and six other students. If he gives everyone a whole sheet, two people will be left with no paper. He then draws a picture of the five sheets of paper. Then he draws a line down the middle of each. If he cuts each sheet in half, there will be 10 pieces of paper. There are seven children. That leaves three extra pieces. What will he do with the extras? He decides that it would be a good idea to have the three sheets in reserve in case someone makes a mistake.

The first problem is a *routine problem*. It follows a predictable pattern and can be solved correctly without actually reading the whole question carefully. The second is called a *nonroutine problem*. There is more than one step, and the problem must be read carefully. Brent has centered on the word "altogether" and stopped with the addition of the two girls' pennies. He misses the question asked, which is, "Once you know there are 31 pennies, is that enough money to buy a 35¢ candy bar?" The current focus in mathematics problem solving is on providing more opportunities for solving nonroutine problems, including those that occur in naturalistic situations such as the problem in the third example. Note that the third problem is multistepped: subtract five from seven, draw a picture, draw a line down the middle of each sheet, count the halves, decide if there are enough, subtract seven from 10, and decide what to do with the three extras. This last problem really has no one right answer. For example, Brent could have left two of the children out, or he could have given three children whole sheets and four children halves. Real problem-solving skills go beyond simple one-step problems.

Note that when dealing with each of the problems, the children went through a process of self-generated questions. This process is referred to as **heuristics**. There are three common types of self-generated questions:

◆ Consider a similar but simpler problem as a model.

◆ Use symbols or representations (build concrete representations; draw a picture or a diagram; make a chart or a graph).

◆ Use means-ends analysis such as identifying the knowns and the unknowns, working backward, setting up intermediate goals, analyzing the situation.

We often provide children with a learned idea or heuristic such as a series of problem-solving steps. Unfortunately, if the rules are too specific, they will not transfer (note Brent's focus on the key word), but if they are very general, how will you know if the idea is mastered? It is important to note that to apply a heuristic such as developing the relevant charts, graphs, diagrams, pictures, or doing needed operations requires a strong grounding in the basics such as counting, whole number operations, geometry, and so on.

Researchers have been concerned with whether heuristics can be taught and with what successful problem solvers do that leads to their success. It has been found that general heuristics cannot be taught. When content is taught with heuristics, content knowledge improves, not problem-solving ability. From studying successful problem solvers it has been discovered that they know the content and organize it in special ways. Therefore, content and problem solving should be taught together, not first one and then the other. Good problem solvers think in ways that are qualitatively different from poor problem solvers. Children must learn how to think about their thinking and manage it in an organized fashion. Heuristics is this type of learning, not just learning some lists of strategies that might not always work. Children have to learn to consciously do the following.

1. Assess the situation and decide exactly what is being asked.
2. Organize a plan that will get them to their goals.
3. Execute the plan using appropriate strategies.
4. Verify the results: behaviors that evaluate the outcomes of the plans.

It is important that children deal with real problems that might not have clearly designated unknowns, that might contain too much or too little information, that can be solved using more than one method, have no one right answer (or even no answer), that combine processes, have multiple steps that necessitate some trial and error, and that take considerable time to solve. Unfortunately, most textbook problems are of the routine variety where the unknown is obvious, only the necessary information is provided, the solution procedure is obvious, there is only one correct answer, and the solution can be arrived at quickly. Children must

learn that their first approach to solving a problem might be erroneous but that if they keep trying, a solution will materialize. It is essential that students have the opportunity to share possible solutions with their peers. If children have the opportunity to explain solutions to others, they will clarify the problem and be better able to explain problems to themselves.

Formal problem solving can be introduced using **contrived problems**, that is, problems devised or selected by teachers. This procedure provides an opportunity for the teacher to model problem-solving behavior by posing the problem and then acting out the solution. The children can then be asked to think of some variations.

Skinner (1990) presented the first problems to her five-year-olds in book form to integrate mathematics and reading/language arts. The tiny books were on sturdy cardboard with an illustration and one sentence on a page. They were held together with spiral binding. Skinner encouraged students to use manipulatives such as Unifix Cubes® to aid in solutions or to act out their solutions. Eventually, the students moved into dictating problems and then into writing. By age seven, they were creating most of their own problems. Research indicates that working with concrete materials and drawing and/or writing explanations of solutions for problems are the best support for improving problem-solving skills.

Assessment

Assessment of children's problem-solving expertise is not an easy task. It demands that teachers be creative and flexible. Development of problem-solving skills is a long-term activity; it is not learned in one lesson. It must be focused on the process of problem solving, not just the answers. Therefore, you must provide children with problem-solving situations and observe how they meet them, interview students, have small groups of children describe how they solved problems, and have students help each other solve problems.

Note the following as students work on problems:

◆ Do they attack the problem in an organized fashion; that is, do they appear to have a logical strategy?
◆ If one strategy does not work, do they try another?

◆ Are they persistent in sticking with the problem until they arrive at what they believe is a satisfactory solution?

◆ How well do they concentrate on the problem-solving task?

◆ Do they use aids such as manipulatives and drawings?

◆ Do their facial expressions indicate interest, involvement, frustration, puzzlement?

Behaviors noted can be recorded with anecdotal records or on checklists.

Interviews will be emphasized as a format for assessment throughout the text. The interview is also an excellent way to look at problem-solving behavior. Present the child with a problem or have the child invent a problem and let the child find a solution, describing what she is thinking as she works. Make a tape recording or take notes.

Instruction

Researchers agree that children should experience a variety of problem-solving strategies so that they do not approach every problem in the same stereotyped way. They should be given problems that are at their developmental level. Natural and informal methods of instruction should begin the exploration of problem solving. For example, ask how many children are in the classroom today, how many glasses of juice we will need at Kate's table, and so on.

To be effective problem solvers, children need time to mull over problems, to make mistakes, to try various strategies, and to discuss problems with their friends. When teaching in the kindergarten and primary grades, if you are required to use a textbook, check the problems carefully. If you find that most of the problems are routine, you will have to obtain some nonroutine problems or devise some yourself. You may use the criteria that follow:

◆ Devise problems that contain extra information or that lack necessary information.

1. George bought two bags of cookies with six cookies in each bag for 10¢ a bag. How many cookies did George buy? (Price is extra information.)

2. John's big brother is six feet tall. How much will John have to grow to be as big as his brother? (We don't know John's height.)

◆ Devise problems that involve estimation or that do not have clearly right or wrong answers.

1. Vanessa has $1. She would like to buy a pen that costs 49¢ and a notebook that costs 39¢. Does she have enough money? (Yes/no rather than numerical answer)

2. How many times can you ride your bike around the block in 10 minutes? In one hour? In a week? In a month? (Estimation)

◆ Devise problems that apply mathematics in practical situations such as shopping, cooking, or building.

◆ Base problems on things children are interested in, or make up problems that are about students in the class (giving them a personal flavor).

◆ Devise problems that require more than one step and provide for application of logic, reasoning, and testing out of ideas.

◆ Ask questions that will require the children to make up a problem.

◆ Design problems that require more than one step.

◆ Provide opportunities to solve problems that will provide data for decision making.

1. There are 25 students in the third-grade class. The students are planning a party to celebrate the end of the school year. They have to decide on a menu, estimate the cost, and calculate how much money each of them will have to contribute.

Collect resources that children can use for problem solving. Gather statistics that children can work with (such as the weather information from the daily newspaper). Use children's spontaneous questions (How far is it to the zoo?). Provide children with problems such as described by Marilyn Burns (1998). Literature (see Unit 15) provides a wealth of information for problem solving. Have children write problems that other children can try to solve. Calculators can be very helpful tools for problem solving. Children can try out more strategies because of the time they save that might have been spent in tedious hand calculations.

Microcomputers can also be used for problem solving. LOGO programming is a problem-solving activity in itself. Remember, have children work in pairs or small groups. Software is described and referred to in each of the units on mathematics and science content.

The conventional problem-solving strategies taught (Reys, Linquist, Lambdin, Smith, & Suydam, 2001) have been as follows:

- ◆ Understand the problem.
- ◆ Devise a plan for solving it.
- ◆ Carry out your plan.
- ◆ Look back to examine the solution obtained.

However, start by letting children develop their own solutions. They will gradually become more direct in their solutions. Through modeling, new strategies can be introduced. Reys et al. (2001) suggest several such strategies.

1. Act out the problem. That is, use real objects or representations to set up the problem and go through the steps for solution. This is the type of activity used to introduce whole number operations.

2. Make a drawing or a diagram. Stress that these pictures need to be very simple, including only the important elements. For example:

George wants to build a building with his blocks that is triangular shaped with seven blocks in the bottom row. How many blocks will he need? Drawing:

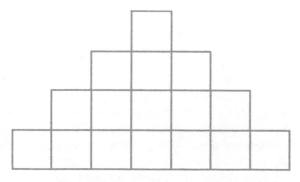

George will need 16 blocks.

Theresa's mother's van has three rows of seats. One row holds three passengers, the next two, and the back row holds four. Can 10 passengers and the driver ride comfortably? Drawing:

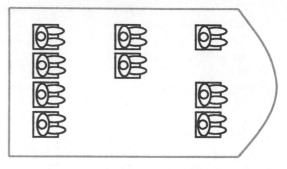

The van holds eight passengers and the driver. Ten passengers and the driver would be crowded.

3. Look for a pattern. (See Unit 28.)
4. Construct a table. (See Unit 31.)
5. Account systematically for all possibilities. That is, as different strategies are tried or different calculations made, keep track of what has been used.

Below is a map showing all the roads from Jonesville to Clinton. Find as many different ways as you can to get from Jonesville to Clinton without ever backtracking.

Jonesville

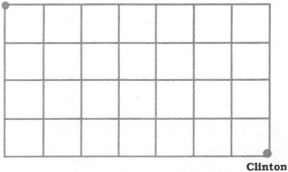

Clinton

6. Guess and check. Make an educated guess based on attention to details of the problem and past experience. Some problems demand trial and error and best guess to solve.

Using only the numbers one through nine, fill the squares so that the sum in every row and column is 15.

7. Work backward. In some problems, the endpoint is given, and the problem solver must work backward to find out how the endpoint was reached. A maze is a concrete example of this type of problem.

   Chan's mother bought some apples. She put half of them in her refrigerator and gave two to each of three neighbors. How many apples did she buy?

8. Identify wanted, given, and needed information. Rather than plunging right into calculations or formulating conclusions, the problem solver sorts out the important and necessary information from the extraneous factors or has to collect additional data. Taking a poll is a common way of collecting data to make a decision.

   Trang Fung says that most of the girls would like to have pepperoni pizza at the slumber party. Sara claims that most of the girls prefer hamburger. To know how much of each to order, they set up a chart, question their friends, and tally their choices.

9. Write an open sentence. That is, make the problem into a number sentence. This process is not easy and is too frequently the only strategy included in some textbooks.

10. Solve a simpler or similar problem. Sometimes large numbers or other complications get in the way of seeing how to solve a problem. Sometimes making a similar problem can help the child discover the solution. For example, in the problem below, the amounts could be changed to "Derrick has $4 and Brent $6."

If Derrick has saved $4.59 and Brent has saved $6.37, how much more money has Brent saved?

Sometimes problems have to be broken down into smaller parts. If a problem is put in the child's own words, sometimes a strategy will be clarified.

11. Change your point of view. Is the strategy being used based on incorrect assumptions? Stop and ask, "What is really being said in this problem?"

All these strategies will not be learned right away. They will be introduced gradually and acquired throughout the elementary grades. Prekindergarten through fourth grade hold a crucial role for providing the foundations for problem solving.

Estimation

Estimation is arriving at an approximation of the answer to a problem. Estimation should be taught as a unique strategy. Estimation should be mental and not be checked to see how accurate it is. Later on, children can apply estimation after computation to help decide if a computed answer is a reasonable one. First, however, the concept must be developed. At the primary level, the most common problems for applying estimation involve length or numerosity and are solved through visual perception. Children might guess how wide the rug is or how many objects are in a container. Computational estimation is usually introduced near the end of the primary period, that is, in the third grade.

There are a number of strategies that can be used for estimation. At the introductory levels, students work with concrete situations. For example, they might explore by estimating how many trucks could be parked in their classroom or how many shoes will fit in the closet. Children can select some benchmarks for measurement such as a body part; that is, they could estimate how many hands wide the hallway is. Another example would be estimating how many beans would fill a jar using a one-cup measure that holds 100 beans as the benchmark. Keeping the same jar and changing the size or type of objects placed in it will help children build on their prior knowledge and increase their estimation skills.

Two strategies might be used for more advanced estimation. The *front-end* strategy is one that young children can use. This strategy focuses on the first number on the left when developing an estimate. For example:

37	To estimate the sum, focus on the left column
43	first. Note that there are nine 10s, which
+24	would be 90. Then look at the right column.

Obviously, the answer is more than 90 and noting that the right column adds up to more than 10, an estimate of $90 + 10 = 100$ is reached.

Another strategy is called *clustering*. Clustering can be used when numbers are close in value. For example, estimate the total attendance in class for the week.

Class attendance

Monday	27	1. There were about
Tuesday	29	30 students each day.
Wednesday	31	
Thursday	32	
Friday	30	2. $5 \times 30 = 150$, the estimated
		total for the week

Rounding is a strategy that is helpful for mental computation. Suppose you wondered how many primary children had eaten lunch at school this week. You found out that there were 43 first graders, 38 second graders, and 52 third graders.

Number of Primary

Students Eating Lunch		Round	Add
First graders	43	40	40
Second graders	38	40	40
Third graders	52	50	50
			130
			(estimate)

There are two additional strategies that are much more complex and would be used by more advanced students beyond the elementary grades. *Compatible numbers* strategy involves more complex rounding. *Special numbers* strategy is one that overlaps several strategies. For the most part, primary children will be using only the noncomputational and the front-end strategies. The important point is that children begin early to realize that mathematics is not just finding the one right answer but can also involve making good guesses or estimates.

Summary

This unit has described six steps that provide a guide for what to teach and how to teach it. Following these steps can minimize guesswork. The steps are (1) assess, (2) choose objectives, (3) plan experiences, (4) select materials, (5) teach, and (6) evaluate.

Problem solving and inquiry are processes that underlie all instruction in mathematics and science. Problem solving is first on the list of mathematics processes as developed by the National Council of Teachers of Mathematics. Inquiry is the focus promoted by the National Science Teachers Association. Problem solving and inquiry emphasize the process rather than the final product (or correct answer). The important factor is that during the early childhood years, children gradually learn a variety of problem-solving strategies and when and where to apply them. For young children, problems develop out of their everyday naturalistic activities. It is critical that children have opportunities to solve many nonroutine math problems, that is, problems that are not just simple and straightforward with obvious answers, but those that will stretch their minds. It is also important that they are afforded the opportunity to investigate science problems in areas of interest. Both assessment and evaluation should focus on the process rather than the answers. Both observation and interview techniques may be used.

Problem-solving instruction for young children begins with their natural explorations in the environment. It requires time and careful guidance as teachers move from teacher-initiated to child-initiated problems.

KEY TERMS

problem solving	plan experiences	routine problems
inquiry	select materials	nonroutine problems
assess	teach	heuristics
choose objectives	evaluate	contrived problems

SUGGESTED ACTIVITIES

1. Interview two teachers who teach prekindergarten, kindergarten, and/or primary. Have them describe their mathematics and science programs. Find out how they address each of the steps in teaching described in this unit.

2. Observe in a prekindergarten, kindergarten, or primary classroom. Write a description of the math and science activities/experiences observed. Could you fit what you observed into the steps described in the text? How?

3. Start a section on problem solving in your Activity File. As you progress through the text, look through the units that involve problem solving. If you find some routine problems, rewrite them as nonroutine problems. Look through other resources for additional problem ideas. Write some problems of your own. Look through your favorite science and social studies units and develop some problems that fit the unit themes.

4. Look through the problem-solving activities in a kindergarten, first-, second-, or third-grade mathematics textbook. Categorize the problems as *routine* or *nonroutine*. Report your findings to the class.

5. Select or create three nonroutine math problems. Have the students in the class try to solve them. Have them write a description of the steps they take and the strategies they use. Have them compare their strategies with those described in the unit and with each other.

6. Try some estimation activities with four-, five , six-, seven-, and/or eight-year-olds.

REVIEW

A. List in order the six steps for instruction described in this unit.

B. Define each of the steps listed in A.

C. Read each of the following descriptions and label them with the correct step name:

1. From her Activity File, the teacher selects two cards from the Classification section.

2. Mrs. Brown has just interviewed Joey and discovered that he can count accurately through 12. He then continues, "15, 14, 19, 20." She thinks about what the next step in instruction should be for Joey.

3. The teacher is seated at the table with Fwang. "Fwang, you put three red teddy bears and two blue teddy bears together in one group. Then you wrote, 3 + 2 = 5. Explain to me how you figured out how to solve the problem."

4. During the first month of school, Mrs. Garcia interviews each of her students individually to find out which concepts and skills they know.

5. Mr. Black has set up the sand table, and the children are using standard-size measuring cups to pour and measure sand to learn the relationship between the different size cups.

6. Katherine needs to work on A-B-A-B type patterns. Her teacher pulls out three cards from the Pattern section of her Activity File.

7. Mr. Wang looks through the library of computer software for programs that require logical thinking strategies.

D. Describe the advantages of following the instructional steps suggested in this unit.

E. Read the description of Miss Conway's method of selecting objectives and activities. Analyze and evaluate her approach.

> Miss Conway believes that all her students are at about the same level in their mathematics and science capabilities and knowledge. She has a math and science program that she has used for 15 years and that she believes is satisfactory. She assumes that all students enter her class at the same level and leave knowing everything she has taught.

F. Write an *R* for routine problems and an *N* for nonroutine problems.

___ 1. Larry has four pennies, and his dad gave him five more pennies. How many pennies does Larry have now?

___ 2. Nancy's mother has five cookies. She wants to give Nancy and her friend Jody the same number of cookies. How many cookies will each girl receive?

___ 3. Larry has four small racing cars. He gives one to his friend Fred. How many does he have left?

___ 4. Nancy has three dolls. Jody has six. How many more dolls does Jody have?

___ 5. Tom and Tasha each get part of a candy bar. Does one get more candy? If so, which one?

G. Explain what a heuristic is.

H. Put an X by the statements that are correct.

___ 1. If children have the heuristics mastered, mastery of the content is not important.

___ 2. Good and poor problem solvers have about the same heuristic skills.

___ 3. Expert problem solvers are skilled at thinking about thinking. They can assess the situation, decide what is being asked, organize a plan, carry out the plan, and verify the results in an organized fashion.

___ 4. Most textbooks today include plenty of nonroutine problems to solve.

___ 5. Having children work in small groups to solve problems is the most productive instructional approach.

___ 6. If a child has to explain a problem to someone else, it will clarify the problem for him.

I. List three techniques that can be used to assess children's problem-solving skills.

J. Critique the following instructional situation:

> "We are going to do some more math problems today. I will pass out the problems to you. You will have 15 minutes to complete them. Do not talk to your neighbors. Follow the steps on the board." The following steps are listed on the board:

> 1. Understand   3. Follow the plan
> 2. Plan   4. Check

There are no manipulatives in evidence, and there is no room on the paper for drawing pictures or diagrams.

K. List the five processes that are included in the mathematics standards.

L. In the third grade math center there are two glass jars filled with marbles. One jar is tall and thin. The other jar is short and fat. There are some three-by-five-inch cards and a shoebox next to the jars. There is a sign that reads

---

TODAY'S ESTIMATION EXERCISE

Remember, don't count!

How many marbles are in the BIG jar?

How many marbles are in the SMALL jar?

Does one jar have more, or do they both have the same amount?

On a card write:

1. Your name

2. Number of marbles in the BIG jar

3. Number of marbles in the SMALL jar

4. Put your card in the shoebox.

Evaluate this activity. How would you follow up on the information collected?

REFERENCES

Burns, M. (1998, January/February). Math in action. Raccoon math: A story for numerical reasoning. *Instructor*, 86–88.

National Council of Teachers of Mathematics. (2000). *Principles and standards for school mathematics.* Reston, VA: Author. (http://www.nctm.org)

Reys, R. E., Lindquist, M. M., Lambdin, D. V., Smith, N. L., & Suydam, M. N. (2001). *Helping children learn mathematics.* New York: John Wiley.

Skinner, P. (1990). *What's your problem?* Portsmouth, NH: Heinemann.

FURTHER READING AND RESOURCES

Artzt, A. F., & Newman, C. M. (1990). *How to use cooperative learning in the mathematics class.* Reston, VA: National Council of Teachers of Mathematics.

Assessing learning in preschool and primary programs. (1993). *Young Children, 48*(5, Special Section), 20–47.

Baker, A., & Baker, J. (1991). *Counting on a small planet.* Portsmouth, NH: Heinemann.

Baroody, A. J., & Wilkins, J. L. M. (1999). The development of informal counting, number, and arithmetic skills and concepts. In J. V. Coplcy (Ed.), *Mathematics in the early years* (pp. 48–65). Reston, VA: National Council of Teachers of Mathematics and Washington, DC: National Association for the Education of Young Children.

Bird, E. (1999). What's in the box? A problem-solving lesson and a discussion about teaching. *Teaching Children Mathematics, 5,* 504–507.

Blake, S., Hurley, S., & Arenz, B. (1995). Mathematical problem solving and young children. *Early Childhood Education Journal, 23*(2), 81–84.

Frakes, C., & Kline, K. (2000). Early childhood corner. Teaching young mathematicians: The challenges and rewards. *Teaching Children Mathematics, 6,* 376–381.

Ginsburg, H. P., Inoue, N., & Seo, K. (1999). Young children doing mathematics (pp. 88–99). In J. V. Copley (Ed.), *Mathematics in the early years* (pp. 48–65). Reston, VA: National Council of Teachers of Mathematics and Washington, DC: National Association for the Education of Young Children.

Greenberg, P. (1993). How and why to teach all aspects of preschool and kindergarten math naturally, democratically, and effectively (For teachers who don't believe in academic programs, Who do believe in education excellence, and Who find math boring to the max)—Part I. *Young Children, 48*(4), 75–84.

Greenes, C. (1999). Ready to learn: Developing young children's mathematical powers (pp. 39–47). In J. V. Copley (Ed.), *Mathematics in the early years* (pp. 48–65). Reston, VA: National Council of Teachers of Mathematics and Washington, DC: National Association for the Education of Young Children.

Hankes, J. E. (1996). An alternative to basic-skills remediation. *Teaching Children Mathematics, 2*(8), 452–458.

Hembree, R., & Marsh, H. (1992). Problem solving in early childhood: Building foundations. In R. J. Jensen (Ed.), *Research ideas for the classroom: Early childhood mathematics* (pp. 151–170). New York: Macmillan.

Hiebert, J., Carpenter, T. P., Fennema, E., Fuson, K., Human, P., Murray, H., Olivier, A., & Wearne, D. (1996). Problem solving as a basis for reform in curriculum and instruction: The case of mathematics. *Educational Researcher, 25*(4), 12–21.

Kamii, C., & Houseman, L. B. (1999). *Children reinvent arithmetic* (2nd ed.). New York: Teachers College.

Lind, K. K. (1999). Science in early childhood: Developing and acquiring fundamental concepts and skills. In *Dialogue on early childhood sciences, mathematics, and technology education.* Washington, DC: American Association for the Advancement of Science.

Martens, M. L. (1999). Productive questions: Tools for supporting constructivist learning. *Science and Children, 36*, 24–27, 53–54.

Menon, R. (1996). Mathematical communication through student-constructed questions. *Teaching Children Mathematics, 2*(9), 530–532.

Methany, D. (2001). Consumer investigations: What is the "best" chip? *Teaching Children Mathematics, 7*, 418–420.

Mewborn, D. S., & Huberty, P. E. (1999). Questioning your way to the standards. *Science and Children, 6*, 226–227, 243–246.

Myren, C. L. (1996). Encouraging young children to solve problems independently. *Teaching Children Mathematics, 3*(2), 72–76.

Olson, M. (1998). Problem solvers: Responses to the "Decoration delight" problem. *Teaching Children Mathematics, 5*, 243–245.

Perlmutter, J. C., Bloom, L., & Burrell, L. (1993). Whole math through investigations. *Childhood Education, 70*(1), 20–24.

Richardson, K. (1984). *Developing number concepts using Unifix Cubes*. Menlo Park, CA: Addison-Wesley.

Richardson, K. (1999). *Developing number concepts: Planning guide*. White Plains, NY: Dale Seymour.

Richardson, K. (1999). *Developing number concepts: Counting, comparing and pattern*. White Plains, NY: Dale Seymour.

Richardson, K. (1999). *Developing number concepts: Addition and subtraction*. White Plains, NY: Dale Seymour.

Richardson, K. (1999). *Developing number concepts: Place value, multiplication and division*. White Plains, NY: Dale Seymour.

Schwartz, S. (1995). Authentic mathematics in the classroom. *Teaching Children Mathematics, 1*(9), 580–584.

Steffe, L. P. (Ed.). (1994). Special issue: Mathematical learning in computer microworlds. *Journal of Research in Early Childhood Education, 8*(2).

Stiff, L. V. (Ed.). (1999). *Developing mathematical reasoning in grades K–12*. Reston, VA: National Council of Teachers of Mathematics.

Stofac, V. J., & Wesley, A. (1987). *Logic problems for primary people* (Books 1–3). Sunnyvale, CA: Creative Publications.

Warfield, J. (2001). Teaching kindergarten children to solve word problems. *Early Childhood Education Journal, 28*, 161–167.

White, W. (2001). *C* is for change. *Science and Children, 38*, 35–39.

Williams, C. V., & Kamii, C. (1986). How do children learn by handling objects? *Young Children, 42*(1), 23–26.

UNIT 4
Assessing the Child's Developmental Level

OBJECTIVES

After reading this unit, you should be able to:

◆ Explain the National Council of Teachers of Mathematics' basic assessment standards.

◆ Explain how to find the child's level of concept development.

◆ Explain the value of commercial assessment instruments for concept assessment.

◆ Make a developmental assessment task file.

◆ Be able to assess the concept development level of young children.

◆ Understand how to record, report, and evaluate using naturalistic/performance-based assessment.

◆ Explain the advantages of portfolio assessment.

Children's levels of concept development are determined by seeing which concept tasks they are able to perform independently. The first question in teaching is "Where is the child now?" To find the answer to this question, the teacher assesses. The teacher gives the child tasks to complete and problems to solve (such as those described in Unit 3). She observes what the child does as he solves the problems and records the answers he gives. This information is used to guide the next steps in teaching. The long-term objective for young children is to be sure that they have a strong foundation in basic concepts that will take them through the transition into the concrete operational stage when they begin to deal seriously with abstract symbols in math and independent investigations in

science. Following the methods and sequence in this text helps reach this goal and at the same time achieves some further objectives.

◆ Builds a positive feeling in the child toward math and science

◆ Builds confidence in the child that he can do math and science activities

◆ Builds a questioning attitude in response to his curiosity regarding math and science problems

The National Council of Teachers of Mathematics' (NCTM) Assessment Principle (2000, p. 22) states that "Assessment should support the learning of important mathematics and furnish useful information to both teachers and students." It should be an integral part of instruction, not just something done to students at the end of instruction. Assessment should include the following elements.

◆ Assessment should enhance children's learning by being a part of everyday instruction.
◆ Assessment tasks that are similar to or the same as the instructional tasks can indicate to students exactly what they should be able to know and do.
◆ Student communication skills can be enhanced when assessment involves observations, conversations, interviews, oral reports, and journals.
◆ Evaluation guides (or **rubrics**) can clarify for the students exactly what their strengths and weaknesses are and enable their self-assessment.

Assessment should be integrated into everyday activities so it is not an interruption but a part of the instructional routine. Assessment should provide both teacher and student with valuable information. There should not be overreliance on formal paper and pencil tests, but information should be gathered from a variety of sources. "Many assessment techniques can be used by mathematics teachers, including open-ended questions, constructed-response tasks, selected response items, performance tasks, observations, conversations, journals and portfolios" (p. 23). In this text the focus is on observations, interviews, and portfolios of children's work, which may include problem solutions, journal entries, results of conversations, and others. It is also important to take heed of the equity principle and diversify assessment approaches to meet the needs of diverse learners such as English language learners, gifted students, and students with learning disabilities.

NCTM (1995) also advocates decreased attention to a number of traditional assessment elements.

◆ Assessing what students do not know, comparing them with other students, and/or using assessments to track students relative to apparent capability
◆ Having assessment be simply counting correct answers on tests for the sole purpose of assigning grades

◆ Focusing on assessment of students' knowledge of only specific facts and isolated skills
◆ Using exercises or word problems requiring only one or two skills
◆ Excluding calculators, computers, and manipulatives from the assessment process
◆ Evaluating teacher success only on the basis of test scores

NCTM (1989) has this to say about the assessment of young children: "methods should consider the characteristics of the students themselves. . . . At this stage, when children's understanding is often closely tied to the use of physical materials assessment tasks that allow them to use such materials are better indicators of learning" (p. 202).

Assessment Methods

Observation and interview are assessment methods the teacher uses to determine the child's level of development. Examples of both of these methods were included in Unit 3. More are provided in this unit. Assessment is appropriately done through observations and interviews using teacher-developed assessment tasks. Commercial instruments used for initial screening may also supply useful information but are limited in scope for the everyday assessment needed for planning. Initial screening instruments usually cover a broad range of areas and provide a profile that indicates overall strengths and weaknesses. These strengths and weaknesses can be looked at in more depth by the classroom teacher for information needed to make normal instructional decisions or by a diagnostic specialist (i.e., school psychologist or speech and language therapist) where an initial screening indicates some serious developmental problem. Individually administered screening instruments should be the only type used with young children. Child responses should require the use of concrete materials and/or pictures, verbal answers, or motoric responses such as pointing or rearranging some objects. Paper and pencil should be used only for assessment of perceptual motor development (i.e., tasks such as name writing, drawing a person, or copying shapes).

Booklet-type paper and pencil tests administered to groups or individuals are inappropriate until children are well into concrete operations, can deal with abstract symbols, and have well-developed perceptual motor skills.

Observational Assessment

Observation is used to find out how children use concepts during their daily activities. Observation can be done during naturalistic, informal, and structured activities. The teacher has in mind the concepts the children should be using. Whenever she sees a concept reflected in a child's activity, she writes down the incident and places it in the child's record folder. This helps her plan future experiences.

Throughout this book, suggestions are made for behaviors that should be observed. The following are examples of behaviors as the teacher would write them down for the child's folder.

- Brad (18 months old) dumped all the shape blocks on the rug. He picked out all the circles and stacked them up. Shows he can sort and organize.
- Cindy (four years old) carefully set the table for lunch all by herself. She remembered everything. Cindy understands one-to-one correspondence.
- Chris (three years old) and George (five years old) stood back to back and asked Cindy to check who was taller. Good cooperation—it is the first time Chris has shown an interest in comparing heights.
- Mary (five years old), working on her own, put the right number of sticks in juice cans marked with the number symbols 0 through 20. She is ready for something more challenging.
- Last week I set out a tub of water and a variety of containers of different sizes in the mathematics and science center. The children spent the week exploring the materials. Trang Fung and Sara seemed especially interested in comparing the amount of liquid that could be held by each container. I gave each of them a standard one-cup measure and asked them to estimate how many cups of water would fill each container.

Then I left it up to them to measure and record the actual amounts. They did a beautiful job of setting up a recording sheet and working together to measure the number of cups of water each container would hold. They then lined up the containers from largest to smallest volume, which demonstrated their understanding of ordering or seriation.

- Today I read Derrick's (second grader) math journal. Yesterday's entry included a chart showing the names and amounts of each type of baseball card in his collection. He also wrote his conclusions as to which players and teams were his favorites as evidenced by the number of cards. Derrick is skilled at organizing data and drawing conclusions and understands the concepts of more and less.
- Ann and Jason (eight-year-olds) argue about which materials will float and sink. They asked their teacher if they could test their theories. They got the water, collected some objects, and set up a chart to record their predictions and then the names of the items that sink and those that float. This demonstrates understanding of how to develop an investigation to solve a problem.

Observational information may also be recorded on a **checklist**. For example, concepts can be listed, and each time the child is observed demonstrating one of the behaviors the date can be put next to that behavior. Soon there will be a profile of the concepts the child demonstrates spontaneously (Figure 4–1).

Interview Assessment

The individual interview is used to find out specific information in a direct way. The teacher can present a task to the child and observe and record the way the child works on the task and the solution she arrives at for the problem presented by the task. The rightness and wrongness of the answer are not as important as how the child arrives at the answer. Often a child starts out on the right track but gets off somewhere in the middle of the problem. For example, Kate (age three) is asked to match four saucers with four cups. This is an example of one-to-one correspondence. She does

CONCEPT ACTIVITY OBSERVATION CHECKLIST

Child's Name _____ Birth Date _____

School Year _____ Grade/Group _____

Concept Activities *(Concepts and activities are described in the text)*	Dates Observed
Selects math center	
Selects science center	
Selects cooking center	
Selects math concept book	
Selects science book	
Selects sand or water	
Sets the table correctly	
Counts spontaneously	
Sorts play materials into logical groups	
Uses comparison words (i.e., *bigger, fatter,* etc.)	
Builds with blocks	
Works with part/whole materials	
Demonstrates an understanding of order and sequence	
Points out number symbols in the environment	
Demonstrates curiosity by asking questions, exploring the environment, and making observations	
Uses concept words	

FIGURE 4–1 Concept observation checklist.

this task easily. Next she is asked to match five cups with six saucers, "Here are some cups and saucers. Find out if there is a cup for every saucer." She puts a cup on each saucer. Left with an extra saucer, she places it under one of the pairs. She smiles happily. By observing the whole task, the teacher can see that Kate does not feel comfortable with the concept of "one more than." This is normal for a preoperational three-year-old. She finds a way to do away with the problem by putting two saucers under one cup. She understands the idea of matching one to one but cannot have things out of balance. Only by observing the whole task can the teacher see the reason for what appears to be a "wrong" answer to the task.

For another example, Tim, age six, has been given access to 20 Unifix Cubes,® 10 red and 10 blue. His teacher asks him to count the red cubes and then the blue cubes, which he does with care and accuracy. Next, she asks him to see how many combinations of 10 he can make using the red cubes and the blue cubes. To demonstrate she counts out nine blue cubes and adds one red cube to her group to make 10. She tells him to write and/or draw each combination that he finds. His teacher watches as he counts out eight blue cubes and two red cubes. He then draws on his paper seven blue squares and two red squares.

Finally, in the second-grade class, Theresa's teacher notices that Theresa is not very accurate in her work. The class is working on two-digit addition and subtraction with no regrouping, and Theresa's teacher is concerned that Theresa will be totally lost when they move on to regrouping. He decides to assess her process skills by having her show him with Unifix Cubes® how she perceives the problems. For $22 + 31$ she takes 22 cubes and 31 cubes and makes a pile of 53. For $45 - 24$ she takes a pile of 45 and adds 24 more cubes. Her teacher realizes that Theresa is not attentive to the signs for plus and minus. He also decides she needs to work on place value and grouping by 10s and ones.

If Kate's, Tim's, and Theresa's answers were observed only at the endpoint and recorded as right or wrong, the crux of their problems would be missed. Only the individual interview offers the opportunity to observe a child solve a problem from start to finish without distractions or interruptions.

An important factor in the one-to-one interview is that it must be done in an accepting manner by the adult. She must value and accept the child's answers whether they are right or wrong from the adult point of view. If possible, the interview should be done in a quiet place where there are no other things that might take the child's attention off the task. The adult should be warm, pleasant, and calm. Let the child know that he is doing well with smiles, gestures (nods of approval, a pat on the shoulder), and specific praise ("You are very careful when you count the cubes"; "I can see you know how to match shapes"; "You work hard until you find an answer"; and so on).

If people other than one of the teachers do the assessment interviews, the teacher should be sure that they spend time with the children before the interviews. Advise a person doing an interview to sit on a low chair or on the floor next to where the children are playing. Children are usually curious when they see a new person. One may ask, "Who are you? Why are you here?" The children can be told, "I am Ms. X. Someday I am going to give each of you a turn to do some special work with me. It will be a surprise. Today I want to see what you do in school and learn your names." If the interviewer pays attention to the children and shows an interest in them and their activities, they will feel comfortable and free to do their best when the day comes for their assessment interview.

If the teacher does the assessment herself, she also should stress the special nature of the activity for her and each child: "I'm going to spend some time today doing some special work with each of you. Everyone will get a turn."

Assessment Task File

Each child and each group of children is different. The teacher needs to have on hand questions to fit each age and stage she might meet in individual young children. She also needs to add new tasks as she discovers more about children and their development. A card file or loose-leaf notebook of assessment tasks should be set up. Such a file or notebook has three advantages.

◆ The teacher has a personal involvement in creating her own assessment tasks and is more likely to use them, understand them, and value them.

◆ The file card or loose-leaf notebook format makes it easy to add new tasks and revise or remove old ones.

◆ There is room for the teacher to use her own creativity to add new questions and make materials.

Use the tasks in each unit and in Appendix A to begin the file. Other tasks can be developed as the student proceeds through the units in this book and through her future career with young children. Directions for each task can be put on five-by-eight-inch plain white file cards. Most of the tasks will require the use of concrete materials and/or pictures. Concrete materials can be items found around the home and center. Pictures can be purchased or cut from magazines and readiness-type workbooks and glued on cards.

The basic materials needed are a five-by-eight-inch file card box, five-by-eight-inch unlined file cards, five-by-eight-inch file dividers or a loose-leaf notebook with dividers, a black pen, a set of colored markers, a ruler, scissors, glue, clear Contac® or laminating material, and preschool/kindergarten readiness workbooks with artwork.

In Appendix A each assessment task is set up as it would be on a five-by-eight-inch card. Note that on each card what the adult says to the child is always printed in CAPITAL LETTERS so the instructions can be found and read easily. The tasks are set up developmentally from the sensorimotor level (birth to age two) to the preoperational level (ages two to seven) to early concrete operations (ages six to eight). The ages are flexible relative to the stages and are given only to serve as a guide for selecting the first tasks to present to each child.

Each child is at his own level. If the first tasks are too hard, the interviewer should start at a lower level. If the first tasks are quite easy for the child, the interviewer should start at a higher level. Figure 4–2 is a sample recording sheet format that could be used to keep track of each child's progress. Some teachers prefer an individual sheet for each child; others prefer a master sheet for the whole class. The names and numbers of the tasks to be assessed are entered in the first column. Several columns are provided for entering the date and the level of progress (+, accomplished; √, needs some help; –, needs a lot of help) for children who need repeated periods of instruction. The column on the right is for comments on the process used by the child that might give some clues as to specific instructional needs.

Assessment Tasks

The assessment tasks included in each content unit and in Appendix A represent the concepts that must be acquired by young children from birth through the primary grades. Most of the tasks require an individual interview with the child. Some tasks are observational and require recording of activities during playtime or work time. The infant tasks and observations assess the development of the child's growing sensory and motor skills. As was discussed in Unit 1, these sensory and motor skills are basic to all later learning.

The assessment tasks are divided into nine developmental levels. *Levels one and two* are tasks for the child in the sensorimotor stage. *Levels three through five* include tasks of increasing difficulty for the prekindergarten child. The *Level six* tasks are those things that the child can usually do when he enters kindergarten between the ages of five and six. This is the level he is growing toward during his prekindergarten years. Some children will be able to accomplish all these tasks by age five; others not until six or over. *Level seven* summarizes the math words that are usually a part of the child's natural speech by age six. *Level eight* is included as an assessment for advanced prekindergartners and for children in centers that have a kindergarten program. The child about to enter first grade should be able to accomplish the tasks at *Level six* and *Level eight*. He should also be using most of the concept words correctly. *Level nine* includes tasks to be accomplished during the primary grades.

Example of an Individual Interview

The following is a part of the *Level five* assessment interview as given to Bob (four and one-half years old). A corner of the storage room has been made into

DEVELOPMENTAL TASKS RECORDING SHEET

Child's Name _____ Birth Date _____

School Year _____ School _____ Teacher _____

Grade/Group _____ Person Doing Assessment _____

Levels: +, accomplishes; √, partial; −, cannot do task

Task	Levels			Comments
	Date	Date	Date	

Comments:

FIGURE 4–2 Recording sheet for developmental tasks.

an assessment center. Mrs. Ramirez comes in with Bob. "You sit there, and I'll sit here, Bob. We have some important things to do." They both sit down at a low table, and Mrs. Ramirez begins.

An interview does not have to include any special number of tasks. For the preoperational child, the teacher can begin with matching and proceed through the ideas and skills one at a time so that each interview can be quite short if necessary.

If the person doing the interviewing has the time for longer sessions and the children are able to work for a longer period of time, the following can serve as suggested maximum amounts of time.

- Fifteen to 20 minutes for two-year-olds
- Thirty minutes for three-year-olds
- Forty-five minutes for four-year-olds
- Up to an hour with five-year-olds and older

Mrs. Ramirez:	Bob's Response:
HOW OLD ARE YOU?	"I'm four." (He holds up four fingers.)
COUNT TO 10 FOR ME, BOB. (Mrs. Ramirez nods her head up and down.)	"One, two, three, four, five, six, seven, eight, nine, 10 . . . I can go some more. Eleven, 12, 13, 20!"
HERE ARE SOME BLOCKS. HOW MANY ARE THERE? (She puts out 10 blocks.)	(He points, saying) "One, two, three, four, five, six, seven, eight, nine, 10, 11, 12." (He points to some more than once.)
GOOD, YOU COUNTED ALL THE BLOCKS, BOB. NOW COUNT THESE. (She puts out 5 blocks.)	(He counts, pushing each one he counts to the left.) "One, two, three, four, five."
(She puts the blocks out of sight and brings up five plastic horses and riders.) FIND OUT IF EACH RIDER HAS A HORSE.	(Bob looks over the horses and riders. He lines up the horses in a row and then puts a rider on each.) "Yes, there are enough."
FINE, YOU FOUND A RIDER FOR EACH HORSE, BOB. (She puts the riders and horses away. She takes out some inch cube blocks. She puts out two piles of blocks: five yellow and two orange.)	
DOES ONE GROUP HAVE MORE?	"Yes." (He points to the yellow.)
OKAY. (She puts out four blue and three green.)	
DOES ONE GROUP HAVE LESS?	(He points to the green blocks.)
GOOD THINKING.	
(She takes out five cutouts of bears of five different sizes.) FIND THE BIGGEST BEAR.	"Here it is." (He picks the biggest.)
FIND THE SMALLEST BEAR.	(He points to the smallest.)
PUT ALL THE BEARS IN A ROW FROM BIGGEST TO SMALLEST.	(Bobby works slowly and carefully.) "All done." (Two of the middle bears are reversed.)
(Mrs. Ramirez smiles.)	
GOOD FOR YOU, BOB. YOU'RE A HARD WORKER.	

Record Keeping and Reporting

The records of each child's progress and activities are kept in a **record folder** and a **portfolio**. The record folder contains anecdotal records and checklists, as already described. The portfolio is a purposeful collection of student work that tells the story of the student's efforts, progress, and achievements. It is a systematic collection of material designed to provide evidence of understanding and to monitor growth. Portfolios provide a vehicle for "authentic" assessment—that is, examples of student work done in many contexts. Students and teacher work together to gather work, reflect on it, and evaluate it.

The physical setup for portfolios is a critical place to begin. A box or file with hanging folders is a convenient place to begin. As work accumulates, it can be placed in the hanging folders. At regular intervals, teacher and child go through the hanging files and select work to place in the portfolio. An expanding legal-size file pocket makes a convenient portfolio container. It is important that each piece of work be dated so that growth can be tracked. Sticky notes or self-stick mailing labels can be used to write notations on each piece of work. Labels should include the date, the type of activity, and the reason for selecting each sample.

A critical attribute of a portfolio is that items are *selected* through regularly scheduled student/teacher conferences. Teachers have always kept folders of student work, but portfolios are more focused and contain specially selected work that can be used for assessment. A portfolio offers a fuller picture than traditional assessment does because it provides a vehicle for student reflection and self-evaluation.

Following are some examples of items that might be included in a portfolio.

◆ written or dictated descriptions of the results of investigations
◆ pictures: drawings, paintings, photographs of the child engaged in a significant activity; teacher or student sketches of products made with manipulatives or construction materials such as unit blocks, Unifix Cubes,® buttons, and so on
◆ dictated (from younger children) or written (from older children) reports of activities, investigations, experiences, ideas, plans, and so on
◆ diagrams, graphs, or other recorded data
◆ excerpts from students' math, science, and/or social studies journals
◆ samples of problem solutions, explanations of solutions, problems created, and so on

◆ videotapes and/or audio tapes
◆ journal entries

This material is invaluable for evaluation and for reporting progress to parents. When beginning portfolio assessment, it is wise to start small. Pick one focus such as mathematics or science or even a focus on one area such as problem solving, data from thematic investigations, artwork, writing, and so on. Beginning with a scope that is too broad can make the task overwhelming.

Evaluating a portfolio involves several steps. First, a *rubric* should be developed. A rubric is a list of general statements that define the attributes of the portfolio that should be evaluated, that is, a list of the qualities you believe are important. Rubrics should be developed based on what you are looking for in your class—not on isolated skills but on broad criteria that reflect understanding. The statements will vary with the content focus of the portfolio. Figure 4–3 provides a general format and sample statements. Next,

SAMPLE PORTFOLIO RUBRIC

	Strong, Well Established	Beginning to Appear	Not Yet Observed
1. Can organize and record data			
2. Explores, analyzes, looks for patterns			
3. Uses concrete materials or drawings to aid in solving problems			
4. Investigations and activities help develop concepts			
5. Persistent, flexible, self-directed			
6. Works cooperatively			
7. Enjoys math and science			

FIGURE 4–3   A general format for a rubric.

PORTFOLIO SUMMARY ANALYSIS

CHILD'S NAME _____ DATE _____

OVERALL EVALUATION

STRENGTHS AND WEAKNESSES

FURTHER RECOMMENDATIONS

FIGURE 4–4 Format for portfolio summary analysis.

---

a summary providing an overview should be written (Figure 4–4). If grades must be assigned, then there is a final step: the **holistic evaluation** (Figure 4–5). For a holistic evaluation, the portfolios are grouped into piles such as strong, average, and weak or very strong, strong, high average, low average, somewhat weak, and very weak based on the rubric and the summary. This comparative analysis can then guide grading. See

the reference list for publications that offer additional ideas regarding the development of portfolio assessment practices.

Summary

The focus of assessment in mathematics and science is on assessment integrated with instruction during naturalistic classroom activities and during activities that involve performance of concrete/ hands-on problem solving and child-directed investigations. The major ways to assess the developmental levels of young children are observation, interview, and the collection of materials in a portfolio. Observation is most useful when looking at how children use concepts in their everyday activities. The interview with one child at a time gives the teacher an opportunity to look at very specific ideas and skills.

Guidelines are given for doing an interview. There is a summary of the nine levels of developmental

---

SAMPLE OF HOLISTIC SCORING FORMAT

4   Strong on all the characteristics listed in the rubric.

3   Consistent evidence of the presence of most of the characteristics.

2   Some presence of the characteristics but incomplete communication or presence of ideas, concepts, and/or behaviors.

1   Little or no presence of desired characteristics.

FIGURE 4–5 Sample of a holistic scoring format.

tasks, which are included in Appendix A. A sample of part of an interview shows how the exchange between interviewer and child might progress.

A system for record keeping, reporting, and evaluation using a record folder and a portfolio are described. A holistic approach to evaluation is recommended.

KEY TERMS

assessment	checklist	portfolio
rubrics	record folder	holistic evaluation

SUGGESTED ACTIVITIES

1. Find out what the expectations are for mathematics concept development for students entering kindergarten and/or first grade in your local school system. Compare the school system list with the tasks suggested at *Levels six* and *seven* in the text and in Appendix A. What are the similarities and differences?
2. Get permission to assess the concept development level of two children at different age levels between four and eight. Make assessment cards and obtain materials needed to administer two or three of the tasks to each child. Compare your results and reactions with those of the other students in the class. Make a class list of improvements and suggestions.
3. Find a prekindergarten, kindergarten, or first-grade teacher who has an established portfolio assessment system. Invite the teacher to be a guest speaker in your class.
4. Find three articles in professional journals that discuss assessment/evaluation of young children. What were the main ideas presented? Explain how you will apply these ideas in the future.

REVIEW

A. Explain why it is important to make assessment the first step in teaching.
B. Describe the NCTM guidelines for assessment.
C. Describe the advantages of portfolio assessment.
D. Read incidents 1 and 2, which follow. What is being done in each situation? What should be done?
   1. Ms. Collins is interviewing a child in the school hallway. Other teachers and students are continuously passing by. The child frequently looks away from the materials to watch the people passing by.
   2. Mr. Garcia is interviewing Johnny. Mr. Garcia places five rectangle shapes on the table. Each is the same length but they vary in width.
   Mr. Garcia:
   WATCH WHAT I DO. (Mr. Garcia lines up the rectangles from widest to thinnest.) NOW I'LL MIX THEM UP. YOU PUT THEM IN A ROW FROM FATTEST TO THINNEST. (Mr. Garcia is looking ahead at the next set of instructions. He glances at Johnny with a rather serious expression.)
   Johnny's response:
   (Johnny picks out the fattest and thinnest rectangles. He places them next to each other. Then he examines the other three rectangles and lines them up in sequence next to the first two. He looks up at Mr. Garcia.)
   Mr. Garcia:
   ARE YOU FINISHED?
   Johnny's response:
   (Johnny nods his head yes.)
   Mr. Garcia:
   TOO BAD, YOU MIXED THEM UP.

REFERENCES

National Council of Teachers of Mathematics (NCTM). (1989). *Curriculum and evaluation standards for school mathematics.* Reston, VA: Author.

National Council of Teachers of Mathematics (NCTM). (1995). *Assessment standards for school mathematics.* Reston, VA: Author.

National Council of Teachers of Mathematics (NCTM). (2000). *Principles and standards for school mathematics.* Reston, VA: Author. (http://www.nctm.org)

FURTHER READING AND RESOURCES

Charlesworth, R., Fleege, P. O., & Weitman, C. (1994). Research on the effects of standardized testing on instruction: New directions for policy. *Early Education and Child Development, 5*, 195–212.

Chittenden, E., & Jones, J. (1999). Science assessment in early childhood programs. In *Dialogue on early childhood science, mathematics, and technology education.* Washington, DC: American Association for the Advancement of Science.

Copley, J. V. (1999). Assessing the mathematical understanding of the young child. In J. V. Copley (Ed.), *Mathematics in the early years* (pp. 182–188). Reston, VA: National Council of Teachers of Mathematics and Washington, DC: National Association for the Education of Young Children.

Culbertson, L. D., & Contreras, G. A. (1999). Assessment: Allowing traditional and alternative approaches to co-exist. In M. R. Jalongo (Ed.), *Resisting the pendulum swing* (pp. 49–60). Olney, MD: Association for Childhood Education International.

Garnett, C. M. (1992). One point of view: Testing—Do not disturb? A concerned parent's view of testing. *Arithmetic Teacher, 39*(6), 8–10.

Guha, S., & Doran, R. (1999). Playful activities for young children: Assessment tasks with low reading and writing demands for young children. *Science and Children, 37*(2), 36–40.

Kamii, C. (Ed.). (1990). *Achievement testing in the early grades: The games grown-ups play.* Washington, DC: National Association for the Education of Young Children.

Kamii, C., & Lewis, B. A. (1991). Achievement tests in primary mathematics: Perpetuating lower order thinking. *Arithmetic Teacher, 38*(9), 4–9.

Kohn, A. (2000). *The case against standardized testing: Raising the scores, ruining the schools.* Portsmouth, NH: Heinemann.

Kohn, A. (2001). Fighting the tests: Turning frustration into action. *Young Children, 56*(2), 19–24.

Lambdin, D. W., & Forseth, C. (1996). Seamless assessment/instruction = Good teaching. *Teaching Children Mathematics, 2*, 294–298.

Portfolio news. Published quarterly by Teacher Education Program, University of California at San Diego, 9500 Gilman Drive, La Jolla, CA 92093-0070.

Richardson, K. 1984. *Developing number concepts using Unifix Cubes.®* Menlo Park, CA: Addison-Wesley.

Robinson, G. E., & Bartlett, K. T. (1993). Assessment and evaluation of learning. In R. J. Jensen (Ed.), *Research ideas for the classroom: Early childhood mathematics.* New York: Macmillan.

Robinson, G. E., & Bartlett, K. T. (1995). Assessing mathematical learning. *Teaching Children Mathematics, 2*, 24–27.

Shepardson, D. P. (1997). Developing alternative assessments using the Benchmarks. *Science and Children, 35*(20), 34–40.

Shores, E. F., & Grace, C. (1998). *The portfolio book.* Beltsville, MD: Gryphon House.

St. Clair, J. (1993). Assessing mathematical understanding in a bilingual kindergarten. In N. L. Webb & A. F. Coxford (Eds.), *Assessment in the mathematics classroom, 1993 yearbook* (pp. 65–73). Reston, VA: National Council of Teachers of Mathematics.

Stearns, C., & Courtney, R. (2000). Designing assessments with the standards. *Science and Children, 37*(4), 51–55, 65.

Stenmark, J. K. (Ed.). (1991). *Mathematics assessment: Myths, models, good questions, and practical suggestions*. Reston, VA: National Council of Teachers of Mathematics.

Webb, N. L., & Coxford, A. F. (Eds.). (1993). *Assessment in the mathematics classroom*. Reston, VA: National Council of Teachers of Mathematics.

Wesson, K. A. (2001). The "Volvo effect"—Questioning standardized tests. *Young Children*, *56*(2), 16–18.

UNIT 5
The Basics of Science

OBJECTIVES

After reading this unit, you should be able to:

◆ Define the relative importance of science content, processes, and attitudes in teaching young children.

◆ Explain why science should be taught to young children.

◆ Identify the major areas of science instruction.

◆ List the science attitudes and process skills appropriate to preschool and primary grades.

◆ Select appropriate science topics for teaching science to young children.

Science and Why We Teach It to Young Children

When people think of science, they generally first think of the content of science. Science is often viewed as an encyclopedia of discoveries and technological achievements. Formal training in science classes often promotes this view by requiring memorization of seemingly endless science concepts. Science has been compiling literally millions of discoveries, facts, and data over thousands of years. We are now living in the age that is sometimes described as the "Knowledge Explosion." Consider the fact that the amount of scientific information created between the years 1900 and 1950 equals that which was learned from the beginning of recorded history until the year 1900. Since 1950 the rate of production of scientific information has increased even further. Some scientists estimate that the total amount of scientific information produced now doubles every two to five years.

If you tried to teach all that has been learned in science in preschool and continued daily straight through high school, you would make only a small dent in the body of knowledge. It is simply impossible to learn everything. Despite this, however, far too many teachers approach the task of teaching children science as if it were a body of information that anyone can memorize. The fact is that it is nearly impossible to predict what specific information taught to preschool and primary age students today will be of use to them as they pursue a career through the next century.

It is entirely possible that today's body of science knowledge will change before a child graduates from high school. Scientists are constantly looking at data in different ways and coming to new conclusions. Thus, it cannot be predicted with any certainty which facts will be the most important for students to learn for life in the 21st century. What is known is that people in the next century will have to face new problems that they will attempt to solve. Life, in a sense, is a series of problems. The people who are most successful in future decades will be those who are best equipped to solve the problems they encounter.

This discussion is intended to put the nature of science in perspective. Science in preschool through college should be viewed more as a verb than a noun. It is not so much a body of knowledge as it is a way of thinking and acting. Science is a way of trying to discover the nature of things. The attitudes and thinking skills that have moved science forward through the

centuries are the same attitudes and skills that enable individuals to solve the problems that they encounter in everyday life.

An approach to science teaching that emphasizes the development of thinking and the open-minded attitudes of science would seem to be most appropriate to the instruction of young children. It is also important for the exploration of science topics to be enjoyable. This supports a lifelong learning of science. This unit covers science processes, attitudes, content, and the importance of science in language arts and reading. In 1996 the National Research Council published the *National Science Education Standards*. The standards were designed to support the development of a scientific literate society. The content standards help identify what children at different ages and stages should know and be able to do in the area of science. The standards describe appropriate content for children in kindergarten through the fourth grade . They also identify the processes, skills, and attitudes needed to successfully understand science (Figure 5–1).

National Science Content Standards, Grades K–4

Unifying Concepts and Processes	Science as Inquiry	Physical Science	Life Science
Systems, order, and organization	Abilities necessary to do scientific inquiry	Properties of objects and materials	Characteristics of organisms
Evidence, models, and explanation	Understandings about scientific inquiry	Position and motion of objects	Life cycles of organisms
Change, constancy, and measurement		Light, heat, and electricity and magnetism	Organisms and environments
Evolution and equilibrium			
Form and function			

FIGURE 5–1 National Science Education Standards. Reproduced with permission from National Research Council (1996). *National Science Education Standards.* Washington, DC: National Academy Press.

continued

Earth and Space Science	Science and Technology	Science in Personal and Social Perspectives	History and the Nature of Science
Properties of earth materials	Abilities of technological design	Personal health	Science as a human endeavor
Objects in the sky	Understandings about science and technology	Characteristics and changes in populations	
Changes in earth and sky	Abilities to distinguish between natural objects and objects made by humans	Types of resources	
		Changes in environments	
		Science and technology in local challenges	

FIGURE 5–1 *continued*

Teaching the Processes of Inquiry

The *National Science Education Standards* emphasize that as a result of science investigations in the primary grades, all students should begin to develop the abilities necessary to do even more advanced scientific inquiry in later years. Children discover the content of science by using the processes of science inquiry. This can be done through science investigations, class discussions, reading and writing, and a variety of other teaching strategies. These are the thinking skills and processes necessary to learn science.

Science **process skills** are those that allow students to process new information through concrete experiences (Figure 5–2). They are also progressive, each building on and overlapping with one another. The skills most appropriate for preschool and primary students are the basic skills of **observing**, **comparing**, **classifying**, **measuring**, and **communicating**. Sharpening these skills is essential for coping with daily life as well as for future study in science and mathematics. As students move through the primary grades, mastery of these skills will enable them to perform intermedi-

ate process skills that include gathering and organizing information, **inferring**, and **predicting**. If students have a strong base of primary and intermediate process skills, they will be prepared by the time they reach the intermediate grades to apply those skills to the more sophisticated and abstract skills, such as forming **hypotheses** and separating **variables**, which are required in experimentation.

Grade level suggestions for introducing specific science process skills are given as a general guide for their appropriate use. Because students vary greatly in experience and intellectual development, you may find that your early childhood students are ready to explore higher-level process skills sooner. In such cases you should feel free to stretch their abilities by encouraging them to work with more advanced science process skills. For example, four- and five-year-olds can begin with simple versions of intermediate process skills, such as making a reasonable guess about a physical change (What will happen when the butter is heated?) as a first step toward predicting. They can gather and organize simple data (such as counting the days until the chicks hatch) and make simple graphs like those described in Unit 20 of this text. Giving preoperational

Science Process Skills

Basic Process Skills

1. *Observing.* Using the senses to gather information about objects or events.
2. *Comparing.* Looking at similarities and differences in real objects. In the primary grades, students begin to compare and contrast ideas, concepts, and objects.
3. *Classifying.* Grouping and sorting according to properties such as size, shape, color, use, and so on.
4. *Measuring.* Quantitative descriptions made by an observer either directly through observation or indirectly with a unit of measure.
5. *Communicating.* Communicating ideas, directions, and descriptions orally or in written form such as pictures, maps, graphs, or journals so others can understand what you mean.

Intermediate Process Skills

6. *Inferring.* Based on observations but suggests more meaning about a situation than can be directly observed. When children infer, they recognize patterns and expect these patterns to recur under similar circumstances.
7. *Predicting.* Making reasonable guesses or estimations based on observations and prior knowledge and experiences.

Advanced Process Skills

8. *Hypothesizing.* Devising a statement, based on observations, that can be tested by experiment. A typical form for a hypothesis is, "*If* water is put in the freezer overnight, *then* it freezes."
9. *Defining and controlling variables.* Determining which variables in an investigation should be studied or should be controlled to conduct a controlled experiment. For example, when we find out if a plant grows in the dark, we must also grow a plant in the light.

FIGURE 5–2 Science process skills.

Science Process Skills

Knowledge and concepts are developed through the use of the processes used in inquiry. It is with these processes and skills that individuals think through and study problems and begin to develop an understanding about scientific inquiry.

Observing

The most fundamental of the scientific thinking process is observation. It is only through this process that we are able to receive information about the world around us. The senses of sight, smell, sound, touch, and taste are the means by which our brains receive information and give us the ability to describe something. As young children use their senses in a firsthand exploratory way, they are using the same skills that scientists extend to construct meaning and knowledge in the world.

Sometimes we observe, but we do not always see very much. Teaching strategies that reinforce observation skills require children to observe carefully to note specific phenomena that they might ordinarily overlook. For example, when Mr. Wang's class observes an aquarium, he guides them by asking, "Which fish seems to spend the most time on the bottom of the tank? In what way do the fish seem to react to things like light or shadow or an object in their swimming path?"

Another way to enable children to observe instead of just looking is to incorporate dramatic play. Have the children construct "observation glasses" (Figure 5–3). These can be made using pipe cleaners for the earpieces and plastic rings that hold soft drink cans together.

The children are then told the glasses will let them see amazing things. Essentially, they will be able to see things they have never seen before.

Storybooks and informational books can also encourage the use of process skills. In the popular

children the opportunity to engage in inferring and predicting allows them to refine these skills. Teachers understand young children need repeated experiences in which to become proficient.

FIGURE 5–3 Observation glasses.

book *Bubbles* (1979), Bernie Zubrowski asks children to note the colors they see and to describe the different patterns that bubbles make when viewed from several angles.

Observation is the first step in gathering information to solve a problem. Students will need opportunities to observe size, shape, color, texture, and other observable properties in objects. The following teacher statements and questions facilitate the use of this process: "Tell me what you see," "What do you hear?," "What does this feel like?," and "How would you describe the object?"

Comparing

As children develop skills in observation, they will naturally begin to compare and contrast and identify similarities and differences. The comparing process, which sharpens their observation skills, is the first step toward classifying.

Teachers can encourage children to find likenesses and differences throughout the school day. A good example of this strategy can be seen when, after a walk through a field, Mrs. Red Fox asks her first graders, "Which seeds are sticking to your clothes?" and "How are these seeds alike?"

The comparing process builds upon the process of observing. In addition to observing the characteristics of an object such as a leaf, children learn more about the leaf by comparing it to other leaves. For example, a child finds a leaf and brings it to class to compare with other leaves in the leaf collection. Statements and questions that facilitate the comparing process include, "How are these alike?," "How are these different?," "Which of these is bigger, wetter, etc.?," and "Compare similarities and differences between these two animals." Begin by having children tell you about the characteristics of the objects. Next, have the children compare objects and discuss how and why they feel the objects are similar or different.

Classifying

Classifying begins when children group and sort real objects. The grouping and sorting are done based on the observations they make about the objects' characteristics. To *group*, children need to compare objects and develop subsets. A **subset** is a group that shares a

common characteristic unique to that group. For example, the jar may be full of buttons, but children are likely to begin grouping by sorting the buttons into subgroups of red buttons, yellow buttons, blue buttons, and other colors.

Mrs. Jones has her kindergarten children collect many kinds of leaves. They place individual leaves between two squares of wax paper. Mrs. Jones covers the wax paper squares with a piece of smooth cloth and presses the cloth firmly with a warm steam iron. The leaf is now sealed in and will remain preserved for the rest of the year.

Once the leaves are prepared, the children choose a leaf to examine, draw, and describe. They carefully observe and compare leaves to discover each leaf's unique characteristics. Then, the children classify the leaves into subgroups of common characteristics. Once the children have completed their classifications, have them explain how they made their decisions. The discussion generated will let the teacher gain insight into a child's thinking.

Children initially group by one property, such as sorting a collection of leaves by color, size, shape, and so on. As children grow older and advance in the classification process, objects or ideas are put together on the basis of two or more characteristics that are inherent in the items. Brown-colored animals with four legs, for example, can be grouped with all brown-colored animals, regardless of the number of legs, or they can be grouped with different-colored animals with four legs, or they can be classified with brown-colored animals with four legs. Scientists from all disciplines use organization processes to group and classify their work whether that work involves leaves, flowers, animals, rocks, liquids, or rockets. Statements and questions that facilitate this process include "Put together all of the animals that belong together," "Can you group them in another way?," "How are these animals organized?," and "Identify several ways that you used to classify these animals."

Measuring

Measuring is the skill of quantifying observations. This can involve numbers, distances, time, volumes, and temperature, which may or may not be quantified with standard units. Nonstandard units are involved when children say that they have used two "shakes" of salt while cooking or a "handful" of rice and a "couple" of beans when creating their collage.

Children can also invent units of measure. For example, when given beans to measure objects, Vanessa may say, "The book is 12 beans long," but Ann finds that the same book is 11 beans long. Activities such as this help children see a need for a standard unit of measure—like an inch. Questions that facilitate the measuring process include, "How might you measure this object?," "Which object do you think is heavier?," and "How could you find out?"

Communicating

All humans communicate in some way. Gestures, body postures and positions, facial expressions, vocal sounds, words, and pictures are some of the ways we communicate with each other and express feelings. It is through communication that scientists share their findings with the rest of the world.

In early childhood science explorations, communicating refers to the skill of describing a phenomenon. A child communicates ideas, directions, and descriptions orally or in written form, such as in pictures, dioramas, maps, graphs, journals, and reports. Communication requires that information be collected, arranged, and presented in a way that helps others understand your meaning.

Teachers encourage communication when they ask children to keep logs, draw diagrams or graphs, or otherwise record an experience they have observed. Children respond well to tasks such as recording daily weather by writing down the date, time of day, and drawing pictures of the weather that day. They will enjoy answering questions about their observations such as, "What was the temperature on Tuesday?," "Was the sun out on Wednesday?," "What did you see?," and "Draw a picture of what you see."

Inferring

When children *infer*, they make a series of observations, categorize them, then try to give them some meaning. An inference is arrived at indirectly (not directly, like a simple observation). For example, you look out the window and see the leaves moving on the trees. You infer that the wind is blowing. You have not experienced the wind directly, but based on your observations and prior knowledge and experience, you know that the wind is blowing. In this case, your inference can be tested simply by walking outside.

The process skill of inferring requires that a reasonable assumption of prior knowledge be present. It requires that children infer something that they have not yet seen because it has not happened or because it cannot be observed directly. For this reason, the inferring process is most appropriate for middle-level grades and the science content associated with those grades. However, science content and inferences associated with past experiences such as inferring what animals made a set of tracks, or the loss of water from plants, or the vapor in air can be appropriate for older primary children.

In another example, a teacher prepares four film canisters by filling them with different substances such as sand, chalk, stones, marbles, and paper clips. As the students observe the closed canisters, the teacher asks, "What do you think is inside of these canisters?," "What did you observe that makes you think that?," "Could there be anything else in the canister?," and "How could you find out?"

Predicting

When you predict, you are making a statement about what you expect to happen in the future. You make a reasonable guess or estimation based on observations of data. Keep in mind that this process is more than a simple guess. Children should have the prior knowledge necessary to make a reasonable prediction. Children enjoy simple prediction questions.

After reading *Science in a Vacant Lot* (1970), by Seymour Simon, children can count the number of seeds in a seed package and then predict how many of the seeds will grow into plants. As they prepare to keep a record of how two plants grow (one has been planted in topsoil; the other in subsoil), they are asked, "Which plant do you think will grow better?"

The ability and willingness to take a risk and form a prediction such as "If you race the metal car with the wooden car, the metal car will go faster" is of great importance in developing an awareness and understanding of cause and effect. This awareness can be developed and refined in many situations into the related skill of perceiving a pattern emerging and predicting accurately how it will continue. For example, if children are investigating changes in the shape of a piece of clay as more weight is added, they can be encouraged to look for patterns in their results, which can be recorded by drawing or measuring, and predict what each succeeding result will be. The more predictions children are able to make, the more accurate they become. Always ask children to explain how they arrived at their prediction. By listening to their reasoning you may find that children know more than you think.

Hypothesizing and Controlling Variables = Investigation

To be called an *experiment*, an investigation must contain a hypothesis and control variables. A *hypothesis* is a more formal operation than the investigative questions that young children explore in the preschool and primary grades. A hypothesis is a statement of a relationship that might exist between two variables. A typical form of a hypothesis is: if _____, then _____. With young children, a hypothesis can take the form of a question such as, "What happens if the magnet drops?"

In a formal experiment, variables are defined and controlled. Although experiments can be attempted with primary age children, experimental investigations are most appropriate in the middle and upper grades.

The question of "What is a hypothesis?" has probably caused more confusion than the other science processes. Hypotheses can be described as simply the tentative answers or untried solutions to the questions, puzzles, or problems that scientists are investigating. The major types of hypotheses are varied in character, but they correspond to the types of knowledge or understanding that the investigation aims to develop. Strategies for creating an environment that encourages investigation can be found in Unit 6.

Science as Inquiry

The *National Science Education Standards* emphasize Science as Inquiry, which is divided into abilities children need in order to do scientific inquiry and understandings they should have about scientific inquiry. Inquiry is presented as a step beyond process learning, such as observing, inferring, and predicting. In inquiry, the process skills are required, but students also must combine these skills with scientific knowledge as they use scientific reasoning and critical thinking to develop understanding. According to the standards, engaging students in inquiry serves five essential functions.

◆ It assists in the development of understanding of scientific concepts.
◆ It helps students "know how we know" in science.
◆ It develops an understanding of the nature of science.
◆ It develops the skills necessary to become independent inquirers about the natural world.
◆ It develops the dispositions to use the skills, abilities, and habits of mind associated with science.

Inquiry-oriented instruction, often contrasted with expository methods, reflects the constructivist model of learning and is often referred to as active learning. Osborne and Freyberg (1985) describe the constructivist model of learning as the result of ongoing changes in our mental frameworks as we attempt to make meaning out of our experiences. To develop scientific inquiry skills, kindergarten and primary age children should be able to do the following skills.

◆ Plan and conduct a simple investigation.
◆ Employ simple equipment and tools to gather data.
◆ Use data to construct reasonable explanations.
◆ Communicate the results of the investigations and give explanations.

Additional strategies that encourage students in the active search for knowledge are discussed in Unit 6.

Developing Scientific Attitudes

In some ways, attitudes toward a subject or activity can be as important as the subject itself. Some examples are: individuals who know that cigarette smoking may kill but continue to smoke or people who know that wearing a seat belt greatly improves their chances of surviving an accident and preventing injury but

Curiosity	Checking evidence
Withholding judgment	Positive approach to failure
Skepticism	Positive self-image
Objectivity	Willingness to change
Open-mindedness	Positive attitude toward change
Avoiding dogmatism	Avoiding superstitions
Avoiding gullibility	Integrity
Observing carefully	Humility
Making careful conclusions	

FIGURE 5–4 Scientific attitudes.

choose not to wear it. The same is true with scientific attitudes.

The scientific attitudes of **curiosity**, **skepticism**, positive self-image, and positive approach to failure are highlighted, and other relevant attitudes are listed in Figure 5–4.

Curiosity

Preschool and primary students are obviously not mentally developed to a point where they can think consciously about forming attitudes for systematically pursuing problems, but they can practice behaviors that will create lifelong habits that reflect scientific attitudes.

Curiosity is thought to be one of the most valuable attitudes that can be possessed by anyone. It takes a curious individual to look at something from a new perspective, question something long believed to be true, or look more carefully at an exception to the rule. This approach that is basic to science is natural to young children. They use all their senses and energies to find out about the world around them. Often, years of formalized experiences in school, which allow little time for exploration and questioning, squelch this valuable characteristic. Educational experiences that utilize firsthand inquiry experiences like the learning cycle make use of a child's natural curiosity rather than trying to suppress it.

Skepticism

Do you believe everything that you see? Are you skeptical about some things that you hear? Good! This attitude reflects the healthy skepticism required by both

science and the child's environment. Children need to be encouraged to question, wonder, ask "why," and be cautious about accepting things at face value. Experiences designed around direct observation of phenomena and gathering data naturally encourage children to explore new situations in an objective and open-minded fashion. This type of experience can do much toward developing confidence and a healthy skepticism.

Positive Approach to Failure and Self-Image

A positive approach to failure and a positive self-image are closely related attitudes. Students need the opportunity to ask their own questions and seek their own solutions to problems. At times this may mean that they will pursue dead ends, but often much more is learned in the pursuit than in the correct answer. If children are conditioned to look to adult authority figures to identify and solve problems, they will have a difficult time approaching new problems both as students and as adults.

In the last 20 years, some educators believed that children should not be allowed to experience failure. Educational situations were structured so that every child could be successful nearly all the time. It was reasoned that the experience of failure would discourage students from future study. In the field of science, however, it is as important to find out what does not work as it is to find out what does. In fact, real growth in science tends to happen when solutions do not fit what was predicted. Although students should not be constantly confronted with frustrating learning situations, a positive attitude toward failure may better serve them in developing problem-solving skills. After all, in much of science inquiry, there are no "right" or "wrong" answers.

The remaining science attitudes, *willingness to change*, *positive attitude toward change*, *withholding judgment*, *avoiding superstitions*, *integrity*, and *humility*, are additional important attitudes both to science and functioning as a successful adult. These can be encouraged in science teaching both through the teacher's exhibiting these behaviors and acknowledging students when they demonstrate them. All of these attitudes that support the enterprise of science are also quite valuable tools for young students in approaching life's inevitable problems.

Science and the Development of Literacy

An often-heard question is, "Why take time to teach science to young children?" Many teachers believe that they have too much to do in a day and they cannot afford to take the time to teach science. The answer to why science should be taught is, "You cannot afford *not* to teach science." Piaget's theory leaves no question as to the importance of learning through activity. The Council for Basic Education reports that there is impressive evidence that hands-on science programs aid in the development of language and reading skills. Some evidence indicates that achievement scores increase as a result of such programs. This statement is supported by many researchers. The following are possible explanations for this improvement:

In its early stages, literacy can be supported by giving children an opportunity to manipulate familiar and unfamiliar objects. During science experiences children use the thinking skills of science to match, discriminate, sequence, describe, and classify objects. These perceptual skills are among those needed for reading and writing (Figure 5–5). A child who is able to make fine discriminations between objects will be prepared to discriminate between letters and words of the alphabet. As children develop conventional reading and writing skills, they can apply their knowledge to facilitate their explorations in science by reading background material and recording hypotheses, observations, and interactions.

What better way to allow for children to develop communication skills than to participate in the "action plus talk" of science! Depending on the age level, children may want to communicate what they are doing to the teacher and other students. They may even start talking about themselves. Communication by talking, drawing, painting, modeling, constructing, drama, puppets, and writing should be encouraged. These are natural communication outcomes of hands-on science.

Reading and listening to stories about the world is difficult when you do not have a base of experience. If story time features a book about a hamster named Charlie, it might be difficult to understand what is happening if you have not seen a hamster. However, the communication gap is bridged if children have knowledge about small animals. Once a child has contact with the object represented by the written word, meaning can be developed. Words do not make a lot of sense when you do not have the background experience to understand what you read.

The relationship of language developed in the context of the direct experiences of science is explored in Unit 7 of this text. Ideas for working with experience charts, tactile sensations, listening, writing, and introducing words are included in curriculum integration.

Science also provides various opportunities to determine cause-and-effect relationships. A sense of self-esteem and control over their lives develops when children discover cause-and-effect relationships and when they learn to influence the outcome of events. For example, a child can experience a causal relationship by deciding whether to add plant cover to an

THINKING SKILLS USED DURING SCIENCE EXPERIENCES	THINKING SKILLS NEEDED FOR READING AND WRITING
Matching similar and logical characteristics	Comparing information and events
Discriminating physical observations and data	Discriminating letters and sounds
Sequencing procedures	Arranging ideas and following sequential events
Describing observations	Communicating ideas
Classifying objects	Distinguishing concepts

FIGURE 5–5 Science and reading connection.

aquarium. Predicting the most probable outcome of actions gives children a sense of control, which is identified by Mary Budd Rowe as "fate control." She found that problem-solving behaviors seem to differ according to how people rate on fate control measures. Children scoring high on these measures performed better at solving problems.

Keep in mind that the child who is academically advanced in math and reading is not always the first to solve a problem or assemble the most interesting collection. If sufficient time to work with materials is provided, children with poor language development may exhibit good reasoning. It is a mistake to correlate language skills with mental ability.

Appropriate Science Content

The science content for preschool and primary education is not greatly different from that of any other elementary grade level in that the depth and complexity of the science content and process skills are determined by the developmental level of the child. As already mentioned, the way that science is taught is probably far more important than the science content itself. The four main areas of science emphasis that are common in the primary grades are life science, health science, physical science, and earth and environmental science. Ideally, each of the four main areas should be given a balanced coverage. Appropriate science concepts for the early childhood years can be found throughout the text and specifically in the units dealing with science content.

Life Science

In life science, children in grades kindergarten through 4 are expected to develop an understanding of the characteristics of organisms, the life cycles of organisms, and organisms and environments. The observations and skills needed to gain an understanding of life science in the primary grades and beyond begin with the observations and investigative explorations of prekindergarten children.

Science teaching at this level is traditionally dominated by life science experiences. This is not because it is most appropriate but rather because of tradition. Teaching at early elementary grades has its roots in the nature study and garden school movements of the first half of the 20th century. Many programs and materials for young children concentrate much time on life science to the exclusion of other science content. This can be attributed to teachers seeking to take advantage of children's interest in what makes up their world. Although life science should not be the entire curriculum for young children, it can be an important part of the curriculum. Children are natural observers and enjoy finding out about the living world around them.

Life science investigations lend themselves quite readily to simple observations, explorations, and classifications. As with all science content at this level, hands-on experiences are essential to development of relevant concepts, skills, and attitudes. The areas of content typically covered with young children are plants, animals, and ecology. These experiences should build a foundation for students' understanding of environmental problems and solutions in higher grade levels and in adult life. Intelligent decision making regarding the interaction of science, technology, and the environment may well be a critical factor for survival in the next century. Examples of strategies for teaching appropriate life science content are found in Units 33, 34, 39, and 40.

Health Science

In the *National Science Education Standards* content standard of Science in Personal and Social Perspectives, children are expected to develop an understanding of personal health, characteristics and changes in populations, types of resources, changes in environments, and science and technology in local challenges. Refer to Units 36, 37, 38, 40, and 41 for additional strategies.

The study of health and the human body is receiving increased emphasis in elementary education. Recent concerns about problems of drug abuse, communicable diseases, and the relationship of nutrition and health have given rise to education in both factual information and refusal skills like "saying no." These learnings will help children take action to prevent the spread of disease, maintain a healthy body, and ask the types of questions that will ensure informed decisions.

Young children are curious about their bodies and are eager to learn more about themselves. They will enjoy exploring body parts and their relationships, body systems, foods, and nutrition. Misconceptions and worries that children have can be clarified by learning "all about me" in a variety of hands-on experiences.

Physical Science

In physical science, children in grades kindergarten through four are expected to develop an understanding of properties of objects and materials; position and motion of objects; and light, heat, electricity, and magnetism. Although prekindergarten children are not able to learn the science concepts at this level, they are able to learn the basic fundamental concepts and skills and gain the familiarity with materials needed to prepare them for higher-level thinking.

Young children enjoy pushing on levers, making bulbs light, working with magnets, using a string-and-can telephone, and changing matter. This is the study of physical science—forces, motion, energy, and machines. Teachers will enjoy watching a child assemble an assortment of blocks, wheels, and axles into a vehicle that really works. Physical science activities are guaranteed to make a child's face light up or ask, "How did you do that?"

Sometimes the content of this area is overlooked, which is unfortunate because physical science lends itself quite well to the needs of young children. One advantage of physical science activities is that they are more foolproof than many other activities. For example, if a young child is investigating the growth of plants, many things can go wrong that will destroy the investigation. Plants can die, get moldy, or take so long to give the desired effect that the children lose interest. Physical science usually "happens" more quickly. If something damages the investigation, it can always be repeated in a matter of minutes. Repeatability of activities is a significant advantage in developing a process orientation to science.

Keep in mind that children are growing up in a technological world. They interact daily with technology. It is likely that future lifestyles and job opportunities may depend on skills related to the realm of physical science.

Earth and Space Science

In earth and space science, students in kindergarten through grade four gain an understanding of properties of earth materials, objects in the sky, and changes in the earth and sky.

The study of earth science also allows many opportunities to help children develop process skills. Children are eager to learn about weather and how soil is formed. Air, land, water, rocks, and the sun, moon, and stars are all a part of earth science. Although these topics are attention grabbers, the teacher of young children must be certain to make the phenomena concrete for them to be effective. Hands-on experiences need not be difficult. Try making fossil cookies, weather and temperature charts, parachutes, and rock and cloud observations to teach a concept. Unit 36 gives a number of examples of how the earth sciences can be made appropriate for young children. Refer to Units 33, 34, 37, 39, and 40 for environmental education ideas.

Science and Technology Education

The content standard of Science and Technology focuses on establishing connections between the natural and designed worlds and providing opportunities for children to develop their decision-making skills. By the fourth grade, a child is expected to have gained the ability to distinguish between natural objects and objects made by humans, the ability of technological design, and a basic understanding about science and technology. Strategies for using science and technology education are integrated throughout the text and are emphasized in Units 36 and 40.

History and Nature of Science

In the *National Science Education Standards* content standard of History and Nature of Science, students are expected to develop an understanding of science as a human endeavor. When children are at an early age, teachers should begin to encourage their questions and investigations and when appropriate, offer experiences that involve investigating and thinking about explanations.

Fundamental concepts and principles that underlie this standard have been practiced by people for a long time.

◆ Men and women have made a variety of contributions throughout the history of science and technology.

◆ Although men and women using scientific inquiry have learned much about the objects, events, and phenomena in nature, much more remains to be understood. Science will never be finished.

◆ Many people choose science as a career and devote their entire lives to studying it. Many people derive great pleasure from doing science.

Summary

Our major goal in science education is to develop scientifically literate people who can think critically.

To teach science to tomorrow's citizens, process skills and attitudes must be established as major components of any science content lesson. Facts alone will not be sufficient for children who are born into a technological world. Children interact daily with science. Their toasters pop; their can openers whir; and their televisions, VCRs, and computers are commonplace. Preparation to live in a changing world as productive individuals should begin early in a child's life.

The manipulation of science materials, whether initiated by the child and/or the teacher, creates opportunities for language and literacy development. Hands-on experiences, which emphasize the process skills of science, are essential if the child is to receive the maximum benefits from science instruction. The intent of this book is to tell how to plan and teach these kinds of experiences for young children.

KEY TERMS

National Science Education Standards	measuring	variables
process skills	communicating	subset
observing	inferring	curiosity
comparing	predicting	skepticism
classifying	hypotheses	

SUGGESTED ACTIVITIES

1. The results of science are everywhere. Make a list of all of the science examples that you encountered on your way to class.

2. Recall a typical primary school-day from your past. What type of science activities were introduced? How were the experiences introduced? Compare your experience with that of a child in a classroom you have observed. What are the similarities and differences? Do technological advancements make a difference?

3. Examine the teacher's edition of a recent elementary science textbook at the primary grade level. What science attitudes are claimed to be taught in the text? Decide if there is evidence of these attitudes being taught in either the student or teacher edition of the text.

4. Interview teachers of preschool and primary children to find out what types of science activities they introduce to students. Is the science content balanced? Which activities include the exploration of materials? Record your observations for class discussion.

5. If you were to teach science to urban children, what type of activities would you provide? Apply the question to rural and suburban environments. Would you teach science differently? Why or why not?

6. Pick one of your favorite science topics. Plan how you would include process, attitude, and content.

7. Compare copies of the National Science Education Standards with state and local written expectations. What are the similarities and differences?

REVIEW

A. Discuss how the traditional view of science as a body of knowledge differs from a contemporary view of science as a process of inquiry.
B. How does the knowledge explosion affect the science that is taught to young children?
C. List process skills that should be introduced to all preschool and primary age students.

D. What is meant by the term *healthy skepticism?*
E. What are the four major areas of science content appropriate for early childhood education?
F. Why has health education received increased attention in early childhood education?

REFERENCES

Carter, G. S., & Simpson, R. D. (1989). Science and reading: A basic duo. *Science Teacher, 45*(3), 19–21.

National Research Council. (1996). *National Science Education Standards.* Washington, DC: National Academy Press.

Osborne, M., & Freyberg, P. (1985). *Learning science: Implications of children's knowledge.* Portsmouth, NH: Heinemann.

Simon, S. (1970). *Science in a vacant lot.* New York: Viking Press.

Zubrowski, B. (1979). *Bubbles.* Boston, MA: Little, Brown and Company.

FURTHER READING AND RESOURCES

Enger, S. K., & Yager, R. E. (2001). *Assessing student understanding in science.* Thousand Oaks, CA: Corwin Press.

Forman, G. E., & Hill, F. (1984). *Constructive play: Applying Piaget in the classroom.* Menlo Park, CA: Addison-Wesley.

Forman, G. E., & Kuschner, D. S. (1983). *The child's construction of knowledge.* Washington, DC: National Association for the Education of Young Children.

Harlan, J. (1991). *Science experiences for the early childhood years.* New York: Macmillan.

Harlan, W. (1995). *Teaching and learning primary science* (3rd ed.). London: Paul Chapman Publishing Ltd.

Howe, A. C., & Jones, L. (1993). *Engaging children in science.* New York: Macmillan.

Kamii, C., & Devries, R. (1993). *Physical knowledge in the classroom: Implications of Piaget's theory* (Rev. ed.). Englewood Cliffs, NJ: Prentice-Hall.

Kamii, C., & Lee-Katz, L. (1979). Physics in preschool education: A Piagetian approach. *Young Children, 34,* 4–9.

Lind, K. K. (1991). Science process skills: Preparing for the future. In *Professional handbook: The best of everything.* Morristown, NJ: Silver Burdett & Ginn.

Lind, K. K., & Milburn, M. J. (1988). Mechanized childhood. *Science and Children, 25*(5), 32–33.

Lowery, L. F. (1997). *NSTA pathways to the science standards.* Arlington, VA: National Science Teachers Association.

Mechling, K. R., & Oliver, D. L. (1983). *Science teaches basic skills.* Washington, DC: National Science Teachers Association.

National Science Resources Center. (1997). *Science for all children: A guide for improving elementary science education in your school district.* Washington, DC: National Academy Press.

Rowe, M. B. (1973). *Teaching science as continuous inquiry.* New York: McGraw-Hill.

Sunal, C. S. (1982). Philosophical bases for science and mathematics in early childhood education. *School, Science and Mathematics, 82*(1), 2–10.

Tipps, S. (1982). Making better guesses: A goal in early childhood science. *School Science and Mathematics, 82*(1), 29–37.

Wenham, M. (1995). *Understanding primary science*. London: Paul Chapman Publishing Ltd.

UNIT 6
How Young Scientists Use Concepts

OBJECTIVES

After reading this unit, you should be able to:

◆ Develop lessons using a variety of science process skills such as observing, comparing, measuring, classifying, and predicting.

◆ Apply problem-solving strategies to lessons designed for young students.

◆ Use data collecting and analysis as a basis for designing and teaching science lessons.

◆ Design experiences for young children that enrich their experience at the preoperational level and prepare them for the concrete operational level.

◆ Describe the process of self-regulation.

◆ Describe the proper use of a discrepant event in teaching science.

Concept Formation in Young Children

Young children try very hard to explain the world around them. Do any of the following statements sound familiar?

"Thunder is the sound of the angels bowling."

"Chickens lay eggs, and pigs lay bacon."

"Electricity comes from a switch on the wall."

"The sun follows me when I take a walk."

These are the magical statements of intuitive thinkers. These children use their senses or intuition to make judgments. Their logic is unpredictable, and they frequently prefer to use "magical explanations" to explain what is happening in their world. Clouds become the "smoke of angels," and rain falls because "it wants to help the farmers." These comments are typical of the self-centered view of intuitive children. They think that the sun rises in the morning just to shine on them. It never occurs to them that there may be another explanation. They also have a difficult time remembering more than one thing at a time.

Statements and abilities such as these inspired Jean Piaget's curiosity about young children's beliefs. His search for answers about how children think and learn has contributed to our understanding that learning is an internal process. In other words, it is the child who

"The sun follows me!"

FIGURE 6–1   Children have misconceptions.

brings meaning to the world and not vice versa. These misconceptions of a child are normal. This is what the child believes; thus, this is what is real to the child (Figure 6–1).

The temptation is to try to move children out of their magical stage of development. This is a mistake. Although some misconceptions can be corrected, others have to wait for more advanced thinking to develop. Students cannot be pushed, pulled, or dragged through developmental stages. Instead, the goal is to support the development of young children at their present level of operation. In this way, they have the richness of experiences to take with them when the next level of development naturally occurs.

Enhancing Awareness

When teaching concepts that are too abstract for children to fully understand, try to focus on aspects of the concept that can be understood. This type of awareness can be enhanced by the use of *visual depictions*, *observing*, *drawing*, and *discussion*.

Although some aspects of weather might remain a mystery, understanding can be developed by recording the types of weather that occur in a month. Construct a

large calendar, and put it on the wall. Every day, have a student draw a picture that represents the weather for the day. When the month is completed, cut the calendar into individual days. Then, glue the days that show similar weather in columns to create a bar graph. Ask the children to form conclusions about the month's weather from the graph. In this way, children can relate to weather patterns and visualize that these patterns change from day to day (Figure 6–2).

In a similar way, children will be better prepared for later studies of nutrition if they have some understanding of their own food intake. Graphing favorite foods is a way for children to visually compare and organize what they eat. On poster board make five columns and mount pictures from the basic food groups at the bottom of each column. Discuss which food group each child's favorite food belongs in. Have the children write their initials or attach a picture of themselves in the appropriate food column or draw a picture of their favorite food. Ask, "What do most of us like to eat?" Discuss healthy foods, and make a new chart at the end of the week. Is there a difference in choices? (Figure 6–3)

WEATHER RECORD

| Sunny | Rainy | Cloudy | Windy | Snowy | Foggy |

FIGURE 6–2   "How many cloudy days were there this month?"

FAVORITE FOODS

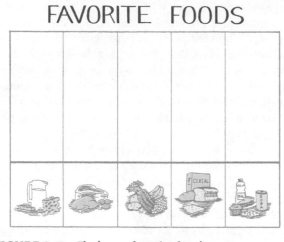

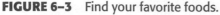

FIGURE 6–3 Find your favorite foods.

FIGURE 6–4 Children notice that the candles are not the same size.

To enhance awareness and to be effective, observations should be done in 10 minutes or less, conducted with a purpose, and brought together by discussions. Unconnected observations do not aid in concept formation. For example, if a purpose is not given for observing two flickering, different-sized candles, children will lose interest within minutes. Instead of telling children to "go look" at two burning candles, ask them to look and to find the difference between the candles. Children will become excited with the discovery that the candles are not the same size (Figure 6–4).

Discussions that follow observations heighten a child's awareness of that observation. A group of children observing a fish tank to see where the fish spends most of its time will be prepared to share what they saw in the tank. However, there may not be agreement.

Differences of opinion about observations stimulate interest and promote discussion. The children are likely to return to the tank to see for themselves what others say they saw. This would probably not happen without the focusing effect of discussion.

Drawing can provide excellent opportunities for observation and discussion. An effective use of drawing to enhance concept development would be to have children draw a tiger from memory before going to the zoo. Strategies like this usually reveal that more information is needed to construct an accurate picture. After visiting the zoo, have the children draw a tiger and compare it with the one drawn before the field trip. Discussion should focus on the similarities and differences between the two drawings. Children will be eager to observe details that they might not otherwise notice about the tigers in the zoo (Figure 6–5).

Teacher Magic and Misconceptions

Children need time to reflect and absorb ideas to fully understand a concept. Misconceptions can occur

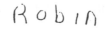

FIGURE 6–5 Robin's drawing of a tiger after a visit to the zoo.

at any stage. Be sure to give them plenty of time to manipulate and explore. For example, when a teacher mixes yellow and blue paints to create green, children might think the result is teacher magic. However, if given the paints and the opportunity to discover green, they might remember that yellow and blue mixed together make green. Because children cannot carry out most operations mentally, they need to manipulate materials to develop concepts. Teachers can enhance a child's understanding by making comments or asking questions that draw attention to a particular event. Using the above example, a teacher might ask, "Why do you think that happened?" or "How did you do that?"

Misconceptions can occur at any stage of development. Some children in the primary grades may be in a transitional stage or have moved into the concrete operation stage of development. Although these students will be able to do much logical thinking, the concepts they work with must still be tied to concrete objects that they can manipulate. Firsthand experiences with materials continue to be essential for learning.

The child in this developmental stage no longer looks at the world through "magical eyes." Explanations for natural events are influenced by other natural objects and events. For example, a child may now say, "The rain comes from the sky" rather than "It rains to help farmers." This linking of physical objects will first appear in the early concrete development stages. Do not be misled by an apparent new awareness. The major factor in concept development is still contingent upon children's need to manipulate, observe, discuss, and visually depict things to understand what is new and different about them. This is true in all of the Piagetian developmental stages discussed in this book.

Self-Regulation and Concept Attainment

Have you ever seen someone plunge a turkey skewer through a balloon? Did you expect the balloon to burst? What was your reaction when it stayed intact? Your curiosity was probably piqued—you wanted to know why the balloon did not burst. Actually, you had just witnessed a **discrepant event** and entered the process of **self-regulation**. This is when

your brain responds to interactions between you and your environment. Gallagher and Reid (1981) describe *self-regulation* as the active mental process of forming concepts. Knowing a little bit about how the brain functions in concept development will help in an explanation of this process. Visualize the human mind with thousands of concepts stored in various sections of the brain, rather like a complex system of mental pigeonholes, much like a postal sorting system or a drawer in a filing cabinet filled with individual file folders. As children move through the world and encounter new objects and phenomena, they assimilate and accommodate new information and store it in the correctly labeled mental category in their minds.

The brain, functioning like a postal worker, naturally classifies and stores information into the appropriate pigeonholes (Figure 6–6). New information is always stored close to all of the related information that has been previously stored. This grouping of closely related facts and phenomena related to a concept is called a **cognitive structure** or schema. In other words, all we know about the color red is stored

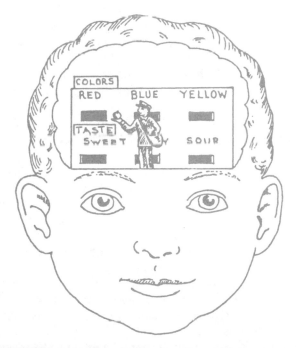

FIGURE 6–6 The brain functions like a postal worker.

in the same area of the brain. Our cognitive structure of red is developed further each time we have a color-related experience. The word *red* becomes a symbol for what we understand and perceive as the color red.

Our understanding of the world is imperfect because sooner or later, there is some point at which true understanding ends and misconceptions exist but go unquestioned. This is because incorrect interpretations of the world are stored alongside correct ones.

Continuing the postal worker analogy: If the information doesn't quite fit into an existing pigeonhole then another pigeonhole must be made.

A point can also be reached where new information conflicts with older information stored in a given cognitive structure. When children realize that they do not understand something they previously thought they understood, they are said to be in what Piaget calls a state of **disequilibrium**. This is where you were when the balloon did not behave as you expected. The balloon did not behave as you expected, and things no longer fit neatly together.

This is the *teachable moment*. When children are perplexed, their minds will not rest until they can find some way to make the new information fit. Because existing structures are inadequate to accommodate all of the existing information, they must continually modify or replace it with new cognitive structures. When in this state, children actively seek out additional information to create the new structure. They ask probing questions, observe closely, and inquire independently into the materials at hand. In this state, they are highly motivated and very receptive to learning. When children have had enough information to satisfy their curiosity and to create a new cognitive structure that explains most or all of the facts, they return to a state of **equilibrium**, where everything appears to fit together. As children move from disequilibrium to equilibrium, two mental activities take place. When confronted with something they do not understand, children fit it into a scheme, something they already know. If this does not work for them, they modify the scheme or make a new one. This is called **accommodation**. **Assimilation** and accommodation work together to help students learn concepts (Figure 6–7).

To make use of the process of self-regulation in your classroom, find out at what point your students misunderstand or are unfamiliar with the topic you are teaching. This will allow you to present information contrary to or beyond their existing cognitive structure and thus put them in a state of disequilibrium, where learning occurs.

Finding out what children know can be done in a number of ways. In addition to referring to the assessment units in this book, listen to children's responses to a lesson or question, or simply ask them to describe their understanding of a concept. For example, before teaching a lesson on animals, ask, "What does an animal look like?" You would be surprised at the number of young children who think that a life-form has to have legs to be considered an animal.

Discrepant Events

A *discrepant event* puts students in disequilibrium and prepares them for learning. They are curious and want to find out what is happening. It is recommended that you take advantage of the natural learning process to teach children what you want them to understand. The following scenes might give you some ideas for discrepant events to improve lessons you plan to teach.

◆ Mr. Wang's second-grade class is working on a unit on the senses. His students are aware of the function of the five senses, but they may not know that the sense of smell plays as large a role in appreciating food as the sense of taste. His students work in pairs with one child blindfolded. The blindfolded students are asked to pinch their noses shut and taste several foods such as bread, raw potatoes, or apples to see if they can identify them.

◆ Students switch roles and try the same investigation with various juices such as apple, orange, tomato, and so on. Most students cannot identify juices. Having experienced this discrepant event, the students will be more interested in finding out about the structures of the nose related to smell. They may be more motivated to conduct an investigation about how the appearance of food affects its taste.

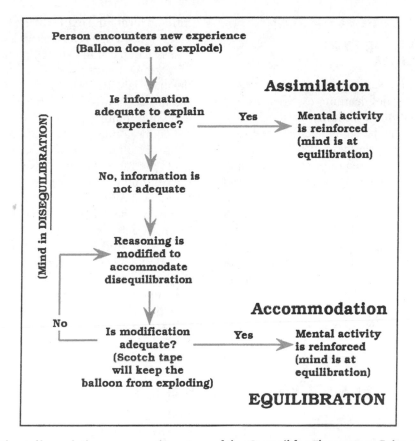

Person encounters new experience
(Balloon does not explode)

(Mind in <u>DISEQUILIBRATION</u>)

Is information
adequate to explain
experience?

Assimilation

Yes → Mental activity
is reinforced
(mind is at
equilibration)

No, information is
not adequate

Reasoning is
modified to
accommodate
disequilibration

No

Is modification
adequate?
(Scotch tape
will keep the
balloon from exploding)

Accommodation

Yes → Mental activity
is reinforced
(mind is at
equilibration)

EQUILIBRATION

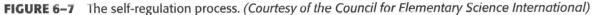

FIGURE 6–7   The self-regulation process. *(Courtesy of the Council for Elementary Science International)*

◆ Mrs. Fox fills two jars with water while her first-grade class watches. She fills one jar to the rim and leaves about an inch of space in the other jar. She puts a lid on each jar and places it on a tray in the school yard on a very cold winter day. Her students return later in the day and find that both have frozen, but the completely filled jar has burst. Students are eager to find out why.

◆ Kindergarten students Ann and Vanessa have been instructed to place two ice cubes in a glass and fill it to the brim with water. The ice cubes float on the water and extend about half an inch above the edge of the glass. Ms. Hebert asks them what will happen when the ice cubes melt. Vanessa thinks the water will overflow because there will be more water. Ann thinks the water

level will drop because the ice cubes will contract when they melt. They watch in puzzlement as they realize that the water level stays the same as the cubes melt (Figure 6–8).

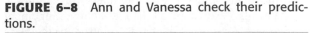

FIGURE 6–8   Ann and Vanessa check their predictions.

Using the Learning Cycle to Build Concepts

You can assist your students in creating new cognitive structures by designing learning experiences in a manner congruent with how children learn naturally. One popular approach is the application of the learning cycle. The learning cycle, described in Unit 1, is based upon the cycle of equilibration originally described by Piaget. The learning cycle, which is used extensively in elementary science education, combines aspects of naturalistic, informal, and structured activity methods—suggested elsewhere in this book—into a method of presenting a lesson.

As you have learned, the discrepant event is an effective device for motivating students and placing them in disequilibrium. The learning cycle can be a useful approach to learning for many of the same reasons. Learning begins with a period of free exploration. During the **exploration phase**, the children's prior knowledge can be assessed. Teachers can assess inquiry skills and gain clues to what the children know about a science concept as they explore the materials. Refer to the Strategies That Encourage Inquiry section in this unit for more information on assessing inquiry. Additionally, any misconceptions the children may have are often revealed during this phase. Exploration can be as simple as giving students the materials to be used in a day's activity at the beginning of a lesson so they can play with them for a few minutes. Minimal or no instructions should be given other than those related to safety, breaking the materials, or logistics in getting the materials. By letting students manipulate the materials, they will explore and very likely discover something they did not know before or something other than what they expected to happen. The following example "Making the Bulb Light" utilizes all three steps of the learning cycle.

MAKING THE BULB LIGHT

Exploration Phase

Mr. Wang placed a wire, a flashlight bulb, and a size D battery on a tray. Each group of three students was given a tray of materials and told to try to figure out a way to make the bulb light. As each group successfully lit the bulb, he asked them if they could find another arrangement of materials that would make the bulbs light. After about 10 minutes, most groups had found at least one way to light the bulb.

Concept Introduction Phase

After playing with the wires, batteries, and bulbs, Mr. Wang had the students bring their trays and form a circle on the floor. He asked the students if they had found out anything interesting about the materials. Jason showed the class one arrangement that worked to light the bulb. To introduce the class to the terms *open*, *closed*, and *short circuit*, Mr. Wang explained to the class that an arrangement that lights is called a closed circuit. Ann showed the class an arrangement that she thought would work but did not. Mr. Wang explained that this is an open circuit. Chad showed the class an arrangement that did not light the bulb but made the wire and battery very warm. Mr. Wang said this was a short circuit. Then he drew an example of each of the three types of circuit on the board and labeled them.

Concept Application Phase

Next, Mr. Wang showed the class a worksheet with drawings of various arrangements of batteries and bulbs. He asked the children to predict which arrangements would not light and form an open circuit; which would form a closed circuit by lighting; and which would heat up the battery and wire, forming a short circuit. After recording their predictions independently, the children returned to their small groups to test each of the arrangements. They recorded the actual answers beside their predictions (Figure 6–9).

After the students completed the task, Mr. Wang called them together. They discussed the results of their investigation, sharing which arrangements of batteries, wire, and bulbs they predicted correctly and incorrectly. Then Mr. Wang reviewed the terms learned during the lesson and asked the students to read a short section of their science text that talked about fire and electrical safety. The reading discussed the dangers of putting metal objects in wall sockets and fingers in light sockets and suggested precautions when flying kites near power lines.

After reading the section aloud, Mr. Wang asked the class if they could see any relationship between the reading and the day's activity. Chad responded that flying a kite into an electrical power line or sticking a dinner fork in a wall socket were similar to what he did when he created a short circuit with the battery and wire. Other students found similar relationships between the reading activity and their lives.

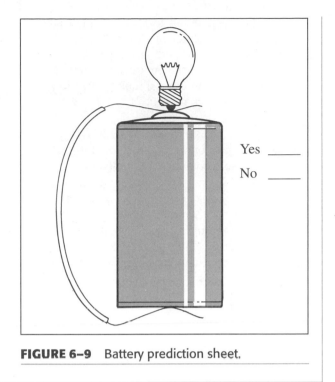

FIGURE 6–9   Battery prediction sheet.

In the preceding activity, you have seen a functioning model of the theory of cognitive development described by Piaget implemented in the classroom. The exploration phase invites assimilation and disequilibrium; the concept development phase provides for accommodation; and as the **concept application phase** expands the concept, reinforcement strategies for retaining the new concept are provided.

Using Part of the Learning Cycle to Build Concepts

Although a formal investigation using the learning cycle is an excellent way to present lessons to children, teaching all lessons in this manner is not desirable. At times, exploration and observation might be the full lesson. Giving students an opportunity to practice their skills of observation is often sufficient for them to learn a great deal about unfamiliar objects or phenomena. In the following scenarios, teachers made use of exploration observations to create lessons.

◆ Mr. Brown constructed a small bird feeder and placed it outside the window of his prekindergarten room. One cold winter day his efforts were rewarded. Students noticed and called attention to the fact that there were several kinds of birds at the feeder. Brad said that they all looked the same to him. Leroy pointed out different characteristics of the birds to Brad. Diana and Cindy noticed that the blue jay constantly chased other birds away from the feeder and that a big cardinal moved away from the feeder as soon as any other bird approached. Students wondered why the blue jay seemed to scare all the other birds and the cardinal seemed to be afraid of even the small birds. They spent several minutes discussing the possibilities.

◆ On Richard's birthday, his preschool teacher, Miss Collins, decided that the class should make a microwave cake to celebrate the occasion. The students helped Miss Collins mix the ingredients and commented on the sequence of events as the cake cooked for seven minutes in the microwave. Richard was the first to observe how bubbles started to form in small patches. Then George commented that the whole cake was bubbling and getting bigger. After removing the cake from the microwave, many children noticed how the cake shrank, got glossy, then lost its gloss as it cooled.

Some lessons can be improved by having children do more than just observing and exploring. These exploration lessons include **data collection** as an instructional focus. Data collection and interpretation are important to real science and real problem solving. Although firsthand observation will always be important, most breakthroughs in science are made in the analysis of carefully collected data. Scientists usually spend much more time searching through stacks of data than peering down the barrel of a microscope or through a telescope.

Data collection for young children is somewhat more abstract than firsthand observation. Therefore, it is important that students have sufficient practice in making predictions, speculations, and guesses with firsthand observations before they begin to collect and interpret data. Nevertheless, young students can benefit from early experience in data collection and interpretation. Initial data collections are usually pictorial in form. Long-term patterns and changes that children cannot easily observe in one setting are excellent beginnings for data collection.

◆ Weather records such as those discussed earlier in the unit can expose children to patterns during any time of the year. After charting the weather with drawings or attaching pictures that represent changing conditions, have children decide which clothing is most appropriate for a particular kind of weather. Drawing clouds, sun, rain, lightning, snow, and so on that correspond to the daily weather and relating that information to what is worn can give students a sense of why data collection is useful.

◆ Growing plants provides excellent opportunities for early data collection. Mrs. Fox's first-grade class charted the progress of bean plants growing in paper cups on the classroom windowsill. Each day students cut a strip of paper the same length as the height of their plant and

glued the strips to a large sheet of newsprint. Over a period of weeks, students could see how their plants grew continuously even though they noticed few differences by just watching them. After pondering the plant data, Dean asked Mrs. Fox if the students could measure themselves with a strip of paper and chart their growth for the rest of the year. Thereafter, Mrs. Fox measured each student once a month. Her students were amazed to see how much they had grown during the year.

Another technique for designing science lessons is to allow students to have input into the process of problem solving and designing investigations. This might be called a *concept introduction lesson* because it utilizes the **concept introduction phase** of the learning cycle as the basis for a lesson. Although initial investigation and problem-solving experiences may be teacher designed, students eventually will be able to contribute to planning their own investigations. Most students probably will not be able to choose a topic and plan the entire investigation independently until they reach the intermediate grades, but their input into the process of planning gives them some ownership of the lesson and increases their confidence to explore ideas more fully. When solving real problems, identifying the problem is often more critical than the skills of attacking it. Students need practice in both aspects of problem solving.

The following examples depict students giving input into the problem to be solved and then helping to design how the problem should be approached.

◆ Mr. Wang's second-grade class had had previous experience in charting the growth of plants. He told his class, "I'd like us to design an investigation about how fast plants grow. What things do you think could affect how fast a plant grows?" As Mr. Wang listed factors on the chalkboard, his students suggested a variety of factors, including the amount of water, fertilizer, sunshine, temperature, type of seed, how much they are talked to, if they are stepped on, and so on. Students came up with possibilities that had never occurred to Mr. Wang. Next, he broke the class into small groups and told each group that it could have several paper cups, seeds, and some potting soil. Each group was asked to choose a factor from the list that it would like to investigate. Then, Mr. Wang helped each group plan its investigation.

◆ Derrick and Brent decided to study the effect of light on their plant. Mr. Wang asked them how they would control the amount of light their plants receive. Brent suggested that they bring a lightbulb to place near the plants so that they could leave the light on all day. Derrick said that he would put the plants in a cardboard box for the hours they were not supposed to receive light. Mr. Wang asked them to think about how many plants they should use. They decided to use three: one plant would receive light all day, one plant would receive no light, and one plant would receive only six hours of light.

Strategies That Encourage Inquiry

The fundamental abilities and concepts that underlie the Science as Inquiry Content Standard of the *National Science Education Standards* lay a groundwork for developing and integrating strategies that encourage inquiry. Young children should experience science in a form that engages them in the active construction of ideas and explanations and enhances their opportunities to develop the skills of doing science. In the early years, when children investigate materials and properties of common objects, they can focus on the process of doing investigations and develop the ability to ask questions. The *National Science Education Standards* suggest the following strategies to engage students in the active search for knowledge.

◆ *Ask a question about objects, organisms, and events in the environment.* Children should be encouraged to answer their questions by seeking information from their own observations and investigations and from reliable sources of information. When possible, children's answers can be compared with what scientists already know about the world.

◆ *Plan and conduct a simple investigation.* When children are in their earliest years, investigations are based on systematic observation. As children develop, they may design and conduct simple investigations to answer questions. However, the idea of a fair test necessary for experimentation may not be possible until the fourth grade. Types of investigations that are appropriate for younger children include describing objects, events, and organisms; classifying them; and sharing what they know with others.

◆ *Employ simple equipment and tools to gather data and extend the senses.* Simple skills such as how to observe, measure, cut, connect, switch, turn on/off, pour, hold, and hook, and simple instruments such as rulers, thermometers, magnifiers, and microscopes should be used in the early years. Children can use simple equipment and can gather data such as observing and recording the attributes of the daily weather. They can also develop skills in the use of computers and calculators.

◆ *Use data to construct a reasonable explanation.* In inquiry, students' thinking is emphasized as they use data to formulate explanations. Even at the earliest grade levels, students learn what counts as evidence and judge the merits of the data and explanations.

◆ *Communicate investigations and explanations.* Students should begin developing the abilities to communicate, critique, and analyze their work and the work of other students. This communication might be spoken or drawn as well as written.

The natural inquiry of young children can be seen as they observe, group, sort, and order objects. By incorporating familiar teaching strategies such as providing a variety of objects for children to manipulate and talking to children as they go about what they are doing with objects, teachers can help children to learn more about their world. Children also can learn about their world through observations and discussions about those observations. When opportunities are provided for children to work individually to construct their own knowledge, they will gain experiences in organizing data and understanding processes. A variety of activities that let children use all of their senses should be offered. In this way, children are allowed to explore at their own pace and to self-regulate their experiences.

Assessing Inquiry Learning

Observation is vital for the teacher as she assesses children's progress. It is essential that the teacher watch carefully as the children group and order materials. Are the materials ordered in a certain way? Do the objects in the group have similar attributes? Are the children creating a random design, or are they making a pattern? Clues to children's thinking can be gained by watching what children do and having them explain what they are doing to each other or to you. In the following example, the teacher makes use of an activity that invites children to manipulate objects to assess their abilities to do scientific inquiry.

Mrs. Raymond has a variety of objects with a number of characteristics, such as size, color, texture, and shape, in her classroom for children to group and sort. She has enough sets of keys, buttons, beans, nuts and bolts, fabric swatches, and wooden shapes for each child to work alone. To expose children to science content, she also has sets of leaves, nuts, bark, twigs, seeds, or other objects related to the science content that she wants to emphasize. As the children group and sort the objects, either by a single characteristic or some other way, Mrs. Raymond observes them carefully and asks them to tell her about the ways they are organizing the objects. The teacher moves around and listens to the individual children as they make decisions. She makes notes in the anecdotal records she is keeping and talks with the children, "Can you put the ones that go together in a pile?" and "How did you decide to put this leaf in the pile?"

Problem Solving in Science

The driving force behind problem solving is curiosity, an interest in finding out. Problem solving is not as much a teaching strategy as it is a student behavior. The challenge for the teacher is to create an environment in which problem solving can occur. Encouragement of problem-solving behavior in a primary classroom can be seen in the following examples.

◆ After his class has studied the movement and structure of the human body, Mr. Brown adds a final challenge to the unit. He has the children work with partners and poses the following situation, asking each pair to come up with a solution to the problem: "You like to play video games, but your family is worried because your wrists seem to be hurting from the motion you use to play the games. Plan a solution to the problem and role-play the family discussion that might take place."

◆ Mr. Wang's class is studying the habitats of animals that live in water and the impact of humans on the environment. One of the problems he poses to the students is to decide what they will do in the following situation: "You are looking forward to an afternoon of fishing at the lake near your home. When you get there you see a sign that was never there before. It says 'No Fishing.' What do you do?"

The asking and answering of questions is what problem solving is all about. When the situations and problems that the students wonder about are perceived as real, their curiosity is stimulated and they want to find an answer. This means a problem is some question or situation that is important to the student and thus gets her attention and enthusiasm focused on the search for a solution.

Problems should relate to and include the children's own experiences. From birth onward, children want to learn and naturally seek out problems to solve. Problem solving through the prekindergarten years focuses on naturalistic and informal learning, which promotes exploration and discovery. In the kindergarten and primary years, a more structured approach can be instituted. For an overall look at implementing a problem-solving approach for kindergarten and primary students, read *What's Your Problem?* (Skinner, 1990).

Research indicates that working with concrete materials and drawing and/or writing explanations of solutions for problems are the best support for improving problem-solving skills. It is important to keep in mind that the process skills discussed in Unit 5 are essential to thinking and acting on a problem.

Four Steps in Problem Solving

While people disagree about the exact number of steps it takes for a learner to solve a problem, there seem to be four basic steps that are essential to the problem-solving process:

1. *Identifying a problem and communicating it in a way that is understood.* This might involve assessing the situation and deciding exactly what is being asked or what is needed.
2. *Determining what the outcome of solving the problem might be.* This step involves the students in organizing a plan that will get them to their goals.
3. *Exploring possible solutions and applying them to the problem.* In this step, the plan is executed using appropriate strategies and materials. Children must learn that their first approach to solving a problem might be erroneous but that if they keep trying, a solution will materialize. It is essential that children have the opportunity to explain their solutions to others; this will help clarify the problem and help them be better able to explain the problem to themselves.
4. *Evaluating the possible solutions and revised solutions* if they do not seem to work as well as hoped. Because there is no one correct answer or way to arrive at an answer, there will be a variety of results. There may, in fact, be no answer to the problem.

Whether the lesson is part of the learning cycle, a culminating activity, or an unstructured experience, keep in mind first and foremost that for problem solving to occur student curiosity must be stimulated with problems that engage, intrigue, and motivate. As students understand and learn how to apply the basic steps of the problem-solving process, they will be able to make connections with their past experiences, while keeping an open mind. The teacher's role is that of a facilitator, using instructional strategies to create a classroom rich with opportunities, where students are enthusiastic about learning and developing the problem-solving skills that will last a lifetime.

Summary

In all of the preschool and primary developmental stages described by Piaget, keep in mind that children's views of the world and concepts are not the same as yours. Their perception of phenomena is from their own perspective and experiences. Misconceptions arise. So, explore the world to expand thinking, and be ready for the next developmental stage. Teach children to observe with all of their senses and classify, predict, and communicate to discover other viewpoints.

There are many possible methods for designing science instruction for young children. The learning cycle is an application of the theory of cognitive development described by Piaget. The learning cycle can incorporate a number of techniques into a single lesson, or each of the components of the learning cycle can be used independently to develop lessons. Other effective methods for designing lessons include discrepant events, data collection and analysis, problem solving, and cooperative planning of investigations. All of these methods emphasize science process skills that are important to the development of concepts in young children.

KEY TERMS

discrepant event	equilibrium	concept application phase
self-regulation	accommodation	data collection
cognitive structure	assimilation	concept introduction phase
disequilibrium	exploration phase	

SUGGESTED ACTIVITIES

1. Interview children to determine their understanding of cause-and-effect relationships. Questions will be effective in gaining insight into the perceptions and misconceptions of young children. Compare remarks with classmates.

2. Brainstorm at least three strategies to prepare children to understand topics such as rain, lightning, clouds, mountains, and night. Pick a topic and prepare a learning experience that will prepare children for future concept development.

3. Pretend you are presenting two lessons about seeds (seeds grow into plants) to a class of first graders. What types of learning experiences will you design for these students? How will you apply Piaget's theory of development to this topic? In what way would you adapt the experiences for a different developmental level?

4. Present a discrepant event to your classmates. After discovering how the event was achieved, analyze the process of equilibration that the class went through. Design a discrepant event that focuses on senses that would be effective for kindergarten age children.

5. The learning cycle has been presented as an effective way to build concepts in young children. What is your concept of the learning cycle, and how will you use it with children? Select a concept, and prepare a learning cycle to teach it.

6. Reflect on your own primary science experiences. What types of learning strategies did you encounter? Were they effective? Why or why not?

REVIEW

A. Describe what is meant by a discrepant event.

B. Why are discrepant events used in science education?

C. List the three major parts of the learning cycle.

D. Describe how cognitive structures change over time.

E. Why is data collection important with young children?

F. Create an example of a discrepant event that you might use with young children on a topic of your choice.

G. Describe strategies you will use to encourage inquiry.

H. Why is problem solving a student behavior?

REFERENCES

Gallagher, J. M., & Reid, D. K. (1981). *The learning theory of Piaget and Inhelder*. Monterey, CA: Brooks/Cole.

Lind, K. K. (2000). *Exploring science in early childhood*. Clifton Park, NY: Delmar Learning.

National Research Council. (1996). *National Science Education Standards*. Washington, DC: National Academy Press.

Skinner, P. (1990). *What's your problem?* Portsmouth, NH: Heinemann.

FURTHER READING AND RESOURCES

Barman, C. (1990). *New ideas about an effective teaching strategy*. Council for Elementary Science International. Indianapolis: Indiana University.

Benham, N. B., Hosticka, A., Payne, J. D., & Yeotis, C. (1982). Making concepts in science and mathematics visible and viable in the early childhood curriculum. *School Science and Mathematics*, *82*(1), 45–64.

Bowman, B. T., Donovan, M. S., & Burns, M. S. (Eds.). (2000). *Eager to learn: Educating our preschoolers*. Washington, DC: National Research Council.

Bredekamp, S., & Rosegrant, T. (1992). *Reaching potentials: Appropriate curriculum and assessment for young children* (Vol. 1). Washington, DC: National Association for the Education of Young Children.

Bredekamp, S., & Rosegrant, T. (1995). *Reaching potentials: Transforming early childhood curriculum and assessment* (Vol. 2). Washington, DC: National Association for the Education of Young Children.

Charlesworth, R. (2000). *Understanding child development* (5th ed.). Clifton Park, NY: Delmar Learning.

Confrey, J. (1990). A review of research on student conceptions in mathematics, science, and programming. In C. Cazden (Ed.), *Review of research in education*. Washington, DC: American Educational Research Association.

Gill, A. J. (1993). Multiple strategies: Product of reasoning and communication. *Arithmetic Teacher, 40*(7), 380–386.

Harlen, W. (Ed.). (1996). *Primary science, taking the plunge: How to teach primary science more effectively*. Portsmouth, NH: Heinemann.

Price, G. G. (1982). Cognitive learning in early childhood education: Mathematics, science, and social studies. In *Handbook of research in early childhood education*. New York: Free Press.

Renner, J. W., & Marek, E. A. (1988). *The learning cycle*. Portsmouth, NH: Heinemann.

Shaw, J. M., & Owen, L. L. (1987). Weather–Beyond observation. *Science and Children*, *25*(3): 27–29.

Sprung, B., Froschl, M., & Campbell, P. B. (1985). *What will happen if . . . ?* New York: Educational Equity Concepts.

Tipps, S. (1982). Making better guesses: A goal in early childhood science. *School Science and Mathematics*, *82*(1): 29–37.

UNIT 7
Planning for Science

OBJECTIVES

After reading this unit, you should be able to:

◆ Develop science concepts with subject area integrations.

◆ Explain and use the strategy of webbing in unit planning.

◆ Identify and develop science concepts in a lesson; design lesson plans for teaching science to children.

◆ Construct evaluation strategies.

Integrating Science into the Curriculum

Concepts will more likely be retained by children if presented in a variety of ways and extended over a period of time. For example, after a trip to the zoo, extend the collective experience by having children dictate a story about their trip or have the children build their own zoo and demonstrate the care and feeding of the animals. The children can also depict the occupations found at the zoo. Other activities could focus on following up pre-visit discussions, directing children to observe specifics at the zoo, such as differences in animal noses. Children might enjoy comparing zoo animal noses with those of their pets by matching pictures of similar noses on a bulletin board. In this way, concepts can continue to be applied and related to past experiences as the year progresses.

Additional integrations might include drawing favorite animal noses, creating plays about animals with specific types of noses, writing about an animal and its nose, and creating "smelling activities." You might even want to introduce reasons an animal has a particular type of nose. One popular idea is to purchase plastic animal noses, distribute them to children, and play a "Mother-May-I"-like game. Say, "If you have four legs and roar, take two giant steps. If you have two legs and quack, take three steps forward" (Figure 7–1).

Think of how much more science can be learned if we make connections between it and other subjects. This requires preparing planned activities and taking advantage of every teachable moment that occurs in your class to introduce children to science.

Opportunities abound for teaching science in early childhood. Consider actively involving children with art, blocks, dramatic play, woodworking, language arts, math, and creative movement. Learning centers are one way to provide excellent integration and provide opportunities for assessment. Centers are discussed in Unit 39 of this book. The following ideas may encourage your thinking.

◆ **Painting**. Finger painting helps children learn to perceive with their fingertips and demonstrates the concept of color diffusion as they clean their hands. Shapes can be recognized by painting with fruit and familiar objects.

◆ **Water center**. Concepts such as volume and conservation begin to be grasped when children

of science integrates especially well with reading and writing. Basic words, object guessing, experience charts, writing stories, and working with tactile sensations all encourage early literacy development.

Children Learn in Different Ways

It is important to provide children with a variety of ways to learn science. Even very young children have developed definite patterns in the way they learn. Observe a group of children engaged in free play: some prefer to work alone quietly; others do well in groups. Personal learning style also extends to a preference for visual or auditory learning. The teacher in the following scenario keeps the wide range of learning styles in mind when planning science experiences.

Ms. Hebert knows that the children in her kindergarten class exhibit a wide range of learning styles and behaviors. For example, Ann wakes up slowly. She hesitates to jump in and explore and prefers to work alone. On the other hand, Vanessa is social, verbal, and ready to go first thing in the morning. As Ms. Hebert plans activities to reinforce the observations of flamingos that her class made at the zoo, she includes experiences that involve both group discussion and individual work. Some of the visual, auditory, and small and large group activities include flamingo number puzzles; drawing and painting flamingos; and acting out how flamingos eat, rest, walk, and honk. In this way, Ms. Hebert meets the diverse needs of the class and integrates concepts about flamingos into the entire week (Figure 7–2). Organizing science lessons with subject matter correlations in mind ensures integration. The following section outlines ways to plan science lessons and units.

Organizing for Teaching Science

To teach effectively, teachers must organize what they plan to teach. How they organize depends largely on their teaching situation. Some school districts require that a textbook series or curriculum guide be used when teaching science. Some have a fully developed program to follow, and others have no established guidelines. Regardless of state or district

FIGURE 7–1 "If you have two legs and quack, take three steps forward."

measure with water and sand. Buoyancy can be explored with boats and sinking and floating objects.

◆ **Blocks**. Blocks are an excellent way to introduce children to friction, gravity, and simple machines. Leverage and efficiency can be reinforced with *woodworking*.

◆ **Books**. Many books introduce scientific concepts while *telling a story*. Books with pictures give views of unfamiliar things and an opportunity to explore detail and infer and discuss.

◆ **Music and rhythmic activities**. These let children experience the movement of air against their bodies. Air resistance can also be demonstrated by dancing with a scarf.

◆ **Manipulative center**. Children's natural capacities for inquiry can be seen when they observe, group, sort, and order objects during periods of play. Children can pair objects, such as animals, and use fundamental skills, such as one-to-one correspondence.

◆ **Creative play**. Dressing, moving, eating, and so on like an animal will provide children with opportunities for expressing themselves. Drama and poetry are a natural integration with learning about living things.

◆ **Playground**. The playground can provide an opportunity to predict weather, practice balancing, and experience friction. The concrete world

FIGURE 7–2 A flamingo lacing card.

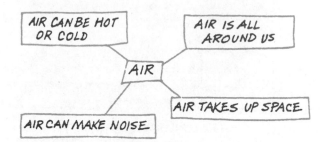

FIGURE 7–3 Begin by making each web of the science concepts you want to teach.

directives, the strategies discussed in this chapter can be adapted to a variety of teaching situations.

Planning for Developing Science Concepts

After assessing what your students know and want to know about a science topic, the first questions to ask when organizing for teaching are "What is the appropriate science content that the children need to know?" and "What is the best way to organize learning experiences?" You might have a general topic in mind, such as air, but do not know where to go from there. One technique that might help organize your thoughts is **webbing**, a strategy borrowed from literature. A web depicts a variety of possible concepts and curricular experiences that you might use to develop concepts. By visually depicting your ideas, you will be able to tell at a glance the concepts covered in your unit. As the web emerges, projected activities can be balanced by subject area (e.g., social studies, movement, art, drama, and math) and by a variety of naturalistic, informal, or structured activities.

Start your planning by selecting what you want children to know about a topic. For example, the topic *air* contains many science concepts. Four concepts

about air that are commonly taught to first graders begin the web depicted in Figure 7–3 and are as follows:

1. Air is all around us.
2. Air takes up space.
3. Air can make noise.
4. Air can be hot or cold.

After selecting the concepts you plan to develop, begin adding appropriate activities to achieve your goal. Look back at Unit 6 and think of some of these strategies that will best help you teach about air. Remember, "messing around" time and direct experience are vital for learning.

The developed web in Figure 7–4 shows at a glance the main concepts and activities that will be included in this unit. You may not want to teach all of these activities, but you will have the advantage of flexibility when you make decisions.

Next, turn your attention to how you will evaluate children's learning. Remember, preschool and primary age children will not be able to verbalize their true understanding of a concept. They simply have not advanced to the formal stages of thinking. Instead, have students show their knowledge in ways that can be observed. Have them explain, predict, show, tell, draw, describe, construct, and so on (Figure 7–5). These are the verbs that indicate an action of some kind. For example, as students explain to you why they have grouped buttons together in a certain way, be assured that the facts are there and so are the concepts, and one day they will come together in a fully developed concept statement. Concept development takes time and cannot be rushed.

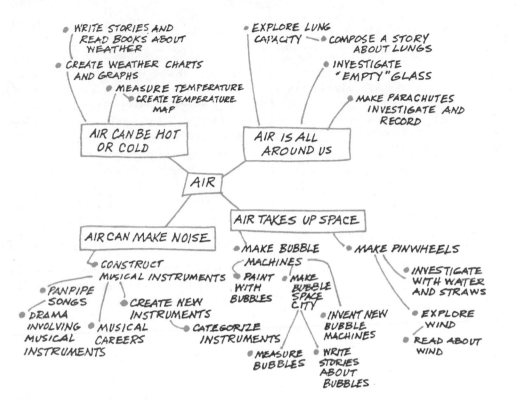

FIGURE 7–4   Example of a webbed unit.

ACTION VERBS

Simple Action Words

arrange	design	match
attempt	distinguish	measure
chart	explain	name
circle	formulate	order
classify	gather	organize
collect	graph	place
compare	identify	point
compile	include	report
complete	indicate	select
contrast	label	sort
count	list	state
define	locate	tell
describe	map	

FIGURE 7–5   Verbs that indicate action.

The webbed unit you have developed is a long-term plan for organizing science experiences around a specific topic. Formal units usually contain overall goals and objectives, a series of lessons, and an evaluation plan. **Goals** are the broad statements that indicate where you are heading with the topic or outcomes you would like to achieve. **Objectives** state how you plan to achieve your goals. Practical teaching direction is provided by daily lesson plans. An evaluation plan is necessary to assess student learning and your own teaching. There are a variety of ways these components can be organized, but Figure 7–6 outlines the essential ingredients. Refer to the Assessment Strategies section of this unit for suggestions on building on children's existing knowledge in designing learning experiences.

Lesson Planning

The **lesson plan** is a necessary component of the unit. It helps you plan the experiences that will aid in

COMPONENTS IN A UNIT PLAN

TOPIC/CONCEPT	What is the topic or concept?
GOAL	Where are you heading?
OBJECTIVE	How do you plan to achieve your goals?
ADVANCED PREPARATION	What do I need to have prepared to teach this lesson?
MATERIALS	What will you need?
LESSONS	What will you teach?
EVALUATION	Did the students learn what you wanted them to learn?

FIGURE 7–6 Components in unit planning.

concept development. The following lesson plan is adaptable and focuses on developing a science concept, manipulating materials, and extending and reinforcing the concept with additional activities and subject area integrations. Refer to Figure 7–7 and Figure 7–8, the bubble machine, for an example of this lesson plan format.

Basic Science Lesson Plan Components

Concept. Concepts are usually the most difficult part of a lesson plan. The temptation is to write an objective or topic title. However, to really focus your teaching on the major concept to be developed, you must find the science in what you intend to teach. For example, ask yourself, "What do I want the children to learn about air?"

Objective. Then ask, "What do I want the children *to do* to help them understand that air takes up space?" When you have decided on the basic experience, be sure to identify the process skills that children will use. In this way, you will be aware of content and process.

Define the teaching process in behavioral terms. State what behavior you want the children to exhibit. This will make evaluation easier because you have stated what you expect the children to accomplish. Although many educators state behavioral objectives with conditions, most teachers find that beginning a statement with "the child should be able to" followed by an action verb is an effective way to state objectives. Some examples follow:

The child should be able to describe the parts of a flower.

The child should be able to construct a diorama of the habitat of a tiger.

The child should be able to draw a picture that shows different types of animal noses.

Materials. For children to manipulate materials, you must decide which materials should be organized in advance of the lesson. Ask, "What materials will I need to teach this lesson?"

Advanced Preparation. These are the tasks that the teacher needs to complete prior to implementing the plan with the children. Teachers should ask themselves, "What do I need to have prepared to teach this lesson?"

Procedure. The procedure section of a lesson plan provides the step-by-step directions for completing the activity with the children. When planning the lesson, try the procedure yourself and ask, "How will this experience be conducted?" You must decide how you will initiate the lesson with children, present the learning experience, and relate the concept to the children's past experiences. Questions that encourage learning should be considered and included in the lesson plan.

It is recommended that an initiating experience begin the lesson. This experience could be the "messing around" with materials stage of the learning cycle, a demonstration or discrepant event, a question sequence that bridges what you intend to teach with a previous lesson or experience. The idea is that you want to stimulate and interest the children about what they are going to do in the lesson.

Extension. To ensure maximum learning of the concept, ways to keep the idea going must be planned. This can be done by extending the concept and building on students' interest with additional learning activities, integrating the concept into other subject areas, preparing learning centers, and so on.

Assessment Strategies

You cannot teach a lesson or unit effectively if you do not plan for assessment. To continue with another lesson before you know what students understand from the current lesson seems pointless. Engaging in ongoing assessment of your own teaching and of student progress is essential to improving teaching

CONCEPT: "Air takes up space. Bubbles have air inside of them."
OBJECTIVE: Construct a bubble-making machine by manipulating materials and
             Observe and describe the bubbles.
MATERIALS: Bubble solution of eight tablespoons liquid detergent and one quart
             gent makes stronger bubbles), straws, four-ounce plastic cups.
ADVANCED PREPARATION:
1. Collect materials.
2. Cut straws into small sections.
3. Mix bubble solution.
PROCEDURE:

Initiating Activity: Demonstrate an assembled bubble machine. Have children observe the machine and
tell what they think is happening.

How to do it: Help children assemble bubble machines. Insert straw into the side of the cup. Pour the
bubble mixture to just below the hole in the side of
the cup. Give children five minutes to explore
blowing bubbles with the bubble machine. Then ask
children to see how many bubbles they can blow.
Ask: "What do your bubbles look like? Describe
your bubbles." Add food coloring for more colorful
bubbles.

   "What happens to your bubbles? Do they burst?
How can you make them last longer?"

   "What do you think is in the bubbles? How can
you tell? What did you blow into the bubble? Can
you think of something else that you blow air into to
make larger?" (balloon)

FIGURE 7–8 Laticia makes a bubble machine.

EVALUATION:
1. Were the children able to blow bubbles?
2. Did they experiment with blowing differing amounts of air?
3. Did the children say things like, "Look what happens when I blow real hard?"
EXTENSION:
1. Have students tell a story about the bubble machine as you record it on chart paper.
2. Encourage children to make bubble books with drawings that depict their bubbles, bubble machines, and
   the exciting time they had blowing bubbles. Encourage the children to write or pretend to write about their
   pictures. Threes and fours enjoy pretending to write; by five or six, children begin to experiment with
   inventing their own spellings. Be sure to accept whatever they produce. Have children read their books to
   the class. Place them in the library center for browsing.
3. Make a bubbles bulletin board. Draw a cluster of bubbles and have students add descriptive words about
   bubbles.
4. Challenge students to invent other bubble machines. (Unit 35 of this book contains activities that teach
   additional concepts of air and bubbles.)

FIGURE 7–7 The bubble machine lesson.

ing. Consider that your major role is to ...dents build concepts, use process skills, and ... incorrect ideas. To do this, students should be ...gaged in meaningful experiences, with the time and ...ools needed to learn. Keep in mind, assessment of students' progress and the guidance of students to self-assessment is at the heart of good teaching.

The *National Science Education Standards* emphasize that the content and form of an assessment task must be congruent with what is supposed to be measured. The task of addressing the complexity of the science content while addressing the importance of collecting data on all aspects of student science achievement can be challenging.

A variety of assessment formats are suggested to determine what students understand and are able to do with their knowledge and how they will apply these learnings. Examples of effective strategies include the use of *teacher recorded observations,* which describe what the students are able to do and the areas that need improvement. *Interviews* or *asking questions* and *interacting* with the children are very effective assessment strategies. *Portfolios* are examples of individual student work that indicate progress, improvement, and accomplishments, and *science journal writing* captures yet another dimension of student understanding. **Performance-based assessment** involves giving one or more students a task to do, which will indicate the student level of understanding of science concepts and thinking skills. Regardless of the assessment strategy used, enough information needs to be provided so that both the student and teacher know what needs to happen for improvement to take place. Additional strategies are discussed in Units 4 and 6 and throughout the text.

Assessment that takes place before teaching is diagnostic in nature and takes place when you assess the children's experiences and ideas about a science concept. For example, when you ask children where they think rain comes from, you are assessing what is known about rain and discovering any misconceptions that might exist.

One effective strategy for science learning is to build upon children's existing knowledge and challenge students' preconceptions and misconceptions. It is important to find out what your students already know, or think they know, about a science topic before you begin teaching. A popular method for finding out

what students already know is the *KWL Strategy,* described by D. Ogle (1986) for literacy and adapted for use in science, in which children are asked what they *know*, what they *want* to know, and what they *learned*. Most teachers begin by recording the children's brainstormed responses to the first two questions on a large piece of paper that has been divided into three columns, each headed by one of the KWL questions. As the responses are recorded, some difference of opinion is bound to occur. This disagreement is positive and can provide a springboard for student inquiry. At this point, potential investigations, projects, or inquiry topics can be added to the curriculum plan. The following scenario describes the KWL strategy in a primary classroom.

Ms. Collins is preparing to teach a unit on pond life. She wants to find out what her students already know about life in ponds, so she gathers the class together and asks, "What do you think lives in a pond?" Students are excited to answer. Richard says that ducks live in a pond. Ms. Collins asks how he knows this, and he tells her he saw one at the lake last summer. On the large piece of chart paper mounted on the board, Ms. Collins writes "ducks" under the heading "What We Know about What Lives in Ponds." Cindy says, "You saw a duck in a lake, but is a pond the same as a lake?" Ms. Collins takes the opportunity to write this question under the heading "What We Want to Know about What Lives in Ponds." Kate wants to know, "Do ducks live in ponds, or do they just swim there sometimes?" Ms. Collins continues to write the questions down, as well as other animals that are suggested. When the process is complete, she asks the students, "How can we find out the answers to your questions?" Richard says they should go to a pond. Cindy responds that she has a book about ponds that she can bring to school to share. Lai reminds the class that there is something about ponds on their computer. Kate says maybe they could ask someone who knows about ponds. Ms. Collins writes the students' suggestions: ask someone, read about it, use the computer, and investigate. Ms. Collins has assessed what her students already know. Now she can make further plans for her unit, including lessons that will address the students' questions.

As teachers assess student progress during teaching, changes in teaching strategies are decided. If one strategy is not working, try something else.

As children work on projects, you will find yourself interacting with them on an informal basis. Listen carefully to children's comments, and watch them manipulate materials. You cannot help but assess how things are going. You might even want to keep a record of your observations or create a chart that reflects areas of concern to you, such as attitudes or interaction between students. When observations are written down in an organized way, they are called *anecdotal records* (Figure 7–9).

If you decide to use anecdotal records, be sure to write down dates and names and to tell students you are keeping track of things that happen. A review of your records will be valuable when you complete the unit. Recording observations can become a habit and provides an additional tool in assessing children's learning and your teaching strategies. Anecdotes are also invaluable resources for parent conferences. Refer to Units 4 and 6 for an example of assessing prior knowledge in inquiry and keeping anecdotal notes.

Responses to oral questions can be helpful in evaluating while teaching. Facial expressions are especially telling. Everyone has observed a blank look that usually indicates a lack of understanding. This look may be because the question asked was too difficult. So, ask an easy question, or present your question in a different manner for improved results.

One way to assess during the after teaching component is to ask questions about the activity in a lesson review. Some teachers write main idea questions on the chalkboard. Then, they put a chart next to the questions and label it "What We Found Out." As the lesson progresses, the chart is filled in by the class as a way of showing progress and reviewing the lesson or unit.

Another strategy is to observe children applying the concept. For example, as the *Three Billy Goats Gruff* (Rounds, 1993) is being read, Joyce comments, "The little billy goat walks just like the goat that we saw at the zoo." You know from this statement that Joyce has some idea of how goats move. (Refer to Units 3 and 4.)

Sometimes students have difficulty learning because an activity doesn't work. One basic rule when teaching science is, "Always do the activity first." This includes noting questions or possible problems you may encounter. If you have trouble, students will too (Figure 7–10).

Evaluating the Unit Plan

How well did you design your unit? Reflect and **evaluate** your unit plan before you begin teaching the unit and ask yourself some questions, such as the following, to help evaluate your work. These questions pull together the major points of this unit.

1. Have you related the unit to the children's prior knowledge and past experiences?
2. Are a variety of science process skills used in the lessons?

RECORDED OBSERVATIONS

Things to record when observing, discussing, or keeping anecdotal records

Cognitive:

How well do the children handle the materials?

Do the children cite out-of-school examples of the science concept?

Is the basic concept being studied referred to as the children go about their day?

Attitude and skill:

Do the children express like or dislike of the topic?

Are there any comments that suggest prejudice?

Do children evidence self-evaluation?

Are ideas freely expressed in the group?

Are there any specific behaviors that need to be observed each time science is taught?

FIGURE 7–9 Keeping anecdotal records.

"Always do the activity first."

FIGURE 7–10 The golden rule.

3. Is the science content developmentally appropriate for the children? How will you know?
4. Have you integrated other subject areas with the science content of the unit?
5. When you use reading and writing activities, do they align with the science content and relate to hands-on learning?
6. Do you allow for naturalistic, informal, and directed activities?
7. Have you included a variety of strategies to engage students in the active search for knowledge (refer to Unit 6)?
8. What opportunities are included for investigation and problem solving?
9. Are both open-ended and narrow questions included?
10. Will the assessment strategies provide a way to determine if children can apply what they have learned?
11. What local resources are included in the unit?

When publishers design a unit, they usually field-test the unit with a population of teachers. In this case, *you* are field-testing the unit as you teach your students. It is important that you keep notes and records on what worked well and what needs to be modified when the lesson is taught again. After teaching the unit you have designed, the *National Science Education Standards* suggest that you take time to reflect on the experience and use assessment data that you have gathered to guide in making judgments about the effectiveness of your teaching. Consider the following categories when making judgments about curricula:

◆ development appropriateness of the science content
◆ student interest in the content
◆ effectiveness of activities in producing the desired learning outcomes
◆ effectiveness of the selected examples
◆ understanding and abilities students must have to benefit from the selected activities and examples

Three Basic Types of Units

Some teachers like to develop *resource units*. The resource unit is an extensive collection of activities and suggestions focusing on a single science topic. The advantage of a resource unit is the wide range of appropriate strategies available to meet the needs, interests, and abilities of the children. As the unit is taught, additional strategies and integrations are usually added. For example, Mrs. Jones knows that she is going to teach a unit on seeds in her kindergarten class. She collects all of the activities and teaching strategies that she can find. When she is ready to teach the seed unit, she selects the activities that she believes are most appropriate.

Teachers who design a *teaching unit* plan to develop a science concept, objectives, materials, activities, and evaluation procedures for a specific group of children. This unit is less extensive than a resource unit and contains exactly what will be taught, a timeline, and the order of activities. Usually, general initiating experiences begin the unit, and culminating experiences end the unit. The specific teaching unit has value and may be used again with other classes after appropriate adaptations have been made. For example, Mr. Wang has planned a two-week unit on batteries and bulbs. He has decided on activities and planned each lesson period of the two weeks.

Extending the textbook in a textbook unit is another possibility. The most obvious limitation of this unit is a school district change in textbooks. A *textbook unit* is designed by outlining the science concepts for the unit and checking the textbook for those already covered in the book or teacher's manual. Additional learning activities are added for concepts not included in the text or sometimes instead of those in the text. Initiating activities to arouse interest in the topic might be needed. One advantage of this unit is using the textbook to better advantage. For example, after doing animal activities, use the text as a resource to confirm or extend knowledge.

Open-Ended and Narrow Questions

Asking questions can be likened to driving a car with a stick shift. When teaching the whole class, start in low gear with a narrow question that can be answered yes or no or with a question that has an obvious answer. This usually puts students at ease. They are happy; they know something. Then, try an open-ended question that has many answers. Open-ended questions stimulate discussion and offer opportunities for thinking. However, if the open-ended question is asked before the class has background information, the children might just stare at you, duck their heads, or exhibit undesirable behavior. Do not panic; quickly shift gears and ask a narrow question. Then, work your way back to what you want to find out.

Teachers who are adept at shifting between narrow and open-ended questions are probably excellent discussion leaders and have little trouble with classroom management during these periods.

Open-ended questions are excellent interest builders when used effectively. For example, consider Ms. Hebert's initiating activity for a lesson about buoyancy.

Ms. Hebert holds a rock over a pan of water and asks a narrow question, "Will this rock sink when dropped in water?" (yes, no) Then, she asks an open-ended question, "How can we keep the rock from sinking into the water?" The children answer, "Tie string around it," "Put a spoon under it," and "Grab it."

As the discussion progresses, the open-ended question leads the children into a discussion about how they can find out if their ideas will work. The teacher provides materials such as plastic containers, clay, and other items for them to use in designing a device that will float the rock.

Good questions excite and motivate children. When questions are posed that are open-ended and do not depend on yes or no answers, children will begin to expand their own capacity for problem solving and inquiry learning.

Summary

Children are more likely to retain science concepts if they are integrated with other subject areas. Making connections between science and other aspects of a child's school-day requires that opportunities for learning be well planned and readily available to children. Learning science in a variety of ways encourages personal learning styles and ensures subject integrations.

The key to effective teaching is organization. Unit and lesson planning provide a way to plan what you want children to learn and how you want them to learn. A planning web is a useful technique for depicting ideas, outlining concepts, and integrating content.

The three basic types of planning units are resource units, teaching units, and textbook units. Teachers utilize whichever unit best suits their classroom needs. By asking open-ended and narrow questions, teachers develop science concepts and encourage higher-order thinking skills in their students.

KEY TERMS

webbing	objectives	performance-based assessment
goals	lesson plan	evaluate

SUGGESTED ACTIVITIES

1. Select an appropriate science concept and work in teams to construct a planning web of the major concepts that are important to know. Add the activities that you plan to use to teach these concepts and suggest appropriate assessment strategies.
2. Select a lesson from a primary level textbook or from a local science curriculum. Compare how the book presents the concept with what you know about how children learn science.
3. Interview a teacher to determine his or her approach to planning, for example, whether a textbook series or curriculum guide is used, how flexibility is maintained, and what assessment techniques are found to be most effective. Ask teachers

to describe how they plan units and lessons and to compare the strategies used the first year of teaching with those they use now. Discuss responses to your questions in a group.

4. Reflect on your past experiences in science classes. Which were the most exciting units? Which were the most boring? Do you remember what made a unit exciting or dull? Or do you primarily remember a specific activity?

5. Observe a primary science lesson. Write down all of the assessment strategies used during the lesson. Analyze the strategies in terms of what you have learned about assessment.

6. Can you integrate a concept in life science with concepts in language arts? After integrating science and language arts, add mathematics, social studies, art, music, and drama.

7. Design a question-asking strategy that will help you assess children's understanding of the sense of taste.

8. Develop an assessment strategy for the bubble machine lesson in Figure 7–7. Your assessment should include questioning strategies and a checklist of behaviors and responses that would guide your anecdotal record keeping.

REVIEW

A. What is webbing, and how can it be applied in designing a science unit?

B. Which process skills are involved in the bubble machine lesson, including extensions?

C. Identify learning cycle components in the bubble machine lesson.

D. What strategies could you use to integrate subject areas into science? Give an example.

E. List the major components of a lesson plan for science and describe the importance of each component.

F. Identify three strategies for determining student progress. In what way will these strategies be used in student assessment?

G. What is a unit? List three basic types of units and describe how they are used.

H. Explain the difference between narrow and open-ended questions and how each is used. What are the strengths and weaknesses of each type?

REFERENCES

Ogle, D. M. (1986). K-W-L: A teaching model that develops active reading of expository text. *The Reading Teacher, 39*(6), 564–570.

Rounds, G. (1993). *Three billy goats gruff*. New York: Holiday House.

FURTHER READING AND RESOURCES

Ferrell, F. (1997). Ponds and technology. *Science and Children 34*(4), 37–39.

Gega, P., & Peters, J. (1997). *Science in elementary education*. Englewood Cliffs, NJ: Prentice Hall.

Harlan, J. (1991). *Science experiences for the early childhood years*. New York: Macmillan.

Jacobson, W. J., & Bergman, A. B. (1990). *Science for children: A book for teachers*. Englewood Cliffs, NJ: Prentice-Hall.

Lind, K. K. (1993). Concept mapping: Making learning meaningful. In *Teacher's desk reference: A professional guide for science educators*. Englewood Cliffs, NJ: Prentice-Hall.

Rice, K. (1986). Soap films and bubbles. *Science and Children 23*(8), 4–9.

Schwartz, J. I. (1991). *Literacy begins at home: Helping your child grow up reading and writing*. Springfield, IL: Charles C. Thomas.

Shavelson, R. J. (1991). Performance assessment in science. *Applied Measurement in Education 4*(4), 347–362.

Townsend, J., & Schiller, P. (1984). *More than a magnet, less than a dollar*. Houston: Evergreen Publishing Company.

Wassermann, S., & Ivany, J. W. G. (1990). *Teaching elementary science*. New York: Harper Collins.

Fundamental Concepts and Skills

UNIT 8
One-to-One Correspondence

OBJECTIVES

After reading this unit, you should be able to:

◆ Explain the NCTM expectations for one-to-one correspondence.

◆ Define one-to-one correspondence.

◆ Identify naturalistic, informal, and structured one-to-one correspondence activities.

◆ Describe five ways to vary one-to-one correspondence activities.

◆ Assess and evaluate children's one-to-one correspondence skills.

NCTM (2000) expectations for one-to-one correspondence relate to rational counting (attaching a number name to each object counted) as described in Unit 9. We believe that placing items in one-to-one correspondence as described in this unit is a supportive concept and skill for rational counting.

One-to-one correspondence is the most fundamental component of the concept of number. It is the understanding that one group has the same number of things as another. For example, each child has a cookie, each foot has a shoe, each person wears a hat. It is preliminary to counting and basic to the understanding of equivalence and to the concept of conservation of number described in Unit 1. Like other mathematics concepts, it can be integrated across the curriculum (Figure 8–1).

Assessment

To obtain information of an informal nature, note the children's behavior during their work, play, and routine activities. Look for one-to-one correspondence that happens naturally. For example, when the child plays train, he may line up a row of chairs so there is one for each child passenger. When he puts his mittens on, he shows that he knows there should be one for each hand; when painting, he checks to be sure he has each paintbrush in the matching color of paint. Tasks for formal assessment are given on page 106 and in Appendix A.

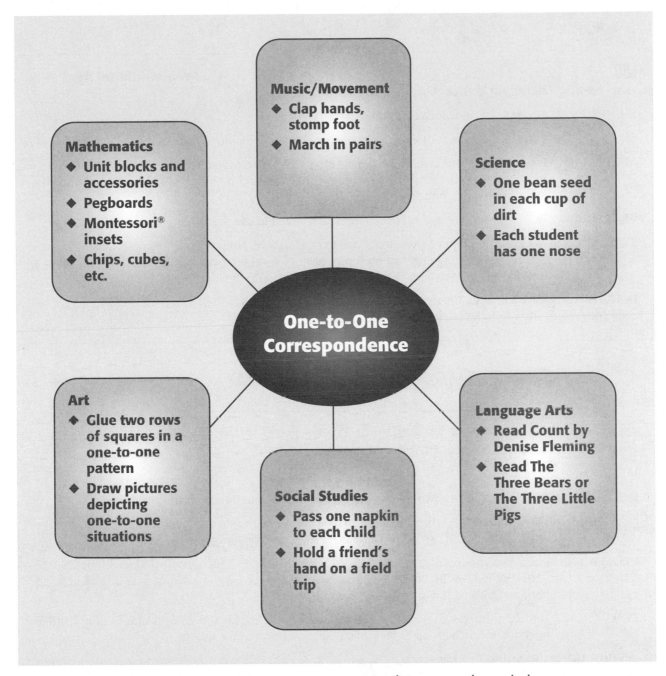

Music/Movement
- Clap hands, stomp foot
- March in pairs

Mathematics
- Unit blocks and accessories
- Pegboards
- Montessori® insets
- Chips, cubes, etc.

Science
- One bean seed in each cup of dirt
- Each student has one nose

One-to-One Correspondence

Art
- Glue two rows of squares in a one-to-one pattern
- Draw pictures depicting one-to-one situations

Social Studies
- Pass one napkin to each child
- Hold a friend's hand on a field trip

Language Arts
- Read Count by Denise Fleming
- Read The Three Bears or The Three Little Pigs

FIGURE 8–1   Integrating one-to-one correspondence across the curriculum.

SAMPLE ASSESSMENT TASK

3A
One-to-one Correspondence: Unit 8

Preoperational Ages 2–3

METHOD: Observation, individuals or groups.

SKILL: Child demonstrates one-to-one correspondence during play activities.

MATERIALS: Play materials that lend themselves to one-to-one activities, such as small blocks and animals, dishes and eating utensils, paint containers and paintbrushes, pegs and pegboards, sticks and stones, and so on.

PROCEDURE: Provide the materials and encourage the children to use them.

EVALUATION: Note if the children match items one to one, such as putting small peg dolls in each of several margarine containers or on top of each of several blocks that have been lined up in a row. Record on checklist, with anecdote and/or photo or video.

INSTRUCTIONAL RESOURCE: Charlesworth, R., and Lind, K. K. (2003). *Math and Science for Young Children* (4th ed.). Clifton Park, NY: Delmar Learning.

SAMPLE ASSESSMENT TASK

6A
One-to-one Correspondence: Unit 8

Preoperational Ages 5–6

METHOD: Interview.

SKILL: The child can place two groups of 10 items each in one-to-one correspondence.

MATERIALS: Two groups of objects of different shapes and/or color (such as pennies and cube blocks or red chips and white chips). Have at least 10 of each type of object.

PROCEDURE: Place two groups of 10 objects in front of the child. FIND OUT IF THERE IS THE SAME AMOUNT (NUMBER) IN EACH GROUP (BUNCH, PILE). If the child cannot do the task, go back and try it with two groups of five.

EVALUATION: The children should arrange each group so as to match the objects one-to-one, or they might count each group to determine equality. Record on checklist.

INSTRUCTIONAL RESOURCE: Charlesworth, R., & Lind, K. K. (2003). *Math and Science for Young Children* (4th ed.). Clifton Park, NY: Delmar Learning.

Naturalistic Activities

One-to-one correspondence activities develop from the infant's early sensorimotor activity. He finds out that he can hold one thing in each hand, but he can put only one object at a time in his mouth. The toddler discovers that five peg dolls will fit one each in the five holes in his toy bus. Quickly he learns that one person fits on each chair, one shoe goes on each foot, and so on. The two-year-old spends a great deal of his playtime in one-to-one correspondence activities. He lines up containers such as margarine cups, dishes, or boxes and puts a small toy animal in each one. He pretends to set the table for lunch. First he sets one place for himself and one for his bear, with a plate for each. Then he gives each place a spoon and a small cup and saucer. He plays with his large plastic shapes and discovers there is a rod that will fit through the hole in each shape.

Informal Activities

There are many opportunities for informal one-to-one correspondence activities each day. There are many times when things must be passed out to a group: food items, scissors, crayons, paper, napkins, paper towels, or notes to go home. Each child should do as many of these things as possible.

Checking on whether everyone has accomplished a task or has what she needs is another chance for informal one-to-one correspondence. Does everyone have a chair to sit on? Does everyone have on two boots or two mittens? Does each person have on his coat? Does each person have a cup of milk or a sandwich? A child can check by matching: "Larry, find out if everyone has a pair of scissors, please."

One-to-one correspondence helps to solve difficulties. For instance, the children are washing rubber dolls in soap suds. Jeanie is crying, "Petey has two dolls and I don't have any." Mrs. Carter comes over. "Petey, more children want to play here now so each one can have only one baby to wash." One-to-one correspondence is often the basis for rules such as, "Only one person on each swing at a time" or "Only one piece of cake for each child today."

Other informal activities occur when children pick out materials made available during free play. These kinds of materials would include pegboards, felt shapes on a flannelboard, bead and inch-cube block patterns, shape sorters, formboards, lotto games, and other commercial materials. Materials can also be made by the teacher to serve the same purposes. Most of the materials described in the next section can be made available for informal exploration both before and after they have been used in structured activities.

Structured Activities

The extent and variety of materials that can be used for one-to-one correspondence activities is almost endless. Referring to Unit 3, remember the six steps from concrete to abstract materials. These steps are especially relevant when selecting one-to-one correspondence materials. Five characteristics must be considered when selecting materials.

◆ perceptual characteristics
◆ number of items to be matched
◆ concreteness
◆ physically joined or not physically joined
◆ groups of the same or not the same number

The teacher can vary or change one or more of the five characteristics and can use different materials. In this way, more difficult tasks can be designed (Figure 8–2).

Perceptual qualities are very important in matching activities. The way the materials to be matched look is important in determining how hard it will be for the child to match them. Materials can differ a great deal on how much the same or how much different they look. Materials are easier to match if the groups are different. To match animals with cages or to find a spoon for each bowl is easier than making a match between two groups of blue chips. In choosing objects, the task can be made more difficult by picking out objects that look more the same.

The number of objects to be matched is important. The more objects in each group, the more difficult it is to match. Groups with fewer than five things are much easier than groups with five or more. In planning activities, start with small groups (fewer than five), and

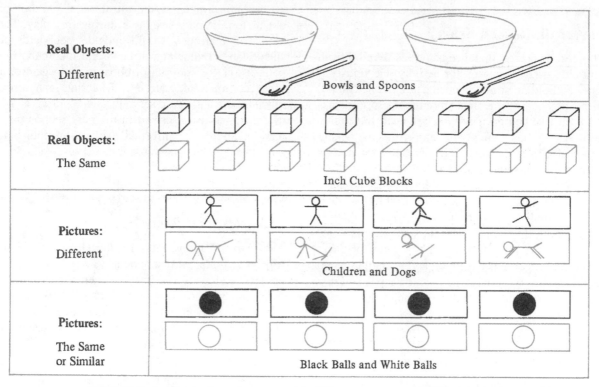

Real Objects: Different	Bowls and Spoons
Real Objects: The Same	Inch Cube Blocks
Pictures: Different	Children and Dogs
Pictures: The Same or Similar	Black Balls and White Balls

FIGURE 8–2 Examples of groups with different perceptual difficulty levels.

work up step by step to groups of nine. When the child is able to place groups of 10 in one-to-one correspondence, he or she has a well-developed sense of the concept.

How close to real materials are is referred to as concreteness (Figure 8–3). Remember from Unit 3 that instruction always should begin with concrete real objects. The easiest and first one-to-one correspondence activities should involve the use of real things such as small toys and other familiar objects. Next, less familiar, more similar objects such as cube blocks, chips, and ice cream bar sticks can be used. The next level would be cutout shapes such as circles and squares, cowboys and horses, or dogs and doghouses. Next would come pictures of real objects and pictures of shapes. Real objects and pictures could also be used. Computer software can be used by young children who need practice in one-to-one correspondence. The following software programs serve this purpose.

◆ Coco's Math Project 1. Singapore, SG: Times Learning Systems Pte Ltd.

◆ Learning with Leeper. Coarsegold, CA: Sierra On-Line, Inc.
◆ Muppetville. Pleasantville, NY: Sunburst Technologies. Learning with Leeper. Coarsegold, CA: Sierra On-Line, Inc.
◆ Let's Go Fishing. Dallas, TX: Learning Technologies, Inc.
◆ Match Up! Lowell, MA: Hayden Software Co.

Learning to hit the computer keys one at a time with one finger is a one-to-one experience in both the kinesthetic and perceptual-motor domains.

It is easier to tell if there is one-to-one correspondence if the objects are joined than if they are not joined. For example, it is easier to tell if there are enough chairs for each child if the children are sitting in them than if the chairs are on one side of the room and the children on the other. In beginning activities, the objects can be hooked together with a line or a string so that the children can more clearly see that there is or isn't a match. In Figure 8–4 each foot is

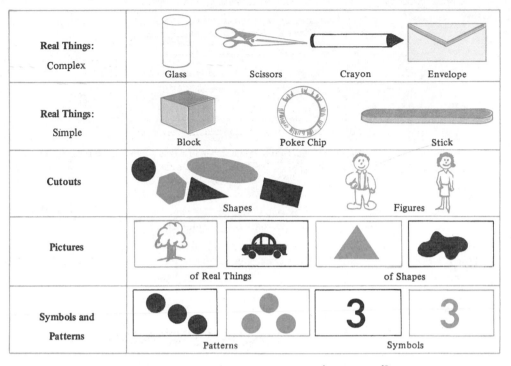

FIGURE 8–3   Concreteness: How close to real?

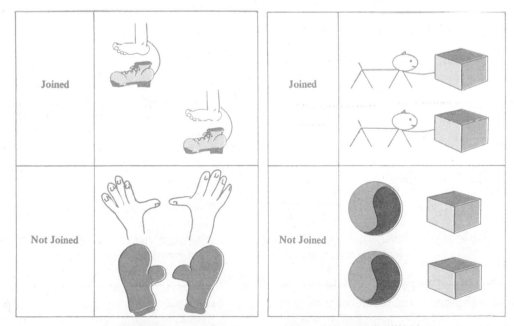

FIGURE 8–4   Joined groups and not joined groups

Can each boy have a ball?

Equal: Same number

Can each dog have a bowl?

Unequal: Not the same number

FIGURE 8–5 Matching equal and unequal groups.

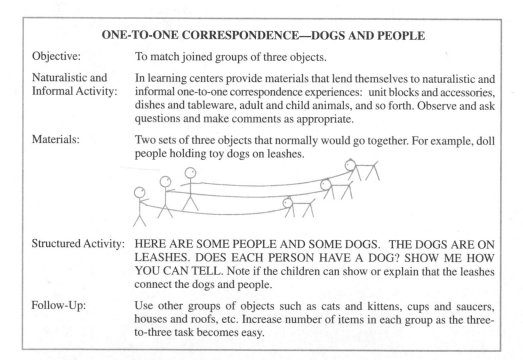

ONE-TO-ONE CORRESPONDENCE—DOGS AND PEOPLE

Objective: To match joined groups of three objects.

Naturalistic and Informal Activity: In learning centers provide materials that lend themselves to naturalistic and informal one-to-one correspondence experiences: unit blocks and accessories, dishes and tableware, adult and child animals, and so forth. Observe and ask questions and make comments as appropriate.

Materials: Two sets of three objects that normally would go together. For example, doll people holding toy dogs on leashes.

Structured Activity: HERE ARE SOME PEOPLE AND SOME DOGS. THE DOGS ARE ON LEASHES. DOES EACH PERSON HAVE A DOG? SHOW ME HOW YOU CAN TELL. Note if the children can show or explain that the leashes connect the dogs and people.

Follow-Up: Use other groups of objects such as cats and kittens, cups and saucers, houses and roofs, etc. Increase number of items in each group as the three-to-three task becomes easy.

FIGURE 8–6 One-to-one correspondence activity card—Dogs and people: Matching objects that are perceptually different.

joined to a shoe and each animal to a bowl. The hands and mittens and balls and boxes are not joined.

Placing unequal groups in one-to-one correspondence is harder than placing equal groups. When the groups have the same number, the child can check to be sure he has used all the items. When one group has more, he does not have this clue (Figure 8–5).

The sample lessons that are given illustrate some basic types of one-to-one correspondence activities. Note that they also show an increase in difficulty by varying the characteristics just described. Each activity begins by presenting the students with a problem to solve. The lessons are shown as they would be put on cards for the Idea File (Figures 8–6 through 8–11).

Evaluation

Informal evaluation can be done by noticing each child's response during structured activities. Also observe each child during free play to see whether he can pass out toys or food to other children, giving one at a time. On the shelves in the housekeeping area, paper shapes of each item (such as dishes, cups, tableware, purses, and so on) may be placed on the shelf where the item belongs. Hang pots and pans on a pegboard with the shapes of each pot drawn on the board. Do the same for blocks and other materials. Notice which children can put materials away by making the right match.

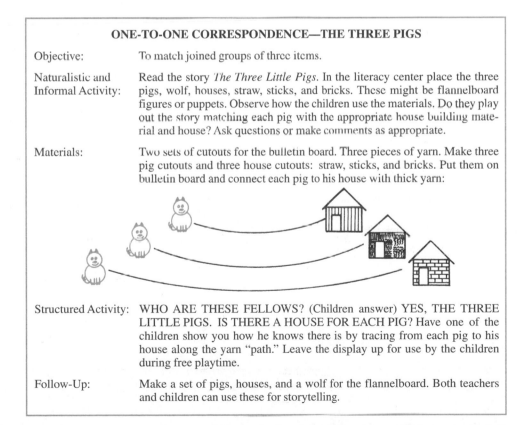

ONE-TO-ONE CORRESPONDENCE—THE THREE PIGS

Objective: To match joined groups of three items.

Naturalistic and Informal Activity: Read the story *The Three Little Pigs*. In the literacy center place the three pigs, wolf, houses, straw, sticks, and bricks. These might be flannelboard figures or puppets. Observe how the children use the materials. Do they play out the story matching each pig with the appropriate house building material and house? Ask questions or make comments as appropriate.

Materials: Two sets of cutouts for the bulletin board. Three pieces of yarn. Make three pig cutouts and three house cutouts: straw, sticks, and bricks. Put them on bulletin board and connect each pig to his house with thick yarn:

Structured Activity: WHO ARE THESE FELLOWS? (Children answer) YES, THE THREE LITTLE PIGS. IS THERE A HOUSE FOR EACH PIG? Have one of the children show you how he knows there is by tracing from each pig to his house along the yarn "path." Leave the display up for use by the children during free playtime.

Follow-Up: Make a set of pigs, houses, and a wolf for the flannelboard. Both teachers and children can use these for storytelling.

FIGURE 8–7 One-to-one correspondence activity card—The three little pigs matching cutouts that are perceptually different.

ONE-TO-ONE CORRESPONDENCE—PENNIES FOR TOYS

Objective:	To match groups of two and more objects.
Naturalistic and Informal Activity:	Set up a store center such as toys, groceries, or clothing. Provide play money pennies. Put a price of 1¢ on each item. Discuss with the students what they might do in the store. Observe and note if they exchange one penny for each item. Make comments and ask questions as appropriate.
Materials:	Ten pennies and 10 small toys (for example, a ball, a car, a truck, three animals, three peg people, a crayon).
Structured Activity:	LET'S PRETEND WE ARE PLAYING STORE. HERE ARE SOME PENNIES AND SOME TOYS. Show the child(ren) two toys. Place two pennies near the toys. DO I HAVE ENOUGH PENNIES TO BUY THESE TOYS IF EACH ONE COSTS ONE PENNY? SHOW ME HOW YOU CAN FIND OUT.
Follow-Up:	Use more toys and more pennies as the children can match larger and larger groups.

FIGURE 8–8   One-to-one correspondence activity card—Pennies for toys: Matching real objects.

ONE-TO-ONE CORRESPONDENCE—PICTURE MATCHING

Objective:	To match groups of pictured things, animals, or people.
Naturalistic and Informal Activity:	Place card sets as described below on a table in one of the classroom learning centers. Observe what the students do with the picture card sets. Do they sort them, match them, and so on? Make comments and ask questions as appropriate.
Materials:	Make or purchase picture cards that show items familiar to young children. Each set should have two groups of 10. Pictures from catalogs, magazines, or readiness workbooks can be cut out, glued on cards, and covered with clear Contac® or laminated. For example, pictures of 10 children should be put on 10 different cards. Pictures of 10 toys could be put on 10 other cards.
Structured Activity:	Present two people and two toys. DOES EACH CHILD HAVE A TOY? SHOW ME HOW YOU CAN FIND OUT. Increase the number of items in each group.
Follow-Up:	Make some more card sets. Fit them to current science or social studies units. For example, if the class is studying jobs, have pilot with plane, drive with bus, etc.

FIGURE 8–9   One-to-one correspondence activity card—Picture matching.

ONE-TO-ONE CORRESPONDENCE—SIMILAR OR IDENTICAL OBJECTS

Objective:	To match 2 to 10 similar and/or identical objects.
Naturalistic and Informal Activity:	Each day in the math center provide opportunity to explore manipulatives such as inch cube blocks, Unifix® Cubes, Lego,® and so on. Observe what the students do with the materials. Note if they do any one-to-one correspondence as they explore. Make comments and ask questions as appropriate.
Materials:	Twenty objects such as poker chips, inch cube blocks, coins, cardboard circles, etc. There may be 10 of one color and 10 of another or 20 of the same color (more difficult perceptually).
Structured Activity:	Begin with two groups of two and increase the size of the groups as the children are able to match the small groups. HERE ARE TWO GROUPS (BUNCHES, SETS) OF CHIPS (BLOCKS, STICKS, PENNIES, ETC.). DO THEY HAVE THE SAME NUMBER, OR DOES ONE GROUP HAVE MORE? SHOW ME HOW YOU KNOW. Have the children take turns using different sizes of groups and different objects.
Follow-Up:	Glue some objects to a piece of heavy cardboard or plywood. Set out a container of the same kinds of objects. Have this available for matching during center time. Also, baggies with groups of objects of varied amounts can be placed in the math center where students can select pairs of objects for matching.

FIGURE 8–10   One-to-one correspondence activity card—Similar or identical objects.

ONE-TO-ONE CORRESPONDENCE—OBJECTS TO DOTS

Objective:	To match zero to nine objects with zero to nine dots.
Naturalistic and Informal Activity:	In the math center provide sets of picture and conventional dominoes and other materials that lend themselves to one-to-one correspondence. Observe what the students do with the materials. Note if they do any one-to-one correspondence as they explore. Make comments and ask questions as appropriate.
Materials:	Ten frozen juice cans or other identical containers, with dots (filled circles) painted in a dark color on each from zero to nine:

Forty-five tongue depressors or ice cream bar sticks.

Structured Activity:	Give each child a can. Put all the sticks in a container where the children can reach them. LOOK AT THE DOTS ON YOUR CAN. PUT THE SAME NUMBER OF STICKS IN YOUR CAN AS THERE ARE DOTS ON YOUR CAN. Have the children check with each other.
Follow-up:	Put the cans and sticks out during free play. Encourage children who have had a hard time in the group to practice on their own.

FIGURE 8–11   One-to-one correspondence activity card—Matching number of objects to number of dots.

Using the same procedures as in the assessment tasks, a more formal check can be made regarding what the children have learned. Once children can do one-to-one with 10 objects, try more—see how far they can go.

Summary

The most basic number skill is one-to-one correspondence. Starting in infancy, children learn about one-to-one relationships. Sensorimotor and early preoperational children spend much of their playtime in one-to-one correspondence activities.

Many opportunities for informal one-to-one correspondence activities are available during play and daily routines. Materials used for structured activities with individuals and/or small groups should be made available for free exploration also.

Materials and activities can be varied in many ways to make one-to-one correspondence fun and interesting. Once children have a basic understanding of the one-to-one concept, they can apply the concept to higher-level activities involving equivalence and more and less.

The World Wide Web contains a multitude of resources for teaching strategies in mathematics and other content areas. A list of Web addresses is included in Appendix B. Examples of resources found on the Web are included for each mathematics concept described in the text.

Example World Wide Web Activities

◆ Buttons to Buttonholes from Amy at http://www.perpetualpreschool.com/mathideas.html
◆ Sticker Matching from Stephanie at http://www.perpetualpreschool.com/mathideas.html

---

KEY TERMS

one-to-one correspondence   rational counting   concreteness

SUGGESTED ACTIVITIES

1. Present a toddler (18 months to two years old) with a plastic container and some small (but safe) objects, such as empty wooden thread spools or plastic lids. Observe how he uses the materials. Note whether anything the child does might indicate the development of the concept of one-to-one correspondence.

2. Collect the materials for one or more of the structured activities described in this unit. Try the activities with two or more children ages four or five. Describe to the class what the children do.

3. Develop your own one-to-one correspondence game. Play the game with a young child. Share the game with the class. Are there any improvements you would make?

4. Make copies of the structured activities, and add them to your Idea File. Add one or two more activities that you create or find suggested in another resource.

5. Discuss with the class what you might do if a five-year-old didn't appear to have the concept of one-to-one correspondence above two groups of three.

6. If available observe a young child interacting with one of the software items listed in this unit. Note if the activity appears to support the child's ability to engage in one-to-one correspondence.

7. Select a one-to-one correspondence activity from the Internet. Assemble any materials needed and use the activity with a small group of pre-K or kindergarten students.

REVIEW

A. Explain how you would define one-to-one correspondence when talking with a parent.

B. Determine which of the following one-to-one correspondence activities is naturalistic, informal, or structured. Give a reason for your decision.

1. Mr. Conklin has six cat pictures and six mouse pictures. "Patty, does each cat have a mouse to chase?"

2. Kathy lines up five red blocks in a row. Then she places a smaller yellow block on each red block.

3. Candy puts one bootie on each of her baby doll's feet.

4. Mindy passes one glass of juice to each child at her table.

5. Mrs. Garcia shows five-year-old José two groups of 10 pennies. "Find out if both groups of pennies have the same amount, or if one group has more."

C. Give examples of several ways that one-to-one correspondence activities may be varied.

D. Look at the following pairs of groups of items. Decide which one in each pair would be more difficult to place in one-to-one correspondence.

1. (a) five red chips and five yellow chips
   (b) 12 white chips and 12 orange chips

2. (a) four feet and four shoes
   (b) four circles and four squares

3. (a) two groups of seven
   (b) a group of seven and a group of eight

4. (a) cards with pictures of knives and forks
   (b) real knives and forks

REFERENCE

National Council of Teachers of Mathematics. (2000). *Principles and standards for school mathematics.* Reston, VA: Author. (http://www.nctm.org)

FURTHER READING AND RESOURCES

AIMS Educational Products. AIMS Education Foundation, P.O. Box 8120, Fresno, CA 93747-8120.

Baratta-Lorton, M. (1972). *Workjobs.* Menlo Park, CA: Addison-Wesley.

Burk, D., Snider, A., & Symonds, P. (1988). *Box it or bag it mathematics: Kindergarten teachers resource guide.* Portland, OR: The Math Learning Center.

Copley, J. V. (2000). *The young child and mathematics.* Washington, DC: National Association for the Education of Young Children.

Copley, J. V. (Ed.). (1999). *Mathematics in the early years.* Washington, DC: National Association for the Education of Young Children.

Richardson, K. (1984). *Developing number concepts using Unifix Cubes.*® Menlo Park, CA: Addison-Wesley.

Richardson, K. (1999). *Developing number concepts: Planning guide.* Parsippany, NJ: Dale Seymour.

Schwartz, S. L. (1995). Authentic mathematics in the classroom. *Teaching Children Mathematics, 1*(9), 580–584.

Stone, A., & Russell, S. J. (1990). *Counting: Ourselves and our families.* Palo Alto, CA: Dale Seymour.

UNIT 9
Number Sense and Counting

OBJECTIVES

After reading this unit, you should be able to:

◆ Explain the NCTM expectations for number.

◆ Describe the concept of number sense and its relationship to counting.

◆ Define rote and rational counting and explain their relationship.

◆ Identify examples of rote and rational counting.

◆ Teach counting using naturalistic, informal, and structured activities appropriate to each child's age and level of maturity.

The NCTM (2000) expectations for number focus on children in prekindergarten through grade 2 counting with understanding and recognizing "how many?" in sets of objects. The children are also expected to develop understanding of the relative position and size of whole numbers, ordinal and cardinal numbers, and their connections to each other. Finally, they are expected to develop a sense of whole numbers and be able to represent and use them in many ways. These expectations should be achieved through real-world experiences and through using physical materials.

Included in the NCTM standards is the standard that children should develop whole number skills that enable them to "construct number meanings through real-world experiences and the use of physical materials; understand our number system by relating, counting, grouping, and (eventually) place-value concepts; and develop number sense." Number sense and counting can be integrated in other content areas (Figure 9–1).

The concept of number or understanding number is referred to as **number sense**. *Number sense* makes the connection between quantities and counting. Number sense underlies the understanding of more and less, of relative amounts, of the relationship between space and quantity (i.e., number conservation), and parts and wholes of quantities. Number sense enables children to understand important benchmarks such as 5 and 10 as they relate to other quantities. Number sense also helps children estimate quantities and measurements. Counting assists children in the process of understanding quantity. Understanding that the last number

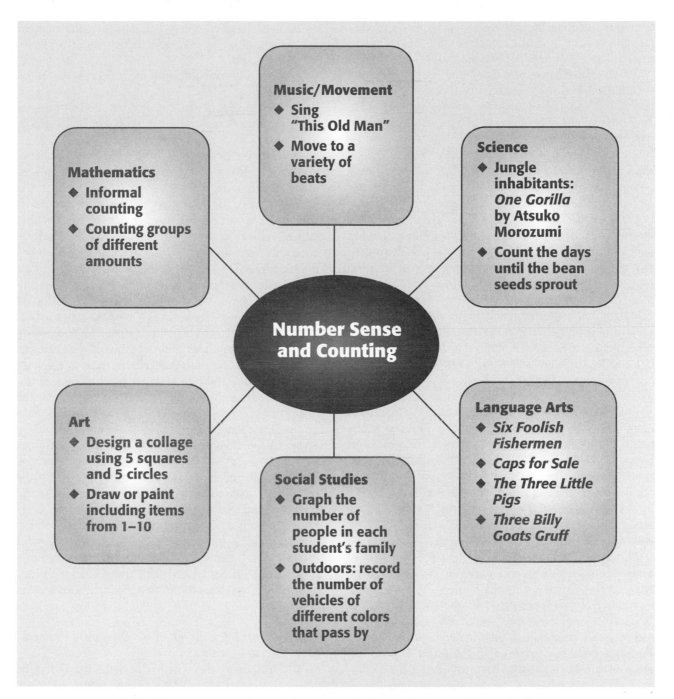

FIGURE 9–1   Integrating number sense and counting across the curriculum.

named is the quantity in the group is a critical fundamental concept. It is the understanding of the "oneness" of one, "twoness" of two, and so on.

When shown a group, seeing "how many" instantly is called subitizing. There are two types of subitizing: perceptual and conceptual. Perceptual subitizing is, when shown a group, one can state how many without counting or grouping. Young children usually learn to subitize up to four items perceptually. That is, when shown a group of four items they can tell you "four" without counting. Conceptual subitizing involves seeing number patterns within a group such as the larger dot patterns on a domino. The viewer may break the eight-dot pattern down into two groups of four, which makes up the whole. Perceptual subitizing is thought to be the basis for counting and cardinality (understanding the last number named is the amount in a group). Conceptual subitizing develops from counting and patterning and helps develop number sense and arithmetic skills. Preschoolers can subitize perceptually. Conceptual subitizing for small quantities usually begins in first grade. Clements (1999) suggests some games that can be played in kindergarten that can bridge into conceptual subitizing.

Quantities from one to four or five are the first to be recognized. Infants can perceive the difference between these small quantities, and children as young as two and one-half or three years may recognize these small amounts so easily that they seem to do so without counting. The concept of number is constructed bit by bit from infancy through the preschool years and gradually becomes a tool that can be used in problem solving.

Number's partner, counting, includes two operations—rote counting and rational counting. *Rote counting* involves reciting the names of the numerals in order from memory. That is, the child who says "One, two, three, four, five, six, seven, eight, nine, 10" has correctly counted in a rote manner from one to 10. *Rational counting* involves matching each numeral name in order to an object in a group. It builds on children's understanding of one-to-one correspondence. Reys, Lindquist, Lambdin, Smith, and Suydam (2001) identify four principles of rational counting.

1. Only one number name may be assigned to each of the objects to be counted.

2. There is a correct order in which the number names may be assigned, that is, one, two, three, and so on.
3. Counting can start with any of the items in the group.
4. The *cardinality rule* states that the last number name used is the number of objects in the group.

As an example, Maria has some pennies in her hand. She takes them out of her hand one at a time and places them on the table. Each time she places one on the table she says the next number name in sequence: "one," places first penny; "two," places another penny; "three," places another penny. She has successfully done rational counting of three objects. Rational counting is a higher level of one-to-one correspondence.

A basic understanding of accurate rote counting and one-to-one correspondence is the foundation of rational counting. The ability to rational count assists children in understanding the concept of number by enabling them to check their labeling of quantities as being a specific amount. It also helps them to compare equal quantities of different things, such as two apples, two children, and two chairs, and to realize that the quantity two is *two*, regardless of what makes up a group. In the long term, number, counting, and one-to-one correspondence all serve as the basis for developing the concept of number conservation, which is usually mastered by age six or seven. Too often the preprimary mathematics program centers on counting with repeated teacher-directed drill and practice. Children need repeated and frequent practice to develop counting skills, but this practice should be of short duration and center on naturalistic and informal instruction. Structured activities should include many applications, such as the examples of data collection that follow:

◆ How many children in the class have brothers? Sisters? Neither?
◆ How many days will it be until the first seed sprouts? Let's make some guesses, and then we'll keep track and see who comes close.
◆ How many days did we mark off before the first egg hatched?
◆ How many carrots do we need so that each rabbit will get one?

◆ How many of the small blocks will balance the big block on the balance scale?

It is a normal expectation that rote counting develops ahead of rational counting. For example, a two- or three-year-old who has a good memory might rote count to 10 but only be able to rational count one or two or three objects accurately. When given a group of more than three to count, a young child might perform as described in the following example: Six blocks are placed in front of a two and one-half-year-old, and she is asked, "How many blocks do you have?" Using her pointer finger, she "counts" and points.

◆ "One, two, three, four, five, six, seven, eight" (pointing at some blocks more than once and some not at all)
◆ "One, two, four, six, three, 10" (pointing to each block only once but losing track of the correct order)

Rational counting is a fairly complex task. To count objects accurately, the child must know the number names in the correct order and be able to coordinate eyes, hands, speech, and memory. This is difficult for the two- or three-year-old because she is still in a period of rapid growth in coordination. She is also limited in her ability to stick to a task. The teacher should not push a child to count more things than he can count easily and with success. Most rational counting experiences should be naturalistic and informal.

By age four or five the rate of physical growth is slowing. Coordination of eyes, hands, and memory is maturing. Rational counting skills should begin to catch up with rote counting skills. Structured activities can be introduced. At the same time, naturalistic and informal activities should continue.

During the kindergarten year, children usually become skilled at rote and rational counting. Many kindergartners are ready to play more complex games with quantities such as counting backward and counting on from a known quantity. Counting backward and counting on lay the foundation for the whole number operations of addition and subtraction. Estimation activities can begin with prekindergartners playing simple games like, "Guess how many beans are in a small jar" or "How many paper clips wide is the

table?," followed by checking their guesses by counting the beans and paper clips.

Kamii, in her book *Number in Preschool and Kindergarten* (1982), particularly emphasizes the necessity of being aware of the coordination of one-to-one correspondence and counting in the development of the concept of number. Four levels of development in counting have been identified by asking children to put out the same number of items as an adult put out using groups of sizes four to eight.

1. Children cannot understand what they are supposed to do.
2. They do a rough visual estimation or copy (that is, they attempt to make their group look like the model).
3. Children do a methodical one-to-one correspondence. It is usually past age five and one-half before children reach this stage.
4. Children count. That is, the child counts the items in the model and then counts out another group with the same amount. Children usually reach this stage at about age seven.

To develop the coordination of the two concepts, it is essential that children count and do one-to-one correspondence using movable objects. It becomes obvious that, among other weaknesses, the use of workbook pages precludes moving the objects to be counted and/or matched. In addition, opportunities should be provided for the children to work together so they can discuss and compare ideas. As the children work individually and/or with others, watch closely and note the thinking process that appears to take place as they solve problems using counting and one-to-one correspondence.

Assessment

The adult should note the child's regular activity. Does he recognize groups of zero to four without counting: "Mary has no cookies," "I have two cookies," "John has four cookies." Does he use rational counting correctly when needed: "Here, Mr. Black, six blocks for you." (Mr. Black has seen him count them out on his own.) For formal assessment, see the tasks on page 120 and those in the Appendix A. Be sure to record naturalistic and informal events.

SAMPLE ASSESSMENT TASK

4G   **Preoperational Ages 3–6**
Rote Counting: Unit 9

METHOD: Interview, individual.

SKILL: Demonstrates the ability to rote count.

MATERIALS: None.

PROCEDURE: COUNT FOR ME. COUNT AS FAR AS YOU CAN. If the child hesitates or looks puzzled, ask again. If the child still doesn't respond, say, ONE, TWO, WHAT'S NEXT?

EVALUATION: Note how far the child counts and the accuracy of the counting. Young children often lose track (i.e., "One, two, three, four, five, six, 10, seven, . . .") or miss a number name. Twos and threes may just count their ages, whereas fours usually can count accurately to 10 and might try the teens and even beyond. By age five or six, children will usually begin to understand the commonalities in the 20s and beyond and move on toward counting to 100. Young children vary a great deal at each age level, so it is important to find where each individual is and move along from there.

INSTRUCTIONAL RESOURCE: Charlesworth, R., and Lind, K. K. (2003). *Math and Science for Young Children* (4th ed.). Clifton Park, NY: Delmar Learning.

SAMPLE ASSESSMENT TASK

4H   **Preoperational Ages 3–6**
Rational Counting: Unit 9

METHOD: Interview, individual or small group.

SKILL: Child demonstrates ability to rational count.

MATERIALS: Thirty or more objects such as cube blocks, chips, or Unifix Cubes.®

PROCEDURE: Place a pile of objects in front of the child (about 10 for a three-year-old, 20 for a four-year-old, 30 for a five-year-old, and as many as 100 for older children). COUNT THESE FOR ME. HOW MANY CAN YOU COUNT?

EVALUATION: Note how accurately the child counts and how many objects are attempted. In observing the process, note the following.
1. Does the child use just his eyes, or does he actually touch each object as he counts?
2. Is some organizational system used, such as lining the objects up in rows, moving the ones counted to the side, and so on?
3. Compare accuracy on rational counting with the child's rote counting ability.

INSTRUCTIONAL RESOURCE: Charlesworth, R., and Lind, K. K. (2003). *Math and Science for Young Children* (4th ed.). Clifton Park, NY: Delmar Learning.

Naturalistic Activities

Number sense is a concept and counting is a skill that are used a great deal by young children in their everyday activities. Once these are in the child's thoughts and activity, he will be observed often in number and counting activities. He practices rote counting often. He may run up to the teacher or parent saying, "I can count—one, two, three." He may be watching a TV program and hear "one, two, three, four. . . ." He may then repeat "one, two. . . ." At first he may play with the number names saying to himself, "one, two, five, four, eight, . . ." in no special order. Listen carefully and note that gradually he gets more of the names in the right order.

Number appears often in the child's activities once he has the idea in mind. A child is eating crackers, "Look at all my crackers. I have two crackers." One and two are usually the first amounts used by children two and three years old. They may use one and two for quite a while before they go on to larger groups. Number names are used for an early form of division. That is, a child has three cookies, which he divides equally with his friends, "One for you, one for you, and one for me." The child is looking at a picture book, "There is one daddy and two babies." The child wants another toy, "I want one more little car, Dad."

Informal Activities

The alert adult can find a multitude of ways to take advantage of opportunities for informal instruction. For example, the child is watching a children's television program. The teacher is sitting next to her. A voice from the TV rote counts by singing, "One, two, three, four, five, six." The teacher says to the child, "That's fun, let's count too." They then sing together. "One, two, three, four, five, six." Or, the teacher and children are waiting for the school bus to arrive. "Let's count as far as we can while we wait. One, two, three. . . ." Because rote counting is learned through frequent but short periods of practice, informal activities should be used most for teaching.

Everyday activities offer many opportunities for informal rational counting and number activities. For instance, the teacher is helping a child get dressed after her nap. "Find your shoes and socks. How many shoes do you have? How many socks? How many feet?" Some children are meeting at the door. The teacher says, "We are going to the store. There should be five of us. Let's count and be sure we are all here."

Table setting offers many chances for rational counting. "Put six placemats on each table." "How many more forks do we need?" "Count out four napkins." Play activities also offer times for rational counting. "Mary, please give Tommy two trucks." A child is looking at his hands, which are covered with fingerpaint: "How many red hands do you have, Joey?"

A more challenging problem can be presented by asking an open-ended question such as, "Get enough napkins for everyone at your table" or "Be sure everyone has the same number of carrot sticks." In these situations, children don't have a clue to help them decide how many they need or how many each person should get but have to figure out for themselves how to solve the problem. Often children will forget to count themselves. This presents an excellent opportunity for group discussion to try to figure out what went wrong. The teacher could follow up such an incident by reading the book *Six Foolish Fishermen* (Elkin, 1968, 1971; see Appendix B), in which the fishermen make the same mistake.

Structured Activities

Rote counting is learned mostly through naturalistic and informal activities. However, there are short, fun things that can be used to help children learn the number names in the right order. There are many rhymes, songs, and finger plays. Songs include those such as "This Old Man," "Johnny Works with One Hammer," and "Five Little Ducks."

A favorite old rhyme is as follows:

> One, two, buckle your shoe.
> Three, four, shut the door.
> Five, six, pick up sticks.
> Seven, eight, shut the gate.
> Nine, 10, a big fat hen.

A finger play can be used.

> ### "Five Little Birdies"
> (*Hold up five fingers. As each bird leaves fly your hand away and come back with one fewer finger standing up*.)
> Five little birdies sitting by the door
> One flew away and then there were four.
> Four little birdies sitting in a tree
> One flew away and then there were three.
> Three little birdies sitting just like you
> One flew away and then there were two.
> One little birdie sitting all alone
> He flew away and then there were none.

More direct ways of practicing rote counting are also good. Clapping and counting at the same time teaches number order and gives practice in rhythm and coordination. With a group, everyone can count at the same time, "Let's count together. One, two, three. . . ." Individual children can be asked, "Count as far as you can."

Groups that have zero to four items are special in the development of rational counting skills. The number of items in groups this size can be perceived without counting. For this reason these groups are easy for children to understand. They should have many experiences and activities with groups of size zero to four before they work with groups of five and more. With structured activities it is wise to start with groups of size two because, as mentioned before, there are so many that occur naturally. For example, the child has two eyes, two hands, two arms, and two legs. Two pieces of bread are used to make a sandwich, and bikes with two wheels are signs of being big. For this reason, activities using two are presented first in the following examples. The activities are set up so that they can be copied onto activity cards for the file.

ACTIVITIES

NUMBER: GROUPS OF TWO

OBJECTIVE: To learn the idea of two.

MATERIALS: The children's bodies, the environment, a flannelboard and/or a magnetic board, pairs of objects, pictures of pairs of objects.

NATURALISTIC AND INFORMAL ACTIVITIES: As children play with materials in the classroom note any occasions when they identify two objects. Ask questions such as, "How many shoes do you need for your dress-up outfit?", "Can two cups of sand fill the bowl?"

STRUCTURED ACTIVITIES:
1. Put several pairs of felt pieces (such as hearts, triangles, or bunnies, for example) on the flannelboard (or magnets on the magnet board). Point to each group in turn: WHAT ARE THESE? HOW MANY ARE THERE?
2. Have the children check their bodies and the other children's bodies for groups of two.
3. Have the children, one at a time, find groups of two in the room.
4. Using rummy cards, other purchased picture cards, or cards you have made, make up sets of cards with identical pairs. Give each child a pack with several pairs mixed up. Have them sort the pack and find the groups of two.
5. Have a container with many objects. Have the children sort out as many groups of two as they can find.

FOLLOW-UP: Have the materials available during center time.

NUMBER: GROUPS OF THREE

OBJECTIVE: To learn the idea of three.

MATERIALS: Flannelboard and/or magnet board, objects, picture cards.

NATURALISTIC AND INFORMAL ACTIVITIES: As children play with materials in the classroom note any occasions when they identify three objects. Ask questions such as, if three children are playing house, "How many cups do you need for your party?", "Can three cups of sand fill the bowl?" to a three-year-old, "How many candles were on your birthday cake?"

STRUCTURED ACTIVITIES: Do the same types of activities using groups of three. Emphasize that three is one more than two.

FOLLOW-UP: Have the materials available during center time.

NUMBER: GROUPS OF ONE

OBJECTIVE: To learn the idea that one is a group.

MATERIALS: Flannelboard and/or magnet board, objects, picture cards.

NATURALISTIC AND INFORMAL ACTIVITIES: As children play with materials in the classroom note any occasions when they identify one object. Ask questions, such as if children are playing house, "How many cups does each person need for the party?", "How many glasses does each person get for milk at lunch?"

STRUCTURED ACTIVITIES: Do the same types of activities using groups of one as were done for groups of two and three.

FOLLOW-UP: Have the materials available during center time.

NUMBER: ZERO

OBJECTIVE: To understand the idea that a group with nothing in it is called *zero*.

NATURALISTIC AND INFORMAL ACTIVITIES: Note if children use the term *zero* during their play activities. Ask questions such as, "If all the sand falls on the floor, how much will be left in the sandbox?", "If you eat all your beans then you will have how many?"

MATERIALS: Flannelboard, magnet board, and objects.

STRUCTURED ACTIVITIES:
1. Show the children groups of things on the flannel board, magnet board, and/or groups of objects. SEE ALL THESE THINGS? Give them a chance to look and respond. NOW I TAKE THEM AWAY. WHAT DO I HAVE NOW? They should respond with "nothing," "all gone," and/or "no more."
2. Put out a group of flannel pieces, magnet shapes, or objects of a size the children all know (such as one, two, three, or four). Keep taking one away. HOW MANY NOW? When none are left say: THIS AMOUNT IS CALLED ZERO. Repeat until they will answer "zero" on their own.

3. Play a silly game. Ask HOW MANY REAL LIVE TIGERS DO WE HAVE IN OUR ROOM? (continue with other things that obviously are not in the room).

FOLLOW-UP: Work on the concept informally. Ask questions: HOW MANY CHILDREN ARE HERE AFTER EVERYONE GOES HOME? (after snack if all the food has been eaten) HOW MANY COOKIES (CRACKERS, PRETZELS, etc.) DO YOU HAVE NOW?

After the children have the ideas of groups of zero, one, two, and three, then go on to four. Use the same kinds of activities. When they have four in mind, then do activities using groups of all five amounts. Emphasize the idea of *one more than* as you move to each larger group.

NUMBER: USING SETS ZERO THROUGH FOUR

OBJECTIVE: To understand groups of zero through four.

MATERIALS: Flannelboard, magnet board, and/or objects.

1. Show the children several groups of objects of different amounts. Ask them to point to sets of one, two, three, and four.
2. Give the children a container of many objects. Have them find sets of one, two, three, and four.
3. Show the children containers of objects (pennies, buttons, etc.). Ask them to find the ones with groups of zero, one, two, three, and four.
4. Give each child four objects. Ask each one to make as many different groups as he can.
5. Ask the children to find out HOW MANY _____ ARE IN THE ROOM? (Suggest things for which there are four or fewer.)

When the children have the idea of groups from zero to four, they can then go on to groups larger than four. Some children are able to perceive five without counting just as they perceive zero through four without actually counting. Having learned the groups of four and fewer, children can be taught five by adding on one more to groups of four. When the children understand five as four with one more and six as five with one more and so on, then more advanced rational counting can begin. That is, children can work with groups of objects where they can find the number only by actually counting each object. Before working with a child on counting groups of six or more, the adult must be sure the child can do the following activities.

◆ Recognize groups of zero to four without counting
◆ Rote count to six or more correctly and quickly
◆ Recognize that a group of five is a group of four with one more added

The following are activities for learning about groups larger than four.

NUMBER/RATIONAL COUNTING: INTRODUCING FIVE

OBJECTIVE: To understand that five is four with one more item added.

MATERIALS: Flannelboard, magnet board, and/or objects.

NATURALISTIC AND INFORMAL ACTIVITIES: Have a variety of manipulatives in the math center. Note how children group the materials and if they mention "how many," such as "I have five red cubes. I need three green cubes." Ask questions such as, "How many white cubes have you hooked together?"

STRUCTURED ACTIVITIES:
1. Show the children a group of four. HOW MANY IN THIS GROUP? Show the children a group of five. HOW MANY IN THIS GROUP? Note how many already have the idea of five. Tell them YES, THIS IS A GROUP OF FIVE. Have them make other groups with the same amount using the first group as a model.
2. Give each child five objects. Ask them to identify how many objects they have.
3. Give each child seven or eight objects. Ask them to make a group of five.

FOLLOW-UP: Have containers of easily counted and perceived objects always available for the children to explore. These would be items such as buttons, poker chips, Unifix Cubes,® and inch cubes. Use books that focus on five, such as *Five Little Ducks* (Raffi: Songs to Read Series, Crown) and *Five Little Monkeys Sitting in a Tree* (E. Christfellow, Clarion).

NUMBER/RATIONAL COUNTING: GROUPS LARGER THAN FIVE

OBJECTIVE: To be able to count groups of amounts greater than five.

MATERIALS: Flannelboard and/or magnet board, objects for counting, pictures of groups on cards, items in the environment.

NATURALISTIC AND INFORMAL ACTIVITIES: Have a variety of manipulatives in the math center. Note how children group the materials and if they mention "how many," such as "I have seven red cubes. I need six green cubes." Ask questions such as, "How many white cubes have you hooked together?", "If you hooked one more cube to your line, how many would you have?"

STRUCTURED ACTIVITIES:
1. One step at a time present groups on the flannel board and magnet board and groups made up of objects such as buttons, chips, ice cream bar sticks, inch cube blocks, etc. Have the children take turns counting them—together and individually.
2. Present cards with groups of six or more, showing cats, dogs, houses, or similar figures. Ask the children as a group or individually to tell how many items are pictured on each card.
3. Give the children small containers with items to count.
4. Count things in the room. HOW MANY TABLES (CHAIRS, WINDOWS, DOORS, CHILDREN, TEACHERS)? Have the children count all at the same time and individually.

FOLLOW-UP: Have the materials available for use during center time. Watch for opportunities for informal activities.

NUMBER/RATIONAL COUNTING: FOLLOW-UP WITH STORIES

OBJECTIVE: To be able to apply rational counting to fantasy situations.

MATERIALS: Stories that will reinforce the ideas of groups of numbers and rational counting skills: Some examples are *The Three Little Pigs, The Three Bears, Three Billy Goats Gruff, Snow White and the Seven Dwarfs, Six Foolish Fishermen.*

ACTIVITIES: As these stories are read to the younger children, take time to count the number of characters who are the same animal or same kind of person. Use felt cutouts of the characters for counting activities and for one-to-one matching (as suggested in Unit 8). Have older children dramatize the stories. Get them going with questions such as HOW MANY PEOPLE WILL WE NEED TO BE BEARS? HOW MANY PORRIDGE BOWLS (SPOONS, CHAIRS, BEDS) DO WE NEED? JOHN, YOU GET THE BOWLS AND SPOONS.

FOLLOW-UP: Have the books and other materials available for children to use during center time.

NUMBER/RATIONAL COUNTING: FOLLOW-UP WITH COUNTING BOOKS

OBJECTIVE: To strengthen rational counting skills.

MATERIALS: Counting books (see list in Appendix B).

ACTIVITIES: Go through the books with one child or small group of children. Discuss the pictures as a language development activity, and count the items pictured on each page.

RATIONAL COUNTING: FOLLOW-UP WITH ONE-TO-ONE CORRESPONDENCE

OBJECTIVE: To combine one-to-one correspondence and counting.

MATERIALS: Flannelboard and/or magnet board and counting objects.

ACTIVITIES: As the children work with the counting activities, have them check their sets that they say are the same number by using one-to-one correspondence. See activities for Unit 8.

FOLLOW-UP: Have materials available during center time.

EXAMPLE WORLD WIDE WEB ACTIVITIES

◆ Let's Count. Counting activities with the numbers from one to 10. Provides pre-K–grade one students practice in counting, using symbols and number names. Link at http://www.math.rice.edu/~lanius/counting/ (Link from Eisenhower National Clearinghouse [ENC])

◆ 100th Day of School Celebration! K–4. Suggestions for Internet and e-mail activities, links to other Web sites, and numerous classroom ideas for making the 100th day of school celebration exciting. Link from Eisenhower National Clearinghouse (ENC) or at http://www.siec.k12.in.us/%7Ewest/proj/100th/

◆ Counting in a Variety of Ways. K–three. Counting in rhythm to music by fives and other skip counting. Link at http://www.lightspan.com

◆ More 100th Day Activities on Teacher2teacher. Link at http://www.mathforum.org.

◆ Magical Number 10. Link at http://www.mathforum.org.

Four- to six-year-olds can play simple group games that require them to apply their counting skills. For example, a bowling game requires them to count the number of pins they knock down. A game in which they try to drop clothespins into a container requires them to count the number of clothespins that land in the container. They can compare the number of pins knocked down or the number of clothespins dropped into the containers by each child. By age six or seven, children can keep a cumulative score using tick marks (lines) such as:

Student	Score
Derrick	//////
Liu Pei	////////
Brent	////
Theresa	//////

Not only can they count, they can compare amounts to find out who has the most and if any of them have the same amount. Older children (see Units 23 and 24) will be interested in writing numerals and might realize that instead of tick marks they can write down the numeral that represents the amount to be recorded.

Students who are skilled at counting enjoy sorting small objects such as colored macaroni, beads, miniature animals, or buttons. At first they might be given a small amount such as 10 items with which to work. They can compare the amounts in each of the groups that they construct as well as compare the amounts in their groups with a partner's. Eventually they can move on to larger groups of objects and to more complex activities such as recording data with number symbols and constructing graphs (see Unit 20). As a special treat, this type of activity can be done with small edibles such as m&m's,® Trix,® Teddy Grahams,® or Gummy Bears.® m&m® activities can be introduced with the book *The m&m's® Counting Book* by Barbara B. McGrath (1994).

Another activity that builds number concepts is the Hundred Days Celebration. Starting the first day of school, using concrete materials, the class records how many days of school have gone by. Attach two large, clear plastic cups to the bulletin board. Use a supply of drinking straws or tongue depressors as recording devices. Each day, count in unison the number of days of school, and add a straw to the cup on the right. Whenever 10 straws are collected, bundle them with a rubber band, and place them in the left-hand cup. Explain that when there are 10 bundles, it will be the 100th day. Ten is used as an informal benchmark. On the 100th day, each child brings a plastic zip-top bag containing 100 items. It is exciting to see what they bring: pieces of dry macaroni, dry beans, pennies, candy, hairpins, and so on. Working in pairs, they can check their collections by counting out groups of 10 and counting how many groups they have. To aid their organization, large mats with 10 circles on each or 10 clear plastic glasses can be supplied. Older fours and kindergartner and primary students enjoy this activity.

Kindergartners can work with simple problem-solving challenges. Schulman and Eston (1998) described a type of problem that kindergartners find intriguing. The children were in the second half of kindergarten and had previously worked in small groups. The basic situation was demonstrated as the "Carrot and raisin" problem.

> Jackie had carrots and raisins on her plate. She had seven items in all. What did Jackie have on her plate?

The children selected orange rods and small stones to represent carrots and raisins, respectively. They were given paper plates to use as work mats. When they had a solution that worked, they recorded it by drawing a picture. As they worked and shared ideas, they realized that many different groupings were surfacing. They recorded all the solutions. Of course, what they were discovering were the facts that compose seven. This same context led to other problems of varying degrees of difficulty (sea stars and hermit crabs in a tide pool, pineapples and pears in a fruit basket, seeds that germinated and seeds that didn't). Some children continued with random strategies while others discovered organized strategies.

Quite a bit of computer software has been designed to reinforce counting skills and the number concept. Five-year-old George sits at the computer deeply involved with *Stickybear Numbers*. Each time he presses the space bar, a group with one fewer appears on the screen. Each time he presses a number, a group with that amount appears. His friend Kate joins him and comments on the pictures. They both count the figures in each group and compare the results. Activity 7 includes a list of software the reader might wish to review.

Evaluation

Informal evaluation can be done by noting the answers given by the children during direct instruction sessions. The teacher should also observe the children during center time and notice whether they apply what they have learned. When they choose to explore materials used in the structured lessons during center time, questions can be asked. For instance, Kate is at the flannelboard arranging the felt shapes in rows. As her teacher goes by, she stops and asks, "How many bunnies do you have in that row?" Or, four children are playing house, and the teacher asks, "How many children in this family?" Formal evaluation can be done with one child by using tasks such as those in Appendix A.

Hundreds collections and graphs can be placed in portfolios. Photos of children working with materials can also be included. Anecdotes and checklists can be used to record milestones in number concept growth and development.

Kathy Richardson (1999, p.7) provides questions to guide evaluation of counting and number sense. Some key questions for counting include:

♦ To what amount can children work with (i.e., five, 10, 12, etc.)

♦ What kinds of errors do the children make? Are they consistent or random?

♦ Do they stick with the idea of one-to-one correspondence as they count?

♦ Are they accurate? Do they check their results?

♦ Do they remember the number they counted to and realize that is the amount in the group (cardinal number)?

Some key questions to consider when evaluating number sense include:

♦ Can the children subitize perceptually, that is, recognize small groups of four or five without counting?

♦ Knowing the amount in one group, can they use that information to figure out how many are in another group?

♦ Can they make reasonable estimates of the amount in a group and revise their estimate after counting some items?

♦ When items are added to a group that they have already counted, do they count on or begin again?

Considering these questions will help you to evaluate if the children understand the concepts of number and number sense.

Summary

Number sense or the number concept connects counting with quantity. Counting, one-to-one correspondence, arranging and rearranging groups, and comparing quantities (see Unit 11) help to develop number sense. The number concept involves an understanding of *oneness, twoness,* and so on. Perceptual subitizing or recognizing groups of four or five or less without counting usually develops during the preschool/kindergarten period. Counting includes two types of skills: rote counting and rational counting. Rote counting is saying from memory the names of the numerals in order. Rational counting is attaching number sense to the number names in numerical order to items in a group to find out the total number of items in the group. There are four principles of rational counting: (1) saying the number names in the correct order; (2) achieving one-to-one correspondence between number name and object; (3) understanding that counting can begin with any object; and (4) understanding that the last number named is the total.

Rote counting is mastered before rational counting. Rational counting begins to catch up with rote counting after age four or five. The number concept is learned simultaneously. Quantities greater than four are not identified until the child learns to rational count beyond four. Counting is learned for the most part through naturalistic and informal activities supported by structured lessons.

KEY TERMS

number sense
subitizing
perceptual subitizing

conceptual subitizing
cardinality

rote counting
rational counting

SUGGESTED ACTIVITIES

1. Try the sample assessment tasks included in this unit with three or four children at different ages between two and one-half and six and one-half years. Record the results, and compare the answers received at each age level.

2. Go to the children's section of the library or a local bookstore. Find three number books (such as those listed in Appendix B). Write a review of each one, giving a brief description and explaining why and how you would use each book.

3. With one or more young children, try one or more of the counting activities suggested in this unit. Evaluate the success of the activity.

4. Add rote and rationale activity cards to your Idea File or Idea Notebook.

 blocks die

5. Make a counting kit by putting together a collection of objects such as shells, buttons, coins, and poker chips. *go up to 10   same   different*

6. Visit one or more preschool or kindergarten classrooms. Record any counting and/or number concept activities or events observed. Decide if each recorded incident should be identified as naturalistic, informal, or structured. Give a reason for each decision.

7. Try to locate some of the computer software listed below, and review it. Use the following criteria suggested by Spencer and Baskin (in Hoot, 1986):

    a. Read the instructions that come with the program, and then try it out. The first time through, take note of your impressions. Was the program interesting? Easy to use?

    b. Go through the program two more times. Are the prompts, questions, and responses logical and clear? Are the graphics, sound, and/or animation of good quality?

    c. If possible, try out each program you reviewed with children. Did they enjoy it? Could they work independently? Would they like to use it again?

    d. Obtain the opinions of teachers and/or parents who have used the program with children.

    e. Write an evaluation of each program, including the following information:

        (1) Program name, manufacturer, and price
        (2) Concept or skill taught
        (3) Brief description
        (4) Your evaluation

Suggested Software

same   Silver paper-clips   different   color paper clips

◆ Balancing Bear. Pleasantville, NY: Sunburst Technology.
◆ Blues 123 Time Activities. Woodinvill, WA: Humongous.
◆ Charlie Brown's 123s. New York: Random House.
◆ Coco's Math Project 1. Singapore, SG: Times Learning Systems Ptd Ltd.
◆ Finger Abacus. Palo Alto, CA: Edutek Corp.
◆ Hands-on-Math, Vols. 1, 2, 3. Nashua, NH: Delta Educational.
◆ Infinity City. Link at http://www.headbone.com: Headbone Interactive.
◆ Introduction to Counting. Agoura, CA: Edu-Ware Services, Inc.
◆ James Discovers Math. Novato, CA: Broderbund.
◆ Kinder Concepts. Farmington, MI: Midwest Software.
◆ Let's Explore the Jungle with Buzzy the Knowledge Bug. Woodinville, WA: Humongous.

- ◆ Millie's Math House. Pleasantville, NY: Sunburst.
- ◆ Sequence. Cambridge, MA: Spinnaker.
- ◆ Stickybear Numbers. Middletown, CT: Weekly Reader Family Software.
- ◆ Unifix Software. Nashua, NH: Delta Educational.

8. Using some manipulatives, show three-, four-, and five-year-olds some groups of two, three, four, and five. Note if they can tell you "how many" in each group without counting.
9. Search the Web for some number and number sense activities. Find some of those suggested in the unit. Try out one of your selections with one or more three- to five-year-old children.

REVIEW

A. Discuss the relationships between number sense, counting, and the understanding of quantities and subitizing.
B. Explain the relationship between rote and rational counting.
C. Describe two examples of rote counting and two examples of rational counting.
D. How should the adult respond in each of the following situations?
   1. Rudy (age three years and six months) looks up at his teacher and proudly recites: "One, two, three, five, seven, 10."
   2. Tony, age two, says, "I have two eyes, you have two eyes."
   3. Molly has been asked to get six spoons for the children at her lunch table. She returns with seven spoons.
   4. Robert is four and one-half. He counts a stack of six Unifix Cubes,® "One, two, three, four, five, seven—seven cubes."
   5. An adult is sitting with some four- and five-year-olds who are waiting for the school bus. She decides to do some informal counting activities.

REFERENCES

Clements, D. H. (1999). Subitizing: What is it? Why teach it? *Teaching Children Mathematics, 5*(7), 400–405.

Elkin, B. (1968, 1971). *Six foolish fishermen*. New York: Scholastic.

Hoot, J. L. (1986). *Computers in early childhood education*. Englewood Cliffs, NJ: Prentice-Hall.

Kamii, C. 1982. *Number in preschool and kindergarten*. Washington, DC: National Association for the Education of Young Children.

McGrath, B. B. (1994). *The m&m's® counting book*. Watertown, MA: Charlesbridge.

National Council of Teachers of Mathematics. (2000). *Principles and standards for school mathematics*. Reston, VA: Author. (http://www.nctm.org)

Reys, R. E., Lindquist, M. M., Lambdin, D. V., Smith, N. L., & Suydam, M. N. (2001). *Helping children learn mathematics*. New York: John Wiley.

Richardson, K. (1999). *Developing number concepts: Planning guide*. Parsippany, NJ: Dale Seymour.

Schulman, L., & Eston, R. (1998). A problem worth revisiting. *Teaching Children Mathematics*, 5(2), 73–77.

FURTHER READING AND RESOURCES

AIMS Educational Products. AIMS Education Foundation, P.O. Box 8120, Fresno, CA 93747-8120.

Baratta-Lorton, M. (1976). *Math their way.* Menlo Park, CA: Addison-Wesley.

Burk, D., Snider, A., & Symonds, P. (1988). *Box it or bag it mathematics: Kindergarten teachers' resource guide.* Portland, OR: The Math Learning Center.

Burton, G. M. (1993). *Curriculum and evaluation standards for school mathematics: Number sense and operations.* Reston, VA: National Council of Teachers of Mathematics.

Copley, J. V. (2000). *The young child and mathematics.* Washington, DC: National Association for the Education of Young Children.

Copley, J. V. (Ed.). (1999). *Mathematics in the early years.* Washington, DC: National Association for the Education of Young Children.

Gelman, R., & Gallistel, C. R. (1986). *The child's understanding of number.* Cambridge, MA: Harvard University Press.

Hanson, E. (1996). Hole math. *Teaching Children Mathematics, 2*(5), 264–268.

Hohmann, C., Carmody, B., & McCabe-Branz, C. (1995). *High/Scope buyer's guide to children's software* (11th ed.). Ypsilanti, MI: High/Scope.

Hopkins, L. (1995). Popping up number sense. *Teaching Children Mathematics, 2*(2), 82–86.

Knecht, P. S. (1991). Making mathematics meaningful with M & Ms®. *Arithmetic Teacher, 38*(9), 50–51.

Lewis, C., & Lewis, T. (1996). Getting acquainted: K–2. *Teaching Children Mathematics, 3*(1), 24.

Myren, C. L. (1996). Encouraging young children to solve problems independently. *Teaching Children Mathematics, 3*(2), 72–76.

Richardson, K. (1984). *Developing number concepts using Unifix Cubes.*® Menlo Park, CA: Addison-Wesley.

Richardson, K. (1999). *Developing number concepts: Counting, comparing, and pattern.* Parsippany, NJ: Dale Seymour.

Russell, S. J., & Stone, A. (1990). *Counting: Ourselves and our families.* Palo Alto, CA: Dale Seymour.

UNIT 10
Logic and Classifying

OBJECTIVES

After reading this unit, you should be able to:

- Explain the NCTM expectations for logic and classifying.
- Describe features of groups.
- Describe the activity of classifying.
- Identify five types of criteria that children can use when classifying.
- Assess, plan, and teach classification activities appropriate for young children.

NCTM (2000) expectations for logic and classifying include being able to sort, classify, and order objects by size, number, and other properties (see also Units 11 and 17) and sort and classify objects according to their attributes and organize data about the objects (see also Unit 20).

In mathematics and science, an understanding of constructing logical grouping and classifying is essential. The NCTM standards identify the importance of connecting counting to grouping. Constructing logical groups provides children with valuable logical thinking experiences. As children construct logical groups, they organize materials by classifying them according to some common criteria. A group may contain from zero (an empty group) to an endless number of things. The youngest children may group by criteria that are not apparent to adults but make sense to them. As children develop, they gradually begin constructing groups for which the criteria are apparent to adults. Children also note common group-

ings that they observe in their environment such as dishes that are alike in pattern go together and cars have four tires plus a spare making a total of five in the group. Logical thinking and classification skills are fundamental concepts that apply across the curriculum (Figure 10–1).

To **add** is to put together or join groups. The four tires on the wheels plus the spare in the trunk equals five tires. To **subtract** is to separate a group into smaller groups. For example, one tire goes flat and is taken off. It is left for repairs, and the spare is put on. A group of one (the flat tire) has been taken away or subtracted from the group of five. There are now two groups: four good tires on the car and one flat tire being repaired.

Before doing any formal addition and subtraction, the child needs to learn about groups and how they can be joined and separated (Figure 10–2). That is, children must practice **sorting** (separating) and **grouping** (joining). This type of activity is called *classification*.

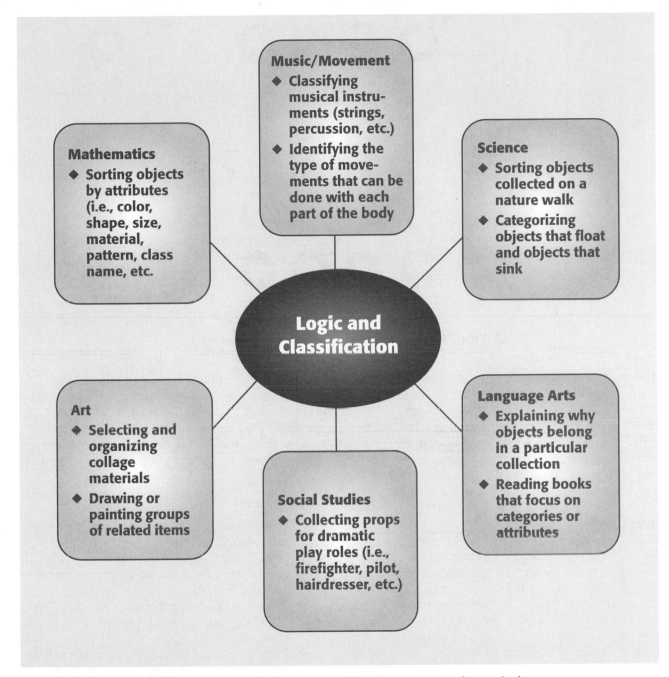

FIGURE 10–1 Integrating logic and classification across the curriculum.

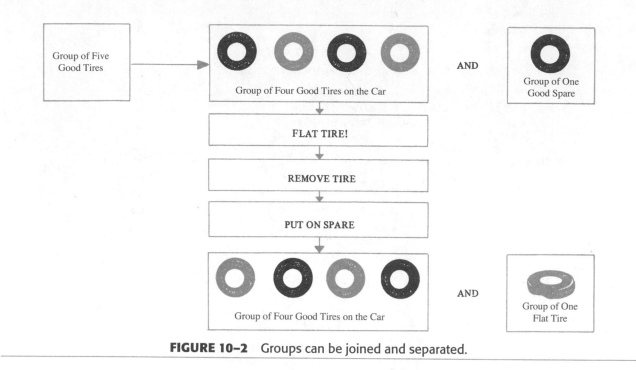

FIGURE 10–2 Groups can be joined and separated.

The child does tasks where he separates and groups things because they belong together for some reason. Things may belong together because they are the same color, or the same shape, do the same work, are the same size, are always together, and so on. For example, a child may have a box of wooden blocks and a box of toy cars (wood, metal, and plastic). The child has two groups: blocks and cars. He then takes the blocks out of the box and separates them by grouping them into four piles: blue blocks, red blocks, yellow blocks, and green blocks. He now has four groups of blocks. He builds a garage with the red blocks. He puts some cars in the garage. He now has a new group of toys. If he has put only red cars in the garage, he now has a group of red toys. The blocks and toys could be grouped in many other ways by using shape and material (wood, plastic, and metal) as the basis for the groups. Figure 10–3 illustrates some possible groups using the blocks and cars.

Young children spend much of their playtime in just such classification activities. As children work busily at these sorting tasks, they simultaneously learn words that label their activity. This happens when another person tells them the names and makes comments: "You have made a big pile of red things." "You have a pile of blue blocks, a pile of green blocks, . . ." "Those are plastic, and those are wood." As children learn to speak, the adult questions them, "What color are these? Which ones are plastic?"

The child learns that things may be grouped together using a number of kinds of common features.

◆ **Color:** Things can go together that are the same color.

◆ **Shape:** Things may all be round, square, triangular, and so on.

◆ **Size:** Some things are big, and some are small; some are fat, and some are thin; some are short, and some are tall.

◆ **Material:** Things are made out of different materials such as wood, plastic, glass, paper, cloth, and metal.

◆ **Pattern:** Things have different visual patterns such as stripes, dots, flowers, or they may be plain (no design).

◆ **Texture:** Things feel different from each other (smooth, rough, soft, hard, wet, dry).

◆ **Function:** Some items do the same thing or are used for the same thing (all are for eating, writing, playing music, for example).

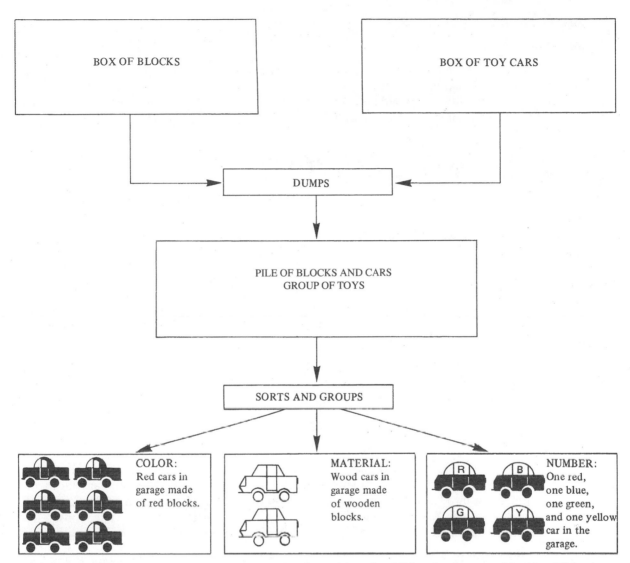

FIGURE 10–3 Classification (forming groups) may be evident in children's play as with this child who sorts blocks and cars in several logical groupings.

◆ **Association:** Some things do a job together (candle and match, milk and glass, shoe and foot) or come from the same place (bought at the store or seen at the zoo) or belong to a special person (the hose, truck, and hat belong to the firefighter).

◆ **Class name:** There are names that may belong to several things (people, animals, food, vehicles, weapons, clothing, homes).

◆ **Common features:** All have handles or windows or doors or legs or wheels, for example.

◆ **Number:** All are groups of specific amounts (see Unit 6) such as pairs; groups of three, four, five, and so on.

Which criteria children select or exactly how they group is not as important as the process of logical thinking that they exercise as they sort and group.

Assessment

The adult should note and record the child's play activities. Does he sort and group his play materials? For example, he might play with a pegboard and put each color peg in its own row; build two garages with big cars in one and small cars in another; when offered several kinds of crackers for snack, he might pick out only triangle shapes; he might say, "Only boys can be daddies—girls are mothers."

More formal assessment can be done using the tasks in Appendix A. Two examples are shown.

SAMPLE ASSESSMENT TASK

5K   **Preoperational Ages 4–6**

Logic and Classifying, Clue Sort: Unit 10

METHOD: Interview.

SKILL: Child is able to classify and form sets using verbal and/or object clues.

MATERIALS: Twenty to 25 objects (or pictures of objects or cutouts) that can be grouped into several possible sets by criteria such as color, shape, size, or category (i.e., animals, plants, furniture, clothing, or toys).

PROCEDURE: Set all the objects in front of the child in a random arrangement. Try the following types of clues.

1. FIND SOME THINGS THAT ARE _____ (Name a specific color, shape, size, material, pattern, function, or class).
2. Hold up one object, picture, or cutout; say, FIND SOME THINGS THAT BELONG WITH THIS. After the choices are made, ask, WHY DO THESE THINGS BELONG TOGETHER?

EVALUATION: Note whether the child makes a conventional logical group and provides a conventional logical reason such as "Because they are cars," "They are all green," "You can eat with them," and so on or a "creative" reason that is logical to the child if not to the adult such as "My mother would like them," "They all have points," "I like these colors, I don't like those," and so on.

INSTRUCTIONAL RESOURCE: Charlesworth, R., and Lind, K. K. (2003). *Math and Science for Young Children* (4th ed.). Clifton Park, NY: Delmar Learning.

SAMPLE ASSESSMENT TASK

5J   **Preoperational Ages 4–6**

Logic and Classifying, Free Sort: Unit 10

METHOD: Interview.

SKILL: Child is able to classify and form sets in a free sort.

MATERIALS: Twenty to 25 objects (or pictures of objects or cutouts) that can be grouped into several possible sets by criteria such as color, shape, size, or category (i.e., animals, plants, furniture, clothing, or toys).

PROCEDURE: Set all the objects in front of the child in a random arrangement. Say, PUT THE THINGS TOGETHER THAT BELONG TOGETHER. If the child looks puzzled, backtrack to the previous task, hold up one item, and say, FIND SOME THINGS THAT BELONG WITH THIS. When a set is completed, say, NOW FIND SOME OTHER THINGS THAT BELONG TOGETHER. Keep on until all the items are grouped. Then point to each group and ask, WHY DO THESE BELONG TOGETHER?

EVALUATION: Note whether the child makes a conventional logical group and provides a conventional logical reason such as "Because they are cars," "They are all green," "You can eat with them," and so on or a "creative" reason that is logical to the child if not to the adult such as "My mother would like them," "They all have points," "I like these colors, I don't like those," and so on.

INSTRUCTIONAL RESOURCE: Charlesworth, R., and Lind, K. K. (2003). *Math and Science for Young Children* (4th ed.). Clifton Park, NY: Delmar Learning.

Naturalistic Activities

Sorting and grouping are some of the most basic and natural activities for the young child. Much of his play is organizing and reorganizing the things in his world. The infant learns the set of people who take care of him most of the time (day-care provider, mother, father, and/or relatives and friends), and others are put in the set of "strangers." He learns that some objects when pressed on his gums makes the pain of growing teeth less. These are his set of teething things.

As soon as the child is able to sit up, he finds great fun in putting things in containers and dumping them out. He can never have too many boxes, plastic dishes, and coffee cans along with safe items such as large plastic beads, table tennis balls, or teething toys (just be sure the items are too large to swallow). With this type of activity, children have their first experiences making sets.

By age three the child sorts and groups to help organize his play activities. He sorts out from his things those that he needs for what he wants to do. He may pick out wild animal toys for his zoo, people dolls for his family play, big blocks for his house, blue paper circles to paste on paper, girls for friends, and so on.

The adult provides the free time, the materials (recycled material is fine as long as it is safe), and the space. The child does the rest.

Informal Activities

Adults can let children know that sorting and grouping activities are of value in informal ways by showing that they approve of what the children are doing. This can be done with a look, smile, nod, or comment.

Adults can also build children's classification vocabulary in informal ways. They can label the child's product and ask questions about what the child has done: "You have used all blue confetti in your picture." "You've used all the square blocks." "You have the pigs in this barn and the cows in that barn." "You painted green and purple stripes today." "Can you put the wild animals here and the farm animals here?" "Separate the spoons from the forks." "See if any of the cleaning rags are dry." "Put the crayons in the can and the pencils in the box." "Show me which things will roll down the ramp." "Which seeds are from your apple? Which are from your orange?" "Put the hamsters in the silver cage and the mice in the brown cage." As the children's vocabularies increase, they will be able to label and describe how and why they are sorting and grouping. In addition, words give them shortcuts for labeling sets.

Structured Activities

Sorting and grouping, which form the basis of classifying sets of things, lend themselves to many activities with many materials. As already mentioned, real objects are used first, then pictures and objects, then cutouts, and then pictures. One-to-one correspondence skills go hand in hand with sorting and grouping. For example, given three houses and three pigs, the child may give each pig a house (three groups) or place the pigs in one group and the houses in another (two groups).

The following activities help children develop the process of constructing groups.

ACTIVITIES

LOGIC AND CLASSIFICATION: COLOR

OBJECTIVE: To sort and group by color.

MATERIALS: Several different objects that are the same color and four objects each of a different color; for example, a red toy car, a red block, a red bead, a red ribbon, a red sock, and so on, and one yellow car, one green ribbon, one blue ball, and one orange piece of paper.

NATURALISTIC AND INFORMAL ACTIVITIES: Provide students with many opportunities to experiment with color. Provide objects and art materials such as crayons, paint, colored paper, and so on. Label the colors: "You have lots of *green* in your picture." "You've used all *red* Lego® blocks." Note when the children label the colors, "Please pass me a piece of *yellow* paper." "I can't find my *orange* crayon." Ask questions such as, "Which colors will you use for your penguins?"

STRUCTURED ACTIVITIES:
1. Hold up one red object, FIND THE THINGS THAT ARE THE SAME COLOR AS THIS. After all the red things have been found: THESE THINGS ARE ALL THE SAME COLOR. TELL ME THE NAME OF THE COLOR. If there is no correct answer: THE THINGS YOU PICKED OUT ARE ALL RED THINGS. Ask, WHAT COLOR ARE THE THINGS THAT YOU PICKED OUT?
2. Put all the things together again: FIND THE THINGS THAT ARE *NOT* RED.

FOLLOW-UP: Repeat this activity with different colors and different materials. During center time put out a container of brightly colored materials. Note if the children put them into groups by color. If they do, ask, WHY DID YOU PUT THOSE TOGETHER? Accept any answer they give but note whether they give a color answer.

LOGIC AND CLASSIFICATION: ASSOCIATION

OBJECTIVE: To form sets of things that go together by association.

MATERIALS: Picture card sets may be bought or made. Each set can have a theme such as one of the following:

1. Pictures of people in various jobs and pictures of things that go with their job:

Worker	Things that go with the worker's job
letter carrier	letter, mailbox, stamps, hat, mailbag, mail truck
airplane pilot	airplane, hat, wings
doctor	stethoscope, thermometer, bandages
Worker	Things that go with the worker's job
trash collector	trash can, trash truck
police officer	handcuffs, pistol, hat, badge, police car
firefighter	hat, hose, truck, boots and coat, hydrant, house on fire
grocer	various kinds of foods, bags, shopping cart

   Start with about three sets, and keep adding more.

2. Things that go together for use:

Item	Goes with
glass tumbler	carton of milk, pitcher of juice, can of soda pop
cup and saucer	coffeepot, teapot, steaming teakettle
match	candle, campfire
paper	pencil, crayon, pen
money	purse, wallet, bank
table	four chairs

   Start with three sets, and keep adding more.

3. Things that are related, such as animals and their babies.

NATURALISTIC AND INFORMAL ACTIVITIES: During center time provide sets of go-together items such as those selected above. Provide both objects and picture sets. Note what the children do with the items. Do they group related items for play? Ask questions such as, "Which things belong together?" "What do you need to eat your cereal?"

STRUCTURED ACTIVITIES:
1. One at a time show the pictures of people or things that are the main clue (the workers, for example) and ask, WHO (WHAT) IS THIS? When they have all been named, show the "go with" pictures one at a time: WHO (OR WHAT) DOES THIS BELONG TO?
2. Give each child a clue picture. Hold each "go with" picture up in turn: WHO HAS THE PERSON (OR THING) THIS BELONGS WITH? WHAT DO YOU CALL THIS?
3. Give a deck of cards to one child: SORT THESE OUT. FIND ALL THE WORKERS AND PUT THE THINGS WITH THEM THAT THEY USE. Or, HERE IS A GLASS, A CUP AND SAUCER, AND SOME MONEY. LOOK THROUGH THESE PICTURES, AND FIND THE ONES THAT GO WITH THEM.

FOLLOW-UP: Have sets of cards available for children to use during center time. Note whether they use them individually or make up group games to play. Keep introducing more sets.

LOGIC AND CLASSIFICATION: SIMPLE SORTING

OBJECTIVE: To practice the act of sorting.

MATERIALS: Small containers such as margarine dishes filled with small objects such as buttons of various sizes, colors, and shapes, or with dried beans, peas, corn; another container with smaller divisions in it (such as an egg carton).

NATURALISTIC AND INFORMAL ACTIVITIES: Notice if children sort as they play. Do they use pretend food when pretending to cook and eat a meal? Do the children playing adult select adult clothing to wear? When provided with animal figures, do children demonstrate preferences? During center time place materials such as those described above on a table. Note how the children sort.

STRUCTURED ACTIVITIES:

1. Have the sections of the larger container marked with a model such as each kind of button or dried bean. The children match each thing from their container with the model until everything is sorted and grouped into new sets in the egg carton (or other large container with small sections).
2. Use the same materials but do not mark the sections of the sorting container. See how the child will sort on his own.

FOLLOW-UP: Have these materials available during center time. Make up more groups using different kinds of things for sorting.

LOGIC AND CLASSIFICATION: CLASS NAMES, DISCUSSION

OBJECTIVE: To discuss groups of things that can be put in the same class and decide on the class name.

MATERIALS: Things that can be put in the same group on the basis of class name, such as

1. animals: several toy animals
2. vehicles: toy cars, trucks, motorcycles
3. clothing: a shoe, a shirt, a belt
4. things to write with: pen, pencil, marker, crayon, chalk

NATURALISTIC AND INFORMAL ACTIVITIES: During center time note if children use class names during their play. Label classes such as, "You like to play with the *horses* when you select from the *animal* collection." Ask questions such as, "Which is your favorite *vehicle*?"

STRUCTURED ACTIVITIES: The same plan can be followed for any group of things.

1. Bring the things out one at a time until three have been discussed. Ask about each
   a. WHAT CAN YOU TELL ME ABOUT THIS?
   b. Five specific questions:
      WHAT DO YOU CALL THIS? (WHAT IS ITS NAME?)
      WHAT COLOR IS IT?
      WHAT DO YOU DO WITH IT? or WHAT DOES IT DO? or WHO USES THIS?
      WHAT IS IT MADE OUT OF?
      WHERE DO YOU GET ONE?

c. Show the three things discussed: WHAT DO YOU CALL THINGS LIKE THIS? THESE ARE ALL (ANIMALS, VEHICLES, CLOTHING, THINGS TO WRITE WITH).
2. Put two or more groups of things together that have already been discussed. Have the children sort them into new groups and tell the class name for each group.

FOLLOW-UP: Put together groups like the ones above that include things from science and social studies.

Classification is one of the most important fundamental skills in science. The following are examples of how classification might be used during science activities.

LOGIC AND CLASSIFICATION: SORTING A NATURE WALK COLLECTION

OBJECTIVE: To sort items collected during a nature walk.

MATERIALS: The class has gone for a nature walk. Children have collected leaves, stones, bugs, etc. They have various types of containers (i.e., plastic bags, glass jars, plastic margarine containers).

NATURALISTIC AND INFORMAL ACTIVITIES: Develop collections with items that children bring in from home such as leaves, worms, bugs, and so on. Place them in the science center. Encourage children to observe birds that may be in the area. If allowed by the school have animals visit, such as children's pets, a person with a guide dog, or a person with a dog trained to do tricks. Have books on nature topics in the library center.

STRUCTURED ACTIVITIES:
1. Have the children spread out pieces of newspaper on tables or on the floor.
2. Have them dump their plants and rocks on the table. Animals and insects purposely collected are in a separate container.
3. LOOK AT THE THINGS YOU HAVE COLLECTED. PUT THINGS THAT BELONG TOGETHER IN GROUPS. TELL ME WHY THEY BELONG TOGETHER. Let the children explore the materials and identify leaves, twigs, flowers, weeds, smooth rocks, rough rocks, light and dark rocks, etc. After they have grouped the plant material and the rocks, have them sort their animals and insects into different containers. See if they can label their collections (i.e., earthworms, ants, spiders, beetles, ladybugs).
4. Help them organize their materials on the science table. Encourage them to write labels or signs using their own spellings, or help them with spelling if needed. If they won't attempt to write themselves, let them dictate labels to you.

FOLLOW-UP: Encourage the children to examine all the collections and discuss their attributes. Have some plant, rock, insect, and animal reference books on the science table. Encourage the children to find pictures of items like theirs in the books. Read what the books tell about their discoveries.

LOGIC AND CLASSIFICATION: SORTING THINGS THAT SINK AND FLOAT

OBJECTIVE: To find out which objects in a collection sink and which float.

MATERIALS: A collection of many objects made from different materials. You might ask each child to bring one thing from home and then add some items from the classroom. Have a large container of water and two empty containers labeled *sink* and *float*. Make a large chart with a picture/name of each item where the results of the explorations can be recorded (Figure 10–4).

NATURALISTIC AND INFORMAL ACTIVITIES: Provide many opportunities for water play. Include items that float and sink. Note the children's comments as they play with the objects. Make comments such as, "Those rocks seem to stay on the bottom while the boat stays on top of the water." Ask questions such as, "What do you think will happen if you put a rock in a boat?"

STRUCTURED ACTIVITIES:

1. Place the materials on the science table, and explain to everyone what the activity is for.
2. During center time let individuals and/or groups of two or three experiment by placing the objects in the water and then in the appropriate container when they float or sink.
3. When the things are sorted, the children can record their names at the top of the next vacant column on the chart and check off which items sank and which floated.
4. After the items have been sorted several times, have the students compare their lists. Do the items float and/or sink consistently? Why?

FOLLOW-UP: The activity can continue until everyone has had an opportunity to explore it. New items can be added. Some children might like to make a boat in the carpentry center.

EXAMPLE WORLD WIDE WEB ACTIVITIES

◆ Color activities see http://www.preschoolbystormie.com
◆ Sorting cards at http://www.preschoolbystormie.com
◆ Spare change (sort money) at http://www.pbs.org/teachersource/math/preschool.shtm
◆ Sorting laundry at http://www.pbs.org/teachersource/math/preschool.shtm
◆ Estimation and classification at http://www.lessonplanspage.com/mathK1.htm
◆ M & M's® Lessons. Link at http://www.lessonplanspage.com/

Sam and Mary are sitting at the computer using the program Gertrude's Secrets. This is a game designed to aid in basic classification skills of matching by specific common criteria. Mary hits a key that is the correct response, and both children clap their hands as a tune plays and Gertrude appears on the screen in recognition of their success. A list of software that helps the development of classification is included in Activity 5.

Evaluation

As the children play, note whether each one sorts and groups as part of his play activities. There should be an increase as they grow and have more experiences with sets and classification activities. They should use more feature names when they speak during work and play. They should use color, shape, size,

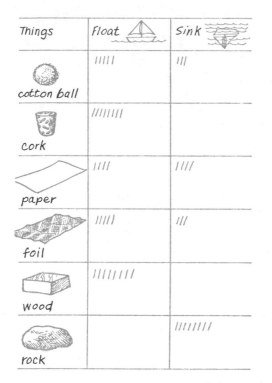

Things	Float ⛵	Sink
cotton ball	/////	///
cork	////////	
paper	////	////
foil	/////	///
wood	////////	
rock		////////

FIGURE 10–4 The students can record the results of their exploration of the floating and sinking properties of various objects.

material, pattern, texture, function, association words, and class names.

1. Tim has a handful of colored candies. "First I'll eat the orange ones." He carefully picks out the orange candies and eats them one at a time. "Now, the reds." He goes on in the same way until all the candies are gone.
2. Diana plays with some small wooden animals. "These farm animals go here in the barn. Richard, you build a cage for these wild animals."
3. Mr. Flores tells Bob to pick out from a box of toys some plastic ones to use in the water table.
4. Mary asks the cook if she can help sort the clean tableware and put it away.

5. George and Sam build with blocks. George tells Sam, "Put the big blocks here, the middle-sized ones here, and the small blocks here."
6. Richard and Diana take turns reaching into a box that contains items that are smooth or rough. When they touch an item, they say whether it is smooth or rough, guess what it is, and then remove it and place it on the table in the smooth or the rough pile.
7. Tanya is working with some containers that contain substances with either pleasant, unpleasant, or neutral odors. On the table are three pictures: a happy face, a sad face, and a neutral face. She puts each of the containers on one of the three faces according to her feelings about each odor.

For more structured evaluation, the sample assessment tasks and the tasks in Appendix A may be used.

Summary

By sorting objects and pictures into groups based on one or more common criteria, children exercise and build on their logical thinking capabilities. The act of putting things into groups by sorting out things that have one or more common feature is called classification.

Classifying is a part of children's normal play. They build a sense of logic that will be the basis of understanding that mathematics makes sense and is not contrived. Children learn that mathematics is natural and flows from their intrinsic curiosity and play. Classifying also adds to their store of ideas and words, and they learn to identify more attributes that can be used as criteria for sorting and grouping.

Naturalistic, informal, and structured classification activities can be done following the sequence of materials from objects, to objects and pictures, to cutouts to picture cards. Books are another excellent pictorial mode for learning class names and members. Computer games that reinforce classification skills and concepts are also available. Logical grouping and classification are essential math and science components.

KEY TERMS

logical grouping	color	function
classifying	shape	association
add	size	class name
subtract	material	common features
sorting	pattern	number
grouping	texture	

SUGGESTED ACTIVITIES

1. Assemble a collection of objects of various sizes, shapes, colors, classes, textures, and uses. Put them in an open container (such as a small plastic dishpan). Present the collection to children of different ages from 18 months through age eight. Tell the children that they may play with the objects. Observe and record what each child does with the objects. Particularly note any classifying and sorting and the criteria used.

2. Find some sorting and classifying activities to include in your Activity File.

3. Devise a sorting and classifying game. Have one or more children play the game. Explain the game to the class, and describe what happened when you tried it out with a child (or children). Ask the class for any suggestions for modifying the game.

4. Visit a prekindergarten, kindergarten, and/or primary classroom. Make a list of all the materials that could be used for sorting and classifying. Write a description of any sorting and/or classifying activities you observe while you are in the classroom. Talk with the teacher. Ask her how she includes sorting and classifying in her program.

5. Using the evaluation criteria in Activity 7, Unit 9, review any of the software listed below that you have access to:
   - ◆ Coco's Math Project 1. Singapore, SG: Times Learning Systems Ptd Ltd.
   - ◆ Dinosaurs. Berkeley, CA: Advanced Ideas, Inc.
   - ◆ Duck's Playground. Coarsegold, CA: Sierra On-Line, Inc.
   - ◆ Early Games Match Maker. Minneapolis, MN: Counterpoint Software, Inc.
   - ◆ Gertrude's Secrets. Fremont, CA: The Learning Company.
   - ◆ Infinity City. Link at http://www.headbone.com: Headbone Interactive.
   - ◆ Let's Explore the Jungle with Buzzy the Knowledge Bug. Woodville, WA: Humongous.
   - ◆ Match Up! Lowell, MA: Hayden Software Co.
   - ◆ Micro Habitats. Pleasantville, NY: Reader's Digest Software, Microcomputer Software Division.
   - ◆ Soc Pix. Circle Pines, MN: American Guidance Service.
   - ◆ Thinkin' things 1. Redmond, WA: Edmark.

6. Surf the Web for logic and classification activities. Locate the ones listed in this unit or find some others. Try out an activity with some young children.

REVIEW

A. Explain what is meant by the terms *logical group* and *classification*. Relate your definitions to the NCTM expectations.

B. Decide which features, as described in this unit, are being used in each of the incidents below:
1. "Find all the things that are rough."
2. "Pour the milk into Johnny's glass."
3. "Put on warm clothes today."
4. Tina says, "There are leaves on all of the trees. Some are green, some are brown, some are orange, and some are yellow."
5. "Find all the things that you can use to write and draw."
6. Carlos makes a train using only the red cube blocks.
7. Tony is putting the clean silverware away. He carefully places the knives, spoons, and forks in the appropriate sections of the silverware container.
8. Fong makes a design using square parquetry blocks.
9. "Please get me six paper napkins."
10. "I'll use the long blocks, and you use the short blocks."
11. Mrs. Smith notices that Tom is wearing a striped shirt and checked pants.

REFERENCE

National Council of Teachers of Mathematics. (2000). *Principles and standards for school mathematics.* Reston, VA: Author. (http://www.nctm.org)

FURTHER READING AND RESOURCES

AIMS Educational Products. AIMS Education Foundation, P.O. Box 8120, Fresno, CA 93747-8120.

Baratta-Lorton, M. (1976). *Math their way.* Menlo Park, CA: Addison-Wesley.

Baratta-Lorton, M. (1979). *Workjobs II.* Menlo Park, CA: Addison-Wesley.

Burk, D., Snider, A., & Symonds, P. (1988). *Box it or bag it mathematics: Kindergarten teachers' resource guide.* Portland, OR: The Math Learning Center.

Copley, J. V. (2000). *The young child and mathematics.* Washington, DC: National Association for the Education of Young Children.

Copley, J. V. (Ed.). (1999). *Mathematics in the early years.* Washington, DC: National Association for the Education of Young Children.

Isenberg, J., & Jacobs, J. (1981). Classification: Something to think about. *Childhood Education, 57*(5).

McGrath, B. B. (1994). *The m&m's® brand counting book.* Watertown, MA: Charlesbridge.

Richardson, K. (1999). *Developing number concepts: Counting, comparing and pattern.* Parsippany, NJ: Dale Seymour.

Richardson, K. (1999). *Developing number concepts: Planning guide.* Parsippany, NJ: Dale Seymour.

Russell, S. J., & Stone, A. (1990). *Counting: Ourselves and our families.* Palo Alto, CA: Dale Seymour.

UNIT 11

Comparing

OBJECTIVES

After reading this unit, you should be able to:

◆ Explain the NCTM expectations for comparison.

◆ List and define comparison terms.

◆ Identify the concepts learned from comparing.

◆ Do informal measurement and quantity activities with children.

◆ Do structured measurement and quantity comparing activities with children.

The NCTM expecations (2000) include relating physical materials and pictures to mathematical ideas; understanding the attributes of length, capacity, weight, area, volume, time, and temperature; and developing the process of measurement. Development of measurement relationships begins with simple comparisons of physical materials and pictures. The expectation is that students will be able to describe qualitative change, such as Mary is taller than Jenny. Figure 11–1 shows how comparing might be integrated across the content areas.

When comparing, the child finds a relationship between two things or groups of things on the basis of some specific characteristic or attribute. One type of attribute is an informal measurement such as size, length, height, weight, or speed. A second type of attribute is quantity comparison. To compare quanti- ties, the child looks at two groups of objects and decides if they have the same number of items or if one group has more. Comparing is the basis of ordering (see Unit 17) and measurement (see Units 18 and 19).

Some examples of measurement comparisons are listed next.

◆ John is taller than Mary.
◆ This snake is long. That worm is short.
◆ Father bear is bigger than baby bear.

Examples of number comparisons are shown as follows:

◆ Does everyone have two gloves?
◆ I have more cookies than you have.
◆ We each have two dolls—that's the same.

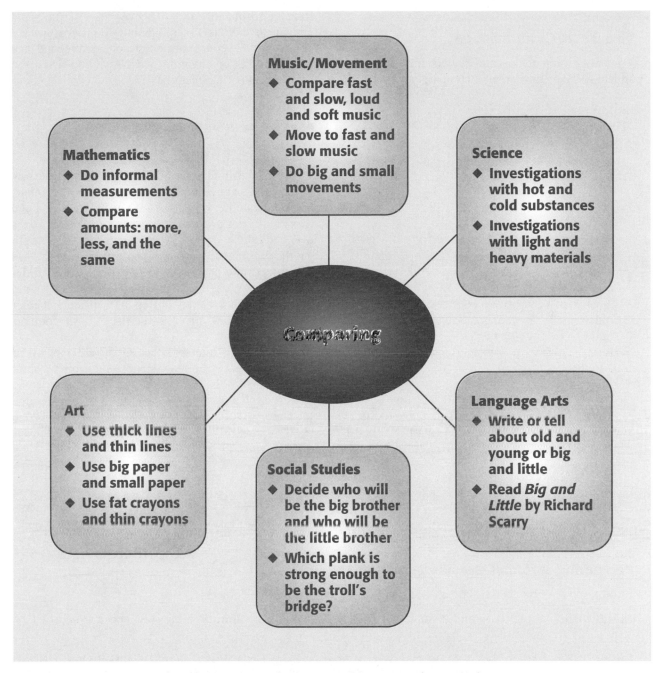

FIGURE 11–1 Integrating comparing across the curriculum.

The Basic Comparisons

To make comparisons and understand them, the child learns the following basic comparisons.

◆ Informal Measurement

large	small
big	little
long	short
tall	short
fat	skinny
heavy	light
fast	slow
cold	hot
thick	thin
wide	narrow
near	far
later	sooner (earlier)
older	younger (newer)
higher	lower
loud	soft (sound)

◆ Number

more	less/fewer

The child also finds that sometimes there is no difference when the comparison is made. That is, the items are the same size, same length, same age, and so on.

Relative to quantity they discover there is the same amount (or number) of things in two groups that are compared. The concept of one-to-one correspondence and the skills of counting and classifying assist the child in comparing quantities.

Assessment

During the child's play, the teacher should note any of the child's activities that might show he is comparing. For example, when a bed is needed for a doll and two shoe boxes are available, does he look the boxes over carefully and place the doll in each box in turn to get the doll into a box that is the right size? If he has two trucks, one large and one small, does he build a bigger garage for the larger truck? The adult should also note with children old enough to talk whether they use the words given in the list of basic comparisons.

In individual interview tasks, the child is asked questions to see if he understands and uses the basic comparison words. The child is presented with some objects or pictures of things that differ or are the same in relation to some attributes or number and is asked to tell if they are the same or different. Tasks (see Appendix A) are like these.

SAMPLE ASSESSMENT TASK

5D   **Preoperational Ages 4–5**
Comparing, Informal Measurement: Unit 11

SKILL: The child will be able to point to big (large) and small objects.

MATERIALS: A big block and a small block (a big truck and a small truck, a big shell and a small shell, etc.).

PROCEDURE: Present two related objects at a time and say, FIND (POINT TO) THE BIG BLOCK. FIND (POINT TO) THE SMALL BLOCK. Continue with the rest of the object pairs.

EVALUATION: Note if the child is able to identify big and small for each pair.

INSTRUCTIONAL RESOURCE: Charlesworth, R., and Lind, K. K. (2003). *Math and Science for Young Children* (4th ed.). Clifton Park, NY: Delmar Learning.

SAMPLE ASSESSMENT TASK

4D   **Preoperational Ages 3–4**
Comparing, Number: Unit 11

SKILL: The child will compare groups and identify which group has more or less (fewer).

MATERIALS: Two dolls (toy animals or cutout figures) and 10 cutout poster board cookies.

PROCEDURE: Place the two dolls (toy animals or cutout figures) in front of the child. Say, WATCH, I'M
                     GOING TO GIVE EACH DOLL (or _____) SOME COOKIES. Put two cookies in front of one doll
                     and six in front of the other. Say, SHOW ME THE DOLL (_____) THAT HAS MORE COOKIES.
                     Now pick up the cookies, and put one cookie in front of one doll and three in front of the
                     other. Say, SHOW ME THE DOLL (_____) THAT HAS FEWER COOKIES. Repeat with different
                     amounts.

EVALUATION: Note whether the child consistently picks the correct amounts. Some children might under-
                     stand *more* but not *fewer*. Some might be able to discriminate if there is a large difference
                     between groups, such as two vs. six, but not small differences, such as four vs. five.

INSTRUCTIONAL RESOURCE: Charlesworth, R., and Lind, K. K. (2003). *Math and Science for Young Children* (4th ed.). Clifton Park, NY: Delmar Learning.

Before giving the number comparison tasks, the teacher should be sure the child has begun to match, count, and classify.

Naturalistic Activities

The young child has many contacts with comparisons in her daily life. At home mother says, "Get up, it's *late*. Mary was up *early*. Eat *fast*. If you eat slowly, we will have to leave before you are finished. Have a *big* bowl for your cereal; that one is too *small*." At school the teacher says, "I'll pick up this *heavy* box; you pick up the *light* one." "Sit on the *small* chair, that one is too *big*." "Let's finish this story." "Remember, the father bear's porridge was too *hot*, and the mother bear's porridge was too *cold*."

As the child uses materials, she notices that things are different. The infant finds that some things can be grabbed and held because they are *small* and *light*, while others cannot be held because they are *big* and *heavy*. As she crawls about, she finds she cannot go behind the couch because the space is too *narrow*. She can go behind the chair because there is a *wide* space between the chair and the wall. The young child begins to build with blocks and finds that there are *more small* blocks in her set of blocks than there are *large* ones. She notices that there are people in her environment who are big and people who are small in relation to her. One of the questions most often asked is "Am I a big boy?" or "Am I a big girl?"

Informal Activities

Small children are very concerned about size and number, especially in relation to themselves. They want to be bigger, taller, faster, and older. They want to be sure they have the same, not less—and if possible more—of things that the other child has. These needs of the young child bring about many situations where the adult can help in an informal way to aid the child in learning the skills and ideas of comparing.

Informal measurements are made in a concrete way. That is, the things to be compared are looked at, felt, lifted, listened to, and so on, and the attribute is labeled.

◆ Eighteen-month-old Brad tries to lift a large box of toy cars. Mr. Brown squats down next to him, holding out a smaller box of cars, "Here, Brad, that box is too big for your short arms. Take this small box."

◆ Three-year-olds, Kate and Chris, run up to Mrs. Raymond, "We can run fast. Watch us. We can run faster than you. Watch us." Off they go across the yard while Mrs. Raymond watches and smiles.

◆ Five-year-olds, Sam and George, stand back to back. "Check us, Mr. Flores. Who is taller?" Mr. Flores says, "Stand by the mirror, and check yourselves." The boys stand by the mirror, back to back. "We are the same," they shout. "You are taller than both of us," they tell their teacher.

◆ It is after a fresh spring rain. The children are on the playground looking at worms. Comments are heard: "This worm is longer than that one." "This worm is fatter." Miss Collins comes up. "Show me your worms. Sounds like they are different sizes." "I think this small, skinny one is the baby worm," says Richard.

Comparative number is also made in a concrete way. When comparing sets of things, just a look may be enough if the difference in number is large.

◆ "Teacher! Juanita has all the spoons and won't give me one!" cries Tanya.

If the difference is small the child will have to use his skill of matching (one-to-one correspondence). He may physically match each time, or he may count— depending on his level of development.

◆ "Teacher! Juanita has more baby dolls than I do." "Let's check," says Mr. Brown. "I already checked," says Tanya. "She has four, and I have three." Mr. Brown notes that each girl has four dolls. "Better check again," says Mr. Brown. "Here, let's see. Put each one of your dolls next to one of Juanita's, Tanya." Tanya matches them up. "I was wrong. We have the same."

A child at a higher level of development could have been asked to count.

To promote informal learning, the teacher must put out materials that can be used by the child to learn comparisons on his own. The teacher must also be ready to step in and support the child's discovery by using comparison words and giving needed help with comparison problems that the child meets in his play and other activities.

Structured Activities

Most children learn the idea of comparison through naturalistic and informal activities. For those who do not, more formal experiences can be planned. There are many commercial materials available individually and in kits that are designed to be used to teach comparison skills and words. Also, the environment is full of things that can be used. The following are some basic types of activities that can be repeated with different materials.

Mr. Flores introduced his class of four- and five-year-olds to the concept of comparing involving opposites by using books, games, and other materials. To support their understanding of the opposite concepts, he has shown the students how to use the computer software Stickybear Opposites (see Activity 4). This program is controlled by two keys, making it a natural for two children working together cooperatively. George and Cindy can be observed making the seesaw go *up* and *down*, watching the plant grow from *short* to *tall*, and comparing the eight (*many*) bouncing balls with the three (*few*) bouncing balls.

ACTIVITIES

COMPARISONS: INFORMAL MEASUREMENTS

OBJECTIVES: To gain skill in observing differences in size, speed, temperature, age, and loudness. To learn the words associated with differences in size, speed, temperature, age, and loudness.

MATERIALS: Use real objects first. Once the child can do the tasks with real things, then introduce pictures and chalkboard drawings.

Comparison	Things to Use
large-small and big-little	buttons, dolls, cups, plates, chairs, books, records, spools, toy animals, trees, boats, cars, houses, jars, boxes, people, pots, and pans
long-short	string, ribbon, pencils, ruler-meter stick, yardstick, snakes, worms, lines, paper strips
tall-short	people, ladders, brooms, blocks, trees, bookcases, flagpoles, buildings
fat-skinny	people, trees, crayons, animals, pencils, books
heavy-light	same size but different weight containers (such as shoe boxes or coffee cans taped shut filled with items of different weights)
fast-slow	toy cars or other vehicles for demonstration, the children themselves and their own movements, cars on the street, music, talking
hot-cold	containers of water, food, ice cubes, boiling water, chocolate milk and hot chocolate, weather
thick-thin	paper-cardboard, books, pieces of wood, slices of food (bologna, cucumber, carrot), cookie dough
wide-narrow	streets, ribbons, paper strips, lines (chalk, crayon, paint), doorways, windows
near-far	children and fixed points in the room, places in the neighborhood, map
late-sooner (earlier)	arrival at school or home, two events
older-younger (newer)	people: babies, younger and older children, adults of different ages; any things brought in that have not been in the environment before
higher-lower	swings, slides, jungle gyms, birds in trees, airplanes flying, windows, stairs, elevators, balconies, shelves
loud-soft	voices singing and talking, claps, piano, drums, records, doors slamming

NATURALISTIC AND INFORMAL ACTIVITIES: Observe children as they use a variety of classroom materials. Take note of their vocabulary—do they use any of the terms listed above? Notice if they do any informal measurements or comparisons as they interact with materials. Comment on their activities: "You built a *tall* building and a *short* building." "You can pour the *small* cup of water into the *big* bowl." Ask questions such as, "Which clay snake is *fat* and which is *skinny*?" "Who is *taller*, you or your sister?"

STRUCTURED ACTIVITIES: The basic activity involves the presentation of the two opposites to be compared. They can be objects, cutouts, or pictures—whatever is most appropriate. Then ask the comparison question. For example:

◆ The teacher places two pieces of paper in front of the children. Each piece is 1 inch wide. One is 6 inches long, and the other is 12 inches long. LOOK CAREFULLY AT THESE STRIPS OF PAPER. TELL ME WHAT IS DIFFERENT ABOUT THEM. If there is no response, ARE THEY THE SAME LENGTH OR ARE THEY DIFFERENT

LENGTHS? If no one responds with long(er) or short(er), SHOW ME WHICH ONE IS LONGER (SHORTER). Provide a variety of objects and ask the children to select two and tell which is longer and which is shorter.

◆ The teacher places two identical coffee cans on the table. One is filled with sand; the other is empty. They are both taped closed so the children cannot see inside. PICK UP EACH CAN. TELL ME WHAT IS DIFFERENT ABOUT THEM. If there is no response or an incorrect response, hold each can out in turn to the child. HOLD THIS CAN IN ONE HAND AND THIS ONE IN THE OTHER. (point) THIS CAN IS HEAVY; THIS CAN IS LIGHT. NOW, YOU SHOW ME THE HEAVY CAN; THE LIGHT CAN. If the child has a problem he should do more activities that involve this concept.

The variety of experience that can be offered with many things that give the child practice exploring comparisons is almost endless.

FOLLOW-UP: On a table, set up two empty containers (so that one is tall, and one is short; one is fat, and one is thin; or one is big, and one is little) and a third container filled with potentially comparable items such as tall and short dolls, large and small balls, fat and thin cats, long and short snakes, big and little pieces of wood, and so on. Have the children sort the objects into the correct empty containers.

COMPARISONS: NUMBER

OBJECTIVE: ◆ To enable the child to compare groups that are different in number.
  ◆ To enable the child to use the terms *more, less, fewer*, and *same number*.

MATERIALS: Any of the objects and things used for matching, counting, and classifying.

NATURALISTIC AND INFORMAL ACTIVITIES: Notice if children use any of the comparison vocabulary during their daily activities, "He has *more* red Unifix Cubes® than I do." "I have *fewer* jelly beans than Mark". Ask questions such as, "Does everyone have the *same number* of cookies?" Make comments such as, "I think you need *one more* dress for your dolls."

STRUCTURED ACTIVITIES: The following basic activities can be done using many different kinds of materials.
1. Set up a flannelboard with many felt shapes or a magnet board with many magnet shapes. Put up two groups of shapes: ARE THERE AS MANY CIRCLES AS SQUARES? (RED CIRCLES AS BLUE CIRCLES? BUNNIES AS CHICKENS?) WHICH GROUP HAS MORE? HOW MANY CIRCLES ARE THERE? HOW MANY SQUARES? The children can point, tell with words, and move the pieces around to show that they understand the idea.
2. Have cups, spoons, napkins, or food for snack or lunch. LET'S FIND OUT IF WE HAVE ENOUGH _____ FOR EVERYONE. Wait for the children to find out. If they have trouble, suggest they match or count.
3. Set up any kind of matching problems where one group has more things than the other: cars and garages, firefighters and fire trucks, cups and saucers, fathers and sons, hats and heads, cats and kittens, animals and cages, and so on.

FOLLOW-UP: Put out groups of materials that the children can use on their own. Go on to cards with pictures of different numbers of things that the children can sort and match. Watch for chances to present informal experiences.
◆ Are there more boys or girls here today?
◆ Do you have more thin crayons or more fat crayons?
◆ Do we have the same number of cupcakes as we have people?

EXAMPLE WORLD WIDE WEB ACTIVITY

◆ Pumpkin numbers game at http://www.lessonplanspage.com/mathK1.htm
◆ Manipulative ideas at http://www.perpetualpreschool.com

Evaluation

The teacher should note whether the child can use more comparing skills during his play and routine activities. Without disrupting his activity, the adult asks questions as the child plays and works.

◆ Do you have more cows or more chickens in your barn?
◆ (Child has made two clay snakes) Which snake is longer? Which is fatter?
◆ (Child is sorting blue chips and red chips into bowls) Do you have more blue chips or more red chips?
◆ (Child is talking about his family) Who is older, you or your brother? Who is taller?

The assessment tasks in Appendix A may be used for formal evaluation interviews.

Summary

Comparing involves finding the relationship between two things or two groups of things. An informal measurement may be made by comparing two things. Comparing two groups of things incorporates the use of one-to-one correspondence, counting, and classifying skills to find out which sets have more, less/fewer, or the same quantities. Naturalistic, informal, and structured experiences support the learning of these concepts.

KEY TERMS

comparing   informal measurement   quantity comparison

SUGGESTED ACTIVITIES

1. Prepare the materials needed for the assessment tasks in this unit. Interview two or more children. Based on their responses, plan comparison activities that fit their level of development. Do the activities with the children. Record their responses and report the results in class.
2. Find some comparison activities to include in your Activity File or Activity Notebook.
3. Observe some three-, four-, and five-year-olds during play activities. Record any instances where they use comparison words and/or do comparisons.
4. Using the guidelines in Activity 7, Unit 9, evaluate some of the following software.

◆ Coco's Math Project 1. Singapore, SG: Times Learning Systems Ptd Ltd.
◆ Comparison Kitchen. Allen, TX: Developmental Learning Materials.
◆ Juggles Rainbow. Menlo Park, CA: The Learning Company.
◆ Millie's Math House. Pleasantville, NY: Sunburst.
◆ Stickybear Opposites. Middletown, CT: Weekly Reader Family Software.

5. On the Web find the activity suggested in this unit or another activity that provides comparison experiences. Try it out with one or more young children.

REVIEW

A. Explain with examples the two aspects of comparing: informal measurement and number/quantity comparisons. Relate your examples to the NCTM expectations for comparison.

B. Decide which type of comparison (number, speed, weight, length, height, or size) is being made in the examples that follow:
   1. This block is longer than your block.
   2. My racing car is faster than your racing car.
   3. My doll is bigger than Janie's doll.
   4. Mother gave you one more apple slice than she gave me.
   5. I'll take the heavy box, and you take the light box.
   6. My mom is taller than your mom.

C. Give two examples of naturalistic, informal, and structured comparison activities.

REFERENCE

National Council of Teachers of Mathematics. (2000). *Principles and standards for school mathematics.* Reston, VA: Author. (http://www.nctm.org)

FURTHER READING AND RESOURCES

AIMS Educational Products. AIMS Education Foundation, P.O. Box 8120, Fresno, CA 93747-8120.

Baratta-Lorton, M. (1972). *Workjobs.* Menlo Park, CA: Addison-Wesley.

Baratta-Lorton, M. (1976). *Mathematics their way.* Menlo Park, CA: Addison-Wesley.

Burk, D., Snider, A., & Symonds, P. (1988). *Box it or bag it mathematics: Kindergarten teachers' resource guide.* Portland, OR: The Math Learning Center.

Copley, J. V. (2000). *The young child and mathematics.* Washington, DC: National Association for the Education of Young Children.

Copley, J. V. (Ed.). (1999). *Mathematics in the early years.* Washington, DC: National Association for the Education of Young Children.

McGrath, B. B. (1995). *The m&m's® brand counting book.* Watertown, MA: Charlesbridge.

Papert, S. (1994). *The children's machine.* New York: Basic Books.

Porter, J. (1995). Balancing acts: K–2. *Teaching Children Mathematics, 1*(7), 430.

Richardson, K. (1984). *Developing number concepts using Unifix Cubes.®* Menlo Park, CA: Addison-Wesley.

Richardson, K. (1999). *Developing number concepts: Counting, comparing, and pattern.* Parsippany, NJ: Dale Seymour.

Richardson, K. (1999). *Developing number concepts: Planning guide.* Parsippany, NJ: Dale Seymour.

UNIT 12
Early Geometry: Shape

OBJECTIVES

After reading this unit, you should be able to:

◆ Explain the NCTM expectations for shape as the foundation of beginning geometry.

◆ Describe naturalistic, informal, and structured shape activities for young children.

◆ Assess and evaluate a child's knowledge of shape.

◆ Help children learn shape through haptic, visual, and visual-motor experiences.

During the preprimary years children should be able to reach the first expectation for geometry (NCTM, 2000): recognize, name, build, draw, compare, and sort two- and three-dimensional shapes. This beginning knowledge of geometry can be integrated with other content areas as illustrated in Figure 12–1. Geometry for young children is more than naming shapes: it is understanding the attributes of shape and applying them to problem solving. Geometry also includes spatial sense, which is the focus of Unit 13.

Each object in the environment has its own shape. Much of the play and activity of the infant during the sensorimotor stage centers on learning about shape. The infant learns through looking and through feeling with hands and mouth. Babies learn that some shapes are easier to hold than others. They learn that things of one type of shape will roll. They learn that some things have the same shape as others. Young children see and feel shape differences long before they can describe these differences in words. In the late sensorimotor and early preoperational stages, the child spends a lot of time matching and classifying things. Shape is often used as the basis for these activities.

Children also enjoy experimenting with creating shapes. Three-dimensional shapes grow out of their exploration of plastic materials such as play dough, clay, and slime. When they draw and paint, children create many kinds of two-dimensional shapes from the stage of controlled scribbles to representational drawing and painting. Their first representative drawings usually consist of circles and lines. Young children enjoy drawing blob shapes, cutting them out, and gluing them on another piece of paper.

As children move into the middle of the preoperational period they begin to learn that some shapes have specific names such as **circle**, **triangle**, **square**, **cylinder**, and **sphere**. First children learn to describe the basic characteristics of each shape in their own

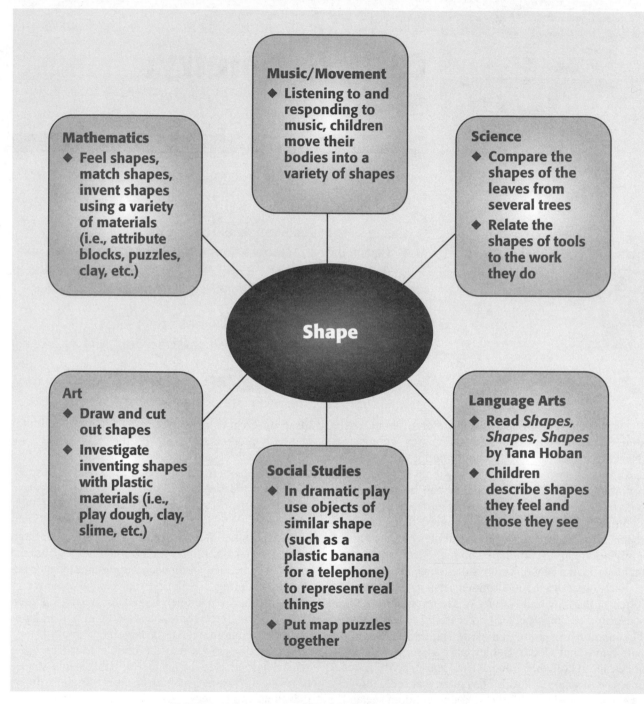

Mathematics
◆ Feel shapes, match shapes, invent shapes using a variety of materials (i.e., attribute blocks, puzzles, clay, etc.)

Music/Movement
◆ Listening to and responding to music, children move their bodies into a variety of shapes

Science
◆ Compare the shapes of the leaves from several trees
◆ Relate the shapes of tools to the work they do

Shape

Art
◆ Draw and cut out shapes
◆ Investigate inventing shapes with plastic materials (i.e., play dough, clay, slime, etc.)

Social Studies
◆ In dramatic play use objects of similar shape (such as a plastic banana for a telephone) to represent real things
◆ Put map puzzles together

Language Arts
◆ Read *Shapes, Shapes, Shapes* by Tana Hoban
◆ Children describe shapes they feel and those they see

FIGURE 12–1   Integrating shape across the curriculum.

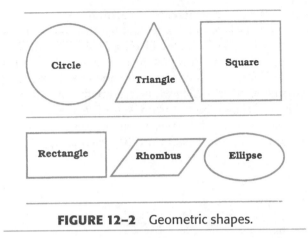

FIGURE 12–2 Geometric shapes.

Lego® and so on provide opportunities for exploration. Preschoolers are just beginning to develop definitions of shapes which probably are not solidified until after age six (Hannibal, 1999). When working with shapes it is important to use a variety of models of each category of shape so children generalize and perceive there is not just one definition. For example, triangles with three equal sides are the most common models so children frequently do not perceive right triangles, isosceles triangles, and so forth as real triangles (Figure 12–4). Many preschoolers do not see that squares are a type of rectangle. After experience with many shape examples and discussion of attributes, children begin to see beyond the obvious and generalize to related shapes.

words, such as "four straight sides" or "curved line" or "it has points." Gradually, the conventional geometry vocabulary is introduced. Children need opportunities to freely explore both two- and three-dimensional shapes. Examples of some two-dimensional shapes are illustrated in Figure 12–2. Examples of some three-dimensional shapes (cylinder, sphere, **triangular prism**, and **rectangular prism**) are illustrated in Figure 12–3. Children need time to freely explore the properties of shapes. Unit blocks, attribute blocks,

Assessment

Observational assessment can be done by noticing whether the child uses shape to organize his world. As the child plays with materials, the adult should note whether he groups things together because the shape is the same or similar. For example, a child plays with a set of plastic shape blocks. There are triangles,

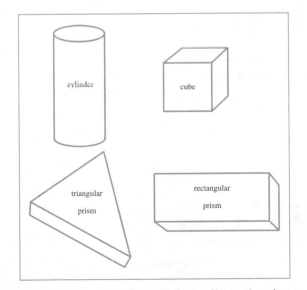

FIGURE 12–3 Examples of three-dimensional geometric figures.

FIGURE 12–4 Triangles come in many varieties.

squares, and circles. Some are red, blue, green, yellow, and orange. Sometimes he groups them by color, sometimes by shape. A child is playing with pop beads of different colors and shapes. Sometimes he makes strings of the same shape; sometimes, of the same color. The child may use some shape names in everyday conversation.

The individual interview tasks for shape center on discrimination, labeling, matching, and sorting. *Discrimination* tasks assess whether the child can see that one form has a different shape from another form. *Labeling* tasks assess whether the child can find a shape when the name is given and whether he can name a shape when a picture is shown to him. At a higher level, he finds shapes in pictures and in his environment. *Matching* would require the child to find a shape like one shown to him. A *sorting* task would be one in which the child must separate a mixed group of shapes into groups (see Unit 10). Two sample tasks follow.

SAMPLE ASSESSMENT TASK

4E   **Preoperational Ages 3–4**
Shape, Identification: Unit 12

METHOD: Interview.

SKILL: When provided with shapes of varying types, size, and colors the child will be able to label and describe them using his/her current knowledge.

MATERIALS: A variety of shapes, both two- and three-dimensional. Select items from small unit blocks, cube block sets, tangrams, attribute blocks, and/or make cardboard cutouts, cover cylindrical containers and small boxes with Contac® paper, etc. Have 15 to 20 different objects.

PROCEDURE: Lay out the materials in front of the child. TELL ME ABOUT THESE SHAPES. DO YOU HAVE ANY NAMES FOR ANY OF THESE SHAPES? WHAT MAKES THE SHAPE A (name of shape)? ARE ANY OF THE SHAPES THE SAME IN ANY WAY? HAVE YOU SEEN ANYTHING ELSE WITH THIS SHAPE? AT SCHOOL? OUTSIDE? AT HOME? (Either one the child selected or one you selected) WHAT KIND OF A PICTURE CAN YOU MAKE WITH THESE SHAPES?

EVALUATION: Note if the child has labels for any of the shapes, if he makes any connections to familiar items in the environment, if he can make a picture with them that is logical, and, overall, if he appears to have noticed the attributes of shape in the environment. Whether or not he uses conventional labels at this point is not important.

INSTRUCTIONAL RESOURCE: Charlesworth, R., and Lind, K. K. (2003). *Math and Science for Young Children* (4th ed.). Clifton Park, NY: Delmar Learning.

SAMPLE ASSESSMENT TASK

5E   **Preoperational Ages 5–6**
Shape, Geometric Shape Recognition: Unit 12

METHOD: Interview.

SKILL: The child can identify shapes in the environment.

MATERIALS: The natural environment.

PROCEDURE: After having had experience with a variety of two- and three-dimensional shapes the follow-
                     ing can be used to assess the child's ability to recognize and generalize. LOOK AROUND THE
                     ROOM. FIND AS MANY SHAPES AS YOU CAN. CAN YOU FIND (a square, a triangle, a rectan-
                     gle, a cylinder, a sphere, a circle, a rectangular prism, etc.)?

EVALUATION: Note how observant the child is. Does he/she note the obvious shapes such as windows,
                     doors, and tables? Does he/she look beyond the obvious? How many shapes and which
                     shapes is he/she able to find?

INSTRUCTIONAL RESOURCE: Charlesworth, R., and Lind, K. K. (2003). *Math and Science for Young Children*
(4th ed.). Clifton Park, NY: Delmar Learning.

Naturalistic Activities

Naturalistic activities are most important in the learning of shape. The child perceives the idea of shape through sight and touch. The infant needs objects to look at, to grasp, and to touch and taste. The toddler needs different things of many shapes to use as he sorts and matches. He needs many containers (bowls, boxes, coffee cans) and many objects (such as pop beads, table tennis balls, poker chips, and empty thread spools). He needs time to fill containers with these objects of different shapes and to dump the objects out and begin again. As he holds each thing, he examines it with his eyes, hands, and mouth.

The older preoperational child enjoys a junk box filled with things such as buttons, checkers, bottle caps, pegs, small boxes, and plastic bottles that he can explore. The teacher can also put out a box of *attribute blocks* (wood or plastic blocks in geometric shapes). Geometric shapes and other shapes can also be cut from paper and/or cardboard and placed out for the child to use. Figure 12–5 shows some blob shapes that can be put into a box of shapes to sort.

In dramatic play, the child can put to use his ideas about shape. The preoperational child's play is representational. He uses things to represent something else that he does not have at the time. He finds something that is close to the real thing, and it is used to represent the real thing. Shape is usually one of the elements used when the child picks a representational object.

◆ A stick or a long piece of wood is used for a gun.
◆ A piece of rope or old garden hose is used to put out a pretend fire.
◆ The magnet board shapes are pretend candy.
◆ A square yellow block is a piece of cheese.
◆ A shoe box is a crib, a bed, or a house—as needed.

FIGURE 12–5 Blob shapes: you can make up your own.

◆ Some rectangular pieces of green paper are dollars, and some round pieces of paper are coins.
◆ A paper towel roll is a telescope for looking at the moon.
◆ A blob of play dough is a hamburger or a cookie.

Informal Activities

The teacher can let the child know that he notices her use of shape ideas in activities through comments and attention. He can also supply her with ideas and objects that will fit her needs. He can suggest or give the child a box to be used for a bed or a house, some blocks or other small objects for her pretend food, or green rectangles and gray and brown circles for play money.

Labels can be used during normal activities. The child's knowledge of shape can be used too.

◆ "The forks have sharp points; the spoons are round and smooth."
◆ "Put square placemats on the square tables and rectangular placemats on the rectangular tables."
◆ "We'll have triangle shaped crackers today."
◆ As a child works on a hard puzzle, the teacher takes her hand and has her feel the empty space with the index finger, "Feel this shape and look at it. Now find the puzzle piece that fits here."
◆ As the children use clay or play dough, the teacher says, "You are making lots of shapes. Kate has made a ball, which is a sphere shape; Jim, a snake, which is a cylinder shape; and Diana, a pancake which is a circle shape."
◆ During cleanup time, the teacher says, "Put the square rectangular prism blocks here and the other rectangular prism blocks over there."

The teacher can pay attention and respond when the child calls his attention to shapes in the environment. The following examples show that children can generalize; they can use what they know about shape in new situations.

◆ "Ms. Moore, the door is shaped like a rectangle." Ms. Moore smiles and looks over at George. "Yes, it is. How many rectangles can you find on the door?" "There are big wide rectangles on the sides and thin rectangles on the ends and the top and bottom."
◆ "The plate and the hamburger look round like circles." "They do, don't they?" comments Mr. Brown.
◆ "Where I put the purple paint, it looks like a butterfly." Mr. Flores looks over and nods.
◆ "The roof is shaped like a witch's hat." Miss Conn smiles.
◆ Watching a variety show on TV, the child asks, "What are those things that are shaped like bananas?" (Some curtains over the stage are yellow and do look just like big bananas!) Dad comments laughingly, "That is funny. Those curtains look like bananas."

Structured Activities

Structured activities are designed to help children see the attributes that are critical to each type of shape. These activities should provide more than learning the names of a limited number of models. Models should vary. For example, every figure should not have a horizontal base. Some examples should be rotated as in Figure 12–4. Some nonexamples should be provided for comparison. Preoperational children need to learn that orientation, color, and size are irrelevant to the identification of the shape. Clements and Sarama (2000, p. 487) suggest that children can be helped to learn what is relevant and what is irrelevant through the following kinds of activities.

◆ identifying shapes in the classroom, school, and community
◆ sorting shapes and describing why they believe a shape belongs to a group
◆ copying and building with shapes using a wide range of materials

Children need both haptic and visual experiences to learn discrimination and labeling. These experiences can be described as follows:

◆ *Haptic activities* use the sense of touch to match and identify shapes. These activities involve experiences where the child cannot see to solve a problem but must use only his sense of touch. The items to be touched are hidden from view. The things may be put in a bag or a box or wrapped in cloth or paper. Sometimes a clue is given. The child can feel one thing and then find another that is the same shape. The child can be shown a shape and then asked to find one that is the same. Finally, the child can be given just a name (or label) as a clue.

◆ *Visual activities* use the sense of sight. The child may be given a visual or a verbal clue and asked to choose from several things the one that is the same shape. Real objects or pictures may be used.

◆ *Visual-motor activities* use the sense of sight and motor coordination at the same time. This type of experience includes the use of puzzles, formboards, attribute blocks, flannelboards, magnet boards, Colorforms,® and paper cutouts, which the child moves about on his own. He may sort the things into sets or arrange them into a pattern or picture. Sorting was described in Unit 10. Examples of making patterns or pictures are shown in Figure 12–6.

As the child does haptic, visual, and visual-motor activities, the teacher can use labels (words such as *round, circle, square, triangle, rectangle, shape, cor-*

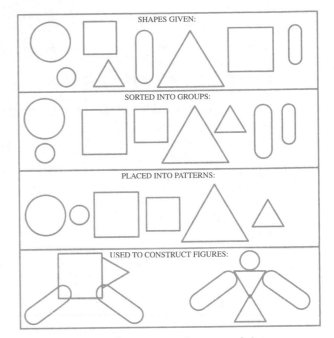

FIGURE 12-6 Shapes can be sorted into groups, placed into a pattern, or made into figures.

ners, points, cone, cylinder, rectangular prism, and so on). The following activities are some examples of basic types of shape experiences for the young child.

ACTIVITIES

SHAPE: FEELING BOX

OBJECTIVE: To give the child experiences that will enable him to use his sense of touch to label and discriminate shapes.

MATERIALS: A medium-sized cardboard box covered with plain Contac® paper with a hole cut in the top big enough for the child to put his hand in but small enough so the child cannot see inside; some familiar objects, such as a toy car, a small wooden block, a spoon, a small coin purse, a baby shoe, a pencil, and a rock.

NATURALISTIC AND INFORMAL ACTIVITIES: During daily center time the children should have opportunities to become acquainted with the objects listed above during their play activities. During their play the teacher should comment on the objects, supplying the names such as, "You have used the *rectangular square prism blocks* to build a garage for your *car.*"

STRUCTURED ACTIVITIES:

1. Show the children each of the objects. Be sure they know the name of each one. Have them pick up each object and name it.
2. Out of their sight, put the objects in the box.
3. Then do the following:
   ◆ Have another set of identical objects. Hold them up one at a time: PUT YOUR HAND IN THE BOX. FIND ONE LIKE THIS.
   ◆ Have a set of identical objects. Put each one in an individual bag: FEEL WHAT IS IN HERE. FIND ONE JUST LIKE IT IN THE BIG BOX.
   ◆ Use just a verbal clue: PUT YOUR HAND IN THE BOX. FIND THE ROCK (CAR, BLOCK, ETC.).
   ◆ PUT YOUR HAND IN THE BOX. TELL ME THE NAME OF WHAT YOU FEEL. BRING IT OUT, AND WE'LL SEE IF YOU GUESSED IT.

FOLLOW-UP: Once the children understand the idea of the "feeling box," a "mystery box" can be introduced. In this case, familiar objects are placed in the box, but the children do not know what they are. They must then feel them and guess what they are. Children can take turns. Before a child takes the object out, encourage him to describe it (smooth, rough, round, straight, bumpy, it has wheels, and so on). After the child learns about geometric shapes, the box can be filled with cardboard cutouts, attribute blocks, or three-dimensional models.

SHAPE: DISCRIMINATION OF GEOMETRIC SHAPES

OBJECTIVE: To see that geometric shapes may be the same or different from each other.

MATERIALS: Any or all of the following may be used:
◆ Magnet board with magnet shapes of various types, sizes, and colors
◆ Flannelboard with felt shapes of various types, shapes, and colors
◆ Attribute blocks (blocks of various shapes, sizes, and colors)
◆ Cards with pictures of various geometric shapes in several sizes (they can be all outlines or solids of the same or different colors)
◆ Three-dimensional models

NATURALISTIC AND INFORMAL ACTIVITIES: During the daily center time provide opportunities for the children to explore the materials. Note if they use any shape words, sort the shapes, match the shapes, make patterns, or make constructions. Ask them to describe what they have done. Comment, using shape words.

STRUCTURED ACTIVITIES: The activities are matching, classifying, and labeling.
◆ Matching: Put out several different shapes. Show the child one shape. Then say, "FIND ALL THE SHAPES LIKE THIS ONE. Tell me why those belong together."
◆ Classifying: Put out several different kinds of shapes. Then say, "PUT ALL THE SHAPES THAT ARE THE SAME KIND TOGETHER. Tell me how you know those shapes are all the same kind."
◆ Labeling: Put out some shapes—several kinds. Then say, "FIND ALL THE TRIANGLES (SQUARES, CIRCLES, ETC.), or TELL ME THE NAME OF THIS SHAPE." (Point to one at random.)

FOLLOW-UP: Do individual and small group activities. Do the same basic activities with different materials.

SHAPE: DISCRIMINATION AND MATCHING GAME

OBJECTIVE: To practice matching and discrimination skills (for the child who has had experience with the various shapes already).

MATERIALS: Cut out some shapes from cardboard. The game can be made harder by the number of shapes used, the size of the shapes, and the number of colors. Make six bingo-type cards (each one should be different) and a spinner card, which includes all the shapes used.

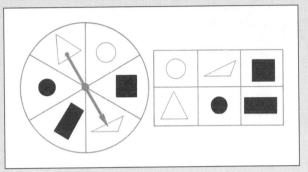

ACTIVITIES:
1. Give each child a bingo card.
2. Have each child in turn spin the spinner. If he has the shape on his card that the spinner points to, he can cover the shape with a paper square or put a marker on it.

FOLLOW-UP: Once the rules of the game are learned the children can play it on their own.

SHAPE: ENVIRONMENTAL GEOMETRY

OBJECTIVE: To see that there are geometric shapes all around in the environment.

MATERIALS: The classroom, the school building, the playground, the home, and the neighborhood.

ACTIVITIES:
1. Look for shapes on the floor, the ceiling, doors, windows, materials, clothing, trees, flowers, vehicles, walls, fences, sidewalks, and so on.
2. Make a shape table. Cover the top, and divide it into sections. Mark each section with a sample shape. Have the children bring things from home and put them on the place on the table that matches the shape of the thing that they bring.
3. Make "Find the Shape" posters (see Figure 12–7).

EXAMPLE WORLD WIDE WEB ACTIVITIES.

Evaluate these activities relative to the unit material.

◆ Hokey Pokey with shapes. Link at http://www.lessonplanspage.com/
◆ Shape plans by the month can be found at Stormie's Web site at http://www.preschoolbystormie.com

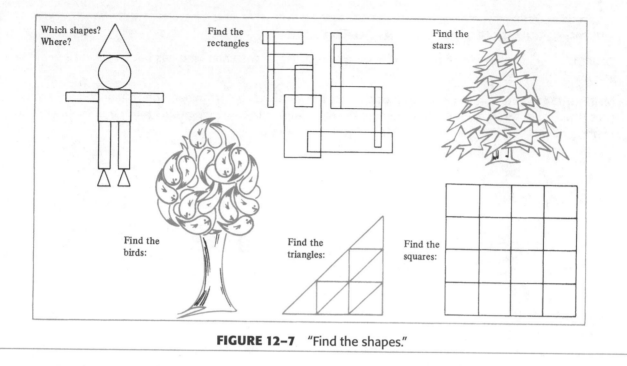

FIGURE 12–7 "Find the shapes."

Evaluation

Through observing during center time and during structured experiences, the teacher can see whether the child shows an increase in ideas regarding shape. She observes whether the child uses the word *shape* and other shape words as he goes about his daily activities. When he sorts and groups materials, the teacher notices whether he sometimes uses shape as the basis for organizing. The adult gives the child informal tasks such as "Put the box on the square table," "Fold the napkins so they are rectangle shapes," "Find two boxes that are the same shape," "Look carefully at the shapes of your puzzle pieces," and "Make a design with these different shaped tiles."

After a period of instruction, the teacher may use interview tasks such as those in Appendix A.

Summary

Each thing the child meets in the environment has shape. The child explores his world and learns in a naturalistic way about the shape of each object in it. Adults help by giving the child things to view, hold, and feel. Adults also teach the child words that describe shapes and the names of geometric shapes such as square, circle, triangle, cylinder, triangular prism, and so on. Through exploration of shapes and spatial relations (see Unit 13) the foundation of geometry is laid.

KEY TERMS

circle	cylinder	rectangular prism
triangle	sphere	
square	triangular prism	

SUGGESTED ACTIVITIES

1. Do an assessment of a child's concept of shape. Plan and do some activities with the child that will enhance his shape understanding. Report on your evaluation of the results.
2. Make or assemble some materials for a haptic activity. Have the class use the materials and give you feedback. Make any needed changes, and add the activity to your file or notebook.
3. Maria Montessori created some haptic activities. Research her method in the library and by visiting a Montessori school. Write an evaluation of her materials.
4. In a preprimary classroom, place some shape materials out where the children can explore them informally. Record what the children do, and share the results with the class.
5. Using the guidelines from Activity 7, Unit 9, evaluate one or more of the following computer programs designed to reinforce shape concepts.

◆ James Discovers Math. Novato, CA: Broderbund.
◆ Hands-on-Math, Vols. 1,2,3. Nashua, NH: Delta Educational.
◆ Millie's Math House (Mouse House). Redmond, WA: Edmark.
◆ Muppet Math. Pleasantville, NY: Sunburst Technology.
◆ Shape and Color Rodeo. Allen, TX: Developmental Learning Materials.
◆ Shape Up! Pleasantville, NY: Sunburst Communications.
◆ Stickers. Minneapolis, MN: Springboard Software, Inc.
◆ Stickybear Shapes. Middletown, CT: Weekly Reader Family Software.
◆ Thinkin' Things. Redmond, WA: Edmark.

REVIEW

A. Below is a description of four-year-old Maria's activities on a school day. Identify the shape activities she experiences, and decide whether each is naturalistic, informal, or structured.

Maria's mother wakes her up at 7:00 a.m. "Time to get up." Maria snuggles her teddy bear, Beady. His soft body feels very comforting. Mom comes in and gets her up and into the bathroom to wash her face and brush her teeth. "What kind of cereal do you want this morning?" Maria responds, "Those round ones, Cheerios.®" Maria rubs her hands over the slippery surface of the soap before she rubs it on her face.

Maria goes into the kitchen where she eats her cereal out of a round bowl. Occasionally, she looks out the window through its square panes. After breakfast, Maria gets dressed, and she and her mother drive to school. Along the way, Maria notices a stop sign, a railroad crossing sign, a school zone sign, buildings with many windows, and other cars and buses.

At the Child Development Center, Maria is greeted by her teacher. She hangs her coat in her cubby and runs over to where several of her friends are building with unit blocks. Maria builds, using combinations of long blocks, short blocks, rectangular blocks, square blocks, and curved blocks. She makes a rectangular enclosure and places some miniature animals in it.

Next, Maria goes to the Art Center. She cuts out a large and small circle and four rectangles. She glues them on a larger sheet of paper. "Look," she says to her teacher, "I made a little person."

The children gather around Miss Collins for a group activity. "Today we will see what kinds of shapes we can make with our bodies." Individually and in small groups, the children form a variety of shapes with their bodies.

For snack, the children have cheese cut into cubes and elliptical crackers. Following snack, Maria goes to a table of puzzles and formboards and selects a geometric shape formboard. After successfully completing the formboard, Maria selects the shape blocks. She sorts and stacks them according to shape. "Look, I made a stack of triangles and a stack of squares."

B. Give an example of shape discrimination, shape labeling, shape matching, and shape sorting.

C. Decide whether each of the following is an example of discrimination, labeling, matching, or sorting.

1. The child is shown an ellipse. "Tell me the name of this kind of shape."
2. The children are told to see how many rectangular prisms they can find in the classroom.
3. The teacher passes around a bag with an unknown object inside. Each child feels the bag and makes a prediction as to what is inside.
4. The teacher holds up a cylinder block and tells the children to find some things that are the same shape.
5. A child is fitting shapes into a shape matrix board.
6. A small group of children is playing shape lotto.

REFERENCES

Clements, D. H., & Sarama, J. (2000). Young children's ideas about geometric shapes. *Teaching Children Mathematics*, 6(8), 482–488.

Hannibal, M. A. (1999). Young children's developing understanding of geometric shapes. *Teaching Children Mathematics*, 5(6), 353–357.

National Council of Teachers of Mathematics. (2000). *Principles and standards for school mathematics*. Reston, VA: Author. (http://www.nctm.org)

FURTHER READING AND RESOURCES

AIMS Educational Products. AIMS Education Foundation, P.O. Box 8120, Fresno, CA 93747–8120.

Burk, D., Snider, A., & Symonds, P. (1988). *Box it or bag it mathematics: Kindergarten teachers' resource guide*. Portland, OR: The Math Learning Center.

Copley, J. V. (2000). *The young child and mathematics*. Washington, DC: National Association for the Education of Young Children.

Copley, J. V. (Ed.). (1999). *Mathematics in the early years*. Washington, DC: National Association for the Education of Young Children.

Del Grande, J. (1993). *Curriculum and evaluation standards for school mathematics: Geometry and spatial sense*. Reston, VA: National Council of Teachers of Mathematics.

Fleege, P., & Crocker, B. (1992). Hands-on slime. *Science and Children*, 30(1), 36–38.

Flores, A. (1995). Bilingual lessons in early grades geometry. *Teaching Children Mathematics, 1* 420–424.

Geometry and geometric thinking. (1999). *Teaching Children Mathematics* 5(6) [Focus issue].

Holly, K. (1995). Shape up! *Teaching Children Mathematics, 2*(4), 226.

Lamphere, P. (1995). Geoboard patterns and figures. *Teaching Children Mathematics, 1*(5), 282–283.

Linquist, M. M., & Clements, D. H. (2001). Principles and standards. Geometry must be vital. *Teaching Children Mathematics*, *7*(7), 409–415.

McGrath, B. B. (1994). *The m&m's® brand counting book*. Watertown, MA: Charlesbridge.

National Council of Teachers of Mathematics (NCTM). (1989). *Curriculum and evaluation standards for school mathematics*. Reston, VA: Author. (http://www.nctm.org)

Richardson, K. (1999). *Developing number concepts: Planning guide*. Parsippany, NJ: Dale Seymour.

UNIT 13
Early Geometry: Spatial Sense

OBJECTIVES

After reading this unit, you should be able to:

◆ Explain the NCTM expectations for prekindergarten through grade two spatial sense.

◆ Define the five spatial sense concepts and tell how each answers specific questions.

◆ Assess and evaluate a child's spatial concepts.

◆ Do informal and structured spatial activities with young children.

NCTM (2000) lists several expectations relative to young children's understanding and application of spatial relationships as one of the foundations of early geometry. Young children are expected to describe, name, and interpret relative positions in space and apply ideas about relative position; describe, name, and interpret direction and distance in navigating space and apply ideas about direction and distance; and find and name locations with simple relationships such as "near to" and "in." A sense of spatial relationships along with an understanding of shape (Unit 12) is fundamental to "interpreting, understanding, and appreciating our inherently geometric world" (NCTM, 1989, p. 48). Spatial sense experiences can integrate across content areas (Figure 13–1).

Assessment

A great deal about the child's concept of space can be learned through observation. The adult notes the child's use of space words.

Does he respond with an appropriate act when he is told the following?

◆ Put the book *on* the table.
◆ Please *take off* your hat.
◆ You'll find the soap *under* the sink.
◆ Stand *behind* the gate.
◆ Sit *between* Kate and Chris.
◆ Move *away from* the hot stove.
◆ It's on the table *near* the window.

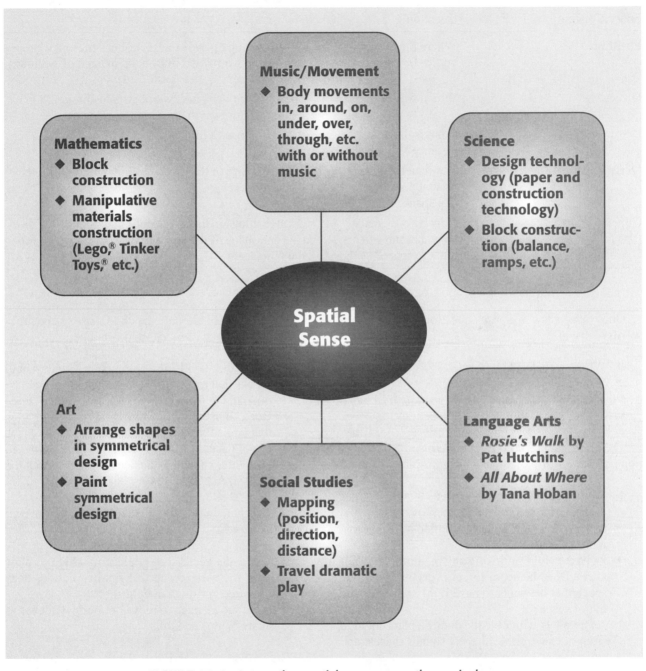

FIGURE 13–1   Integrating spatial sense across the curriculum.

Space Concept	Question	Answers
Position	Where (am I, are you, is he)?	on-off; on top of-over-under; in-out; into-out of; top-bottom; above-below; in front of-in back of-behind; beside-by-next to; between
Direction	Which way?	up-down; forward-backward; around-through; to-from; toward-away from; sideways; across
Distance	What is the relative distance?	near-far; close to-far from
Organization and Pattern	How can things be arranged so they fit in a space?	arrange things in the space until they fit, or until they please the eye
Construction	How is space made? How do things fit into the space?	arrange things in the space until they fit; change the size and shape of the space to fit what is needed for the things

Does she answer space questions using space words?

◆ Where is the cat? *On* the bed.
◆ Where is the cake? *In* the oven.
◆ Which way did John go? He went *up* the ladder.
◆ Where is your house? *Near* the corner.

The adult should note the child's use of organization and pattern arrangement during his play activities.

◆ When he does artwork, such as a collage, does he take time to place the materials on the paper in a careful way? Does he seem to have a design in mind?
◆ Does the child's drawing and painting show balance? Does he seem to get everything into the space that he wants to have it in, or does he run out of space?
◆ As he plays with objects, does he place them in straight rows, circle shapes, square shapes, and so on?

The teacher should note the child's use of construction materials such as blocks and containers:

◆ Does the child make structures with small blocks that toys such as cars and animals can be put into?
◆ Does he use the large blocks to make buildings that large toys and children can get into?
◆ Can he usually find the right sized container to hold things (such as a shoe box that makes the right sized bed for his toy bear)?

The teacher should note the child's use of her own body in space.

◆ When she needs a cozy place in which to play, does she choose one that fits her size, or does she often get stuck in tight spots?
◆ Does she manage to move her body without too many bumps and falls?

The individual interview tasks for space center on relationships and use of space. The following are examples of interview tasks.

SAMPLE ASSESSMENT TASK

3G   **Preoperational Ages 2–3**
Space, Position: Unit 13

METHOD: Interview.

SKILL: Given a spatial relationship word, the child is able to place objects relative to other objects
                     on the basis of that word.

MATERIALS: A small container such as a box, cup, or bowl and an object such as a coin, checker, or chip.

PROCEDURE: PUT THE (_____) IN THE BOX (or CUP or BOWL). Repeat using other space words:
                     ON, OFF OF, OUT OF, IN FRONT OF, NEXT TO, UNDER, OVER.

EVALUATION: Note if the child is able to follow the instructions and place the object correctly relative to the
                     space word used.

INSTRUCTIONAL RESOURCE: Charlesworth, R., and Lind, K. K. (2003). *Math and Science for Young Children* (4th ed.). Clifton Park, NY: Delmar Learning.

SAMPLE ASSESSMENT TASK

4F   **Preoperational Ages 3–4**
Space, Position: Unit 13

METHOD: Interview.

SKILL: Child will be able to use appropriate spatial relationship words to describe positions in
                     space.

MATERIALS: Several small containers and several small objects; for example, four small plastic glasses
                     and four small toy figures such as a fish, dog, cat, and mouse.

PROCEDURE: Ask the child to name each of the objects so you can use his name for them if it is different
                     from your names. Line up the glasses in a row. Place the animals so that one is *in*, one *on*,
                     one *under*, and one *between* the glasses. Then say, TELL ME WHERE THE FISH IS. Then, TELL
                     ME WHERE THE DOG IS. Then, TELL ME WHERE THE CAT IS. Finally, TELL ME WHERE THE
                     MOUSE IS. Frequently, children will insist on pointing. Say, DO IT WITHOUT POINTING. TELL
                     ME WITH WORDS.

EVALUATION: Note whether the child responds with position words and whether or not the words used
                     are correct.

INSTRUCTIONAL RESOURCE: Charlesworth, R., and Lind, K. K. (2003). *Math and Science for Young Children* (4th ed.). Clifton Park, NY: Delmar Learning.

Naturalistic Activities

It is through everyday motor activities that the child first learns about space. As she moves her body in space, she learns position, direction, and distance relationships and about the use of the space. Children in the sensorimotor and preoperational stages need equipment that lets them place their own bodies on, off, under, over, in, out, through, above, below, and so on. They need places to go up and down, around and through, and sideways and across. They need things that they can put in, on, and under other things. They need things that they can place near and far from other things. They need containers of many sizes to fill; blocks with which to build; and paint, collage, wood, clay, and such, which can be made into patterns and organized in space. Thus, when the child is matching, classifying, and comparing, she is learning about space at the same time.

The child who crawls and creeps often goes under furniture. At first she sometimes gets stuck when she has not judged correctly the size space under which she will fit. As she begins to pull herself up, she tries to climb on things. This activity is important not only for her motor development but for her spatial learning. However, many pieces of furniture are not safe or are too high. An empty beverage bottle box with the dividers still in it may be taped closed and covered with some colorful Contac® paper. This makes a safe and inexpensive place to climb. The adults can make several, and the child will have a set of large construction blocks. It has been stated in other units that the child needs safe objects to aid in developing basic concepts. Each time the child handles an object, she may learn more than one skill or idea. For instance, Juanita builds a house with some small blocks. The blocks are different colors and shapes. First Juanita picks out all the blue rectangular prisms and piles them three high in a row. Next she picks all the red rectangular prisms and piles them in another direction in a row. Next she piles orange rectangular prisms to make a third side to her structure. Finally, she lines up some yellow cylinders to make a fourth side. She places two pigs, a cow, and a horse in the enclosure. Juanita has sorted by color and shape. She has made a structure with space for her farm animals (a class) and has put the animals *in* the enclosure.

With the availability of information on outer space flight in movies and on television, children might demonstrate a concept of outer space during their dramatic play activities. For example, they might build a space vehicle with large blocks and fly off to a distant planet or become astronauts on a trip to the moon.

Children begin to integrate position, direction, distance, organization, pattern, and construction through mapping activities. Early mapping activities involve developing more complex spaces such as building houses and laying out roads in the sand or laying out roads and buildings with unit blocks. Or the activity could be playing with commercial toys that include a village printed on plastic along with houses, people, animals, and vehicles that can be placed on the village. Provided with these materials, children naturally make these types of constructions, which are the concrete beginnings of understanding maps.

Informal Activities

Spatial sense is an area where there are many words to be learned and attached to actions. The teacher should use spatial words (as listed earlier in the unit) as they fit into the daily activities. She should give spatial directions, ask spatial questions, and make spatial comments. Examples of directions and questions are in the assessment section of this unit. Spatial comments would be as follows.

- Bob is at the *top* of the ladder.
- Cindy is *close* to the door.
- You have the dog *behind* the mother in the car.
- Tanya can move the handle *backward* and *forward*.
- You children made a house big enough for all of you. (construction)
- You pasted all the square shapes on your paper. (organization and pattern)

Jungle gyms, packing crates, ladders, ramps, and other equipment designed for large muscle activity give the child experiences with space. They climb *up*, *down*, and *across*. They climb *up* a ladder and crawl or slide *down* a ramp. On the jungle gym they go *in* and *out*, *up* and *down*, *through*, *above*, *below*, and *around*. They get *in* and *out* of packing crates. On swings they go *up* and *down* and *backward* and *forward* and see the world *down below*.

With the large blocks, boxes, and boards, they make structures that they can get *in* themselves. Chairs and tables may be added to make a house, train, airplane, bus, or ship. Props such as a steering wheel, firefighter or police hats, ropes, hoses, discarded radios, and so on inspire children to build structures on which to play. With small blocks, children make houses, airports, farms, grocery stores, castles, trains, and so on. They then use their toy animals, people, and other objects in spatial arrangements, patterns, and positions. They learn to fit their structures into space available: on the floor, on a large table, or on a small table. They might also build space vehicles and develop concrete mapping representations in the sand or with blocks. The teacher can ask questions about their space trip or their geographic construction: "How far is it to the moon?" or "Show me the roads you would use to drive from Richard's house to Kate's house."

As the child works with art materials, he plans what to choose to glue or paste on his paper. A large selection of collage materials such as scrap paper, cloth, feathers, plastic bits, yarn, wire, gummed paper, cotton balls, bottle caps, and ribbon offer a child a choice of things to organize on the space he has. As he gets past the first stages of experimentation, the child plans his painting. He may paint blobs, geometric shapes, stripes, or realistic figures. He enjoys printing with sponges or potatoes. All these experiences add to his ideas about space.

Structured Activities

Structured activities of many kinds can be done to help the child with her ideas about space and her skills in the use of space. Basic activities are described for the three kinds of space relations (position, direction, and distance) and the two ways of using space (organization/pattern and construction).

Mrs. Red Fox's first graders enjoy Stickybear Townbuilder (see Activity 6), a computer program that provides them with the raw material for actually building their own town. Buildings and pieces of road are included. Towns can even be saved on a disk and revisited. A cursor car can be used to take a trip around the town. This experience gives practice with basic spatial relationships and an introduction to maps.

ACTIVITIES

SPACE: RELATIONSHIPS, PHYSICAL SELF

OBJECTIVE: To help the child relate his position in space to the positions of other people and things.

MATERIALS: The child's own body, other people, and things in the environment.

NATURALISTIC AND INFORMAL ACTIVITIES: Children should be encouraged to use their bodies in gross motor activity such as running, climbing, jumping, lifting, pulling, and so on. They should be assisted in motor control behaviors such as defining their own space and keeping a safe distance from others.

STRUCTURED ACTIVITIES:

1. Set up an obstacle course using boxes, boards, ladders, tables, chairs, and like items. Set it up so that by following the course, the children can physically experience position, direction, and distance. This can be done indoors or outdoors. As the child proceeds along the course, use space words to label his movement: "Leroy is going *up* the ladder, *through* the tunnel, *across* the bridge, *down* the slide, and *under* the table. Now he is *close to* the end."

2. Find Your Friend
   Place children in different places: sitting or standing on chairs or blocks or boxes, under tables, sitting three in a row on chairs facing different directions, and so on. Have each child take a turn to find a friend.
   FIND A FRIEND WHO IS ON A CHAIR (A BOX, A LADDER).
   FIND A FRIEND WHO IS UNDER A TABLE (ON A TABLE, NEXT TO A TABLE).
   FIND A FRIEND WHO IS BETWEEN TWO FRIENDS (BEHIND A FRIEND, NEXT TO A FRIEND).
   FIND A FRIEND WHO IS SITTING BACKWARDS (FORWARDS, SIDEWAYS).
   FIND A FRIEND WHO IS ABOVE ANOTHER FRIEND (BELOW ANOTHER FRIEND).
   Have the children think of different places they can place themselves. When they know the game, let the children take turns saying the FIND statements.
3. Put Yourself Where I Say
   One at a time give the children instructions for placing themselves in a position.
   CLIMB UP THE LADDER.
   WALK BETWEEN THE CHAIRS.
   STAND BEHIND TANYA.
   GET ON TOP OF THE BOX.
   GO CLOSE TO THE DOOR (GO FAR FROM THE DOOR).
   As the children learn the game, they can give the instructions.
4. Where Is Your Friend?
   As in Activity 2, "Find Your Friend," place the children in different places. This time ask WHERE questions. The child must answer in words. As WHERE IS (child's name)? Child answers, "Tim is under the table," or "Mary is on top of the playhouse."

FOLLOW-UP: Set up obstacle courses for the children to use during playtime both indoors and outdoors.

SPACE: RELATIONSHIPS, OBJECTS

OBJECTIVE: To be able to relate the position of objects in space to other objects.

MATERIALS: Have several identical containers (cups, glasses, boxes) and some small objects such as blocks, pegs, buttons, sticks, toy animals, people.

NATURALISTIC AND INFORMAL ACTIVITIES: Note how children play with objects during center time. Do they stack their blocks? Do they put dolls in beds? Do they place vehicles in structures? Comment on their placements: "The red block is *on* two green blocks." "The doll is *in* the bed." Give instructions: "Sit *next to* Mary," "Put the placemat *under* the dishes," "Put this brush *in* the red paint." Note if the children are able to comply.

STRUCTURED ACTIVITIES:
1. Point To
   Place objects in various spatial relationships such as shown below.

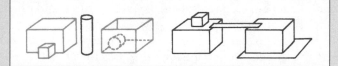

   POINT TO (OR SHOW ME) THE THING THAT IS (IN, ON, UNDER, BETWEEN, BEHIND, etc.) A BOX.

2. Put the

Set some containers out. Place some objects to the side. Tell the child PUT THE (object name IN, ON, THROUGH, ACROSS, UNDER, NEAR) THE CONTAINER.

3. Where Is?

Place objects as in 1 above and/or around the room. Ask, WHERE IS (object name)? TELL ME WHERE THE (object name) IS. Child should reply using a space word.

FOLLOW-UP: Repeat the activity using different objects and containers. Leave the materials out for the children to use during center time.

SPACE: USE, CONSTRUCTION

OBJECTIVE: To organize materials in space in three dimensions through construction.

MATERIALS: Wood chips, polythene, cardboard, wire, bottle caps, small empty boxes (i.e., tea, face cream, toothpaste, frozen foods, etc.), and other waste materials that can be recycled for construction projects, glue, cardboard, and/or plywood scraps.

NATURALISTIC AND INFORMAL ACTIVITIES: Provide children with time to build with construction toys (unit blocks, LEGO®, Unifix Cubes®, etc.) during center time. Also provide experiences in making a variety of collages, which provide the children with experiences in organizing materials and using glue.

STRUCTURED ACTIVITY: Give the child a bottle of glue, a roll of masking tape, and a piece of cardboard or plywood for a base. Let him choose from the scrap materials things to use to build a structure on the base. Encourage him to take his time, plan, and choose carefully which things to use and where to put them.

FOLLOW-UP: Keep plenty of waste materials on hand so that children can make structures when they are in the mood.

SPACE: USE, CONSTRUCTION

OBJECTIVE: To organize materials in space in three dimensions through that construction.

MATERIALS: Many kinds of construction materials can be purchased that help the child to understand space and also improve eye-hand coordination and small muscle skills. Some of these are listed:

1. Lego®: Jumbo for the younger child, regular for the older child or one with good motor skills
2. Tinker Toys®
3. Bolt-it®
4. Snap-N-Play® blocks
5. Rig-A-Jig®
6. Octons®, Play Squares® (and other things with parts that fit together)

NATURALISTIC AND INFORMAL ACTIVITIES: Once the child understands the ways that the toys can be used, he can be left alone with the materials and his imagination.

SPACE: MAPPING

OBJECTIVE: To integrate basic space concepts through simple mapping activities.

MATERIALS: Make a simple treasure map on a large piece of poster board. Draw a floor plan of the classroom, indicating major landmarks (such as the learning centers, doors, windows, etc.) with simple drawings. Draw in some paths going from place to place. Make a brightly colored treasure chest from a shoe box. Make a matching two-dimensional movable treasure chest that can be placed anywhere on the floor plan.

NATURALISTIC AND INFORMAL ACTIVITIES: Children should have opportunities for sand play and unit block play with a variety of vehicles. Note if they construct roads, bridges, tunnels, and so on. Ask, "Where does your road go?" They should have a miniature house with miniature furniture to arrange. Ask, "How do you decide where to place the furniture?" Include maps as a dramatic play prop. Note if children find a way to use the maps in their play. How do they use them? Does their activity reflect an understanding of what a map is for?

STRUCTURED ACTIVITY: Hide the treasure chest somewhere in the room. Place the small treasure chest on the floor plan. Have the children discuss the best route to get from where they are to the treasure using only the paths on the floor plan. Have them try out their routes to see if they can discover the treasure.

FOLLOW-UP: Let class members hide the treasure and see if they are able to place the treasure chest correctly on the floor plan. Let them use trial and error when hiding the treasure, marking the spot on the plan, and finding the treasure. Make up some other games using the same basic format. Try this activity outdoors. Supply some adult maps for dramatic play and observe how children use them.

EXAMPLE WORLD WIDE WEB ACTIVITY

◆ About Space. Space Includes Shadows (matching figures with their shadows). An Annenberg Project. Link at http://www.learner.org/teacherslab/

Evaluation

Informal evaluation can be done through observation. The teacher should note the following as the children proceed through the day.

◆ Does the child respond to space words in a way that shows understanding?
◆ Does she answer space questions and use the correct space words?
◆ Do her artwork and block building show an increase in pattern and organization?
◆ Does the child handle her body well in space?
◆ Does her use of geoboards, parquetry blocks, color inch cubes, and/or pegboards show an increase in organization and pattern?

After children have done several space activities, the teacher can assess their progress using the interview tasks in Appendix A.

Summary

Spatial sense is an important part of geometry. The child needs to understand the spatial relationship between his body and other things. He must also understand the spatial relationship between things around him. Things are related through position, direction, and distance.

The child also needs to be able to use space in a logical way. He learns to fit things into the space available and to make constructions in space.

KEY TERMS

position
direction

distance
organization and pattern

construction

SUGGESTED ACTIVITIES

1. Observe some young children on the playground using large motor equipment such as the jungle gym, slides, or tricycles. Note instances that reflect children's concepts of space as listed in the chart at the beginning of the unit and in the assessment tasks included in the unit.

2. Observe some young children in their classroom playing with blocks and other construction materials. Note instances that reflect children's concepts of space as listed in the chart at the beginning of the unit and in the assessment tasks included in the unit.

3. Design a piece of large motor equipment (i.e., jungle gym or slide) that offers children a variety of spatial experiences. Explain where and how these experiences might take place.

4. Pretend you have been provided with a budget of $300. Select from a catalog the construction toys you would purchase. Provide a rationale for each selection.

5. Add two or more space activities to your file or notebook.

6. Review one of the following computer programs using the guidelines suggested in Activity 7, Unit 9.
   - Arrow Graphics. St. Louis, MO: Milliken Publishing Co.
   - My Make Believe Castle. Highgate Springs, VT: LOGO Computer Systems, Inc.
   - Spatial Relations. Pleasantville, NY: Sunburst Technology. (Available in English and Spanish versions)
   - Stickybear Town Builder. Middletown, CT: Weekly Reader Family Software.
   - Trudy's Time and Place House. Pleasantville, NY: Sunburst Technology.

REVIEW

A. Describe how a teacher can assess children's concepts of space through observing their play.

B. Decide which of the following examples are
   a. Position
   b. Direction
   c. Distance
   d. Organization
   e. Construction
   f. Mapping

   1. Several children are building with blocks. "Is Carl's building closer to Kate's or to Bob's?"
   2. Lego® construction materials.
   3. "How can we get all these trucks into this garage?"
   4. Mario works with the trucks until he manages to park them all in the garage he has built.
   5. Mary is next to Carlo and behind Jon.
   6. "Are we closer to the cafeteria or to the playground? Let's measure on our school floor plan."
   7. Parquetry blocks.
   8. "Let's play 'London Bridge.'"
   9. "Where am I?" is the central question.
   10. "Which way?" is the focus question.
   11. Geoboards are useful in the development of which spatial concept?
   12. "We don't have enough room for everyone who wants to play house. What can we change?"
   13. "Let's act out *The Three Billy Goats Gruff*."
   14. In the sandbox, the children are building tunnels and roads.
   15. As Angelena swings she chants, "Up and down, up and down."

C. Explain how the NCTM expectations for spatial sense relate to each of the examples in question B.

REFERENCES

National Council of Teachers of Mathematics. (1989). *Curriculum and evaluation standards for school mathematics.* Reston, VA: Author. (http://www.nctm.org)

National Council of Teachers of Mathematics. (2000). *Principles and standards for school mathematics.* Reston, VA: Author. (http://www.nctm.org)

FURTHER READING AND RESOURCES

AIMS Educational Products. AIMS Education Foundation, P.O. Box 8120, Fresno, CA 93747–8120.

Andrews, A. B. (1996). Developing spatial sense—a moving experience. *Teaching Children Mathematics, 5,* 290–293.

Burk, D., Snider, A., & Symonds P. (1988). *Box it or bag it mathematics*: *Kindergarten teachers' resource guide.* Portland, OR: The Math Learning Center.

Clements, D. H. (2000). Young children's ideas about geometric shapes. *Teaching Children Mathematics, 6*(8), 482–487.

Copley, J. V. (2000). *The young child and mathematics.* Washington, DC: National Association for the Education of Young Children.

Copley, J. V. (Ed.). (1999). *Mathematics in the early years.* Washington, DC: National Association for the Education of Young Children.

Del Grande, J. (1993). *Curriculum and evaluation standards for school mathematics: Geometry and spatial sense.* Reston, VA: National Council of Teachers of Mathematics.

Geometry and geometric thinking. (1999). *Teaching Children Mathematics, 5*(6). [Focus issue].

Haugland, S. (1993). Computers and young children: The outstanding developmental software. *Day Care and Early Education, 21*(2).

Hewitt, K. (2001). Blocks as a tool for learning: A historical and contemporary perspective. *Young Children, 56*(1), 6–12.

Hirsch, E. S. (Ed.) (1996). *The block book* (3rd ed.). Washington, DC: National Association for the Education of Young Children.

Hoot, J. L. (1986). *Computers in early childhood education.* Englewood Cliffs, NJ: Prentice-Hall.

Johnson, P. (1992). *Pop-up paper engineering.* London: Falmer.

Lambdin, D. V., & Lambdin, D. (1995). Connecting mathematics and physical education through spatial awareness. In P. A. House & A. F. Coxford (Eds.), *Connecting mathematics across the curriculum,* 147–151. Reston, VA: National Council of Teachers of Mathematics.

Linquist, M. M., & Clements, D. H. (2001). Principles and standards. Geometry must be vital. *Teaching Children Mathematics, 7*(7), 409–415.

Reifel, S. (1984). Block construction: Children's developmental landmarks in representation of space. *Young Children, 40*(1), 61–67.

Richardson, K. (1999). *Developing number concepts: Planning guide.* Parsippany, NJ: Dale Seymour.

Tickle, L. (1990). *Design technology in primary classrooms.* London: Falmer.

UNIT 14
Parts and Wholes

OBJECTIVES

After reading this unit, you should be able to:

◆ Explain and apply the NCTM expectations for part/whole relationships.

◆ Describe the three types of part/whole relationships.

◆ Assess and evaluate a child's knowledge of parts and wholes.

◆ Do informal and structured part/whole activities with young children.

Young children have a natural understanding and interest in **parts** and **wholes** that can be used later as a bridge to understanding **fractions**. NCTM (2000) expectations include that young children will develop a sense of whole numbers and represent them in many ways by breaking groups down into smaller parts. They will also understand and represent commonly used fractions such as one-quarter, one-third, and one-half. They learn that objects and their own bodies are made up of special (unique) parts, that sets of things can be divided into parts, and that whole things can be divided into smaller parts.

They learn about special parts.

◆ Bodies have parts (arms, legs, head).

◆ A car has parts (engine, doors, steering wheel, seats).

◆ A house has parts (kitchen, bathroom, bedroom, living room).

◆ A chair has parts (seat, legs, back).

They learn that groups of things can be divided.

◆ They pass out cookies for snack.

◆ They deal cards for a game of picture rummy.

◆ They give each friend one of their toys with which to play.

◆ They divide their blocks so each child may build a house.

They learn that whole things can be divided into parts.

◆ One cookie is broken in half.

◆ An orange is divided into several segments.

◆ A carrot or banana is sliced into parts.

◆ The contents of a bottle of soda pop are put into two or more cups.

◆ A large piece of paper is cut into small pieces.

The young child centers on the number of things he sees. Two-year-old Pete breaks up his graham cracker into small pieces. "I have more than you," he says to Tim, who has one whole graham cracker also. Pete does not see that although he has more pieces of cracker he does not have more crackers. Ms. Moore shows Chris a whole apple. "How many apples do I have?" "One," says Chris. "Now watch," says Ms. Moore as she cuts the apple into two pieces. "How

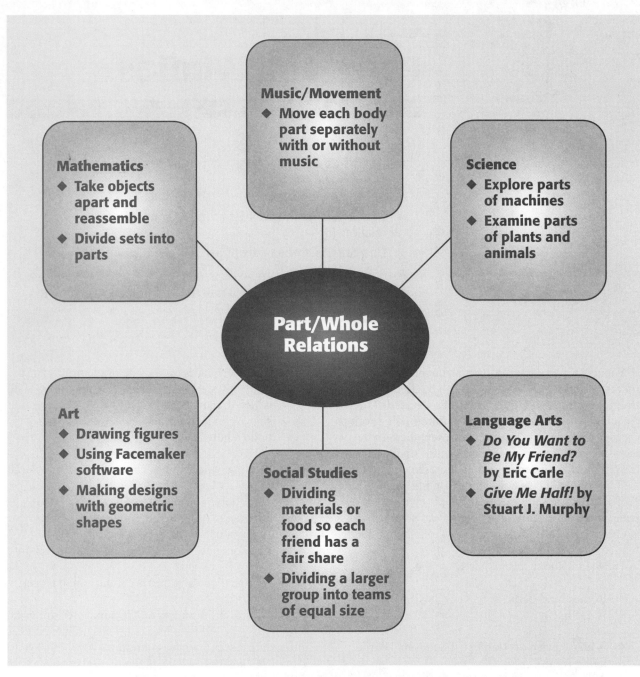

FIGURE 14–1 Integrating part/whole concepts across the curriculum.

many apples do I have now?" "Two!" answers Chris. As the child enters concrete operations, he will see that a single apple is always a single apple even though it may be cut into parts.

Gradually the child is able to see that a whole is made up of parts. He also begins to see that parts may be the same (equal) in size and amount or different (unequal) in size and amount. He compares number and size (see Unit 11) and develops the concepts of more, less, and the same. These concepts are prerequisites to the understanding of fractions, which are introduced in the primary grades. An understanding of more, less, and the same underlies learning that objects and sets can be divided into two or more equal parts and still maintain the same amount. Part/whole concepts can be integrated into other content areas (Figure 14–1).

Assessment

The teacher should observe as the child works and plays whether she uses the words *part* and *whole*. The teacher should note whether the child uses them correctly. The teacher should note her actions.

◆ Does she try to divide items to be shared equally among her friends?
◆ Will she think of cutting or breaking something in smaller parts if there is not enough for everyone?
◆ Does she realize when a part of something is missing (such as the wheel of a toy truck, the arm of a doll, the handle of a cup)?

Interview questions would be like the following tasks.

SAMPLE ASSESSMENT TASK

3H
Parts and Wholes, Missing Parts: Unit 14

Preoperational Ages 2–3

METHOD:	Interview.
SKILL:	Child is able to tell which part(s) of objects and/or pictures of objects are missing.
MATERIALS:	Several objects and/or pictures of objects and/or people with parts missing. Following are some examples:
Objects:	A doll with a leg or an arm missing A car with a wheel missing A cup with a handle broken off A chair with a leg gone A face with only one eye A house with no door
Pictures:	Mount pictures of common things on poster board. Parts can be cut off before mounting.
PROCEDURE:	Show the child each object or picture. LOOK CAREFULLY. WHICH PART IS MISSING FROM THIS?
EVALUATION:	Note if the child is able to tell which parts are missing in both objects and pictures. Does he have the language label for each part? Can he perceive what is missing?

INSTRUCTIONAL RESOURCE: Charlesworth, R., and Lind, K. K. (2003). *Math and Science for Young Children* (4th ed.). Clifton Park, NY: Delmar Learning.

SAMPLE ASSESSMENT TASK

5F   **Preoperational Ages 4–5**
Parts and Wholes, Parts of a Whole: Unit 14

METHOD: Interview.

SKILL: The child can recognize that a whole divided into parts is still the same amount.

MATERIALS: Apple and knife.

PROCEDURE: Show the child the apple. HOW MANY APPLES DO I HAVE? After you are certain the child understands that there is one apple, cut the apple into two equal halves. HOW MANY APPLES DO I HAVE NOW? HOW DO YOU KNOW? If the child says "Two," press the halves together and ask, HOW MANY APPLES DO I HAVE NOW? Then cut the apple into fourths and eighths, following the same procedure.

EVALUATION: If the child can tell you that there is still one apple when it is cut into parts, she is able to mentally reverse the cutting process and may be leaving the preoperational period.

INSTRUCTIONAL RESOURCE: Charlesworth, R., and Lind, K. K. (2003). *Math and Science for Young Children* (4th ed.). Clifton Park, NY: Delmar Learning.

SAMPLE ASSESSMENT TASK

6D   **Preoperational Ages 5–6**
Parts and Wholes, Parts of Sets: Unit 14

METHOD: Interview.

SKILL: The child can divide a set of objects into smaller groups.

MATERIALS: Three small dolls (real or paper cutouts) and a box of pennies or other small objects.

PROCEDURE: Have the three dolls arranged in a row. I WANT TO GIVE EACH DOLL SOME PENNIES. SHOW ME HOW TO DO IT SO EACH DOLL WILL HAVE THE SAME AMOUNT.

EVALUATION: Note how the child approaches the problem. Does he give each doll one penny at a time in sequence? Does he count out pennies until there are three groups with the same amount? Does he divide the pennies in a random fashion? Does he have a method for finding out if each has the same amount?

INSTRUCTIONAL RESOURCE: Charlesworth, R., and Lind, K. K. (2003). *Math and Science for Young Children* (4th ed.). Clifton Park, NY: Delmar Learning.

Naturalistic Activities

The newborn infant is not aware that all her body parts are part of her. Her early explorations lead her to find out that her hand is connected via an arm to her shoulder and those toes she sees at a distance are hooked to her legs. As she explores objects, she learns that they have different parts also. As she begins to sort and move objects about, she learns about parts and wholes of sets.

The following are some examples of the young child's use of the part/whole idea.

◆ Two-year-old Pete has a hotdog on his plate. The hotdog is cut in six pieces. He gives two pieces to his father, two to his mother, and keeps two for himself.
◆ Three-year-old Jim is playing with some toy milk bottles. He says to Ms. Brown, "You take two like me."
◆ Three-year-old Kate is sitting on a stool in the kitchen. She sees three eggs boiling in a pan on the stove. She points as she looks at her mother. "One for you, one for me, and one for Dad."
◆ Tanya is slicing a carrot. "Look, I have a whole bunch of carrots now."
◆ Juanita is lying on her cot at the beginning of nap time. She holds up her leg. "Mrs. Raymond, is this part of a woman?"
◆ Bob runs up to Mr. Brown. "Look! I have a whole tangerine."

Informal Activities

Many times during the day the teacher can help children develop their understanding of parts and wholes. The teacher can use the words *part*, *whole*, divide, and half.

◆ "Today, everyone gets *half* of an apple and *half* of a sandwich."
◆ "Too bad; *part* of this game is missing."
◆ "Take this basket of crackers, and *divide* them up so everyone gets some."
◆ "No, we won't cut the carrots up. Each child gets a *whole* carrot."
◆ "Give John *half* the blocks so he can build too."
◆ "We have only one apple left. Let's *divide* it up."
◆ "Point to the *part* of the body when I say the name."

The child can be given tasks that require him to learn about parts and wholes. When the child is asked to pass something, to cut up vegetables or fruit, or to share materials, he learns about parts and wholes.

Structured Activities

The child can be given structured experiences in all three types of part/whole relationships. Activities can be done that help the child become aware of special parts of people, animals, and things. Other groups of activities involve dividing sets into smaller sets. The third type of activity gives the child experiences in dividing wholes into parts.

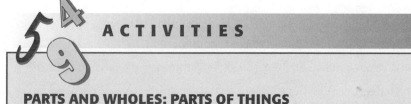

ACTIVITIES

PARTS AND WHOLES: PARTS OF THINGS

OBJECTIVE: To learn the meaning of the term *part* as it refers to parts of objects, people, and animals.

MATERIALS: Objects or pictures of objects with parts missing.

NATURALISTIC AND INFORMAL ACTIVITIES: Provide students time to play with a wide variety of toys and other objects. Label the parts, such as doll body parts, parts of vehicles, furniture, and so on, as fits naturally occurring situations. For example, "You put a shoe on each of the doll's feet," "There are four wheels on the truck," "You found all the pieces of the puzzle," and so on. Ask questions such as, "Which toys have wheels?" "Which toys have arms and legs?" Comment on sharing such as, "That is really nice that you gave your friend some of your blocks." Note the examples earlier in the unit.

STRUCTURED ACTIVITIES:

1. The Broken Toys
   Show the child some broken toys or pictures of broken toys. WHAT'S MISSING FROM THESE TOYS? After the child tells what is missing from each toy, bring out the missing parts (or pictures of missing parts). FIND THE MISSING PART THAT COMES WITH EACH TOY.
2. Who (or What) Is Hiding?
   The basic game is to hide someone or something behind a screen so that only a part is showing. The child then guesses who or what is hidden. The following are some variations.
   a. Two or more children hide behind a divider screen, a door, or a chair. Only a foot or a hand of one is shown. The other children guess whose body part can be seen.
   b. The children are shown several objects. The objects are then placed behind a screen. A part of one is shown. The child must guess which thing the part belongs to. (To make the task harder, the parts can be shown without the children knowing first what the choices will be.)
   c. Do the same type of activity using pictures.
      ◆ Cut out magazine pictures (or draw your own), and mount on cardboard. Cut a piece of construction paper to use to screen most of the picture. Say, LOOK AT THE PART THAT IS SHOWING. WHAT IS HIDDEN BEHIND THE PAPER?
      ◆ Mount magazine pictures on construction paper. Cut out a hole in another piece of construction paper of the same size. Staple the piece of paper onto the one with the picture on it so that a part of the picture can be seen. Say, LOOK THROUGH THE HOLE. GUESS WHAT IS IN THE PICTURE UNDER THE COVER.

FOLLOW-UP: Play *What's Missing Lotto* game (Childcraft) or *What's Missing? Parts & Wholes, Young Learners' Puzzles* (Teaching Resources) (Company addresses are in Unit 39.) Read and discuss books such as *Tail Toes Eyes Ears Nose* by Marilee Robin Burton and those listed in the web in Figure 14–1.

PARTS AND WHOLES: DIVIDING GROUPS

OBJECTIVE: To give the child practice in dividing sets into parts (smaller groups).

MATERIALS: Two or more small containers and some small objects such as pennies, dry beans, or buttons.

NATURALISTIC AND INFORMAL ACTIVITIES: Provide the children with opportunities to explore small objects and containers. Note how they use the materials. Do they put materials together that are the same or similar (see Unit 10)? Do they count items? Do they compare groups? Do they put some similar items in different containers? Note the examples earlier in the unit.

STRUCTURED ACTIVITIES: Set out the containers (start with two and increase the number as the child is able to handle more). Put the pennies or other objects in a bowl next to the containers. DIVIDE THESE UP SO EACH CONTAINER HAS SOME. Note whether the child goes about the task in an organized way and whether he tries to put the same number in each container. Encourage the children to talk about what they have done. DO THEY ALL HAVE THE SAME AMOUNT? DOES ONE HAVE MORE? HOW DO YOU KNOW? IF YOU PUT ALL THE PENNIES BACK IN THE SAME CONTAINER, WOULD YOU STILL HAVE THE SAME AMOUNT? LET'S DO IT AND CHECK THE AMOUNT. Note if the children realize that the total amount does not change when the objects in the group are separated. That is, can they conserve number?

FOLLOW-UP: Increase the number of smaller sets to be made. Use different types of containers and different objects.

PARTS AND WHOLES

OBJECTIVE: To divide whole things into two or more parts.

MATERIALS: Real things or pictures of things that can be divided into parts by cutting, tearing, breaking, or pouring.

NATURALISTIC AND INFORMAL ACTIVITIES: Children should have plenty of opportunities to explore puzzles, construction toys, fruits such as oranges, etc. Talk about the parts and wholes as in the examples earlier in the unit.

STRUCTURED ACTIVITIES:
1. Have the children cut up fruits and vegetables for snack or lunch. Be sure the children are shown how to cut so as not to hurt themselves. Be sure also that they have a sharp knife so the job is not frustrating. Children with poor coordination can tear lettuce, break off orange slices, and cut the easier things such as string beans.
2. Give the child a piece of paper. Have her cut it or tear it. Then have her fit the pieces back together. Have her count how many parts she made.
3. Give the child a piece of play dough or clay. Have her cut it with a dull knife or tear it into pieces. How many parts did she make?
4. Use a set of plastic measuring cups and a larger container of water. Have the children guess how many of each of the smaller cups full of water will fill the one-cup measure. Let each child try the one-fourth, one-third, and one-half cups, and count how many of each of these cups will fill the one cup.

FOLLOW-UP: Purchase or make some more structured part/whole materials* such as
1. Fraction Pies: circular shapes available in rubber and magnetic versions.
2. Materials that picture two halves of a whole.
   Halves to Wholes® (DLM)
   Match-ups® (Childcraft and Playskool)
3. Puzzles that have a sequence of difficulty with the same picture cut into two, three, and more parts:
   Basic Cut Puzzles® (DLM)
   Fruit and Animal Puzzles® (Teaching Resources)
4. Dowley Doos® take-apart transportation toys (Lauri)

*Addresses are in Unit 39.

EXAMPLE WORLD WIDE WEB ACTIVITIES

◆ Edible Fractions and Fraction Plates. Link at http://mathforum.org
◆ Orange Slices. Link at http://mathforum.org
◆ Red Fruits at http://www.preschoolstormie.com.scolors.html.
◆ Logo Puzzles from Elizabeth at http://www.perpetualpreschool.com/mathideas.html

---

Diana, age five, is delighted with Facemaker (Spinnaker, see Activity 5), a computer program that enables her to select from a variety of head parts and clothing to create a figure of her choice. When she has finished creating her cartoon figure, she signals the printer, and her creation is printed out for her to keep. This experience gives Diana practice with creating a whole from parts in an imaginative way.

Evaluation

The adult should observe and note if the child shows increased use of part/whole words and more skills in his daily activities:

◆ Can he divide groups of things into smaller groups?

◆ Can he divide wholes into parts?
◆ Does he realize that objects, people, and animals have parts that are unique to each?

Summary

Young children have a natural interest in parts and wholes. This interest and the ideas learned are the foundations of learning about fractions.

The child learns that things, people, and animals have parts. She learns that sets can be divided into parts (sets with smaller numbers of things). She learns that whole things can be divided into smaller parts or pieces.

Experiences in working with parts and wholes help the young child move from preoperational centering to the concrete view and to understanding that the whole is no more than the sum of all its parts.

KEY TERMS

parts	fractions	half
wholes	divide	

SUGGESTED ACTIVITIES

1. Observe in a Montessori classroom. Write a description of all the materials that are designed to teach the concept of part/whole.
2. Assess the part/whole concept of one or more young children. Based on the results, plan some part/whole activities. Do the activities with the children. Evaluate the results.
3. Add part/whole activities to your file/notebook.
4. If the school budget allocated $100 for part/whole materials, decide what would be top priority purchases.

5. Using guidelines from Activity 7, Unit 9, evaluate one or more of the following computer programs that are designed to reinforce the concept of parts and wholes.

◆ Dr. Seuss Fix Up the Mixedup Puzzle. Greenwich, CT: CBS Software.
◆ Facemaker. Cambridge, MA: Spinnaker Software.
◆ Infinity City. Link at http://www.headbone.com: Headbone Interactive.

◆ Mr. and Mrs. Potato Head. New York: Random House.

◆ Stickers. Minneapolis, MN: Springboard Software, Inc.

◆ Tonk in the Land of Buddy-Bots. Northbrook, IL: Mindscape, Inc.

REVIEW

A. Decide which of the following categories the items below fit into: (a) things, people, and animals have parts; (b) sets can be divided into parts; and (c) whole things can be divided into smaller parts or pieces.
1. Chris shares his doughnut.
2. Pieces of a cat puzzle.
3. Tina gives Fong some of her crayons.
4. Larry tears a piece of paper.
5. Pete takes half of the clay.
6. Kate puts the yellow blocks in one pile and the orange blocks in another.
7. A teddy bear's leg.
8. Juanita takes the fork from the place setting of utensils.

B. Describe the types of experiences and activities that support the child's development of the concept of parts and wholes.

C. Explain how the child's knowledge of parts and wholes can be assessed through observation and interview.

D. Decide which of the NCTM expectations for parts and wholes match the examples in question A.

REFERENCE

National Council of Teachers of Mathematics. (2000). *Principles and standards for school mathematics*. Reston, VA: Author. (http://www.nctm.org)

FURTHER READING AND RESOURCES

AIMS Educational Products. AIMS Education Foundation, P.O. Box 8120, Fresno, CA 93747-8120.

Beaty, J. J., & Tucker, W. H. (1987). *The computer as a paintbrush*. Columbus, Ohio: Merrill.

Burk, D., Snider, A., & Symonds, P. (1988). *Box it or bag it mathematics: Kindergarten teachers' resource guide*. Portland, OR: The Math Learning Center.

Copley, J. V. (2000). *The young child and mathematics*. Washington, DC: National Association for the Education of Young Children.

Copley, J. V. (Ed.). (1999). *Mathematics in the early years*. Washington, DC: National Association for the Education of Young Children.

Richardson, K. (1999). *Developing number concepts: Planning guide*. Parsippany, NJ: Dale Seymour.

Riddle, M., & Rodzwell, B. (2000). Fractions: What happens between kindergarten and the army? *Teaching Children Mathematics, 7*(4), 202–206.

Shade, D. D. (1994). Computers and young children: New frontiers in computer hardware and software *or* what computer should I buy? *Day Care and Early Education, 21*(3).

Watanabe, T. (1996). Ben's understanding of one-half. *Teaching Children Mathematics, 8*, 460–464.

UNIT 15
Language and Concept Formation

OBJECTIVES

After reading this unit, you should be able to:

◆ Explain the importance of language to the NCTM process expectations.

◆ Explain two ways to describe a child's understanding of concept words.

◆ Describe the whole language philosophy as it applies to mathematics and science.

◆ Use literature, writing, drawing, and speaking to support the development of mathematics and science language.

The NCTM (2000) standards include expectations in five process areas: **problem solving**, **reasoning**, **communications**, **connections**, and **representation**. *Problem solving* was discussed in Unit 3 as the major process focus in mathematics. For the youngest mathematicians problem solving is the major means for building mathematical knowledge. Problems usually arise from daily routines, play activities and materials, and from stories. As children work with the materials and activities already described, they figure things out using the processes of reasoning, communications, connections, and representation. Logical *reasoning* develops in the early years and is especially important in working with classification and with patterns. Reasoning enables students to draw logical conclusions, apply logical classification skills, explain their thinking, justify their problem solutions and processes, apply patterns and relationships to arrive at solutions, and make sense out of mathematics and science. *Communication* with oral,

written, and pictorial language provides the means for explaining problem-solving and reasoning processes. Children need to provide a description of what they do and why they do it and what they have accomplished. They need to use the language of mathematics in their explanations. The important *connections* for the young mathematicians are the ones between the naturalistic and informal mathematics they learn first and the formal mathematics they learn in school. Concrete objects can serve as the bridge between informal and formal mathematics. Young children can "*represent* their thoughts about, and understanding of, mathematical ideas through oral and written language, physical gestures, drawings, and invented and conventional symbols" (NCTM, 2000, p. 136).

What the child does and what the child says tells the teacher what the child knows about math and science. The older the child gets, the more important concepts become. The language the child uses and how she uses it provide clues to the teacher as to the conceptual development of the child. However, children may imitate adult use of words before the concept is highly developed. The child's language system is usually well developed by age four; that is, by this age, children's sentences are much the same as an adult's. Children are at a point where their vocabulary is growing very rapidly.

The adult observes what the child does from infancy through age two and looks for the first understanding and the use of words. Between two and four the child starts to put more words together into longer sentences. She also learns more words and what they mean.

In assessing the young child's concept development, questions are used. Which is the big ball? Which is the circle? The child's understanding of words is checked by having her respond with an appropriate action.

◆ "Point to the big ball."
◆ "Find two chips."
◆ "Show me the picture in which the boy is on the chair."

These tasks do not require the child to say any words. She need only point, touch, or pick up something. Once the child demonstrates her understanding of math words by using gestures or other nonverbal answers, she can move on to questions she must answer with one or more words. The child can be asked the same questions as before in a way that requires a verbal response.

◆ (The child is shown two balls, one big and one small.) "What is different about these balls?"
◆ (The child is shown a group of objects.) "How many are there in this group?"
◆ (The child is shown a picture of a boy sitting on a chair.) "Where is the boy?"

The child learns many concept words as she goes about her daily activities. It has been found that by the time a child starts kindergarten, she uses many concept words she has learned in a naturalistic way. Examples have been included in each of the previous units (8 through 14). The child uses both comments and questions. Comments would be as follows.

◆ "Mom, I want two pieces of cheese."
◆ "I have a *bunch* of birdseed."
◆ "Mr. Brown, this chair is *small*."
◆ "*Yesterday* we went to the zoo."
◆ "The string is *long*."
◆ "This is the *same* as this."
◆ "The foot fits *in* the shoe."
◆ "This cracker is a *square* shape."
◆ "Look, some of the worms are *long* and some are *short*, some are *fat* and some are *thin*."
◆ "The *first* bean seed I planted is *taller* than the *second* one."
◆ "Outer space is *far* away."

Questions would be like these.

◆ "How *old* is he?"
◆ "*When* is Christmas?"
◆ "*When* will I grow as *big* as you?"
◆ "*How many* are coming for dinner?"
◆ "Who has *more*?"
◆ "What *time* is my TV program?"
◆ "Is this a school *day*, or is it *Saturday*?"
◆ "What makes the bubbles when the water gets *hot*?"
◆ "Why does this roller always go *down* its ramp *faster* than that roller goes *down* its ramp?"
◆ "Why are the leaves turning *brown* and *red* and *gold* and falling *down on* the ground?"

The answers that the child gets to these questions can help increase the number of concept words she knows and can use.

The teacher needs to be aware of using concept words during center time, lunch, and other times when a structured concept lesson is not being done. She should also note which words the child uses during free times.

The teacher should encourage the child to use concept words even though she may not use them in an accurate, adult way, for example:

◆ "I can count—one, two, three, five, 10."
◆ "Aunt Helen is coming after my last nap." (Indicates future time)

◆ "I will measure my paper." (Holds ruler against the edge of the paper)

◆ "Last night Grandpa was here." (Actually several days ago)

◆ "I'm six years old." (Really two years old)

◆ "I have a million dollars." (Has a handful of play money)

Adults should accept the child's use of the words and use the words correctly themselves. Soon the child will develop a higher-level use of words as she is able to grasp higher-level ideas. For the two- or three-year-old, any group of things more than two or three may be called a *bunch*. Instead of using *big* and *little*, the child may use family words: "This is the mommy block" and "This is the baby block." Time (see Unit 19) is one concept that takes a long time to grasp. A young child may use the same word to mean different time periods. The following examples were said by a three-year-old.

◆ "*Last night* we went to the beach." (Meaning last summer)

◆ "*Last night* I played with Chris." (Meaning yesterday)

◆ "*Last night* I went to Kenny's house." (Meaning three weeks ago)

For this child, *last night* means any time in the past. One by one he will learn that there are words that refer to times past such as last summer, yesterday, and three weeks ago.

Computer activities can also add to vocabulary. The teacher uses concept words when explaining how to use the programs. Children enjoy working at the computer with friends and will use the concept words in communication with each other as they work cooperatively to solve the problems presented by the computer.

Many concept words have already been introduced, and more will appear in the units to come. The prekindergarten child continually learns words. The following presents those concept words that most children can use and understand by the time they complete kindergarten. However, caution must be taken in assessing children's actual understanding of the concept words they use. The use of a concept word does not by itself indicate an understanding of the concept. Children imitate behavior they hear and see. Real

understanding can be determined through an assessment interview.

Concept Words

The words that follow have appeared in Units 8 through 14.

◆ **One-to-one correspondence:** one, pair, more, each, some, group, bunch, set, amount

◆ **Number and counting:** zero, one, two, three, four, five, six, seven, eight, nine, 10, how many, count, group, one more than, next, number, computer

◆ **Logic and classifying:** groups; descriptive words for color, shape, size, materials, pattern, texture, function, association, class names, and common features; belong with; goes with; is used with; put with; the same

◆ **Comparing:** more, less, big, small, large, little, long, short, fat, skinny, heavy, light, fast, slow, cold, hot, thick, thin, wide, narrow, near, far, later, sooner, earlier, older, younger, newer, higher, lower, loud, soft (sound)

◆ **Geometry (shape):** circle, square, triangle, rectangle, ellipse, rhombus, shape, round, point, square prism (cube), rectangular prism, triangular prism, cylinder, pyramid

◆ **Geometry (spatial sense):** *where* (on, off, on top of, over, under, in, out, into, out of, top, bottom, above, below, in front of, in back of, behind, beside, by, next to, between); *which way* (up, down, forward, backward, around, through, to, from, toward, away from, sideways, across); *distance* (near, far, close to, far from); map, floor plan

◆ **Parts and wholes:** part, whole, divide, share, pieces, some, half, one-quarter, one-third

Words that will be introduced later include:

◆ **Ordering:** first, second, third; big, bigger, biggest; few, fewer, fewest; large, larger, largest; little, littler, littlest; many, more, most; thick, thicker, thickest; thin, thinner, thinnest; last, next, then

- **Measurement of volume, length, weight, and temperature:** little, big, medium, tiny, large, size, tall, short, long, far, farther, closer, near, high, higher, thin, wide, deep, cup, pint, quart, gallon, ounces, milliliter, kiloliter, liter, foot, inch, kilometer, mile, meter, centimeter, narrow, measure, hot, cold, warm, cool, thermometer, temperature, pounds, grams, kilograms, milligrams

- **Measurement of time and sequence:** morning, afternoon, evening, night, day, soon, week, tomorrow, yesterday, early, late, a long time ago, once upon a time, minute, second, hour, new, old, already, Easter, Kwanza, Christmas, Passover, Hanukkah, June 10th, Pioneer Days, Cinco de Mayo, birthday, now, year, weekend, clock, calendar, watch, when, time, date, sometimes, then, before, present, soon, while, never, once, sometime, next, always, fast, slow, speed, Monday and other days of the week, January and other months of the year, winter, spring, summer, fall

- **Practical:** money, cash register, penny, dollar, buy, pay, change, cost, check, free, store, map, recipe, measure, cup, tablespoon, teaspoon, boil, simmer, bake, degrees, time, hours, minutes, freeze, chill, refrigerate, pour, mix, separate, add, combine, ingredients

Words can be used before they are presented in a formal structured activity. The child who speaks can become familiar with words and even say them before he understands the concepts they stand for.

- **Primary-level words:** addition, subtraction, number facts, plus, add, minus, take away, total, sum, equal, difference, amount, altogether, in all, are left, number line, place value, rename, patterns, ones, 10s, 100s, digit, multiplication, division, equation, times, divide, product, even, odd, fractions, halves, fourths, thirds, wholes, numerator, denominator, measure, inches, feet, yards, miles, centimeter, meter, kilometer

The Whole Language Philosophy and Mathematics and Science

The emphasis on communication, reasoning, and making connections in mathematics and science relates naturally to the **whole language philosophy** in reading and language arts. Just as mathematics and science are turning toward a conceptual emphasis (vs. memorization, drill, and learning basic facts and formulas), reading and language arts have turned to an approach referred to as *whole language*, which integrates written and spoken language into meaningful contexts. Reading and writing are learned through active involvement in the context of meaningful experiences with literature, drama, music, science, mathematics, and social studies. Immersion in language and print; opportunities and resources such as materials, time, space, and activities; meaningful communication; a teacher who is a communication role model; acceptance of children as readers and writers; and the expectation that children will become literate are the critical elements in the whole language approach (Raines & Canady, 1990). In the whole language classroom, children listen to good literature, experiment with writing, and learn to read naturally. They explain and discuss, record data, and write about their explorations in science and mathematics. Refer to Unit 3 for applications to problem solving. Through these activities, children develop their spoken and written language vocabulary in a meaningful context.

Literature and Mathematics and Science

There has been a tremendous growth in the use of children's literature as a springboard to curriculum integration in mathematics and science instruction. While there have long been many books that include mathematics and science concepts (see Appendix B), there has recently been an increasing number of literature-centered activities described in the major journals, books that present thematic activities centered on pieces of literature, and a number of books containing annotated lists of mathematics-related children's books. Examples of such literature have been included in previous units and more will be included in future units. The Further Reading and Resource section of this unit includes references to articles describing mathematics and science studies, which focus on children's literature.

An example of a book used as a focus for mathematics, science, and writing is described by Charlesworth and Lind (1995). In Claudia Wangsgaard's first-grade classroom in Kaysville, Utah, the students kept math journals, writing about their solutions to math problems. For example, one day's math activities centered on the book *One Gorilla* by Atsuko Morozumi. The narrative starts with one gorilla, who wanders through each page; the book includes scenes in the jungle as well as in other locations. Jungle and nonjungle inhabitants are introduced in groups in numerical order up to 10: two butterflies and one gorilla among the flowers, three budgies and one gorilla in the house, four squirrels and one gorilla in the woods, and so on. The students discussed each illustration, locating the gorilla and counting the other creatures.

The class then divided up into groups of four to work cooperatively on the following problem: *How many creatures were there altogether in this story?* The students used a variety of materials: large sheets of blank paper, tubs of Unifix Cubes,® pencils, and crayons. Mrs. Wangsgaard circulated from group to group, providing help as needed. When everyone was finished, the class members reassembled. A reporter from each small group explained the group results, summarizing what was recorded on the group's poster. Several communication procedures were used such as drawing the number of Unifix Cubes® or making marks to tally the number of creatures. Each group also wrote its procedure. For example:

> We did unafick cubes and then we did tally Marcks and there were 56. *Jason, Caitlin, Malorie, and Kady* (p. 171)

This activity provided for cooperative learning and communication of thinking through concrete representations, drawings, and written and oral language. Figure 15–1 illustrates how this activity might be included in a planning web for an extended study of jungle inhabitants using the book *One Gorilla* as the focus.

Books for Emergent Readers

Zaner-Bloser publishes sets of easy readers that provide beginning readers with the opportunity to apply their math and science process skills. Each book is related to the NCTM standards. *Harry's Math Books*, authored by Sharon Young, present problems related to real life experiences in simple repetitive text for the early reader. For example, *The Shape Maker* (Young, 1997) relates making cutout shapes to a kite-making project. *At The Park* (Young, 1998) moves from identifying circles in the environment to a circle of friends holding hands. *Six Pieces of Cake* (Young, 1998) relates a whole cake to its parts as pieces are distributed one by one. Other books in the series include concepts such as numeracy and counting skills, skip-counting forward and backward, using fractions, using ordinal numbers, comparing and ordering, sorting and classifying, and performing early operations. The teacher guide suggests extension activities based on each book.

The emergent science series also provides meaningful stories, directions for hands-on science investigations, and correlations with national standards. Topics include animals, cycles of life, earth, self-care, water, light and sound, insects, weather, space, and forces and motion, all with accompanying teacher guides.

As resources increase on the Web, ideas for literature-related mathematics are increasing. Following are some examples.

EXAMPLE WORLD WIDE WEB ACTIVITIES

- Inch measuring using the book *Inch by Inch* by Leo Lionni (1960), Scholastic, at http://www.mathforum.org/measurement.html
- Nonstandard measuring using the book *Miss Nelson Is Missing!* by Harry Allard (1977), Houghton. Link to http://www.mathforum.org/measurement.html
- Eric Carle has written many classic mathematics-related books such as *The Very Hungry Caterpillar* and has his own Web site at www.eric-carle.com

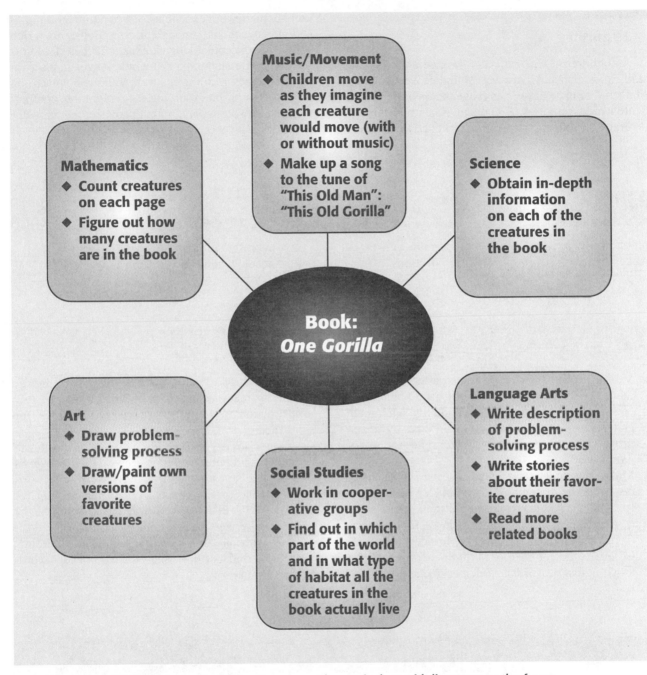

Music/Movement
- ◆ Children move as they imagine each creature would move (with or without music)
- ◆ Make up a song to the tune of "This Old Man": "This Old Gorilla"

Mathematics
- ◆ Count creatures on each page
- ◆ Figure out how many creatures are in the book

Science
- ◆ Obtain in-depth information on each of the creatures in the book

**Book:
One Gorilla**

Art
- ◆ Draw problem-solving process
- ◆ Draw/paint own versions of favorite creatures

Social Studies
- ◆ Work in cooperative groups
- ◆ Find out in which part of the world and in what type of habitat all the creatures in the book actually live

Language Arts
- ◆ Write description of problem-solving process
- ◆ Write stories about their favorite creatures
- ◆ Read more related books

FIGURE 15–1 An integration across the curriculum with literature as the focus.

Summary

As children learn math and science concepts and skills, they also add many words to their vocabularies. Math and science have a language that is basic to their content and activities. Language is learned through naturalistic, informal, and structured activities. Computer activities are excellent for promoting communication between and among children. Books are a rich source of conceptual language that matches children's growing understanding. The whole language philosophy of literacy learning fits well with the emphasis on processes of problem solving, representation, communication, reasoning, and making connections in mathematics and science.

KEY TERMS

problem solving
reasoning

communications
connections

representation
whole language philosophy

SUGGESTED ACTIVITIES

1. Visit a prekindergarten, a kindergarten, and a primary classroom. Observe for at least 30 minutes in each room. Write down every child and adult math and science word used. Compare the three age groups and teachers for number and variety of words used.
2. Make the concept language assessment materials described in Appendix A. Administer the tasks to four-, five-, and six-year-old children. Make a list of the concept words recorded in each classroom. Count the number of times each word was used. Compare the number of different words and the total number of words heard in each classroom.
3. In the library, research the area of whole language and its relationship to mathematics and science instruction. Write a report summarizing what you learned.
4. Observe some young children doing concept development computer activities. Record their conversations, and note how many concept words they use.
5. Select one of the concept books included in the resource list in this unit or from the list in Appendix B. Familiarize yourself with the content. Read the book with one or more young children. Question them to find out how many of the concept words they can use.

REVIEW

A. Explain how language learning relates to science and mathematics concept learning.
B. Describe how a whole language approach to instruction might increase the concept vocabulary of young children.
C. Describe how the five mathematics process expectations relate to young children's learning.

REFERENCES

Charlesworth, R., & Lind, K. K. (1995). Whole language and primary grades mathematics and science: Keeping up with national standards. In S. Raines (Ed.), *Whole language across the curriculum: Grades 1, 2, 3* (pp. 146–178). New York: Teachers College.

National Council of Teachers of Mathematics. (2000). *Principles and standards for school mathematics.* Reston, VA: Author. (http://www.nctm.org)

Raines, S. C., & Canady, R. J. (1990). *The whole language kindergarten.* New York: Teachers College Press.

Young, S. (1998). *At the park.* Columbus, OH: Zaner Bloser.

Young, S. (1998). *Six pieces of cake.* Columbus, OH: Zaner Bloser.

Young, S. (1997). *The shape maker.* Columbus, OH: Zaner Bloser.

FURTHER READING AND RESOURCES

Aram, R. J., Whitson, S., & Dieckhoff, R. (2001). Habitat sweet habitat. *Science and Children, 38*(4), 23–27.

Bertheau, M. (1994). The most important thing is. . . . *Teaching Children Mathematics, 1,* 112–115.

Burns, M. (1992). *Mathematics and literature (K–3).* White Plains, NY: Cuisinaire Co. of America.

Burns, M., & Silbey, R. (2001, April). Math journals boost real learning. *Instructor,* 18–20.

Butterworth, S., & Cicero, A. M. L. (2001). Storytelling: Building a mathematics curriculum from the culture of the child. *Teaching Children Mathematics, 7*(7), 396–399.

Chapman, S. A. (2000). The M.O.O.K. Book: Students author a book about mathematics. *Teaching Children Mathematics, 6*(6), 388–390.

Communications. (1995). *Teaching Children Mathematics, 1*(6) [Focus issue].

Copley, J. V. (2000). *The young child and mathematics.* Washington, DC: National Association for the Education of Young Children.

Copley, J. V. (Ed.). (1999). *Mathematics in the early years.* Washington, DC: National Association for the Education of Young Children.

Ducolon, C. K. (2000). Quality literature as a springboard to problem solving. *Teaching Children Mathematics, 6*(7), 442–446.

Ellis, B. F. (2001).The cottonwood. *Science and Children, 38*(4), 42–46.

Fleege, P. O., & Thompson, D. R. (2000). From habits to legs: Using science-themed counting books to foster connections. *Teaching Children Mathematics, 7*(2), 74–78.

Flores, A. (1995). Bilingual lessons in early grades geometry. *Teaching Children Mathematics, 1,* 420–424.

Fox, B., Guenther, J., & Lubarski, D. (1994). Student-authored minimath. *Teaching Children Mathematics, 1,* 208–212.

Gee, T. C., & Olson, M. W. (1992). Let's talk trade books. *Science and Children, 29*(6), 13–14.

Ginsburg, H. P., & Seo, K. (2000). Preschoolers' mathematical reading. *Teaching Children Mathematics, 7*(4). 226–229.

Harms, J. M., & Lettow, L. J. (2000). Poetry and environment. *Science and Children, 37*(6), 30–33.

Harris, J. (1999). Interweaving language and mathematics literacy through a story. *Teaching Children Mathematics, 5*(9), 520–524.

Hellwig, S. J., Monroe, E. E., & Jacobs, J. S. (2000). Making informed choices: Selecting children's trade books for mathematics instruction. *Teaching Children Mathematics, 7*(3), 138–143.

Hopkins, L. (1995). Popping up number sense. *Teaching Children Mathematics, 2,* 82–86.

Hopkins, M. H. (1993). IDEAS (math and literature). *Arithmetic Teacher, 40*(9), 512–519.

Jaberg, P. (1995). Assessment and *Geraldine's Blanket. Teaching Children Mathematics, 1,* 514–517.

Karp, K. S. (1994). Telling tales: Creating graphs using multicultural literature. *Teaching Children Mathematics, 1,* 87–91.

Lowe, J. L., & Matthew, K. I. (2000). Puppets and prose. *Science and Children, 37*(8), 41–45.

Lubinski, C. A., & Thiessen, D. (1996). Exploring measurement through literature. *Teaching Children Mathematics, 2,* 260–263.

Maguire, B. E. (1992). Introducing Mr. I. M. Treeless. *Science and Children, 29*(7), 21–22.

Martinez, J. G. R., & Martinez, N. C. (2000, January). Teaching math with stories. *Teaching Pre-K-8,* 54–56.

Matthews, M., Gee, D., & Bell, E. (1995).Science learning with a multicultural emphasis. *Science and Children, 32*(6), 20–23, 54.

Mayer, D. A. (1995). How can we best use children's literature in teaching science concepts? *Science and Children, 32*(6), 16–19, 43.

McMath, J., & King, M. A. (1994). Using picture books to teach mathematical concepts. *Day Care and Early Education, 21*(3), 18–22.

National Council of Teachers of Mathematics. (1989). *Curriculum and evaluation standards for school mathematics.* Reston, VA: Author.

Norwood, K. S., & Carter, G. (1994). Journal writing: An insight into students' understanding. *Teaching Children Mathematics, 1,* 146–148.

O'Connell, S. R. (1995). Newspapers: Connecting the mathematics classroom to the world. *Teaching Children Mathematics, 1,* 268–274.

Outstanding science trade books for children— 2001. (2001). *Science and Children, 38*(6), 27–34.

Outstanding science trade books for children for 2000. (2000). *Science and Children, 37*(6), 19–25.

Outstanding science trade books for children for 1995. (1995). *Science and Children, 32*(6), 24–29.

Outstanding science trade books for children in 1991. (1992). *Science and Children, 29*(6), 20–27.

Owens, L. L., Love, F. E., & Shaw, J. M. (1999). How big is big? How small is small? *Science and Children, 36*(7), 36–39.

Piccirilli, R. (1996). *Write about math!* Jefferson City, MO: Scholastic.

Rice, D. C., Dudley, A. P., & Williams, C. S. (2001). How do you choose science trade books? *Science and Children, 38*(6), 18–22.

Richardson, K. (1999). *Developing number concepts: Planning guide.* Parsippany, NJ: Dale Seymour.

Scarnati, J. T., & Weller, C. J. (1992). The write stuff. *Science and Children, 29*(4), 28–29.

Schneider, S. (1995). Scrumptious activities in the stew. *Teaching Children Mathematics, 1,* 548–552.

Schon, I. (1992). Ciencia en Español. *Science and Children, 29*(6), 18–19, 46.

Schon, I. (2001). Libros de ciencias en Español. *Science and Children, 38*(6), 23–26.

Schon, I. (2000). Libros de ciencias en Español. *Science and Children, 37*(6), 26–29.

Schon, I. (1995). Libros de ciencias en Español. *Science and Children, 32*(6), 30–32.

Schon, I. (1994). Libros de ciencias en Español. *Science and Children, 31*(6), 38–40.

Schon, I. (1994). Recent noteworthy books in Spanish for young children. *Young Children, 49*(6), 81–82.

Smith, J. (1995). Threading mathematics into social studies. *Teaching Children Mathematics, 1,* 438–444.

Taylor, G. M. (1999). Reading, writing, arithmetic— Making connections. *Teaching Children Mathematics, 6*(3), 190–197.

Thiessen, D., Matthias, M., & Smith, J. (1998). *The wonderful world of mathematics: A critically annotated list of children's books in mathematics* (2nd ed.). Reston, VA: National Council of Teachers of Mathematics.

Tiedt, I. M. (1999). Library of conservation. *Science and Children, 37*(3), 18–21.

Weinberg, S. (1996). Going beyond ten black dots. *Teaching Children Mathematics, 2,* 432–435.

Welchman-Tischler, R. (1992). *How to use children's literature to teach mathematics.* Reston, VA: National Council of Teachers of Mathematics.

Whitin, D. J. (1994). Literature and mathematics in preschool and primary: The right connection. *Young Children, 49*(2), 4–11.

Whitin, D. J., & Wilde, S. (1992). *Read any good math lately? Children's books for mathematical learning, K–6.* Portsmouth, NH: Heinemann.

Journals such as *Teaching Children Mathematics*, *Childhood Education*, *Dimensions*, *Science and Children* and *Young Children* have book review columns in each issue. Many of the books reviewed apply math and science concepts.

UNIT 16
Fundamental Concepts in Science

OBJECTIVES

After reading this unit, you should be able to:

◆ Design lessons that integrate fundamental science and math concepts.

◆ Develop naturalistic, informal, and structured activities that utilize science and math concepts.

The *National Science Education Standards* emphasize that, for children, the essence of learning lies not in memorizing fact, but carrying out the processes of inquiry—asking questions; making observations; and gathering, organizing, and analyzing data. The concepts and skills that children construct during the preprimary period are essential to investigating science problems.

The fundamental concepts and skills of one-to-one correspondence, number sense and counting, sets and classifying, comparing, shape, space, and parts and wholes are basic to developing the abilities needed for scientific inquiry. This unit shows how the concepts presented in Units 8 through 14 of this book can be explored and used in science with children in the sensorimotor and preoperational period of development. Recommendations can be found in Unit 4, and individual assessments are in Appendix A.

One-to-One Correspondence

When doing one-to-one correspondence, children are pairing and learning basic concepts about how things are alike or different. At an early age, the pairings are made on the basis of single attributes inherent in objects (e.g., shape, color, and so on), and objects are arranged in various piles or in a chained linear sequence. This skill must be developed for grouping, sorting, and classifying to take place.

Science topics such as animals and their homes lend themselves well to matching activities. Not only are children emphasizing one-to-one correspondence by matching one animal to a particular home, they are also increasing their awareness of animals and their habitats. The questions that teachers ask will further reinforce the process skills and science content contained in the activities. The following science-related activities work well with young children.

1. Create a bulletin board background of trees (one tree should have a cavity), a cave, a plant containing a spiderweb, and a hole in the ground. Hang a beehive from a branch, and place a nest on another branch. Ask the children to tell you where each of the following animals might live: owl, bird, bee, mouse, spider, and bear. Place the animal by the appropriate home. Then, make backgrounds and animals for each child, and let the children paste the animal where it might live (Figure 16–1). Ask, "do you think a plant is a good place for a spider to spin a web?" "why do you think so?" (Outdoor insects can land in the web.) Have the children describe the advantages of living in the different homes.

2. Another popular animal matching activity involves the preparation of six animals and six homes. These animals and homes may be used as a cut-and-paste activity or put in a posters and folder games format that can be used repeatedly

FIGURE 16–2 Cut out the pictures of animals and homes. Mount them on cardboard for the children to match.

in centers. In the matching activity, the children must cut out a home and paste it in the box next to the animal that lives there. For example, a bee lives in a beehive, a horse in a barn, an ant in an anthill, a bird in a nest, a fish in an aquarium, and a child in a human home (Figure 16–2). Ask, "why would an ant live in the ground?" Emphasize that animals try to live in places that offer them the best protection or source of food. Discuss how each is suited to its home.

3. Counters are effective in reinforcing the fundamental concept of one-to-one correspondence. For example, when the children study about bears, make and use bear counters that can be put into little bear caves. As the children match the bear to its cave, they understand that there are the same number of bears as there are caves. Lead the children in speculating why bears might take shelter in caves (convenient, will not be disturbed, hard to find, good place for baby bears to be born, and so on).

4. Children enjoy working with felt shapes. Cut out different-sized felt ducks, bears, ponds, and caves for children to match on a flannelboard. If children have the materials available, they will be likely to play animal matching games on their own, such as, "Match the baby and adult

FIGURE 16–1 "Find a home for the bear."

animals," or "Line up all of the ducks, and find a pond for each one." Have children compare the baby ducks with the adult ducks by asking, "in what ways do the babies look like their parents?" "how are they alike?" "can you find any differences?" Emphasize camouflage as the primary reason that baby animals usually blend in with their surroundings. The number of animals and homes can be increased as the children progress in ability.

5. After telling the story *Goldilocks and the Three Bears*, draw three bears of different sizes without noses. Cut out noses that will match the blank spaces, and have the children match the nose to the bear (Figure 16–3). You might want to do this first as a group, and then have the materials available for the children to work with individually. Point out that larger bears have bigger noses.

One-to-one correspondence and the other skills presented in this unit cannot be developed in isolation of content. Emphasize the science concepts and process skills as you utilize animals as a means of developing fundamental skills. Further animal matching and sorting activities can be created by putting pic-

tures into categories of living and nonliving things, invertebrates, and reptiles, amphibians, birds, and fish.

When comparing major groups of animals—reptiles, for example—try to include as many representatives of the group as possible. Children can study pictures of turtles (land turtles are called tortoises, and some freshwater turtles are called terrapins), snakes, lizards, alligators, and crocodiles and match them to their respective homes. The characteristics of each reptile can be compared and contrasted. The possibilities for matching, counting, comparing, and classifying animals are limitless and are a natural math and science integration.

Number Sense and Counting

Emphasizing science content while learning number concepts enables children to relate these subjects to their everyday lives and familiar, concrete examples. The following example shows a kindergarten class using concrete experiences to reinforce counting and the concept that apples grow on trees.

When Mrs. Jones teaches an apple unit in the fall, she sorts apples of different sizes and colors. Then she has the children count the apples before they cook them to make applesauce and apple pies. Children can also taste different types of apples, graph their choices, and count to see which apple the class likes best.

For additional number concept extensions, she uses a felt board game that requires the children to pick apples from trees. For this activity, she creates two rows of apple trees with four felt trees in each row. The trees are filled with one to nine apples and the numerals are at the bottom of each row. As the children play with the game, Mrs. Jones asks, "How many apples can you pick from each tree?" As Sam picks apples off a tree, he counts aloud, "one, two, three, four, five—I picked five apples from the apple tree." He smiles and points to the numeral five (Figure 16–4).

When doing science activities, do not miss opportunities to count. The following activities emphasize counting.

1. If bugs have been captured for study, have your children count the number of bugs in the bug

FIGURE 16–3 "Which nose belongs to Baby Bear?"

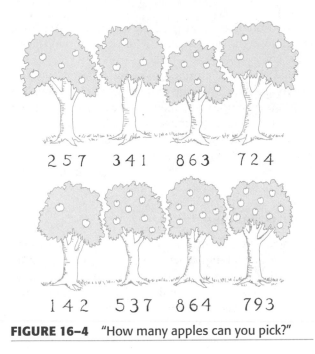

2 5 7　　3 4 1　　8 6 3　　7 2 4

1 4 2　　5 3 7　　8 6 4　　7 9 3

FIGURE 16–4 "How many apples can you pick?"

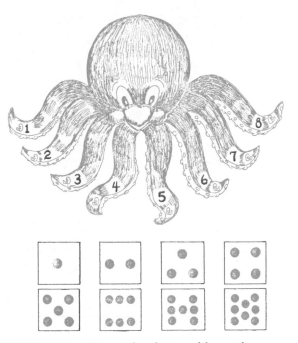

FIGURE 16–5 "Count the dots and hang the square on the correct tentacle."

keeper. Keep in mind that insects can be observed for a couple of days but should be released to the area in which they were originally found.

2. Take advantage of the eight tentacles of an octopus to make an octopus counting board. Enlarge an octopus on a piece of poster board, and attach a curtain hook to each tentacle above a number. Make circles with dots (one to eight) to hang on hooks. Ask children to count the number of tentacles that the octopus has. Explain that all octopuses have eight tentacles. Discuss how an octopus uses its armlike tentacles. Then, have children count the dots on the squares and put the squares on the hook over the correct number (Figure 16–5).

3. A fish tank bulletin board display emphasizes counting and prepares children for future activities in addition. Prepare construction-paper fish, a treasure chest, rocks, and plants and attach them to a 12″ × 20″ rectangle made from light blue oak tag. Glue some of the fish, the treasure chest, rocks, and plants to the blue background. Then, using thumbtacks, attach a 13″ × 21″ clear plastic rectangle to the top of the light blue oak tag to create a fish tank bulletin board. Before the students arrive the next day, put more fish in

the tank. Then ask, "How many fish are swimming in the tank?" Each day, add more fish, and ask the class, "How many fish are swimming in the tank today?" "How many were swimming in the tank yesterday?" "Are there more fish swimming in the tank today, or were there more yesterday?" Use as many fish as are appropriate for your students (Figure 16–6).

4. Read Ruth Brown's *Ten Seeds* (2001). Count the seeds and animals on each page as you read with the children. Then ask, "What happened to the seeds that the child planted?" Next, reread the story while having the children watch for a change in either the seed or plant.

Children love to count. They count informally and with direction from the teacher. Counting cannot be removed from a context—you have to count something. As children count, emphasize the science in which they are counting. If children are counting the number of baby ducks following an adult duck, lead the children in speculating where the ducks might be going and what they might be doing.

FIGURE 16–6 "Create a fish tank bulletin board for counting fish."

Sequencing and Ordinal Position

Science offers many opportunities for reinforcing sequencing and ordinal position. Observing the life cycle of a butterfly is a good way to learn about the life of an insect. Like all insects, butterflies go through four distinct life stages: (1) egg, (2) larva (the caterpillar that constantly eats), (3) pupa (the caterpillar slowly changes inside of a chrysalis), and (4) adult (the butterfly emerges from the chrysalis). Pictures of each of these stages can be mounted on index cards, matched with numerals, and put in sequence. Children will enjoy predicting which stage they think will happen next and comparing this to what actually happens.

Animal Movement

Children can be encouraged to learn how different animals move as they learn one-to-one correspondence and practice the counting sequence.

Arrange the children in a line. Have them stamp their feet as they count, raising their arms in the air to emphasize the last number in the sequence. A bird might move this way, raising its wings in the air in a threatening manner or in a courtship dance (Figure 16–7). Have children change directions without losing the beat by counting "one" as they turn. For example,

"One, two, three, four (up go the arms, turn); one, two, three, four (up go the arms, turn); one, two, three, four," and so on.

Now, have the children move to different parts of the room. Arm movements can be left out, and the children can tiptoe, lumber, or sway, imitating the ways various animals move. A bear has a side-to-side motion, a monkey might swing its arms, and an elephant its trunk. This activity is also a good preparation strategy for the circle game suggested in the next paragraph.

A Circle Game

Practice in counting, sequencing, one-to-one correspondence, looking for patterns, and the process skills of predicting are involved in the following circle game, which focuses attention on the prediction skills necessary in many science activities. Rather than be the source of the "right" answer, Mrs. Jones allows the results of the game to reveal this. For maximum success, refer to the move-like-an-animal activity in the previous section of this unit.

Mrs. Jones asks six children to stand in a circle with their chairs behind them. The child designated as the "starter," Mary, wears a hat and initiates the counting. Mary counts one and each child counts off in sequence, one, two, three, and so on. The child who says the last number in the sequence (six) sits down. The next child begins with one and again the last sits down. The children go around and around the circle,

FIGURE 16–7 "Move your arms like a bird."

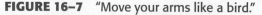

skipping over those sitting down, until only one child is left standing.

Mrs. Jones repeats the activity exactly, starting with the same child and going in the same direction using the same sequence, neither adding nor removing any children. She asks the children to predict who they think will be the last one standing. Mrs. Jones accepts all guesses equally, asking, "Who has a different idea?" until everyone who wishes has guessed. She repeats the activity so children can check their predictions. Then the activity is repeated, but this time Mrs. Jones says, "Whisper in my ear who you think will be the last child standing." The kindergarten teacher plans to repeat this game until every child can predict correctly who will be the one left standing.

The game can be played with any number of players and with any length number sequence. Rather than evaluate the children's predictions, Mrs. Jones uses the predictions as a good indication of children's development. Try this game; you will be surprised by children's unexpected predictions.

Sets and Classifying

A *set* is a group of things with common features that are put together by the process of classifying. Children classify when they sort (separate) and group (join) things because they belong together for some reason. Although classification requires grouping by more than one characteristic and usually takes place when children are older, in young children the grouping process is usually called classification. The following classification activities develop analytical thinking and encourage clear expression of thought in a variety of settings.

1. One way to encourage informal classifying is to keep a button box. Children will sort buttons into sets on their own. Ask, "How do these go together?" Let the children explain.
2. Kindergarten age children can classify animals into **mammals**, reptiles, and amphibians by their body coverings. They can use pictures, plastic animals, or materials that simulate the body coverings of the animals.
3. Children can classify colors with color-coordinated snacks. As children bring in snacks, help

them classify the foods by color. Some examples might include
Green: lettuce, beans, peas
Yellow: bananas, lemonade, corn, cake
Orange: carrots, oranges, cheese
White: milk, cottage cheese, bread
Red: ketchup, cherry-flavored drinks, apples, jams, tomatoes
Brown: peanut butter, whole wheat bread, chocolate

4. Display a collection of plant parts such as stems, leaves, flowers, fruit, and nuts. Have the children sort all of the stems into one pile, all of the leaves into another, and so on. Ask a child to explain what was done. Stress that things that are alike in some way are put together to form a group. Then, have the children re-sort the plant parts into groups by properties such as size (small, medium, and large).
5. Children might enjoy playing a sorting game with objects or pictures of objects. One child begins sorting a collection of objects. After he is halfway through, the next child must complete the activity by identifying the properties the first child used and continue sorting with the same system.

Using Charts and Lists in Classification

The following example shows a first-grade teacher using classification activities to help make her class aware of the technological world around them.

First, Mrs. Red Fox has the children look around the classroom and name all the **machines** that they can see. She asks, "Is a chair a machine?" Dean answers, "No, it does not move." Mrs. Red Fox follows up with an open question, "Do you know what is alike about machines?" Mary and Judy have had experience in the machine center and say, "Machines have to have a moving part." This seems to jog Dean's memory, and he says, "And I think they have to do a job." (A *machine* is the term for a device that, by applying and transferring forces, enables people to do something they cannot do unaided. Most hand tools, such as screwdrivers, levers, and hammers, are examples of simple machines and whenever possible should be investigated by actually working with them.) Mrs. Red Fox writes down all of the suggestions in a list called

"Machines in Our Classroom." The children add the pencil sharpener, a door hinge, a light switch, a water faucet, a record player, and an aquarium to the list. Mrs. Red Fox then asks the children to describe what the machines do, and how they make work easier. After discussing the machines found in the classroom, the students talk about the machines that are in their homes.

The next day the children brainstorm, make a list called "Machines in Our Home," and hang it next to the classroom machine list. When the lists are completed, Mrs. Red Fox asks the children, "Do you see any similarities between the machines found at home and the machines found in our classroom?" Trang Fung answers, "There is a clock in our classroom, and we have one in the kitchen, too." Other children notice that both places have faucets and sinks. When the teacher asks, "What differences do you see between the machines found at home and at school?" Dean notices that there isn't a telephone or a bicycle at school, and Sara did not find a pencil sharpener in her home.

Mrs. Red Fox extends the activity by giving the children old magazines and directing them to cut out pictures of machines to make a machine book. The class also decides to make a large machine collage for the bulletin board.

Comparing

When young children compare, they look at similarities and differences with each of their senses. Children are able to detect small points of difference and, because of this, enjoy spotting mistakes and finding differences between objects. Activities such as observing appearances and sizes, graphing, and dressing figures give experience in comparing.

1. Compare appearances by discussing likeness between relatives, dolls, or favorite animals. Then, make a block graph (see Unit 20) to show the different hair colors in the room or any other characteristics that interest your students.
2. Size comparisons seem to fascinate young children. They want to know who is the biggest, oldest, tallest, shortest. Compare the lengths of hand spans and arm spans and lengths of paces and limbs. Have a few facts ready. Children will want to know which animals are the biggest, smallest, run the fastest, and so on. They might even decide to test which paper towel is the strongest or which potato chip is the saltiest.
3. Clothes can be compared and matched to paper dolls according to size, weather conditions, occupations, and activities such as swimming, playing outdoors, or going to a birthday party. This comparison activity could be a regular part of a daily weather chart activity.

Comparing and Collecting

What did you collect as a child? Did you collect baseball cards, leaves, small cereal box prizes, shells, or pictures of famous people? Chances are you collected something. This is because young children are natural scientists; they are doing what comes naturally. They collect and organize their environment in a way that makes sense to them. Even as adults, we still retain the natural tendency to organize and collect.

Consider for a moment: Do you keep your coats, dresses, shoes, slacks, and jewelry in separate places? Do the spoons, knives, forks, plates, and cups have their own space in your house? In all likelihood, you have a preferred spot for each item. Where do you keep your soup? The cans are probably lined up together. Do you have a special place just for junk? Some people call such a place a junk drawer. Take a look at your house or room as evidence that you have a tendency to think like scientists and try to bring the observable world into some sort of structure.

In fact, when you collect, you may be at your most scientific. As you collect, you combine the processes of observation, comparison, classification, and measurement, and you think like a scientist thinks. For example, when you add a leaf to your collection, you observe it and compare it with the other leaves in your collection. Then, you ask yourself, "Does this leaf measure up to my standards?" "Is it too big, small, old, drab?" "Have insects eaten its primary characteristics?" You make a decision based on comparisons between the leaf and the criteria you have set.

Similarities and Differences

Finding similarities, concepts, or characteristics that link things together may be even more difficult than identifying differences in objects. For example, dogs, cats, bears, lizards, and mice are all animals. But to gain an understanding of a concept, children need to develop the idea that some similarities are more important than others. Even though the lizard has four legs and is an animal, the dog, cat, bear, and mouse are more alike because they are mammals. Unit 34 shows ways of teaching differences in animals.

In addition to quantitative questions such as "How long?" and "How many?" qualitative questions are necessary to bring about keener observations of similarities and differences. Observe the contrast in Chris's responses to his teacher in the following scenario.

Mrs. Raymond asks Chris, "How many seeds do you have on your desk?" Chris counts the seeds, says "Eight," and goes back to arranging the seeds. Mrs. Raymond then asks Chris, "Tell me how many ways your seeds are alike and how they are different." Chris tells his observations as he closely observes the seeds for additional differences and similarities. "Some seeds are small, some seeds are big, some have cracks, some feel rough." Chris's answers began to include descriptions of shape, size, color, texture, structure, markings, and so on. He is beginning to find order in his observations.

Everyday Comparisons

Comparisons can help young children become more aware of their environment; following are some examples.

1. Go for a walk, and have children observe different trees. Ask them to compare the general shape of the trees and the leaves. Let them feel the bark and describe the differences between rough or smooth, peeling, thin or thick bark. As the children compare the trees, discuss ways that they help people and animals (home, shelter, food, shade, and so on).

2. Activities that use sound to make comparisons utilize an important way that young children learn. Try comparing winter sounds with summer sounds. Go for a walk in the winter or summer and listen for sounds. For example, the students in Mrs. Hebert's class heard their boots crunching in snow, the wind whistling, a little rain splashing, and a few even noticed a lack of sound on their winter walk. Johnny commented that he did not hear any birds. This initiated a discussion of where the birds might be and what the class could do to help the birds that remained in the area all winter.

3. The sense walk can be extended by separating the children into three groups and asking each of the groups to focus on a different sense; that is, one group focuses on the *sounds* of spring, another on the *smells* of spring, and the other group uses their sense of *sight*. As the teacher records children's responses on the Spring Sense Walk experience chart, she will be able to assess the children's observation and comparison skills.

4. Insect investigations are natural opportunities for comparison questions and observation. Take advantage of the young children's curiosity, and let them collect four or five different insects for observation. Mr. Wang's class collected insects on a field trip. Theresa found four different kinds of insects. She put them carefully in a jar with leaves and twigs from the area in which she found them and punched holes in the jar lid (Figure 16–8). Mr. Wang helped her observe differences, such as size and winged or wingless, and similarities, such as six legs, three body parts, and two antennae. All insects have these characteristics. If your captive animal does not have these, it is not an insect. It is something else.

5. Snack time is a good time to compare the changes in the color and texture of vegetables before and after they are cooked. Ask, "How do they look different?" When you make butter ask, "What changes do you see in the cream?" Make your own lemonade with fresh lemons and ask, "What happens to the lemons?" Then let the children taste the lemonade before and after sugar is added. Ask, "How does sugar change the taste of the lemonade?"

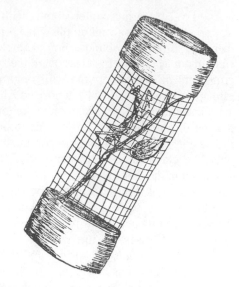

FIGURE 16–8 A bug collector.

Shape

Learning activities relating to shape are essential in the *description of the physical environment*, which is a part of any aspect of science. These descriptions are not possible without an understanding of spatial relationships, which include the study of shapes, symmetry, time, and motion.

Most things have a shape. Children identify and classify objects by their shapes. Basic two-dimensional geometric shapes include the circle, triangle, square, and rectangle. Each of these shapes is constructed from a straight line. The following scenario is a fundamental kindergarten lesson that introduces shapes and applies them to how children learn.

Mrs. Jones arranges children in groups and gives each child a different sponge shape. After the children have had time to explore the outer edges of their sponge shape, she picks up one of the shapes and asks, "How many sides does this shape have?" Mary and Lai answer, "Three." Mrs. Jones says, "Hold your shape up if it is just like my shape." She makes sure that each child gets a chance to examine each shape. If the shape has sides, the children count the sides of the shape aloud. Then she asks all children who have circles to hold them up and pass them to other members of the group for examination. Yarn is passed out and the children begin to duplicate the shapes on the tabletop.

The next day, Mrs. Jones asks George to pick up a shape from the table. He selects a circle. Mrs. Jones asks George if he can find a shape in the room that matches the circle (clock, button, table, pan, record). Sam and Mary take turns finding triangle shapes (sailboat sails, diagonally cut sandwiches), and Lai finds square shapes (floor tiles, crackers, cheese slices, napkins, paper towels, bulletin boards, books, tables). Then, each child stands next to the shape and identifies its name. Mrs. Jones leads the group in shape matching until everyone finds and reports objects of each shape.

To extend the activity, Mrs. Jones has the children use their sponge shapes to paint pictures. She prepares the paint by placing a wet paper towel in a pie tin and coating the towel with tempera paint. The towel and paint work like a stamp pad in which to dip damp sponge shapes. After the children complete their pictures, she asks, "Which shapes have you used in your picture?"

More Shape Activities

The following activities integrate shape with other subject areas.

1. Construction-paper shapes can be used to create fantasy animal shapes such as the shape from outer space, or the strangest insect shape ever seen. Have the children design an appropriate habitat and tell the background for their imaginary shape creature.
2. Take students on a shape walk to see how many shapes your children can find in the objects they see. Keep a record. When you return to your classroom, make a bar graph. Ask the children to determine which shape was seen most often.
3. Shape books are an effective way of reinforcing the shape that an animal has. For example, after viewing the polar bears, make a book in the shape of a polar bear. Children can paste pictures in the book, create drawings of what they saw, and dictate or write stories about bears. Shape books can be covered with wallpaper or decorated in the way that the animal appears.

Shape and the Sense of Touch

Young children are ardent touchers; they love to finger and stroke different materials. The following activities are a few ways that touch can be used to classify and identify shapes.

1. A classic touch bag gives children a chance to recognize and match shapes with their sense of touch. Some children might not want to put their hands into a bag or box. Be sure to use bright colors and cheerful themes when decorating a touch bag or box. A touching apron with several pockets is an alternative. The teacher wears the apron, and students try to identify what is in the pockets.

2. Extend this activity by making pairs of tactile cards with a number of rough- and smooth-textured shapes. Have the children close their eyes and match the cards with partners. Ask, "Can you find the cards that match?" and "How do you know they match?" Or, play "Mystery Shapes" by cutting different shapes out of sandpaper and mounting them on cards. Ask the children to close their eyes, feel the shape, and guess what it is.

3. Students will enjoy identifying shapes with their feet, so you can make a foot feely box. Students will probably infer that they can feel things better with their fingertips than with their toes. A barefoot trail of fluffy rugs, a beach towel, ceramic tiles, bubble packing wrap, a pillow, and a window screen would be a good warm-up activity for identifying shapes with feet. Students should describe what they feel as they walk over each section of the trail (Figure 16–9).

FIGURE 16–9 Taking a tactile walk.

"The big gray one next to the sunken treasure chest."

This is the conversation of two children playing a game with identical boards and pieces. One child gives directions and follows them, placing the piece in the correct position on a hidden game board. Another child, after making sure he understands the directions, chooses a piece and places it on the board. Then the first child continues with another set of directions: "Put the clam under that other rock."

The children are having fun, but there's more to their game than might first appear. A great deal about the child's concept of space can be learned through observation once the child responds to directions such as up-down, on-off, on top of, over-under, in front of, behind, and so on. Is care taken to place the objects on the paper in a careful way?

Space

Although young children are not yet ready for the abstract level of formal thinking, they can begin thinking about space and shape relationships. The following science board game being played in a primary classroom is a good example of this relationship.

"Put the starfish on top of the big rock."

"Which rock do you mean?"

Bird's-Eye View

Children sometimes have difficulty with concepts involved in reading and making maps. One reason for this is that maps demand that they look at things from an unusual perspective: a bird's-eye view of spatial relations. To help children gain experience with this perspective, try the following strategy.

Ask children to imagine what it's like to look down on something from high above. Say, "When a bird looks down as it flies over a house, what do you think it sees?" You will need to ask some directed questions for young children to appreciate that objects will look different. "What would a picnic table look like to a bird?" "Does your house look the same to the bird in the air as it does to you when you're standing on the street?" Next have the children stand on a stepladder and describe a toy that is on the ground.

Then tell the children to stand and look down at their shoes. Ask them to describe what they can see from this perspective. Then ask them to draw their bird's-eye view. Some children will be able to draw a faithful representation of their shoes; others may be able only to scribble what they see. Give them time to experiment with perspective, and if they are having difficulty getting started, have them trace the outlines of their shoes on a piece of drawing paper. Ask, "Do you need to fill in shoelaces or fasteners?" "What else do you see?" Put the children's drawings on their desks for open house. Have parents locate their child's desk by identifying the correct shoes.

This lesson lends itself to a simple exercise that reinforces a new way of looking and gives parents a chance to share what is going on at school. Ask children to look at some familiar objects at home (television, kitchen table, or even the family pet) from their new bird's-eye perspective and draw one or two of their favorites (Figure 16–10). When they bring their drawings to school, other children can try to identify the objects depicted.

FIGURE 16–10   Katie's cat from a bird's-eye view.

On the Playground

Playground distance can be a good place to start to get children thinking about space. Use a stopwatch to time them as they run from the corner of the building to the fence. Ask, "How long did it take?" Then, have the children walk the same route. Ask, "Did it take the same amount of time?" Discuss the differences in walking and running and moving faster or slower over the same space.

Parts and Wholes

After students are used to identifying shapes, introduce the concept of balanced proportions called *symmetry*. **Bilateral symmetry** is frequently found in nature. *Bilateral* means that a line can be drawn through the middle of the shape and divide it into two. Each of the shapes the students have worked with to this point can be divided into two matching halves (Figure 16–11). Point out these divisions on a square, circle, and equilateral triangle. Provide lots of pictures of animals, objects, and other living things. Have the children show where a line could be drawn through each picture. Ask, "How might your own body be divided like this?" Provide pictures for the children to practice folding and drawing lines.

Food activities commonly found in early childhood classrooms provide many opportunities for demonstrating parts and wholes. For example, when working with apples, divide them into halves or fourths. Ask, "How many apples will we need for everyone to receive a piece?" When you cut open the apples, let the children count the number of seeds inside. If you are making applesauce, be sure the children notice the difference between a whole cup of apples or sugar and a half cup. A pizza would be a natural food to order and talk about. Ask, "Can you eat the whole pizza?" or "Would you like a part of the pizza?"

During snack time, ask each student to notice how his or her sandwich has been cut. Ask, "What shape was your sandwich before it was cut?", "What shape are the two halves?", and "Can you think of a different way to cut your sandwich?" Discuss the whole sandwich and parts of a sandwich.

FIGURE 16–11 A bear has symmetry.

Instructional Technology

There are several programs, found in many schools, that teachers can use as an additional tool for teaching fundamental concepts. Although not a substitute for manipulating materials, using the computer can reinforce concepts that have already been introduced, especially as children become familiar with the use of a computer as a tool.

Teachers can create all sorts of computerized activities to reinforce fundamental concepts and skills in science. Teachers can use the ClarisWorks program to create an activity in which the child must place objects in some correct order, match objects, or follow some directions requiring spatial skills. This is done by creating "stationary files," which become an untitled document that is renamed and saved. Each child can open the same file, do the activity, and save the completed activity in her own name; the teacher's original Claris-

Works file is not affected. Children can share each other's work by bringing up the file. In the Claris-Works file example in Figure 16–12, the child must click on the baby animal and drag it over to the corresponding mother animal. ClarisWorks 4.0 comes with a clipart "library" for this purpose.

Sammy's Science House is an example of a software program that already has a section called "The Workshop" as part of the program. In this section children choose the pieces that will make whatever object is displayed. Another section of Sammy's Science House is called "The Sorting Station." In this activity, children sort plants and animals into the correct category, either "plant" or "animal." ThemeWeavers: Animals is another software package that uses beginning math concepts and skills to explore science.

Summary

One-to-one correspondence is the most basic number skill. Children can increase their awareness of this skill and science concept as they do science-related matching activities such as putting animals with their homes and imitating animal movement.

Animal and plant life cycles offer many opportunities for reinforcing sequencing and ordinal position, and number concepts can be emphasized with familiar concrete examples of counting.

Sets are composed of items put together in a group based on one or more common criteria. When children put objects into groups by sorting out items that share some feature, they are classifying. Comparing requires that children look for similarities and differences with each of their senses. Activities requiring observation, measuring, graphing, and classifying encourage comparisons.

Adults help children learn shape when they give them things to view, hold, and feel. Each thing that the child meets in the environment has a shape. The child also needs to use space in a logical way. Things must fit into the space available. As children make constructions in space, they begin to understand the spatial relationship between themselves and the things around them.

The idea of parts and wholes is basic to objects, people, and animals. Sets and wholes can be divided

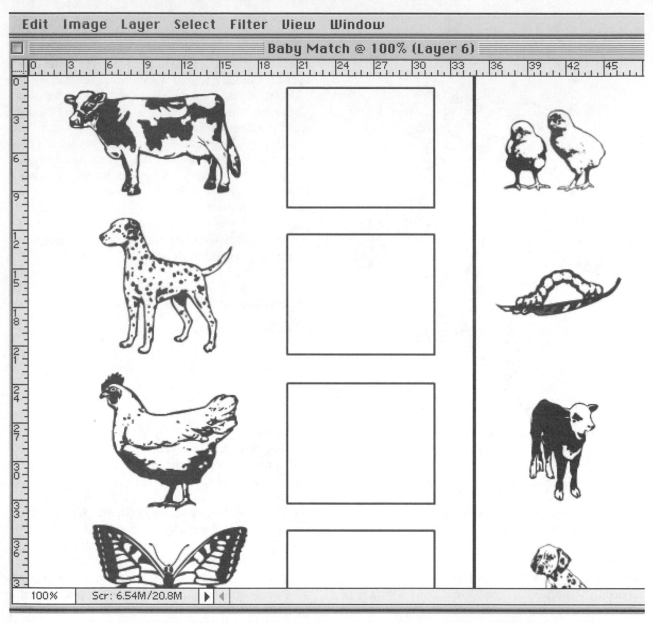

FIGURE 16–12 "Can you match the baby animals to the mother animals?"

into smaller parts or pieces. The concept of bilateral symmetry is introduced when children draw a line through the middle of a shape and divide it into two halves.

Naturalistic, informal, and structured experiences support the learning of these basic science and math skills. A variety of evaluation techniques should be used. Informal evaluation can be done simply by observing the progress and choices of the child. Formal tasks are available in Appendix A.

KEY TERMS

invertebrates	terrapins	mammals
reptiles	larva	machine
amphibians	pupa	bilateral symmetry
tortoises	chrysalis	

SUGGESTED ACTIVITIES

1. How will you evaluate children's learning? How will you assess if children are developing science and math concepts and skills?

2. Select a science topic such as air, and identify possible ways the science and the math concepts in this unit can be integrated with the curriculum.

3. Choose one or more of the fundamental concepts discussed in this unit to teach to a student or a small group of students. Align the concepts and skills with the science content being emphasized in the class. Videotape the lesson and assess the extent to which the student or students understand the concepts.

4. Describe your childhood collection to the class. Discuss the basis for your interest and where you kept your collection. Do you continue to add to this collection?

5. Begin a nature collection. Mount and label your collection, and discuss ways that children might collect objects in a formal way. Refer to Unit 33 of this book for nature collection suggestions.

6. Observe a group of students doing a science activity. Record the informal math and science discoveries they make.

7. Design a questioning strategy that will encourage the development of classification and encourage student discussion. Try the strategy with children. Develop questioning strategies for two more of the concepts and skills presented in this unit.

8. Gain access to a computer with ClarisWorks and create a "stationary file" that teaches or reinforces one of the fundamental concepts and skills discussed in this unit and previous units. Once your work is saved on the stationary file, open it and see that it has a name and is not an "untitled" document. Try your activity with a child, asking her to save her work with her name as the document title. Save the student work to a diskette and share the work with classmates. Discuss ways these files can be useful with children.

9. Using the evaluation criteria found in the Online Resources, review any of the following software that you have access to.
   ◆ Sammy's Science House Redmond, WA: Edmark. (PreK–2)
   ◆ ClarisWorks. Santa Clara, CA: Claris. (all ages)
   ◆ ClarisWorks for Kids. Santa Clara, CA: Claris. (ages five and six)

10. Develop a science activity and have a partner identify science and math concepts the children would learn.

REVIEW

A. Match each term to an activity that emphasizes the concept.

_____ Using the sense of touch to match similar objects   a. One-to-one correspondence

_____ Looking down on things from a bird's-eye view   b. Counting

_____ Matching animals to their homes   c. Sets and classifying

_____ Figuring out how many fish are swimming in the tank   d. Comparing

_____ Classifying animals into groups of mammals and reptiles   e. Shape

_____ Duplicating yarn triangles and circles   f. Space

_____ Drawing an imaginary line through the middle of a sandwich   g. Parts and whole

B. Describe how children use math concepts and skills to learn about science.

REFERENCES

Brown, R. (2001). *Ten seeds*. New York, NY: Alfred A. Knopf.

ClarisWorks. Santa Clara, CA: Claris.

ClarisWorks for kids. Santa Clara, CA: Claris.

Sammy's science house. Redmond, WA: Edmark. (PreK–2)

_____ (1995). *Goldilocks and the three bears*. Bedford, MA: Applewood Books.

National Research Council. (1996). *National science education standards*. Washington, DC: National Academy Press.

Themeweavers: Animals. Redmond, WA: Edmark. (PreK–2)

FURTHER READING AND RESOURCES

Abruscoto, J. (1995). *Teaching children science: A discovery approach*. Needham Heights, MA: Allyn & Bacon.

Day, B. (1988). *Early childhood education*. New York: Macmillan.

Harlan, W. (Ed.). (1995). *Primary science, taking the plunge: How to teach primary science more effectively*. Portsmouth, NH: Heinemann.

Hunder-Grundin, E. (1979). *Literacy: A systematic experience*. New York: Harper & Row.

Kamii, C. (1982). *Number in preschool and kindergarten*. Washington, DC: National Association for the Education of Young Children.

Koppel, S., & Lind, K. K. (1985). Follow my lead: A science board game. *Science and Children, 23*(1), 48–50.

Lind, K. K. (1984). A bird's-eye view: Mapping readiness. *Science and Children, 22*(3), 39–40.

Lind, K. K., & Milburn, M. J. (1988). Mechanized childhood. *Science and Children, 25*(5), 39–40.

Markle, S. (1988). *Hands-on science*. Cleveland, OH: The Instructor Publications.

Pugh, A. F., & Dukes-Bevans, L. (1987). Planting seeds in young minds. *Science and Children, 25*(3), 19–21.

Richards, R., Collis, M., & Kincaid, D. (1987). *An early start to science*. London: MacDonald Educational.

Sprung, B., Foschl, M., & Campbell, P. B. (1985). *What will happen if . . . ?* New York: Educational Equity Concepts.

Warren, J. (1984). *Science time*. Palo Alto, CA: Monday Morning Books.

Science Process Skills

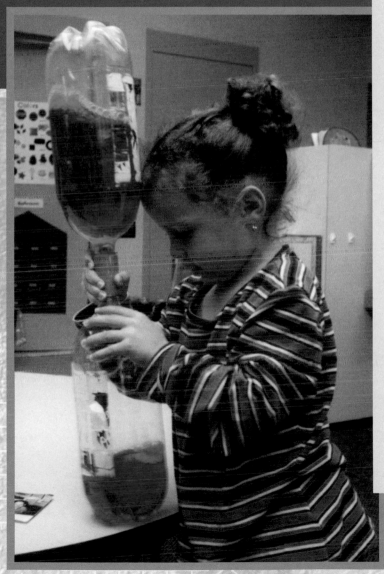

Science Process Skills are those that allow students to process new information through concrete experiences. They are progressive, each building on and overlapping with one another. It is with these processes and skills that individuals think through and study problems and begin to develop an understanding about scientific inquiry.

The Scientific Process Skills most appropriate for preschool and primary students are the basic skills of observing, comparing, classifying, measuring, and communicating (from Figure 5–2 on p. 65).

Observing. Using the senses to gather information about objects or events.

Comparing. Looking at similarities and differences in real objects. In the primary grades, students begin to compare and contrast ideas, concepts, and objects.

Classifying. Grouping and sorting according to properties such as size, shape, color, use, and so on.

Measuring. Quantitative descriptions made by observer either directly through observation or indirectly with a unit of measure.

Communicating. Communicating ideas, directions, and descriptions orally or in written form such as pictures, maps, graphs, or journals so others can understand what you mean.

Strategies That Encourage Inquiry

Young children should experience science in a form that engages them in the active construction of ideas and explanations and enhances their opportunities to develop the skills needed to do science.

The National Science Education Standards suggest the following strategies to engage students in the active search for knowledge.

Ask a question about objects, organisms, and events in the environment. Children should be encouraged to answer their questions by seeking information from their own observations and investigations.

Use data to construct reasonable explanations. In inquiry, students' thinking is emphasized. Even at the earliest ages, students learn what counts as evidence and judge the merits of the data and explanations.

Communicate investigations and explanations. The natural inquiries of young children can be seen as they observe, group, sort, and order objects.

By incorporating familiar teaching strategies such as providing a variety of objects for children to manipulate and talking to children as they go about what they are doing with objects, teachers can help children to learn more about their world.

When children are provided opportunities to work individually to construct their own knowledge, they will gain experiences in organizing data and understanding processes. A variety of activities that let children use all of their senses should be offered. In this way, children are allowed to explore at their own pace and to self-regulate their experiences.

Applying Fundamental Concepts, Attitudes, and Skills

U N I T   17
Ordering, Seriation, and Patterning

OBJECTIVES

After reading this unit, you should be able to:

◆ Define ordering, seriation, and patterning.

◆ List and describe four basic types of ordering activities.

◆ Provide for naturalistic ordering, seriation, and patterning experiences.

◆ Do informal and structured ordering, seriation, and patterning activities with young children.

◆ Assess and evaluate a child's ability to order, seriate, and pattern.

◆ Relate ordering, seriation, and patterning to the NCTM standard for prekindergarten through grade two algebra.

The NCTM (2000, p. 90) standard for prekindergarten through grade two algebra includes the expectations that students will order objects by size, number, and other properties; recognize and extend patterns; and analyze how patterns are developed. Very young children learn repetitive rhymes and songs and hear stories with predictive language. They develop patterns with objects and eventually with numbers. They recognize change such as in the seasons or in their height as they grow.

National Council of Teacher of Mathematics (NCTM) Standard 13 provides that students "recognize, extend, and create a wide variety of patterns" (p. 60). Underlying the concept of patterning are the concepts of comparing, ordering, and seriation.

Ordering is a higher level of comparing (Unit 11). Ordering involves comparing more than two things or more than two groups. It also involves placing things in a sequence from first to last. In Piaget's terms,

ordering is called seriation. Patterning is related to ordering in that children need a basic understanding of ordering to do patterning. Patterning involves making or discovering auditory, visual, and motor regularities. Patterning includes (1) simple patterns such as placing Unifix Cubes® in a sequence by color and/or number, (2) number patterns such as days of the week and patterns on the 100s chart, (3) patterns in nature such as spiderwebs and designs on shells, (4) quilt patterns, and (5) graphs. Movement can also be used to develop pattern and sequence through clapping, marching, standing, sitting, jumping, and the like.

Ordering and seriation start to develop in the sensorimotor stage. Before the age of two, the child likes to work with nesting toys. *Nesting toys* are items of the same shape but of varying sizes so that each one fits into the larger ones. If put into each other in order by size, they will all fit in one stack. Ordering and seriation involve seeing a pattern that follows continuously in equal increments. Other types of patterns involve repeated sequences that follow a preset rule. Daily routine is an example of a pattern that is learned early; that is, infants become cued into night and day and to the daily sequence of diaper changing, eating, playing, and sleeping. As they experiment with rattles, they might use a regular pattern of movement that involves motor, auditory, and visual sequences repeated over and over. As the sensorimotor period progresses, toddlers can be observed lining up blocks, placing a large one, then a small one, large, small or red, green, yellow, red, green, yellow.

An early way of ordering is to place a pattern in one-to-one correspondence with a model as in Figure 17–1. This gives the child the idea of ordering. Next, he learns to place things in ordered rows on the basis of length, width, height, and size. At first the child can think of only two things at one time. When ordering by length, he places sticks in a sequence such as shown in Figure 17–1(C). As he develops and practices, he will be able to use the whole sequence at once and place the sticks as in Figure 17–1(D). As the child develops further, he becomes able to order by other characteristics, such as color shades (dark to light), texture (rough to smooth), and sound (loud to soft).

Once the child can place one set of things in order, he can go on to double seriation. For double seriation he must put two groups of things in order. This is a use of matching, or one-to-one correspondence (Unit 8).

Sets of things can also be put in order by the number of things in each set. By ordering scts, each with one more thing than the others, the child learns the concept (idea) of **one more than**. In Figure 17–2, some cards with different numbers of dots are shown. In 17–2(A), the cards are mixed. In 17–2(B), the cards have been put in order so that each set has one more dot than the one before.

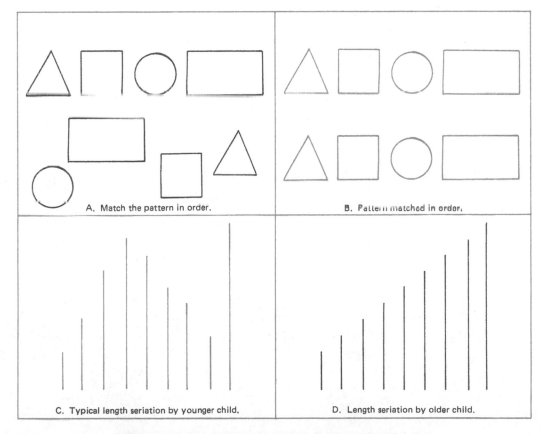

A. Match the pattern in order.

B. Pattern matched in order.

C. Typical length seriation by younger child.

D. Length seriation by older child.

FIGURE 17–1 Ordering by pattern and seriating by size.

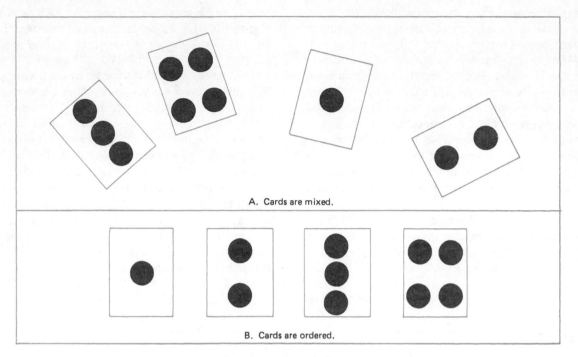

A. Cards are mixed.

B. Cards are ordered.

FIGURE 17-2 Ordering sets.

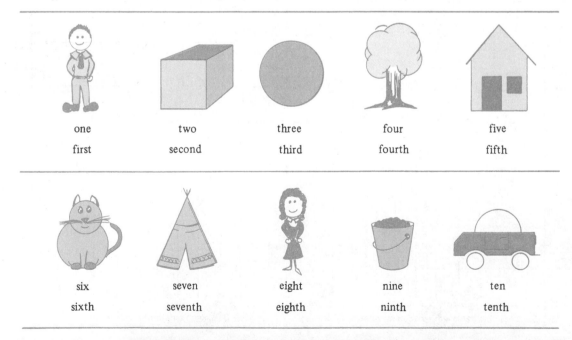

| one | two | three | four | five |
| first | second | third | fourth | fifth |

| six | seven | eight | nine | ten |
| sixth | seventh | eighth | ninth | tenth |

FIGURE 17-3 Counting numbers and ordinal numbers.

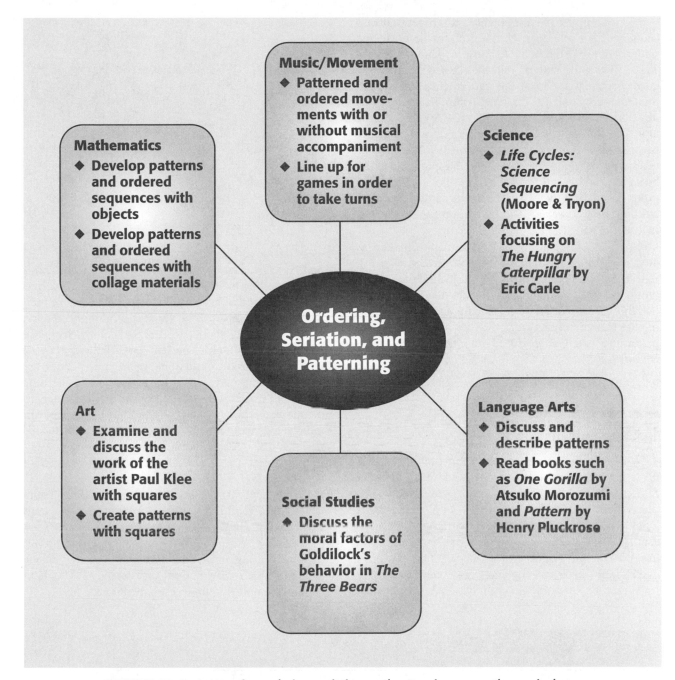

Music/Movement
- Patterned and ordered movements with or without musical accompaniment
- Line up for games in order to take turns

Mathematics
- Develop patterns and ordered sequences with objects
- Develop patterns and ordered sequences with collage materials

Science
- *Life Cycles: Science Sequencing* (Moore & Tryon)
- Activities focusing on *The Hungry Caterpillar* by Eric Carle

Ordering, Seriation, and Patterning

Art
- Examine and discuss the work of the artist Paul Klee with squares
- Create patterns with squares

Social Studies
- Discuss the moral factors of Goldilock's behavior in *The Three Bears*

Language Arts
- Discuss and describe patterns
- Read books such as *One Gorilla* by Atsuko Morozumi and *Pattern* by Henry Pluckrose

FIGURE 17–4   Integrating ordering, seriation, and patterning across the curriculum.

More complex patterns involve the repetition of a sequence. For example, children might be presented with a pile of shapes such as those depicted in Figure 17–1, shown the pattern, and then asked to select the correct shapes to repeat the pattern in a line (rather than matching underneath, one to one). Patterns can be developed with Unifix Cubes,® cube blocks, beads, alphabet letters, numerals, sticks, coins, and many other items. Auditory patterns can be developed by the teacher with sounds such as hand clapping and drum beats or motor activities such as the command to jump, jump, and then sit. To solve a pattern problem, children have to be able to figure out what comes next in a sequence.

Ordering and patterning words are those such as next, last, biggest, smallest, thinnest, fattest, shortest, tallest, before, and after. Also included are the ordinal numbers: first, second, third, fourth, and so on to the last thing. Ordinal relations as compared with counting are shown in Figure 17–3. Ordering, seriation, and patterning can be integrated into the content areas (Figure 17–4).

Assessment

While the child plays, the teacher should note activities that might show the child is learning to order things. Notice how she uses nesting toys. Does she place them in each other so she has only one stack? Does she line them up in rows from largest to smallest? Does she use words such as *first* ("I'm first") and *last* ("He's last") on her own? In her dramatic play, does she go on train or plane rides where chairs are lined up for seats and each child has a place (first, sec-

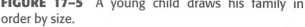

FIGURE 17–5 A young child draws his family in order by size.

ond, last)? Seriation may be reflected in children's drawings. For example, in Figure 17–5 a child has drawn a picture of his family members in order of their height. Paint chips can be seriated from light to dark, such as from light pink to dark burgundy. Sequence stories (such as a child blowing up a balloon) can be put on cards for the child to put in order.

Also during play, watch for evidence of patterning behavior. Patterns might appear in artwork such as paintings or collages; in motor activity such as movement and dance; in musical activity such as chants and rhymes; in language activities such as acting out patterned stories (e.g., *The Three Billy Goats Gruff* or *Goldilocks and the Three Bears*); or with manipulative materials such as Unifix Cubes,® Teddy Bear Counters,® Lego,® building blocks, attribute blocks, beads for stringing, Geoboards,® and so on.

Ask the child to order different numbers and kinds of items during individual interview tasks as in the examples that follow and in Appendix A. The following are examples of three assessment tasks.

S A M P L E   A S S E S S M E N T   T A S K

5G **Preoperational Ages 4–5**
Ordering, Sequential/Ordinal Number: Unit 17

METHOD: Interview.

SKILL: Child can order up to five objects relative to physical dimensions and identify the ordinal position of each.

MATERIALS: Five objects or cutouts that vary in equal increments of height, width, length, and overall size dimensions.

PROCEDURE: Start with five objects or cutouts. If this proves to be difficult, remove the objects or cutouts, then put out three and ask the same questions. FIND THE (TALLEST, BIGGEST, FATTEST OR SHORTEST, SMALLEST, THINNEST). PUT THEM ALL IN A ROW FROM TALLEST TO SHORTEST (BIGGEST TO SMALLEST, FATTEST TO THINNEST). If the child accomplishes the task, ask, WHICH IS FIRST? WHICH IS LAST? WHICH IS SECOND? WHICH IS THIRD? WHICH IS FOURTH?

EVALUATION: Note whether the children find the extremes, but mix up the three objects or cutouts that belong in the middle. This is a common approach for preoperational children. Note if children take an organized approach to solving the problem or if they seem to approach it in a disorganized, unplanned way.

INSTRUCTIONAL RESOURCE: Charlesworth, R., and Lind, K. K. (2003). *Math and Science for Young Children* (4th ed.). Clifton Park, NY: Delmar Learning.

SAMPLE ASSESSMENT TASK

6H   **Transitional Ages 5–7**
Ordering, Double Seriation: Unit 17

METHOD: Interview.

SKILL: Child will place two sets of 10 items in double seriation.

MATERIALS: Two sets of 10 objects, cutouts, or pictures of objects that vary in one or more dimensions in equal increments such that one item in each set is the correct size to go with an item in the other set. The sets could be children and baseball bats, children and pets, chairs and tables, bowls and spoons, cars and garages, hats and heads, etc.

PROCEDURE: Suppose you have decided to use hats and heads. First, place the heads in front of the child in random order. Instruct the child to line the heads up in order from smallest to largest. Help can be given such as, FIND THE SMALLEST. GOOD, NOW WHICH ONE COMES NEXT? AND NEXT? If the child is able to line up the heads correctly, then put out the hats in a random arrangement. Tell the child, FIND THE HAT THAT FITS EACH HEAD, AND PUT IT ON THE HEAD.

EVALUATION: Note how the children approach the problem, whether in an organized or haphazard fashion. Note whether they get the whole thing correct or partially correct. If they get a close approximation, go through the procedure again with 7 items or 5 to see if they grasp the concept when fewer items are used. A child going into concrete operations should be able to accomplish the task with two groups of 10. Transitional children may be able to perform the task correctly with fewer items in each group.

INSTRUCTIONAL RESOURCE: Charlesworth, R., and Lind, K. K. (2003). *Math and Science for Young Children* (4th ed.). Clifton Park, NY: Delmar Learning.

SAMPLE ASSESSMENT TASK

6I   **Transitional Period Ages 5–7**
Ordering, Patterning: Unit 17

METHOD: Interview.

SKILL: Child can copy, extend, and describe patterns made with concrete objects.

MATERIALS: Color cubes, Unifix Cubes,® Teddy Bear Counters,® attribute blocks, small toys, or other objects that can be placed in a sequence to develop a pattern.

PROCEDURE: 1. Copy patterns: One at a time, make patterns of various levels of complexity (each letter stands for one type of item such as one color of a color cube, one shape of an attribute block, or one type of toy). For example, A-B-A-B could be red block–green block–red block–green block or big triangle–small triangle–big triangle–small triangle. Using the following series of patterns, tell the child to MAKE A PATTERN JUST LIKE THIS ONE. (If the child hesitates, point to the first item and say, START WITH ONE LIKE THIS.)
    a. A-B-A-B
    b. A-A-B-A-A-B
    c. A-B-C-A-B-C
    d. A-A-B-B-C-C-A-A-B-B-C-C
  2. Extend patterns: Make patterns as in 1, but this time say, THIS PATTERN ISN'T FINISHED. MAKE IT LONGER. SHOW ME WHAT COMES NEXT.
  3. Describe patterns: Make patterns as in 1 and 2. Say, TELL ME ABOUT THESE PATTERNS. (WHAT COMES FIRST? NEXT? NEXT?) IF YOU WANTED TO CONTINUE THE PATTERN, WHAT WOULD COME NEXT? NEXT?
  4. If the above tasks are easily accomplished, then try some more difficult patterns such as
    a. A-B-A-C-A-D-A-B-A-C-A-D
    b. A-B-B-C-D-A-B-B-C-D
    c. A-A-B-A-A-C-A-A-D

EVALUATION: Note which types of patterns are easiest for the children. Are they more successful with the easier patterns? With copying? With extending? With describing?

INSTRUCTIONAL RESOURCE: Charlesworth, R., and Lind, K. K. (2003). *Math and Science for Young Children* (4th ed.). Clifton Park, NY: Delmar Learning.

Naturalistic Activities

Just as children's natural development guides them to sort things, it also guides them to put things in order and to place things in patterns. As children sort they often put the items in rows or arrange them in patterns. For example, Kate picks out blocks that are all of one size, shape, and color and lines them up in a row. She then adds to the row by lining up another group of blocks of the same size, shape, and color. She picks out blue blocks and yellow blocks and lines them up, alternating colors. Pete is observed examining his mother's measuring cups and spoons. He lines them up from largest to smallest. Then he makes a pattern: cup-spoon-cup-spoon-cup-spoon-cup-spoon.

As speech ability increases, the child uses order words. "I want to be *first*." "This is the *last* one." "Daddy Bear has the *biggest* bowl." "I'll sit in the *middle*." As he starts to draw pictures, he often draws mothers, fathers, and children and places them in a row from smallest to largest.

Informal Activities

Informal teaching can go on quite often during the child's daily play and routine activities. The following are some examples.

◆ Eighteen-month-old Brad has a set of mixing bowls and measuring cups to play with on the kitchen floor. He puts the biggest bowl on his head. His mother smiles and says, "The *biggest* bowl fits on your head." He tries the smaller bowls, but they do not fit. Mom says, "The *middle-sized* bowl and the *smallest* bowl don't fit, do they?" She sits down with him and picks up a measuring cup. "Look, here is the cup that is the *biggest*. These are *smaller*." She lines them up by size. "Can you find the *smallest* cup?" Brad proceeds to put the cups one in the other until they are in one stack. His mother smiles, "You have them all in *order*."

◆ Five-year-old George, four-year-old Richard, and three-year-old Jim come running across the yard to Mr. Brown. "You are all fast runners." "I was *first*," shouts George. "I was *second*," says Richard. "I was *third*," says Jim. George shouts, "You were *last*, Jim, 'cause you are the *littlest*." Jim looks mad. Mr. Brown says, "Jim was both *third* and *last*. It is true Jim is the *littlest* and the *youngest*. George is the *oldest*. Is he the *biggest*?" "No!" says Jim, "He's *middle size*."

◆ Mary has some small candies she is sharing with some friends and her teacher. "Mr. Brown, you and I get five because we are the *biggest*. Diana gets four because she's the *next* size. Pete gets three. Leroy gets two, and Brad gets one. Michael doesn't get any 'cause he is a baby." "I see," says Mr. Brown, "you are dividing them so the *smallest* people get the least and the *biggest* get the most."

◆ Mrs. Red Fox tells her first graders that she would like them to line up boy-boy-girl-girl.

◆ Second grader Liu Pei decides to draw a picture each day of her bean sprout that is the same height as it is that day. Soon she has a long row of bean sprout pictures, each a little taller than the one before. Mr. Wang comments on how nice it is to have a record of the bean sprout's growth from the day it sprouted.

◆ Miss Collins tells the children, "You have to take turns on the swing. Tanya is *first* today."

These examples show how comments can be made that help the child see her own use of order words and activities. Many times in the course of the day, opportunities come up where children must take turns. These times can be used to the fullest for teaching order and ordinal number. Many kinds of materials can be put out for children that help them practice ordering. Some of these things are self-correcting.

Structured Activity

Structured experiences with ordering and patterning can be done with many kinds of materials. These materials can be purchased, or they can be made by the teacher. Things of different sizes are easy to find at home or school. Measuring cups and spoons, mixing bowls, pots and pans, shoes, gloves, and other items of clothing are easy to get in several different sizes. Paper and cardboard can be cut into different sizes and shapes. Paper towel rolls can be made into cylinders of graduated sizes. The artistic teacher can draw pictures of the same item in graduated sizes. Already drawn materials such as Richardson's (1999) Unifix® cube train patterns, counting boards, or working-space papers can be used for patterning. The following are basic activities that can be done with many different kinds of objects, cutouts, and pictures.

ACTIVITIES

ORDERING AND PATTERNING: THE BASIC CONCEPT

OBJECTIVE: To help the child understand the idea of order and sequence.

MATERIALS: Large colored beads with a string for the teacher and each child.

NATURALISTIC AND INFORMAL ACTIVITIES: Have the container of beads available during center time. As the children explore the beads, note if they develop patterns based on color. Comment such as, "First you lined up the blue beads and then the red beads"; "You lined up two yellow, two red, and two blue beads."

STRUCTURED ACTIVITIES: The beads are in a box or bowl where they can be reached by each child. Say, WATCH ME. I'M GOING TO MAKE A STRING OF BEADS. Start with three beads. Add more as each child learns to do each amount. Lay the string of three beads down where each child can see it: NOW YOU MAKE ONE LIKE MINE. WHICH KIND OF BEAD SHOULD YOU TAKE FIRST? When the first bead is on: WHICH ONE IS NEXT? When two are on: WHICH ONE IS NEXT?
Use patterns of varying degrees of complexity.

1. A-B-A-B
2. A-B-C-A-B-C
3. A-A-B-A-A-C-A-A-D
4. Make up your own patterns.

FOLLOW-UP:

1. Make a string of beads. Pull it through a paper towel roll so that none of the beads can be seen. Say, I'M GOING TO HIDE THE BEADS IN THE TUNNEL. NOW I'M GOING TO PULL THEM OUT. WHICH ONE WILL COME OUT FIRST? NEXT? NEXT? and so on. Then pull the beads through and have the children check as each bead comes out.
2. Dye some macaroni with food coloring. Set up a pattern for a necklace. The children can string the macaroni to make their own necklaces in the same pattern.

ORDERING/SERIATION: DIFFERENT SIZES, SAME SHAPE

OBJECTIVE: To make comparisons of three or more items of the same shape and different sizes.

MATERIALS: Four to 10 squares cut with sides 1 inch, 1¼ inch, 1½ inch, and so on.

NATURALISTIC AND INFORMAL ACTIVITIES: Have a container of the squares and other shapes in a sequence of sizes available during center time. Note how the children use the shapes. Do they sequence them by size? Comment such as, "You put the biggest square first"; "You put all the same sizes in their own piles."

STRUCTURED ACTIVITY: Lay out the shapes. HERE ARE SOME SQUARES. STACK THEM UP SO THE BIGGEST IS ON THE BOTTOM. Mix the squares up again. NOW, PUT THEM IN A ROW STARTING WITH THE SMALLEST.

FOLLOW-UP: Do the same thing with other shapes and materials.

ORDERING/SERIATION: LENGTH

OBJECTIVE: To make comparisons of three or more things of the same width but different lengths.

MATERIALS: Sticks, strips of paper, yarn, string, Cuisinaire Rods®, drinking straws, or anything similar cut in different lengths such that each one is the same difference in length from the next one.

NATURALISTIC AND INFORMAL ACTIVITIES: Have containers of each type of material available during center time. Some of the items could be placed in the art center to be used for collages. Note how the children explore the materials. Do they line them up in sequence? Comment such as, "You put the largest (smallest) first"; "Tell me about what you made."

STRUCTURED ACTIVITY: Put the sticks out in a mixed order. LINE THESE UP FROM SHORTEST TO LONGEST (LONGEST TO SHORTEST). Help if needed. WHICH ONE COMES NEXT? WHICH ONE OF THESE IS LONGEST? IS THIS THE NEXT ONE?

FOLLOW-UP: Do this activity with many different kinds of materials.

ORDERING/SERIATION: DOUBLE SERIATION

OBJECTIVE: To match one-to-one two or more ordered sets of the same number of items.

MATERIALS: *Three Bears* flannelboard figures or cutouts made by hand: mother bear, father bear, baby bear, Goldilocks, three bowls, three spoons, three chairs, and three beds.

NATURALISTIC AND INFORMAL ACTIVITIES: Have the flannelboard and story pieces available during center time. Note how the children use the material. Do they tell the story? Do they line up the pieces in sequence? Comment if they hesitate, "What comes next in the story?" Note if they sequence and/or match the materials by size, "You matched up each bear with his/her chair, bowl, bed."

STRUCTURED ACTIVITY: Tell the story. Use all the order words biggest, middle-sized, smallest, next. Follow up with questions: WHICH IS THE BIGGEST BEAR? FIND THE BIGGEST BEAR'S BOWL (CHAIR, BED, SPOON). Use the same sequence with each character.

FOLLOW-UP: Let the children act out the story with the felt pieces or cutouts. Note if they use the order words; if they change their voices; and if they match each bear to the right bowl, spoon, chair, and bed.

ORDERING: SETS

OBJECTIVE: To order groups of one to five objects.

MATERIALS: Glue buttons on cards, or draw dots on cards so there are five cards.

NATURALISTIC AND INFORMAL ACTIVITIES: Have the cards available during center time. Note if the children sequence them from one to five items. Comment such as, "Tell me how many buttons (dots) there are on each card"; "Which cards have more than one?"

STRUCTURED ACTIVITY: Lay out the cards. Put the card with one button in front of the child. HOW MANY BUTTONS ON THIS CARD? Child answers. Say, YES, THERE IS ONE BUTTON. FIND THE CARD WITH ONE MORE BUTTON. If child picks out the card with two, say, YOU FOUND ONE MORE. NOW FIND THE CARD WITH ONE MORE BUTTON. Keep on until all five are in line. Mix the cards up. Give the stack to the child. LINE THEM ALL UP BY YOURSELF. START WITH THE SMALLEST GROUP.

FOLLOW-UP: Repeat with other materials. Increase the number of groups as each child learns to recognize and count larger groups. Use loose buttons (chips, sticks, or coins), and have the child count out her own groups. Each set can be put in a small container or on a small piece of paper.

ORDER: ORDINAL NUMBERS

OBJECTIVE: To learn the ordinal numbers *first, second, third,* and *fourth.* (The child should be able to count easily to four before he does these activities.)

MATERIALS: Four balls or beanbags, four common objects, four chairs.

NATURALISTIC AND INFORMAL ACTIVITIES: Have the materials available during center time or gym time as appropriate. Note how the children use them. Note if they figure out that they must take turns. Comment such as, "You are doing a good job taking turns. Mary is first, José is second, Larry is third, and Jai Li is fourth."

STRUCTURED ACTIVITIES:

1. Games requiring that turns be taken can be used. Just keep in mind that young children cannot wait very long. Limit the group to four children, and keep the game moving fast. For example, give each of the four children one beanbag or one ball. Say, HOW MANY BAGS ARE THERE? LET'S COUNT. ONE, TWO, THREE, FOUR. CAN I CATCH THEM ALL AT THE SAME TIME? NO, I CAN'T. YOU WILL HAVE TO TAKE TURNS: YOU ARE FIRST, YOU ARE SECOND, YOU ARE THIRD, AND YOU ARE FOURTH. Have each child say his number, "I am (first, second, third, and fourth)." OKAY, FIRST, THROW YOURS. (Throw it back.) SECOND, THROW YOURS. (Throw it back.) After each has had his turn, have them all do it again. This time have them tell you their ordinal number name.
2. Line up four objects. Say, THIS ONE IS FIRST, THIS ONE IS SECOND, THIS ONE IS THIRD, THIS ONE IS FOURTH. Ask the children: POINT TO THE (FOURTH, FIRST, THIRD, SECOND).
3. Line up four chairs. WE ARE GOING TO PLAY BUS (PLANE, TRAIN). Name a child, _____ YOU GET IN THE THIRD SEAT. Fill the seats. Go on a pretend trip. NOW WE WILL GET OFF. SECOND SEAT GET OFF. FIRST SEAT GET OFF. FOURTH SEAT GET OFF. THIRD SEAT GET OFF.

FOLLOW-UP: Make up some games that use the same basic ideas. As each child knows first through fourth, add fifth, then sixth, and so on.

PATTERNING: AUDITORY

OBJECTIVE: To copy and extend auditory patterns.

MATERIALS: None needed.

NATURALISTIC AND INFORMAL ACTIVITIES: Note if the children engage in spontaneous chants and rhymes. Encourage them by joining in their rhythmic activities.

STRUCTURED ACTIVITIES: Start a hand-clapping pattern. Ask the children to join you. LISTEN TO ME CLAP. Clap, clap, (pause), clap (repeat several times). YOU CLAP ALONG WITH ME. Keep on clapping for 60 to 90 seconds so everyone has a chance to join in. Say, LISTEN. WHEN I STOP, YOU FINISH THE PATTERN. Do three repetitions, then stop. Say, YOU DO THE NEXT ONE. Try some other patterns such as "Clap, clap, slap the elbow" or "Clap, stamp the foot, slap the leg."

FOLLOW-UP: Help the children develop their own patterns. Have them use rhythm instruments to develop patterns (such as drumbeat, bell jingle, drumbeat, sound cans).

PATTERNING: OBJECTS

OBJECTIVE: To copy and extend object patterns.

MATERIALS: Several small plastic toys such as vehicles, animals, peg people; manipulatives such as Unifix Cubes,® inch cubes, or attribute blocks; or any other small objects such as coins, bottle caps, eating utensils, or cups.

NATURALISTIC AND INFORMAL ACTIVITIES: Provide opportunities to explore many kinds of materials such as those listed above. After the children have had some structured pattern activities, note if they develop patterns during their independent activity periods. Do they call your attention to their pattern constructions? Will they describe their constructions when you ask them to?

STRUCTURED ACTIVITIES: Have the children explore ways to make patterns with the objects. Have them see how many different kinds of patterns they can make.

FOLLOW-UP: Find additional ideas for pattern activities in the references listed in Further Reading and Resources for this unit.

PATTERNING: EXPLORING PATTERNS IN SPACE

OBJECTIVE: To organize materials in space in a pattern.

MATERIALS: Many kinds of materials are available that will give the child experiences in making patterns in space. Some of these are listed.
1. Geoboards are square boards with attached pegs. Rubber bands of different colors can be stretched between the pegs to form patterns and shapes.
2. Parquetry and pattern blocks are blocks of various shapes and colors that can be organized into patterns.
3. Pegboards are boards with holes evenly spaced. Individual pegs can be placed in the holes to form patterns.
4. Color inch cubes are cubes with 1-inch sides. They come in sets with red, yellow, blue, green, orange, and purple cubes.

NATURALISTIC AND INFORMAL ACTIVITIES: Provide time for exploration of materials during center time. Note the patterns the children construct. Do they call your attention to their pattern constructions? Will they describe their constructions when you ask them to?

STRUCTURED ACTIVITIES:

1. The children can experiment freely with the materials and create their own patterns.
2. Patterns can be purchased or made for the children to copy.

FOLLOW-UP: After the children have been shown how they can be used, the materials can be left out for use during center time.

PATTERNING: ORGANIZING PATTERNS IN SPACE

OBJECTIVE: To organize materials in space in a pattern.

MATERIALS: Construction paper, scissors, and glue.

NATURALISTIC AND INFORMAL ACTIVITIES: Children should have many opportunities, both naturalistic and informal and structured, and many opportunities to work in small groups before being assigned the following activity.

STRUCTURED ACTIVITY: Provide a poster-size piece of construction paper. Provide an assortment of precut construction paper shapes (i.e., squares, triangles, circles, etc.). Suggest that the children, working in small groups, create as many different patterns as they can and glue them on the big piece of paper.

FOLLOW-UP: Offer the activity several times. Use different colors for the shapes, use different sizes, and change the choice of shapes.

EXAMPLE WORLD WIDE WEB ACTIVITIES

◆ Captain Birdwell's Treasure at http://www.pbkids.org/clifford/labelingandpatterningideas
◆ Trudy (3-14-00) provides coloring book seriation materials at http://www/perpetualpreschool.com/mathideas.html

---

George, a kindergartner, is enjoying using Match, a computer program that provides experience in sequencing designs. When he finishes with Match, he asks if he can change to Dr. Seuss Fix Up the Mixed-up Puzzle, which also includes some sequencing activities.

Evaluation

Note whether the children use more ordering and patterning words and so more ordering and patterning activities during play and routine activities. Without disrupting the children's activities, ask questions or make comments and suggestions.

◆ Who is the biggest? (the smallest?)
◆ (As the children put their shoes on after their nap) Who has the longest shoes? (the shortest shoes?)
◆ Who came in the door first today?
◆ Run fast. See who can get to the other side of the gym first.
◆ (The children are playing train) Well, who is in the last seat? She must be the caboose. Who is in the first seat? She must be the engineer.
◆ Everyone can't get a drink at the same time. Line up with the shortest person first.

◆ Great, you found a new pattern to make with the Unifix Cubes®!
◆ Sam made some patterns with the ink pad and stamps.

Richardson (1999, pp. 78–79) suggests noting if children can

◆ copy patterns
◆ extend patterns
◆ create patterns
◆ analyze a given pattern

The assessment tasks in Appendix A can be used for individual evaluation interviews.

Summary

When more than two things are compared, the process is called ordering or seriation. There are four basic types of ordering activities. The first is to put things in sequence by size. The second is to make a one-to-one match between two sets of related things. The third is to place sets of different numbers of things in order from the least to the most. The last is ordinal numbers. Ordinal numbers are first, second, third, and so on.

Patterning is related to ordering and includes auditory, visual, and physical motor sequences that are repeated. Patterns may be copied, extended, or verbally described.

KEY TERMS

ordering   seriation   patterning   one more than

SUGGESTED ACTIVITIES

1. Observe children at school. Note those activities that show the children are learning order and patterning. Share your observations with the class.
2. Add ordering and patterning activities to your Activity File.
3. Assemble the materials needed to do the ordering and patterning assessment tasks in this unit. Try out the tasks with several young children. What did the children do? Share the results with the class.
4. Plan and do one or more ordering and/or patterning activities with a small group of preschool and/or kindergarten students.
5. Look through two or three educational materials catalogs. Pick out 10 materials you think would be best to use for ordering and/or patterning activities.
6. Using the evaluation system from Activity 7, Unit 9, evaluate one or more of the following computer programs in terms of each program's value for learning about ordering and/or patterning.

◆ Blues 123 Time Activities. Woodinville, WA: Humongous.
◆ Dr. Seuss Fix Up the Mixed-up Puzzle. Greenwich, CT: CBS Software.
◆ Match (in Kindercomp). Cambridge, MA: Spinnaker Software.
◆ Millie's Math House. Redmond, WA: Edmark.
◆ Muppet Math. Pleasantville, NY: Sunburst Technologies.
◆ Soc Order. Circle Pines, MN: American Guidance Service.
◆ Spatial Relationships (English and Spanish versions). Pleasantville, NY: Sunburst Technologies.
◆ Thinkin' Things 1. Redmond, WA: Edmark.

REVIEW

A. List at least seven of the major characteristics of ordering/seriation.

B. Describe the major characteristics of patterning.

C. Decide whether the descriptions below are examples of the following ordering and patterning behaviors: (a) size sequence, (b) one-to-one comparison, (c) ordering sets, (d) using ordinal words or numbers, (e) basic concept of ordering, (f) using double seriation, (g) patterning.

1. Child arranges tokens in groups: one in the first group, two in the second, three in the third, and so on.

2. Pablo says, "I'm last."

3. Maria lines up sticks of various lengths from shortest to longest.

4. Kate is trying to place all the nesting cups inside each other in order by size.

5. Child chants, "Ho, ho, ho. Ha, ha, ha. Ho, ho, ho. Ha, ha, ha."

6. Jim strings blue beads in this manner: large-small-large-small-large-small.

7. Fong places a white chip on each red chip.

8. Nancy places the smallest flower in the smallest flowerpot, the middle-sized flower in the middle-sized flowerpot, and the largest flower in the largest flowerpot.

9. Mr. Mendez says, "Today we will line up with the shortest child first."

10. Child parks cars: yellow car, blue car, yellow car, blue car.

11. Tanja tells Josie, "I'm first this time."

12. In the Montessori class, the pink tower is constructed with the largest cube at the bottom, the next smaller cube second, and so on until all the cubes are used.

D. Summarize the NCTM expectations for algebra that are described in this unit.

REFERENCES

Moore, J. E., & Tryon, L. (1986). *Life cycles. Science sequencing* (2nd ed.). Monterey, CA: Evan Moor.

National Council of Teachers of Mathematics. (2000). *Principles and standards for school mathematics.* Reston, VA: Author. (http://www.nctm.org)

Richardson, K. (1999). *Developing number concepts: Counting, comparing, and pattern (Book 1).* Parsippany, NJ: Dale Seymour.

FURTHER READING AND RESOURCES

AIMS Educational Products. AIMS Education Foundation, P.O. Box 8120, Fresno, CA 93747-8120.

Teaching Children Mathematics. See monthly "Ideas" columns.

Baratta-Lorton, M. (1976). *Math their way*. Menlo Park, CA: Addison-Wesley.

Coburn, T. G. (1993). *Curriculum and evaluation standards for school mathematics: Patterns*. Reston, VA: National Council of Teachers of Mathematics.

Copley, J. V. (2000). *The young child and mathematics*. Washington, DC: National Association for the Education of Young Children.

Copley, J. V. (Ed.). (1999). *Mathematics in the early years*. Washington, DC: National Association for the Education of Young Children.

Economopoulos, K. (1998). What comes next? The mathematics of pattern in kindergarten. *Teaching Children Mathematics*, *5*(4), 230–233.

May, L. (1996). Teaching math: Searching for patterns. *Teaching K–8, 27*(3), 21.

Richardson, K. (1984). *Developing number concepts using Unifix Cubes.*® Menlo Park, CA: Addison-Wesley.

Richardson, K. (1999). *Developing number concepts: Planning guide*. Parsippany, NJ: Dale Seymour.

UNIT 18
Measurement: Volume, Weight, Length, and Temperature

OBJECTIVES

After reading this unit, you should be able to:

◆ Explain how measurement develops in five stages.

◆ Assess and evaluate the measurement skills of a young child.

◆ Do informal and structured measurement with young children.

◆ Provide for naturalistic measurement experiences.

◆ Explain the NCTM standard for measurement as it applies to preschool/kindergarten children.

The NCTM (2000, p.102) expectations for children in the beginning stages of measurement include recognizing the attributes of length, volume, weight, and time and comparing and ordering objects according to these attributes. Time is addressed in Unit 19. Also included in this unit are the attributes of temperature. By the time they reach kindergarten, young children are expected to understand measurement with non-standard units such as multiple copies of objects of the same size (e.g., paperclips). Measurement connects geometry and number and builds on children's experiences with comparisons (Unit 11). Length is the major focus for the younger children, but experiences with volume, weight, and temperature are also important. Estimation is an important measurement tool in the early stages.

Measurement is one of the most useful math skills. *Measurement* involves assigning a number to things so they can be compared on the same attributes. Numbers can be assigned to attributes such as volume, weight, length, and temperature. For example, the child drinks *one cup* of milk. Numbers can also be given to time measurement. However, time is not an attribute of things and so is presented separately (Unit 19). Standard units such as pints, quarts, liters, yards, meters, pounds, grams, and degrees tell us exactly how much (*volume*); how heavy (*weight*); how long, wide, or deep (*length*); and how hot or cold (*temperature*). A number is put with a standard unit to let a comparison be made. Two quarts contain more than one quart, two pounds weigh less than three pounds, one meter is shorter than four meters, and 30° is colder than 80°.

Stages of Development

The concept of measurement develops through five stages as outlined in Figure 18–1. The first stage is a **play stage**. The child imitates older children and adults. She plays at measuring with rulers, measuring cups, measuring spoons, and scales as she sees others do. She pours sand, water, rice, beans, and peas from one container to another as she explores the properties of volume. She lifts and moves things as she learns about weight. She notes that those who are bigger than she can do many more activities and has her first concept of length (height). She finds that her short arms cannot always reach what she wants them to reach (length). She finds that she has a preference for cold or hot food and cold or hot bathwater. She begins to learn about temperature. This first stage begins at birth and continues through the sensorimotor period into the preoperational period.

The second stage in the development of the concept of measurement is the one of making **comparisons** (Unit 11). This is well under way by the preoperational stage. The child is always comparing: bigger-smaller, heavier-lighter, longer-shorter, and hotter-colder.

The third stage, which comes at the end of the preoperational period and at the beginning of concrete operations, is one in which the child learns to use what are called **arbitrary units**; that is, anything the child has can be used as a unit of measure. She will try to find out how many coffee cups of sand will fill a quart milk carton. The volume of the coffee cup is the arbitrary unit. She will find out how many toothpicks long her foot is. The length of the toothpick is the arbitrary unit. As she goes through the stage of using arbitrary units, she learns concepts she will need to understand standard units.

When the child enters the period of concrete operations, she can begin to see the need for standard units. She can see that to communicate with someone else in a way the other person will understand, she must use the same units the other person uses. For example, the child says that her paper is nine thumbs wide. Another person cannot find another piece of the same width unless the child and the thumb are there to measure it. But, if she says her paper is eight and one-half inches wide, another person will known exactly the width of the paper. In this case, the thumb is an arbitrary unit, and the inch is a *standard unit*. The same is true for other units. Standard measuring cups and spoons must be used when cooking in order for the recipe to turn out correctly. If any coffee cup or teacup and any spoon are used when following a recipe, the measurement will be arbitrary and inexact, and the chances of a successful outcome will be poor. The same can be said of building a house. If nonstandard measuring tools are used, the house will not come out as it appears in the plans, and one carpenter will not be communicating clearly with another.

The last stage in the development of the concept of measurement begins in the concrete operations period. In this last stage, the child begins to use and understand the standard units of measurement such as inches, meters, pints, liters, grams, and degrees.

Obviously, prekindergartners and most kindergartners are still exploring the concept of measurement. Prekindergartners are usually in stages one (play and imitation) and two (making comparisons). The kindergartners begin in stage two and move into stage three (arbitrary units). During the primary grades, students begin to see the need for standard units (stage four) and move into using standard units (stage five). Measurement can be integrated into the other content areas (Figure 18–2).

Piagetian Stage	Age	Measurement Stage
Sensorimotor and Preoperational	0–7	1. Plays and imitates 2. Makes comparisons
Transitional: Preoperational to Concrete Operations	5–7	3. Uses arbitrary units
Concrete Operations	6+	4. Sees need for standard units 5. Uses standard units

FIGURE 18–1   Stages in the development of the concept of measurement.

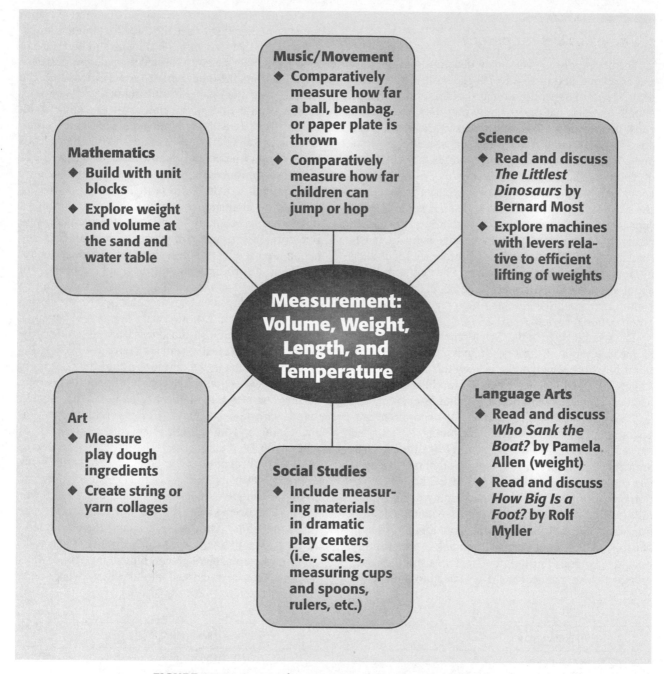

Music/Movement
- ◆ Comparatively measure how far a ball, beanbag, or paper plate is thrown
- ◆ Comparatively measure how far children can jump or hop

Science
- ◆ Read and discuss *The Littlest Dinosaurs* by Bernard Most
- ◆ Explore machines with levers relative to efficient lifting of weights

Mathematics
- ◆ Build with unit blocks
- ◆ Explore weight and volume at the sand and water table

Measurement: Volume, Weight, Length, and Temperature

Art
- ◆ Measure play dough ingredients
- ◆ Create string or yarn collages

Social Studies
- ◆ Include measuring materials in dramatic play centers (i.e., scales, measuring cups and spoons, rulers, etc.)

Language Arts
- ◆ Read and discuss *Who Sank the Boat?* by Pamela Allen (weight)
- ◆ Read and discuss *How Big Is a Foot?* by Rolf Myller

FIGURE 18–2 Integrating measurement across the curriculum.

How the Young Child Thinks about Measurement

To find out why standard units are not understood by young children in the sensorimotor and preoperational stages, Piaget must be reviewed. Remember from the first unit that the young child is fooled by appearances. He believes what he sees before him. He does not keep old pictures in mind as he will do later. He is not yet able to conserve (or save) the first way something looks when its appearance is changed. When the ball of clay is made into a snake, he thinks the volume (the amount of clay) has changed because it looks smaller to him. When the water is poured into a differently shaped container, he thinks there is more

or less—depending on the height of the glass. Because he can focus on only one attribute at a time, the most obvious dimension determines his response.

Two more examples are shown in Figure 18–3. In the first task, the child is fooled when a crooked road is compared with a straight road. The straight road looks longer (*conservation of length*). In the second task, size is dominant over material, and the child guesses that the Ping-Pong ball weighs more than the hard rubber ball. He thinks that since the table tennis ball is larger than the hard rubber ball, it must be heavier.

The young child becomes familiar with the words of measurement and learns which attributes can be measured. He learns mainly through observing older children and adults as they measure. He does not need to be taught the standard units of measurement

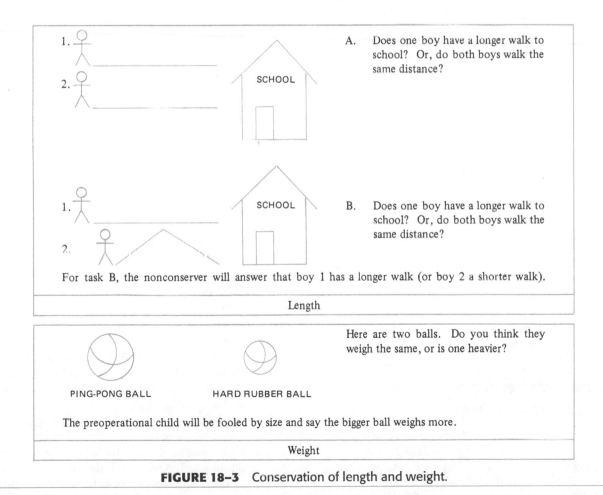

FIGURE 18–3   Conservation of length and weight.

in a formal way. The young child needs to gain a feeling that things differ on the basis of "more" and "less" of some attributes. He gains this feeling mostly through his own observations and firsthand experimental experiences.

Assessment

To assess measurement skills in the young child, the teacher observes. He notes whether the child uses the term *measure* in the adult way. He notes whether she uses adult measuring tools in her play as she sees adults use them. He looks for the following kinds of incidents.

- ◆ Mary is playing in the sandbox. She pours sand from an old bent measuring cup into a bucket and stirs it with a sand shovel. "I'm measuring the flour for my cake. I need three cups of flour and two cups of sugar."
- ◆ Juanita is seated on a small chair. Kate kneels in front of her. Juanita has her right shoe off. Kate puts Juanita's foot on a ruler. "I am measuring your foot for your new shoes."
- ◆ The children have a play grocery store. George puts some plastic fruit on the toy scale. "Ten pounds here."
- ◆ Tim is the doctor, and Bob is his patient. Tim takes an imaginary thermometer from Bob's mouth. "You have a hot fever."

Individual interviews for the preoperational child may be found in Unit 11. For the child who is near concrete operations (past five years of age), the conservation tasks in Appendix A and in Unit 1 may be used to determine if children are conservers and probably ready to use standard units of measurement.

Naturalistic Activities

Young children's concepts of measurement come, for the most part, from their natural, everyday experiences exploring the environment, discovering its properties, and thus constructing their own knowledge. The examples in the assessment section of this unit demon-

strate how children's play activities reflect their concepts of measurement. Mary has seen and may have helped someone make a cake. Kate has been to the shoe store and knows the clerk must measure the feet before he brings out a pair of shoes to try on the customer. George has seen the grocer weigh fruit. Tim knows that a thermometer tells how "hot" a fever is. The observant young child picks up these ideas on his own without being told specifically that they are important.

The child uses his play activities to practice what he has seen adults do. He also uses play materials to learn ideas through trial and error and experimentation. Water, sand, dirt, mud, rice, and beans teach the child about volume. As he pours these substances from one container to another, he learns about *how much*, or amount. The child can use containers of many sizes and shapes: buckets, cups, plastic bottles, dishes, bowls, and coffee cans. Shovels, spoons, strainers, and funnels can also be used with these materials. When playing with water, the child can also learn about weight if he has some small objects like sponges, rocks, corks, small pieces of wood, and marbles, which may float or sink. Any time a child tries to put something in a box, envelope, glass, or any other container, he learns something about volume.

The child can begin to learn the idea of linear measure (length, width, height) and area in his play. The unit blocks that are usually found in the early childhood classroom help the child learn the idea of units. He will soon learn that each block is a unit of another block. Two, four, or eight of the small blocks are the same length when placed end to end as one of the longest blocks. As he builds enclosures (houses, garages, farmyards, and so on), he is forced to pick his blocks so that each side is the same length as the one across from it.

The child learns about weight and balance on the teeter-totter. He soon learns that it takes two to go up and down. He also learns that it works best when the two are near the same weight and are the same distance from the middle.

The child makes many contacts with temperature. He learns that his soup is hot, warm, and then as it sits out, cold. He likes cold milk and hot cocoa. He learns that the air may be hot or cold. If the air is hot, he may wear just shorts or a bathing suit. If the air is cold, he will need a coat, hat, and mittens.

Informal Activities

The young child learns about measurement through the kinds of experiences just described. During these activities there are many opportunities for informal teaching. One job for the adult as the child plays is to help her by pointing out properties of materials that the child may not be able to find on her own. For instance, if a child says she must have all the long blocks to make her house large enough, the teacher can show her how several small blocks can do the job. She can show the child how to measure how much string will fit around a box before she cuts off a piece to use.

The teacher can also take these opportunities to use measurement words such as the names of units of measurement and the words listed in Unit 15. She can also pose problems for the child.

◆ How can we find out if we have enough apple juice for everyone?
◆ How can we find out how many paper cups of milk can be poured from a gallon container?
◆ How can we find out if someone has a high fever?
◆ How can we find out without going outside if we need to wear a sweater or coat?

◆ How can we find out who is the tallest boy in the class? The heaviest child?
◆ How many of these placemats will fit around the table?
◆ Who lives the longest distance from school?

It is the teacher's responsibility to provide environmental opportunities for the exploration and discovery of measurement concepts.

Structured Activities

The young child learns most of his basic measurement ideas through his play and home activities that come through the natural routines of the day. He gains a feeling for the need for measurement and learns the language of measurement. Structured activities must be chosen with care. They should make use of the child's senses. They should be related to what is familiar to the child and expand what he already knows. They should pose problems that will show him the need for measurement. They should give the child a chance to use measurement words to explain his solution to the problem. The following are examples of these kinds of experiences and the naturalistic and informal experiences that serve as their foundation.

ACTIVITIES

MEASUREMENT: VOLUME

OBJECTIVES:
◆ To learn the characteristics of volume
◆ To see that volume can be measured
◆ To learn measurement words used to tell about volume (more, less, too big, too little, the same)

MATERIALS:
◆ Sandbox (indoors and/or out), water table (or sink or plastic dishpans)
◆ Many containers of different sizes: bottles, cups, bowls, milk cartons, cans (with smooth edges), boxes (for dry materials)
◆ Spoons, scoops, funnels, strainers, beaters
◆ Water, sand, rice,* beans,* peas,* seeds, or anything else that can be poured

NATURALISTIC AND INFORMAL ACTIVITIES: Allow plenty of time for experimenting with the materials listed above during center time. Note if children are into the pretend play measurement stage, are making comparisons, or if they mention any standard units. Ask questions or make comments such as, "How many of the blue cups of sand will fill up the purple bowl?"; "Which bottle will hold more water?"; "You filled that milk carton up to the top."

STRUCTURED ACTIVITIES:

1. Have several containers of different kinds and sizes. Fill one with water (or sand or rice or peas or beans). Pick out another container. Ask the children: IF I POUR THIS WATER FROM THIS BOTTLE INTO THIS OTHER BOTTLE, WILL THE SECOND BOTTLE HOLD ALL THE WATER? After each child has made her prediction, pour the water into the second container. Ask a child to tell what she saw happen. Continue with several containers. Have the children line them up from the one that holds the most to the one that holds the least.

2. Pick out one standard container (coffee cup, paper cup, measuring cup, tin can). Have one or more larger containers. Say, IF I WANT TO FILL THE BIG BOWL WITH SAND AND USE THIS PAPER CUP, HOW MANY TIMES WILL I HAVE TO FILL THE PAPER CUP AND POUR SAND INTO THE BOWL? Write down the children's predictions. Let each child have a turn to fill the cup and pour sand into the bowl. Record by making slash marks how many cups of sand are poured. Have the children count the number of marks when the bowl is full. Compare this amount with what the children thought the amount would be. This can be done with many different sets of containers.

FOLLOW-UP: Do the same types of activities using different sizes of containers and common objects. For example, have a doll and three different-sized boxes. Have the children decide which box the doll will fit into.

*Some educators feel it is inappropriate to use food for play—be cautious.

MEASUREMENT: WEIGHT

OBJECTIVES:

◆ To learn firsthand the characteristics of weight
◆ To learn that weight and size are different attributes (big things may have less weight than small things)
◆ To learn that light and heavy are relative ideas

MATERIALS:

◆ Things in the classroom or brought from home, e.g., manipulatives, paper clips, buttons, crayons, pencils, small toys
◆ A teeter-totter, a board and a block, a simple pan balance
◆ Sand, sugar, salt, flour, sawdust, peas, beans, rice
◆ A ball collection with balls of different sizes and materials: ball bearings, table tennis, golf, solid rubber, foam rubber, Styrofoam, balsa wood, cotton, balloons

NATURALISTIC AND INFORMAL ACTIVITIES: During center time provide opportunities for the children to experiment with a simple pan balance using a variety of materials. Note if they use any weight vocabulary (such as heavy or light). Ask them to explain their actions. Outdoors or in the gym provide a teeter-totter. Note how they find ways to balance. Ask them what happens when children of different weights or different numbers of children sit on each end.

STRUCTURED ACTIVITIES:

1. Have the child name things in the room that he can lift and things he cannot lift. Which things can he not lift because of size? Which because of weight? Compare things such as a stapler and a large paper bag (small and heavy and large and light). Have the children line up things from heaviest to lightest.

2. Have the children experiment with the teeter-totter. How many children does it take to balance the teacher? Make a balance with a block and a board. Have the child experiment with different things to see which will make the board balance.

3. A fixed-position pan balance can be used for firsthand experiences with all types of things.
    a. The child can try balancing small objects such as paper clips, hair clips, bobby pins, coins, toothpicks, cotton balls, and so on in the pans.
    b. Take the collection of balls. Pick out a pair. Have the child predict which is heavier (lighter). Let him put one in each pan to check his prediction.
    c. Put one substance such as salt in one pan. Have the child fill the other pan with flour until the pans balance. IS THE AMOUNT (VOLUME) OF FLOUR AND SALT THE SAME?
    d. Have equal amounts of two different substances such as sand and sawdust in the balance pans. DO THE PANS BALANCE?

FOLLOW-UP: Make some play dough with the children. Have them measure out one part flour and one part salt. Mix in some powder tempera. Add water until the mixture is pliable but not too sticky. See Unit 22 for cooking ideas. Read *Who Sank the Boat?* by Pamela Allen.

MEASUREMENT: LENGTH AND HEIGHT

OBJECTIVES:
- To learn firsthand the concepts of length and height
- To help the child learn the use of arbitrary units

MATERIALS:
- The children themselves
- Things in the room that can be measured, e.g., tables, chairs, doors, windows, shelves, books
- Balls of string and yarn, scissors, construction paper, markers, beans, chips, pennies, other small counters, pencils, toothpicks, ice cream bar sticks, unit blocks

NATURALISTIC AND INFORMAL ACTIVITIES: During center time note if the children engage in any comparison or play length measurement activities. Unit blocks are especially good for naturalistic and informal measurement explorations. For example, when using unit blocks notice if children appear to use trial and error to make their blocks fit as they wish. Comment, "You matched the blocks so your house has all the sides the same length."

STRUCTURED ACTIVITIES:

1. Present the child with problems where she must pick out something of a certain length. For example, a dog must be tied to a post. Have a picture of the dog and the post. Have several lengths of string. Have the child find out which string is the right length. Say, WHICH ROPE WILL REACH FROM THE RING TO THE DOG'S COLLAR?

2. LOOK AROUND THE ROOM. WHICH THINGS ARE CLOSE? WHICH THINGS ARE FAR AWAY?

3. Have several children line up. Have a child point out which is the tallest, the shortest. Have the children line up from tallest to shortest. The child can draw pictures of friends and family in a row from shortest to tallest.

4. Draw lines on construction paper. HOW MANY BEANS (CHIPS, TOOTHPICKS, OR OTHER SMALL THINGS) WILL FIT ON EACH LINE? WHICH LINE HAS MORE BEANS? WHICH LINE IS LONGEST? Gradually use paper with more than two lines.
5. Put a piece of construction paper on the wall from the floor up to about 5 feet. Have each child stand next to the paper. Mark her height, and write her name by her height. Check each child's height each month. Note how much each child grows over the year.
6. Have an arbitrary unit such as a pencil, a toothpick, a stick, a long block, or a piece of yarn or string. Have the child measure things in the room to see how many units long, wide, or tall the things are.

FOLLOW-UP: Keep the height chart out so the children can look at it and talk about their heights. Read *The Littlest Dinosaurs* by Bernard Most and *How Big Is a Foot?* by Rolf Myller.

MEASUREMENT: TEMPERATURE

OBJECTIVES:
◆ To give the child firsthand experiences that will help him learn that temperature is the relative measure of heat
◆ To learn that the thermometer is used to measure temperature
◆ To experience hot, warm, and cold as related to things, to weather, and to the seasons of the year

MATERIALS: Ice cubes, hot plate, teakettle or pan, pictures of the four seasons, poster board, markers, scissors, glue, construction paper, old magazines with pictures, real thermometers (body, inside, and outside).

NATURALISTIC AND INFORMAL ACTIVITIES: Note children's comments regarding temperature. Make comments such as, "Be careful, the soup is very hot"; "It's cold today, you must button up your coat." Ask questions such as, "Do we need to wear mittens or gloves today?"

STRUCTURED ACTIVITIES:
1. Have the children decide whether selected things in the environment are hot, cold, or warm: ice and boiling water, the hot and cold water taps, the radiators, the glass in the windows, their skin, for example.
2. Show pictures of summer, fall, winter, and spring. Discuss the usual temperatures in each season. What is the usual weather? What kinds of clothes are worn? Make a cardboard thermometer. At the bottom put a child in heavy winter clothes, above put a child in a light coat or jacket, then a child in a sweater, then one in short sleeves, then one in a bathing suit. Each day discuss the outside temperature relative to what was worn to school.
3. Give the children scissors and old magazines. Have them find and cut out pictures of hot things and cold things. Have them glue the hot things on one piece of poster board and the cold things on another.
4. Show the children three thermometers: one for body temperature, one for room temperature, and one for outdoor use. Discuss when and where each is used.

FOLLOW-UP: Each day the outside temperature can be discussed and recorded in some way (such as in the second listed activity or on a graph as discussed in Unit 20).

EXAMPLE WORLD WIDE WEB ACTIVITIES.

◆ Cooking Zoo Food—Volume. Link at http://www.lessonplanspage.com/ScienceMathZooFood-MeasurementK
◆ Melting Snow—Temperature. Link at http://www.lessonplanspage.com/ScienceMathMeltingSnowThermometer
◆ Inch measuring using the book *Inch by Inch* by Leo Lionni (1960), Scholastic. Link at http://www.mathforum.org/paths/measurement/inchbyinch.html
◆ Nonstandard measuring using the book *Miss Nelson Is Missing!* by Harry Allard (1977), Houghton. Link at http://www.mathforum.org/paths/measurement/nonstand.html

---

Young children will also enjoy working with the computer program *How to Weigh an Elephant*, which presents problems in weight, volume, and mass designed for children ages four to seven.

Evaluation

The adult should note the children's responses to the activities given them. She should observe them as they try out the materials and note their comments. She must also observe whether they are able to solve everyday problems that come up by using informal measurements such as comparisons. Use the individual interviews in this unit and in Appendix A.

Summary

The concept of measurement develops through five stages. Preoperational children are in the early stages: play, imitation, and comparing. They learn about measurement mainly through naturalistic and informal experiences that encourage them to explore and discover. Transitional children move into the stage of experimenting with arbitrary units. During the concrete operations period, children learn to use standard units of measurement.

KEY TERMS

measurement	weight	play stage
length	temperature	comparisons
volume	standard units	arbitrary units

SUGGESTED ACTIVITIES

1. Observe young children during group play. Note and record any measurement activities that you observe. Identify the stage of measurement understanding that is represented by each activity observed.

2. In class, discuss ways in which children can be encouraged at home and at school to develop concepts of measurement.

3. Plan two or three measurement activities. Assemble the necessary materials, and use the activities with a group of young children.

4. Look through an early childhood school supply catalog. Make a list of the measurement materials you would purchase if you had $300 to spend.

5. Add several measurement activities to your file/notebook.

6. Use the evaluation scheme in Activity 7, Unit 9, to evaluate any of the following software programs.

   ◆ Coco's Math Project 1. Singapore, SG: Times Learning Systems Pte Ltd.
   ◆ Balancing Bear. Pleasantville, NY: Sunburst Technology.
   ◆ How to Weigh an Elephant. Dallas, TX: Panda/Learning Technologies.

   Find out if there is any other measurement software for young children.

REVIEW

A. List the five stages of measurement in order.
B. Describe each of the five stages of measurement.
C. Identify the level of measurement described in each of the following incidents.
   1. Johnny says, "My block building is bigger than yours."
   2. Linda checks the thermometer. "It's 32° today—very cold!"
   3. Cindy, Juanita, and Li pour dry beans in and out of an assortment of containers.
   4. "I weigh 60 pounds. How much do you weigh?"
   5. "Dad, it would take two of my shoes to make one as long as yours."
D. Explain how a young child's measurement skills can be assessed.
E. Describe the NCTM (2000) expectations for measurement for preschool/kindergarten children.

REFERENCE

National Council of Teachers of Mathematics. (2000). *Principles and standards for school mathematics.* Reston, VA: Author. (http://www.nctm.org)

FURTHER READING AND RESOURCES

AIMS Educational Products. AIMS Education Foundation, P.O. Box 8120, Fresno, CA 93747-8120.

Baratta-Lorton, M. (1976). *Mathematics their way*. Menlo Park, CA: Addison-Wesley.

Burghardt, B., & Heilman, G. (1994). Math by the month: Water matters. *Teaching Children Mathematics*, *1*, 24.

Copley, J. V. (2000). *The young child and mathematics*. Washington, DC: National Association for the Education of Young Children.

Copley, J. V. (Ed.). (1999). *Mathematics in the early years*. Washington, DC: National Association for the Education of Young Children.

Dyche, S. E. (1992). In step with the metric system. *Science and Children*, *29*(8), 22–23.

Lehman, J. R. (1994). Measure up to science. *Science and Children, 31*(5), 30–31.

Lubinski, C. A., & Thiessen, D. (1996). Exploring measurement through literature. *Teaching Children Mathematics, 2*, 260–263. (*How big is a foot* by R Myller)

McGregor, J. (1996). Math by the month: How do you measure up?: K–2. *Teaching Children Mathematics, 3*, 84.

National Council of Teachers of Mathematics (NCTM). (1989). *Curriculum and evaluation standards for school mathematics*. Reston, VA: Author.

Porter, J. (1995). Math by the month: Balancing acts. *Teaching Children Mathematics, 1*, 430.

Richardson, K. (1999). *Developing number concepts: Planning guide*. Parsippany, NJ: Dale Seymour.

Schwartz, S. L. (1995). Developing power in linear measurement. *Teaching Children Mathematics, 1*, 412–416.

Shimabukuro, M. A., & Fearing, V. (1993). How does your garlic grow? *Science and Children*, *30*(8), 8–11.

Shipley, L. M. (1994). Math by the month: Long distance. *Teaching Children Mathematics, 1*, 162.

West, S., & Cox, A. (2001). *Sand and water play*. Beltsville, MD: Gryphon House.

U N I T   1 9

Measurement: Time

OBJECTIVES

After reading this unit, you should be able to:

◆ Describe what is meant by time sequence.

◆ Describe what is meant by time duration.

◆ Explain the three kinds of time.

◆ Do informal and structured time measurement activities with young children.

◆ Explain the NCTM (2000) expectations for preschool and kindergarten students' understanding of time.

The NCTM standards (2000) for measurement include expectations for the understanding of time. Preschool and kindergarten children are learning the attributes of time such as sequence and duration. *Sequence* of time has to do with the order of events. It is related to the ideas about ordering presented in Unit 17. While the child learns to sequence things in patterns, he also learns to sequence events. He learns small, middle-sized, and large beads go in order for a pattern sequence. He gets up, washes his face, brushes his teeth, dresses, and eats breakfast for a time sequence. *Duration* of time has to do with how long an event takes (seconds, minutes, hours, days, a short time, a long time).

Kinds of Time

There are three kinds of time a child has to learn. Time is a hard measure to learn. The child cannot see it and feel it as she can weight, volume, length, and temperature. There are fewer clues to help the child. The young child relates time to three things: personal experience, social activity, and culture.

In her *personal experience*, the child has her own past, present, and future. The past is often referred to as "When I was a baby." "Last night" may mean any time before right now. The future may be "After my night nap" or "When I am big." The young child has difficulty with the idea that there was a time when mother and dad were little and she was not yet born.

Time in terms of *social activity* is a little easier to learn and makes more sense to the young child. The young child tends to be a slave to order and routine. A change of schedule can be very upsetting. This is because time for her is a sequence of predictable events. She can count on her morning activities being the same each day when she wakes up. Once she gets to school, she learns that there is order there too: first she takes off her coat and hangs it up, next she is greeted by her teacher, then she goes to the big playroom to play, and so on through the day.

A third kind of time is **cultural time**. It is the time that is fixed by clocks and calendars. Everyone learns this kind of time. It is a kind of time that the child probably does not really understand until she is in the concrete operations period. She can, however, learn the language (seconds, minutes, days, months, and so on) and the names of the timekeepers (clock, watch, calendar). She can also learn to recognize a timekeeper when she sees one.

Language of Time

To learn time is as dependent on language as any part of math. Time and sequence words are listed in Unit 15. They are listed again in this unit for easy reference.

- ◆ **General words:** time, age
- ◆ **Specific words:** morning, afternoon, evening, night, day, noon
- ◆ **Relational words:** soon, tomorrow, yesterday, early, late, a long time ago, once upon a time, new, old, now, when, sometimes, then, before, present, while, never, once, next, always, fast, slow, speed, first, second, third, and so on
- ◆ **Specific duration words:** clock and watch (minutes, seconds, hours); calendar (date, days of the week names, names of the month, names of seasons, year)
- ◆ **Special days:** birthday, Passover, Juneteenth, Cinco de Mayo, Easter, Christmas, Thanksgiving, vacation, holiday, school day, weekend

Time concept experiences can be integrated into the other content areas (Figure 19–1).

Assessment

The teacher should observe the child's use of time language. She should note if he makes an attempt to place himself and events in time. Does he remember the sequence of activities at school and at home? Is he able to wait for one thing to finish before going on to the next? Is he able to order things (Unit 17) in a sequence?

The following are examples of the kinds of interview tasks that are included in Appendix A.

SAMPLE ASSESSMENT TASK

5H   **Preoperational Ages 4–5**
Time, Labeling and Sequence: Unit 19

METHOD: Interview.

SKILL: Shown pictures of daily events, the child can use time words to describe the action in each picture and place the pictures in a logical time sequence.

MATERIALS: Pictures of daily activities such as meals, nap, bath, playtime, bedtime.

PROCEDURE: Show the child each picture. Say, TELL ME ABOUT THIS PICTURE. WHAT'S HAPPENING? After the child has described each picture, place all the pictures in front of him, and tell the child,

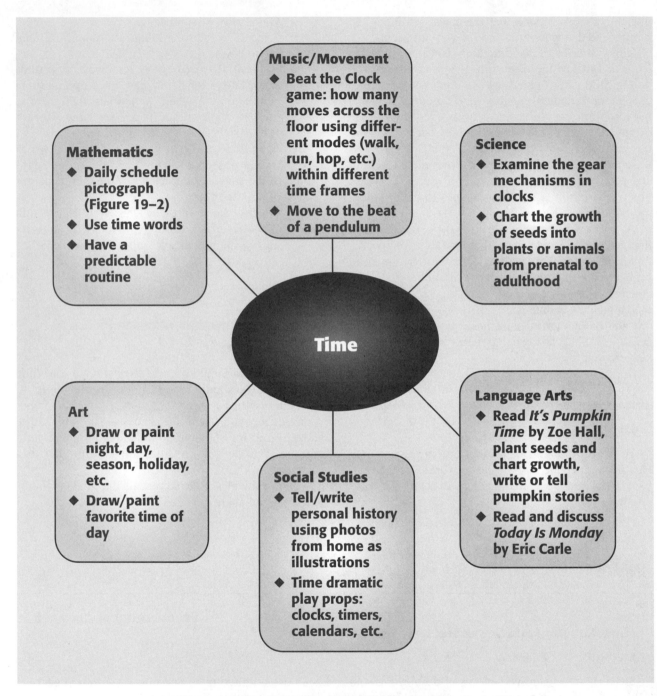

FIGURE 19–1 Integrating time experiences across the curriculum.

PICK OUT (SHOW ME) THE PICTURE OF WHAT HAPPENS FIRST EACH DAY. After a picture is selected, ask WHAT HAPPENS NEXT? Continue until all the pictures are lined up.

EVALUATION: When describing the pictures, note whether the child uses time words such as breakfast time, lunchtime, playtime, morning, night, etc. Note whether a logical sequence is used in placing the pictures in order.

INSTRUCTIONAL RESOURCE: Charlesworth, R., and Lind, K. K. (2003). *Math and Science for Young Children* (4th ed.). Clifton Park, NY: Delmar Learning.

SAMPLE ASSESSMENT TASK

4I   **Preoperational Ages 3–6**
Time, Identify Clock or Watch: Unit 19

METHOD: Interview.

SKILL: The child can identify a clock and/or watch and describe its function.

MATERIALS: One or more of the following timepieces: conventional clock and watch, digital clock and watch. Preferably at least one conventional and one digital should be included. If real timepieces are not available, use pictures.

PROCEDURE: Show the child the timepieces or pictures of timepieces. Ask, WHAT IS THIS? WHAT DOES IT TELL US? WHAT IS IT FOR? WHAT ARE THE PARTS, AND WHAT ARE THEY FOR?

EVALUATION: Note whether the child can label watch(es) and clock(s), how much she is able to describe about the functions of the parts (long and short hands, second hands, alarms set, time changer, numerals). Note also if the child tries to tell time. Compare knowledge of conventional and digital timepieces.

INSTRUCTIONAL RESOURCE: Charlesworth, R., and Lind, K. K. (2003). *Math and Science for Young Children* (4th ed.). Clifton Park, NY: Delmar Learning.

Naturalistic Activities

From birth on, children are capable of learning time and sequence. In an organized, nurturing environment, infants learn quickly that when they wake up from sleep, they are held and comforted, their diapers are changed, and then they are fed. The first sense of time duration comes from how long it takes for each of these events. Infants soon have a sense of how long they will be held and comforted, how long it takes for a diaper change, and how long it takes to eat. Time for the infant is a sense of sequence and of duration of events.

The toddler shows his understanding of time words through his actions. When he is told "It's lunchtime," he runs to his high chair. When he is told it is time for a nap, he may run the other way. He will notice cues that mean it is time to do something new: toys are being picked up, the table is set, or Dad appears at the door. He begins to look for these events that tell him that one piece of time ends and a new piece of time is about to start.

As spoken language develops, the child will use time words. He will make an effort to place events and himself in time. It is important for adults to listen and respond to what he has to say. The following are some examples.

◆ Eighteen-month-old Brad tugs at Mr. Flores's pants leg, "Cookie, cookie." "Not yet Brad. We'll have lunch first. Cookies are after lunch."

◆ Linda (20 months of age) finishes her lunch and gets up. "No nap today. Play with dollies." Ms. Moore picks her up, "Nap first. You can play with the dolls later."

◆ "Time to put the toys away, Kate." Kate (30 months old) answers, "Not now. I'll do it a big later on."

◆ Chris (three years old) sits with Mrs. Raymond. Chris says, "Last night we stayed at the beach house." "Oh yes," answers Mrs. Raymond, "You were at the beach last summer, weren't you?" (For Chris anything in the past happened "last night.")

◆ Mr. Flores is showing the group a book with pictures of the zoo. Richard (four years old) comments, "I want to go there yesterday." Mr. Flores says, "We'll be going to the zoo on Friday."

◆ Cindy (six years old) says, "One time, when I was real small, like three or something, _____." Her teacher listens as Cindy relates her experience.

It is very important for the young child to have a predictable and regular routine. It is through this routine that the child gains his sense of time duration and time sequence. It is also important for him to hear time words and to be listened to when he tries to use his time ideas. It is especially important that his own time words be accepted. For instance Kate's "a big later on" and Chris's "last night" should be accepted. Kate shows an understanding of the future and Chris of the past even though they are not as precise as an adult would be.

Informal Activities

The adult needs to capitalize on the child's efforts to gain a sense of time and time sequence. Reread the situations given as examples in the section before this (Naturalistic Activities). In each, the adults do some informal instruction. Mr. Flores reminds Brad of the coming sequence. So does Ms. Moore, and so does the adult with Kate. Mrs. Raymond accepts what Chris

says while at the same time she uses the correct time words "last summer." It is important that adults listen to and expand on what children say.

The adult serves as a model for time-related behavior. The teacher checks the clock and the calendar for times and dates. The teacher uses the time words in the Language of Time section. She makes statements and asks questions.

◆ "*Good morning*, Tom."
◆ "*Goodnight*, Mary. See you *tomorrow*."
◆ "What did you do over the *weekend*?"
◆ "Who will be our guest for lunch *tomorrow*?"
◆ "*Next week* on *Tuesday* we will go to the park for a picnic."
◆ "Let me check the *time*. No wonder you are hungry. It's almost *noon*."
◆ "You are the *first* one here *today*."

Children will observe and imitate what the teacher says and does before they really understand the ideas completely.

An excellent tool for informal classroom time instruction is a daily picture/word schedule placed in a prominent place. Figure 19–2 is an example of such a schedule. Children frequently ask, "When do we _____?," "What happens after this?," and so on. Teachers can take them to the pictorial schedule and help them find the answer for themselves. "What are we doing now?" "Find (activity) on the schedule." "What comes next?" Eventually, children will just have to be reminded to "Look at the schedule," and they will answer their questions by themselves.

Structured Activities

Structured time and sequence activities include sequence patterns with beads, blocks, and other objects; sequence stories; work centering around the calendar; and work centering around clocks. Experiences with pattern sequence and story sequence can begin at an early age. The infant enjoys looking at picture books, and the toddler can listen to short stories and begin to use beads and clocks to make her own sequences. The more structured pattern, story, calendar, clock, and other time activities described next are for children older than four and one-half.

DAILY SCHEDULE

8:00 A.M.—8:30 A.M.
Breakfast

8:30 A.M.—9:00 A.M.
Playtime
Outdoors or in Gym

9:00 A.M.—9:15 A.M.
Group Meeting

9:15 A.M.—10:30 A.M.
Center Activities

10:30 A.M.—10:45 A.M.
Snack

10:45 A.M.—11:15 A.M.
Playtime
Outdoors or in Gym

FIGURE 19–2   A picture/word daily schedule supports the development of the concept of time sequence (continued on next page).

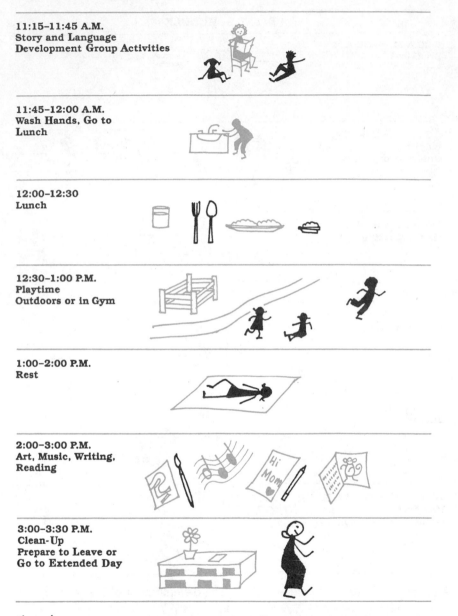

11:15–11:45 A.M.
Story and Language
Development Group Activities

11:45–12:00 A.M.
Wash Hands, Go to
Lunch

12:00–12:30
Lunch

12:30–1:00 P.M.
Playtime
Outdoors or in Gym

1:00–2:00 P.M.
Rest

2:00–3:00 P.M.
Art, Music, Writing,
Reading

3:00–3:30 P.M.
Clean-Up
Prepare to Leave or
Go to Extended Day

FIGURE 19–2   *continued*

ACTIVITIES

TIME: SEQUENCE PATTERNS

OBJECTIVE: To be able to understand and use the sequence idea of *next*.

MATERIALS: Any real things that can be easily sequenced by category, color, shape, size, etc. Some examples are listed.
◆ Wooden beads and strings
◆ Plastic eating utensils
◆ Poker chips or buttons or coins
◆ Shapes cut from cardboard
◆ Small toy animals or people

NATURALISTIC AND INFORMAL ACTIVITIES: Having had opportunities to explore the objects listed above, the children should be familiar with the names of all the items and be able to identify their colors. For example, a child selects all the horses from a container of animals: "You have all the horses: brown ones (teacher points), black (teacher points), and white (teacher points)."

STRUCTURED ACTIVITIES: In this case, plastic eating utensils are used as the example. There are knives (K), forks (F), and spoons (S) in three colors (C_1, C_2, and C_3). The teacher sets up a pattern to present to the child. Many kinds of patterns can be presented. Any of the following may be used:
◆ Color: C_1-C_2-C_1-C_2 . . .
   C_2-C_3-C_3-C_2-C_3-C_3 . . .
◆ Identity: K-F-S-K-F-S . . .
   K-S-S-K-S-S . . .

Say to the child: THIS PATTERN IS KNIFE, FORK, SPOON (or whatever pattern is set up). WHAT COMES NEXT? When the child has the idea of pattern, then set up the pattern and say, THIS IS A PATTERN. LOOK IT OVER. WHAT COMES NEXT?

FOLLOW-UP: Do the same activity with some of the other materials suggested. Also try it with the magnet board, flannelboard, and chalkboard.

TIME: SEQUENCE STORIES

OBJECTIVE: To learn sequences of events through stories.

MATERIALS: Picture storybooks* that have clear and repetitive sequences of events, such as
◆ *The Gingerbread Man*
◆ *The Three Little Pigs*
◆ *The Three Billy Goats Gruff*
◆ *Henny Penny*
◆ *Caps for Sale*
◆ *Brown Bear, Brown Bear*
◆ *Polar Bear, Polar Bear*

NATURALISTIC AND INFORMAL ACTIVITIES: Place the books in the library center where children can make selections during center time, rest time, or book time. Note which children appear to be familiar with the stories as they turn the pages pretending to read to themselves, a friend, or a doll or stuffed animal.

STRUCTURED ACTIVITIES: Read the stories several times until the children are familiar with them. Begin by asking, WHAT HAPPENS NEXT? before going on to the next event. Have the children say some of the repeated phrases such as "Little pigs, little pigs, let me come in," "Not by the hair on my chinny-chin-chin," "Then I'll huff and I'll puff and I'll blow your house in." Have the children try to repeat the list of those who chase the Gingerbread Man. Have them recall the whole story sequence.

FOLLOW-UP: Obtain some sequence story cards, such as Life Cycles Puzzles and Stories® from Insect Lore, or Lakeshore's Logical Sequence Tiles® and Classroom Sequencing Card Library.® Encourage children to reenact and retell the stories and events that are read to them. Encourage them to pretend to read familiar storybooks. This kind of activity helps with comprehending the stories and the sequences of events in them.

*References in Appendix B

TIME: SEQUENCE ACTIVITY, GROWING SEEDS

OBJECTIVE: To experience the sequence of the planting of a seed and the growth of a plant.

MATERIALS: Radish or lima bean seeds, Styrofoam cups, sharp pencil, 6-inch paper plate, some rich soil, a tablespoon.

NATURALISTIC AND INFORMAL ACTIVITIES: During center time provide dirt and small shovels, rakes, pots, and so on in the sand and water table. Talk with the children about what else they might need in order to grow something. Note if they talk about planting seeds.

STRUCTURED ACTIVITIES:
1. Give the child a Styrofoam cup. Have her make a drainage hole in the bottom with the sharp pencil.
2. Set the cup on the paper plate.
3. Have the child put dirt in the cup up to about an inch from the top.
4. Have the child poke three holes in the dirt with her pointer finger.
5. Have her put one seed in each hole and cover the seeds with dirt.
6. Have the child put in 1 tablespoon of water.
7. Place the pots in a sunny place, and watch their sequence of growth.
8. Have the children water the plants each day. Have them record how many days go by before the first plant pops through the soil.

FOLLOW-UP: Plant other types of seeds. Make a chart, or obtain a chart that shows the sequence of growth of a seed. Discuss which steps take place before the plant breaks through the ground. In the fall use the book *It's Pumpkin Time* by Zoe Hall (Scholastic) to introduce a seed project and how we get the pumpkins we carve for Halloween.

TIME: THE FIRST CALENDAR

OBJECTIVE: To learn what a calendar is and how it can be used to keep track of time.

MATERIALS: A one-week calendar is cut from poster board with sections for each of the seven days identified by name. In each section, tabs are cut with a razor blade to hold signs made to be slipped under the tabs to indicate special times and events or the daily weather. These signs may have pictures of birthday cakes, items seen on field trips, umbrellas to show rainy days, the sun to show fair days, and so on.

NATURALISTIC AND INFORMAL ACTIVITIES: In the writing center or in the dramatic play center, place a number of different types of calendars. Note if the children know what they are and if they use them in their pretend play activities. Ask them to explain how they are using them. Where else have they seen calendars? Who uses them?

STRUCTURED ACTIVITIES: Each day the calendar can be discussed. Key questions may include:
◆ WHAT IS THE NAME OF TODAY?
◆ WHAT IS THE NAME OF YESTERDAY?
◆ WHAT IS THE NAME OF TOMORROW?
◆ WHAT DAY COMES AFTER_____?
◆ WHAT DID WE DO YESTERDAY?
◆ DO WE GO TO SCHOOL ON SATURDAY AND SUNDAY?
◆ HOW MANY DAYS UNTIL_____?
◆ HOW MANY DAYS OF THE WEEK DO WE GO TO SCHOOL?
◆ WHAT DAY OF THE WEEK IS THE FIRST DAY OF SCHOOL?
◆ WHAT DAY OF THE WEEK IS THE LAST DAY OF SCHOOL?

CAUTION: You do not have to ask every question every day. The calendar is still an abstract item for young children. See the cautionary article by Sidney Schwartz (1994) listed in the unit references.

FOLLOW-UP: Read *Today Is Monday* by Eric Carle (Scholastic). Discuss which foods the students like to eat on each day of the week. They could draw/dictate/write their own weekly menus.

TIME: THE USE OF THE CLOCK

OBJECTIVE: To find out how we use the clock to tell us when it is time to change activity.

MATERIALS: School wall clock and a handmade or a purchased large clock face such as that made by the Judy Company.

NATURALISTIC AND INFORMAL ACTIVITIES: Place a large wooden toy clock in the dramatic play center. Note if the children use it as a dramatic play prop. Do they use time words? Do they make a connection to the clock on the classroom wall or to the daily schedule picture?

STRUCTURED ACTIVITY: Point out the wall clock to the children. Show them the clock face. Let them move the hands around. Explain how the clock face is made just like the real clock face. Show them how you can set the hands on the clock face so that they are the same as the ones on the real clock. Each day set the clock face for important times (such as cleanup, lunch, time to get up from the nap, etc.). Explain that when the real clock and the clock face have their hands in the same place, it will be time to (do whatever the next activity is).

FOLLOW-UP: Do this every day. Soon each child will begin to catch on and check the clocks. Instead of asking "When do we get up from our nap?," they will be able to check for themselves.

TIME: BEAT THE CLOCK GAME

OBJECTIVE: To learn how time limits the amount of activity that can be done.

MATERIALS: Minute Minder® or similar timer.

NATURALISTIC AND INFORMAL ACTIVITIES: Note how children react to time limit warnings (e.g., five minutes until cleanup). Use a signal (bell, buzzer, dim the lights, etc., as a cue). Note if the children react with an understanding of time limits (five minutes to clean up the room).

STRUCTURED ACTIVITIES: Have the child see how much of some activity can be done in a set number of minutes, for example, three to five.
1. How many pennies can be put in a penny bank one at a time?
2. How many times can he bounce a ball?
3. How many paper clips can he pick up one at a time with a magnet?
4. How many times can he move across the room: walking, crawling, running, going backward, sideways, etc. Set the timer for three to five minutes. When the bell rings the child must stop. Then count to find out how much was accomplished.

FOLLOW-UP: Try many different kinds of activities and different lengths of time. Have several children do the tasks at the same time. Who does the most in the time given?

TIME: DISCUSSION TOPICS FOR LANGUAGE

OBJECTIVE: To develop time word use through discussion.

MATERIALS: Pictures collected or purchased. The following book may be used for this purpose:
Rutland, J. (1976). *Time*. New York: Grosset and Dunlap.
Pictures could show the following.
◆ Day and night
◆ Activities that take a long time and a short time
◆ Picture sequences that illustrate times of day, yesterday, today, and tomorrow
◆ Pictures that illustrate the seasons of the year
◆ Pictures that show early and late

NATURALISTIC AND INFORMAL ACTIVITIES: During center time place the time pictures on a table. Observe as the children examine the pictures. Note if they use any time words. Ask them to describe the pictures.

STRUCTURED ACTIVITIES: Discuss the pictures using the key time words.

FOLLOW-UP: Put pictures on the bulletin board that the children can look at and talk about during their free playtime.

EXAMPLE WORLD WIDE WEB ACTIVITIES.

◆ Today's the day at http://www.pbs.org/arthur/useandmakeacalendar
◆ It's about time at http://www.pbs.org/kids/noddy/makeclocks

Evaluation

The teacher should note whether the child's use of time words increases. He should also note whether her sense of time and sequence develops to a more mature level: Does she remember the order of events? Can she wait until one thing is finished before she starts another? Does she talk about future and past events? How does she use the calendar? The clock? The sequence stories? The teacher may use the individual interview tasks in this unit and in Appendix A.

Summary

The young child can begin to learn that time has duration and that time is related to sequences of events. The child first relates time to his personal experience and to his daily sequence of activities. It is not until the child enters the concrete operations period that he can use units of time in the ways that adults use them.

The young child learns his concept of time through naturalistic and informal experiences for the most part. When he is around the age of four and one-half or five, he can do structured activities also.

KEY TERMS

sequence
duration
personal experience
social activity
cultural time

Time words: general
      specific
      relational
      specific duration
      special days

SUGGESTED ACTIVITIES

1. Observe some young children engaged in group play. Record any examples of time measurement that take place. Which stages of measurement did each incident represent?
2. In class, discuss some ways that time measurement skills can be developed through home and school activities.
3. Plan and gather materials for at least one time sequence and one time measurement activity. Do the activities with a small group of young children. Report the results in class.
4. Use the evaluation scheme in Activity 7, Unit 9, to evaluate one of the following selections.

   Changes around Us. Pleasantville, NY: Sunburst Technologies. (K–2). Explores the seasons and the growing cycles of plants and animals.

   Trudy's Time and Place House. Pleasantville, NY: Sunburst Technologies. Includes clocks, calendars, directions and maps.
5. Add some time measurement activities to your file/notebook.

REVIEW

A. Describe and compare time sequence and time duration.

B. Decide if the children's comments below reflect (a) time sequence, (b) time duration, or (c) neither sequence nor duration:
1. A child playing with a ball says, "The ball went up high."
2. Mario asks his dad, "Please read me a bear story at bedtime."
3. Janie says, "I stayed with Grandma for three nights."
4. Lindsey says, "I love to play with Daddy for hours and hours."
5. Li says, "It's lunchtime, everybody."
6. Donny says, "This box weighs a million tons."
7. Tina sighs, "It took me a long time to draw the pictures in my dog book."

C. Explain the three kinds of time. Include an example of each type.

D. Decide which of the words in the list below are (a) general time words, (b) specific time words, (c) relational words, (d) specific duration words, or (e) special day words:
1. yesterday
2. three hours
3. this afternoon
4. Easter
5. twice
6. four years old
7. birthday
8. two minutes
9. today

E. Explain the NCTM (2000) expectations for preschool/kindergarten time understanding.

REFERENCE

National Council of Teachers of Mathematics. (2000). *Principles and standards for school mathematics.* Reston, VA: Author. (http://www.nctm.org)

FURTHER READING AND RESOURCES

AIMS Educational Products. AIMS Education Foundation, P.O. Box 8120, Fresno, CA 93747-8120.

Church, E. B. (1997). "Is it time yet?" *Early Childhood Today* (January), 33–34.

Copley, J. V. (2000). *The young child and mathematics.* Washington, DC: National Association for the Education of Young Children.

Copley, J. V. (Ed.). (1999). *Mathematics in the early years.* Washington, DC: National Association for the Education of Young Children.

Czerniak, C. M. (1993). The Jurassic spark. *Science and Children, 31*(2), 19–22.

Daugherty, B. (1993). The great bone search. *Science and Children, 31*(2), 14–16.

Friederitzer, F. J., & Berman, B. (1999). The language of time. *Teaching Children Mathematics, 6*(4), 254–259.

Pliske, C. (2000). Natural cycles: Coming full circle. *Science and Children, 37*(6), 35–39, 60.

Richardson, K. (1999). *Developing number concepts: Planning guide.* Parsippany, NJ: Dale Seymour.

Schwartz, S. (1994). Calendar reading: A tradition that begs remodeling. *Teaching Children Mathematics* (1), 104–109.

Schwartz, S. (1995). Authentic mathematics in the classroom. *Teaching Children Mathematics* (1), 580–584.

Seefeldt, C., & Tinnie, S. (1985). Dinosaurs: The past is present. *Young Children, 40*(4), 20–24.

Shimabukuro, M. A., & Fearing, V. (1993). How does your garlic grow? *Science and Children, 30*(8), 8–11.

Srulowitz, F. (1992). Diary of a tree. *Science and Children, 29*(5), 19–21.

Timberlake, P. (1986). Time concepts in the classroom: What is today? *Dimensions, 15*(1), 5–7.

Young, S. L. (1990). Ideas: Dinosaur data. *Arithmetic Teacher, 38*(1), 23–33.

UNIT 20
Interpreting Data Using Graphs

OBJECTIVES

After reading this unit, you should be able to:

◆ Explain the use of graphs.

◆ Describe the three stages that young children go through in making graphs.

◆ List materials to use for making graphs.

◆ Describe the NCTM (2000) expectations for preschool/ kindergarten level graphing activities and understanding.

The NCTM (2000, p.108) expectations for data analysis for prekindergarten and kindergarten focus on children sorting and classifying objects according to their attributes, organizing data about the objects, and describing the data and what they show. "The main purpose of collecting data is to answer questions when the answers are not immediately obvious" (NCTM, 2000, p.109). Children's questions should be the major source of data. The beginnings of data collection are included in the fundamental concepts learned and applied in classifying in a logical fashion (Unit 10).

Data collection activities can begin even before kindergarten as students collect sets of data from their real life experiences and depict the results of their data collection in simple graphs. Consider the following example as it takes place in Ms. Moore's classroom:

Ms. Moore hears George and Sam talking in loud voices. She goes near them and hears the following discussion.

George: "More kids like green than blue."
Sam: "No! No! More like blue!"

George: "You are all wrong."
Sam: "I am not. You are wrong."

Ms. Moore goes over to the boys and asks, "What's the trouble, boys?" George replies, "We have to get paint to paint the house Mr. Brown helped us build. I say it should be green. Sam says it should be blue."

Sam insists, "More kids like blue than green."

Ms. Moore asks, "How can we find out? How do we decide on questions like who will be our next president?" George and Sam looked puzzled. Then George says, "I remember when Mom and Dad voted. We could have the class vote." Sam agreed that this would be a good idea. Ms. Moore then asked them how they might have all the students vote. They were afraid that if they asked for a show of hands their classmates might just copy whoever voted first. Ms. Moore than suggested that they put out a green box and a blue box and a bowl of green and blue cube blocks. George's eyes lit up. "I see then each person could vote by putting either a blue block in the blue box or a green block in the green box." Sam agreed.

After setting up the boxes and blocks, Sam and George go around the room. They explain the problem to each child. Each child comes over to the table. They each choose one block of the color they like better and place the block in the matching box. When the voting is completed, George and Sam empty the boxes and stack the blocks as shown in Figure 20–1.

Ms. Moore asks the boys what the vote shows. Sam says, "The green stack is higher. More children like the idea of painting the house green." "Good," answers Ms. Moore, "would you like me to write that down for you?" Sam and George chorus, "Yes!"

"I have an idea," says George, "Let's make a picture of this for the bulletin board so everyone will know. Will you help us, Ms. Moore?"

Ms. Moore shows them how to cut out squares of green and blue paper to match each of the blocks used. The boys write "green" and "blue" on a piece of white paper and then paste the green squares next to the word "green" and the blue squares next to the word "blue." Ms. Moore shows them how to write the title: "Choose the Color for the Playhouse." Then they glue

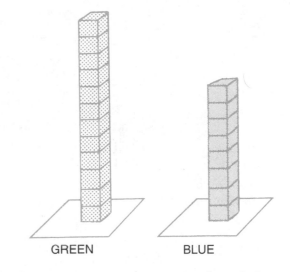

FIGURE 20–1   A three-dimensional graph that compares children's preferences for green or blue.

the description of the results at the bottom. The results can be seen in Figure 20–2.

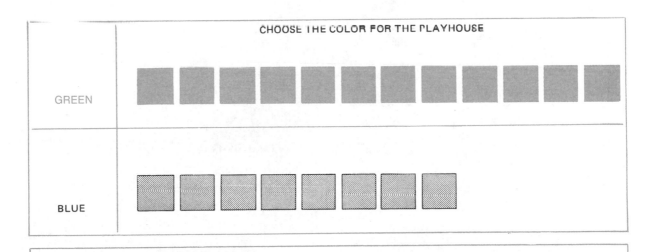

FIGURE 20–2   The color preference graph is copied using squares of green and blue paper, and the children dictate their interpretation.

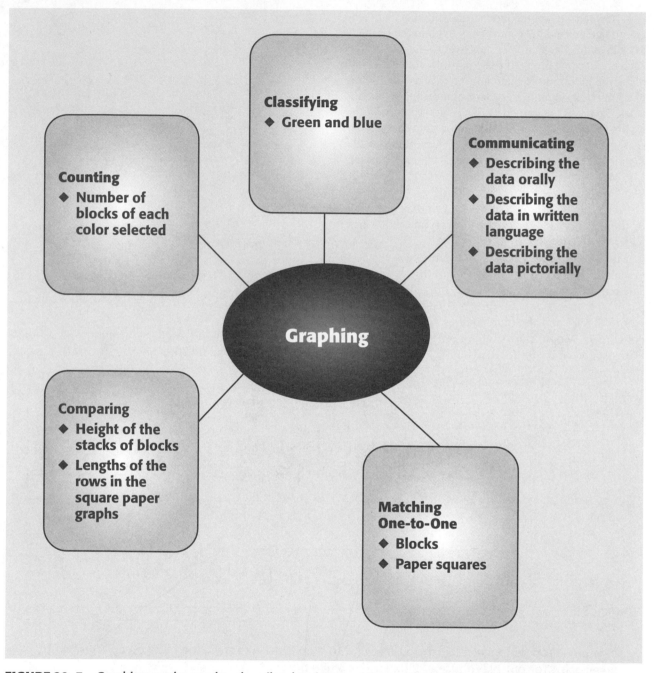

FIGURE 20–3 Graphing can be used to describe data in any of the content areas and provides an opportunity to apply fundamental concepts and skills.

In the preceding example, the teacher helped the children solve their problem by helping them make two kinds of graphs. Graphs are used to show visually two or more comparisons in a clear way. When a child makes a graph, he uses basic skills such as classification, counting, comparing quantities, one-to-one matching, and communicating through describing data. By making a concrete structure or a picture that shows some type of information, they visualize a variety of different quantities. Graphing provides an opportunity to apply several fundamental concepts and skills as illustrated in Figure 20–3.

Stages of Development for Making and Understanding Graphs

The types of graphs that young children can construct progress through five stages of development. The first three stages are described in this unit. The fourth is included in Unit 25 and the fifth in Unit 31. In stage one, object graphs, the child uses real objects to make her graph. Sam and George used cube blocks. At this stage only two things are compared. The main basis for comparison is one-to-one correspondence and visualization of length and height.

In stage two, picture graphs, more than two items are compared. In addition, a more permanent record is made—such as when Sam and George in an earlier example glued squares of paper on a piece of paper for the bulletin board. An example of this type of graph is shown in Figure 20–4. The teacher has lined off 12 columns on poster board (or large construction paper). Each column stands for one month of the year. Each child is given a paper circle. Crayons, water markers, glue, and yarn scraps are available so each child can draw her own head and place it on the month for her birthday. When each child has put her "head" on the graph, the children can compare the months to see which month has the most birthdays.

In stage three, square paper graphs, the children progress through the use of more pictures to block charts. They no longer need to use real objects but can start right off with cutout squares of paper. Figure 20–5 shows this type of graph. In this stage, the children work more independently.

April has the most birthdays. There are four.
March and October have no birthdays.
Three months have three.
One month has two.
Five months have one.

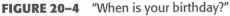

FIGURE 20–4   "When is your birthday?"

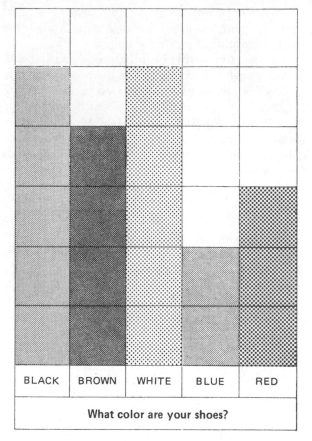

BLACK	BROWN	WHITE	BLUE	RED

What color are your shoes?

FIGURE 20–5 A block graph made with paper squares.

Discussion of a Graph

As the children talk about their graphs and dictate descriptions for them, they use concept words. They use words such as

less than	the same as
more than	none
fewer than	all
longer, longest	some
shorter, shortest	a lot of
the most	higher
the least	taller

Materials for Making Graphs

There are many kinds of materials that can be used for the first stage graphs. An example has been shown in which cube blocks were used. Other materials can be used just as well.

At first it is best to use materials that can be kept in position without being knocked down or pushed apart by young children. Stands can be made from dowel rods. A washer or curtain ring is then placed on the dowel to represent each thing or person (Figure 20–6[A]). Strings and beads can be used. The strings can be hung from hooks or a rod; the lengths are then compared (Figure 20–6[B]). Unifix Cubes® (Figure 20–6[C]) or pop beads (Figure 20–6[D]) can also be used.

Once the children have worked with the more stable materials, they can use the cube blocks and any other things that can be lined up. Poker chips, bottle caps, coins, spools, corks, and beans are good for this type of graph work (Figure 20–7).

At the second stage, graphs can be made with these same materials but with more comparisons made. Then the child can go on to more permanent recording by gluing down cutout pictures or markers of some kind (Figure 20–8).

At the third stage, the children can use paper squares. This prepares the way for the use of squared paper. (This will be included in Unit 25.)

Topics for Graphs

Any type of student question can be researched and the information put into graphical form. For example, a group of kindergartners collected information about their school bus (Colburn & Tate, 1998) while another group of young children studied a tree that grows on their campus (El Harim, 1998).

Once children start making graphs, they often think of problems to solve on their own. The following are some comparisons that might be of interest:

◆ number of brothers and sisters
◆ hair color, eye color, clothing colors

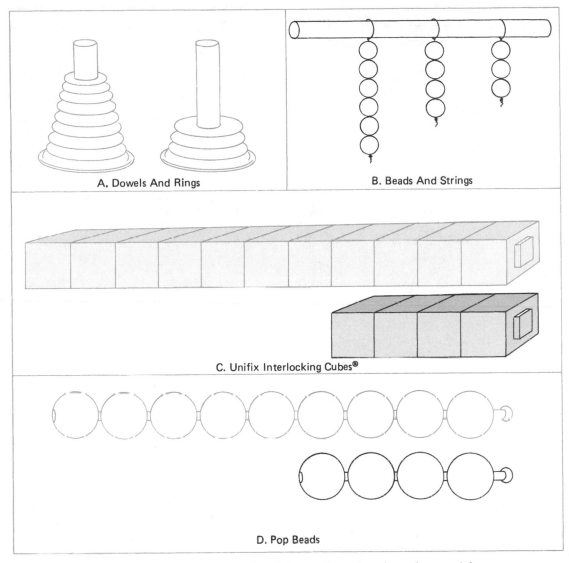

A. Dowels And Rings

B. Beads And Strings

C. Unifix Interlocking Cubes®

D. Pop Beads

FIGURE 20–6   Four examples of three-dimensional graph materials.

- kinds of pets children have
- heights of children in the class
- number of children in class each day
- sizes of shoes
- favorite TV programs (or characters)
- favorite foods
- favorite colors
- favorite storybooks

- type of weather each day for a month
- number of cups of water or sand that will fill different containers
- time, in seconds, to run across the playground
- number of baby hamsters class members predict that their female hamster will bear
- number of days class members predict that it will take for their bean seeds to sprout

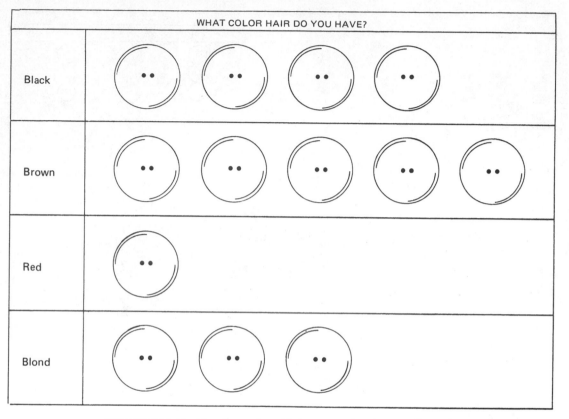

FIGURE 20–7   Graph made with buttons glued to cardboard.

- data obtained regarding sinking and floating objects (Unit 10)
- comparison of the number of seeds found in an apple, an orange, a lemon, and a grapefruit
- students' predictions regarding items that will be attracted and not attracted by magnets
- frequency with which different types of insects are found on the playground
- distance that rollers will roll when ramps of different degrees of steepness are used
- comparison of the number of different items that are placed in a balance pan to weigh the same as a standard weight
- frequency count of each color in a bag of m&m's,® Skittles,® or Trix®
- frequency with which the various combinations of yellow and orange show up when the counters (orange on one side and yellow on the other) are shaken and tossed out on the table.

Summary

Making graphs provides a means for use of some of the basic math skills in a creative way. Children can put into a picture form the results of classifying, comparing, counting, and measuring activities. Graphs also serve as a means of integrating mathematics with other content areas such as science and social studies

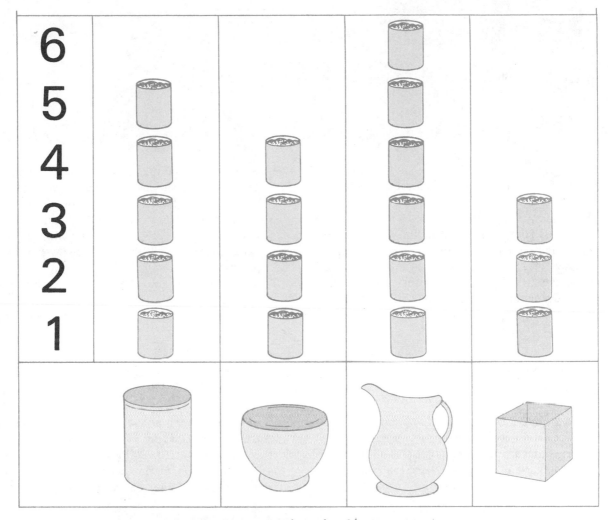

FIGURE 20–8 Graph made with paper cutouts.

through providing a vehicle for depicting and analyzing data.

The first graphs are three dimensional and made with real objects. The next are made with pictures and the next with paper squares. Children can discuss the results of their graph projects and dictate a description of the meaning of the graph to be put on the bulletin board with the graph.

KEY TERMS

graphs
stage one, object graphs

stage two, picture graphs
stage three, square paper graphs

SUGGESTED ACTIVITIES

1. Interview several prekindergarten and kindergarten teachers. Find out if and how they use graphs in their classrooms. Report your findings in class.
2. With a small group of four-, five-, and/or six-year-olds, discuss some topics that might be of interest for collecting some information and making a graph. Then make the graph with the group. Bring the graph to class, and explain the process to the class.
3. Use the evaluation scheme in Activity 7, Unit 9, to evaluate one of the following graphing software programs:

Graphers. Pleasantville, NY: Sunburst Technologies. Data are supplied for making a variety of graphs. Products can be printed out.

Muppet Math. Pleasantville, NY: Sunburst Technologies. Simple program that includes graphing experiences as well as experiences with shapes, patterns, and counting.

Find out if there is any other graphing software for young children.

4. Add ideas for graphs to your Activity File/ Notebook.

REVIEW

A. Explain the importance and values of graph making.
B. There are three levels of making and understanding graphs that are appropriate for prekindergarten and kindergarten students. Name and describe each of these stages.

C. Sketch out a graph at each of the three beginning stages of graph making.
D. Describe the NCTM (2000) expectations for preschool and kindergarten students constructing and analyzing information displayed in graphs.

REFERENCES

Colburn, K., & Tate, P. (1998). The big, yellow laboratory. *Science and Children, 36*(1), 22–25.

El Harim, J. L. (1998). A *tree*mendous learning experience. *Science and Children, 35*(8), 26–29.

National Council of Teachers of Mathematics. (2000). *Principles and standards for school mathematics.* Reston, VA: Author. (http://www.nctm.org)

FURTHER READING AND RESOURCES

AIMS Educational Products. AIMS Education Foundation, P.O. Box 8120, Fresno, CA 93747-8120.

Barnett, C. S. (1991). Ideas: Sneaker data. *Arithmetic Teacher, 38*(5), 26–33.

Copley, J. V. (2000). *The young child and mathematics.* Washington, DC: National Association for the Education of Young Children.

Copley, J. V. (Ed.). (1999). *Mathematics in the early years.* Washington, DC: National Association for the Education of Young Children.

Curcio, F. R., & Folkson, S. (1996). Exploring data: Kindergarten children do it their way. *Teaching Children Mathematics, 2,* 382–385.

Helm, J. H. (1997, January). On the path to math. *Early Childhood Today,* 9.

Irons, C., & Irons, R. (1991). Ideas levels K–2: What's the weather? *Arithmetic Teacher, 39*(2), 26, 29.

Lamphere, P. (1994). Classroom data. *Teaching Children Mathematics, 1,* 28–31.

Litton, N. (1995). Graphing from A to Z. *Teaching Children Mathematics, 2,* 220–223.

McGrath, B. B. (1994). *The m&m's® brand counting book.* Watertown, MA: Charlesbridge.

National Council of Teachers of Mathematics (NCTM). (1989). *Curriculum and evaluation standards for school mathematics.* Reston, VA: Author.

Olson, M., & Easley, B. (1996). Math by the month: It could be! . . . Well, Maybe? *Teaching Children Mathematics, 2,* 358.

Pearlman, S., & Pericak-Spector, K. (1995). Graph that data! *Science and Children, 32*(4), 35–37.

Richardson, K. (1999). *Developing number concepts: Planning guide.* Parsippany, NJ: Dale Seymour.

Russell, S. J., & Stone, A. (1990). *Counting: Ourselves and our families.* Palo Alto, CA: Dale Seymour.

Schwartz, S. L. (1995). Authentic mathematics in the classroom. *Teaching Children Mathematics,* 1, 580–584.

Spurlin, Q. (1995). Put science in a bag. *Science and Children, 32*(4), 19–22.

Young, S. L. (1990). Ideas: Dinosaur data. *Arithmetic Teacher, 38*(1), 23–33.

Young, S. L. (1990). Ideas: Popcorn data. *Arithmetic Teacher, 38*(2), 24–33.

Young, S. L. (1990). Ideas: Ball data. *Arithmetic Teacher, 38*(3), 23–32.

Young, S. L. (1991). Ideas: Pizza math. *Arithmetic Teacher, 38*(8), 26–33.

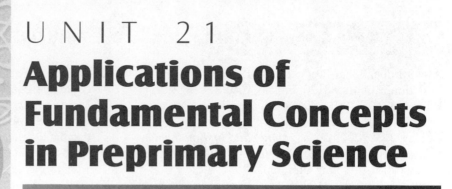

UNIT 21

Applications of Fundamental Concepts in Preprimary Science

OBJECTIVES

After reading this unit, you should be able to:

◆ Apply the concepts and skills related to ordering and patterning, measuring, and graphing to science lessons and units at the preprimary level.

◆ Design science lessons that include naturalistic, informal, and structured activities.

The *National Science Education Standards* emphasize the inquiring nature of children and the responsibility of teachers to provide appropriate classroom settings for children to carry out inquiry investigations. This unit presents activities, lessons, and scenarios that focus on the fundamental concepts, attitudes, and skills of ordering and patterning, measuring, and graphing as they apply to experiences in preprimary science investigations.

Ordering and Patterning

Underlying the concept of patterning are the concepts of comparing and ordering. Ordering is a higher level of comparing because ordering involves comparing more than two things or more than two sets. It also involves placing things in a sequence from

first to last. In Piaget's terms, this ordering is called seriation. Children must have some understanding of seriation to do the more advanced skill of patterning.

Ordering and patterning build on the skills of comparing. If children have not had prior experience in comparing, they will not be ready to order and find patterns. The following activities involve using a science emphasis in shape, animals, color, and sound while making or discovering visual, auditory, and motor regularities.

1. **Sun, moon, and stars.** Use your flannelboard to help children recognize patterns in flannel figures of the moon, sun, and star shapes. Start the activity by discussing the shapes in the night sky. Then, place the moon, sun, and star shapes in a pattern on the flannelboard. Make a game of placing a figure in the pattern and having the children decide which figure comes next. As the

FIGURE 21–1   Cindy creates a pattern.

children go through the process of making a pattern with the flannel figures, they are also reinforcing the concept of shapes existing in the night sky (Figure 21–1).

The natural patterns found in the night sky are an ideal observational activity for young children. When the sun goes down and the child can see the moon and stars, it is time to observe the night sky. Observing the changes in the sky from day to night reinforces the patterns that children learn at a very young age. Children may also be aware of the changes in the shape of the moon and want to draw those shapes.

2. **Animal patterns.** Make patterns for shapes that go together in some way such as zebra, tiger, leopard (wild animals), or pig, duck, and cow (farm animals). After introducing children to the pattern game described above, have them manipulate tagboard animal shapes in the same way.

3. **Changing colors.** Create original patterns in necklaces by dyeing macaroni with food color. Children will be fascinated by the necklace and by the change in the appearance of the macaroni. Have children help prepare the macaroni: mix one tablespoon of alcohol, three drops of food coloring, and a cup of macaroni in a glass jar. Screw the lid on tightly, and take turns shak-

ing the jar. Then, lay the macaroni out on a piece of newspaper to dry overnight. Do this for each color you select. Have children compare the macaroni before and after dyeing and describe the similarities and differences.

4. **Stringing macaroni.** To help children string macaroni, tie one end through a piece of tagboard. Then, have students practice stringing the macaroni on the string. When they are comfortable, let each invent a pattern of colors. The pattern is then repeated over and over until the necklace is completed. Have the children say aloud the patterns they are stringing, for example, "Red, blue, yellow; red, blue, yellow," until they complete the necklace. In this way, the auditory pattern is reinforced as well as the visual pattern. To extend this activity, have children guess each other's patterns, tell patterns, and try to duplicate patterns. Children will enjoy wearing their creations when they dress up for a Thanksgiving feast (Figure 21–2).

Sound Patterns

In the following scenario, Mrs. Jones introduces sound patterns to her kindergarten children.

Mrs. Jones brings out plastic bells. She selects three widely varied tones, rings them for the children, and asks, "Can you tell me what you hear?" Jane responds, "Bells, I hear bells!" The teacher asks, "Do any of the bells sound different?" "Yes," the children say. "In what way do they sound different?" Mrs. Jones asks. "Some sound like Tinkerbell, and some do not,"

FIGURE 21–2   Macaroni necklaces make a pattern.

George responds. After giving the children a chance to ring the bells, Mrs. Jones puts out a red, a yellow, and a blue construction paper square on a table. She asks, "Will someone put the bell with the highest sound on the red card?" After Lai completes the task, Mrs. Jones asks the children to find a bell that has a low sound, and finally, one with the lowest sound. Each bell has its own color square.

Patterns can be found in the sounds that rubber bands make. Construct a rubber band banjo by placing three different widths of rubber bands around a cigar box, the open end of a coffee can, milk carton, or margarine tub. Have children experiment with the rubber band "strings" of varying length, and see if they notice differences in sound. Playing around with strings and homemade instruments helps prepare children for future concept development in sound.

Rhythmic patterns can be found in classic poems and songs such as "There Was a Little Turtle." Have children add actions as they sing the song.

> There was a little turtle
> He lived in a box
> He swam in a puddle
> He climbed on the rocks
> He snapped at a mosquito
> He snapped at a flea
> He snapped at a minnow
> And he snapped at me.
> He caught the mosquito
> He caught the flea
> He caught the minnow
> But he didn't catch me.

Making Patterns with a Computer Program

A number of computer programs exist that allow children to draw. Most of these have "stamps" that children can use in their pictures. For example, a child might choose a "stamp" of a tree, a person, a heart, or a star. Children enjoy selecting stamps and colors for making patterns. Children can work in pairs to repeat each other's patterns or design new ones. KidWare, KidWorks, and Kid Pix are three programs that seem to be popular with children and adults.

Measurement: Volume, Weight, Length, Temperature

The *National Science Education Standards* emphasize that the meaning of measurement and how to use measurement tools are a part of any investigation. These ideas are introduced frequently throughout the early years.

Measurement is basically a spatial activity that must include the manipulation of objects to be understood. If children are not actively involved with materials as they measure, they simply will not understand measurement. Water and sand are highly sensory science resources for young children. Both substances elicit a variety of responses to their physical properties, and they can be used in measurement activities. Keep in mind that for sand and water to be effective as learning tools, long periods of "messing around" with the substances should be provided. For further information on the logistics of handling water and sand and a discussion of basic equipment needs, see Unit 39 of this book. The following activities and lessons use sand and water as a means of introducing measurement.

1. **Fill it up.** Put out containers and funnels of different sizes and shapes, and invite children to pour liquid from one to the other. Aspects of pouring can be investigated. Ask, "Is it easier to pour from a wide- or narrow-mouthed container?," "Do you see anything that could help you pour liquid into a container?," and "Does the funnel take longer? Why?" Add plastic tubing to the water center. Ask, "Can a tube be used to fill up a container?" and "Which takes longer?" (Figure 21–3).

2. **Squeeze and blow.** Plastic squeeze bottles or turkey basters will encourage children to find another way to fill the containers. After the children have manipulated the baster and observed air bubbling out of it, set up the water table for a race. You will need table tennis balls, tape, and basters. The object is to move the ball across the water by squeezing the turkey baster. Children should practice squeezing the baster and moving the balls across the water. Place a piece of tape down the center of the table lengthwise,

FIGURE 21–3 "Can a tube be used to fill a container?"

FIGURE 21–4 Children explore volume by weighing sand.

and begin. Use a piece of string to measure how far the ball is moved. Compare the distances with the length of string. Ask, "How many squeezes does it take to cover the distance?"

3. **A cup is a cup.** Volume refers to how much space a solid, liquid, or gas takes up or occupies. For example, when a one-cup measure is full of water, the volume of water is one cup. Volume can be compared by having children fill small boxes or jars with sand or beans. Use sand in similar containers, and compare the way the sand feels. Compare the heft of a full container with an empty container. Use a balance scale to dramatize the difference. If you do not have a commercial balance, provide a homemade balance and hanging cups. Children will begin to weigh different levels of sand in the cups. Statements such as, "I wonder if sand weighs more if I fill the container even higher?" can be overheard. Let children check predictions and discuss what they have found (Figure 21–4).

4. **Sink or float.** Comparisons between big-little and heavy-light are made when children discover that objects of different sizes sink and float. Make a chart to record observations. After discussing what the terms *sink* and *float* mean, give the children a variety of floating and non-floating objects to manipulate. Ask, "What do you think will float? Big corks? Small marbles?" As children sort objects by size and shape and test whether they sink or float, they

are discovering science concepts and learning about measurement (Figure 21–5).

Ms. Moore has her class predict, "Will it sink or float?" Her materials include a leaf, nail, balloon, cork, wooden spoon, and metal spoon. She makes a chart with columns labeled *sink* and *float* and has the children place the leaf and so on where they think they will go.

Cindy excitedly floats the leaf. "It floats, it floats!" she says. Because Cindy correctly predicts that the leaf would float, the leaf stays in the *float* column on the chart. Diana predicts that the metal spoon will float. "Oh, it's not

FIGURE 21–5 "Will it sink or float?"

floating. The metal spoon is sinking." Diana moves the metal spoon from the *float* column to the *sink* column on the chart. In this way, children can predict and compare objects as they measure weight and buoyancy (Figure 21–6).

5. **Little snakes.** Many children in preschool and kindergarten are not yet conserving length. For example, they still think that a stick may vary in length if it is changed in some way. Therefore, use care in assessing your students' developmental stages. The child must be able to conserve for measurement activities to make sense. In the following scenario, a teacher of young children assesses the conservation of length while relating length to animals.

Mrs. Raymond reinforces the shape/space concept by giving each child in her class two pipe cleaners. She instructs them to place the pipe cleaners side by side and asks, "Which pipe

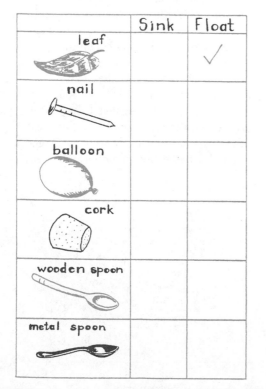

FIGURE 21–6 "Do you think the leaf will sink or float?"

cleaner is longer?" Then she tells the children to bend one of the pipe cleaners and asks, "Which is longer now?" She repeats this several times, having the children create different shapes.

Then the children make the pipe cleaners into little snakes by gluing small construction paper heads on one end of each pipe cleaner. Mrs. Raymond shows the children pictures of a snake that is coiled and one that is moving on the ground (try to find pictures of the same kind of snake). She asks, "Is the coiled snake shorter?" "Yes," the children say. "Let's see if we can make our pipe cleaners into coiled snakes," instructs Mrs. Raymond. "Oh," says Jimmie, "this really looks like a coiled snake."

The teacher asks the students to lay out the other pipe cleaners to resemble a moving snake and asks, "Which is longer?" There are a variety of responses as the children manipulate the pipe cleaner snakes to help them understand that the coiled and moving snakes are the same lengths. Then, have the children glue a small black construction paper end on the end of the pipe cleaners. Let them practice coiling and coiling the "snakes" and discuss how snakes move. Ask, "Can you tell how long a snake is when it is coiled up?" and "Was your coiled-up snake longer than you thought?"

6. **A big and little hunt.** Height, size, and length can be compared in many ways. For example, Mrs. Jones takes her children on a big and little hunt.

After taking the children outside, Mrs. Jones has them sit in a circle and discuss the biggest and smallest things that they can see. Then she asks them, "Of all the things we have talked about, which is the smallest?" George and Mary are certain that the leaves are the smallest, but Sam and Lai do not agree. "The blades of grass are smaller," Sam observes. "Are they?" Mrs. Jones asks. "How can we tell which is smaller?" "Let's put them beside each other," Mary suggests. The children compare the length of each item and discuss which is longer and wider.

7. **Body part measures.** Children enjoy measuring with body parts, such as a hand or foot length. Ask, "How many feet is it to the door?"

and let the children count the number of foot lengths they must take. Or ask, "How many hands high are you?"

Give children pieces of string and have them measure head sizes. Then take the string, and measure other parts of their bodies. Compare their findings.

8. **How long will it take to sink?** Let children play for five minutes with dishpans of water, a kitchen scale, a bucket of water, and an assortment of objects. Then, give the children plastic tubes to explore and measure. As one child drops a marble into a plastic tube filled with water, count in measured beats the amount of time that the marble takes to sink. Ask, "Will it sink faster in cold water or hot water?"

9. **Hot or not.** The following activities and questions correlate with science and, in many cases, integrate into the curriculum of a preschool or kindergarten.

◆ Take an outdoor walk to see what influences the temperature. "Is it warmer or colder outside?"

◆ Visit a greenhouse. Predict what the temperature will be inside the greenhouse; discuss the reasons for these predictions.

◆ Notice differences in temperature in different areas of the supermarket. Ask, "Are some areas colder?" and "Which is the warmest area of the supermarket?"

◆ Melt crayons for dripping on bottles and painting pictures. Notice the effect of heat on the crayons. Ask, "Have you ever felt like a melted crayon?" and "Act out the changes in a melting crayon with your bodies."

◆ Put some finger paints in the refrigerator. Have children compare how the refrigerated paints and room-temperature paints feel on their hands.

◆ Ask, "What happens to whipped cream as we finger paint with it?" Have children observe the whipped cream as it cools off and melts.

◆ Ask, "What happens to an ice cream cone as you eat it?" and "Why do you think this happens?"

Communicating with Graphs

When children make graphs, they use the basic process skills of observing, classifying, comparing, and measuring visually communicated information. In fact, the act of making a graph is in itself the process of communication. A graph is a way of displaying information so that predictions, inferences, and conclusions can be made. Refer to Unit 20 for helpful hints on introducing graphs to children and problem-solving topics that result in graph making.

When using graphs, it is essential that the meaning of the completed graph is clear to the children. With questions and discussion, it is possible for a graph to answer a question, solve a problem, or show data so that something can be understood. In the following scenario, Mrs. Jones uses common kitchen sponges to provide children with an opportunity to manipulate and construct two types of graphs.

Mrs. Jones distributes sponges of different colors to her kindergarten class. After allowing children time to examine the sponges, she suggests that they stack the sponges by color. As the sponges are stacked, a bar graph is naturally created. Mrs. Jones lines up each stack of sponges and asks, "Which color sponge do we have the most of?" Lai says, "The blue stack is the tallest. There are more blue sponges." "Good," answers Mrs. Jones. "Can anyone tell me which stack of sponges is the smallest?" "The yellow ones," says Mary. The children count the number of sponges in each stack and duplicate the three-dimensional sponge graph by making a graph of colored oak tag sponges. The children place pink, blue, yellow, and green oak tag sponges that Mrs. Jones has prepared in columns of color on a tagboard background. In this way, children learn in a concrete way the one-to-one correspondence that a bar graph represents.

Mrs. Jones follows up the graphing activity with other sponge activities. Sam says, "Sponges in my house are usually wet." "Yes," chorus the children. George says, "Our sponges feel heavier, too." The children's comments provide an opportunity to submerge a sponge in water and weigh it. The class weighs the wet and dry sponges, and an experience chart of observations is recorded. The next day, Sam brings in a sponge with bird seed on it. He says, "I am going to keep it damp and see what happens."

Calendar Graph

Calendars are another way to reinforce graphing, the passage of time, and one-to-one correspondence. Mrs. Carter laminates small birthday cakes, and then writes each child's name and birth date on the paper cake with a permanent marker. At the beginning of the year, she shows the children the chart and points out which cake belongs to them. At the beginning of each month, the children with birthdays move their cakes to the calendar. Various animals, trees, and birds can be substituted for cakes (Figure 21–7).

Pets

Graphs can be used to compare sets and give early literacy experiences. Make a list of the pets that your children have. Divide a bristol board into columns to represent every pet named. Cover the board with clear laminate film. Make labels with pet categories such as dogs, cats, snakes, fish, lizards, turtles, and so on. Glue the labels to clothespins. Then, place a labeled clothespin at the top of each column. Have the children write their names in the appropriate column (Figure 21–8).

Favorite Foods

Divide a poster board into columns and paste or draw a picture of each food group at the top of each column. Allow each child to draw a picture of their favorite food and paste it under the appropriate column. Velcro can also be used to attach the pictures, or the children can write their names under their choice.

Graphing Attractions

Simple magnets can be fun to explore. A real object graph can be made with ruled bristol board. Rule the board into columns to equal the number of magnets. Trace the shape of a magnet at the top of each column. Attach a drapery hook below each picture and proceed like Mrs. Carter.

After letting the children explore metal objects such as paper clips, Mrs. Carter places a pile of paper clips on the table along with different types of magnets. She invites Cindy to choose a magnet and see

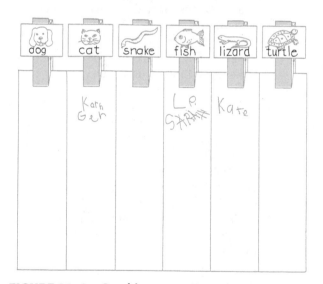

FIGURE 21–7 Calendars reinforce graphing, time, and one-to-one correspondence.

FIGURE 21–8 Graphing our pets.

how many paper clips it will attract. Cindy selects a horseshoe-shaped magnet and hangs paper clips from the end, one at a time, until the magnet no longer attracts any clips. "Good," says Mrs. Carter. "Now, make a chain of the paper clips that your magnet attracts." After Cindy makes the paper clip chain, Mrs. Carter directs her to hang it on the drapery hook under the drawing of the horseshoe-shaped magnet.

"I bet the magnet that looks like a bar will attract more paper clips," predicts Richard. He selects the rod magnet and begins to attract as many paper clips as he can. Then, he makes a chain and hangs it on the drapery hook under the rod magnet. The process is repeated until each child in the group has worked with a magnet. Mrs. Carter makes no attempt to teach the higher-level concepts involved in magnetic force; rather, her purpose is to increase the children's awareness and give them some idea of what magnets do.

In this scenario, children observe that magnets can be different shapes and sizes (horseshoe, rod, disk, the letter U, ring, and so on) and attract a different amount of paper clips. They also have a visual graphic reminder of what they have accomplished. When snack time arrives, Mrs. Carter prepares a plate of metallic-paper-wrapped chocolate candy balls and a jar of peanut butter. She gives each child two large pretzel sticks. The children dip the pretzels into the peanut butter and then "attract" the metallic candy, imitating the way the magnets attracted the paper clips.

Summary

When more than two things are ordered and placed in sequence, the process is called seriation. If children understand seriation, they will be able to do the more advanced skills of patterning. Patterning involves repeating auditory, visual, or physical motor sequences.

Children begin to understand measurement by actively manipulating measurement materials. Water and sand are highly sensory and are effective resources for young children to develop concepts of volume, temperature, length, and weight. Time measurement is related to sequencing events. The use of measurement units will formalize and develop further when children enter the concrete operations period.

Graph making gives children an opportunity to classify, compare, count, measure, and visually communicate information. A graph is a way of displaying information so that predictions, inferences, and conclusions can be made.

KEY TERMS

comparing   ordering   patterning

SUGGESTED ACTIVITIES

1. Interview a preprimary teacher about the kinds of problems and challenges encountered when teaching about ordering and patterning, measurement, and graphing. Ask the teacher to discuss ways that he has overcome or modified the challenges of applying fundamental concepts in preprimary science. Share the interview results with your classmates and compare strategies used by different teachers. Videotape or tape record yourself in a similar teaching situation; this can help to clearly illustrate a problem.
2. To measure is to match things. Observe and record every comparison that one child makes in a day. Record all forms of measuring that you observe this child performing. Teachers will probably tell you that children are not very interested in measuring for its own sake, so find the measuring in the child's everyday school life.
3. Reflect on measurement in your own life. What did you measure this morning? In groups, brainstorm all of the measuring that you did on your way to class. Predict the types of measuring that you will do tonight. Then reflect on ordering, patterning, and graphing in the same way.

4. Design a lesson that emphasizes one of the concepts and skills discussed in this unit. Teach the lesson to a class, and note the reactions of the children to your teaching. Discuss these reactions in class. "Did you teach what you intended to teach?," "How do you know your lesson was effective?," and "If not, why not, and how could the lesson be improved?"

5. Use the evaluation scheme in Activity 7, Unit 9, to evaluate the following programs.

- ◆ KidWare. Redmond, WA: Edmark.

- ◆ KidWorks. Torrance, CA: Davidson & Associates, Inc. (Pre-K–2)
- ◆ Kid Pix. Novato, CA: Broderbund Software, Inc.

Design a lesson that would integrate one of these computer programs into the classroom environment. Try teaching the lesson to a child who has had experience manipulating objects in patterns and evaluate the results. What factors do you think need to be taken into account when using computers in this way?

REVIEW

A. What is seriation? Why must children possess this skill before they are able to pattern objects?

B. Which activities might be used to evaluate a child's ability to compare and order?

C. How will you teach measurement to young children?

D. Explain how graphing assists in learning science concepts.

REFERENCE

National Research Council. (1996). *National Science Education Standards*. Washington, DC: National Academy Press.

FURTHER READING AND RESOURCES

Baratta-Lorton, M. (1976). *Mathematics their way.* Menlo Park, CA: Addison-Wesley.

Baratta-Lorton, M. (1994). *Twentieth anniversary edition mathematics their way.* Reading, MA: Addison-Wesley.

Burk, D., Snider, A., & Symonds, P. (1988). *Box it or bag it mathematics: Kindergarten teachers' resource guide.* Portland, OR: The Math Learning Center.

Council for Elementary Science International Sourcebook IV. (1986). *Science experiences for preschoolers.* Columbus, OH: SMEAC Information Reference Center.

Forman, G. E., & Kuschner, D. (1983). *Child's construction of knowledge.* Washington, DC: National Association for the Education of Young Children.

Fowlkes, M. A. (1985). Funnels and tunnels. *Science and Children*, 22(6), 28–29.

Hill, D. M. (1977). *Mud, sand and water.* Washington, DC: National Association for the Education of Young Children.

James, J. C., & Granovetter, R. F. (1987). *Water works.* Lewisville, NC: Kaplan Press.

McIntyre, M. (1984). *Early childhood and science.* Washington, DC: National Science Teachers Association.

Phillips, D. G. (1982). Measurement or mimicry? *Science and Children*, 20(3), 32–34.

Rockwell, R. E., Sherwood, E. A., & Williams, R. A. (1986). *Hug a tree.* Beltsville, MD: Gryphon House, Inc.

Shaw, E. L. (1987). Students and sponges—Soaking up science. *Science and Children*, 25(1), 21.

Warren, J. (1984). *Science time.* Palo Alto, CA: Monday Morning Books.

UNIT 22

Integrating the Curriculum through Dramatic Play and Thematic Units and Projects

OBJECTIVES

After reading this unit, you should be able to:

◆ Describe how children apply and extend concepts through dramatic play.

◆ Describe how children apply and extend concepts through thematic units and projects.

◆ Encourage dramatic role-playing that promotes concept acquisition.

◆ Recognize how dramatic role-playing and thematic units and projects promote interdisciplinary instruction and learning.

◆ Use dramatic play and thematic units and projects as settings for science investigations, mathematical problem solving, social learning, and language learning.

◆ Connect the math and science standards to integrated curriculum.

The mathematics (NCTM, 2000) and science standards (National Research Council, 1996) focus on content areas skills and understandings and processes that can be applied across the curriculum. Problem solving, reasoning, communication, connections, and hands-on learning can be applied and experienced through *dramatic play*, *thematic and project approaches*, and integrated curriculum. Play is the major medium through which children learn (Unit 1). They experiment with grown-up roles, explore materials, and develop rules for their actions. Curriculum that meets the national standards can be implemented through the use of thematic units and projects that integrate mathematics, science, social studies, language arts, music, and movement. Themes may be teacher selected (Isbell, 1995) and/or child selected (Helm & Katz, 2001; Katz & Chard, 1989). Integrated curriculum can also support state standards (Akerson, 2001; Clark, 2000; Decker, 1999).

Integrated curriculum can easily include mathematics. Remember that mathematics is composed of fundamental concepts that are used for thinking in all the content areas (Whitin & Whitin, 2001). These concepts are used to investigate the world. According to Whitin and Whitin (2001), authentic, real-world learning experiences can be provided to children through the use of two strategies: (1) having children make direct observations and (2) posing questions or wonders based on these observations (p. 1). For example, a first-grade class went outside in February to look for insects. They wondered why they did not find any. This question led to the study of the life cycles of insects, which applied their knowledge of time. A month later there were insects in abundance. The students took measurements (length) to find out how far grasshoppers can jump. Their observations caused them to wonder why spiders made webs in corners (spatial relations). Eventually, the class made a map of the best places to find bugs. This type of activity exemplifies a student-selected project that applies mathematics to answer questions developed from observation (Whitin & Whitin, 2001).

The purpose of this unit is to demonstrate how dramatic play and thematic units can enrich children's acquisition of concepts and knowledge, not only in science and mathematics but also in the other content areas. Furthermore, these areas offer rich settings for social learning, science investigations, and mathematical problem solving. In Unit 1 the commonalities between math and science were described. Unit 7 provided a basic unit plan and examples of science units that incorporate math, social studies, language arts, fine arts, motor development, and dramatic play. Units 33 through 38 include integrated units and activities for the primary level. This unit emphasizes the natural play of young children as the basis for developing thematic units that highlight the potentials for an interdisciplinary curriculum for young children.

Concepts and skills are valuable to children only if they can be used in everyday life. Young children spend most of their waking hours involved in play. Play can be used as a vehicle for the application of concepts. Young children like to feel big and do "big person" things. They like to pretend they are grown up and want to do as many grown-up things as they can. Role-playing can be used as a means for children to apply what they know as they take on a multitude of grown-up roles.

Dramatic role-playing is an essential part of thematic units. For example, using food as the theme for a unit could afford opportunities not only for applying concepts and carrying out science investigations and mathematics problem solving but also for children to try out adult roles and do adult activities. Children can grow food and shop for groceries; plan and prepare meals, snacks, and parties; serve food; and enjoy sharing and eating the results of their efforts. Opportunities can be offered that provide experiences for social education as children learn more about adult tasks, have experiences in the community, and learn about their own and other cultures. Teachers can use these experiences to assess and evaluate through observation.

Butterworth and Lo Cicero (2001) described a project that grew from the interests of four- and five-year-old Latino children in a transitional kindergarten class. The teachers used the Reggio Emilia approach (Edwards, Gandini, & Forman, 1998) in developing the project. That is, they began with the children's culture. In this case they had the children tell stories about their trips to the supermarket, and these stories were transformed into math problems. The market provided a setting that led the children naturally to talk about quantity and money. After presenting their stories, the children re-enacted them through dramatic play. They pretended to buy fruit and to take it home to eat. Setting the table naturally posed problems in rational counting and one-to-one correspondence. The project continued on into more complex problems and other types of child-selected dramatic play.

Dramatic Role-Playing

When children are engaged in dramatic role-playing, they practice what it is like to be an adult. They begin with a simple imitation of what they have observed. Their first roles reflect what they have seen at home. They bathe, feed, and rock babies. They cook meals, set the table, and eat. One of their first outside experiences is to go shopping. This experience is soon reflected in dramatic play. They begin by carrying things in bags, purses, and other large containers. At first, they carry around anything that they can stuff in their containers. Gradually, they move into using more realistic props such as play money and empty food containers. Next, they might build a store with big blocks and planks. Eventually, they learn to play cooperatively with other children. One child might be the mother, another the father, another the child, and another the store clerk. As the children move toward this stage, teachers can provide more props and background experiences that will expand the raw material children have for developing their role-playing. Problem-solving skills are refined as children figure out who will take which role, provide a location for the store and home, and develop the rules for the activity.

Children can learn about adult roles through field trips to businesses such as restaurants, banks, the post office, and stores both in the local neighborhood and in the extended community. Museums, construction sites, hospitals, fire stations, and other places offer experiences that can enrich children's knowledge of adult roles. Books, tapes, films, and classroom visitors can also provide valuable experiences for children. Following such experiences, props can be provided to support children's dramatic role-playing. Each type of business or service center can be set up in the classroom with appropriate props.

Some examples of dramatic play centers and props follow:

◆ A toy store could be set up by having the children bring old toys from home, which they could pretend to buy and sell.
◆ A grocery store can also be set up using items that might otherwise be discarded, such as empty food containers that the children could bring from home. The children could make food from play dough, clay, or papier-mâché. Plastic food replicas can be purchased.
◆ A clothing store can be organized into children's, ladies', and men's departments; children

can bring discarded clothing and shoes from home.
◆ A jewelry store can be stocked with old and pretend jewelry (such as macaroni necklaces and cardboard watches).
◆ Services centers such as the post office, fire station, police station, automobile repair shop, hospital, beauty shop, and the like can be stocked with appropriate props.
◆ Transportation vehicles such as space vehicles, automobiles, trucks, and buses can be built with large blocks, with lined-up chairs, and with commercially made or teacher-made steering wheels and other controls.
◆ A zoo, veterinarian's office, circus, farm, or pet shop could be set up. Have children bring stuffed animals from home to live in the zoo, visit the vet, act in the circus, live on the farm, or be sold in the pet shop. Classify the animals as to which belong in each setting. Children can predict which animals eat the most, are dangerous to humans, are the smartest, and so on. Provide play money to pay for goods and services.
◆ Health and medical service centers can be organized. Provide props for medical play. Tie these in with discussions of good nutrition and other health practices. The children can "pay the bill" for the services.
◆ Space science vehicles can be created. Provide props for space travel (e.g., a big refrigerator carton that can be made into a spaceship, paper bag space helmets, and so on). Provide materials for making mission control and for designing other planetary settings.
◆ Water environments can be created. Provide toy boats, people, rocks for islands, and the like. Discuss floating and sinking. Outdoors, use water for firefighter play and for watering the garden. Have a container (bucket or large dishpan) that can be a fishing hole, and have waterproof fish with a safety pin or other metal object attached so they can be caught with a magnet fish bait. Investigate why the magnet/metal combination makes a good combination for pretend fishing. Count how many fish each child catches.
◆ Simple machines can be set up. Vehicles, a packing box elevator, a milk carton elevator on

a pulley, a plank on rollers, and so on make interesting dramatic play props, and their construction and functioning provide challenging problems for investigation.

Concepts are applied in a multitude of play activities such as those just described. The following are some examples:

◆ One-to-one correspondence can be practiced by exchanging play money for goods or services.
◆ Sets and classifying are involved in organizing each dramatic play center in an orderly manner, for example, placing all the items in the drugstore in the proper place.
◆ Counting can be applied to figuring out how many items have been purchased and how much money must be exchanged.
◆ Comparing and measuring can be used to decide if clothing fits, to determine the weight of fruits and vegetables purchased, to check a sick person's temperature, and to decide on which size box of cereal or carton of milk to purchase.
◆ Spatial relations and volume concepts are applied as items purchased are placed in bags, boxes, and/or baskets and as children discover how many passengers will fit in the space shuttle or can ride on the bus.
◆ Number symbols can be found throughout dramatic play props, for example, on price tags, play money, telephones, cash registers, scales, measuring cups and spoons, thermometers, rulers, and calculators.

Money is a basic part of most of these activities. For advanced preprimary and primary children who have a beginning understanding of earning and spending money, the computer program Duck's Playground can offer entertainment and practice in working and earning money. This program is available from Sierra On-Line, Inc., Coarsegold, California.

Pocket calculators are excellent props for dramatic play. Children can pretend to add up their expenses, costs, and earnings. As they explore calculators, they will learn how to use them for basic mathematical operations. Methods for introducing calculators are described in Section 4. (See resources in Figure 22–1.)

A Thematic Unit Example: Food

A thematic unit that focuses on food can involve many science, mathematics, social studies, language arts, art, music, and movement experiences. As scientists, children observe the growth of food, the physical changes that take place when food is prepared, and the effects of food on growth of humans and animals. They also compare the tastes of different foods and categorize them into those they like and those they dislike and into sweet and sour; liquid and solid; "junk" and healthful; and groups such as meat/dairy products, cereals/ breads, and fruits/vegetables.

As mathematicians, children pour, measure, count, cut wholes into parts, and divide full pans or full bowls into equal servings. They count the strokes when mixing a cake, make sure the oven is on the correct temperature setting, and set the clock for the required baking time. At the store, they exchange money for food and weigh fruits and vegetables. They count the days until their beans sprout or the fruit ripens.

Through food experiences, children learn much about society and culture. They can make foods from different cultures. They learn where food is grown, how it is marketed, and how it must be purchased with money at the grocery store. They cooperate with each other and take turns when preparing food. Then they share what they make with others.

Children can sing about food and draw their food-related experiences. They can move like an eggbeater, like a stalk of wheat blowing in the wind, or like a farmer planting seeds. The following are some examples of dramatic play, mathematics, and science food experiences.

Food and Dramatic Play

In the home living center at school, children purchase, cook, serve, and eat food as part of their role playing. It was suggested in Unit 18 that a simple measuring activity could be to make flour and salt dough. The dough can be made into pretend food to use as dramatic play props.

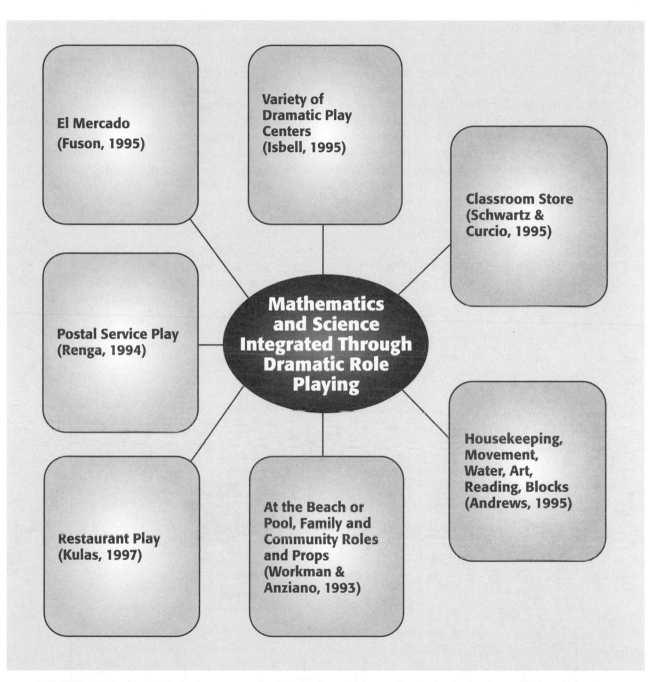

FIGURE 22–1   Examples of resources for integrating mathematics and science through dramatic play.

Food and Math

Cooking activities are a rich source of mathematics experiences. Following a recipe provides a sequencing activity. Each ingredient must be measured exactly using a standard measuring tool. The correct number of cups, tablespoons, eggs, and so on must be counted out. Baked foods must be cooked at the correct temperature for the prescribed amount of time. Some foods are heated, while others are placed in the refrigerator or freezer. When the food is ready to eat, it must be divided into equal portions so that each person gets a fair share. A simple pictograph recipe can help children to be independent as they assemble ingredients (Figure 22–2).

Children who live in the country or who have a garden have additional opportunities to apply math concepts to real life experiences. They can count the number of days from planting until the food is ready to be picked. They can measure the growth of the plants at regular intervals. The number of cucumbers harvested and the weight of the potatoes can be measured. If the child lives where livestock can be kept, the daily number of eggs gathered can be counted, the young calf can be weighed each week, and the amount of money collected for products sold can be counted.

Setting the table at the home living center or for a real meal is an opportunity for applying math skills. The number of people to be seated and served is calculated and matched with the amount of tableware and the number of chairs, napkins, and placemats needed. Putting utensils and dishes away is an experience in sorting things into sets. Pictographs can be used to provide clues about where each type of item should be placed.

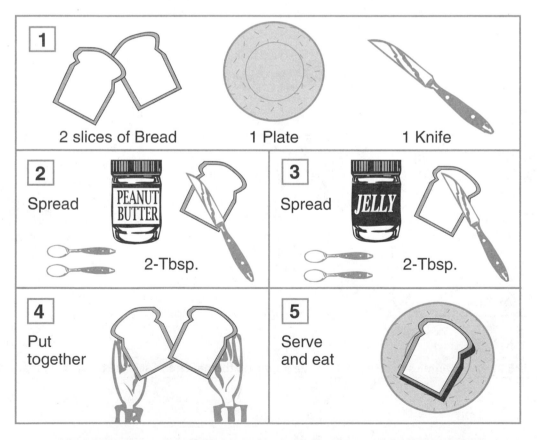

1 2 slices of Bread   1 Plate   1 Knife

2 Spread PEANUT BUTTER 2-Tbsp.

3 Spread JELLY 2-Tbsp.

4 Put together

5 Serve and eat

FIGURE 22–2 A pictograph for making a peanut butter and jelly sandwich.

Food and Science

Each of the activities described under the Food and Math section also involves science. Children can be asked to predict what will happen when the wet ingredients (oil and milk) are mixed with the dry ingredients (flour, baking powder, and salt) when making the play dough biscuits. They can then make the mixture; observe and describe its texture, color, and density; and compare their results with their predictions. Next, they can predict what will happen when the dough is baked in the oven. When it is taken out, they can observe and describe the differences that take place during the baking process. They can be asked what would happen if the oven is too hot or if the biscuits are left in too long.

If the children have the opportunity to see eggs produced, this can lead to a discussion of where the eggs come from and what would happen if the eggs were fertilized. They could observe the growth from seed to edible food as vegetables are planted, cultivated, watered, and picked. Applesauce exemplifies several physical changes: from whole to parts, from solid chunks to soft lumps, and to smooth and thick as cutting, heating, and grinding each have an effect. Children can also note the change in taste before and after the sugar is added. Stone soup offers an opportunity for discussion of the significance of the stone. What does the stone add to the soup? Does a stone have nutrients? What really makes the soup taste good and makes it nutritious?

Food and Social Studies

Each of the activities described also involves social studies. City children might take a trip to the farm. For example, a trip to an orchard to get apples for applesauce is an enriching and enjoyable experience. They might also take a trip to the grocery store to purchase the ingredients needed in their recipes. Then they can take turns measuring, cutting, adding ingredients, or whatever else is required as the cooking process proceeds. Stone soup is an excellent group activity because everyone in the class can add an ingredient. Invite people from different cultures to bring foods to class and/or help the children make their special foods. Children can note similarities and differences across cultures.

Other Thematic Unit, Project, and Learning Center Resources

As can be seen by looking through the resource list at the end of the unit, there are many topics that can serve as the focus for thematic units and projects that include mathematics and science integrated with other content areas. A few examples will be mentioned. *Maths in Context* (Edwards, 1990) starts with mathematics and provides ideas for units as diverse as dragons and Christmas. *Counting on a Small Planet* (Baker & Baker, 1991) contains activities for environmental mathematics. *The Whole Language Kindergarten* (Raines & Canady, 1990) has a whole language focus. *Science Centers A to Z* (Kerr, 1993) provides ideas for a variety of themes and activities. *Integrated Curriculum and Developmentally Appropriate Practice: Birth to Age Eight* (Hart, Burts, & Charlesworth, 1997) provides an overview of integrated curriculum from the view of each of the major content areas. The journals *Teaching Children Mathematics* (formerly *Arithmetic Teacher*) and *Science and Children* are rich sources of ideas. Several articles from these sources are also listed.

Summary

Dramatic play and thematic units and projects provide math, science, and social studies experiences that afford children an opportunity to apply concepts and skills. They can predict, observe, and investigate as they explore these areas. As children play home, store, and service roles, they match, count, classify, compare, measure, and use spatial relations concepts and number symbols. They also practice the exchange of money for goods and services. Through dramatic play they try out grown-up roles and activities.

Through thematic units and projects, mathematics and science can be integrated with other content areas. The thematic experiences provide real life connections for abstract concepts. For teachers, these activities offer valuable opportunities for naturalistic and informal instruction as well as time to observe children and assess their ability to use concepts in everyday situations.

KEY TERMS

integrated curriculum   thematic units   dramatic role-playing
play   projects

SUGGESTED ACTIVITIES

1. Observe young children at play in school. Note if any concept experiences take place during dramatic role-playing or while doing thematic activities. Share what you observe with your class.
2. Add a section for dramatic play and thematic resources to your Activity File/Notebook.
3. Review several cookbooks (the ones suggested in this unit or some others) and examine recipes recommended for young children. Explain to the class which recipe books you think are most appropriate for use with young children.
4. Use the evaluation scheme in Activity 7, Unit 9, to evaluate any of the following software.
   Dinosaurs. Redmond, WA: Microsoft Corp.

   The Jungle. Woodinville, WA: Humongous.
   Learn about Life Science: Plants. Pleasantville, NY: Sunburst. (K–2).
   Learn about Life Science: The Senses. Pleasantville, NY: Sunburst Technologies. (K–2).
   Learn about Physical Science: Simple Machines. Pleasantville, NY: Sunburst Technologies. (K–2).
   Where in the World Is Carmen Sandiego? Junior Detective. (Pre-K–3). Novato, CA: Broderbund.
   Find out whether there is any other software that could be used to support a thematic unit or project.
5. Add to your Activity File five food experiences that enrich children's concepts and promote application of concepts.

REVIEW

A. Briefly answer each of the following questions.
   1. Why should dramatic role-playing be included as a math, science, and social studies concept experience for young children?
   2. Why should food activities be included as math, science, and social studies concept experiences for young children?
   3. How can teachers encourage dramatic role-playing that includes concept experiences?
   4. Describe four food activities that can be used in the early childhood math, science, and social studies program.
   5. Explain how thematic units promote an integrated curriculum.
B. Describe the props that might be included in three different dramatic play centers.
C. Describe the relationship between integrated curriculum and the math and science standards.

REFERENCES

Akerson, V. L. (2001). Teaching science when your principal says "Teach language arts." *Science and Children*, *38*(7), 42–47.

Andrews, A. G. (1995). The role of self-directed discovery time in the development of mathematics concepts. *Teaching Children Mathematics, 2*, 116–120.

Baker, A., & Baker, J. (1991). *Counting on a small planet*. Portsmouth, NH: Heinemann.

Butterworth, S., & Lo Cicero, A. M. (2001). Storytelling: Building a mathematics curriculum from the culture of the child. *Teaching Children Mathematics*, *7*(7), 396–399.

Clark, A. M. (2000). Meeting state standards through the project approach. *Eric/EECE Newsletter*, *12*(1), 1–2.

Decker, K. A. (1999). Meeting state standards through integration. *Science and Children*, *36*(6), 28–32, 69.

Edwards, C., Gandini, L., & Forman, G. (Eds.). (1998). *The hundred languages of children: The Reggio Emilia approach—Advanced reflections*. Greenwich, CT: Ablex.

Edwards, D. (1990). *Maths in context: A thematic approach*. Portsmouth, NH: Heinemann.

Fuson, K. C. (1996, April). *Latino children's construction of arithmetic understanding in urban classrooms that support thinking*. "El Mercado" project used as a focus. Presentation at the annual meeting of the American Educational Research Association, New York City. For a copy of the paper: pterando@nwu.edu relative to the subject of AERA Latino.

Hart, C. H., Burts, D. C., & Charlesworth, R. (Eds.). (1997). *Integrated curriculum and developmentally appropriate practice: Birth to age eight*. Albany, NY: SUNY Press.

Helm, J. H., & Katz, L. G. (2001). *Young investigators: The project approach in the early years*. New York: Teachers College.

Isbell, R. (1995). *The complete learning center book*. Beltsville, MD: Gryphon House.

Katz, L. G., & Chard, S. C. (1989). *Engaging children's minds: The project approach*. Norwood, NY: Ablex.

Kerr, S. (1993). *Science centers A to Z*. Wheeling, IL: Look At Me Productions.

Kulas, L. L. (1997). May I take your order? *Teaching Children Mathematics, 3*, 230–234.

National Council of Teachers of Mathematics. (2000). *Principles and standards for school mathematics*. Reston, VA: Author. (http://www.nctm.org)

National Research Council. (1996). *National science education standards*. Washington, DC: National Academy Press.

Raines, C. S., & Canady, R. J. (1990). *The whole language kindergarten*. New York: Teachers College.

Renga, S. (1994). Moving the mail. *Arithmetic Teacher, 41*(8), 463.

Schwartz, S. L., & Curcio, F. R. (1995). Learning mathematics in meaningful contexts: An action-based approach in the primary grades. In P. A. House (Ed.), *Connecting mathematics across the curriculum: 1995 Yearbook* (116–123). Reston, VA: National Council of Teachers of Mathematics.

Whitin, D., & Whitin, P. (2001). Where is the mathematics in interdisciplinary studies? *Dialogues* [On-line serial]. Available: http://www.nctm.org/dialogues/2001-01

FURTHER READING AND RESOURCES

Theme, Project, and Integration

Charlesworth, R. (1997). Mathematics in the developmentally appropriate curriculum. In C. H. Hart, D. C. Burts, & R. Charlesworth (Eds.), *Integrated curriculum and developmentally appropriate practice: Birth to age eight.* Albany, NY: SUNY Press.

Charlesworth, R., & Lind, K. (1995). Whole language and the mathematics and science standards. In S. Raines (Ed.), *Whole language in grades 1, 2, and 3.* New York: Teachers College Press.

Corwin, R. B. (1993). Ideas: Using webs. *Arithmetic Teacher, 40*(6), 325–337.

Cook, H., & Matthews, C. E. (1998). Lessons from a "living fossil." *Science and Children, 36*(3), 16–19.

Copley, J. V. (2000). *The young child and mathematics.* Washington, DC: National Association for the Education of Young Children.

Copley, J. V. (Ed.). (1999). *Mathematics in the early years.* Washington, DC: National Association for the Education of Young Children.

Draznin, Z. (1995). *Writing math: A project-based approach.* Glenview, IL: Goodyear Books.

Fioranelli, D. (2000). Recycling into art: Integrating science and art. *Science and Children, 38*(2), 30–33.

Hamm, M., & Adams, D. (1998). What research says. Reaching across disciplines. *Science and Children, 36*(1), 45–49.

House, P. A., & Coxford, A. F. (Eds.). (1995). *Connecting mathematics across the curriculum.* Reston, VA: National Council of Teachers of Mathematics.

Huffman, A. B. (1996). Beyond the weather chart: Weathering new experiences. *Young Children, 51*(5), 34–37.

Irons, C., & Irons, R. (1991). Ideas: Toy shop numbers and other things in the environment. *Arithmetic Teacher, 39*(4), 18–25.

Krogh, S. (1995). *The integrated early childhood curriculum.* New York: McGraw-Hill.

Lind, K. K. (1997). Science in the developmentally appropriate integrated curriculum. In C. H. Hart, D. C. Burts, & R. Charlesworth (Eds.), *Integrated curriculum and developmentally appropriate practice: Birth to age eight.* Albany, NY: SUNY Press.

McLaughlin, C. W., Hampton, L., & Moxham, S. (1999).Shining light on photosynthesis. *Science and Children, 36*(5), 26–31.

Moses, B. E., & Proudfit, L. (1992). Ideas: Math and music. *Arithmetic Teacher, 40*(4), 215–225.

Owens, K. (2001). An integrated approach for young students. *Dialogues* [On-line serial]. Available: http://www.nctm.org/dialogues/2001-01

Patton, M. M., & Kokoski, T. M. (1996). How good is your early childhood science, mathematics, and technology program? Strategies for extending your curriculum. *Young Children, 51*(5), 38–44.

Piazza, J. A., Scott, M. M., & Carver, E. C. (1994). Thematic webbing and the curriculum standards in primary grades. *Arithmetic Teacher, 41*, 294–298.

Richardson, K. (1999). *Developing number concepts: Planning guide.* Parsippany, NJ: Dale Seymour.

Rothenberg, B. S. (1996). The measure of music: K–2. *Teaching Children Mathematics, 2*, 408.

Schnur-Laughlin, J. (1999). Pantry math. *Teaching Children Mathematics, 6*(4), 216–218.

Skinner, P. (1990). *What's your problem?* Portsmouth, NH: Heinemann.

Trepanier-Street, M. (2000). Multiple forms of representation in long-term projects: The garden project. *Childhood Education, 77*(1), 19–25.

Vacc, N. N., Ervin, C., & Travis, S. (1995). Beyond the classroom. *Teaching Children Mathematics, 1*, 494–497.

Vandas, S. (1991). Water: The resource that gets used and used and used for everything! *Science and Children, 28*(8), 8–9.

Warner, L., & Morse, P. (2001). Studying pond life with primary-age children: The project approach in action. *Childhood Education, 77*(3), 139–143.

Wasserman, S. (2000). *Serious players in the primary classroom* (2nd ed.). New York: Teachers College.

Cooking and Food

Albyn, C. L., & Webb, L. S. (1993). *The multicultural cookbook for students.* Phoenix, AZ: Oryx.

Christenberry, M. A., & Stevens, B. (1984). *Can Piaget cook?* Atlanta, GA: Humanics.

Dahl, K. (1998). Why cooking in the curriculum? *Young Children, 53*(1), 81–83.

Faggella, K., & Dixler, D. (1985). *Concept cookery.* Bridgeport, CT: First Teacher Press.

Howell, N. M. (1999). Cooking up a learning community with corn, beans and rice. *Young Children, 54*(5), 36–38.

McClenahan, P., & Jaqua, I. (1976). *Cool cooking for kids.* Belmont, CA: Fearon-Pitman.

Metheny, D., & Hollowell, J. (1994). Food for thought. *Teaching Children Mathematics, 1*, 164.

Owen, S., & Fields, A. (1994). Eggs, eggs, eggs. *Teaching Children Mathematics, 1*, 92–93.

Partridge, E., Austin, S., Wadlington, E., & Bitner, J. (1996). Cooking up mathematics in the kindergarten. *Teaching Children Mathematics, 2*, 492–495.

Rothstein, G. L. (1994). *From soup to nuts: Multicultural cooking activities and recipes.* New York: Scholastic.

Taylor, S. I., & Dodd, A. T. (1999). We can cook! Snack preparation with toddlers and twos. *Early Childhood Education Journal, 27*(1), 29–33.

Wanamaker, N., Hearn, K., & Richarz, S. (1979). *More than graham crackers.* Washington, DC: National Association for the Education of Young Children.

Young, S. L. (1991). Ideas: Pizza math. *Arithmetic Teacher, 38*(8), 26–33.

Project/Thematic Resources Online

◆ http://www.lightspan.com has resources for units/projects

◆ http://www.preschoolbystormie.com has integrated units

◆ Also see http://www/lessonplanspage.com/mathk-1

Symbols and Higher-Level Activities

U N I T 2 3
Symbols

OBJECTIVES

After reading this unit, you should be able to:

◆ List the six number symbol skills.

◆ Describe four basic types of self-correcting number symbol materials.

◆ Set up an environment that supports naturalistic and informal number symbol experiences.

◆ Do structured number symbol activities with children.

Number symbols are called numerals. Each numeral represents an amount and acts as a shorthand for recording *how many*. The young child sees numerals all around (Figure 23–1). He has some idea of what they are before he can understand and use them. He sees that there are numerals on his house, the phone, the clock, and the car license plate. He may have one or more counting books. He may watch a children's TV program where numeral recognition is taught. Sometime between the age of two and the age of five a child learns to name the numerals from zero to 10.

However, the child is usually four or more when he begins to understand that each numeral stands for a group of things of a certain amount that is always the same. He may be able to tell the name of the symbol "3" and count three objects, but he may not realize that the "3" can stand for the three objects or the cardinal meaning of three. This is illustrated in Figure 23–2.

It can be confusing to the child to spend time on drill with numerals until he has had many concrete experiences with basic math concepts. Most experiences with numerals should be naturalistic and informal.

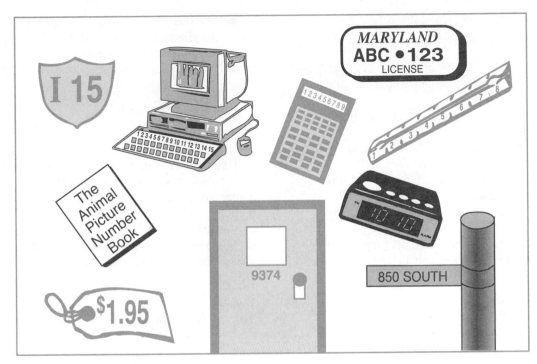

FIGURE 23–1   Numerals are everywhere in the environment.

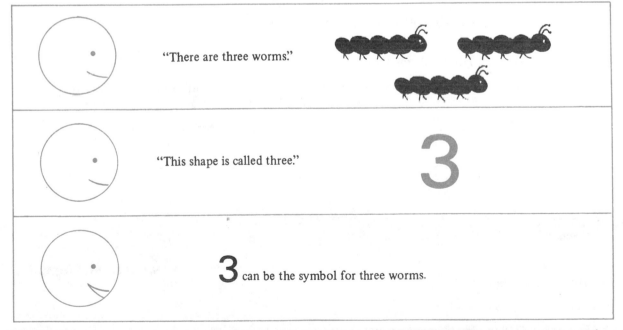

FIGURE 23–2   The child counts the objects, learns the symbol, and realizes that the symbol can represent the set.

The Number Symbol Skills

There are six number symbol skills that young children acquire during the preoperational period.

◆ She learns to recognize and say the name of each numeral.
◆ She learns to place the numerals in order: 0-1-2-3-4-5-6-7-8-9-10.
◆ She learns to associate numerals with sets: "1" goes with one thing.
◆ She learns that each numeral in order stands for one more than the numeral that comes before it. (That is, two is one more than one, three is one more than two, and so on.)

◆ She learns to match each numeral to any set of the size that the numeral stands for and to make sets that match numerals.
◆ She learns to reproduce (write) numerals.

The first four skills are included in this unit. The last two are the topics for Unit 24.

Assessment

The teacher should observe whether the child shows an interest in numerals. Does he repeat the names he hears on television? Does he use self-correcting materials that are described in the part of this unit on informal learning and teaching? What does he do when he uses these materials? Individual interviews would include the types of tasks that follow.

SAMPLE ASSESSMENT TASK

4J   **Preoperational Ages 3–6**
Symbols, Recognition: Unit 23

METHOD: Interview.

SKILL: Child is able to recognize numerals 0 to 10 presented in sequence.

MATERIALS: 5″ × 8″ cards with one numeral from 0 to 10 written on each.

PROCEDURE: Starting with 0, show the child each card in numerical order from 0 to 10. WHAT IS THIS? TELL ME THE NAME OF THIS.

EVALUATION: Note if the child uses numeral names (correct or not), indicating she knows the kinds of words associated with the symbols. Note which numerals she can label correctly.

INSTRUCTIONAL RESOURCE: Charlesworth, R., and Lind, K. K. (2003). *Math and Science for Young Children* (4th ed.). Clifton Park, NY: Delmar Learning.

SAMPLE ASSESSMENT TASK

5L   **Preoperational Ages 4–6**
Symbols, Sequencing: Unit 23

METHOD: Interview.

SKILL: Child is able to sequence numerals from 0 to 10.

MATERIALS: 5″ × 8″ cards with one numeral from 0 to 10 written on each.

PROCEDURE: Place all the cards in front of the child in random order. PUT THESE IN ORDER. WHICH COMES FIRST? NEXT? NEXT?

EVALUATION: Note whether the child seems to understand that numerals belong in a fixed sequence. Note how many are placed in the correct order and which, if any, are labeled.

INSTRUCTIONAL RESOURCE: Charlesworth, R., and Lind, K. K. (2003). *Math and Science for Young Children* (4th ed.). Clifton Park, NY: Delmar Learning.

SAMPLE ASSESSMENT TASK

6J   **Preoperational Ages 5 and Older**
Symbols, One More Than: Unit 23

METHOD: Interview.

SKILL: Child is able to identify numerals that are "one more than."

MATERIALS: 5″ × 8″ cards with one numeral from 0 to 10 written on each.

PROCEDURE: Place the numeral cards in front of the child in order from 0 to 10. TELL ME WHICH NUMERAL MEANS ONE MORE THAN TWO. WHICH NUMERAL MEANS ONE MORE THAN SEVEN? WHICH NUMERAL MEANS ONE MORE THAN FOUR? (If the child answers these, then try LESS THAN.)

EVALUATION: Note whether the child is able to answer correctly.

INSTRUCTIONAL RESOURCE: Charlesworth, R., and Lind, K. K. (2003). *Math and Science for Young Children* (4th ed.). Clifton Park, NY: Delmar Learning.

Naturalistic Activities

As the young child observes his environment, he sees numerals around him. He sees them on clocks, phones, houses, books, food containers, television programs, money, calendars, thermometers, rulers, measuring cups, license plates, and on many other objects in many places. He hears people say

◆ My phone number is 622-7732.
◆ My house number is 1423.
◆ My age is 6.
◆ I have a $5 bill.
◆ The temperature is 78°.
◆ Get a 5-pound bag of rabbit food.
◆ We had 3 inches of rain today.
◆ This pitcher holds 8 cups of juice.

Usually children start using the names of the number symbols before they actually match them with the symbols.

◆ Tanya and Juanita are ready to take off in their spaceship. Juanita does the countdown, "Ten, nine, eight, three, one, blast off!"
◆ Tim asks Ms. Moore to write the number 7 on a sign for his race car.
◆ Sam notices that the thermometer has numbers written on it.

◆ Diana is playing house. She takes the toy phone and begins dialing, "One-six-two. Hello dear, will you please stop at the store and buy a loaf of bread?"

◆ "How old are you, Pete?" "I'm six," answers two-year-old Pete.

◆ "One, two, three, I have three dolls."

◆ Tanya is playing house. She looks up at the clock. "Eight o'clock and time for bed," she tells her doll. (The clock really says 9:30 a.m.)

Children begin to learn number symbols as they look and listen and then imitate in their play what they have seen and heard.

Informal Activities

During the preoperational period, most school activities with numerals should be informal. Experimentation and practice in perception with sight and touch are most important. These experiences are made available by means of activities with self-correcting manipulative materials. **Self-correcting materials** are those the child can use by trial and error to solve a problem without adult assistance. The material is made in such a way that it can be used with success with very little help. **Manipulative materials** are things that have parts and pieces that can be picked up and moved by the child to solve the problem presented by the materials. The teacher observes the child as she works. He notes whether the child works in an organized way, and whether she sticks with the material until she has the task finished.

There are four basic types of self-correcting manipulative math materials that can be used for informal activities. These materials can be bought, or they can be made. The four basic groups of materials are those that teach discrimination and matching, those that teach sequence (or order), those that give practice in association of symbols with sets, and those that combine association of symbols and sets with sequence. Examples of each type are illustrated in Figures 23–3 through 23–5.

The child can learn to discriminate one numeral from the other by sorting packs of numeral cards. She can also learn which numerals are the same as she

matches. Another type of material that serves this purpose is a lotto-type game. The child has a large card divided equally into four or more parts. She must match individual numeral cards to each numeral on the big card. These materials are shown in Figure 23–3 (A and B). She can also experiment with felt, plastic, magnetic, wooden, rubber, and cardboard numerals.

There are many materials that teach sequence or order. These may be set up so that parts can only be put together in such a way that when the child is done, she sees the numerals are in order in front of her. An example would be the Number Worm® by Childcraft (Figure 23–4 [A]). Sequence is also taught through the use of a number line or number stepping-stones. The Childcraft giant Walk-On Number Line® lets the child walk from one numeral to the next in order (Figure 23–4 [B]). The teacher can set out numerals on the floor (such as Stepping Stones® from Childcraft) that the child must step on in order (Figure 23–4 [C]). There are also number sequence wooden inset puzzles (such as Constructive Playthings' Giant Number Puzzle® and Number Art Puzzle®).

The hand calculator lends itself to informal exploration of numerals. First, show the students how to turn the calculator on and off. Tell them to watch the display window and then turn on the calculator. A 0 will appear. Explain that when they first turn on their calculators a 0 will always appear. Then tell them to turn on their calculators and tell you what they see in the window. Have them practice turning their calculators on and off until you are sure they all understand this operation. Next, tell them to press **1**. Ask them what they see in the window. Note if they tell you they see the same number. Next, have them press **2**. A 2 will appear in the window next to the 1. Show them that they just need to press the **C** key to erase. Then let them explore and discover on their own. Help them by answering their questions and posing questions to them such as, "What will happen if _____?"

Many materials can be purchased that help the child associate each numeral with the set that goes with it. Large cards that can be placed on the bulletin board (such as Childcraft Poster Cards®) give a visual association (Figure 23–5 [A]). Numerals can be seen and touched on textured cards, which can be bought (such as Didax Tactile Number Cards®). Numeral cards can be made using sandpaper for the sets of dots

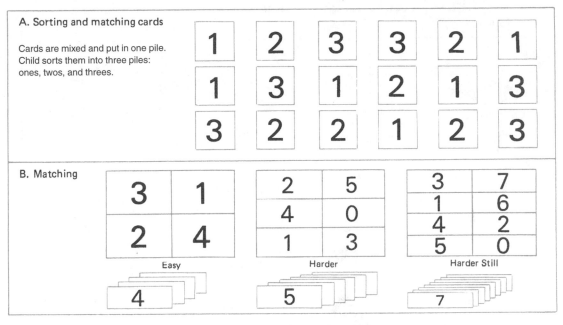

A. Sorting and matching cards

Cards are mixed and put in one pile. Child sorts them into three piles: ones, twos, and threes.

1	2	3	3	2	1
1	3	1	2	1	3
3	2	2	1	2	3

B. Matching

| 3 | 1 |
| 2 | 4 |

Easy

4

2	5
4	0
1	3

Harder

5

3	7
1	6
4	2
5	0

Harder Still

7

FIGURE 23–3 Sorting and matching.

FIGURE 23–4 Materials that help the child learn numeral sequence.

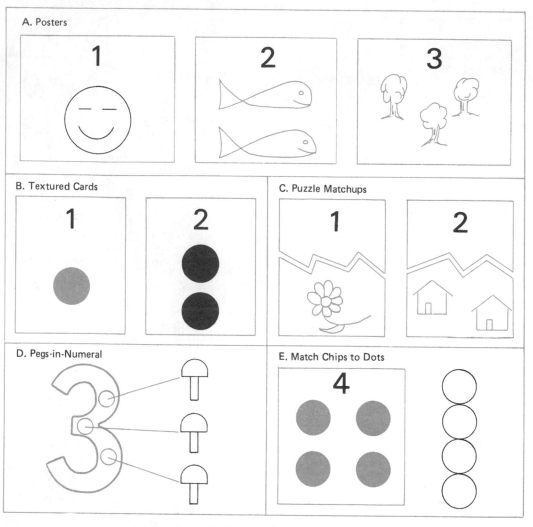

FIGURE 23–5 Numeral and set association.

and for the numerals (Figure 23–5 [B]). Other materials require the child to use visual and motor coordination. She may have to match puzzlelike pieces (such as Math Plaques® from Childcraft, Figure 23–5 [C]). She may put pegs in holes (such as Peg Numerals® from Childcraft, Figure 23–5 [D]). Unifix® inset pattern boards require the same type of activity. The teacher can make cards that have numerals and dots the size of buttons or other counters. The child could place a counter on each dot (Figure 23–5 [E]).

Materials that give the child experience with sequence and association at the same time are also available. These are shown in Figure 23–6. It can be seen that the basis of the materials is that the numerals are in a fixed order, and the child adds some sort of counter that can be placed only in the right amount. Unifix® stairs are like the inset patterns but are stuck together (Figure 23–6 [A]). Other materials illustrated are counters on rods (Figure 23–6 [B]), pegs in holes (Number-Ite® from Childcraft, Figure 23–6 [C]), or 1–5 pegboard (Figure 23–6 [D]).

The teacher's role with these materials is to show the child how they can be used and then step back and watch. After the child has learned to use the materials independently, the teacher can make comments and ask questions.

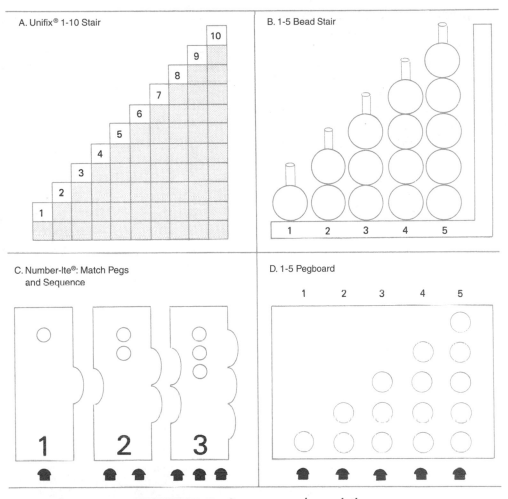

FIGURE 23–6   Sequence and association.

◆ How many pegs are on this one?
◆ Can you tell me the name of each numeral?
◆ You put in the four pegs that go with that numeral 4.
◆ How many beads are there here? (point to stack of one) How many here? (stack of two, and so on)
◆ Good, you separated all the numerals into piles. Here are all 1s, and here are all 2s.

Numerals can also be introduced informally as part of daily counting activities. For example, the class can keep track of the first 100 days of school (see Unit 9). Children can make a 100-number line around

the room. They add the appropriate numeral each day to a number line strip after they have agreed on how many straws they have accumulated. The strip should be wide enough so that large-sized numerals (that the students can easily see) can be glued or written on it.

1	2	3	4	5	6	7	8	9	10

The children can draw special symbols representing special days, such as birthdays, Halloween, Thanksgiving, and so on, below the appropriate numeral on the line. The number line then serves as a timeline recording the class history. A weekly or monthly calendar may also be placed on the bulletin board next to the 100-days display. Calendars were introduced in Unit 19.

Most children will learn through this informal use of materials to recognize and say the name of each numeral, to place the numerals in order, to see that each numeral stands for one more than the one before it, and to associate numerals with amounts. However, some children will need the structured activities described next.

Structured Activities

By the time young children finish kindergarten, they should be able to do the following activities.

◆ Recognize the numerals from 0 to 10
◆ Place the numerals from 0 to 10 in order
◆ Know that each numeral represents a group one larger than the numeral before (and one less than the one that comes next)

◆ Know that each numeral represents a set of things

Numeral	Amount in Set
0	
1	X
2	XX
3	XXX
4	XXXX
5	XXXXX
6	XXXXXX
7	XXXXXXX
8	XXXXXXXX
9	XXXXXXXXX
10	XXXXXXXXXX

They may not always match the right numeral to the correct amount, but they will know that there is such a relationship. The five-year-old child who cannot do one or more of the tasks listed needs some structured help.

Most of the computer programs described in Unit 9 include numeral recognition. Knowing Numbers by

ACTIVITIES

NUMERALS: RECOGNITION

OBJECTIVE: To learn the names of the number symbols.

MATERIALS: Write the numerals from 0 to 10 on cards.

NATURALISTIC AND INFORMAL ACTIVITIES: Place the cards in the math center for exploration. Note if children label and/or sequence the numerals or in any way demonstrate a knowledge of the symbols and what they mean. Ask questions such as, "What are those?" "Do they have names?"

STRUCTURED ACTIVITY: This is an activity that a child who can name all the numbers can do with a child who needs help. Show the numerals one at a time in order. THIS NUMERAL IS CALLED _____. LET'S SAY IT TOGETHER: _____. Do this for each numeral. After 10, say, I'LL HOLD THE CARDS UP ONE AT A TIME. YOU NAME THE NUMERAL. Go through once. Five minutes at a time should be enough.

FOLLOW-UP: Give the child a set of cards to review on his own.

NUMERALS: SEQUENCE AND ONE MORE THAN

OBJECTIVE: To learn the sequence of numerals from 0 to 10.

MATERIALS: Flannelboard or magnet board, felt or magnet numerals, felt or magnet shapes (such as felt primary cutouts, or magnetic geometric shapes).

NATURALISTIC AND INFORMAL ACTIVITIES: Place the numerals and shapes in the math center for exploration. Note if the children make groups and place numerals next to the groups. Ask questions such as, "How many does this numeral mean?"; "Why does this numeral go next to this group?"; "Tell me about your groups."

STRUCTURED ACTIVITY: Put the 0 up first at the upper left-hand corner of the board. WHAT IS THIS NUMERAL CALLED? If the child cannot tell you, say: THIS IS CALLED 0. Put the 1 numeral up next to the right. WHAT IS THIS NUMERAL CALLED? If the child cannot tell you, say: THIS IS 1. SAY IT WITH ME. ONE. Continue to go across until the child does not know two numerals in a row. Then, go back to the beginning of the row. TELL ME THE NAME OF THIS NUMERAL. YES, 0. WHAT IS THE NAME OF THE NEXT ONE? YES, IT IS 1, SO I WILL PUT ONE RABBIT HERE. Put one rabbit under the 1. THE NEXT NUMERAL IS ONE MORE THAN 1. WHAT IS IT CALLED? After the child says 2 on his own or with your help, let him pick out two shapes to put on the board under the 2. Keep going across until you have done the same with each numeral he knows, plus two that he does not know.

FOLLOW-UP: Have the child set up the sequence. If he has trouble, ask: WHAT COMES NEXT? WHAT IS ONE MORE THAN _____? Leave the board and the numerals and shapes out during playtime. Encourage the children who know how to do this activity to work with a child who does not.

NUMERALS: RECOGNITION, SEQUENCE, ASSOCIATION WITH GROUPS, ONE MORE THAN

OBJECTIVE: To help the child to integrate the concepts of association with groups, with one more than, while learning the numeral names and sequence.

MATERIALS: Cards with numerals 0 to 10 and cards with numerals and sets 0 to 10.

NATURALISTIC AND INFORMAL ACTIVITIES: Place the cards in the math center for exploration. Note if the children make matches and/or sequences. Ask, "Can you tell me about what you are doing with the cards?"

STRUCTURED ACTIVITIES:
1. I'M GOING TO PUT DOWN SOME CARDS. EACH ONE HAS A NUMERAL ON IT. THEY GO UP TO 10. SAY THE NAMES WITH ME IF YOU KNOW THEM.
2. HERE IS ANOTHER SET OF CARDS WITH NUMERALS. Give the cards with numerals and sets to the child. MATCH THESE UP WITH THE OTHER CARDS. LET'S SAY THE NAMES AS YOU MATCH.

FOLLOW-UP: Let the child do this activity on his own. Encourage him to use the self-correcting materials also.

EXAMPLE WORLD WIDE WEB ACTIVITY

◆ Count with me at http://www.pbs.org/teachersource/math/preschool.shtm

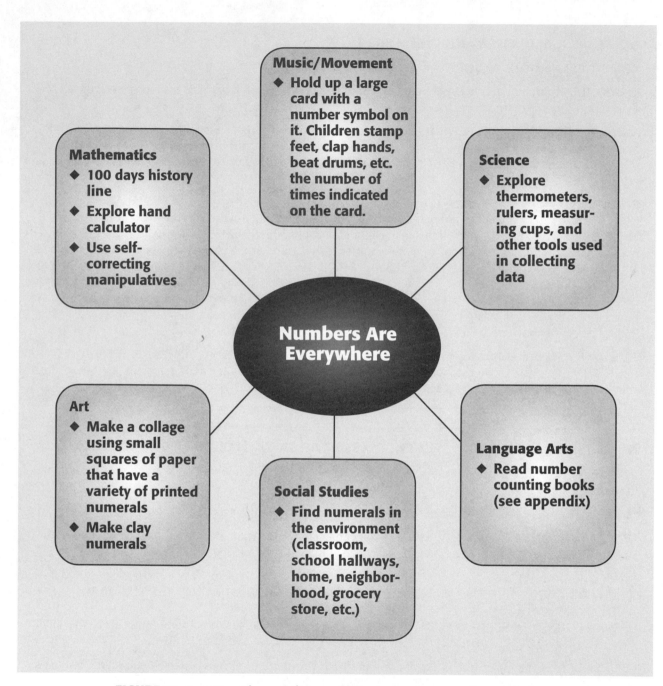

FIGURE 23–7 Integrating number symbol experiences across the curriculum.

Learning Well and Sequence, part of the Kindercomp software from Spinnaker, also provide experiences with numeral recognition. Sequence takes more advanced students up into two- and three-digit numerals. Number symbols can be incorporated in other content areas (Figure 23–7).

Evaluation

The teacher may question each child as she works with the self-correcting materials. He should note which numerals she can name and if she names them in sequence. He may interview her individually using the assessment questions in this unit and in Appendix A.

Summary

Numerals are the symbols used to represent amounts. The name of each numeral must be learned. The sequence, or order, must also be learned. The child needs to understand that each numeral represents a group that is one larger than the one before (and one less than the one that comes next).

Most children learn the properties and purposes of numerals through naturalistic and informal experiences. There are many excellent self-correcting materials that can bought or made for informal activities. Any structured activities should be brief.

KEY TERMS

numerals
cardinal meaning

self-correcting materials
manipulative materials

SUGGESTED ACTIVITIES

1. Observe children to see how they use numerals. Share your experience with your class.
2. Interview preschool and kindergarten teachers to find out how they teach number symbols. Share your findings with the class.
3. Add numeral activities to your Activity File/Notebook.
4. Make a number symbol game. Try it out with four- and five-year-olds. Report to the class on the children's responses. *notecards with numbers and matching game*
5. Go to a school supply or toy store, and evaluate the developmental appropriateness of the number symbol materials you find. *notecards with objects*
6. Use the evaluation system described in Activity 7, Unit 9, to review and evaluate one of the following software programs:

   ◆ Knowing Numbers. Roslyn Heights, NY: Learning Well.
   ◆ Millie's Math House. Redmond, WA: Edmark.
   ◆ Number Meanings and Counting. Pleasantville, NY: Sunburst Technologies. (Pre–K-1). Demonstrates how numbers can be represented in a variety of ways, that is, numerals, tallies, words, or drawings.
   ◆ Numbers Undercover. Pleasantville, NY: Sunburst Technologies. (K–3). Applies numbers to time, measuring, counting, and money problems.
   ◆ Piggy in Numberland. Santa Cruz, CA: Learning in Motion. (Pre–K). Eleven activities deal with 25 math concepts.
   ◆ Sequence from Kindercomp. Cambridge, MA: Spinnaker Software.

REVIEW

A. Respond to each of the following.
  1. Explain what numerals are.
  2. List and define the six number symbol skills.
  3. Explain what is meant by self-correcting manipulative materials.
  4. Describe and sketch examples of the four basic types of self-correcting number symbol manipulative materials.
  5. Describe the teacher's role in the use of self-correcting number symbol materials.
B. What type of number symbol knowledge might children gain from each of the following numeral materials?
  1. Magnet board 0–5 numerals and various magnetic animals
  2. Matchmates® (match plaques)
  3. A set of 11 cards containing the number symbols 0 to 10
  4. Lotto® numeral game
  5. Number Worm®
  6. Pegs-in-Numerals®
  7. Unifix 1–10 Stair®
  8. Walk on Line®
  9. Number-Ite®
  10. 1-2-3 Puzzle®
  11. Hand calculator
  12. Personal computer

FURTHER READING AND RESOURCES

AIMS Educational Products. AIMS Education Foundation, P.O. Box 8120, Fresno, CA 93747-8120.

Baratta-Lorton, M. (1972). *Workjobs*. Menlo Park, CA: Addison-Wesley.

Baratta-Lorton, M. (1976). *Mathematics their way*. Menlo Park, CA: Addison-Wesley.

Box it or bag it mathematics (K–2). Portland, OR: The Math Learning Center. (800-575-8130) (http://www.mlc.pdx.edu)

Bridges in mathematics (K–2). Portland, OR: The Math Learning Center. (800-575-8130) (http://www.mlc.pdx.edu)

Copley, J. V. (2000). *The young child and mathematics*. Washington, DC: National Association for the Education of Young Children.

Copley, J. V. (Ed.). (1999). *Mathematics in the early years*. Washington, DC: National Association for the Education of Young Children.

National Council of Teachers of Mathematics. (2000). *Principles and standards for school mathematics*. Reston, VA: Author. (http://www.nctm.org)

Richardson, K. (1999). *Developing number concepts: Counting, comparing, and pattern (Book 1)*. Parsippany, NJ: Dale Seymour.

Richardson, K. (1999). *Developing number concepts: Planning guide*. Parsippany, NJ: Dale Seymour.

Wakefield, A. P. (1998). *Early childhood number games*. Boston: Allyn & Bacon.

UNIT 24
Groups and Symbols

OBJECTIVES

After reading this unit, you should be able to:

◆ Describe the three higher-level tasks that children do with groups and symbols.

◆ Set up an environment that provides for naturalistic and informal groups and symbols activities.

◆ Plan and do structured groups and symbols activities with young children.

◆ Assess and evaluate a child's ability to use math groups and symbols.

The activities in this unit build on many of the ideas and skills presented in earlier units: matching, numbers and counting, sets and classifying, comparing, ordering, and symbols.

The experiences in this unit will be most meaningful to the child who can do the following activities:

◆ match things one-to-one and match groups of things one-to-one

◆ recognize groups of one to four without counting and count groups up to at least 10 things accurately

◆ divide large groups into smaller groups and compare groups of different amounts

◆ place groups containing different amounts in order from least to most

◆ name each of the numerals from zero to 10

◆ recognize each of the numerals from zero to 10

◆ be able to place each of the numerals in order from zero to 10

◆ understand that each numeral stands for a certain number of things

◆ understand that each numeral stands for a group of things one more than the numeral before it and one less than the numeral after it

When the child has reached the objectives in the preceding list, she can then learn to do the following activities:

◆ Match a symbol to a group; that is, if she is given a set of four items, she can pick out or write the numeral 4 as the one that goes with that group.

◆ Match a group to a symbol; that is, if she is given the numeral 4 she can make or pick out a group of four things to go with it.

◆ Reproduce symbols; that is, she can learn to write the numerals.

Moving from working with groups alone to groups and symbols and finally to symbols alone must be done carefully and sequentially. In *Workjobs II* (1979), Mary Baratta-Lorton describes three levels of increasing abstraction and increasing use of symbols: the concept level, connecting level, and symbolic level. These three levels can be pictured as follows:

Concept Level	ΔΔΔΔ	Number sense—child has concept of amounts
Connecting Level	ΔΔΔΔ4	Child connects group amount with numeral
Symbolic Level	4	Child understands numeral is the symbol for an amount

Units 9, 10, and 11 worked at the concept level. In Unit 23 the connecting level was introduced informally. The major focus of this unit is the connecting level. In Unit 25 the symbolic level will be introduced.

Assessment

If the children can do the assessment tasks in Units 8 through 14, 17, and 23, then they have the basic skills and knowledge necessary to connect groups and symbols. In fact, they may be observed doing some symbol and grouping activities on their own if materials are made available for exploration in the math center. The following are some individual interview tasks.

SAMPLE ASSESSMENT TASK

6M   **Preoperational/Concrete Ages 5–7**
Groups and Symbols, Match Symbols to Groups: Unit 24

METHOD: Interview.

SKILL: Child will be able to match symbols to groups using numerals from 0 to 10 and groups of amounts 0 to 10.

MATERIALS: 5″ ¥ 8″ cards with numerals 0 to 10, 10 objects (e.g., chips, cube blocks, buttons).

PROCEDURE: Lay out the cards in front of the child in numerical order. One at a time show the child sets of each amount in this order: 2, 5, 3, 1, 4. PICK OUT THE NUMERAL THAT TELLS HOW MANY THINGS ARE IN THIS GROUP. If the child does these correctly, go on to 7, 9, 6, 10, 8, 0 using the same procedure.

EVALUATION: Note which groups and symbols the child can match. The responses will indicate where instruction can begin.

INSTRUCTIONAL RESOURCE: Charlesworth, R., and Lind, K. K. (2003). *Math and Science for Young Children* (4th ed.). Clifton Park, NY: Delmar Learning.

SAMPLE ASSESSMENT TASK

6L   **Preoperational/Concrete Ages 5–7**
Groups and Symbols, Match Groups to Symbols: **Unit 24**

METHOD: Interview.

SKILL: Child will be able to match groups to symbols using groups of amounts 0 to 10 and numerals from 0 to 10.

MATERIALS: 5" ¥ 8" cards with numerals 0 to 10, 60 objects (e.g., chips, cube blocks, coins, buttons).

PROCEDURE: Lay out the numeral cards in front of the child in a random arrangement. Place the container of objects within easy reach. MAKE A GROUP FOR EACH NUMERAL. Let the child decide how to organize the materials.

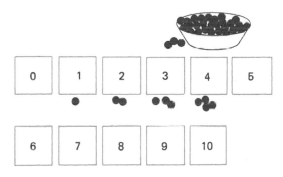

EVALUATION: Note for which numerals the child is able to make groups. Note how the child goes about the task. For example, does he sequence the numerals from 0 to 10? Does he place the objects in an organized pattern by each numeral? Can he recognize some amounts without counting? When he counts does he do it carefully? His responses will indicate where instruction should begin.

INSTRUCTIONAL RESOURCE: Charlesworth, R., and Lind, K. K. (2003). *Math and Science for Young Children* (4th ed.). Clifton Park, NY: Delmar Learning.

SAMPLE ASSESSMENT TASK

6K
Groups and Symbols, Write/Reproduce Numerals: Unit 24

Preoperational/Concrete Ages 5–7

METHOD: Interview.

SKILL: Child can reproduce (write) numerals from 0 to 10.

MATERIALS: Pencil, pen, black marker, black crayon, white paper, numeral cards from 0 to 10.

PROCEDURE: HERE IS A PIECE OF PAPER. PICK OUT ONE OF THESE (point to writing tools) THAT YOU WOULD LIKE TO USE. NOW, WRITE AS MANY NUMBERS AS YOU CAN. If the child is unable to write from memory, show him the numeral cards. COPY ANY OF THESE THAT YOU CAN.

EVALUATION: Note how many numerals the child can write and if they are in sequence. If the child is not able to write the numerals with ease, this indicates that responding to problems by writing is not at this time an appropriate response. Have him do activities in which movable numerals or markers can be placed on the correct answers.

INSTRUCTIONAL RESOURCE: Charlesworth, R., and Lind, K. K. (2003). *Math and Science for Young Children* (4th ed.). Clifton Park, NY: Delmar Learning.

Naturalistic Activities

As the child learns that groups and symbols go together, this will be reflected in her daily play activities.

◆ Mary and Dean have set up a grocery store. Dean has made price tags, and Mary has made play money from construction paper. They have written numerals on each price tag and piece of money. Sam comes up and picks out a box of breakfast cereal and a carton of milk. Dean takes the tags, "That will be $4." Sam counts out four play dollar bills. Dean takes a piece of paper from a note pad and writes a "receipt." "Here, Sam."

◆ Brent has drawn a picture of a birthday cake. There are six candles on the cake and a big numeral 6. "This is for my next birthday. I will be six."

◆ The flannelboard and a group of primary cutouts have been left out in a quiet corner.

George sits deep in thought as he places the numerals in order and counts out a group of cutouts to go with each numeral.

Each child uses what she has already learned in ways that she has seen adults use these skills and concepts.

Informal Activities

The child can work with groups and numerals best through informal experiences. Each child needs a different amount of practice. By making available many materials that the child can work with on his own, the teacher can help each child have the amount of practice he needs. Each child can choose to use the group of materials that he finds the most interesting.

Workjobs (Baratta-Lorton, 1972) and *Workjobs II* (Baratta-Lorton, 1979) are excellent resources for groups and symbols activities and materials. The basic activities for matching symbols to groups and groups to symbols involve the use of the following kinds of materials.

1. Materials where the numerals are "fixed" and counters are available for making the groups. These are called counting trays and may be made or purchased. They may be set up with the numerals all in one row or in two or more rows.

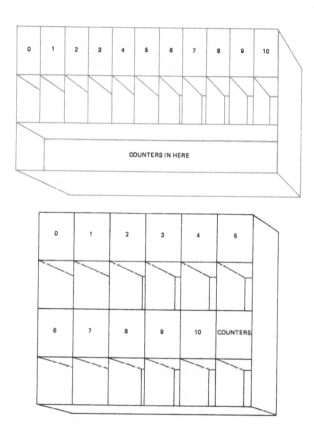

2. Materials where there are movable containers on which the numerals are written and counters of some kind. There might be pennies and banks, cups and buttons, cans and sticks, and similar items.

3. Individual numeral cards with a space for the child to make a group to match.

4. Groups of real things or pictures of things that must be matched to numerals written on cards.

Each child can be shown each new set of materials. He can then have a turn to work with them. If the teacher finds that a child has a hard time, she can give him some help and make sure he takes part in some structured activities.

Informal experiences in which the child writes numerals come up when the child asks how to write his age, phone number, or address. Some children who are interested in writing may copy numerals that they see in the environment—on the clock and calendar or on the numeral cards used in matching and group-making activities. These children should be encouraged and helped if needed. The teacher can make or buy a group of sandpaper numerals. The child can trace these with his finger to get the feel of the shape and the movement needed to make the numeral. Formal writing lessons should not take place until the child's fine muscle coordination is well developed. For some children this might not be until they are seven or eight years of age.

Structured Activities

Structured activities with symbols and groups for the young child are done in the form of games. One type of game has the child match groups and numerals using a theme such as "Letters to the Post Office" or "Fish in the Fishbowl." A second is the basic board game. A third type of game is the lotto or bingo type. In each case, the teacher structures the game. However, once the children know the rules, two or more can play on their own. One example of each game is described. With a little imagination, the teacher can think of variations. The last three activities are for the child who can write numerals.

ACTIVITIES

GROUPS AND SYMBOLS: FISH IN THE FISHBOWL

OBJECTIVE: To match groups and symbols for the numerals 0 through 10.

MATERIALS: Sketch 11 fishbowls about 7" × 10" on separate pieces of cardboard or poster board. On each bowl write one of the numerals from 0 to 10. Cut out 11 fish, 1 for each bowl. On each fish, put dots—from 0 on the first to 10 on the last.

NATURALISTIC AND INFORMAL ACTIVITIES: Place the fish and fish bowls in the math center for the children to explore. Note if they make any matches as they play with them. Do they notice the dots and numerals and attempt to make matches? If they make matches, ask them to tell you about them.

STRUCTURED ACTIVITY: Play with two or more children. Line up the fishbowls (on a chalk tray is a good place). One at a time, have each child choose a fish, sight unseen. Have her match her fish to its own bowl.

FOLLOW-UP:
1. Make fish with other kinds of sets such as stripes or stars.
2. Line up the fish, and have the children match the fishbowls to the right fish.

GROUPS AND SYMBOLS: BASIC BOARD GAMES

OBJECTIVE: To match groups and symbols.

MATERIALS: The basic materials can be purchased or can be made by the teacher. Basic materials would include:
◆ A piece of poster board (18" × 36") for the game board
◆ Clear Contac® or laminating material
◆ Marking pens
◆ Spinner cards, plain 3" × 5" file cards, or a die
◆ Place markers (chips, buttons, or other counters)

Materials for three basic games are shown: The game boards can be set up with a theme for interest such as the race car game. Themes might be "Going to School," "The Road to Happy Land," or whatever the teacher's or children's imaginations can think of.

NATURALISTIC AND INFORMAL ACTIVITIES: Put the games out, one at a time, during center time. Note if any of the children are familiar with these types of games. Take note of what they do. Do they know about turn taking? Do they know how to use the spinners and count the jumps? Do they make up rules?

STRUCTURED ACTIVITY: The basic activity is the same for each game. Each child picks a marker and puts it on START. Then each in turn spins the spinner (or chooses a card or rolls the die) and moves to the square that matches.

FOLLOW-UP:
1. The children can learn to play the games on their own.

2. Make new games with new themes. Make games with more moves and using more numerals and larger groups to match.
3. Let the children make up their own rules.

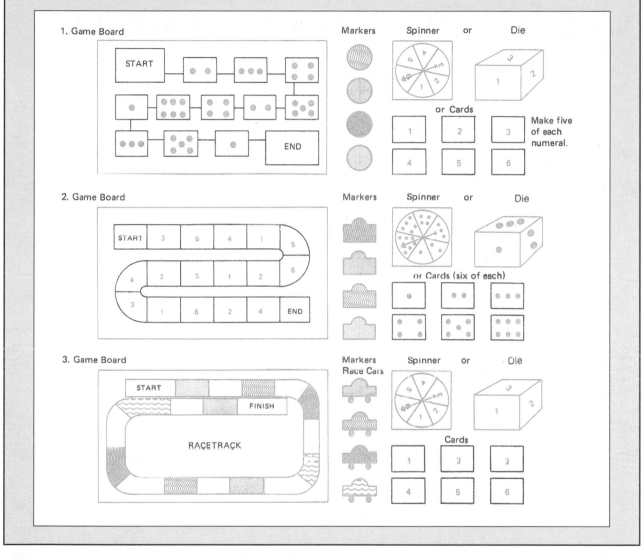

GROUPS AND SYMBOLS: LOTTO AND BINGO GAMES

OBJECTIVE: To match groups and symbols.

MATERIALS: For both games, there should be six basic game cards, each with six or more squares (the more squares, the longer and harder the game). For lotto, there is one card to match each square. For bingo, there must also be markers to put on the squares. For bingo, squares on the basic game cards are repeated; for lotto, they are not.

NATURALISTIC AND INFORMAL ACTIVITIES: Put the games out, one at a time, during center time. Note if any of the children are familiar with these types of games. Take note of what they do. Do they know about turn taking? Do they know how to use the materials and make matches? Do they recognize the numerals on the bingo cards? Do they make up rules?

STRUCTURED ACTIVITIES:

1. Lotto Game

   Each child receives a basic game card. The matching cards are shuffled and held up one at a time. The child must call out if the card has her mark on it (dot, circle, triangle) and then match the numeral to the right group. The game can be played until one person fills her card or until everyone does.

2. Bingo Game

   Each child receives a basic game card. She also receives nine chips. The matching set cards are shuffled. They are held up one at a time. The child puts a chip on the numeral that goes with the group on the card. When someone gets a row full in any direction, the game starts again.

FOLLOW-UP: More games can be made using different picture groups and adding more squares to the basic game cards. Bingo cards must always have the same odd number of squares up and down and across (three-by-three, five-by-five, seven-by-seven).

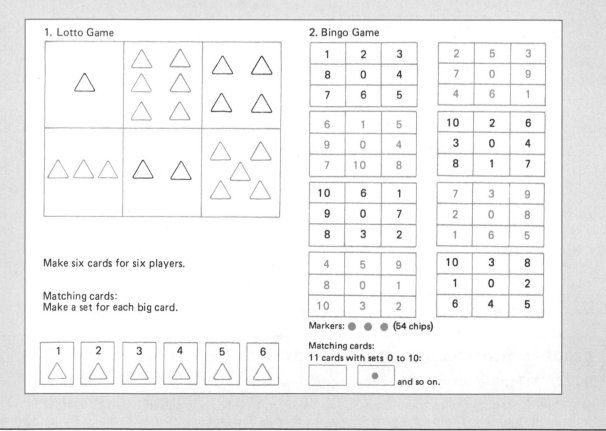

GROUPS AND SYMBOLS: MY OWN NUMBER BOOK

OBJECTIVE: To match groups and symbols.

MATERIALS: Booklets made with construction paper covers and several pages made from newsprint or other plain paper, hole puncher and yarn or brads to hold book together, crayons, glue, scissors, and more paper or stickers.

NATURALISTIC AND INFORMAL ACTIVITIES: The children should have had opportunities to make their own books in the writing center. They should also have had number books read to them and have explored them independently.

STRUCTURED ACTIVITY: The child writes or asks the teacher to write a numeral on each page of the book. The child then puts a set on each page. Sets can be made using
1. Stickers
2. Cutouts made by the child
3. Drawings done by the child

FOLLOW-UP: Have the children show their books to each other and then take the books home. Also read to the children some of the number books listed in Appendix B.

GROUPS AND SYMBOLS: WRITING NUMERALS TO MATCH GROUPS

OBJECTIVE: To write the numeral that goes with a group.

MATERIALS: Objects and pictures of objects, chalk and chalkboard, crayons, pencils, and paper.

NATURALISTIC AND INFORMAL ACTIVITIES: Children should have explored many numerals and groups and numeral materials. Numeral models should be available in the writing center for the children to observe and copy.

STRUCTURED ACTIVITY: Show the child some objects or pictures of objects. WRITE THE NUMERAL THAT TELLS HOW MANY _____ THERE ARE. The child then writes the numeral on the chalkboard or on a piece of paper.

FOLLOW-UP: Get some clear acetate. Make some set pictures that can be placed in acetate folders for the child to use on her own. Acetate folders are made by taking a piece of cardboard and taping a piece of acetate of the same size on with some plastic tape. The child can write on the acetate with a nonpermanent marker and then erase her mark with a tissue or a soft cloth.

EXAMPLE WORLD WIDE WEB ACTIVITIES

◆ Count With Me at http://www.pbs.org/teachersource/math
◆ Fishing for Numbers. (Pre-K and K). Practice number recognition and counting by matching the number on the fishing pole to the number of fish in the lake. Link at http://www.lightspan.com

Counting books are another resource for connecting groups and symbols. In most counting books the numerals are included with each set to be counted. Caution must be taken in selecting counting books. Ballenger, Benham, and Hosticka (1984) suggest the following criteria for selecting counting books.

1. Be sure the numerals always refer to how many and not to ordinal position or sequence.
2. The numeral names should also always refer to how many.
3. The narrative on the page should clearly identify the set of objects that the numeral is associated with.
4. The illustrations of objects to be counted and connected to the numeral on each page should be clear and distinct.
5. When ordinals are being used, the starting position (e.g., first) should be clearly identified.
6. When identifying ordinal positions, the correct terms should be used (e.g., first, second, third).
7. When numerals are used to indicate ordinal position, they should be written as 1st, 2nd, 3rd, and so on.
8. The numerals should be uniform in size (not small numerals for small groups and larger numerals for larger groups).
9. The book should emphasize the concept of one-to-one correspondence.
10. When amounts above 10 and their associated numerals are illustrated, the amounts should be depicted as a group of 10 plus the additional items.

Computers and calculators can also be used for helping children acquire the groups and symbols connection. Most of the software listed in Units 9 and 23 as supportive of counting and symbol recognition also connects groups and symbols. These programs should also be evaluated with the same criteria suggested for books. Students could play games with their calculators such as closing their eyes, pressing a key, identifying the numeral, and then selecting or constructing a group that goes with the numeral. There are also many self-correcting computer/calculator-type toys available that children enjoy using.

Groups and symbol activities may be included in other content areas. See Figure 24–1 for examples.

Evaluation

With young children most of the evaluation can be done by observing their use of the materials for informal activities. The adult can also notice how the children do when they play the structured games.

For children about to enter first grade, an individual interview should be done using the assessment interviews in this unit and in Appendix A.

Summary

When the child works with groups and symbols, he puts together the skills and ideas learned earlier. He must match, count, classify, compare, order, and associate written numerals with groups.

He learns to match groups to symbols and symbols to groups. He also learns to write each number symbol. The child uses mostly materials that can be used informally on his own. He can also learn from more structured game kinds of activities, number books, computer games, and calculator activities.

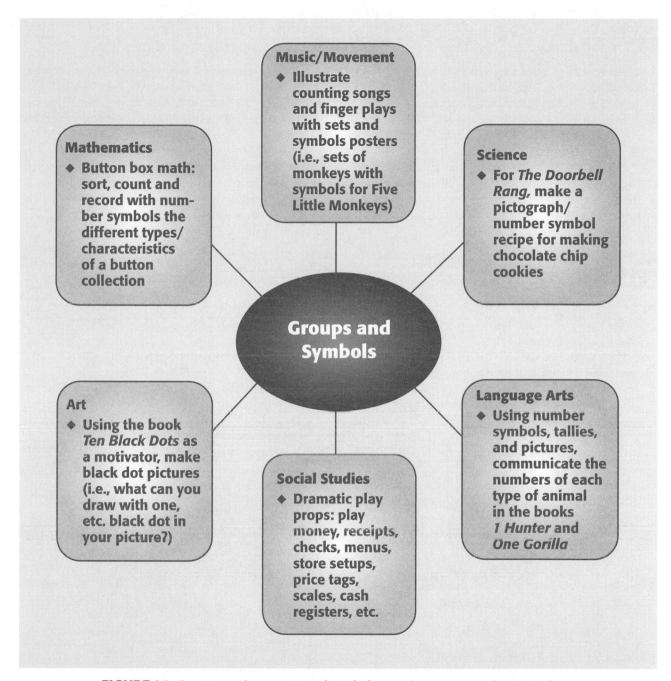

FIGURE 24–1   Integrating groups and symbols experiences across the curriculum.

SUGGESTED ACTIVITIES

1. Observe prekindergarten, kindergarten, and first-grade students during work and play. Note instances where they match groups and symbols.
2. Add groups and symbols assessment tasks to your Assessment File/Notebook and activities to your Activity File/Notebook.
3. Make groups and symbols instructional materials. Use them with prekindergarten, kindergarten, and first-grade students. Share the results with the class.
4. Look through some early childhood materials catalogs for groups and symbols materials. If you had $300 to spend, which would you purchase?
5. Review one or more computer programs listed in Units 9 and 23 using the procedure suggested in Activity 7, Unit 9 and the criteria suggested for children's counting books in this unit.
6. Go to a bookstore, the children's literature library, and/or your local public library. Identify three or more counting books and evaluate them using the criteria suggested by Ballenger et al.

*look at activity box
use those

REVIEW

A. List and describe the skills a child should have before doing the activities suggested in this unit or in higher-level units.
B. Decide which of the following incidents are examples of (a) matching a symbol to a group, (b) reproducing symbols, or (c) matching a group to a symbol:
   1. Mario is writing down his phone number.
   2. Kate selects three Unifix Cubes® to go with the numeral 3.
   3. Fong selects the magnetic numeral 6 to go with the six squares on the magnet board.
C. Describe three kinds of materials that are designed to be used for matching symbols to groups and groups to symbols.
D. If four-year-old John tells you he wants to know how to write his phone number, what should you do?
E. Describe two structured groups and symbols activities.
F. List some materials that young children could use for reproducing symbols.
G. Describe two informal groups and symbols activities young children might be engaged in.
H. What criteria should be used when selecting books and software to use in helping children acquire the groups and symbols connection?

REFERENCES

Ballenger, M., & Hosticka, A. (1984, September/ October). Children's counting books. *Childhood Education*, 30–35.

Baratta-Lorton, M. (1972) *Workjobs*. Menlo Park, CA: Addison-Wesley.

Baratta-Lorton, M. (1979) *Workjobs II*. Menlo Park, CA: Addison-Wesley.

FURTHER READING AND RESOURCES

AIMS Educational Products. AIMS Education Foundation, P.O. Box 8120, Fresno, CA 93747-8210.

Baratta-Lorton, M. (1976). *Mathematics their way*. Menlo Park, CA: Addison-Wesley.

Box it or bag it mathematics (K–2). Portland, OR: The Math Learning Center. (800-575-8130) (http://www.mlc.pdx.edu)

Bridges in mathematics (K–2). Portland, OR: The Math Learning Center. (800-575-8130) (http://www.mlc.pdx.edu)

Copley, J. V. (2000). *The young child and mathematics*. Washington, DC: National Association for the Education of Young Children.

Copley, J. V. (Ed.). (1999). *Mathematics in the early years*. Washington, DC: National Association for the Education of Young Children.

National Council of Teachers of Mathematics. (2000). *Principles and standards for school mathematics*. Reston, VA: Author. (http://www.nctm.org)

Richardson, K. (1984). *Developing number concepts using Unifix Cubes.*® Menlo Park, CA: Addison-Wesley.

Richardson, K. (1999). *Developing number concepts: Counting, comparing, and pattern (Book 1)*. Parsippany, NJ: Dale Seymour.

Richardson, K. (1999). *Developing number concepts: Planning guide*. Parsippany, NJ: Dale Seymour.

Wakefield, A. P. (1998). *Early childhood number games*. Boston: Allyn & Bacon.

Also see the games and materials resources suggested in Unit 23 and the books suggested in Appendix B.

U N I T 2 5
Higher-Level Activities and Concepts

OBJECTIVES

After reading this unit, you should be able to:

◆ List the eight areas in which higher-level concept activities are described in the unit.

◆ Describe the three higher levels of classification.

◆ Plan higher-level activities for children who are near the stage of concrete operations.

The experiences in this unit include further applications of skills that children learned through the activities in the previous units. These experiences support more complex application of the processes of problem solving, reasoning, communication connections, and representation (NCTM, 2000; see Unit 15). They are appropriate for preschool/kindergarten students who are developing at a fast rate and can do the higher-level assessment tasks with ease or for the older students who still need concrete experiences. The nine areas presented are algebraic thinking, **classification**, **shape**, **spatial relations**, **concrete whole number operations**, **graphs**, **symbolic level** activities, **quantities above 10**, and **estimation**.

Assessment

Assessment determines where the children are in their zones of proximal development (ZPD, Unit 1). That is, where they can work independently and where they can complete tasks with support from scaffolding by an adult or a more advanced peer.

The teacher looks at the child's level in each area. Then he makes a decision as to when to introduce these activities. When introduced to one child, any one activity could capture the interest of another child who might be at a lower developmental level. Therefore, it is not necessary to wait for all the children to be at the highest level to begin. Children at lower levels can participate in these activities as observers and as contributors. The higher-level child can serve as a model for the lower-level child. The lower-level child might be able to do part of the task following the leadership of the higher-level child. For example, if a floor plan of the classroom is being made, the more advanced child might design it while everyone draws a picture of a piece of furniture to put on the floor plan. The more advanced child might get help from the less advanced child when she makes a graph. The less advanced child can count and measure; the more advanced child records the results. Children can work in pairs to solve concrete addition, subtraction, multiplication, and division problems. They can move into higher levels of symbol use and work with numerals and quantities greater than 10. They can also work together exploring calculators and computer software.

Algebraic Thinking

Algebra is viewed by many people as a blockade in their progress in understanding mathematics. It is seen as the mindless abstract manipulation of symbols. NCTM is promoting a new vision of algebra as "a way of thinking, a method of seeing and expressing relationships" (Moses, 1997). It is seen as a way of thinking that goes beyond numerical reasoning and that can begin in the elementary grades.

For preprimary-level children, algebraic thinking is reflected in their discovery of patterns as they sort and group objects, combine groups and count totals, build with blocks, and use objects as symbolic representations. As young children explore these materials, they construct generalizations that reflect an increasing understanding of patterns and relationships (Curcio & Schwartz, 1997).

Children figure out how to balance their block buildings. They discover that 10 groups of 10 is 100.

Exploring with a pan balance, they find that if they put certain objects on each side, the pans will balance. They find that groups will break down into smaller sets and still be the same number. These discoveries are the outcome of the beginnings of algebraic thinking. As children move into higher-level activities, it is important to continue to provide them with opportunities for exploration and discovery. Algebraic reasoning is also supported by science inquiry activities.

Classification

The higher levels of classification are called **multiple classification, class inclusion,** and **hierarchical classification.** Multiple classification requires the child to classify things in more than one way and to solve matrix problems. Figures 25–1 and 25–2 illustrate these two types of multiple classification. In Figure 25–1, the child is shown three shapes, each in three

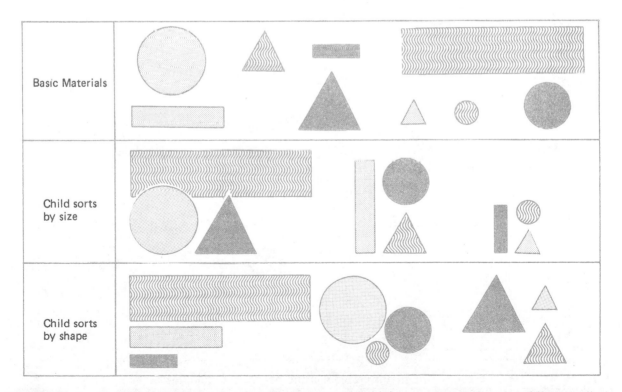

FIGURE 25–1 *Multiple classification* involves sorting one way and then sorting again using different criteria.

sizes and in three colors. He is asked to put the ones together that belong together. He is then asked to find another way to divide the shapes.

The preoperational child will not be able to do this. He centers on his first sort. Some games are suggested that will help the child move to concrete operations.

Matrix problems are illustrated in Figure 25–2. A simple two-by-two matrix is shown in Figure 25–2(A). In this case, size and number must both be considered to complete the matrix. The problem can be made more difficult by making the matrix larger (there are always the same number of squares in each row, both across and up and down). Figure 25–2(B) part shows a four-by-four matrix. The easiest problem is to fill in part of a matrix. The hardest problem is to fill in a whole blank matrix as is illustrated in Figure 25–2(C).

The preoperational child cannot see that one class may be included within another (*class inclusion*). For example, the child is shown 10 flowers: two roses and

eight daisies. The child can divide the flowers into two groups: roses and daisies. He knows that they are all flowers. When asked if there are more flowers or more daisies, he will answer "More daisies." He is fooled by what he sees and centers on the greater number of daisies. He is not able to hold in his mind that daisies are also flowers. This problem is shown in Figure 25–3.

Hierarchical classification has to do with classes being within classes. For example, black kittens ⇒ kittens ⇒ house cats ⇒ cats ⇒ mammals. As can be seen in Figure 25–4, this forms a *hierarchy*, or a series of ever-larger classes. Basic-level concepts are usually learned first. This level includes categories such as dogs, monkeys, cats, cows, and elephants as illustrated in Figure 25–4. Superordinate-level concepts such as mammals, furniture, vehicles, and so on are learned next. Finally, children learn subordinate categories such as domestic cats and wildcats or types of chairs such as dining room, living room, rocking, kitchen, folding, and so on.

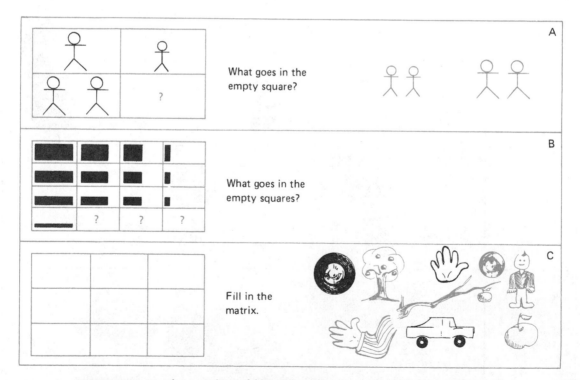

FIGURE 25–2 The matrix problem is another type of multiple classification.

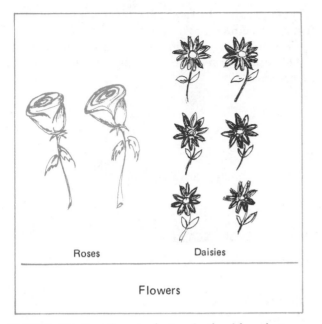

Another interesting aspect of young children's concept learning is their view of which characteristics the members of a class have in common. Although preoperational-level children tend to be perceptually bound when they attempt to solve many types of conceptual problems, they are able to classify on category membership when shown things that are perceptually similar. For example, four-year-olds were shown pictures of a blackbird; a bat, which looked much like the blackbird; and a flamingo. They were told that the flamingo gave its baby mashed-up food, and the bat gave its baby milk. When asked what the blackbird fed its baby, they responded that it gave its baby mashed-up food. In this case the children looked beyond the most obvious physical attributes.

Another type of characteristic that is interesting to ask young children about is their view of what is inside members of a class. When young children are asked if members of a class all have the same "stuff" inside, preschoolers tend to say that yes, they have; that is, all dogs, people, chairs, and dolls are the same inside. Children are aware of more than just observable similarities. By second grade, they can discriminate

FIGURE 25–3 *Class inclusion* is the idea that one class can be included in another.

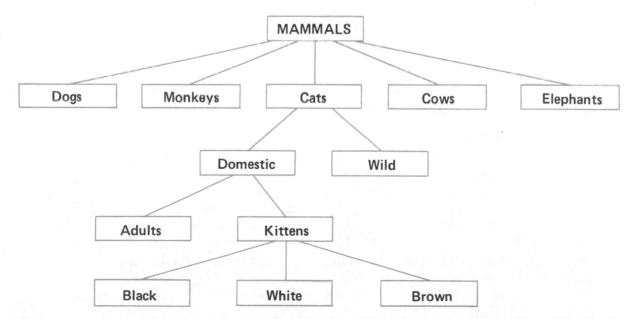

FIGURE 25–4 In a *hierarchical classification*, all things in each lower class are included in the next higher class.

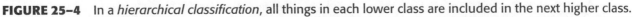

between natural and synthetic items; that is, they realize that living things such as dogs, people, or apples are, for the most part, the same inside as other dogs, people, or apples, although the insides of different types of chairs, dolls, or other manufactured items are not necessarily the same. For the younger children, category membership overwhelms other factors.

The following activities will help the transitional child (usually ages five to seven) to enter concrete operations.

ACTIVITIES

HIGHER-LEVEL CLASSIFICATION: MULTIPLE CLASSIFICATION, RECLASSIFY

OBJECTIVE: To help the transitional child learn that groups of objects or pictures can sometimes be sorted in more than one way.

MATERIALS: Any group of objects or pictures of objects that can be classified in more than one way, for example, pictures or cardboard cutouts of dogs of different colors (brown and white), sizes (large and small), and hair lengths (long and short).

ACTIVITY: Place the dogs in front of the child. WHICH DOGS BELONG TOGETHER or ARE THEY THE SAME? Note whether she groups by size, color, or hair length. NOW, WHAT IS ANOTHER WAY TO PUT THEM IN SETS? CAN THEY BE PUT LIKE (name another way)? Put them in one pile again if the child is puzzled. OKAY, NOW TRY TO SORT THE _____ FROM THE _____. Repeat using different criteria each time.

FOLLOW-UP: Make other sets of materials. Set them up in boxes where the child can get them out and use them during free playtime. Make some felt pieces to use on the flannelboard.

HIGHER-LEVEL CLASSIFICATION: MULTIPLE CLASSIFICATION, MATRICES

OBJECTIVE: To help the transitional child see that things may be related on more than one criterion.

MATERIALS: Purchase or make a matrix game. Start with a two-by-two matrix and gradually increase the size (three-by-three, four-by-four, and so on). Use any of the criteria from Unit 10 such as color, size, shape, material, pattern, texture, function, association, class name, common feature, or number. Make a game board from poster board or wood. Draw or paint permanent lines. Use a flannelboard, and make the lines for the matrix with lengths of yarn. An example of a three-by-three board is shown. Start with three-dimensional materials, then cutouts, then cards.

ACTIVITIES: Start with the matrix filled except for one space, and ask the child to choose from two items the one that goes in the empty space. WHICH ONE OF THESE GOES HERE? After the item is placed, say, WHY DOES IT BELONG THERE? Once the child understands the task, more spaces can be left empty until it is left for the child to fill in the whole matrix.

FOLLOW-UP: Add more games that use different categories and larger matrices.

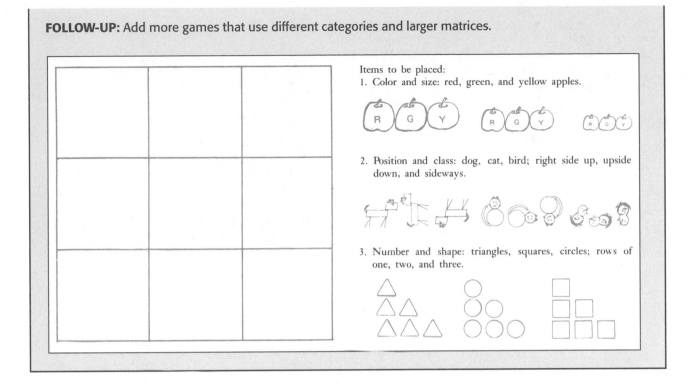

Items to be placed:
1. Color and size: red, green, and yellow apples.

2. Position and class: dog, cat, bird; right side up, upside down, and sideways.

3. Number and shape: triangles, squares, circles; rows of one, two, and three.

HIGHER-LEVEL CLASSIFICATION: CLASS INCLUSION

OBJECTIVE: To help the transitional child see that a smaller set may be included within a larger set.

MATERIALS: Seven animals. Two kinds should be included (such as horses and cows, pigs and chickens, dogs and cats). There should be four of one animal and three of the other. These can be cutouts or toy animals.

ACTIVITY: Place the animals within an enclosure (a yarn circle or a fence made of blocks). WHO IS INSIDE THE FENCE? Children will answer "horses," "cows," "animals." SHOW ME WHICH ONES ARE HORSES (COWS, ANIMALS). ARE THERE MORE HORSES OR MORE ANIMALS? HOW DO YOU KNOW? LET'S CHECK (use one-to-one correspondence).

FOLLOW-UP: Play the same game. Use other categories such as plants, types of material, size, and so on. Increase the size of the sets.

HIGHER-LEVEL CLASSIFICATION: HIERARCHICAL

OBJECTIVE: To help the transitional child see that each thing may be part of a larger category (or set of things).

MATERIALS: Make some sets of sorting cards. Glue pictures from catalogs and/or workbooks onto file cards or poster board. The following are some that can be used.

◆ One black cat, several house cats, cats of other colors, one tiger, one lion, one panther, one bobcat, one dog, one horse, one cow, one squirrel, one bear
◆ One duck, three swans, five other birds, five other animals
◆ One teaspoon, two soupspoons, a serving spoon, two baby spoons, three forks, two knives

ACTIVITIES: Place the cards where they can all be seen. Give the following instructions.

1. FIND ALL THE ANIMALS. FIND ALL THE CATS. FIND ALL THE HOUSE CATS. FIND ALL THE BLACK CATS. Mix up the cards, and lay them out again. PUT THEM IN SETS THE WAY YOU THINK THEY SHOULD BE. When the child is done, WHY DID YOU PUT THEM THAT WAY? Mix them up, and lay them out. IF ALL THE ANIMALS WERE HUNGRY, WOULD THE BLACK CAT BE HUNGRY? IF THE BLACK CAT IS HUNGRY, ARE ALL THE ANIMALS HUNGRY?

2. FIND ALL THE ANIMALS. FIND ALL THE BIRDS. FIND THE WATERBIRDS. FIND THE DUCK. Mix up the cards, and lay them out again. PUT THEM IN SETS THE WAY YOU THINK THEY SHOULD BE. When the child is done, WHY DO THEY BELONG THAT WAY? Mix them up, and lay them out again. IF ALL THE BIRDS WERE COLD, WOULD THE DUCK BE COLD? IF THE DUCK WERE COLD, WOULD ALL THE WATERBIRDS BE COLD? IF ALL THE ANIMALS WERE COLD, WOULD THE WATERBIRDS BE COLD?

3. FIND ALL THE THINGS THAT WE EAT WITH. FIND ALL THE KNIVES. FIND ALL THE FORKS. FIND ALL THE SPOONS. Mix them up, and lay them out again. PUT THEM IN SETS THE WAY YOU THINK THEY BELONG. When the child is done, WHY DO THEY BELONG THAT WAY? Mix them up, and lay them out again. IF ALL THE SPOONS ARE DIRTY, WOULD THE TEASPOON BE DIRTY? IF ALL THE THINGS WE EAT WITH WERE DIRTY, WOULD THE BIG SPOON BE DIRTY? IF THE TEASPOON IS DIRTY, ARE ALL THE OTHER THINGS WE EAT WITH DIRTY TOO?

FOLLOW-UP: Make up other hierarchies. Leave the card sets out for the children to sort during play. Ask them some of the same kinds of questions informally.

HIGHER-LEVEL CLASSIFICATION: MULTIPLE CLASSIFICATION

OBJECTIVE: To help the transitional child learn to group things in a variety of ways using logical reasoning.

MATERIALS: *What to Wear?* (1998), an emergent reader book by Sharon Young. The book depicts a boy who has two shirts, two pairs of shorts, and two caps, with each item a different color. The problem presented to the reader is figuring out how many different outfits the boy can put together.

ACTIVITIES: The *Teacher Guide for Harry's Math Books™* Set B (1998) suggests a number of activities that can be done to support the concepts in *What to Wear?* For example

1. Have the children discuss ways clothes can be sorted such as school clothes/play clothes/dress-up clothes or clean clothes/dirty clothes.

2. Use cutouts to see that although there are only two of each type of clothing in the book, more than two outfits can be constructed.

3. Make connections with other areas such as meal combinations with two main dishes, two vegetables, two potatoes, two desserts, and two drinks.

4. Have the students draw the eight different outfits that can be derived from the book.

FOLLOW-UP: Provide real clothing in the dramatic play center. Note how many combinations of outfits the students can put together.

Shape

Once the child can match, sort, and name shapes she can also reproduce shapes. This can be done informally. The following are some materials that can be used:

Geoboards can be purchased or made. A *geoboard* is a square board with headed screws or pegs sticking up at equal intervals. The child is given a supply of rubber bands and can experiment in making shapes by stretching the rubber bands between the nails.

A container of pipe cleaners or straws can be put out. The children can be asked to make as many different shapes as they can. These can be glued onto construction paper. Strips of paper, toothpicks, string, and yarn can also be used to make shapes.

Pattern blocks are an important material for children to use in exploring shape (Wilson, 2001). For beginners, puzzle frames are usually provided that indicate the shapes to be used to fill the frame. For more advanced students, frames are provided where the pattern block shapes are partially indicated. Children who can select pieces to fill in the puzzle without trial and error may be provided puzzle frames with no hints as to which pattern block shapes will fill the frame. Children who master these advanced frames can be offered the challenge of filling the frames in more than one way.

Spatial Relations

Children can learn more about space after playing the treasure hunt game described in Unit 13 by reproducing the space around them as a floor plan or a map. Start with the classroom for the first map. Then move to the whole building, the neighborhood, and the town or city. Be sure the children have maps among their dramatic play props.

HIGHER-LEVEL ACTIVITIES: SPATIAL RELATIONS, FLOOR PLANS

OBJECTIVE: To relate position in space to symbols of position in space.

MATERIALS: Large piece of poster board or heavy paper, markers, pens, construction paper, glue, crayons, scissors, some simple sample floor plans.

ACTIVITY:
1. Show the children some floor plans. WHAT ARE THESE? WHAT ARE THEY FOR? IF WE MAKE A FLOOR PLAN OF OUR ROOM, WHAT WOULD WE PUT ON IT? Make a list.
2. Show the children a large piece of poster board or heavy paper. WE CAN MAKE A PLAN OF OUR ROOM ON HERE. EACH OF YOU CAN MAKE SOMETHING THAT IS IN THE ROOM, JUST LIKE ON OUR LIST. THEN YOU CAN GLUE IT IN THE RIGHT PLACE. I'VE MARKED IN THE DOORS AND WINDOWS FOR YOU. As each child draws and cuts out an item (a table, shelf, sink, chair) have her show you where it belongs on the plan and glue it on.

FOLLOW-UP: After the plan is done, it should be left up on the wall so the children can look at it and talk about it. They can also add more things to the plan. The same procedure can later be used to make a plan of the building. Teacher and children should walk around the whole place. They should talk about which rooms are next to each other and which rooms are across from each other. Sticks or straws can be used to lay out the plan.

HIGHER-LEVEL ACTIVITIES: SPATIAL RELATIONS, MAPS

OBJECTIVE: To relate position in space to symbols of position in space.

MATERIALS: Map of the city, large piece of poster board or heavy paper, marking pens, construction paper, glue, crayons, scissors.

ACTIVITY: Show the children the map of the city (or county in a rural area). Explain that this is a picture of where the streets would be if the children were looking down from a plane or a helicopter. Mark each child's home on the map with a small label with her name. Mark where the school is. Talk about who lives closest and who lives farthest away. Each child's address can be printed on a card and reviewed with her each day. The teacher can help mark out the streets and roads. The children can then cut out and glue down strips of black paper for the streets (and/or roads). Each child can draw a picture of her home and glue it on the map. The map can be kept up on the wall for children to look at and talk about. As field trips are taken during the year, each place can be added to the map.

FOLLOW-UP: Encourage the children to look at and talk about the map. Help them add new points of interest. Help children who would like to make their own maps. Bring in maps of the state, the country, and the world. Try to purchase United States and world map puzzles.

HIGHER LEVEL ACTIVITIES: SHAPE AND SPACE FROM THE INTERNET

About Shape and About Space. About Shape includes Quilts, Taxicab Treasure Hunt (searching through city blocks), and Corner to Corner (diagonal of a square). About Space includes I Took a Trip on a Train (matching a map with snapshots), Pilot Plans and Silhouettes (designing a structure), and Shadows (matching figures with their shadows). An Annenberg Project, there is a link from http://www.learner.org/teacherslab/math/geometry/space/

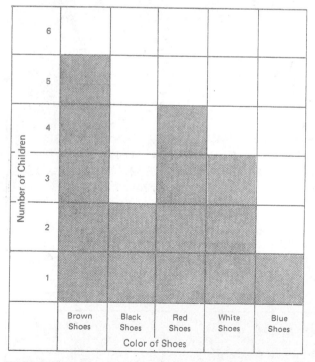

FIGURE 25–5 Square paper graphs can be made by the child who has had many experiences with simpler graphs.

Graphs

The fourth level of graphs introduces the use of squared paper. The child may graph the same kind of things as discussed in Unit 20. He will now use squared paper with squares that can be colored in. These should be introduced only after the child has had many experiences of the kinds described in Unit 20. The squares should be large. A completed graph might look like the one shown in Figure 25–5.

Concrete Whole Number Operations

Once children have a basic understanding of one-to-one correspondence, number and counting, and comparing, they can sharpen their problem-solving skills with concrete whole number operations. That is, they can solve simple addition, subtraction, division, and multiplication problems using concrete materials. You can devise some simple problems to use as models as described in Unit 3. Some examples are in the box that follows. Provide the children with 10 counters (pennies, chips, Unifix Cubes,® and so on) or the real items or replicas of the real items described in the problems. The children will gradually catch on and begin devising their own problems, such as those described by Skinner (1990).

As children grow and develop and have more experiences with whole number operations, they learn more strategies for solving problems. They gradually stop using the less efficient strategies and retain the more efficient ones. For example, four- and five-year-olds usually begin addition with the *counting all* strategy. That is, for a problem such as "John has three cars and Kate gives him two more. How many does John have now?," the four- or five-year-old will count all the cars (one-two-three-four-five). Fives will gradually change to *counting on*; that is, considering that John has three cars, they then count on two more (four-five). Even older children who are using recall $(3 + 2 = 5)$ will check with counting all and counting on. When observing children working with division, note whether or not they make use of their concept of one-to-one correspondence (for example, when giving three people equal numbers of cookies, note whether they pass out the cookies one at a time, consecutively to each of the three recipients).

One More Child by Sharon Young (1998) takes the emergent reader through the process of adding on one from one to four. This affords an opportunity to see the logic that when you add one more, the total is the next number in order. The students can use objects or a calculator to continue adding ones. Suggest they add several ones and discover how many they obtain. The book *Six Pieces of Cake* (1998) takes the emergent reader through the subtraction process in which one-by-one pieces of cake are taken off a plate.

The Symbolic Level

Children who can connect groups (or sets) and symbols (Unit 24), identify numerals 0 to 9, and do concrete addition and subtraction problems can move to the next step, which is connecting groups (or sets) and symbols in addition and subtraction.

As children continue to create their own problems and work on teacher-created problems, they can be encouraged to communicate their findings. Suggest that they draw, write, and use numerals to show their results. They can use cards with numerals written on them and gradually write the numerals themselves. Children can work in pairs on problems and trade problems with other students.

ADDITION:
- If Mary has three pennies and her mother gives her one more penny, how many pennies will Mary have?
- George wants two cookies for himself and two for Richard. How many cookies should he ask for?

SUBTRACTION:
- Mary has six pennies. She gives three pennies to her sister. How many does she have now?
- George has six cookies. He gives Richard three. How many does he have left?

MULTIPLICATION:
- Mary gives two pennies to her sister, two to her brother, and two to her friend Kate. How many pennies did she give away?
- Tanya had three friends visiting. Mother said to give each one three cookies. How many cookies should Tanya get from the cookie jar?

DIVISION:
- Lai has three dolls. Two friends come to play. How many dolls should she give each friend so they will each have the same number?
- Lai's mother gives her a plate with nine cookies. How many cookies should Lai and each of her friends take so they each have the same number?

Problems can be devised with stories that fit thematic topics.

As the children work with these concrete symbol/ set addition and subtraction problems, they will begin to store the basic facts in their memories and retrieve them without counting. They can then do problems without objects. Just have the objects on hand in case they are needed to check the answers.

Excellent resources for games and materials are *Workjobs II* (Baratta-Lorton, 1979), *Mathematics Their Way*, (Baratta-Lorton, 1976), *The Young Child and Mathematics* (Copley, 2000), *Developing Number Concepts: Addition and Subtraction, Book 2* (Richardson, 1999), and *Developing Number Concepts Using Unifix Cubes*® (Richardson, 1984). In *What's Your Problem?* (Skinner, 1990) a means is provided for encouraging children to develop their own problems. Unit 27 provides a more detailed description of the procedure for introducing the symbols needed for whole number operations.

Calculators are also useful as tools for experimentation. Children will learn to make connections between problem solving and the signs on the calculator (i.e., +, −, and =).

Quantities above Ten

Once children can count 10 objects correctly, can identify the numerals 1 to 10, have a good grasp of one-to-one correspondence, and can accurately count by rote past 10, they are ready to move on to counting quantities above 10. They can acquire an understanding of quantities above 10 through an exploration of the relationship of groups of 10 with additional amounts. For example, they can count out 10 Unifix Cubes® and stick them together. Then they can pick one more Unifix Cube.® Ask if they know which number comes after 10. If they cannot provide an answer, tell them that 11 comes after 10. Have them take another cube. Ask if they know what comes after 11. If they do not know the answer, tell them 12. Go as far as they can count by rote accurately. When they get to 20, have them put their cubes together, lay them next to the first 10, and compare the number of cubes in the two rows. See if they can tell you that there are two 10s. Give them numeral cards for 11 to 19.

See if they can discover that the right-hand numeral matches up with how many more than 10 that numeral stands for.

Once the children understand through 19, they can move on to 20, 30, 40, and so on. By exploring the number of 10s and 1s represented by each numeral, they will discover the common pattern from 20 to 99; that is, that the 2 in 20 means two 10s, and no 1s, the 2 in 21 means two 10s and the 1 means one 1, and so on, and the same pattern holds true through 99.

Estimation

Estimation for young children involves making a sensible and reasonable response to the problem of how many are in a quantity or how much in a measurement something is. It is the "process of thinking about a 'how many' or 'how much' problem and possible solutions" (Lang, 2001, p. 463). Children might estimate how many objects (e.g., candies, teddy bears, screws, etc.) are in a jar or how many shoes tall the bookcase is. In order to come up with a reasonable response children need to have developed number, spatial, and measurement sense. Without these prerequisite concepts they will make wild guesses rather than reasonable estimates.

Lang (2001) suggests several ways to assist children so they can make reasonable estimates. A *referent* can be used such as, "If I know how tall John is, I can estimate how tall the bookcase is if he stands next to it." *Chunking* involves taking a known measurement and using it as a guide for estimating a larger measurement. For example, if the children know how long 10 Unifix Cubes® are, they can use this information to estimate the length of the table in cubes. Unitizing is another type of chunking where, if one part is known, then the whole can be estimated. For example, if a cup of pennies fills a jar half full, then two cups will fill the whole jar. If the number of pennies in the jar is known, then the number to fill the jar can be estimated. It is important that children understand the language of comparison (Units 11 and 15) in order to give and receive communications regarding their estimates.

Computer Software

Young children will enjoy exploring computer software (see Activity 5) that reinforces higher-level concepts and skills. Alligator Alley is an arcade-type game where a correct answer to a math problem placed on an apple results in the alligator eating the apple. Practice in the introductory steps of graphing can be obtained by playing Bumble Games. The Peanuts characters motivate children as they play a matching memory game, which builds skills in addition and subtraction in Peanuts Math Matcher.

Software for the more advanced student can provide challenges. Primary Graphing and Probability Workshop, Grades K–2 can be used by the not-yet-reader, because directions are provided with icons. Primary Geometry Workshop, Grades K–2 provides activities involving making, using, and measuring geometric shapes. Geometric shapes can be manipulated in a variety of ways using Logic Blocks.

KEY TERMS

classification
shape
spatial relations
concrete whole number operations
graphs

symbolic level
quantities above 10
estimation
algebra
multiple classification

class inclusion
hierarchical classification
geoboard

SUGGESTED ACTIVITIES

1. Observe in a kindergarten classroom. Note any behaviors that suggest that any of the children are ready for higher-level concept activities. Share your observations with the class.
2. Interview one or more kindergarten teachers. Ask them to describe the concept activities available for students who are entering the concrete operations period.
3. In a kindergarten or first grade, identify one or more transitional-level students. Plan and prepare two higher-level activities to try with them. Share the results with the class.
4. Include higher-level concept activities in your Activity File/Notebook.
5. Review some computer software that supports higher-level concepts and skills. Use the evaluation format suggested in Activity 7, Unit 9. Some suggested software follows:
   - ◆ Alligator Alley. Allen, TX: DLM (SRA, McGraw Hill).
   - ◆ Animals in Their World. Pleasantville, NY: Sunburst Technologies. (classification)
   - ◆ Beginning Math Concepts. Bedford Hills, NY: Orange Cherry Media Software.
   - ◆ Bumble Games. Fremont, CA: The Learning Company.
   - ◆ Coco's Math Project 1. Singapore, SG: Times Learning Systems Pte Ltd. (Ages four to 10). Involves number, grouping, shapes, weight, matching, and more.
   - ◆ The Graph Club (K–4). Watertown, MA: Tom Snyder. Provides for creating a variety of graphs from simple to complex.
   - ◆ Hey Taxi! Chatsworth, CA: OL—Opportunities for Learning.
   - ◆ Muppetville. Pleasantville, NY: Sunburst Communications. (shapes, symbols, colors, numbers)
   - ◆ My Make Believe Castle. Highgate Springs, VT: LOGO Computer Systems, Inc. (K–2). Populating a castle involves logical thinking, sequencing, and reasoning about spatial relations.
   - ◆ Peanuts Math Matcher. Chatsworth, CA: OL—Opportunities for Learning.

- Piggy in Numberland. Santa Cruz, CA: Learning in Motion. (Pre-K). Eleven activities deal with 25 math concepts.
- Primary Geometry Workshop, Grades K–2. (1991). Glenview, IL: Scott, Foresman, & Co. (reviewed in *Arithmetic Teacher*, April 1992)
- Primary Graphing and Probability Workshop, Grades K–2. (1991). Glenview, IL: Scott, Foresman & Co. (reviewed in *Arithmetic Teacher*, March 1993)
- Soc Sort and Soc Match. Circle Pines, MN: American Guidance Service.
- Unifix® Software (also available in Lab Pack with manipulatives). Rowley, MA: Didax.

REVIEW

A. Describe areas in this unit that provide higher-level concept activities.

B. Characterize the three higher levels of classification.

C. Which of the examples below can be identified as (a) multiple classification, (b) class inclusion, or (c) hierarchical classification?
  1. Basset hound, dog, animal
  2. Matrix that varies horizontally by size and vertically by color
  3. Two cars and three airplanes; are there more airplanes or more vehicles?
  4. Texture, weight, and material
  5. Markers, pens, pencils, things you can write with
  6. Three apples and one banana—are there more apples or more fruit?

D. Read the following descriptions of situations carefully. Identify the higher-level activity the child seems to be engaged in, and suggest how the teacher should respond.
  1. Kate says, "Donny lives on the other side of the street from me."
  2. Liu takes the Unifix Cubes® and places them in groups of three.
  3. Cindy takes some cube blocks and some toy cars and places them on the balance scale.
  4. Bret points to the orange in the picture book and says, "Look at that round orange."
  5. Liu says that chocolate ice cream is the best. Kate says vanilla is best. Kate insists that most children like vanilla ice cream better than chocolate.
  6. "John, give me two more blocks so that I will have six, too."
  7. Mrs. Jones notices that Sam is laboriously drawing four oranges and five apples. Then he writes a numeral 4 by the oranges and the number 5 by the apples. Finally he writes in invented spelling, "thrs 9 froots."
  8. Mrs. Carter notices that five-year-old George can rote count to 99 accurately.
  9. Tanya explains that all people have blood, bones, and fat inside, but all dolls are filled with cotton.
  10. We counted out 20 jelly beans in this scoop. How can we use that information to estimate how many jelly beans this jar will hold when full?

REFERENCES

Baratta-Lorton, M. (1976). *Mathematics their way*. Menlo Park, CA: Addison-Wesley.

Baratta-Lorton, M. (1979). *Workjobs II*. Menlo Park, CA: Addison-Wesley.

Copley, J. V. (2000). *The young child and mathematics*. Washington, DC: National Association for the Education of Young Children.

Curcio, F. R., & Schwartz, S. L. (1997). What does algebraic thinking look like with preprimary children? *Teaching Children Mathematics*, *3*(6), 296–300.

Lang, F. K. (2001). What is a "good guess" anyway? Estimation in early childhood. *Teaching Children Mathematics*, *7*(8), 462–466.

Moses, B. (1997). Algebra for a new century. *Teaching Children Mathematics, 3*(6), 264–265.

National Council of Teachers of Mathematics. (2000). *Principles and standards for school mathematics*. Reston, VA: Author. (http://www.nctm.org)

Richardson, K. (1999). *Developing number concepts: Addition and subtraction, Book 2*. Parsippany, NJ: Dale Seymour.

Richardson, K. (1999). *Developing number concepts: Using Unifix Cubes®*. Menlo Park, CA: Addison-Wesley.

Skinner, P. (1990). *What's your problem?* Portsmouth, NH: Heinemann.

Wilson, D. C. (2001). Patterns of thinking in pattern block play. *Building Blocks News, 3*, 2.

Young, S. (1998). *Harry's Math Books,™ Set B, Teacher Guide*. Columbus, OH: Zaner-Bloser.

Young, S. (1998). *One more child*. Columbus, OH: Zaner-Bloser.

Young, S. (1998). *Six pieces of cake*. Columbus, OH: Zaner-Bloser.

Young, S. (1998). *What to wear?* Columbus, OH: Zaner-Bloser.

FURTHER READING AND RESOURCES

AIMS Educational Products. AIMS Education Foundation, P.O. Box 8120, Fresno, CA 93747-8120.

Behounek, L. J., Rosenbaum, L. B., & Burcalow, J. V. (1988). Our class has twenty-five teachers. *Arithmetic Teacher, 36*(4), 10–13.

Box it or bag it mathematics (K–2). Portland, OR: The Math Learning Center. (800-575-8130) (http://www.mlc.pdx.edu)

Bridges in mathematics (K–2). Portland, OR: The Math Learning Center. (800-575-8130) (http://www.mlc.pdx.edu)

Clements, D. H., & Sarama, J. (2000). Predicting pattern blocks on and off the computer. *Teaching Children Mathematics, 6*(7), 458–461.

Clements, D. H., Swaminathan, S., Hannibal, M. A. Z., & Sarama, J. (1999). Young children's concepts of shape. *Journal for Research in Mathematics Education, 30*(2), 192–212.

Copley, J. V. (Ed.). (1999). *Mathematics in the early years*. Washington, DC: National Association for the Education of Young Children.

Falkner, K. P., Levi, L., & Carpenter, T. R. (1999). Children's understanding of equality: A foundation for algebra. *Teaching Children Mathematics, 6*(4), 232–236.

Fitzsimmons, P. F., & Goldhaber, J. (1997). Siphons, pumps, and missile launchers: Inquiry at the water tables. *Science and Children, 34*(4), 16–19.

Hembree, R., & Marsh, H. (1992). Problem solving in early childhood: Building foundations. In R. J. Jensen (Ed.), *Research ideas for the classroom: Early childhood mathematics* (pp. 151–170). New York: Macmillan.

Holly, K. A. (1997). Math by the month: Patterns and functions. *Teaching Children Mathematics, 3*(6), 312.

Richardson, K. (1999). *Developing number concepts: Planning guide*. Parsippany, NJ: Dale Seymour.

Stice, C. F., & Alvarez, M. C. (1987). Hierarchical concept mapping in the early grades. *Childhood Education, 64*, 86–96.

Willoughby, S. (1997). Functions from kindergarten through sixth grade. *Teaching Children Mathematics, 3*(6), 314–318.

UNIT 26
Higher-Level Activities Used in Science Units and Activities

OBJECTIVES

After reading this unit, you should be able to:

◆ Plan and do structured lessons in sets and symbols, classification, and measurement.

◆ Apply the concepts, skills, and attitudes found in math to lessons in science.

◆ Design higher-level lessons that develop science concepts for children closer to the concrete level of development.

Sets, Symbols, and Classification

Children in the transitional stage apply and develop fundamental concepts in sets and symbols, classification, shape, spatial relations, measurement, and graphs as they are exposed to higher-level experiences. As they near the concrete operational level of development, they will continue to develop these concepts. The higher-level experiences described in this unit offer opportunities to build on many of the ideas presented in Units 23 through 25 of this book.

Vegetable Time

Although children will be asked to bring vegetables from home for this lesson, you will need to prepare a variety of vegetables for maximum learning. Seed and garden catalogs and magazine pictures can provide illustrations of how the vegetables grow. Three major categories of vegetables that work well with children are *leaf* and *stem vegetables* (cabbage, lettuce, spinach, mustard, parsley), *root vegetables* (sweet potatoes, carrots, beets, turnips, onions), and *seed vegetables* (cucumbers, peas, beans, corn, soybeans). Mrs. Red Fox conducts the following activity in the fall with her first-grade class.

First, she invites the children to join her on a rug to examine the different vegetables. Then she asks her class to describe the vegetables in front of them. They answer, "Long, rough, smooth, peeling, hard, scratchy, lumpy, bumpy, crunchy, white, orange." Mrs. Red Fox holds up a potato and asks, "Can someone describe this potato?" "I can," Trang Fung says. "The potato is bumpy and brown." "Good," says Mrs. Red Fox. "Who can find another vegetable that is bumpy?" "A pea is a little bumpy," suggests Sara. Mrs. Red Fox writes the word *bumpy* on a card and groups the potato and pea together. Then she holds up a carrot and asks, "Is there another vegetable that looks like this one?" Dean studies the assortment of vegetables and says, "How about the pumpkin?" "Yes, the pumpkin and the carrot are both orange." Mrs. Red Fox writes the word *orange* on a card and places the carrot and pumpkin together with the card. The children continue to classify by characteristics until each vegetable is in a group. Mrs. Red Fox refrigerates the vegetables overnight and readies them for a series of activities that emphasize a variety of concepts.

1. *Where do they grow?* The class discusses how the different vegetables looked while they were growing. After all, for all the children know, potatoes come from produce sections of supermarkets, and corn comes from a can. The children have fun matching the vegetable with pictures of the vegetable growing. Mrs. Red Fox makes a game of matching actual vegetables with how they look as they grow.

2. *Digging for potatoes.* After matching actual vegetables with pictures of growing vegetables, children practice digging for potatoes. Mrs. Red Fox fills the sandbox with rows of potatoes, and children take turns digging. Carrots, beets, and turnips are planted with their leafy tops above the soil, and children take turns gardening.

3. *What is inside?* Bowls of peas are set out to be opened and explored, and the idea of starting a garden begins to occur to children.

4. *Under, on, and above.* Mrs. Red Fox makes a bulletin board backdrop of a garden, and the children match cutout vegetables to where they grow. Onions are placed *under the ground*; peas, beans, and corn are shown *above the ground*; and lettuce, cabbage, and parsley are displayed *on the ground.*

5. *Patterns.* Children place the vegetables in patterns. Trang Fung made a pattern of potatoes, pumpkins, celery, and cucumbers. She said, "Bumpy, bumpy, bumpy, smooth. Look at my pattern. Dean, can you make a pattern?" Dean began his own pattern. "I am not going to tell you my pattern," said Dean. He laid out mustard, carrots, peas, cabbage, potato, and beans. Trang Fung smiled and continued the pattern. "On the ground, under the ground, and above the ground, spinach, onion, corn," she said.

6. *Vegetable prints.* As the week continued, some children wondered if the insides of the vegetables were alike and different, too. So, Mrs. Red Fox cut up several vegetables and let the children explore printing with vegetables. She poured tempera paint on sponges for a stamp pad. Then the children dipped the vegetable in paint and printed on construction paper. Mrs. Red Fox labeled some of the prints with vegetable words and hung them up for decoration. The prints were then classified by color and characteristics. Some children made patterns with their prints and asked others to guess the pattern and which vegetable made the pattern.

Stone Soup

Children can also learn about the vegetable members of the vegetable and fruit group through literature and cooking. After vegetables are identified as members of the vegetable and fruit food group, read the book *Stone Soup* (Paterson, 1981) and act out the story on the flannelboard.

Print the recipe on poster board (see Unit 22), add picture clues, and have the children wash vegetables for cooking. The children will quickly learn to use vegetable peelers and table knives as they cut the vegetables into small pieces. Then, act out the story once again. This time, really add the stone and vegetables to a crockpot to cook for the day. Bouillon cubes, salt, and pepper will spice up the soup. Do not be surprised if younger children think that the stone made all of the soup.

Prepare a set of cards with pictures of the ingredients, and have students put the cards in the correct sequence of the cooking activity. The children will want to make an experience chart of preparing the stone soup. They could even graph their favorite parts of the soup (Figure 26–1).

FIGURE 26–1   "What did we add to the soup first? Then what did we add?"

Animal Sets

Stuffed animals are familiar to the children and can be grouped in many ways. One way is to group stuffed animals on a table by sets: a group of one, two, three, and so on. Ask the children to draw the set of animals at their table on a piece of white paper. After the children have drawn the animals, include early literacy experiences by having them dictate or write a story about the animals. Staple the drawings at each table into a book. The children at each table have made an animal book of ones, twos, and so on. Read each book with the children and make all books available for independent classroom reading.

More First Mapping Experiences

The everyday experience of reading maps is abstract and takes practice to develop. The following mapping activities include the use of symbols and build on the early "Bird's-Eye View" mapping experiences in Unit 21 and the mapping experiences suggested in Units 13 and 25.

1. *Tangible mapping.* Children will not be able to deal with symbols on maps if they have not had experience with tangible mapping. Observe children as they create roads, valleys, and villages in clay or at the sand table. Keep in mind the perspective of *looking down* as children place objects on a huge base map. Such a map can be made from oilcloth and rolled up when not in use.

2. *Pictorial mapping.* Take children to the top of a hill or building, and ask them to draw what they see. This activity can emphasize spatial relations and relative locations. After you have returned from a field trip, discuss what was seen on the bus ride. Use crayons or paint to construct a mural of the trip.

3. *Semipictorial mapping.* Children will use more conventional symbols when they construct a semipictorial map. As they discover that pictures take up a lot of room, they search for symbols to represent objects. Colors become symbolic and can be used to indicate water and vegetation.

4. *Base map.* The base map contains the barest minimum detail filled in by the teacher, that is, outline, key streets, and buildings. This is a more abstract type of map; thus the area must be known to the child. Add tangible objects to the abstract base, that is, toy objects and pictures. A flannel base map is a variation.

5. *Caution.* Never use one map to do many things. If your mapping experience tries to do too much, children cannot rethink the actual experience and relationships. Each mapmaking experience must fulfill some specific purpose. Each map must represent something in particular that children look for and understand.

6. *Start small*. Begin with maps of the children's block constructions. Next, move to mapping a center in the classroom before moving to something larger. Gradually increase the size of the space you are planning to map. Remember to discuss directionality.

Exploring Pumpkins: October Science

If you live where pumpkins grow, take a field trip to purchase some; if not, buy some at the grocery. You will need a pumpkin for each child. Plan to organize the children in groups with an adult helper. The following activities use the senses to apply and integrate the skills and fundamental concepts used in measuring, counting, classifying, and graphing into the exploration of pumpkins.

Time to Explore

Give children time to examine their pumpkins and their stems. Ask, "How does the pumpkin feel?," "How does it smell?," and "Do all pumpkins have stems?" Later, when the pumpkins are carved, encour-age the children to describe the differences in texture between the inside and outside of their pumpkins.

Ask, "Which pumpkin is the heaviest?" and "Who has the lightest pumpkin?" After the children decide, bring out a scale, and make an accurate measurement. The children probably cannot comprehend what the scale means or read the numbers, but they like to weigh things anyway. Tape the weight (mass) on the bottom of each pumpkin. Then, when jack-o'-lanterns are created, the children can compare the difference in mass.

Have children measure the circumference of a pumpkin with yarn. Ask, "Where shall we put the yarn on the pumpkin?" and "Why?" Instruct the children to wrap the yarn around the middle of the pumpkin. Then, help children cut the yarn and label it. Write the child's name on masking tape and attach it to the yarn length. After the children have measured their pumpkins and labeled their yarn, have them thumbtack the yarn length to a bulletin board. Ask, "Which pumpkin is the smallest around the middle?," "Which is the largest?," and "How can you tell?" Have the children refer to the yarn graph. Some kindergarten children might be ready to lay the yarn length along a measuring stick and draw horizontal bar graphs instead of yarn ones (Figure 26–2).

FIGURE 26–2 "How big is your pumpkin?"

Children will want to measure height as well as circumference. The major problem to solve will probably be where to measure from—the top of the stem or the indentation where the stem was. This time, cut a piece of yarn that fits around the height of the pumpkin. Label the yarn, and attach it to pieces of masking tape. Order the yarn lengths from shortest to tallest. Ask, "Which yarn is the longest?" and "Can you tell me who has the tallest pumpkin?"

Observing Pumpkins

Mrs. Jones has kindergarten children count the number of curved lines along the outside of the pumpkin. She asks, "How many lines are on your pumpkin?" She instructs the children to help each other. One child places a finger on the first line of the pumpkin and another child counts the lines. Then Mrs. Jones asks, "Do all the pumpkins have the same number of lines?" "No," answers Mary. "My pumpkin has more lines than Lai's pumpkin." Some children even begin to link the number of lines with the size of the pumpkin as they compare findings.

Mrs. Jones asks, "How does your pumpkin feel?" George says his pumpkin is rough, but Sam insists that his is smooth. "Yes," Mrs. Jones observes. "Some pumpkins are rough, and some are smooth." "Are they the same color?" This question brings a buzz of activity as the children compare pumpkin color. Mrs. Jones attaches the name of each child to his or her pumpkin and asks the children to bring their pumpkins to the front table. She asks the children to group the pumpkins by color variations of yellow, orange, and so on. Some of the children are beginning to notice other differences in the pumpkins such as brown spots and differences in stem shapes.

The children gather around Mrs. Jones as she carves a class pumpkin. She carefully puts the seeds and pulp on separate plates and asks the children to compare the inside color of the pumpkin with the outside color. She asks, "What colors do you see?" and "What colors do you see inside of the pumpkin?" "I see a lighter color," Mary says. "Do all pumpkins have light insides?" George is more interested in the stringy fibers. "This looks like string dipped in pumpkin stuff." "I am glad you noticed, George," Mrs. Jones comments. "The stringy stuff is called fiber. It is part of the pumpkin." Students learn the word *pulp* and also compare the seeds for future activities.

Children will also notice that *pumpkins smell.* Ask them to describe the smell of their pumpkins. Have them turn their pumpkins over and smell all parts. Then ask them to compare the smell of the inside of their pumpkins with the outside rind and with the seeds, fiber, and pulp. "Does the pumpkin smell remind you of anything?" Record dictated descriptions and create an experience chart of pumpkin memories. Ask, "What do you think of when you smell pumpkins?"

As children make jack-o'-lantern faces, discuss the shapes they are using. Then, ask them to draw faces on the surfaces of their pumpkins using a felt-tip pen. Closely supervise children as they carve their pumpkins. Instruct them to cut away from their bodies. They will need help in holding the knife, and their participation might be limited to scooping out the pumpkin. Note: Apple corers work well for these experiences and are easier to use.

After the jack-o'-lanterns are cut and have been admired, Mrs. Jones begins a measurement activity. She asks, "How can we tell if the pumpkin is lighter than it was before it was carved?" "Lift it," say the children. "Yes," says Mrs. Jones, "that is one way to tell, but I want to know for sure." George suggests, "Let's use the scale again." But before the pumpkins are weighed, Mrs. Jones asks the children to whisper a prediction in her ear. She asks, "Do you think the pumpkin will weigh more or less after it has been carved and the seeds and pulp removed? Whisper 'More,' 'Less,' or 'The same.'" As the children respond, Mrs. Jones writes their responses on paper pumpkins and begins a more, less, and the same graph of predictions (Figure 26–3).

Last but not least in a series of pumpkin activities is tasting. Pumpkin pulp can be made into pumpkin bread or, for science and Halloween party time, make drop cookies with raisins for eyes, nose, and mouth. Or, for a tasty snack, cut some of the pumpkin pulp into chunks for cooking. Once cooked, dot the pieces with butter, and add a dash of nutmeg.

Try roasting some pumpkin seeds. Have the children wash the seeds to remove the pulp and fiber. The seeds can be dried between layers of paper towels, then roasted in a single layer on a cookie sheet. Bake in a 350° oven for 30 to 40 minutes. The children can tell when the seeds are ready by their pale brown color. To make a comparison lesson, show them seeds

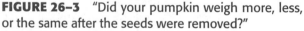

FIGURE 26–3 "Did your pumpkin weigh more, less, or the same after the seeds were removed?"

that you have previously roasted, and invite them to tell you when the color of the roasting seeds matches yours. Cool the seeds, then have a snack. Before cooking the seeds have each child count the seeds found in his or her pumpkin and compare to see which pumpkin has the most? Least? If the seeds are not being eaten they can be dried and used for counting and making sets.

Measuring the World around Us

Playgrounds, yards, and sidewalks provide many opportunities for measuring in science. The following activities emphasize the science and measurement in outdoor adventures.

1. *How far will it blow?* After talking about air and how it moves, take the children outside to determine how far the wind will blow dandelion seeds. Draw bull's-eye-like circles on the playground with chalk. Label the circles. Have a child stand in the middle of the circle and hold a mature dandelion up to the wind. Record which direction the wind blows the seeds and the circle in which most of them landed. This would be a good time to discuss wind as a way of dispersing seeds. If dandelions are not available small pieces of tissue paper with seeds drawn on them can be used.

2. *Weed watch.* Place a stick next to a growing plant such as a dandelion or similar weed. Have the children mark the height of the weed on the stick. Check the weed each day for a week and see how tall it gets. (You might have to talk to the groundskeeper before trying this activity.) Children enjoy seeing the weeds grow. Discuss differences and possible factors in weed growth.

3. *How long does it take?* After students have had time to explore the water center, select some of the containers used in the center. Lead the children to an area that has pinecones, acorns, or other natural objects available. Recall the amount of time it took to fill the containers with water. Then, give a container to each group of children and instruct them to fill it with specific objects. Note the time that it takes to fill the containers. Vary the activity by assigning different groups of contrasting objects, that is, small, big, rough, and so on, with which to fill the containers.

4. *Line them up.* Have children count the objects that they have collected in the containers. Ask each group to line up the objects. Compare the number of objects that it took to fill each container. If the objects collected were different, compare the number of each type of object that was needed to fill the container.

5. *How can we tell?* Children will probably find many ways to compare objects they have found. After they have examined and compared their objects visually, encourage them to weigh several of the objects. Ask, "Which container is the heaviest?" and "How can we tell?" A balance

provides an objective measure. Balance the content of one container (acorns) against the content of another (walnuts). Have children predict which will be heavier. Some might want to draw a picture of what they think will happen.

Popcorn Time

Children will sequence events as they act out a favorite snack. Have two or three children become popcorn by asking them to crouch down in the middle of a masking tape circle or hula hoop. As you pour imaginary oil on them, have the rest of the class make sizzling noises and wait for them to pop. When ready, each child should jump up, burst open like a popcorn kernel, and leap out of the popper circle. Children will want to take turns acting out the popcorn sequence.

Then, place a real popcorn popper on a sheet in the middle of the floor. Seat the children around the popper, remove the popcorn lid, and watch the popcorn fly. Before eating the popcorn, measure how far the popcorn popped with Unifix Cubes® or string. (Be careful of the hot popper.) Ask, "Which popcorn flew the farthest?" and "Which flew the shortest?"

Spatial Relations

Inside and Outside

Young children are curious about their bodies. They are familiar with outside body parts, which they can see and touch, but they are just beginning to notice that things happen inside their bodies. To increase this awareness and reinforce the concepts of inside and outside, Mrs. Jones has children look at, feel, and listen to what is going on inside of their bodies in the following scenario.

Mrs. Jones fills a garbage bag with an assortment of items—a wound-up alarm clock, rubber balls, a book, a few sticks, and a bunch of grapes in a small sandwich bag (Figure 26–4). She places the bag on a chair in the front of the room, allowing it to drape down to show the outlines of some of the objects inside. She asks, "What is on the chair?" George says, "A garbage bag." "Is anything on the chair besides the bag?" asks the teacher. "No," the children respond. Mrs. Jones invites

FIGURE 26–4   "Do you feel anything inside of the bag?"

the children to gather around the bag and feel it. She asks, "Do you hear or feel anything?" "Yes," Mary says. "I feel something sharp." "And squishy," adds Sam. George is certain that he hears a clock ticking, and Lai feels a round and firm object that moves.

After the children guess what might be in the bag, Mrs. Jones opens it and shows the children what was inside. "Did you guess correctly?" "I did," says George. "I heard something ticking." "Good," answers Mrs. Jones. "How did you know that sticks were in the bag?" Mary says, "I could feel them poking through the plastic." "Yes," Sam adds, "the grapes must have been the squishy stuff."

After the children discuss the contents of the bag, Mrs. Jones takes the bag off the chair, asks the children to return to their places, and invites Mary to sit in the chair. She asks, "Now, what is on the chair?" The class choruses, "Mary." "Yes, Mary is on the chair," says Mrs. Jones. "How is Mary like the bag?" After a few responses, George says, "Mary has something inside of her, too." The children come up to look at Mary, but do not touch her. Mrs. Jones asks, "Do you see what's inside showing through the way it did with the bag?" The children notice bones, knuckles, the funny bone, kneecap, and some veins. Mrs. Jones asks

Mary to flex her arm muscles so the children can see muscles moving beneath her skin.

Mrs. Jones encourages the children to discover other muscles and feel them working. She has them stretch out on mats on the floor, curl up tightly, then slowly uncurl. "What have your muscles done?" Then she has them stretch out like a cat and curl up into a ball. Facial muscles are fun for the children. Mrs. Jones asks them to find and use all the muscles that they can on their faces. They wiggle noses, flutter eyelids, tighten jaws, and raise eyebrows. The teacher asks, "Does your tongue have muscles in it?" "How do you know?" Finally, the children move to music as they focus on what is happening inside their bodies. Mrs. Jones has them dancing like marionettes, stiffly with a few joints moving; then bending and curling the way rag dolls do; and finally, dancing like people, with muscles, joints, and bones controlling their movements.

The children are fascinated with the thought of something important inside of them. They make toy stethoscopes from funnels and rubber tubing and take turns finding and listening to their heartbeats. Some begin to count the beats; others enjoy tapping a finger in time with the sound of their hearts.

Mrs. Jones has the children simulate the way a heart works by folding their hands one over the other and squeezing and releasing them rhythmically. (This motion is somewhat like the way the heart muscles move to expand and contract the heart, pushing blood through.) She has them place their clasped hands close to their ears and asks, "What do you hear?," "Is this squeezing sound like the soft thumping you heard through the stethoscope?," and "How is it different?"

Assessment Tasks

If they can do the assessment tasks for Units 8 through 25, children will have the basic skills and knowledge necessary to connect sets and symbols and successfully complete higher-level learning activities. The following example is a strategy many teachers use when children have made differing progress in classification, shape, spatial relations, measurement, and graphing.

As different concepts and activities are introduced to one child or a group of children, any one activity could capture the interest of children who might be at a lower developmental level. Therefore, it is not necessary to wait for all the children to be at the highest level to begin. Children at lower levels can participate in these activities as observers and contributors. Or the lower-level children might be able to do part of the task following the leadership of the higher-level child. Children can work in pairs to solve problems and can move into higher levels of symbol and measurement use as well as explore calculators and computer software together. Most activities in science promote working in teams and sharing roles and responsibilities. This makes science an especially appropriate way to address differing levels of development.

Technology

Technology can be used to expand and supplement your science program. It can and should be used to enhance the understanding of beginning math and science concepts. The two main uses of technology in early childhood classes are software and the Internet. Software is usually used to support the acquisition and practice of concepts and skills. The Internet is often used to research topics of interest, connect with people in other locations, and illustrate concepts that children are unable to experience directly.

Appropriate software should reinforce what children are learning in the classroom. It should not be used as the sole method of instruction or take the place of actual hands-on experience. When choosing software teachers should ask themselves the questions that follow:

1. Does the software ask children to engage in activities appropriate for their age?
2. Is the software interactive? The more interactive or choices a child is able to make, the more appropriate it will be.
3. Does the software come in multiple languages and utilize diverse populations in their graphics?
4. Does the software have a range of complexity that can be tailored to individual children?

Some examples of appropriate software are Sammy's Science House and KidWare.

The Internet is another form of technology that is often used in early childhood classrooms. Before accessing the Internet be sure the computers in the classroom are equipped with filtering software so the children will not be exposed to undesirable Web sites. If the school or center is networked, one should always check to see if the server is protected with a firewall that will filter inappropriate Web sites.

Internet Web sites should be used to reinforce topics under study. For example, if the class is unable to visit a pumpkin patch, then do a virtual tour. If the class is studying weather, then the class can track the changes in weather by logging on to http://www.weather.com.

Summary

Children in the transitional stage develop fundamental concepts in sets and symbols, classification, shape, spatial relations, measurement, and graphs as they are exposed to higher-level experiences. As children near the concrete operational level of development, they continue to need hands-on exploration.

Science activities at this level allow children to pull together skills and ideas learned earlier. Most children incorporate these skills through naturalistic and informal experiences. Structured activities are also appropriate but should be brief.

SUGGESTED ACTIVITIES

1. Design a graphing experience for transitional children. Select an appropriate science topic, describe procedures, and develop a questioning strategy. Share the lessons in groups, and teach the lesson to a class.

2. Accompany a class on a field trip or walk around the block. Make a picture map of the field trip. Record the types of comments children make as they recall their trip. What types of objects made an impression on the children? Are the comments in keeping with what you know about children and the way they think?

3. Select a computer program for young children that emphasizes one of the concepts or skills discussed in this unit. Try the program yourself and develop a lesson that uses this program. What kinds of experiences will children need to have to use this program? What science concepts or skills will be taught or reinforced? What kinds of follow-up ex-

periences will be needed? Following are suggested computer programs.

- Computergarten. New York: Scholastic. (Pre-K–1).
- Greeting Card option of Print Shop. Novato, CA: Broderbund Software.
- KidWare. Alexandria, VA: MOBIUS
- KidWorks Deluxe. Torrance, CA: Davidson & Associates. (Pre-K–2)
- Micros for Micros: Estimation. Berkeley, CA: Lawrence Hall of Science. (K–2)
- Quicktake 150 or 200 Digital Camera. Cupertino, CA: Apple Computer. (All grades)
- Sammy's Science House. Redmond, WA: Edmark. (Pre-K–2)
- ThemeWeavers: Animals. Redmond, WA: Edmark.

Please refer to the computer resources listed in Units 33 through 39 for additional software recommendations.

REVIEW

A. List areas discussed in this unit that have higher-level concept activities.

B. Name three types of mapping activities that can be used with young children. Why use these strategies with children?

C. Why is it essential that children have time to explore materials when learning a science concept?

D. Discuss things a teacher should keep in mind when choosing software.

REFERENCE

Paterson, D. (1981). *Stone soup*. Mahwah, NJ: Troll Associates.

FURTHER READING AND RESOURCES

Buckleitner, W. (1993). *Survey of early childhood software*. Ypsilanti, MI: High/Scope Press.

Burk, D., Snider, A., & Symonds, P. (1988). *Box it or bag it mathematics: Kindergarten teachers' resource guide*. Portland, OR: The Math Learning Center.

Davidson, J. I. (1989). *Children and computers together in the early childhood classroom*. Clifton Park, NY: Delmar Learning..

Haughland, S. W., & Wright, J. L. (1997). *Young children and technology: A world of discovery*. Boston, MA: Allyn & Bacon.

Kamii, C., & Devries, R. (1993). *Physical knowledge in the classroom: Implications of Piaget's theory* (Rev. ed.). Englewood Cliffs, NJ: Prentice Hall.

Lind, K. K. (1984). A bird's-eye view: Mapping readiness. *Science and Children, 22*(3), 39–40.

Lind, K. K. (1985). The inside story. *Science and Children, 22*(4), 122–123.

McIntyre, M. (1984). *Pumpkin science. Early childhood and science*. Washington, DC: National Science Teachers Association.

Rockwell, R. E., Sherwood, E. A., & Williams, R. A. (1986). *Hug a tree*. Mt. Rainier, MD: Gryphon House.

Stronck, D. (Ed.). (1983). *Understanding the healthy body*. Council for Elementary Science International Sourcebook III. Columbus, OH: SMEAC Information Reference Center.

Ukens, L. (Ed.). (1985). *Science experiences for preschoolers*. Council for Elementary Science International Sourcebook IV. Columbus, OH: SMEAC Information Reference Center.

Mathematics Concepts and Operations for the Primary Grades

UNIT 27
Operations with Whole Numbers

OBJECTIVES

After reading this unit, you should be able to:

◆ Define the whole number operations of addition, subtraction, multiplication, and division.

◆ Introduce the whole number operations to primary grade children.

◆ Administer whole number operations assessment tasks.

◆ Introduce whole number operations notation and number sentence format following a three-step process.

◆ Develop instructional activities and materials for whole number operations at the primary level.

This unit looks at arithmetic, which includes the areas that were conventionally the core of the elementary grades mathematics program; that is, the **whole number operations** of addition, subtraction, multiplication, and division (Charlesworth & Senger, 2001). Today, however, the term *mathematics* refers to all the related concepts and skills included in this text, for example, algebra, geometry, number sense, data analysis, and so on. Mathematics is a much more inclusive content area than it used to be.

The NCTM (2000) standard on number and operations includes expectations for the understanding of operations and how they relate to each other and for fluent computation and making reasonable estimates (discussed in Unit 25). During the primary grades, students should reach an understanding of a variety of means for adding and subtracting and the relationship between the two operations, of the effects of adding

and subtracting whole numbers, and understand the situations where multiplication and division are used. Children should develop skill at whole number computation for addition and subtraction, should be able to use the basic addition and subtraction number combinations, and use many different computation tools such as "objects, mental computation, estimation, paper and pencil, and calculators" (p. 78).

Today, the most complex calculations are done with calculators and computers. Further, children are encouraged to use estimation and mental computation. However, children need to learn how to solve problems using conventional and/or invented **algorithms** in order to reach an understanding of each operation. Algorithms are step-by-step procedures for solving problems (Warshauer & Warshauer, 2001, p. 23). Once this understanding is established, more can be accomplished by working on how to set up problems and then using technology to do the calculations. In this unit, methods are described for introducing children to whole number operations and whole number notation at a basic level. Once children understand the concepts, they can move on to more complex operations using calculators and computers to perform calculations.

Children naturally engage in the whole number operations of addition, subtraction, multiplication, and division prior to reaching the primary grades. In previous units (see Units 23, 24, and 25), the beginnings of the whole number operations are described as they grow out of naturalistic and informal experiences. Prior to entering first grade, young children also usually have an understanding of number symbols as they represent quantities. During the primary period (grades one through three), children gradually learn the meaning of **action symbols** such as + (add), − (subtract), × (multiply), ÷ (divide), = (equals), < (less than), and > (greater than).

Teachers are expected to use state and locally developed lists of objectives and selected textbooks to provide a structure for planning instruction. Unfortunately, primary teachers tend to rely too heavily on textbooks, workbooks, and photocopied support materials. Conventionally, students are expected to be able to do paper and pencil arithmetic even though it might be developmentally inappropriate. Opportunities for the use of exploration as a route to the construction of concepts and operations are too seldom observed in the primary classroom. Students usually sit at individual desks with social interaction kept at a minimum (if allowed at all).

Constance Kamii is a major critic of the conventional approach to mathematics instruction in the primary grades. She presents her point of view in her books *Young Children Reinvent Arithmetic* (1985), *Young Children Continue to Reinvent Arithmetic, Second Grade* (1989), and *Young Children Reinvent Arithmetic, Third Grade* (1994). As a Piagetian, she believes that just as our ancestors invented it, children reinvent arithmetic through their own actions and needs rather than learning through what someone else tells them. Children need to reinvent arithmetic through naturalistic and informal exploration with naturally occurring problems and through group games. They should be encouraged to invent their own proce-

dures and use their own thinking. Kamii explains that paper and pencil worksheet approaches remove the child from the logical thinking that is the heart of arithmetic. Kamii's emphasis on group games and social interaction as the basis for the understanding of arithmetic has its roots in Piaget's view that social interaction is essential as a stimulus for construction of knowledge. The following are examples of children solving problems through peer interaction.

- Three nonconservers are going to drink juice. The server pours juice into glass A. Now he must pour equal amounts into glasses B and C, which are different in size and shape from each other and glass A. The children discuss how to do this in a fair manner and arrive at a solution: Use glass A as a measuring cup to fill the other two glasses.
- Derrick has written 7 + 4 = 10, and Brent has written 7 + 4 = 12. Their teacher has them explain to each other why they think that their respective answers are correct. Soon they discover that they are both wrong.

A danger in primary math instruction is that students will be pushed too fast before they have developed the cognitive capacity to understand the logical reasoning underlying the operations. Keep in mind that children must be in the concrete operations period before they can successfully meet primary-level expectations. Beginning in kindergarten, standardized testing is performed each year, and teachers are pressured to teach the concepts and skills that are included in the tests. This pressure leads teachers to instruct arithmetic as a rote memory activity that has no logical meaning to the children. Children should be allowed to move at their own pace through primary math just as they did prior to entering first grade. They should also be allowed to invent their own procedures for solving problems. Herbert Ginsburg (1977) claims that young children naturally invent their own methods and should be able to use and experiment with them. For example, young children usually learn on their own to use counting methods for addition. When adding 2 + 2, the child might say, "One, two, three, four" using fingers or objects. If left on their own, they will eventually stop counting, having internalized 2 + 2 = 4.

Carpenter, Carey, and Kouba (1990) point out that children enter first grade with informal concepts of the whole number operations. They also state the importance of observing the processes children use in solving problems. They believe that symbols should be introduced only to represent concepts that children already know. Instruction should begin with observations of naturalistic and informal activities.

Fuson, Grandau, and Sugiyama (2001) support the importance of informal teaching. "Such informal teaching can be done while children play, eat, get dressed, go up and down stairs, jump, and otherwise move through the day" (Fuson, Grandau, & Sugiyama, 2001, p. 522). During these activities adults and more advanced peers can model mathematical concepts and skills, which children can then combine with understandings obtained during more structured mathematics activities.

In this text, a sequence of concept instruction is described with the caution to the teacher to keep in mind that children move at their own pace. As in previous units, naturalistic, informal, and structured activities are described. Structured activities emphasize the use of concrete materials, with paper and pencil introduced through children's natural interests when they are ready.

Basic Combinations (Facts) and Algorithms

Isaacs and Carroll (1999) pose several questions about the value and purpose of learning the **basic facts** (or combinations) in the early grades. Will making first graders learn the addition facts interfere with their mathematical thinking? What kinds of instructional practices can build understanding and quick recall? Can children learn the facts through problem-solving activities, or is drill and practice needed? Isaacs and Carroll go on to provide answers to these questions. Certainly, knowing the facts is essential to furthering mathematical understanding but drill and practice and timed tests only lead to stress and anxiety. Rather we should build on the knowledge children bring to school and support children in developing strategies

for learning the basic facts. Children enter the primary grades with counting skills and an understanding that quantities can be broken down into parts. Facts can be learned through solving problems using their understanding of counting and parts and wholes. Building concrete models supports understanding and remembering. Having students share strategies will move them toward more efficient ones. Useful practice that is brief and nonstressful such as games, computers, or even flash cards can support the learning of basic facts. Isaacs and Carroll suggest an instructional sequence based on strategies (pp. 511–512).

1. for basic concepts of addition; direct modeling (using objects) and "counting all" for addition
2. the 0 and 1 addition facts; then "counting on" with 2
3. doubles (6 + 6, 8 + 8, etc.)
4. sums of 10 (9 + 1, 8 + 2, etc.)
5. basic concepts of subtraction; direct modeling (using objects)
6. easy subtraction facts (−0, −1, −2 facts); "counting back" to subtract
7. harder addition facts; derived fact strategies such as those near doubles or over 10
8. "counting up" to subtract
9. harder subtraction facts; derived-fact strategies for subtraction (using addition facts, over-10 facts)

Assessment should be process oriented in the primary grades; that is, children can use a number of strategies for solving problems. By the end of third grade and the beginning of fourth grade, children should be able to recall the addition and subtraction facts quickly and automatically.

Algorithms may be thought of as procedures, efficient methods, or rules for computation (Curcio & Schwartz, 1998). Several questions arise when it comes to instructional practice. Should algorithms be taught before, along with, or after children have had the opportunity to invent some of their own strategies? Curcio and Schwartz suggest that we begin with the children's own strategies and through questioning guide their reasoning toward more efficient and possibly conventional methods.

Computational Fluency

An important goal for the primary grades is the development of computational fluency with whole numbers (NCTM, 2000). Russell (2000) provides guidelines for developing computational fluency. Fluency involves three ideas: efficiency, accuracy, and flexibility. Efficiency means the student can proceed directly without getting distracted from his goal. Accuracy depends on being careful and double-checking results. Flexibility means being able to try out more than one strategy for solving problems. Fluency goes beyond memorizing one procedure or algorithm. As they learn more basic facts this knowledge can be applied to recording their methods of problem solving. Children in grades kindergarten through two should be encouraged to invent computational methods as they invent strategies to solve problems (Reys & Reys, 1998).

Action and Relational Symbols

At the primary level, children are usually introduced to the action and relational symbols. *Action symbols* show that some quantities have been or will be acted upon, or changed, in some way (+, −, ×, ÷); relational symbols show that quantities are in some way related (=, <, >). These symbols appear in number sentences that symbolize an operation, such as

◆ 2 + 3 = 5 (two things put together in a group with three things is the same amount as five things).

◆ 5 > 2 (five is more or greater than two).

Kamii (1985, 1989, 1993, 1994) and others have found that young children often learn to deal with these symbols without a genuine understanding of how they relate to real quantities. Children should work with operations mentally through concrete experiences before connecting these operations to symbols and using complete conventional written number sentences such as $1 + 5 = 6, 5 - 3 = 2, 6 > 2$, and so on.

Kamii (1985, 1989) suggests that full number sentences (e.g., $4 + 2 = 6$) should not be introduced until second grade. Children should be encouraged to devise their own notation systems and apply them as a bridge to formal notation. Children need experiences in joining and separating quantities and verbalizing about their actions prior to really understanding what symbols represent. Just filling in blanks in a workbook or marking answers in a standardized test booklet does not indicate that children understand the deeper meaning of number sentences.

In summary, formal number sentences should be introduced gradually. First, children should have extensive exploratory experiences that provide opportunities to invent their own solutions to everyday problems. They should be encouraged to find their own systems of recording solutions using their own notation. Develop the language of number sentences through word problems that come from real-life experiences. Introduce formal number sentences when children have developed to the level where they can understand that number sentences are a shorthand representation for words. Introduce numeral notation first, then operational signs, and finally relational signs. Richardson's books (1984, 1999) are excellent resources for methods and materials that can be used for accomplishing these tasks. Some of these ideas for introducing formal symbolic notation will be described in the discussions that follow.

Instructional Strategies

Fraivillig (2001) outlines instructional strategies for advancing children's mathematical thinking. Effective teaching includes three aspects: eliciting, supporting, and extending children's solution methods. This framework is called advancing children's thinking (ACT). Eliciting (p. 456) involves supporting a variety of solutions for any problem by listening to children, encouraging elaboration, being accepting of errors, promoting collaborative problem solving, and being sure everyone has an opportunity to report. Supporting (p. 457) involves pointing out problems that are similar, providing background knowledge, supporting students as they review their strategies, putting symbolic representations of solutions on the board, and encouraging children to ask for help. Extending (p. 457) requires maintaining high standards and expectations for all children, encouraging the drawing of generalizations, listing all solutions on the board in order to promote reflection, encouraging children to try alternative solutions and more efficient solutions, and promoting enthusiasm for challenge. Overall the learning must take place in a safe environment where all students feel comfortable and respected.

Assessment

Observations and interviews can be used to assess children's progress in constructing operations with whole numbers. Assessment should be done through concrete activities with real-life or pretend situations. Paper and pencil tests are not appropriate for primary students until they can read and comprehend story problems on their own. Assessment examples will be provided as each whole number operation is discussed.

To find out if children are ready to move on to whole number operations, use the assessment interviews in Appendix A, Concrete Operations: Level 8. These tasks include conservation of number; knowledge of symbols and sets and symbols; multiple classification; and class inclusion.

Addition

Constructing the concept of addition involves an understanding that adding is putting together groups of objects to find out how many there are. It also involves learning the application of terms such as total, sum, and equal, as well as the operation signs (+ and =), which represent these terms, and connecting these amounts to symbols. Before children make these connections, they must understand quantity and what happens when quantities are combined.

Assessment

Assessment of children's understanding of addition is more than finding out if they know the so-called number facts. It is important to observe the process each child goes through in dealing with quantities. Observing the process and questioning children regarding what they have done will reveal what they do and do not understand. Their mistakes can be informative and used to help the children develop a more accurate knowledge of arithmetic.

Observations can be made during naturalistic and informal activities. Dean figures out that if he has two dimes and his grandmother gives him four more, he will have six dimes. Liu Pei decides that if there are three children at one table, two at another, and four at a third, she will have to get nine pieces of paper to pass out. Ann realizes that instead of counting everyone to find out if there are enough pencils, she can record the number at each table, find the total, and compare it with the number of pencils in the box.

Observations can also be made during structured activities. Sara's teacher tells her to take groups of six cube blocks and place them in as many combinations of group sizes as she can. Does Sara realize that, however she arranges six objects (in groups of three and three; one and five; two, two, and two; two and four; or six and zero), there are still six altogether? The children are playing a card game called "Double War." Each player has two stacks of cards, which are turned over two cards at a time. The player with the higher sum gets the other player's two cards. The teacher can observe the children's strategies and whether they help each other. He can also suggest that they write and/or draw descriptions of their strategies.

As with the assessment of other math concepts, addition can also be measured using an interview approach. The following is a sample task.

SAMPLE ASSESSMENT TASK

9A
Addition, Combining Sets Up to 10: Unit 27

Concrete Operations Ages 6–8

METHOD: Interview.

SKILL:	Child is able to combine sets to form new sets up to 10.
MATERIALS:	Twenty counters (cube blocks, Unifix Cubes®, chips): 10 of one color and 10 of another.
PROCEDURE:	Have the child select two groups of counters from each color so that the total is 10 or less. Say, PUT THREE YELLOW CUBES OVER HERE AND FIVE BLUE CUBES OVER HERE. Child completes task. Say, NOW TELL ME, IF YOU PUT ALL THE CUBES IN ONE BUNCH, HOW MANY CUBES DO YOU HAVE ALTOGETHER? HOW DO YOU KNOW? Do this with combinations that add up to 1 through 10.
EVALUATION:	Note if the child is able to make the requested groups with or without counting. Note the strategy used by the child to decide on the sum.

1. Does he begin with one and count all the blocks?
2. Does he count on? That is, in the example above, does he put his two small groups together and then say, "Three blocks, four, five, six, seven, eight. I have eight now"?
3. Does he just say, "Eight, because I know that three plus five is eight"?

INSTRUCTIONAL RESOURCE: Charlesworth, R., and Lind, K. K. (2003). *Math and Science for Young Children* (4th ed.). Clifton Park, NY: Delmar Learning.

Instruction

Instruction begins with naturalistic and informal experiences that familiarize children with quantities and how they relate to each other. Students can be guided toward constructing their own concepts if they are provided with games and word or story problems to solve and encouraged to make up their own problems.

In *Young Children Reinvent Arithmetic* (1985), Constance Kamii and Georgia DeClark describe a number of types of games that can support the development of addition concepts. The following are examples of activities.

ACTIVITIES

ADDITION: DOUBLE WAR

OBJECTIVE: Constructing combinations of addends (i.e., 1 + 1, 1 + 2, etc.) up to four.

MATERIALS: Two decks of cards with different patterns on the back.

PLAYING THE GAME: Start using the cards with addends up to four (aces, twos, threes, and fours). Two children play together. To play the game, the children begin with half the cards in each of the two decks, which are stacked facedown next to each other in front of them. Without looking at the cards, they simultaneously turn over the top two cards from each deck. Each finds the total of her two cards. The child with the highest total keeps all four cards.

FOLLOW-UP: Add the cards with the next higher addends as the students become adept with the first four. If the game takes too long, remove some of the smaller addends as the larger are included. Have the students write and/or draw descriptions of their strategies.

ADDITION: BOARD GAMES

OBJECTIVE: Constructing combinations of addends up to six.

MATERIALS: A pair of dice, a marker for each player (four), and a board game. Board games can be purchased or teacher made. Teacher-made games can be designed with themes that fit units in science and social studies. Some basic board game patterns and the materials needed for construction are described in Unit 24. Board games at the primary level can be designed with more spaces than those in Unit 24 because the older students may move farther on each turn and will have longer attention spans.

PLAYING THE GAME: Each player, in turn, rolls the dice, finds the sum of the roll, and moves the marker that many spaces.

FOLLOW-UP: Bring in new games as the students become skilled at playing the old ones. As the students become adept at playing board games, purchase or make some with pitfalls. That is, on some spaces the player might have to move backward or lose a turn (i.e., when a player lands on a red space, the dice are rolled again, and the player moves backward the sum of the dice; or else when a player lands on a certain space, a turn is lost).

The importance of problem solving was described in Unit 3. Placing operations in the context of real-life situations makes them come alive for the students so they can see the practical applications of mathematics. Richardson (1984, 1999) suggests that the children act out stories using real objects from around the room as props. For example, Derrick brings six books from the library center and Theresa brings four. "How many did they bring altogether?" Derrick and Theresa actually demonstrate by going to the library center and obtain-

ADDITION: STORY PROBLEMS

OBJECTIVE: To construct the concept of addition by solving story problems.

MATERIALS: Twenty small toys that fit a current unit. For example:
◆ Miniature dinosaurs during a dinosaur unit
◆ Miniature dogs, cats, horses, etc., during a pet unit
◆ Miniature farm animals during a farm unit
◆ Miniature vehicles during a safety unit

DEVELOPING THE PROBLEMS: Let the students act out the problems as you tell the stories.
◆ FIND THREE PLANT-EATING DINOSAURS. FIND FOUR MEAT-EATING DINOSAURS. HOW MANY DINOSAURS DO YOU HAVE?
◆ MARY HAS SOME PUPPIES. SHE SELLS THREE PUPPIES. NOW SHE HAS TWO PUPPIES LEFT. HOW MANY DID SHE HAVE TO START WITH?
◆ OFFICER SMITH GAVE TICKETS TO THE DRIVERS OF TWO CARS FOR SPEEDING. OFFICER VARGAS GAVE THE DRIVERS OF THREE CARS TICKETS FOR GOING TOO SLOW ON THE INTERSTATE. HOW MANY TICKETS DID THEY GIVE?
◆ FARMER SMITH HAS FIVE HORSES. FARMER VALDEZ HAS THREE MORE HORSES THAN FARMER SMITH. HOW MANY HORSES DOES FARMER VALDEZ HAVE?

FOLLOW-UP: Create problems to fit units and other activities and events.

ing the number of books in the problem. Trang Fung joins Dean and Sara. "How many children were there to start with?" "How many are there now?" Again, the children act out the situation. Richardson (1999) provides resources for acting out story problems with Unifix Cubes® and other objects.

Carpenter et al. (1990) identify four types of addition problems.

Join, Result Unknown. Kim has two cars. Mario gave her five more cars. How many does Kim have altogether?

Separate, Start Unknown. Kim has some cars. She gave two to Mario. Now she has five cars. How many cars did Kim have to start with?

Part-Part-Whole, Whole Unknown. Kim has two yellow cars and five blue cars. How many cars does she have?

Compare, Compare Quantity Unknown. Mario has two cars. Kim has five more cars than Mario. How many cars does Kim have?

The authors caution that textbooks often contain only join and separate problems, when all four types should be introduced. A further caution is that these types are not formulas to be memorized but just problem variations that children need to explore.

As children get more advanced, the numbers can be larger, and more addends can be included. More complex, or nonroutine problems also should be used (see Unit 3).

Once the children have had some experiences with teacher-made problems, they can create their own problems.

ADDITION: CREATING PROBLEMS USING DICE OR A FISHBOWL

OBJECTIVE: The children will create their own addition problems.

MATERIALS: A pair of dice or a container (fishbowl) full of numerals written on small pieces of cardboard cut into fish shapes, objects such as cube blocks, chips, or Unifix Cubes®.

PLAYING THE GAME: Either by rolling the dice or picking two fish, each child obtains two addends. He counts out the amount for each addend and then tells how many objects or fish he has.

FOLLOW-UP: Once students are having an easy time making up problems using the dice or the written numerals as cues, suggest that they write or dictate their favorite problem, draw it, and write or dictate the solution. For example, Brent's dog is expecting pups. He writes, "I have one dog. I hope she has five pups." Then he draws his dog and the five pups. He writes, "Then I will have six dogs."

Using number symbols is referred to as notation. Gradually, number symbols can be connected to problems as you find that the children understand the process of addition and understand class inclusion. Although most first graders can fill in the blanks correctly on worksheets, this does not indicate a real understanding of what notation means. To find out if a child really understands notation, present a problem such as the following.

Show the child several (four, five, or six) counters. Then show how you add some (two, three, or four) more. Then say, "Write on your paper what I did."

Even at the end of first grade you will find very few children who will write the correct notation, that is, 5 + 3 = 8. It is very common for first graders to write the first and last numeral (5 8) or to write all three (5 3 8) and omit the action symbols. They may also be unable to tell you what they did and why. It is very important that the use of notation be an integral part of concrete problem-solving activities.

Richardson (1984, 1999) suggests that formal instruction in connecting symbols to the process of addition begin with modeling of the writing of equations. After acting out a problem such as described previously, write the problem on the chalkboard, explaining that this is another way to record the information. For example, "Another way to write three cows plus six cows makes nine cows is: 3 + 6 = 9 (three plus six equals nine)." Help the children learn what the plus sign means by playing games and doing activities that require the use of the plus sign with the equals sign. For example, try the following activity.

ADDITION: USING NOTATION AT THE CONNECTING LEVEL

OBJECTIVE: Children will connect symbols to problems using numerals and the plus operation symbol.

MATERIALS: Objects to count and one die.

PLAYING THE GAME: Children take turns rolling the die to find out how many to add. For example, a three is rolled. Each child counts out three counters, and the teacher writes 3 + on the board. A five is rolled. The students count out groups of five to put with their groups of three, and the teacher writes 3 + 5.

FOLLOW-UP: After working in small groups with the teacher, students can work independently with problems written on cards: 2 + 3, 4 + 6, and so on. As you go by, observe what they do, and ask them to read the problems to you.

Children sometimes look upon the equals sign as indicating that the answer is coming next rather than understanding that it indicates there is the same amount on each side of the equation. This concept can be clarified using a balance scale to explore equality.

When the children are comfortable with connecting the symbols to the problems and using the plus symbol, they can begin to write the notation themselves. Start with problems in which you write the notation, and have the children copy what you do before they go on to independent work. For example, have everyone pick five groups of five counters each. Then tell them to separate each group of five counters as many ways as they can, and you write the results.

1 + 4 = 5	1	2	1	2	5
2 + 3 = 5	+4	+3		2	+0
1 + 1 + 3 = 5	5	5	+3	+1	5
2 + 2 + 1 = 5			5	5	
5 + 0 = 5					

After you write each equation, have the children write it on a piece of paper and put it next to the counters they have counted out. Follow up by having the students work independently, finding out how many ways they can break the amounts up to six and write the equations. When they are doing well up to six, have them move on to seven and above.

Subtraction

To conceptualize subtraction is to develop an understanding that subtracting involves taking objects away to find out how many are left or comparing groups of objects to find out the difference between them. It also involves learning the application of terms such as minus, difference, and equal, as well as the action signs (− and =), which represent these terms. Subtraction also involves thinking about **more than** (>) and **less than** (<) and the symbols (> and <), which stand for these relationships. It also includes connecting to symbols as a shorthand notation for concrete operations. As with addition, before children make the connections to and between symbols, they must understand quantity and what happens when something is taken away from a group or when two groups are compared.

Assessment

As with addition, assessment of children's understanding of subtraction is more than finding out if they know the so-called number facts. It is important to observe the process each child goes through in dealing with quantities. Observing the process and questioning children regarding what they have done will reveal what they do and do not understand. Their mistakes can be informative to the teacher and used to help the children develop a more accurate knowledge of arithmetic.

Observations can be made during naturalistic and informal activities. Chan figures out that if there are 10 more minutes until school is out and Ms. Hebert says that in five minutes they will start to get ready to leave, that they will have five minutes to get ready. Jason has 10 bean seeds. He decides that he can give Ann four, and the six he will have left will be enough for his seed sprouting experiment. Six children are allowed to work in the science center at one time. Brent notices that there are only four children there now. He suggests to Derrick that they hurry over while there is room for two more. Vanessa observes that there is room for eight children in the library center, while six

at a time may work in the math center. Thus there is room for two more in the library center than in the math center.

Observations can be made during structured activities. Dean is trying to figure out how many different amounts he can take away from five. Mrs. Red Fox notes that Dean is well organized and systematic as he constructs one group of five after another and takes a different amount away until he has the combinations five minus zero, one, two, three, four, and five. Derrick and Liu Pei are playing "Double War." They have to subtract the amount that is smaller from the amount that is larger. Mr. Wang can note whether the children can figure out the correct differences and whether they help each other.

Subtraction can be assessed using an interview approach. The following is a sample task.

SAMPLE ASSESSMENT TASK

9B   **Concrete Operations Ages 6–8**
Subtraction, Sets of 10 and Less: Unit 27

METHOD:　　Interview.

SKILL:　　Child is able to subtract sets to make new sets using groups of 10 and smaller.

MATERIALS:　Twenty counters (cube blocks, Unifix Cubes®, chips): 10 of one color and 10 of another and a small box or other small container.

PROCEDURE: Pick out a group of 10 or fewer counters. Say, I HAVE SEVEN CUBES. I'M GOING TO HIDE SOME IN THE BOX. (Hide three in the box.) NOW HOW MANY DO I HAVE LEFT? HOW MANY DID I HIDE? If the child cannot answer, give him seven of the other color cubes and ask him to take three away and tell you how many are left. Do this with amounts of 10 and less. For the less mature or younger child, start with five and less.

EVALUATION: Note if the child is able to solve the problem and the process used. Note whether the child has to count or whether he just knows without counting.

INSTRUCTIONAL RESOURCE: Charlesworth, R., and Lind, K. K. (2003). *Math and Science for Young Children* (4th ed.). Clifton Park, NY: Delmar Learning.

Instruction

Just as with addition, instruction begins with naturalistic and informal experiences that familiarize children with quantities and how they relate to each other. Students can be guided toward constructing

their own concepts if they are provided with games and word or story problems to solve and encouraged to make up their own problems. Once the students evidence an understanding of addition, subtraction can be introduced. Children can work with both addition and subtraction problems so that they can learn the clues for deciding which operation to use.

The game "Double War" can be modified and played as a subtraction game by having the player with the largest difference between her pair of cards keep all four cards. As with addition, begin with numbers up to four, and gradually include higher numbers as the children get adept at the game. Board games can also be purchased or devised that use subtraction as the operation that indicates which way to move. A board game could be made where all the moves are backward. The theme might be running away from a wild animal or going home from a friend's house. Or dice could be thrown, and each move would be the difference between the two.

Of course, word or story problems are an essential ingredient in the instruction of subtraction, just as they are for addition. Problems should be set in real-life contexts and acted out. For example, suppose Derrick and Theresa have brought 10 books from the library center. The activity could be continued by asking children to take different numbers of books back to the library center and finding out how many are left after each trip. Place children in groups of different sizes. If there are five children in this group and three in this group, which group has more? How many more? How will we find out? There are a number of different basic patterns that can be used for subtraction story problems.

Carpenter et al. (1990) have identified seven types of subtraction problems.

Join, Change Unknown. Kim has three cars. How many more cars will she need to have eight all together?

Join, Start Unknown. Kim has some cars. Mario gave her three more cars. Now she has eight cars. How many cars did Kim have to start with?

Separate, Result Unknown. Kim had eight cars. She gave Mario three cars. How many cars does Kim have left?

Separate, Change Unknown. Kim had eight cars. She gave some to Mario. Now she has five cars. How many did she give to Mario?

Part-Part-Whole, Part Unknown. Kim has eight cars. Five are yellow. The rest are green. How many are green?

Compare, Difference Unknown. Kim has eight cars. Mario has three cars. How many more cars does Kim have than Mario?

Compare, Referent Unknown. Kim has eight cars. She has five more cars than Mario. How many cars does Mario have?

As with addition, once the children have experiences with teacher-devised story problems, they can dictate or write their own. The dice/fishbowl game can be modified for subtraction. Children can also dictate or write original problems, draw them, and write or dictate the solutions.

As with addition, subtraction notation can be introduced gradually. Number symbols can be connected to problems as you find the children have an understanding of the process of subtraction. To find out if a child really understands notation, the same type of procedure can be used as for addition. That is, show the child several counters (five, six, or seven). Have her tell you how many you have. Hide one or more of the counters, and ask the child to show you on paper what you did. Do not be surprised if very few end-of-the-first-grade students and many second graders will not be able to write the correct equation.

Formal introduction of subtraction can begin with modeling. Act out a problem, and then explain that there is another way to record the information. Write the number sentence for the problem on the chalkboard. For example, "Another way to write five rabbits take away three rabbits is $5 - 3 = 2$ (five minus three equals two)." Help the children learn what the minus sign means by playing games and doing activities that require the use of the minus sign with the equals sign. For example, try the following activity.

ACTIVITIES

SUBTRACTION: USING NOTATION AT THE CONNECTING LEVEL

OBJECTIVE: The children will connect symbols to problems using numerals and the minus action symbol.

MATERIALS: Objects to count and two dice.

PLAYING THE GAME: The children take turns rolling the dice to find out which numbers to subtract. First they identify the larger number and count out that amount of counters. The teacher writes [larger number –]. Then they remove the smaller number of counters, and the teacher continues [larger number – smaller number]. Then the children identify how many are left in the original pile, and the teacher completes the equation [larger number – smaller number = difference]. For example, they roll six and two. They make a group of six counters. The teacher writes 6 –. Then they remove two counters, and the teacher continues: 6 – 2. Then they identify the difference (four). The teacher finishes the equation: 6 – 2 = 4.

FOLLOW-UP: After working in small groups with the teacher, students can work independently with problems written on cards: 5 – 1, 3 – 2, etc. They can also make up problems using dice or pulling numbers out of a fishbowl. As you observe what the children are doing, stop and ask them to read the problems to you.

As with addition, when the students are comfortable with connecting the symbols to the problems and using the minus symbol, they can begin to write the notation themselves. Start with problems where you write the notation and the children copy you before they go on to independent work. For example, have everyone pick six counters. Have them see what kinds of problems appear as different amounts are taken away. After each problem, take a new group of six so the problems can be compared. You write the results of each take-away on the chalkboard (i.e., 6 – 1 = 5) and have the children copy it on a piece of paper and put it next to the counters they have counted out. Follow up by having the students work independently, finding out how many subtraction problems they can discover starting with groups of different amounts up through six. When they are doing well up to six, have them move on to seven and above.

The notation for greater (more) than (>) and less than (<) is conventionally introduced in first grade along with subtraction but is usually not really understood until grade three. For the most part, students in early primary grades work with *more* and *less* using concrete materials such as those described in Unit 11. As they begin to understand the concepts, the children can apply them to playing games. For example, lotto and bingo boards (see Unit 24) can be used. For bingo the players can roll a die and cover a square on their card containing a number or set that is more than or less than the number rolled. For lotto they would pick a numeral or set card and again cover a card on the board that was either more than or less than the numeral or set on the card. As students become familiar with the action symbols, cards could be used that indicate that they pick an amount or numeral that is > (more or greater than) or < (less than) one of those on the card. They could then move on to using cards that indicate an amount such as [_____ > 2] or [_____ < 5] and thus require the use of addition or subtraction to arrive at a selection.

Multiplication

Conceptualizing multiplication requires that the students understand what equal quantities are. Then they can proceed to learn that multiplication is a shorthand way of adding equal quantities. That is, 4×3 is the same as $3 + 3 + 3 + 3$. Multiplication also involves learning the application of terms such as **factors** (the two numbers that are operated on) and **product** (the result of the operation). Students also learn the action terms **times** and **equals** and connect them to the action signs ($\times$ and $=$). Multiplication with concrete objects was introduced prior to the primary level and continues at this level for most primary students. Notation and the more formal aspects may be introduced toward the end of the primary level, but students are not usually proficient at the most fundamental level until fourth grade.

Assessment

Assessment of children's understanding of multiplication, as with the other whole number operations, is more than finding out if children know the number facts. It is important to observe the process each child goes through in dealing with quantities and ask questions that will provide a view of the thought behind their actions.

Observations can be made during naturalistic and informal activities. Use the terms *rows*, *stacks*, and *groups* to refer to equal sets that will be added. There is no rush to use the term *times*. Many children learn to recite the times tables by heart without any understanding of what *times* really means. First children must understand that when they multiply they are counting groups of objects, not individual objects. Watch for incidents when children work with equal groups. For example, Dean comments that every child at his table has three carrot sticks. Theresa makes sure that each of the six children working in the science center receives four bean seeds to plant. Chan tells Ms. Hebert that he has purchased three miniature dinosaurs for each of the five friends invited to his birthday party. She asks him if he can figure out how many he bought altogether.

Multiplication can also be assessed by using an interview approach. The following is a sample task.

SAMPLE ASSESSMENT TASK

9F
Multiplication, Readiness: Unit 27   **Concrete Operations Ages 7–8**

METHOD: Interview.

SKILL: Child is able to demonstrate readiness for multiplication by constructing equal groups of different sizes from groups of the same size.

MATERIALS: Twenty counters (cube blocks, Unifix Cubes,® chips).

PROCEDURE: Make two groups of six counters each. Ask the child, MAKE THREE GROUPS OF TWO CHIPS (BLOCKS, CUBES) EACH WITH THIS BUNCH OF SIX CHIPS (BLOCKS, CUBES). When the child finishes (right or wrong), point to the other group of counters. NOW MAKE TWO GROUPS OF THREE WITH THESE CHIPS (BLOCKS, CUBES).

EVALUATION: Note if the child is able to make the two different subgroups. Children who are not ready for multiplication will become confused and not see the difference between the two tasks.

INSTRUCTIONAL RESOURCE: Charlesworth, R., and Lind, K. K. (2003). *Math and Science for Young Children* (4th ed.). Clifton Park, NY: Delmar Learning.

Instruction

Just as with addition and subtraction, instruction in multiplication begins with naturalistic and informal experiences that familiarize children with quantities and how they relate to each other. Students can be guided toward constructing their own concepts if they are provided with games and word or story problems to solve and encouraged to make up their own problems. Richardson (1984, 1999) suggests that the children should first be asked to look for equal groups in the environment. How many tables have four chairs? How many girls have two barrettes in their hair? How many children have three cookies for dessert? How many parts of the body can they identify that come in groups of two? What parts do cars have that come in groups of four?

Of course, word or story problems are an essential ingredient in the instruction of multiplication just as they are for subtraction and addition. Problems should be set in real-life contexts and acted out. Dean gives four children two crayons each. How many crayons did he pass out? Chan makes three stacks of books. He puts three books in each stack. How many books does he have? Ann gives each of the five people at her table four pieces of paper. How many pieces of paper did she pass out?

Build models of multiplication problems with the students. Counters can be stacked, put in rows, and placed in groups as illustrated in Figure 27–1. For example, working with inch cubes,

◆ make three stacks of four cubes each.
◆ make four rows of five cubes each.
◆ make six groups of two cubes each.

Notation can be introduced gradually. Number symbols can be connected to problems as you find that the children have an understanding of the process of multiplication. Formal introduction of multiplication can begin with modeling. Act out a problem, and then explain that there is another way to record the information. Write the number sentence for the problem on the chalkboard. For example: "Another way to write 'Dean gave four children two crayons each' is [4 groups of 2 = 8]. Another way to write 'Chan has three stacks of three books' is [3 stacks of 3 = 9]." Do

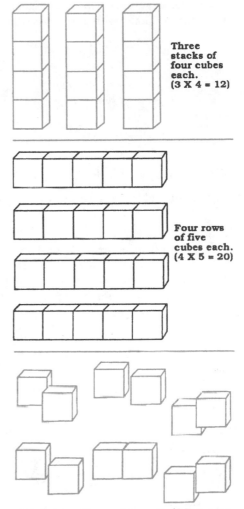

Three stacks of four cubes each. (3 X 4 = 12)

Four rows of five cubes each. (4 X 5 = 20)

Six groups of two cubes each. (6 X 2 = 12)

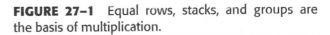

FIGURE 27–1 Equal rows, stacks, and groups are the basis of multiplication.

several problems in this manner. Then introduce the multiplication sign. First model. Explain that there is another shorter way to write problems. Erase "stacks of" or "groups of" and write × in its place. Then write problems on the board and have the children work them out with their counters. Next, have them work out problems and copy you as you write the whole equation, that is [4 × 2 = 8]. Finally, have them make models and write the equations on their own.

The following is an example of an independent activity that can be done with multiplication using notation.

ACTIVITIES

MULTIPLICATION: USING NOTATION AT THE CONNECTING LEVEL

OBJECTIVE: The children will connect symbols to problems using numerals and the times action symbol.

MATERIALS: Counters, a die, several small containers, and a sheet for recording the problems.

ACTIVITY: Children can work on their own writing equations. First they decide how many containers to use. They can roll the die or just pick a number. They line up the cups and then, starting with zero, one at a time, fill the cups and write the resulting equation. For example, if they pick four cups, they would first put zero blocks in each cup and write the equation, then one block in each, two, three, and so on. Their work would look like the illustration that follows.

FOLLOW-UP: Develop some more independent activities using the resources suggested at the end of the unit.

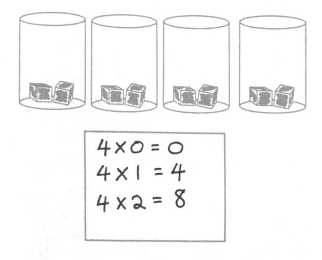

$$4 \times 0 = 0$$
$$4 \times 1 = 4$$
$$4 \times 2 = 8$$

To find out if a child really understands notation, the same type of procedure can be used as was used for addition and subtraction; that is, show the child three or more equivalent groups. Explain that you are going to put the groups together into one group, and ask him to write what you did. For example, if you show three groups of four, he should write [$3 \times 4 = 12$].

Division

Division is an activity that children engage in frequently during their natural everyday activities (see Unit 25). They are encouraged to share equally, and they are often asked to pass out items so that everyone has the same amount. Formal instruction in division is usually introduced toward the end of the primary period during the third grade, but children are not expected to be proficient in doing division problems until the fifth grade. Division is used to solve two types of problems.

◆ Grouping. The process of *grouping* is used to find out how many subgroups of a particular size a larger group contains. For example, George has 15 blocks. He wants to make towers that are five blocks high. How many can he make?

◆ Sharing. *Sharing* is the process of dividing a larger group into a particular number of groups to find out how many items will be included in that number of subgroups. Six children will work in the science center exploring the reaction of different types of items when they are touched by magnets. There are 32 items. How many will each child get? Are there any left over?

The children do not have to distinguish between these types of problems. They serve mainly as a guide for making up problems for them to explore. Eventually they will learn the terminology of division (**dividend** ÷ **divisor** = **quotient**), and if some are left over, **remainder**.

Assessment

Assessment of children's understanding of division focuses on the processes they use to group and to share.

Instruction

Division also begins with naturalistic and informal experiences. Children can be given many tasks that give them division experiences. Passing out items, putting items into groups to be shared, and finding out if there is enough for everyone are opportunities to develop the division concept. Games and story problems can be used as guides in supporting the child's construction of the concept of division as she ventures into more formal activities.

As with the other whole number operations, begin formal instruction by doing concrete problems. As Richardson (1984) suggests, tell the children stories, and have them act them out. Start with real objects from the classroom. For example,

◆ Ann has 16 pieces of paper. Each child in her group needs four pieces. How many children can receive four pieces of paper?
◆ Jason, Chan, and Vanessa want to feed the guinea pig. The guinea pig gets six pellets of food. How many pellets can each child give it?

SAMPLE ASSESSMENT TASK

9I   **Concrete Operations Ages 7–8**
Division, Basic Concept: Unit 27

METHOD: Interview.

SKILL: Child can demonstrate an understanding that division consists of grouping or sharing objects.

MATERIALS: Thirty counters (cube blocks, Unifix Cubes,® chips) and five small containers (such as clear plastic glasses).

PROCEDURE: Put out eight chips and four containers. DIVIDE UP THE CHIPS SO THAT EACH CUP HAS THE SAME AMOUNT. When the chips are divided ask, HOW MANY CUBES DO YOU HAVE IN EACH CUP? The child should respond "Two in each cup" rather than "I have two, two, and two." Try the same procedure with more cups and larger amounts to divide. Then try it with uneven amounts. Note if the child becomes confused or can recognize that there are more than are needed. Also do some sharing problems. That is, for example, put out 16 chips. I WANT TO GIVE THREE FRIENDS THE SAME AMOUNT OF CHIPS. HOW MANY WILL EACH ONE RECEIVE? ARE THERE ANY LEFT OVER?

EVALUATION: Note how the children handle the problem. Do they proceed in an organized fashion? Can they deal with the remainders?

INSTRUCTIONAL RESOURCE: Charlesworth, R., and Lind, K. K. (2003). *Math and Science for Young Children* (4th ed.). Clifton Park, NY: Delmar Learning.

Next, have the children act out similar stories, using counters to represent real objects. Have the children make many models by constructing rows and stacks and dividing them into groups.

ACTIVITIES

DIVISION: MAKING MODELS

OBJECTIVE: The children will construct models of division.

MATERIALS: Counters (cube blocks, Unifix Cubes,® chips) and several 16-ounce clear plastic cups.

ACTIVITY: Using different amounts initially and having the children divide them up into groups of different sizes and into different numbers of groups, have the students do many problems using the following patterns:

1. MAKE A ROW (TRAIN) WITH (number) OF BLOCKS (CUBES, CHIPS). HOW MANY STACKS OF (number) CAN YOU MAKE?
   DIVIDE YOUR ROW (TRAIN) OF (number) INTO (number) OF ROWS. HOW MANY CUBES (BLOCKS, CHIPS) ARE IN EACH ROW?
2. GET (number) CUPS. DIVIDE (number) CUBES INTO EACH CUP SO THAT THERE IS THE SAME AMOUNT OF CUBES IN EACH CUP. Continue with different numbers of cups and counters.

FOLLOW-UP: Develop some more independent activities using the resources suggested at the end of the unit.

Division notation can be introduced with modeling. Act out problems just as you did with the other whole number operations. For example

- "John has 12 crackers." Write [12] on the board. "He has three friends. He wants to give himself and each friend the same number of crackers." Write [12 ÷ 4]. "Each child got three crackers." Write [12 ÷ 4 = 3].
- "The children are going to explore how pendulums work. There are four pendulums and eight children. How many children will have to share each pendulum? Eight children (write 8), divided by four pendulums (write [8 ÷ 4]) equals two children must share each pendulum" (write [8 ÷ 4 = 2]).

After you have modeled several problems, the children can go to the next step by acting out the problems and copying what you write. Next, you can give them problems that they can act out with counters and write the equations themselves. When the children have completed the equations, you can write them on the board and they can check theirs. Check each child's model and equation. Note whether there are any difficulties, and help children figure out how to act out and write the equation correctly. Move on to giving the children written problems (i.e., 10 ÷ 2), and have them act them out using counters. Finally, have them make up their own problems, act them out, draw them, and write them.

To find out if a child really understands notation, use the same procedure as suggested for the other whole number operations. That is, act out division, and ask the children to write what you did. For example, count out 15 counters and divide them into five groups of three. See whether the children can write [15 ÷ 5 = 3] and tell you that 15 divided into five groups makes three in each group.

Integration with Other Content Areas

Whole number operations can be applied in the other major content areas as depicted in Figure 27–2.

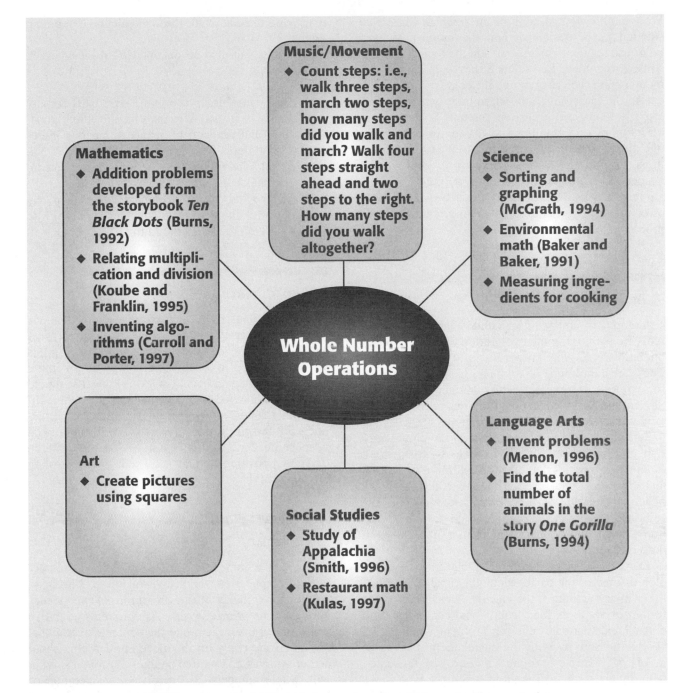

Music/Movement
- Count steps: i.e., walk three steps, march two steps, how many steps did you walk and march? Walk four steps straight ahead and two steps to the right. How many steps did you walk altogether?

Mathematics
- Addition problems developed from the storybook *Ten Black Dots* (Burns, 1992)
- Relating multiplication and division (Koube and Franklin, 1995)
- Inventing algorithms (Carroll and Porter, 1997)

Science
- Sorting and graphing (McGrath, 1994)
- Environmental math (Baker and Baker, 1991)
- Measuring ingredients for cooking

Whole Number Operations

Art
- Create pictures using squares

Social Studies
- Study of Appalachia (Smith, 1996)
- Restaurant math (Kulas, 1997)

Language Arts
- Invent problems (Menon, 1996)
- Find the total number of animals in the story *One Gorilla* (Burns, 1994)

FIGURE 27–2   Integrating whole number operations across the curriculum.

For example, for an art project, students can create squared paper designs, count the number of each color used in their design, and add the total number of squares included. For science they can do environmental math such as graphing the contents of the trash can in the classroom and determining which type of trash is found in the largest amount. Social studies offers many opportunities such as adding up the cost of a meal in a restaurant, dividing food into equal portions, or finding out how many of an item will be needed if each person in the group gets a fixed amount. Books, as previously described in Unit 15, offer many opportunities for solving whole number problems.

Technology

Computers and hand calculators are very useful tools for supporting the exploration of whole number operations and the properties of whole numbers. There are a multitude of computer programs available for working with basic whole number operations. Several are included in the Activities section of this unit. Most of these computer programs are designed to help children remember the basic addition, subtraction, multiplication, and division facts. Many have interesting graphics that catch the children's attention and make drill and practice fun. With the capability of letting the children know right away whether the response is correct, the programs give the children immediate feedback and allow them to move along at their own pace.

During preprimary activities, children have explored some of the basic calculator capabilities. During primary activities, the calculator can be used for further exploration, for checking and comparing with manual calculations, and for problem solutions. A very basic activity with the calculator is the exploration of multiples. Young children are fascinated with rhymes such as "Two, four, six, eight, who do we appreciate?" This type of counting is called **skip counting**. Skip counting in the example defines the multiples of two, that is, all the numbers that result when multiplied by two such as $2 \times 2 = 4$, $2 \times 3 = 6$, $2 \times 4 = 8$, and so on. Children can explore these prop-

erties with the calculator through calculator counting (Figure 27–3).

Activities can also be obtained from the Internet. Two examples are

- Base ten block activities—five-part activity looking at addition, subtraction, multiplication, and division of whole numbers. Grades one through four. Link from Eisenhower National Clearinghouse or http://mason.gmu.edu/~mmankus/whole/base10/baseten.htm
- Al the Alligator (greater than/less than) by Kelly at http://www.lessonplanspage.com/MthGTLT-AlTheAlligator12.htm

Evaluation

Evaluation, just as with assessment, should be done first with concrete tasks, observing both the process and the product. The tasks in Appendix A and in this unit can be used for evaluation as well as for initial assessment. Standardized achievement tests should not be administered until the students have the concepts internalized with concrete activities. For guidelines for testing young children, see the National Association for the Education of Young Children (NAEYC) position statement on standardized testing of young children three through eight years of age.

Summary

The whole number operations of addition, subtraction, multiplication, and division have begun to develop through naturalistic and informal experiences during the preprimary years. As children's cognitive development takes them into the concrete operational level, they are ready for the move into learning about action symbols and written notation. Problem solving with whole numbers also involves consideration of learning basic facts and algorithms and developing computational fluency. Conventionally, children start with addition and subtraction in the beginning of the primary period (grade one). They move on to more complex addition and subtraction and the introduction

COUNT WITH YOUR CALCULATOR

Push Ⓒ ⓪ ⊕ ② ⊜

What do you see? _____

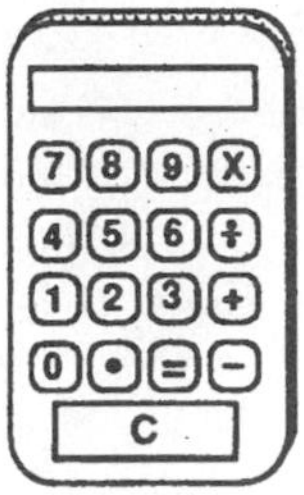

Push ⊜ again

What do you see? _____

What will the calculator show if you

push ⊜ again? _____

Do it. Were you correct? _____

Push ⊜ ⊜ ⊜ .

Guess what the calculator will show each time. _____ _____ _____

What happened? _____

Complete the following. Then use your calculator to see if you are correct.

Push Ⓒ ⓪ ⊕ ③ ⊜

The calculator will show _____

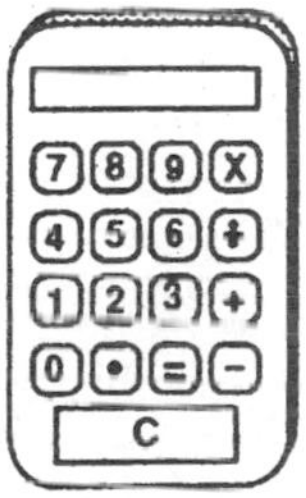

Push

⊜ _____ _____

⊜ _____

⊜ _____

Push Ⓒ ⓪ ⊕ ④ ⊜

The calculator will show _____

Push

⊜ _____

⊜ _____

⊜ _____

FIGURE 27-3 The calculator can be used to count by equal multiples.

of multiplication in the second grade. Division is usually introduced in the third grade. Each operation begins with the informal activities and acting out problems with concrete objects and moves gradually into the use of formal notation and written problems. Story or word problems that put the operations into real-life contexts are the core around which the whole number operations are constructed in the young child's mind.

KEY TERMS

whole number operations
algorithms
action symbols
basic facts
computational fluency
relational symbols
number sentences
total

sum
equal
nonroutine problems
notation
more than (>)
less than (<)
factors
product

times
dividend
divisor
quotient
remainder
skip counting

SUGGESTED ACTIVITIES

1. Develop at least two of the independent activities suggested by Kathy Richardson and/or the group games described by Constance Kamii in their respective books. Add the instructions to your Activity File. If possible, try out the activities with one or more primary grade children. Report to the class regarding what you developed, whom you tried it with, what happened, and how well you believe it worked.

2. Do a comparison of concrete and paper and pencil modes of math assessment. Select three whole number operations assessment tasks from this unit or Appendix A. Devise a paper and pencil test that includes the same kinds of problems. Use the interview tasks with two primary students. Return a week later and use the conventional paper and pencil test with the same two students. Take careful notes on the process used by the students to solve the problems. Write a report describing the two types of assessment tasks; the results, including the students' performance; and your comparison and evaluation of the two methods of assessment.

3. Observe in two or more primary classrooms during times when math activities are occurring. Report to the class, including a description of what you observed, how the instruction compared with the methods described in this unit, and suggestions for any changes you would make if you were teaching in those classrooms.

4. Review some whole number operations software using the format described in Activity 7, Unit 9. You might try one of the following programs if available.

- Animated Arithmetic. DelValle, TX: Flix Productions Animated Educational Software. Provides drill and practice with whole number arithmetic.

- Animated Math for Windows! DelValle, TX: Flix Productions Animated Educational Software. Practice on addition and subtraction facts to 10. (K–2).

- Balancing Bear. Pleasantville, NY: Sunburst Technologies. (English/Spanish).

- Challenge Math. Pleasantville, NY: Sunburst.

- Coco's Math Project 1. Singapore, SG: Times Learning Systems Pte Ltd. Includes problems in addition, subtraction, multiplication, reasoning, and equations.

- Fizz and Martina's Math Adventure Series: Buddies for Life. (Grades 1 and 2). Watertown, MA: Tom Snyder. Supports skills in addition and subtraction of one-digit numbers, communication, and teamwork.

- Gold Medal Math. Norwalk, CT: EdVenture Software. Practice in whole number computation with an Olympic theme.

- Hands-On Math: Learning with Computers and Math Manipulatives. Newbury Park, CA: Ventura Educational Systems.

◆ Hop to It!. Pleasantville, NY: Sunburst.
◆ Learning in Motion Series: Assess Math! Santa Cruz, CA: Learning in Motion. Teachers can use this software to create assessment materials.
◆ M*A*T*H Circus. (Grades K–8). Greygum Educational Software (see http://www.terc.edu). Circus theme includes problems that apply reasoning and problem solving using whole number operations.
◆ Math Blaster1: In Search of Spot. Knowledge adventure (see http://www.terc.edu). Includes sections on number sense and computation in addition, subtraction, multiplication, and division.
◆ Math Quest with Aladdin. Disney interactive (see http://www.terc.edu). A game based on the Disney film Aladdin. Includes whole number operations.
◆ Math Rabbit. Fremont, CA: The Learning Company.

◆ Math Workshop. Pleasantville, NY: Sunburst. Includes games that apply whole number operations and computation.
◆ Mental Math Games, Series 1. (1992). Sandy, UT: Waterford Institute.
◆ Muppet Math™. Pleasantville, NY: Sunburst.
◆ Number Connections. Pleasantville, NY: Sunburst.
◆ Pearson Educational Software Math—2&4. Austin, TX: Pearson Publishing, Kamico Instructional Media. (Grades 2–10). Hundreds of questions and tutorials.
◆ Sidewalk Sneakers. Pleasantville, NY: Sunburst
◆ Splish, Splash Math. Pleasantville, NY: Sunburst. (Grades K–2). Reinforces basic addition and subtraction.
◆ Unifix® Software. Nashua, NH: Delta Education.

REVIEW

A. Explain why it is essential that children have the opportunity to construct their own whole number algorithms.
B. Match the action symbols in Column I with the words they stand for in Column II.

Column I	Column II
1. +	a. multiply, times
2. –	b. equals
3. ×	c. more than or greater than
4. ÷	d. add, plus
5. =	e. less than
6. <	f. divide
7. >	g. subtract, minus

C. Select the statements that are correct.
1. Constance Kamii believes that children learn arithmetic by being told about it.
2. Kamii believes that group games are excellent vehicles for supporting the construction of math concepts.
3. Paper and pencil worksheets are excellent for helping children develop the logic of arithmetic.
4. Kamii believes that children should always work alone at their desks when learning math.
D. Explain why standardized testing is a threat to the development of logical thinking.
E. When introducing whole number sentences (equations), a three-stage sequence should be followed. List the steps.
F. Explain briefly the instructional processes for addition, subtraction, multiplication, and division.

REFERENCES

Baker, A., & Baker, J. (1991). *Counting on a small planet*. Portsmouth, NH: Heinemann.

Carpenter, T., Carey, D., & Kouba, V. (1990). A problem-solving approach to the operations. In J. N. Payne (Ed.), *Mathematics for the young child* (pp. 111–131). Reston, VA: National Council of Teachers of Mathematics.

Carroll, W. M., & Porter, D. (1997). Invented strategies can develop meaningful mathematical procedures. *Teaching Children Mathematics, 3*(7), 370, 374.

Charlesworth, R., & Senger, E. (2001). Arithmetic. In L. S. Grinstein & S. I. Lipsey, Eds., *Encyclopedia of mathematics* (pp. 37–43). New York: Routledge-Falmer.

Curcio, F. R., & Schwartz, S. L. (1998). There are no algorithms for teaching algorithms. *Teaching Children Mathematics, 5*(1), 26–30.

Fraivillig, J. (2001). Strategies for advancing children's mathematical thinking. *Teaching Children Mathematics, 7*(8), 454–459.

Fuson, K. C., Grandau, L., & Sugiyama, P. A. (2001). Achievable numerical understandings for all young children. *Teaching Children Mathematics, 7*(9), 522–526.

Ginsburg, H. (1977). *Children's arithmetic*. New York: D. Van Nostrand.

Isaacs, A. C., & Carroll, W. M. (1999). Strategies for basic-facts instruction. *Teaching Children Mathematics, 5*(9), 508–515.

Kamii, C. K. (1989). *Young children continue to reinvent arithmetic, second grade*. New York: Teachers College.

Kamii, C. K. (1994). *Children reinvent arithmetic, 3rd grade*. New York: Teachers College.

Kamii, C. K., & DeClark, G. (1985). *Young children reinvent arithmetic*. New York: Teachers College.

Kouba, V. L., & Franklin, K. (1995). Multiplication and division: Sense making and meaning. *Teaching Children Mathematics, 1*(9), 574–577.

Kulas, L. (1997). May I take your order? *Teaching Children Mathematics, 3*(5), 230–234.

McGrath, B. B. (1994). *The m&m's® brand counting book*. Watertown, MA: Charlesbridge.

Menon, R. (1996). Mathematical communication through student-constructed questions. *Teaching Children Mathematics, 2*(9), 530–532.

National Association for the Education of Young Children (NAEYC) and National Association of Early Childhood Specialists in State Departments of Education (NAECSSDE). (1991). Guidelines for appropriate curriculum content and assessment in programs serving children ages 3 through 8: A position statement. *Young Children, 46*(3), 21–38.

National Council of Teachers of Mathematics. (2000). *Principles and standards for school mathematics*. Reston, VA: Author. (http://www.nctm.org)

Reys, B. J., & Reys, R. E. (1998). Computation in the elementary curriculum: Shifting the emphasis. *Teaching Children Mathematics, 5*(4), 236–241.

Richardson, K. (1984). *Developing number concepts using Unifix Cubes.®* Menlo Park, CA: Addison-Wesley.

Richardson, K. (1999). *Developing number concepts: Book 2, addition and subtraction*. Parsippany, NJ: Dale Seymour.

Russell, S. J. (2000). Developing computational fluency with whole numbers. *Teaching Children Mathematics, 7*(3), 154–158.

Warshauer, H. K., & Warshauer, M. L. (2001). Algorithms. In L. S. Grinstein & S. I. Lipsey, Eds., *Encyclopedia of mathematics* (pp. 23–24). New York: RoutledgeFalmer.

FURTHER READING AND RESOURCES

Anderson, T. L. (1996). "They're trying to tell me something": A teacher's reflection on primary children's construction of mathematical knowledge. *Young Children, 51*(4), 34–42.

Artzt, A. F., & Newman, C. M. (1990). *How to use cooperative learning in the mathematics class*. Reston, VA: National Council of Teachers of Mathematics.

Box it or bag it mathematics. (K–2). Portland, OR: The Math Learning Center. (800-575-8130) (http://www.mlc.pdx.edu)

Bridges in mathematics. (K–2). Portland, OR: The Math Learning Center. (800-575-8130) (http://www.mlc.pdx.edu)

Burns, M. (1991). Introducing division through problem-solving experiences. *Arithmetic Teacher, 38*(8), 14–18.

Burns, M. (1992). *Math and literature: K–3*. Sausalito, CA: Math Solutions. (Available from Cuisinaire)

Burns, M., & Silbey, R. (2001, April). Math journals boost real learning. *Instructor*, 18–20.

Clements, D. H. (1999). Subitizing: What is it? *Teaching Children Mathematics, 5*(7), 400–405.

Clements, D. H., Swaminathan, S., Hannibal, M. A. Z., & Sarama, J. (1999). Young children's concepts of shape. *Journal for Research in Mathematics Education, 30*(2), 192–212.

Copley, J. V. (2000). *The young child and mathematics*. Washington, DC: National Association for the Education of Young Children.

Copley, J. V. (Ed.). (1999). *Mathematics in the early years*. Washington, DC: National Association for the Education of Young Children.

Dempsy. D., & Marshall, J. (2001). Dear Verity, Why are all the dictionaries wrong? *Phi Delta Kappan, 82*(6), 457–459.

Drosdeck, C. C. (1995). Promoting calculator uses in elementary classrooms. *Teaching Children Mathematics, 1*(5), 300–305.

Fosnot, C. T., & Dolk, M. (2001). *Young mathematicians at work: Constructing number sense, addition, and subtraction*. Portsmouth, NH: Heinemann.

Fuson, K. C., Carroll, W. M., & Drueck, J. V. (2000). Achievement results for second and third graders using the *Standards*-based curriculum *Everyday Mathematics. Journal for Research in Mathematics Education, 31*(3), 277–295.

Jensen, R. J. (Ed.) (1993). *Research ideas for the classroom: Early childhood mathematics*. New York: Macmillan.

Kamii, C., Lewis, B. A., & Booker, B. M. (1998). Instead of teaching missing addends. *Teaching Children Mathematics, 4*(8), 458–461.

Kamii, C. K., Lewis, B. A., & Livingston, S. J. (1993). Primary arithmetic: Children inventing their own procedures. *Arithmetic Teacher, 41*(4), 200–203.

Kline, K. (1998). Kindergarten is more than counting. *Teaching Children Mathematics, 5*(2), 84–87.

May, L. (1996, October). *Creative questioning. Teaching K–8*, 25.

National Council of Teachers of Mathematics (NCTM). (1989). *Curriculum and evaluation standards for school mathematics*. Reston, VA: Author.

O'Connell, S. (2000). *Introduction to problem solving: Strategies for the elementary math classroom*. Portsmouth, NH: Heinemann.

Page, A. (1994). Helping students understand subtraction. *Teaching Children Mathematics, 1*(3), 140–143.

Parker, J., & Widmer, C. C. (1992). Teaching mathematics with technology: Computation and estimation. *Arithmetic Teacher, 40*(1), 48–51.

Prescott, J. O. (2001, April). We love math! *Instructor*, 24–27, 76.

Richardson, K. (1999). *Developing number concepts: Planning guide*. Parsippany, NJ: Dale Seymour.

Skinner, P. (1990). *What's your problem?* Portsmouth, NH: Heinemann.

Smith, J. J. (1996). Counting on company row. *Teaching Children Mathematics, 3*, 34–38.

Wakefield, A. P. (1998). *Early childhood number games*. Boston: Allyn & Bacon.

Willson, K. J. (1991). Calculators and word problems in the primary grades. *Arithmetic Teacher, 38*(9), 12–14.

See the monthly issues of *Teaching Children Mathematics* for activities, materials, and reviews of computer software.

UNIT 28
Patterns

OBJECTIVES

After reading this unit, you should be able to:

◆ Describe patterning as it applies to primary age mathematics.

◆ Explain why the cognitive developmental level of primary children makes looking for patterns an especially interesting and appropriate activity.

◆ Assess primary grade children's understanding of patterning.

◆ Plan and teach patterning activities for primary children.

As described in Unit 17, the NCTM (2000, p. 90) standard for prekindergarten through grade two algebra includes the expectations that students will order objects by size, number and other properties; recognize and extend patterns; and analyze how patterns are developed. Very young children learn repetitive rhymes and songs and hear stories with predictive language. They develop patterns with objects and eventually with numbers. They recognize change, such as in the seasons or in their height as they grow. During the primary grades children make a transition into more complex patterning activities such as comparing patterns, learning number patterns, extending complex patterns, and gaining an understanding of equality (that two quantities are the same amount).

Ordering, or putting things into a sequence, is basic to patterning. Patterning is the process of discovering auditory, visual, and motor regularities.

There are many regularities in the number system that children must understand. During the primary years, children work with more complex problems with concrete materials, connect concrete patterns to symbols, and learn to recognize some of the patterns and higher-level sequences in the number system.

This unit focuses on extending the concept of patterning to more complex patterns and connecting symbols and patterns. It also describes activities for looking at patterns in the environment.

Assessment

Look back at Unit 17 for a description of naturalistic and informal patterning behaviors that can be observed during children's activities. By the primary grades children should be able to copy and extend patterns with ease. During the primary grades they develop the ability to extend patterns further, make more complex patterns, become more adept at describing patterns with words, build their own patterns, and see patterns in numbers. See Unit 17 for a sample assessment task procedure for pattern copying, extending patterns, and describing patterns and more difficult extensions. The following are examples of higher-level assessment tasks.

SAMPLE ASSESSMENT TASK

9K   **Concrete Operations Ages 6–8**
Patterns, Extension in Three Dimensions: Unit 28

METHOD: Interview.

SKILL: The child can extend complex patterns in three dimensions by predicting what will come next.

MATERIALS: Inch or centimeter cubes, Unifix Cubes®, or other counters that can be stacked.

PROCEDURE: Present the child with various patterns made of stacked counters. Ask the child to describe the pattern and to continue it as far as he can. Stack the blocks as follows one pattern at a time:

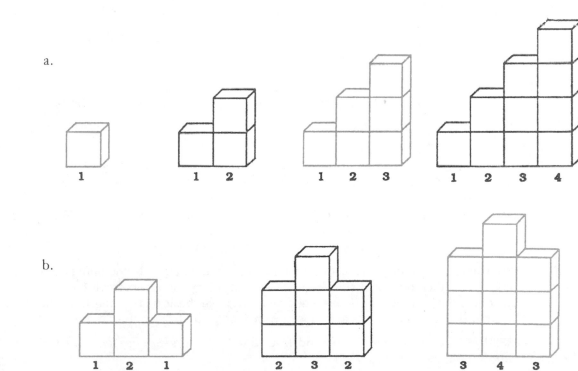

c.

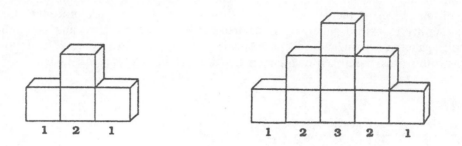

1 2 1   1 2 3 2 1

For each pattern ask, TELL ME ABOUT THIS PATTERN. WHAT COMES NEXT? HOW DO YOU KNOW? CONTINUE THE PATTERN FOR ME.

EVALUATION: Note whether the child can continue each pattern and state his rationale. Note where the child might need further help and practice.

INSTRUCTIONAL RESOURCE: Charlesworth, R., and Lind, K. K. (2003). *Math and Science for Young Children* (4th ed.). Clifton Park, NY: Delmar Learning.

SAMPLE ASSESSMENT TASK

9M
Patterns, Multiple Numbers: Unit 28
                                             Concrete Operations Ages 7–9

METHOD: Interview.

SKILL: The child can use a 00 to 99 chart to discover and predict number multiple patterns.

MATERIALS: Inch or centimeter cubes, Unifix Cubes®, or other counters, and a 00 to 99 chart (Figure 28–1).

PROCEDURE: Start a pattern using multiples of two blocks. Tell the child, CIRCLE OR MARK THE AMOUNT IN MY GROUP ON THE CHART. If the child has a problem, show her the 02, and circle it for her if necessary. Next to the group of two blocks construct a group of four blocks. Use the same procedure as above. Continue up to 10. Then say, SHOW ME WHICH NUMBERS YOU WOULD CIRCLE IF I KEPT CONTINUING WITH THIS PATTERN. When children can predict accurately with multiples of two, try threes, fours, fives, and so on.

EVALUATION: Note whether the children can connect the numbers in the pattern to the numerals on the chart and whether they can predict what comes next. If they cannot accomplish these tasks, note where their errors are: Do they need more help with basic pattern construction? With counting? With connecting sets to symbols? With finding numbers on the chart?

INSTRUCTIONAL RESOURCE: Charlesworth, R., and Lind, K. K. (2003). *Math and Science for Young Children* (4th ed.). Clifton Park, NY: Delmar Learning.

00	01	02	03	04	05	06	07	08	09
10	11	12	13	14	15	16	17	18	19
20	21	22	23	24	25	26	27	28	29
30	31	32	33	34	35	36	37	38	39
40	41	42	43	44	45	46	47	48	49
50	51	52	53	54	55	56	57	58	59
60	61	62	63	64	65	66	67	68	69
70	71	72	73	74	75	76	77	78	79
80	81	82	83	84	85	86	87	88	89
90	91	92	93	94	95	96	97	98	99

FIGURE 28–1 00 to 99 chart.

Activities

Children who have reached concrete operations are in a stage of cognitive development in which they are naturally seeking out the rules and regularities in the world. Patterning activities fit the natural inclinations and interests of children in this stage. While engaged in calendar and 100 days activities, children are challenged to note number patterns and count by multiples (i.e., two, four, six, eight, and so on). They also enjoy arranging paper shapes into quilt patterns. The following examples are activities adapted from Richardson (1984, 1999) and Baratta-Lorton (1976). Patterning examples are also included in Greenes, Cavanagh, Dacey, Findell, and Small (2001).

ACTIVITIES

PATTERNING: INCREASING PATTERNS

OBJECTIVE: To copy and extend patterns using objects.

MATERIALS: Counters such as chips, cube blocks, or Unifix Cubes®; paper; and pencil.

ACTIVITY: The following are examples of patterns that can be developed. In each case, the teacher models the first three elements in the pattern, and then the children are asked to predict what comes next and to extend the pattern as far as they can. The children may write down the pattern in numerals under each element and compare the patterns with both the objects and the numeral representations.

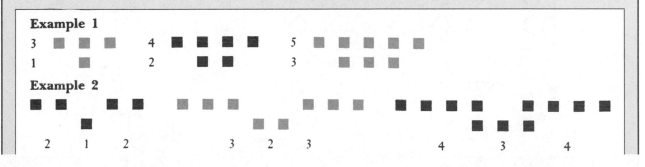

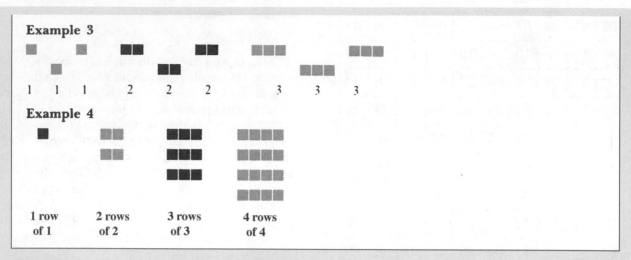

Example 3

1 1 1 2 2 2 3 3 3

Example 4

1 row
of 1   2 rows
of 2   3 rows
of 3   4 rows
of 4

FOLLOW-UP: Have children work with various types of patterns until you believe they have grasped the concept. Then present the higher-level pattern activities that follow.

PATTERNING: TASK CARDS

OBJECTIVE: To copy and extend patterns using task cards.

MATERIALS: Counters such as chips, inch or centimeter cubes, or Unifix Cubes®; task cards with the first three steps in a pattern; for example:

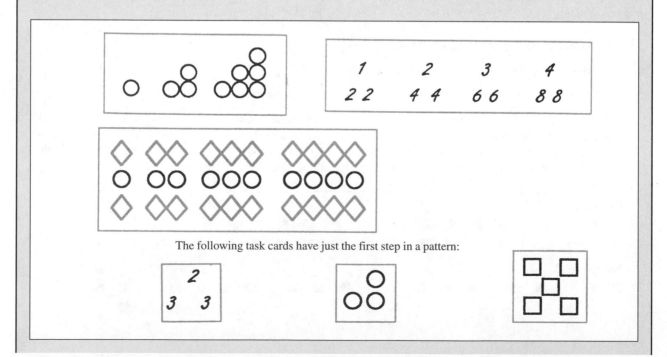

ACTIVITY: Provide the task cards and a good supply of counters. The children copy the models and then proceed to extend the patterns. With the three-step models, the pattern is set. With the one-step models, the children can create their own rules for extending the patterns. Always have them explain their pattern to you.

FOLLOW-UP: When the children have the concept of working from the abstract to the concrete with the task cards, have them create their own patterns, first with objects and then drawing them using the objects as models.

PATTERNING: 00 TO 99 CHART ACTIVITIES

OBJECTIVE: For children who have the concept of place value (see Unit 30) for the 1s and 10s place, 00 to 99 chart activities can be used. The objective is to perceive patterns on the chart in pictorial form.

MATERIALS: Copies of the 00 to 99 chart (see Figure 28–1) and counters.

ACTIVITY: On the chart the children can color in or mark the amounts in their patterns. For example, they made the following pattern.

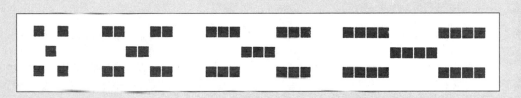

The children then mark off on the chart the amount in each part of the pattern: 5, 10, 15, 20, and so on.

FOLLOW-UP: The children can transfer to the charts from patterns you provide and then move on to patterns that they devise themselves.

PATTERNING: EXPLORING NATURAL MATERIALS

OBJECTIVE: To be able to observe and describe patterns in natural materials.

MATERIALS: Fruits and vegetables such as cabbage, onion, orange, lemon, grapefruit, and apple; magnifying glass; pencil; and paper.

ACTIVITY: Let the children explore and examine the whole fruits and vegetables. Encourage them to describe what they see and feel. Suggest that they examine them with the magnifying glass and draw them if they wish. After a few days, ask them to predict what each item looks like inside. Then cut each one in half. Talk about what they discover. Compare what they see with what they predicted. Suggest that they draw the inside patterns.

FOLLOW-UP: Have each child use his or her pictures to make a "What's inside?" book. The children can write or dictate what they know about each item.

PATTERNING: MULTIPLES GRAPHS

OBJECTIVE: To collect data regarding natural patterns and depict the data on graphs.

MATERIALS:

1. Number line templates. These templates are made from heavy tagboard. The numbers are written across. A hole is cut or punched below each one so that the numbers can be copied.

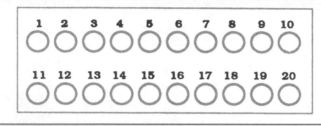

2. Large sheets of manila paper, rulers, crayons, markers, and picture magazines.

ACTIVITY: With the children discuss a question such as

◇   How many eyes do five people have among them?
◇   How many legs do three chairs have among them?

Have the children draw lines about 3 to 4 inches apart on a large piece of manila paper with their rulers. Have them copy their number line at the bottom of the paper using a template. Have them draw or cut out and paste pictures on their paper as depicted in Figure 28–2. Then have them record the number of eyes (legs) down the right side of the paper and circle the corresponding numerals on the number line. Ask them to examine the number line and describe the pattern they have made.

FOLLOW-UP: Have the children think of other items that they could graph in multiples to create patterns.

PATTERNING: DIVISION

OBJECTIVE: To make division patterns.

MATERIALS: Large pieces of paper (11″ × 18″), smaller pieces of paper (4¼″ × 5½″), scissors, crayons or markers, and glue.

ACTIVITY: With the whole group, start with a large piece of paper. Have a child cut it in half and give the half to another child. Have each child cut the paper in half and give one part away. Keep a record of the number of cuts and the number of children until everyone has a piece of paper. Next give each child a large piece of paper and a small piece of paper. Have them glue the smaller piece at the top of the larger sheet (Figure 28–3). Have them take another small piece, cut it in half, and glue the two parts on the large paper below the first whole piece (Figure 28–3). Have them take another small piece, cut it in half, and then cut each half in half. Glue these four parts on the large sheet. Let them continue as long as they wish. Have them record the number of pieces in each row on the right-hand side of the chart.

FOLLOW-UP: Have the more advanced children cut three parts each time and see what kind of pattern they make.

FIGURE 28–2 Multiples graph.

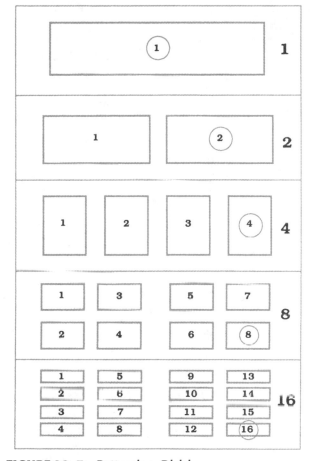

FIGURE 28–3 Patterning: Division.

Other patterning activities can be developed using manipulatives such as pattern blocks. Pattern blocks come in a variety of sizes, thicknesses, and colors. There are many supplementary materials available such as tracing templates, stickers, rubber stamps, puzzles (see the Creative Publications catalog, address in Unit 39). You can also make your own materials. Pattern blocks can be used to make quilt designs. Patterning activities can also be developed from children's literature (see Appendix B for book list). As with other concepts, patterning activities can be integrated across the curriculum. (Figure 28–4).

As already described in Unit 27, calculator activities are interesting ways to look at number patterns. After some practice with patterns as suggested in Unit 27, have the children discover and extend patterns with their calculators; for example.

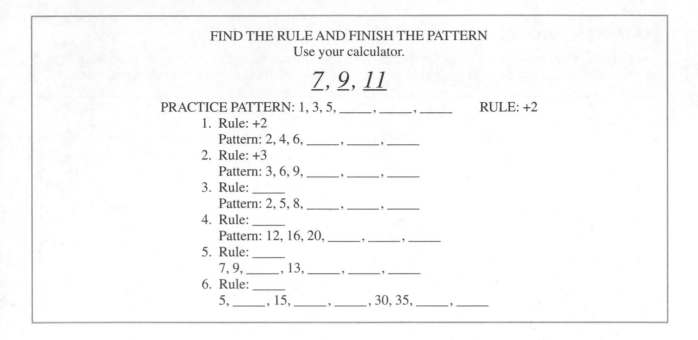

FIND THE RULE AND FINISH THE PATTERN
Use your calculator.

$\underline{7}, \underline{9}, \underline{11}$

PRACTICE PATTERN: 1, 3, 5, _____, _____, _____   RULE: +2

1. Rule: +2
   Pattern: 2, 4, 6, _____, _____, _____
2. Rule: +3
   Pattern: 3, 6, 9, _____, _____, _____
3. Rule: _____
   Pattern: 2, 5, 8, _____, _____, _____
4. Rule: _____
   Pattern: 12, 16, 20, _____, _____, _____
5. Rule: _____
   7, 9, _____, 13, _____, _____, _____
6. Rule: _____
   5, _____, 15, _____, _____, 30, 35, _____, _____

Make up some more patterns for the children to explore with calculators.

Clements and Sarama (2000) describe the Predict and Cover activity, which can be done both on and off the computer. First the children explore pattern blocks, developing their own designs. Then they are provided with specific shapes and asked to predict and then select pattern blocks to cover the shapes provided. Students also can do this activity on the computer with Shape Up! (Sunburst, 1995), Tenth Planet Explores Math (Tenth Planet, 1997), and Exploring Mathematics with Manipulatives (EDC, 1992) as recommended by Clements and Sarama. Several advantages of doing the activity on the computer are: children can use as many blocks as they wish, work can be saved and retrieved, children can design their own puzzles, and tasks are broken down in ways that clarify mathematical mental actions. A variety of computer manipulatives can be found at http://www.tenthplanet.com.

As with other math concepts, pattern computer software is available. See the activities at the end of this unit and at the end of Unit 17 for suggestions.

Evaluation

Note how the children deal with the suggested pattern activities. Use the assessment tasks in the appendix for individual evaluation interviews.

Summary

Primary-level children extend the work they did with patterning at earlier levels. Now they begin to identify and work with patterns in the number system as they connect numerals to patterns and develop number patterns using counting and calculators. Number patterns are the basis for multiplication and division.

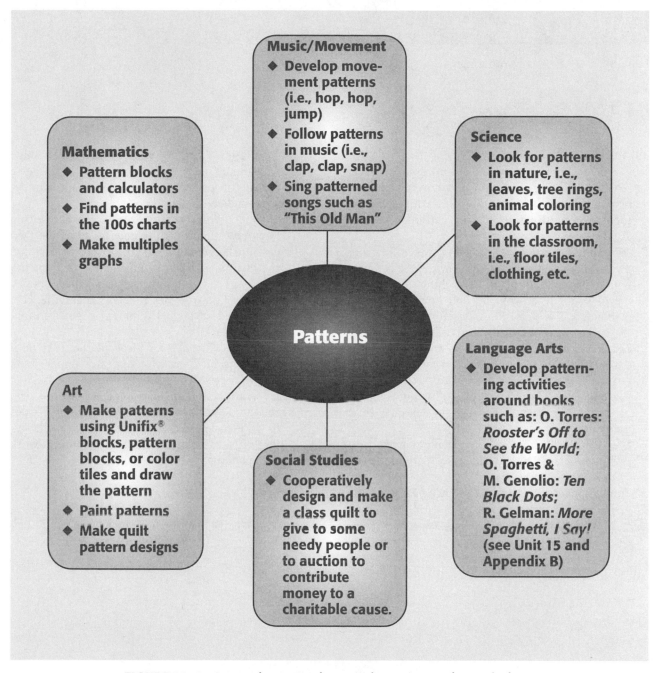

Mathematics
- ◆ Pattern blocks and calculators
- ◆ Find patterns in the 100s charts
- ◆ Make multiples graphs

Music/Movement
- ◆ Develop movement patterns (i.e., hop, hop, jump)
- ◆ Follow patterns in music (i.e., clap, clap, snap)
- ◆ Sing patterned songs such as "This Old Man"

Science
- ◆ Look for patterns in nature, i.e., leaves, tree rings, animal coloring
- ◆ Look for patterns in the classroom, i.e., floor tiles, clothing, etc.

Patterns

Art
- ◆ Make patterns using Unifix® blocks, pattern blocks, or color tiles and draw the pattern
- ◆ Paint patterns
- ◆ Make quilt pattern designs

Social Studies
- ◆ Cooperatively design and make a class quilt to give to some needy people or to auction to contribute money to a charitable cause.

Language Arts
- ◆ Develop patterning activities around books such as: O. Torres: *Rooster's Off to See the World*; O. Torres & M. Genolio: *Ten Black Dots*; R. Gelman: *More Spaghetti, I Say!* (see Unit 15 and Appendix B)

FIGURE 28–4 Integrating patterning experiences across the curriculum.

KEY TERMS

equality   ordering   patterning

SUGGESTED ACTIVITIES

1. Administer the sample assessment tasks to a first grader, a second grader, and a third grader. Write a report describing what you did, how the children responded, and how they compared with each other. Include suggestions for further activities for each child.

2. Assemble the materials for one or more of the suggested instructional activities. Try out the activities with a small group of primary children. Report to the class on what you did and how the children responded. Evaluate the children's responses and the appropriateness of the activities. Describe any changes you would make when using these activities another time.

3. Using the evaluation system from Activity 7, Unit 9, evaluate one or more of the following computer programs relative to its value for learning about patterning.

    Exploring Mathematics with Manipulatives. Boca Raton, FL: EDC. A variety of activities using onscreen manipulatives.

    Tenth Planet Explores Geometry. Pleasantville, NY: Tenth planet. A variety of onscreen geometry activities.

Math Blaster 1: In Search of Spot. Knowledge Adventure (see http://www.terc.edu). Includes a variety of problems which focus on number sense and computation.

Math Quest with *Aladdin*. Disney interactive (see http://www.terc.edu). A game based on the Disney film *Aladdin*. Includes problems in addition, subtraction, multiplication, division, geometry, problem-solving, logic, attributes, and patterns.

Sequencing Fun! (Grades K–2). Pleasantville, NY: Sunburst. Use logical thinking to put information in order.

Shape Up! (Grades K–8). Pleasantville, NY: Sunburst. Five different two- and three-dimensional environments for exploration and creation of geometric shapes, patterns, and pictures.

Sunbuddy Series: Numbers Undercover. (Grades K–3). Pleasantville, NY: Sunburst. Uses the setting of Max's Detective Agency. Includes work with patterns.

REVIEW

A. Describe patterning as it applies to primary age mathematics. Give at least one example.

B. Explain why the cognitive developmental level of primary children makes looking for patterns an especially appropriate and interesting activity.

C. Match the types of activities to the examples that follow:
1. Copy and extend patterns using objects.
2. Copy and extend patterns using task cards.
3. Observe and describe patterns in natural materials.
4. Collect data from naturally occurring objects, and depict the data on a graph.
5. Make a division pattern.

Examples:
a. Chan carefully draws the pattern that appears in half of an orange.

b. Sara examines three groups of blocks and proceeds to create the group she believes should come next.

c. Theresa draws lines across a large sheet of paper, copies her number line with a template, then looks through a magazine for animals with four legs.

d. Vanessa has a large sheet of paper and several smaller sheets. First she glues one small sheet at the top of the large sheet and writes the numeral 1 to the right.

e. Brent examines some patterns drawn on a card. Then he takes some Unifix Cubes®, makes the same designs, and adds two more.

D. Describe how a 00 to 99 chart might be used to assist in illustrating number multiple patterns.

REFERENCES

Baratta Lorton, M. (1976). *Mathematics their way.* Menlo Park, CA: Addison-Wesley.

Clements, D. H., & Sarama, J. (2000). Predicting pattern blocks on and off the computer. *Teaching Children Mathematics, 6*(7), 458–462.

Greenes, C., Cavanagh, M., Dacey, L., Findell, C., & Small, M. (2001). *Navigating through algebra in prekindergarten–grade 2.* Reston, VA: National Council of Teachers of Mathematics.

National Council of Teachers of Mathematics. (2000). *Principles and standards for school mathematics.* Reston, VA: Author. (http://www.nctm.org)

Richardson, K. (1984). *Developing number concepts using Unifix Cubes.*® Menlo Park, CA: Addison-Wesley.

Richardson, K. (1999). *Developing number concepts, book 1. Counting, comparing and pattern.* Parsippany, NJ: Dale Seymour.

FURTHER READING AND RESOURCES

AIMS Educational Products. AIMS Education Foundation, P.O. Box 8120, Fresno, CA 93747-8120.

Armstrong, B. E. (1995). Teaching patterns, relationships, and multiplication as worthwhile mathematical tasks. *Teaching Children Mathematics, 1*, 446–450.

Box it or bag it mathematics. (K–2). Portland, OR: The Math Learning Center. (800-575-8130) (http://www. mlc.pdx.edu)

Bresser, R., & Sheffield, S. (1996, November/December). Bringing out the math in popular subjects. *Instructor*, 52–53.

Bresser, R., & Sheffield, S. (1997, March). Double your math fun with these function activities. *Instructor*, 66–67.

Bridges in mathematics. (K–2). Portland, OR: The Math Learning Center. (800-575-8130) (http://www. mlc.pdx.edu)

Copley, J. V. (2000). *The young child and mathematics*. Washington, DC: National Association for the Education of Young Children.

Copley, J. V. (Ed.). (1999). *Mathematics in the early years*. Washington, DC: National Association for the Education of Young Children.

Filliman, P. (1999). Patterns all around. *Teaching Children Mathematics, 5*(5), 282–283.

Holly, K. A. (1997). Patterns and functions. *Teaching Children Mathematics, 3*, 312–313.

MacDonald, S. (2001). *Block play: The complete guide to learning and playing with blocks*. Belltsville, MD: Gryphon House.

May, L. (1996, November/December). Searching for patterns. *Teaching K–8*, 21.

National Council of Teachers of Mathematics (NCTM). (1989). *Curriculum and evaluation standards for school mathematics*. Reston, VA: Author.

Richardson, K. (1999). *Developing number concepts: Planning guide*. Parsippany, NJ: Dale Seymour.

Speer, W. R., & Brahier, D. J. (1995). What comes nex_? *Teaching Children Mathematics, 2*, 100–101.

UNIT 29
Fractions

OBJECTIVES

After reading this unit, you should be able to:

◆ Explain how the concept of fractions is based on an understanding of part/whole relationships.

◆ Explain why primary children should not be rushed into using fraction notation.

◆ Assess primary children's understanding of the concept of fractions.

◆ Plan and teach fraction lessons appropriate for primary children.

In Unit 14, it was explained that young children have a natural understanding and interest in **parts** and **wholes** that can be used later as a bridge to understanding **fractions**. NCTM (2000, p. 78) expectations include that young children will develop a sense of whole numbers and represent them in many ways by breaking groups down into smaller parts. By the end of second grade they should understand and be able to represent commonly used fractions such as ¼, ⅓, and ½.

As described in Unit 14 the fundamental concept of *parts* and *wholes* is the basis for the understanding of fractions. Through naturalistic, informal, and structured experiences, preprimary children become familiar with three aspects of the part/whole concept: things have special parts, a whole object can be divided into parts, and sets of things can be divided into smaller sets. They also become familiar with the application of

the terms *more*, *less*, and *same*. During the primary level, young children expand on the concrete activities that they engaged in during the preprimary level. It is important not to introduce notation and symbols too soon. Even nine year-olds have difficulty with fractions at the symbolic level. This would indicate that for most children fraction symbols cannot safely be introduced until the end of the primary period (the latter part of grade three) and may not be fully understood until well into the intermediate level (grade four or higher). Fraction problems cannot be solved by counting as can whole number problems. This factor makes them much more abstract and thus more difficult.

At the presymbolic level, work with fractions should be limited to **halves**, **thirds**, and **fourths**. These are the fractions we deal with most frequently in life, and if children develop an understanding of them, they should be able to transfer this knowledge to fractions in general. Children can learn fraction terminology relative to concrete experiences without being concerned with the corresponding symbols. Terms such as *one-half*, *one-third*, and *one-fourth* can be associated with parts of concrete objects and subgroups of large groups of concrete objects. During the primary period, children continue to work with fractions as part/whole relationships. They can work with volume, regions, length, and sets. Experiences with foods (such as cutting up a carrot) and cooking (measuring ingredients) involve volume. Regions are concrete and easy to work with. They involve working with shapes such as circles, rectangles, squares, and triangles. Lengths can also be divided into parts. Long, narrow pieces of paper, string, thread, and ribbon are useful for this type of activity. When working with groups, a whole group of objects serves as the unit to be divided into smaller subgroups.

Payne, Towsley, and Huinker (1990, pp. 175–200) sum up the sequence in the development of conceptual knowledge of fractions. Three- through five-year-old children, as you have already seen, work with the concept of parts and wholes. Five- through eight-year-olds work on equal parts and oral (*not* written) names. That is, children learn to use terms such as *halves*, *thirds*, *fourths*, and the like. They also use terms such as *part*, pieces, *whole*, and almost whole.

Assessment

In Unit 14, both observational and interview tasks for assessment of part/whole concepts were described. When children understand that a whole can be divided into parts, that when a quantity is divided its whole is conserved, and that the size of each part gets smaller as the number of equal divisions increases, then they are ready to understand fractions. If children evidence some of the behaviors described in Unit 14 as indicating an understanding of the part/whole concept and are able to respond successfully to the Unit 14 assessment tasks, then try the following kinds of higher-level assessment tasks.

SAMPLE ASSESSMENT TASK

9N   **Concrete Operations Ages 6–8**
Fractions, Equivalent Parts: Unit 29

METHOD: Interview.

SKILL: The child can divide a rectangle into smaller equal parts.

MATERIALS: A supply of paper rectangles of equal size ($8\frac{1}{2}'' \times 2\frac{3}{4}''$) in four different colors and a pair of scissors.

PROCEDURE: Show the child a paper rectangle. THIS IS A RECTANGLE. Place two more rectangles (color #2) below the first one. HERE ARE TWO MORE RECTANGLES. ARE ALL THREE THE SAME SIZE? Be sure the child agrees. Let him compare them to be sure. NOW I'M GOING TO FOLD ONE OF THE RECTANGLES (color #2) SO BOTH PARTS ARE THE SAME. Fold the rectangle. NOW YOU FOLD THIS OTHER ONE (also color #2) JUST LIKE I DID. Offer assistance if necessary. The three rectangles should look like this:

Color #1

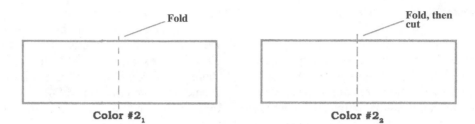

ARE THE PARTS OF (color #2) RECTANGLE THE SAME SIZE AS THE PARTS OF THIS ONE? (also color #2) SHOW ME HOW YOU KNOW. I'M GOING TO CUT THIS ONE (second color #2) ON THE FOLD. HOW MANY PARTS DO I HAVE NOW? IF I PUT THEM BACK TOGETHER, WILL THEY BE THE SAME SIZE AS THIS WHOLE RECTANGLE? AS YOUR (color #1) RECTANGLE? WHAT IS A SPECIAL NAME FOR THIS AMOUNT OF THE WHOLE RECTANGLE? Point to the half. If the response is one-half, go through the procedure again with one-third and one-fourth, using colors #3 and #4, respectively.

EVALUATION: Note whether the child has to check on the equivalency of the three rectangles. Can he keep in mind that the parts still equal the whole, even when cut into two or more parts? Does he know the terms *one-half*, *one-third*, and/or *one-fourth*?

INSTRUCTIONAL RESOURCE: Charlesworth, R., and Lind, K. K. (2003). *Math and Science for Young Children* (4th ed.). Clifton Park, NY: Delmar Learning.

SAMPLE ASSESSMENT TASK

90   **Concrete Operations Ages 6–8**
Fractions, One-Half of a Group: Unit 29

METHOD: Interview.

SKILL: The child can divide a set of objects into smaller groups when given directions using the term *one-half*.

MATERIALS: Ten counters (cube blocks, chips, Unifix Cubes®, or other concrete objects).

PROCEDURE: Place the counters in front of the child. I HAVE SOME (name of counters). DIVIDE THESE SO THAT WE EACH HAVE ONE-HALF OF THE GROUP. If the child completes this task easily, go on to nine counters and ask her to divide the group into thirds. Then go on to eight counters, and ask her to divide the group into fourths.

EVALUATION: Note the method used by the child. Does she use counting, or does she pass the counters out: "One for you and one for me"? Does she really seem to understand the terms *one-half*, *one-fourth*, and *one-third*?

INSTRUCTIONAL RESOURCE: Charlesworth, R., and Lind, K. K. (2003). *Math and Science for Young Children* (4th ed.). Clifton Park, NY: Delmar Learning.

Activities

In Unit 14, naturalistic and informal activities were emphasized as the foundation for structured experiences. These activities should be encouraged and continued. Primary children need to continue to have time to explore materials and construct their concept of parts and wholes through their own actions on the environment. There are many materials that children can explore independently in developing the foundations for the understanding of fractions. Any of the usual kinds of counting objects can be organized as a group, which can then be divided (or partitioned) into smaller groups. Some materials for dividing single objects or shapes into parts are illustrated in Figure 29–1. The examples include Fit-a-Fraction® (Lakeshore), Fraction Circles® and Skittles® (Nienhuis-Montessori), and Fractional Wood Fruit Plate® (ETA). Figure 29–2 illustrates materials that promote the construction and comparison of parts and wholes. These materials include Unit Blocks (Community Playthings), Cuisinaire Rods® (Cuisinaire of America), puzzles (Lakeshore), and Lego® (Lakeshore).

Following are structured activities that can be used to develop fraction concepts.

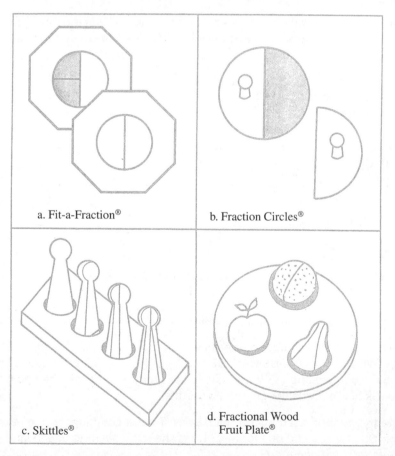

a. Fit-a-Fraction®

b. Fraction Circles®

c. Skittles®

d. Fractional Wood Fruit Plate®

FIGURE 29–1 Examples of materials that can be used to explore how whole things can be divided into equal parts.

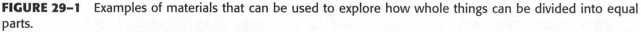

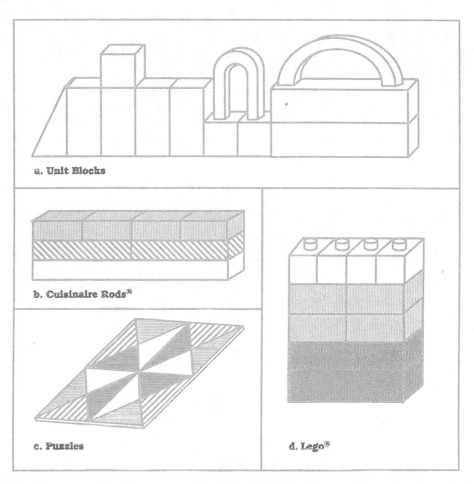

FIGURE 29–2 Materials that promote the construction and comparison of parts and wholes.

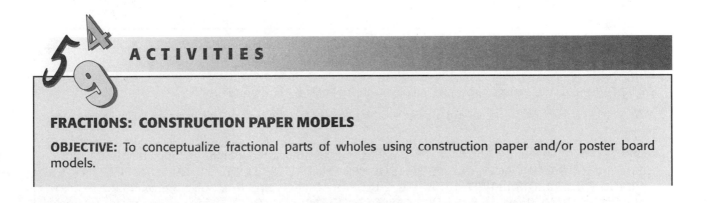

ACTIVITIES

FRACTIONS: CONSTRUCTION PAPER MODELS

OBJECTIVE: To conceptualize fractional parts of wholes using construction paper and/or poster board models.

MATERIALS: Make your own models out of construction paper and/or poster board. Use a different color for each fractional part; for example, a blue whole circle, a red circle the same size cut into halves, a yellow circle cut into thirds, and a green circle cut into fourths.

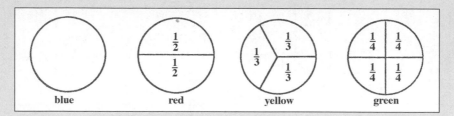

The same colors can be used to make a set of fraction rectangles and a set of fraction squares.

ACTIVITY: Let the children explore the sets of fraction models. After they have worked with them several times, ask them some questions such as

◆ What have you learned about those shapes?
◆ How many red pieces make a circle the same size as the blue circle? How many yellow pieces? How many green pieces?
◆ Use the same procedure with the rectangles and the squares.

FOLLOW-UP: Label the parts as halves, thirds, and fourths of the wholes. Provide the students with matching construction paper shapes, and have them make their own models by folding. Start with rectangles and squares.

FRACTIONS: COMPARING SIZES

OBJECTIVE: To compare sizes of halves, thirds, and fourths.

MATERIALS: Same as in previous activity.

ACTIVITY: Put out the models one set at a time. Ask the children, WHICH IS LARGER—A HALF, A THIRD, OR A FOURTH? HOW MANY FOURTHS MAKE ONE-HALF?

FOLLOW-UP: Provide models of other fractions for children who have a good understanding of halves, fourths, and thirds.

FRACTIONS: PARTS OF GROUPS

OBJECTIVE: To divide groups of objects into subgroups of halves, thirds, and fourths.

MATERIALS: Draw, color, and cut out a mother rabbit, four child rabbits, and 12 carrots (see Figure 29–3 for patterns).

ACTIVITY: Place the mother rabbit, two child rabbits, and 4 carrots in front of the children. MOTHER RABBIT HAS 4 CARROTS AND WANTS TO GIVE EACH OF HER CHILDREN HALF OF THE CARROTS. HELP HER BY DIVIDING THE CARROTS BETWEEN THE TWO CHILDREN SO EACH HAS HALF. Give the child time to complete the task. NOW SUPPOSE SHE HAS 4 CARROTS AND FOUR CHILDREN (bring out two more children).

FIGURE 29–3   Patterns for the "Parts of Groups" activity.

SHOW ME HOW THEY CAN SHARE THE CARROTS SO EACH HAS ONE-FOURTH OF THE CARROTS. As long as the children are interested, continue the activity using different numbers of child rabbits and different amounts of carrots. Emphasize that the carrots must be shared so that it is fair to everyone.

FOLLOW-UP: Make other sets of materials (such as children and apples, dogs and bones). Move on to other fractions when the children can do these problems easily.

FRACTIONS: LIQUID VOLUME

OBJECTIVE: To compare fractional parts of liquid volume.

MATERIALS: Several sets of standard measuring cups, color coded, if available; a pitcher of water. If color-coded cups are not available, mark each size with a different color (i.e., 1 cup with blue, ½ cup with red, ⅓ cup with yellow, ¼ cup with green).

ACTIVITY: Give each child a set of measuring cups. Let them examine the set and tell you what they notice. After discussion and examination, have everyone pick up their 1-cup size and their ½-cup size. HOW MANY OF THESE SMALL CUPS OF WATER WILL FILL THE LARGE CUP? Let the children predict. FILL YOUR SMALL CUP WITH WATER. POUR THE WATER IN YOUR LARGE CUP. IS THE LARGE CUP FULL? POUR IN ANOTHER

SMALL CUP OF WATER. IS THE LARGE CUP FULL NOW? HOW MANY OF THE SMALLER CUPS WERE NEEDED TO FILL THE LARGER CUP? Follow the same procedure with the $\frac{1}{3}$- and $\frac{1}{4}$-size cups.

FOLLOW-UP: Reverse the procedure. Starting with the full 1-cup measure, have the children count how many $\frac{1}{2}$, $\frac{1}{3}$, and $\frac{1}{4}$ cupfuls it takes to empty the full cup. Do the same activity using rice, birdseed, or sand instead of water.

FRACTIONS: LENGTH

OBJECTIVE: To compare fractional parts of lengths.

MATERIALS: Cuisinaire Rods®.

ACTIVITY: Provide the children with a basket full of Cuisinaire Rods®. After they have had an opportunity to explore the rods, suggest that they select a long rod and find out which lengths of rods can be placed next to it to show halves, thirds, and fourths.

FOLLOW-UP: Follow the same procedure with whole straws and straws cut into halves, fourths, and thirds. Try the activity with other materials such as string, ribbons, and paper strips.

FRACTIONS: USING LITERATURE

OBJECTIVE: To analyze the fractional components of relevant children's literature as an application of the concept of fractions.

MATERIALS: Children's trade books that contain fractional concepts, writing and drawing implements, paper, chalk, and chalkboard.

ACTIVITY: Read books such as *When the Doorbell Rang* (P. Hutchins, 1986, Greenwillow). Provide problem situations such as making a chart showing how as more children come, each gets fewer cookies. Have the children draw pictorial representations of what is happening. For further suggestions and a list of additional books see the following articles and others listed in Unit 15.

    Conaway, B., & Midkiff, R. B. (1994). Connecting literature, language and fractions. *Arithmetic Teacher, 8,* 430–434.

    Lubinski, C. A, & Otto, A. D. (1997). Literature and algebraic reasoning. *Teaching Children Mathematics, 3,* 290–295.

FOLLOW-UP: Use additional books. Children will become more independent and see more and more ways of looking at fractions.

FRACTIONS: STORY PROBLEMS

OBJECTIVE: To have the children create and solve fraction story problems.

MATERIALS: One or more model problems; paper, pencils, crayons, markers, and scissors; chart paper for model problems.

ACTIVITY: Have the students brainstorm real-life situations in which things have to be divided into equal parts. Encourage them to write or dictate their own problems, draw a picture of the problem, and write out the solution. If they cannot come up with their own problems, provide one or two models that they can work through with you. Here are some models (have each problem written on chart paper):

1. TWO CHILDREN FOUND SIX PENNIES. ONE CHILD TOOK THREE PENNIES. WHAT FRACTIONAL PART OF THE PENNIES WAS LEFT FOR THE OTHER CHILD? Draw two stick figure children. Draw six pennies on another piece of paper. Glue three pennies by one child and three by the other. WHAT PART OF THE PENNIES DOES EACH CHILD HAVE? YES, ONE-HALF. Write: "Each child has one-half of the pennies" (Figure 29–4).

2. BRENT INVITES THREE FRIENDS OVER FOR PIZZA. IF EACH CHILD GETS A FAIR SHARE, HOW WILL THE PIZZA LOOK WHEN IT IS CUT UP? Give each child a paper pizza. Ask them to fold the pizzas into the right size and number of parts. Cut up one of the pizzas, and glue the parts on the chart. Write: "Each child gets one-fourth."

FOLLOW-UP: Encourage the children to create and illustrate their own fraction problems.

Q: "Two children found six pennies. One child took three pennies. What fractional part of the pennies was left for the other child?"

A: "Each child has one-half of the pennies."

FIGURE 29–4 The teacher can write and illustrate a model story problem that involves the partitioning of a set.

FRACTIONS: GEOBOARD SHAPES

OBJECTIVE: To divide geoboard shapes into equal parts.

MATERIALS: Geoboards, geoboard shape patterns, and rubber bands.

ACTIVITY: Have the children make rectangles and squares on their geoboards with rubber bands, then divide the shapes into equal parts using additional rubber bands.

FOLLOW-UP: Question the children regarding how they know that their shapes are divided into equal parts. Note whether they use the number of geoboard nails as a clue to making their parts equal.

EXAMPLE WORLD WIDE WEB ACTIVITIES

◆ Edible Fractions on Fraction Plates. Link at http://www.mathforum.org/
◆ Learn Fractions with Cuisinaire Rods. Link at http://www.crpc.rice.edu/CRPC/GirlTECH/silha/Lessons/cuisen2.html or type in "cuisinaire" in search

---

For the more advanced students, notation can be introduced.

Show them how one-half can be written as ½, which means one part out of two. Then ask how they think they might write one-third as one part out of three, two-thirds as two parts out of three, and so on. Have them write the numerical fractions that match the parts of some of the materials suggested earlier in the unit.

Some children will enjoy using computer software that sharpens their knowledge of fractions. Third graders Vanessa and Jason enjoy racing cars and find the fraction problem-solving activities in Grand Prix (Random House) very challenging.

The connection between fractions and decimals can be made through further concrete activities. Avoid placing any emphasis on decimal points. Work with 10ths and 100ths using models and diagrams in the same manner as you did with the larger fractions. Show through models how $\frac{1}{10}$ and $\frac{1}{100}$ can also be written .1 and .01. By fourth grade, if students have a strong conceptual foundation, they can move into operations with fractions and decimals.

Fraction concepts can be integrated into the other content areas as depicted in Figure 29–5.

Evaluation

Continue to note whether the children apply what they have learned about fractions during their everyday activities. Be sure to provide situations in which individual items or groups of items have to be shared equally with others. Note whether the children can use their concept of fractions in these situations. Also note if they apply their concept of fractions during measuring experiences that are a part of food preparation and science investigations. Administer the assessment tasks described in Appendix A.

Summary

During the primary years, young children expand their informal concept of parts and wholes of objects and groups to the more formal concept of fractions, or equal parts. Primary children learn the vocabulary of fractions and work with fractions at the concrete level. Usually they do not go beyond halves, thirds, and fourths, and most of them are not ready to understand fraction notation until the latter part of the primary period. It is important not to rush young children into the abstract use of fractions until they are ready because fractions are much more difficult to work with than whole numbers.

KEY TERMS

part(s)	halves	pieces
whole(s)	thirds	almost whole
fractions	fourths	

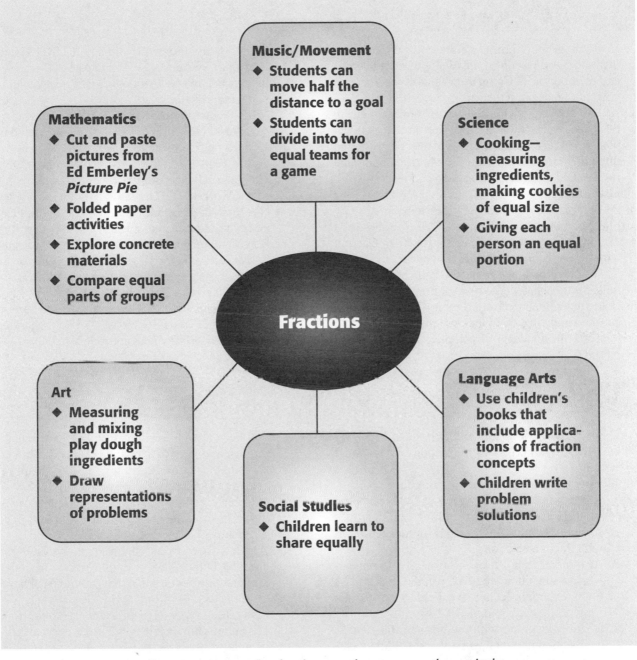

FIGURE 29–5 Integrating fraction experiences across the curriculum.

SUGGESTED ACTIVITIES

1. Visit one or more primary classrooms during math instruction on fractions. Take note of the materials and methods used. Compare what you observe with what is suggested in the text.
2. Assess a primary child's level of development in the concept of fractions. Prepare an instructional plan based on the results. Prepare the materials, and implement the lesson with the child. Evaluate the results. Did the child move ahead as a result of your instruction?
3. Be sure to add fraction activities to your Activity File/Notebook.
4. Try out some of the activities suggested in this unit with primary children of different ages.
5. If the school budget allotted $50 for fraction materials, decide what would be your priority purchases.
6. Using the guidelines from Activity 7, Unit 9, evaluate the following computer programs designed to reinforce the concept of fractions.

◆ Coco's Math Project 1. Singapore, SG: Times Learning Systems Pte Ltd. (Ages 4 to 10). Involves number, grouping, shapes, weight, matching, fractions, and more.
◆ Math Blaster 1: In Search of Spot. Knowledge adventure (see http://www.terc.edu). Includes sections on fractions.
◆ Math Team. (Grades K–3). Toronto, ON: Philsoft. Includes comparison of fractions.
◆ Math Workshop. (Grades 1–6). Pleasantville, NY: Sunburst. Includes addition and multiplication of fractions using music.
◆ Representing Fractions. (Grades 2–4). Pleasantville, NY: Sunburst. A garden theme is used to represent the relationship between a whole number and its parts.
◆ Tenth Planet Number Investigations Series: Equivalent Fractions. (Grades 3–4). Pleasantville, NY: Sunburst. Introduces equivalent fractions.

REVIEW

A. Explain why primary children should not be rushed into working with fraction and decimal notation.
B. Identify the statements that are correct.
   1. At the presymbolic level, work with fractions should be limited to halves, thirds, and fourths.
   2. Fraction terminology should be introduced along with fraction notation.
   3. At the presymbolic level, primary children can work with volume, regions, lengths, and sets.
   4. Food experiences are excellent opportunities for working with volume.
   5. Begin assessment with the tasks in this unit. It can be assumed that primary-level children can already do the lower-level tasks included in Unit 14.
   6. Primary children still need exploratory experiences before being presented with structured fraction activities.
   7. Primary children are too young to make the connections between fractions and decimals.

C. Label the following examples as (a), partitioning (dividing) into sets; (b), a whole object can be divided into equal parts; or (c), a liquid can be divided into equal parts.
   1. Liu Pei carefully folds rectangular pieces of paper in half and then in half again and cuts accurately on each line.
   2. Ann has six crackers. She wants to be sure that she and both of her friends receive an equal amount. She decides that they should each have two crackers.
   3. Jason has a one-cup measure of milk. Ms. Hebert tells him that they will need one-half cup of milk for their recipe. Jason selects a smaller cup that says ½ on the handle and fills it with milk from the larger cup.
   4. Trang Fung is experimenting with the Fit-a-Fraction® set.

REFERENCES

Emberley, E. (1984). *Picture pie: A circle drawing book*. Boston: Little Brown.

National Council of Teachers of Mathematics. (2000). *Principles and standards for school mathematics*. Reston, VA: Author. (http://www.nctm.org)

Payne, J. N., Towsley, A., & Huinker, D. (1990). Fractions and decimals. In J. N. Payne (Ed.), *Mathematics for the young child* (pp. 175–200). Reston, VA: National Council of Teachers of Mathematics.

FURTHER READING AND RESOURCES

AIMS Educational Products. AIMS Education Foundation, P.O. Box 8120, Fresno, CA 93747-8120.

Anderson, C. L., Anderson, K. M., & Wenzel, E. J. (2000). Oil and water don't mix but they do teach fractions. *Teaching Children Mathematics, 7*(3), 174–178.

Box it or bag it mathematics (K–2). Portland, OR: The Math Learning Center. (800-575-8130) (http://www.mlc.pdx.edu)

Bridges in mathematics (K–2). Portland, OR: The Math Learning Center. (800 575-8130) (http://www.mlc.pdx.edu)

Carey, D. A. (1992). The patchwork quilt: A context for problem solving. *Arithmetic Teacher, 40*(4), 199–203.

Copley, J. V. (2000). *The young child and mathematics*. Washington, DC: National Association for the Education of Young Children.

Copley, J. V. (Ed.). (1999). *Mathematics in the early years*. Washington, DC: National Association for the Education of Young Children.

Dorgan, K. (1994). What textbooks offer for instruction in fraction concepts. *Teaching Children Mathematics, 1*, 150–155.

Empson, S. B. (1995). Using sharing to help children learn fractions. *Teaching Children Mathematics, 2*, 110–114.

Langford, K., & Sarullo, A. (1993). Introductory common and decimal fraction concepts. In R. J. Jensen (Ed.), *Research ideas for the classroom: Early childhood mathematics* (pp. 223–247). New York: Macmillan.

National Council of Teachers of Mathematics (NCTM). (1989). *Curriculum and evaluation standards for school mathematics*. Reston, VA: Author.

Ortiz, E. (2000). A game involving fraction squares. *Teaching Children Mathematics, 7*(4), 218–222.

Richardson, K. (1999). *Developing number concepts: Planning guide*. Parsippany, NJ: Dale Seymour.

Riddle, M., & Rodzwell, B. (2000). Fractions: What happened between kindergarten and the army. *Teaching Children Mathematics, 7*(4), 202–206.

Witherspoon, M. L. (1993). Fractions: In search of meaning. *Arithmetic Teacher, 40*(8), 482–485.

UNIT 30
Numbers above 10 and Place Value

OBJECTIVES

After reading this unit, you should be able to:

◆ Define place value, renaming, and regrouping.

◆ Identify developmentally appropriate place value and two-digit whole number operations instruction.

◆ Assess children's understanding of numbers above 10 and of place value.

◆ Provide developmentally appropriate place value and addition and subtraction instruction with two-digit numbers.

As described in Unit 27, the NCTM (2000, p. 78) standard on number and operations includes expectations for the understanding of operations and how they relate to each other and for fluent computation and making reasonable estimates (discussed in Unit 25). During the primary grades, students should reach an understanding of a variety of means for adding and subtracting and the relationship between the two operations, understand the effects of adding and subtracting whole numbers, and understand the situations where multiplication and division are used. Children should develop skill at whole number computation for addition and subtraction, be able to use the basic addition and subtraction number combinations, and use many different computation tools such as "objects, mental computation, estimation, paper and pencil, and calculators" (p. 78). This unit proceeds into working

with numbers above 10 and addition and subtraction of double-digit whole numbers.

During the latter part of the preoperational period (see Unit 25), children who are adept at manipulating quantities up to 10 can move on to working with quantities above 10. Through manipulation of groups of 10 and quantities between zero and 10, children move through the teens and up to 20. Some will pick up the pattern of the 20s, 30s, and so on up through the 90s. As children enter concrete operations, they perfect their informal knowledge of numbers above 10 and move on to whole number operations with numbers above 10. To fully understand what they are doing when they use whole number operations involving numbers above 10, they must be able to conceptualize **place value**. Place value pertains to an understanding that the same numeral represents different amounts depending on which position it is in. For example, consider the numbers *3*, *30*, and *300*. In the first instance, *3* stands for three 1s and is in the 1s' place. In 30, *3* stands for three 10s and is in the 10s' place. In 300, *3* stands for three 100s and is in the 100s' place. In each of these cases, 0 indicates there is no quantity in the place that it holds. In the number 32, *3* is in the 10s' place, and *2* is in the 1s' place. An understanding of place value underlies the understanding of certain **trading** rules that govern place value and enable whole number operations to be accomplished. Following are examples of some trading rules.

◆ Ten ones can be traded for one 10.
◆ One 10 can be traded for 10 ones.
◆ Ten 10s can be traded for 100.
◆ One hundred ones can be traded for 100.

The place-value concept enables us to represent any value using only 10 digits (zero to nine).

Place value is one of the most difficult concepts for young children to grasp. Being able to rote and rational count above 10 is only a beginning step on the way to an understanding of place value. Children need many counting experiences (as described in Unit 9) and many experiences with concrete models to develop the place-value concept. All too often children are rushed into the place-value operations involved in **regrouping** (what used to be referred to as borrowing and carrying) as a rote memory activity without the necessary underlying conceptualization. Through an understanding of place value, children will realize that when they take one from the 10's column they are actually taking one group of 10 and that when they add numbers in the ones' column and arrive at a sum above nine that the amount they move to the 10's column represents one or more groups of 10. Understanding place value will also help them to see that the placement of numerals is critical in determining value. For example, *sixty-eight* can be written as 68, six 10s and eight ones, and 60 + 8 but *not* 86. The sequence for writing numbers follows fixed rules just like a word sentence. That is, "Ball boy the throws" does not follow the conventions of correctly written English. In the same fashion, *one hundred twenty-one* is not written as 10021. How to guide children to an understanding of this concept is the focus of this unit.

Assessment

Understanding place value is a difficult task for young children. They will normally flounder for a while, seeming to understand the concept in some situations and not in others. Teachers should be patient and accepting and give the children time and appropriate experiences. The following are examples of assessment tasks that can be used to discover where the children are on the road to understanding two-digit numbers and the concept of place value.

SAMPLE ASSESSMENT TASK

9P   **Concrete Operations Ages 7–8**
Place Value, Groups of 10: Unit 30

METHOD: Interview.

SKILL: Child is able to count groups of 11 or more objects and tell how many 10s are in the groups.

MATERIALS: A container of 100 counters (e.g., chips, cubes, or sticks).

PROCEDURE: Place the container of counters in front of the child. Say, HERE ARE A BUNCH OF COUNTERS. COUNT OUT AS MANY OF THEM AS YOU CAN. If the child counts out 11 or more ask, HOW MANY 10s DO YOU THINK YOU HAVE? HOW MANY 1s?

EVALUATION: If the child answers correctly, then she probably has the concept of place value for 10s. If she answers incorrectly, this indicates that although she may be able to rational count groups of objects greater than 10, she does not yet understand the meaning of each of the numerals in her response.

INSTRUCTIONAL RESOURCE: Charlesworth, R., and Lind, K. K. (2003). *Math and Science for Young Children* (4th ed.). Clifton Park, NY: Delmar Learning.

SAMPLE ASSESSMENT TASK

9Q   **Concrete Operations Ages 7–8**
Place Value, Grouping to Identify an Amount: Unit 30

METHOD: Interview.

SKILL: The child is able to form two or more subgroups of 10 objects, each with some remaining from the original group and tell how many he has without counting each individual object.

MATERIALS: A container of 100 counters (e.g., chips, cubes, or sticks).

PROCEDURE: Place a pile of counters (start with about 35) in front of the child. MAKE AS MANY GROUPS OF 10 AS YOU CAN. HOW MANY (counters) DO YOU HAVE ALTOGETHER?

EVALUATION: Note if the child can come up with the answer by counting the number of groups of 10 and adding on the number of ones, or if he has to count each object to be sure of the total. If the child can determine the answer without counting by ones, this is an indication that he is developing the concept of place value.

INSTRUCTIONAL RESOURCE: Charlesworth, R., and Lind, K. K. (2003). *Math and Science for Young Children* (4th ed.). Clifton Park, NY: Delmar Learning.

On the average, first graders can learn to read, write, and understand two-digit numbers, second graders three-digit numbers, and third graders four-digit numbers. However, there will be a broad range of normal variation within any particular group. The best rule of thumb in assessment is to be sure children understand one-digit numbers before going on to two-digit, two before three, and so on.

Activities

The following activities are adapted from the selection of resources listed at the end of the unit. Young children need many experiences in manipulating objects relative to numerals greater than 10 and place value before proceeding to whole number operations with two-digit numbers. Start with counting activities such as those suggested in Unit 9. Then move on to the kinds of activities described in the following pages. The first two activities focus on constructing an understanding of the properties of amounts greater than 10.

ACTIVITIES

NUMERALS GREATER THAN 10: CONSERVATION OF LARGE NUMBERS

OBJECTIVE: To understand, when given a group of more than 10 objects, that the number of objects remains the same no matter how they are arranged.

MATERIALS: Each child will need a container with 50 or more counters (i.e., cubes, chips, or sticks) and a place-value board, as suggested by Richardson (1984) in *Developing Number Concepts Using Unifix Cubes®* (p. 212). A place-value board is a piece of paper divided into two sections so that groups can be placed on one side and loose counters on the other side. To make a place-value board, take a 9″ × 12″ piece of paper or tagboard, and glue or staple a 6″ × 9″ piece of colored paper on one half. Draw a picture in the upper right-hand corner of the white side so the child will know how to place the board in the correct position.

Unifix Cubes® are excellent for this activity because they can be snapped together. However, cubes or chips that can be stacked or sticks that can be held together with a rubber band may also be used.

ACTIVITY: Tell the children to put some amount of counters greater than 10 on the white side of their place-value board. Suggest the children work in pairs so they can check each other's counting. When they agree that they have the same amount, say, MAKE A GROUP OF 10 (counters) AND PUT IT ON THE (color) SIDE OF YOUR BOARD. HOW MANY LOOSE (counters) DO YOU HAVE LEFT? HOW MANY (counters) DO YOU HAVE ALTOGETHER? Note how many children realize that they still have the same number of counters. Ask, DO YOU HAVE ENOUGH (counters) TO MAKE ANOTHER 10? Note if they respond correctly. If they do make another 10, ask again how many loose cubes they have and if the total is still the same. To connect their arrangements to number symbols, write the arrangements on the board.

3 tens and 4 ones

2 tens and 14 ones

FOLLOW-UP: The same activity could be done using containers to put the counters in. Each container could be labeled 10. If small counters such as tiny chips, bottle caps, or beans are used, this would be a more efficient way to keep the groups separated. See Richardson's books (1984, 1999) for additional variations on this activity.

NUMERALS GREATER THAN 10: MEASURING

OBJECTIVE: To work with large numbers through nonstandard measurement activities (see Unit 18 for background information).

MATERIALS: Small objects that can be used as nonstandard units, paper and pencil to record measurements, and measurement cards (suggested by Richardson, 1984). Each measurement card depicts something in the classroom that can be measured.

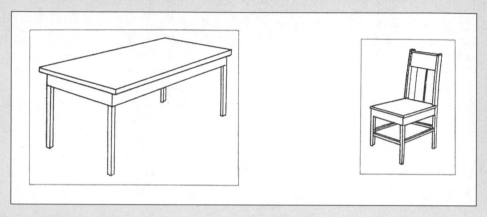

ACTIVITY: The children measure the items with the objects, group the objects into 10s, then figure out how many they have used. They record the results on their paper.

The chair is 24 paper clips tall.

The table is 36 paper clips wide.

FOLLOW-UP: Have the children measure the same items using different nonstandard units and compare the number of units. See Richardson's books (1984, 1999) for further activities.

Once the children have a good understanding of counting and subdividing groups greater than 10, they are ready for activities that gradually move them into the complexities of place value.

PLACE VALUE: CONSTRUCTING MODELS OF TWO-DIGIT NUMBERS

OBJECTIVE: To develop models of two-digit numbers using the place-value board.

MATERIALS: Place-value board (described in previous activity) and a supply of cards with individual numerals zero to nine written on each card. Provide the child(ren) with at least two sets of numerals and a supply of counters that can be readily stacked, snapped, or bundled into groups of 10. One child working alone will need 100 counters. If children are working in small groups and sharing the counters, add 50 counters per child.

ACTIVITY: Have the children put the place-value boards in front of them. Provide them with an ample supply of numerals in a small container and place the container of counters where it is convenient for everyone to reach. CLOSE YOUR EYES AND PICK TWO NUMERALS. PUT ONE ON YOUR BOARD ON THE (color) SIDE AND ONE ON YOUR BOARD ON THE WHITE SIDE. MAKE A MODEL OF THE NUMERAL YOU HAVE SELECTED.

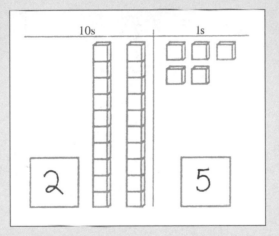

FOLLOW-UP: Have the students repeat this activity with different number combinations. Have them work alone, in pairs, and/or in small groups. Have them do the same activity using base 10 blocks after they have been introduced. (Base 10 blocks will be described later.) The same activity can be adapted to work with 100s and 1,000s when the children are ready. The activity could also be done using spinners, one for each place value.

PLACE VALUE: ESTIMATION WITH COMMON ITEMS

OBJECTIVE: To estimate amounts and apply knowledge of place value to finding out how close the estimate is.

MATERIALS: A container of common items such as a bag of peanuts, dry beans, or cotton balls; a box of paper clips, rubber bands, or cotton swabs; a jar of bottle tops, clothespins, pennies, or other common items; some small cups, bowls, or plastic glasses; flip-chart numerals or paper and pencil to write results. (Flip-chart numerals can be made by writing numerals zero to nine on cards, punching two holes at the top of each card, and putting the cards on rings.)

ACTIVITY: *Estimating* is the math term for guessing or predicting the answer to a math problem. Show the children the container of objects. Let them hold it, examine it, but not open it. LOOK CLOSELY AT THIS (item). HOW MANY (items) DO YOU THINK ARE IN THIS (container)? You record or have the children record each child's guess. Open the container. COUNT OUT GROUPS OF 10 (item) AND PUT THEM IN THE (cups, glasses, and so on). FIND OUT HOW MANY GROUPS OF 10 THERE ARE ALTOGETHER. EACH TIME YOU COUNT OUT 10, TURN OVER A NUMBER ON YOUR FLIP CHART, or if the children can write, WRITE THE NUMBER THAT TELLS HOW MANY 10s YOU HAVE.

FOLLOW-UP: Once the children catch on, put out the estimate of the week. Children can record their guesses on a chart. Then on Friday they can open the container and find out the actual amount. A graph can be made showing the distribution of estimates.

	10s	20s	30s	40s	50s	60s
4					59	
3			39		56	64
2		27	39	45	55	63
1		25	32	40	51	60

See *Mathematics Their Way* (Baratta-Lorton, 1976), Chapters 11 and 12, for more ideas.

Base 10 blocks provide a different kind of model for working with the place-value concept. It is important that children work with a variety of types of materials in model construction so that they do not think there is just one way to view place value with concrete materials. So far we have described making models with discrete items. Base 10 blocks depict each place with a solid model. Units (or 1s) are individual cubes, rods (or 10s) are the equivalent of 10 unit cubes stuck together in a row, flats (or 100s) are the equivalent of 10 rods stuck together, and cubes (or 1,000s) are the equivalent of 10 flats stacked and glued together. See the illustration to the right.

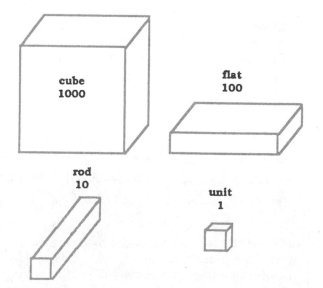

PLACE VALUE: BASE 10 BLOCKS

OBJECTIVE: To work with place value using base 10 blocks.

MATERIALS: A classroom set of base 10 blocks.

ACTIVITY: The base 10 blocks can be used for the activities previously described by adding on another step. Each time the child makes a group of 10, she can record this by selecting a rod. She can then count the rods at the end to find out how many groups of 10 she has found.

FOLLOW-UP: Many auxiliary materials can be purchased that provide activities with base 10 blocks besides those that come with the Teacher's Guide. Base 10 blocks and teachers' guides can be purchased from suppliers such as Dale Seymour, Creative Publications, ETA, Cuisinaire, and DIDAX Educational Resources (see addresses in Unit 39).

Trading is another procedure for working with place value. Primary children need many experiences counting piles of objects, trading for groups of 10, and describing the results. Once they can do these activities with ease, they can move on to regrouping and renaming. Too often they are pushed into regrouping and renaming without an adequate conceptual base built on counting and constructing many groups of 10 and relating them and any ones remaining to written numerals. Regrouping happens when one or more items are added or taken away so that an amount moves to the next 10, next 100, next 1,000, and so on. That is, a group might break down into two 10s and six units, or 26. Five more units are added so there are now 11 units. Ten units are then moved to the 10s' place, leaving one in the 1s' place. There are now three 10s and one unit, or 31. Renaming of the group has also occurred. It has now been *renamed* 31.

Reverse trading would take place if units were removed. For example, if seven units were to be taken away from the three 10s and one unit, a 10 would be moved over to the units, making 11 units, and seven units could then be removed, leaving two 10s and four ones, or 24. Primary grade children need to do many trading activities with concrete materials before moving on to paper and pencil computations. These trades can be practiced with concrete items such as cubes and chips or the beads on an abacus or with solids such as base 10 blocks. Chip trading materials can be purchased from Dale Seymour.

PLACE VALUE: TRADING ACTIVITIES

OBJECTIVE: To construct the concepts of regrouping and renaming through trading activities.

MATERIALS: A supply of paper squares: 100 reds (units) and 30 blues (10s) and a place-value board with a 1s' and 10s' place.

ACTIVITY: Have the children put their place-value boards in front of them. Place a supply of red and blue paper squares where they can be easily reached. THE RED SQUARES ARE 10s, AND THE BLUE SQUARES ARE 1s. Hold up a large 27. SHOW ME HOW YOU CAN MAKE A MODEL OF THIS NUMBER ON YOUR BOARD. Have the children try several examples. When you are sure they understand that the reds are 1s and the blues are 10s, go on to regrouping. Go back to 27. MAKE 27 ON YOUR BOARDS AGAIN. NOW, SUPPOSE SOMEONE GIVES YOU FIVE MORE 1s. TAKE FIVE MORE. WHAT HAPPENS TO YOUR 1s? Encourage them to describe what happens. Remind them that there cannot be more than nine in the 1s' place. Eventually someone will realize that 32 should be modeled with three 10s and two 1s. Have the children discuss what they might do to get a model that has three 10s and two 1s by trading. SUPPOSE YOU TRADE 10 BLUES FOR 1 RED. WHERE

SHOULD THE RED BE PLACED? Once everyone has the red in the 10s' place, ask, SUPPOSE SOMEONE NEEDS FOUR 1s. HOW COULD YOU GIVE THEM FOUR? Encourage them to discuss this problem with each other and ask you questions until someone discovers that another trade will have to be made. Have everyone trade in a blue for 10 reds, take 4 away, and note that they now have 2 blues and 8 reds (28).

FOLLOW-UP: Create some story problems and have the children solve them using trading. Then move on to adding and taking away two-digit quantities. Also provide students with pairs of two-digit numbers and have them invent problems using the numbers.

EXAMPLE WORLD WIDE WEB ACTIVITIES

◆ 100th Day of School Celebration! (K–4). Suggestions for Internet and e-mail activities, links to other Web sites, and numerous classroom ideas for making the 100th Day of School Celebration exciting. Link from Eisenhower National Clearinghouse or http://www/siec.k12.in.us/%7Ewest/proj/100th/

◆ Base ten block activities link from Eisenhower National Clearinghouse or http://www.mason.gmu.edu/whole/base10/baseten.htm

◆ Place value activities can be found at http://www.lessplanspage.com/math23.htm

When the children practice trading to regroup and rename on their place-value boards, they are actually adding and subtracting informally. Richardson's book (1984) explains how to carry this activity over to addition and subtraction of two-digit numbers. Richardson (*Developing Number Concepts Using Unifix Cubes®*) believes that it is confusing to begin two-digit addition and subtraction with numbers that do not have to be regrouped, such as

$$
\begin{array}{cccc}
22 & 53 & 46 & 18 \\
+35 & +14 & -34 & -13 \\
\hline
57 & 67 & 12 & 5 \\
\end{array}
$$

This type of addition and subtraction may lead children to believe that adding or subtracting with two digits is exactly the same operation as with one digit and results in responses such as those below.

$$
\begin{array}{cccc}
25 & 48 & 72 & 37 \\
+16 & +34 & -35 & -28 \\
\hline
311 & 712 & 43 & 11 \\
\end{array}
$$

Note in these examples that the children have added or subtracted each column as though it were an individual one-digit problem. Introduce two-digit addition as follows:

PUT 26 CUBES
ON YOUR BOARD.

NOW GET 18 CUBES,
AND PUT THEM
NEXT TO YOUR BOARD.

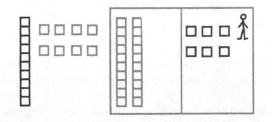

NOW PUT THEM TOGETHER. HOW MANY 10s? HOW MANY ONES?
YES, WE HAVE THREE 10s AND FOURTEEN ONES. DO WE HAVE ENOUGH TO MAKE ANOTHER 10?

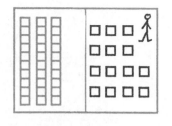

(Give them time to move 10 cubes.)
NOW WE HAVE FOUR 10s AND FOUR 1s. HOW
MANY IS THAT? YES, THAT IS 44.

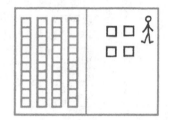

Repeat this process several times with different
pairs of two-digit numbers: Sometimes the sum contains more than nine units, and sometimes it does not.
When the children understand the process without
symbols, connect the symbols by writing them on the
board as you go through the process.

Subtraction of two-digit numbers can be introduced
in parallel fashion. For example, have the children put
out 42 cubes; then tell them they need to take away 25.
They will discover that they have to break up a 10 to
accomplish this task. After doing many examples
without written numbers, go through some problems
in which you connect the quantities to numbers at each
step, thus gradually introducing the notation. Then
have them do mixed sets of problems. Finally, move
on to story problems.

Problems and activities that apply place-value
concepts can be integrated into other content areas.
(Figure 30–1).

Kamii's Approach

The activities suggested in this unit follow a fairly
structured sequence while promoting construction
of concepts through exploration. Constance Kamii
(1993) has been working with primary children using
open-ended activities that provide for more child trial

and error and self-sequencing. Interviewing primary
students who had been through conventional work-
book/textbook instruction, she discovered that they
were able to do regrouping and renaming as a rote
process without really knowing the meaning of the
numbers they were using. For example, when asked to
do a two-digit problem such as 28 + 45, they could
come up with the correct answer:

$$
\begin{array}{r}
1 \\
28 \\
+45 \\
\hline
73
\end{array}
$$

However, when asked what the 1 in 13 means, they
said it meant one rather than 10. Kamii has had greater
success in getting this concept over to primary children using games and letting them discover the relationship of the digits on their own. No workbooks or
worksheets are used and neither are the kinds of concrete activities described in this unit. Problems are
written on the board, children contribute answers, and
every answer is listed. Then the children give their
rationales for their answers. When working with double-digit addition, their natural inclination is to start on
the left. They add the 10s; write the answer; add the
1s; and, if necessary, move any 10s over, erasing the
original answer in the 10s' column. Through trial and
error and discussion, they develop their own method
and construct their own place-value concept. Place
value is not taught as a separate skill needed prior to
doing double-column addition. This method sounds
most intriguing and is more fully described in Kamii
(1989).

Calculators

When children explore calculators for counting,
they notice that the number on the right changes every
time, whereas the other numbers change less frequently. Calculators provide a graphic look at place
value and the relation of each place to those adjacent.
Suggest that the children try + 10 = = = = = and note
what happens; that is, which place changes, and
how much each time? This activity will assist children in seeing what the 10s' place means. Concepts

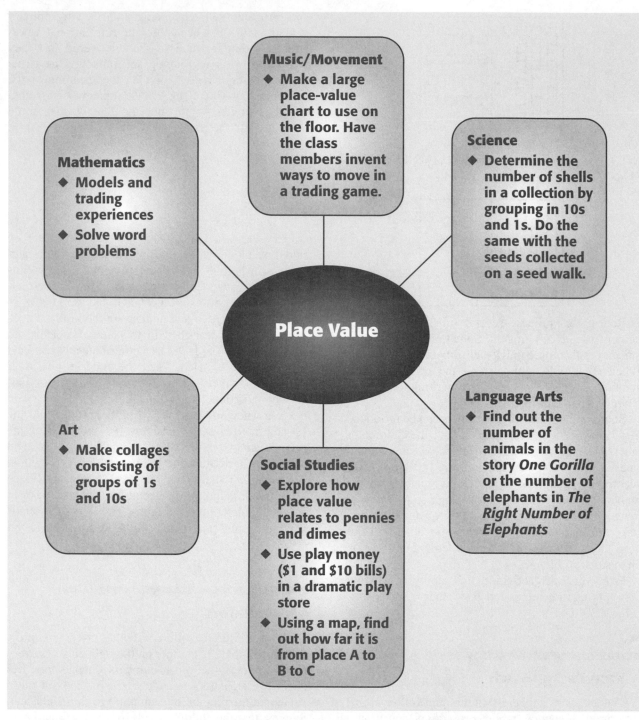

Music/Movement
◆ Make a large place-value chart to use on the floor. Have the class members invent ways to move in a trading game.

Mathematics
◆ Models and trading experiences
◆ Solve word problems

Science
◆ Determine the number of shells in a collection by grouping in 10s and 1s. Do the same with the seeds collected on a seed walk.

Place Value

Art
◆ Make collages consisting of groups of 1s and 10s

Social Studies
◆ Explore how place value relates to pennies and dimes
◆ Use play money ($1 and $10 bills) in a dramatic play store
◆ Using a map, find out how far it is from place A to B to C

Language Arts
◆ Find out the number of animals in the story *One Gorilla* or the number of elephants in *The Right Number of Elephants*

FIGURE 30–1 Integrating experiences with place value and quantities above 10 across the curriculum.

constructed using manipulatives can be reinforced with calculator activities. By adding one to numbers that end in nine and subtracting one from numbers that end in zero, students can see immediately what happens. Suggest that they guess which number follows nine, 29, and 59. Then have them use their calculators to check their predictions. Use the same procedure, except have them predict what will happen if they subtract one from 20, 40, and 70.

Evaluation

An evaluation technique suggested by Kamii (1989, 1993) shows if children really understand place value in two-digit numbers.

Show the child a three-by-five-inch card with 16 written on it. Ask, "What does this say?" After the child says 16, count out 16 chips. With the top of a pen circle the 6 of the 16. "What does this *part* (the 6) mean? show me with the chips what this *part* (the 6) means." Circle the 1 of the 16. "What does this *part* (the 1) mean? show me with the chips what this *part* (the 1) means."

Kamii says that after conventional instruction with workbooks and possibly some manipulatives, all first and second graders can answer correctly regarding the 6, but of the primary children Kamii interviewed, none of the end of first-graders, 33% of end-of-third-graders, and only 50% of end-of-fourth-graders said

that the 1 means 10. Children who learned about place value through constructing it themselves using Kamii's method did considerably better. At the end of the second grade, 66% said that the 1 means 10 and 74% said that the 5 in 54 means 50.

Whichever instructional method you use, be sure to observe very carefully the process each child uses. Be sure to question children frequently about what they are doing to be sure they really understand the concepts and are not just answering in a rote manner.

Summary

Learning about place value and working with two-digit whole number operations that require regrouping and renaming are two of the most difficult challenges faced by the primary-level child. Conventionally, they are taught from a workbook approach with few if any manipulatives to support the instruction. Also, they are conventionally introduced too early and become rote memory activities for those who have the facility to remember the steps necessary to come up with correct answers. Less capable students flounder in a lack of understanding.

Most mathematics educators believe that children learn the concepts and skills needed to understand place value and the processes of regrouping and renaming through practice solving problems using concrete materials. Kamii (1989) takes a different approach, using no concrete materials but guiding children through trial and error and discussion.

KEY TERMS

place value   regrouping   renaming
trading

SUGGESTED ACTIVITIES

1. Visit one or more primary classrooms. Observe the math instruction. Describe the methods observed. Is place value and/or two-digit addition and subtraction being taught? How? Is the method developmentally appropriate? Are the children ready for these concepts? Do they seem to understand?

2. Using Kamii's technique, interview one first grader, one second grader, and one third grader. Describe the results. Compare the performance of the children you interviewed with those interviewed by Kamii. What did you learn from this experience?

3. Review the first-, second-, and third-grade levels of two or more elementary math textbook series. At what level are place value, two-digit addition and subtraction, regrouping, and renaming introduced? What methods of instruction are used? Compare the textbook methods with those described in this unit. What are the similarities and differences? Explain why you would or would not like to use these textbooks.

4. Prepare materials for one of the activities suggested in this unit. Try out the activity with a child or small group of children you believe should be at the right stage for it. Write a report explaining what you did, who you did it with, what happened, and your evaluation of the activity and the children's responses.

5. Using the guidelines from Activity 7, Unit 9, evaluate any of the following software designed to reinforce concepts of place value.
   - Awesome Animated Monster Maker Math. (Grades 1–6). Houghton Mifflin Interactive, link through TERC (http://www.terc.edu). Includes a variety of word problems.
   - Grouping and Place Value. (Grades 1–3). Pleasantville, NY: Sunburst. Experiences with ones, tens, and hundreds designed to develop an understanding of place value.
   - Hands-on-Math, Vols. 1, 2, 3. (Grades K–8). Nashua, NH: Delta Educational. Includes a variety of problems and provides for students to write their own problems.
   - Mighty Math®Carnival Countdown.® (K–2). Pleasantville, NY: Sunburst. Includes one- and two-digit addition and place value.

6. Keep your Activity File/Notebook up-to-date.

REVIEW

A. Define the following terms.
   1. Place value
   2. Regrouping
   3. Renaming
B. Identify which, if any, of the following are descriptions of place value being taught as described in this unit.
   1. A kindergarten teacher is drilling her class on 1s, 10s', and 100s' places using a worksheet approach.
   2. A second-grade teacher gives one of her students 35 Unifix Cubes® and asks him to make as many groups of 10 as he can.
   3. A primary teacher is beginning instruction on two-digit addition with simple problems such as 12 + 41 so the students will not have to regroup and rename right away.
   4. Some primary children are exploring with calculators. Their teacher has suggested they take a list of the numbers 19, 29, 39, and 49, and predict what will happen if 1 is added to each. Then they are to try these operations with their calculators, write down what happens, and share the results with the other children and the teacher.
C. Look back at question B. Explain why you answered as you did.
D. List three kinds of materials that can be used for making place-value models.
E. In what ways does Kamii's approach to teaching

place value differ from what is conventionally done?

F. Check yourself on place value.

1. Identify the number of 100s, 10s, and 1s in each numeral.

	100s	10s	1s
37			
4			
276			

2. In the numeral 3,482, the 4 means ____ , the 8 means ____ , and the 2 means ____ .

3.
```
   1
  67        The 1 above the 6 means:
 +17
  84        _____
```

REFERENCES

Baratta-Lorton, M. (1976). *Mathematics their way.* Menlo Park, CA: Addison-Wesley.

Kamii, C. (1989). *Young children continue to reinvent arithmetic, 2nd grade.* New York: Teachers College.

Kamii, C. , Lewis, B. A., & Livingston, S. J. (1993). Primary arithmetic: Children inventing their own procedures. *Arithmetic Teacher, 41*(4), 200–203.

Morozumi, A. (1990). *One gorilla.* New York: Farrar, Straus, & Giroux.

National Council of Teachers of Mathematics. (2000). *Principles and standards for school mathematics.* Reston, VA: Author. (http://www.nctm.org)

Richardson, K. (1984). *Developing number concepts using Unifix Cubes.*® Menlo Park, CA: Addison-Wesley.

Richardson, K. (1999). *Developing number concepts, book 2: Addition and subtraction.* Parsippany, NJ: Dale Seymour.

Richardson, K. (1999). *Developing number concepts, book 3: Place value, multiplication, and division.* Parsippany, NJ: Dale Seymour.

Sheppard, J. (1990). *The right number of elephants.* New York: Harper Collins.

FURTHER READING AND RESOURCES

AIMS Educational Products. AIMS Education Foundation, P.O. Box 8120, Fresno, CA 93747-8120.

Auriemma, S. H. (1999). How huge is a hundred? *Teaching Children Mathematics, 6*(3), 154–159.

Bove, S. P. (1995). Place value: A vertical perspective. *Teaching Children Mathematics, 1,* 542–546.

Burns, M. (1994). *Math by all means: Place value, grade 2.* White Plains, NY: Cuisinaire.

Box it or bag it mathematics. (K–2). Portland, OR: The Math Learning Center. (800-575-8130) (http://www.mlc.pdx.edu)

Bridges in mathematics. (K–2). Portland, OR: The Math Learning Center. (800-575-8130) (http://www.mlc.pdx.edu)

Copley, J. V. (2000). *The young child and mathematics.* Washington, DC: National Association for the Education of Young Children.

Copley, J. V. (Ed.). (1999). *Mathematics in the early years.* Washington, DC: National Association for the Education of Young Children.

Jensen, R. J. (Ed.). (1993). *Research ideas for the classroom: Early childhood mathematics.* New York: Macmillan.

Jones, G. A., & Thornton, G. A. (1993). Research in review: Children's understanding of place value. A framework for curriculum development and assessment. *Young Children, 48*(5), 12–18.

Reed, K. M. (2000). How many spots does a cheetah have? *Teaching Children Mathematics, 6*(6), 346–349.

Richardson, K. (1999). *Developing number concepts: Planning guide*. Parsippany, NJ: Dale Seymour.

Thompson, C. (1990). Place value and larger numbers. In J. N. Payne (Ed.), *Mathematics for the young child* (pp. 89–108). Reston, VA: National Council of Teachers of Mathematics.

Weinberg, S. (1996). Going beyond *Ten Black Dots*. *Teaching Children Mathematics, 2,* 432–435.

Children's Books

Crews, D. (1986). *Ten black dots*. New York: Mulberry.

Schwartz, D. M. (1985). *How much is a million?* New York: Lothrop, Lee, & Shepard.

Young Children Constructing Math Concepts

Mathematics begins with natural explorations of concrete materials.

Computer software provides opportunities for both individual and group exploration of concepts.

Pegboards provide self-correcting experience with one-to-one correspondence, shape matching, and color classification.

The chalkboard provides a large space for experimenting with writing number symbols.

Construction materials such as Duplo® (and Lego®) provide rich experiences in creating constructions in space.

Coins can be used for exploration in counting, place value, fractions, and standard units of measurement.

Unit blocks provide opportunities for exploring a variety of fundamental and higher level concepts.

Going shopping is a popular dramatic play activity.

Games such as checkers help reinforce understanding of spatial relationships, counting, and turn taking.

Geometry, Data Collection, and Algebraic Thinking

OBJECTIVES

After reading this unit, you should be able to:

◆ List the basic concepts of geometry that young children learn informally at the primary level.

◆ Assess children's readiness for primary-level geometry and data collection experiences.

◆ Plan and carry out developmentally appropriate primary-level geometry, data collection, algebraic thinking, estimation, and probability instruction.

◆ Be able to construct and interpret graphs and tables.

Standards for geometry (Units 12, 13), data analysis (Units 10, 20), and algebra (Units 10, 11, 17, 25) were introduced and the topics discussed previously (NCTM, 2000). The initial level of algebraic thinking lies in the understanding of patterns and relationships. These expectations continue into the primary grades, when children are expected to further their capabilities to recognize, name, build, draw, compare, and sort two- and three-dimensional shapes. Further, they should gain some understanding of symmetry, be able to create mental images of geometric shapes, recognize shapes from different perspectives, relate ideas in geometry to number and measurement, and locate geometric shapes in the environment. Primary-level children are expected to move further in their under-standing of data analysis by being able to describe and explain the meaning of data and make predictions from data. The expectations for understanding probability are at an informal level only.

Weather is the current science topic in Mr. Gonzales's third-grade class in northern Utah. This morning the children are huddled over copies of the past week's weather forecasts that they clipped out of the local morning paper. They are reading the forecast section to find out what kind of information is included and to discuss how they might organize some of the data presented. They note that the day's forecast is included along with the normal highs and lows for that date. There is a regional forecast for Utah and a forecast map and description of the weather for the entire

United States. Selected national and global temperatures along with precipitation and outlook are included in a table. The nation's highs and lows are also reported. The children compile a list of this information and discuss what they can learn and what information might be interesting to record.

Chan's great-great-grandparents came to Utah from Beijing, People's Republic of China. Chan has noticed that Ogden and Beijing are at about the same latitude. He decides to record the high temperatures in Beijing for eight days and compare them with the high temperatures in Ogden for the same time period. First Chan made a chart and then a graph to depict the information from the chart. Then he wrote a description of the information obtained from the graphs. To complete this activity, he applied his mathematical knowledge (measurement, counting, graph making) to an activity that integrates science (the topic of weather), social studies (geography), and reading and language arts (reading and comprehending the article and writing about the information obtained). Figure 31–1 depicts what Chan might have produced.

Groundwork for this type of activity was laid in several previous units: Unit 12 (Early Geometry: Shape), Unit 13 (Early Geometry: Spatial Sense), Unit 20 (Interpreting Data Using Graphs), and Unit 25 (Higher-Level Activities and Concepts). Primary children must have this groundwork before moving on to the activities described in this unit. Children need a basic understanding of shape and space, which they apply to the early graphing and mapping experiences during the preoperational period, to help them to move on to higher-level graphing and geometry concepts. Children should know the basic characteristics of shape and be able to identify geometric shapes such as circles, triangles, squares, rectangles, and prisms when they enter the primary level. They should also have the spatial concepts of position, direction, and distance relationships and be able to use space for making patterns and constructions. During the primary years, they should continue with these basic experiences and be guided to more complex levels.

Geometry is studied in a very general, informal way during the elementary grades. Spatial concepts are reinforced, and the senses are sharpened. During the primary years, geometric concepts continue to be developed mainly at an intuitive level. However, geo-

| Cities | Dates/Temperatures | | | | | | | |
	22	23	24	25	26	27	28	29
Beijing	28	28	37	37	41	41	45	37
Ogden	36	27	26	26	33	33	42	44

High temperatures in Beijing and Ogden, November 27–29

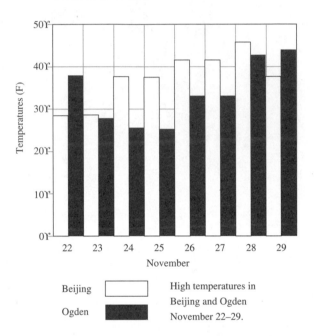

1. Beijing started out colder than Ogden.
2. Beijing gradually got warmer than Ogden.
3. At the end of the eight days, Ogden was warmer than Beijing again.
4. Both cities follow a similar pattern from the high 20s to the low 40s.
5. Both cities are cold in November.
6. Both cities have similar temperatures over time.

FIGURE 31–1   Chan's data table and bar graph.

metric figures are used to teach other concepts, so children should be familiar with them. For example, multiplication is frequently illustrated in a rectangular grid.

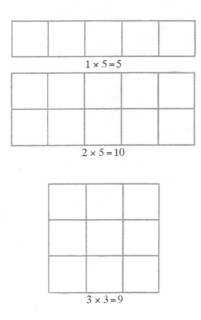

$1 \times 5 = 5$

$2 \times 5 = 10$

$3 \times 3 = 9$

Fractions are commonly illustrated using geometric shapes (see Unit 29), such as the following.

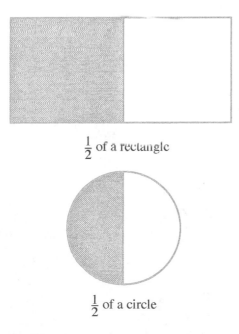

$\frac{1}{2}$ of a rectangle

$\frac{1}{2}$ of a circle

Number lines (which will be described later) are conventionally used to help children visualize greater than, less than, betweenness, and the rules of addition

and subtraction. For example the number line below is used to illustrate that $2 + 3 = 3 + 2$.

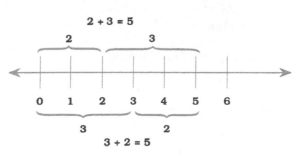

Collecting and organizing data continue to be important applications of mathematics. Graphing is closely related to geometry in that it makes use of geometric concepts such as line and shape. Note that the graphs depicted in this unit and in earlier units are based on squares and rectangles. More advanced graphs are based on circles, and others involve the use of line segments to connect points. Tables are the necessary first step in organizing complex data prior to illustrating it on a graph. Charts are closely related to graphs.

In the 21st century we look at algebra as "a way of thinking, a method of seeing and expressing relationships" (Moses, 1997). Algebra provides a way to organize and generalize the patterns we observe in everyday activities. Through learning how to develop relationships, we can understand the regularities, not just in mathematics, but also in science, history, economics, language, and so on.

Moses (1997) suggests that algebraic thinking can begin in the early primary grades through the use of geometric concepts such as perimeter and involve investigations with square tiles, string, pipe cleaners, and grid paper. Students can identify geometric and number patterns as they explore these relationships. Technology can also be used to support the development of algebraic thinking. The February 1997 issue of *Teaching Children Mathematics* is devoted to this topic. More recently, algebra has been defined in the NCTM standards (2000) and in the navigations publication for prekindergarten through grade two algebra (Greenes, Cavanagh, Dacey, Findell, & Small, 2001).

In summary, knowledge of geometry and construction of graphs, tables, and charts and algebraic thinking are closely related basic tools for organizing data. The remainder of the unit describes geometry, graphing, the use of charts and tables, and algebraic thinking at the primary level. Also described are Lego® and its relationship with **LOGO** programming, estimation, and probability.

Assessment

Readiness for the following primary-level activities should be assessed using the assessment tasks that accompany Units 12 and 13. Readiness is also measured by observing children's capabilities in accomplishing the graphing activities in Unit 20 and the higher-level graphing and spatial relations (mapping) activities in Unit 25. It is not safe to assume that children have had all the prerequisite experiences before they arrive in your primary classroom. You might have to start with these earlier levels before moving on to the activities suggested in this unit.

Activities

This section begins with geometry and mapping. LOGO computer applications to mapping and to robotics are described. The unit then goes on to the topics of charts and tables, algebraic thinking, estimation, and probability.

Geometry

Primary children are not ready for the technicalities of geometry, but they can be introduced informally to some of the basic concepts. They can learn about **points** as small dots on paper or on the chalkboard. **Curves** are introduced as smooth but not straight paths that connect two points during a story or a mapping activity. **Lines** appear as number lines, in measurement activities, and as the sides of geometric figures. Children perceive *angles* (space made by the meeting of two straight lines) in geometric figures. *Congruency* or sameness of size and shape is what children deal with when they match and compare the size and shape of various figures, such as when they sort attribute blocks or make collages from paper shapes. Symmetry (correspondence of parts of a figure on opposite sides of a point, line, or plane) is what children are working with when they do the paper folding suggested in the unit on fractions. The terms *point(s)*, *line(s),* and *curve(s)* may be used with young children without going into the technicalities. The terms *congruency*, *symmetry*, and *angle* will be introduced beyond the primary level and are not essential to working with the concepts informally. The readings and resources at the end of the unit contain a multitude of ideas for activities that will lay the basis for the formal study of geometry. The following are some examples.

ACTIVITIES

GEOMETRY: GEOBOARD ACTIVITIES

OBJECTIVE: To provide experience exploring the qualities of plane figures.

MATERIALS: Geoboards and rubber bands. Geoboards may be purchased or made. A geoboard is a square board with round head screws or smooth, slender cylinders made of plastic placed at equal intervals so that it appears to be made up of many squares of equal size. Commercial geoboards have five rows of five screws each.

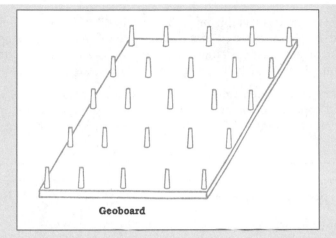

Geoboard

ACTIVITIES:

1. Put out the geoboards and an ample supply of rubber bands of different sizes and colors (special rubber bands may be purchased with the geoboards). Allow plenty of time for the children to explore the materials informally. Suggest that they see how many different kinds of shapes they can make.

2. Give each child a geoboard and one rubber band. MAKE AS MANY DIFFERENT SHAPES AS YOU CAN WITH ONE RUBBER BAND. Encourage children to count the sides of their shapes and to count the number of screws in each side. Suggest that they make a drawing of each shape.

3. Give each child a rubber band and an attribute block. MAKE A SHAPE JUST LIKE THE BLOCK'S SHAPE. Start with squares and rectangles, then triangles and hexagons.

4. On graph paper made to match the geoboard, draw patterns that the children can copy with their rubber bands. For example,

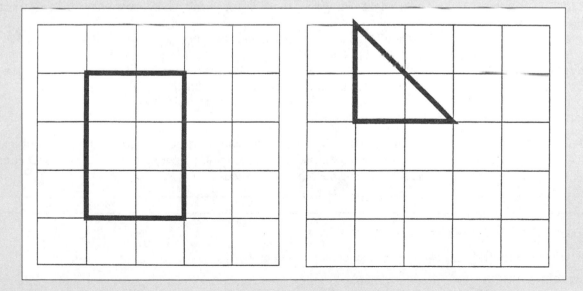

(Commercially made patterns can be purchased also.)

5. Have the children draw patterns on graph paper that matches the size of the geoboards. Demonstrate on the chalkboard first to be sure they realize that they need to make their lines from corner to corner. Have them try out their capabilities on some laminated blank graphs first. Then have them copy their own patterns on the geoboards. Encourage them to exchange patterns with other children.

FOLLOW-UP: Provide more complicated patterns for the children to copy. Encourage those who are capable of doing so to draw and copy more complicated patterns, possibly even some that overlap. Overlapping patterns can be drawn with different colored pencils or crayons and then constructed with rubber bands of matching colors.

GEOMETRY: ACTIVITIES WITH SOLIDS

OBJECTIVE: To explore the characteristics of solid geometric figures.

MATERIALS: A set of geometric solids (available from ETA, Kaplan, Nienhuis Montessori, DIDAX Educational Resources, Creative Publications, Dale Seymour, Cuisinaire etc.).

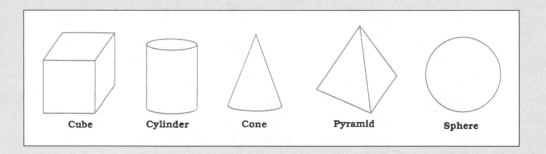

Cube   Cylinder   Cone   Pyramid   Sphere

ACTIVITIES: Let the children explore the solids, noting the similarities and differences. Once they are familiar with them, try the following activities.
Put out three of the objects. Describe one and see if the children can guess which one it is.
◆ IT IS FLAT ALL OVER, AND EACH SIDE IS THE SAME. (cube)
◆ IT IS FLAT ON THE BOTTOM. ITS SIDES LOOK LIKE TRIANGLES. (pyramid)
◆ IT IS FLAT ON THE BOTTOM, THE TOP IS A POINT, AND THE SIDES ARE SMOOTH. (cone)
◆ BOTH ENDS ARE FLAT AND ROUND, AND THE SIDES ARE SMOOTH. (cylinder)
◆ IT IS SMOOTH AND ROUND ALL OVER. (sphere)

FOLLOW-UP: Have the children take turns being the person who describes the geometric solid. Put up a ramp. Have the students predict which solids will slide, which will roll. Then try them out. See if the children realize that some may roll or slide depending how they are placed.

GEOMETRY: SYMMETRY

OBJECTIVE: To provide experiences for exploration of symmetry.

MATERIALS: Construction paper symmetrical shapes. (See Figure 31–2, on page 413, for some patterns.) The following are some suggested shapes. Use your imagination to develop others.

ACTIVITY: Give the children one shape pattern at a time. Have them experiment with folding the shapes until the halves match.

FOLLOW-UP: 1. Have the children use the shapes they have folded to make a three-dimensional collage. PUT GLUE ON JUST ONE HALF OF YOUR FOLDED PAPER.

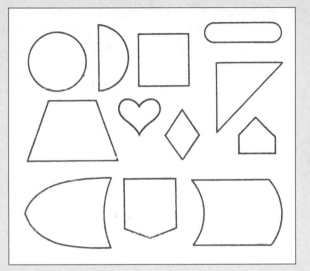

2. Give the children paper squares and rectangles. Show them how they can fold them in the middle and then cut the sides so they come out with a figure that is the same on both halves. These can also be used to make three-dimensional collages.

GEOMETRY: NUMBER LINES

OBJECTIVE: To apply the concept of a line as a visual picture of addition and subtraction and more than and less than.

MATERIALS: A laminated number line for each child, a large laminated number line that can be used for demonstration and/or a permanent number line on the chalkboard, markers (i.e., chips) to mark places on the number lines.

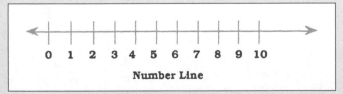

Number Line

ACTIVITIES: The number line can be used to illustrate the following activity.
1. Greater and less than. PUT A MARKER ON THE 4. FIND A NUMBER THAT IS GREATER THAN 4. PUT A MARKER ON IT. Discuss which numbers were selected. How did they know which numbers were greater than four? Go through the same procedure with the other numbers. Then go through the procedure looking for numbers less than a given number.

2. Addition. HOW CAN WE SHOW 2 + 4 ON THE NUMBER LINE? Encourage the children to try to figure it out. If they can't, then demonstrate. FIRST I'LL PUT A MARKER ON 2. NOW I'LL COUNT OVER FOUR SPACES. NOW I'M AT 6. HOW MUCH IS 2 PLUS 4? Have the children try several problems with sums of 10 or less.

3. Subtraction. HOW CAN WE SHOW 5 – 2 ON THE NUMBER LINE? Encourage the children to try to figure it out. If they cannot, then demonstrate. FIRST I'LL PUT A MARKER ON THE 5. NOW WHICH WAY SHOULD I GO TO FIND 5 – 2? Have them try several problems using numbers 10 or less.

FOLLOW-UP: Have the children illustrate equivalent sums and differences on the number line (i.e., 3 + 4 = 1 + 6; 8 – 4 = 7 – 3. The children could also make up number line problems for themselves. Suggest that when they need help with a one-digit problem, they use the number line to find the answer.

GEOMETRY: COMPARING ROAD AND STRAIGHT LINE DISTANCES

OBJECTIVE: To see the relationship between a direct route and the actual route between points on a map. (This activity would be for the more advanced level primary students who have learned how to use standard measurement tools.)

MATERIALS: Maps of your state for everyone in the class, foot rulers, and marking pens.

ACTIVITIES: Have the students explore the maps. See if they can find the legend and if they can tell you what the various symbols mean. Be particularly sure that they know which kinds of lines are roads, how you find out the mileage from one place on the map to another, and how many miles there are to the inch. Spend some time finding out how far it is from your town or city to some of the nearby towns and cities. Have the class agree on two places in the state they would like to visit. Using their rulers and marking pens, have them draw a line from your city to the nearest place selected, from that place to the other location selected, and from there back home. They should then have a triangle. Have everyone figure out the mileage by road and then by direct flight by measuring the lines. Add up the three sides of the triangle. Add up the three road routes. Find the difference between the road trip and the direct route. Discuss why the roads are not as direct as the lines.

FOLLOW-UP: Encourage interested students to compare road and direct distances to other points in the state.

LOGO and Lego®

LOGO computer language can provide experience with geometry at a number of levels. With just a few simple commands and minimal instruction, children can explore, play, and create an infinite number of geometric shapes and designs. With a little more structured approach, they can learn how to plan out patterns ahead of time and use more complex instructional commands. The cursor, referred to as the **turtle** in LOGO, can be moved about in many directions, at different angles, to make straight or curved lines. Prob-

lem-solving skills are developed when children work on figuring out how they will make the turtle go just where they want it to in order to come up with a particular design or figure.

Children's building with Lego® building bricks and their exploration of LOGO are combined in math/science/technology connection with **Lego® Logo**, Lego®Mindstorms, and LEGO Dacta robotics which provides children with the opportunity to explore physics, technology, and mathematics. They have a choice of many projects ranging from a simple traffic light assembly to complex constructions such as

FIGURE 31–2   Patterns for exploring symmetry.

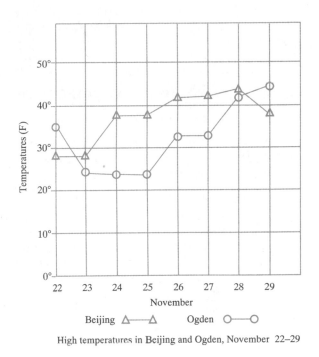

High temperatures in Beijing and Ogden, November 22–29

FIGURE 31–3   Chan's data depicted in a line graph.

bridges, playground rides, construction equipment, and vehicles. In the original version the computer was programmed to control the operation of Lego® machines. More recently National Instruments, LEGO Dacta, and Tufts University have developed a ROBO-LAB system which enables students to write computer programs and transfer them into programmable Lego® bricks (http://www.ceeo.tufts.edu/graphics/robolab). Even kindergartners can create their own robot designs. Lego®Mindstorms includes many robotics products with sets for building *Star Wars* robots and many others (http://mindstorms.com). With the invention of the programmable bricks, the robots no longer need to be bound to the computer.

Making Graphs

Graphing includes constructing graphs, reading information on graphs, and interpreting what the information on a graph means. The data used for making graphs need to be something of interest to the students. In Unit 20, there is a list of possible graphing subjects that young children might enjoy working on. Other

subjects will grow out of their current interests and activities.

The four most popular types of graphs are picture graphs, bar graphs or histograms, **line graphs**, and circle or pie graphs. The graphs described earlier fall into the first two categories and are the easiest for young children to construct and interpret. Circle or pie graphs are beyond the primary level. Some primary-level children can begin to work with line graphs.

Line graphs demand concrete operational thinking because more than one aspect of the data must be focused on at the same time. Line graphs are made on a squared paper grid and apply the basic skills that children would learn by first doing the squared paper activities with the geoboard. They are especially good for showing variations such as rainfall, temperature, and hours of daylight. In Figure 31–3, Chan's temperature data are translated from the bar graph to the line graph. Note that the left side and the bottom are called the **axes**, and each must be labeled. In this case, the left side is the temperature axis and the bottom is the days-of-the-week axis. To find the correct point for each temperature on each day, the child has to find the

ACTIVITIES

GRAPHING: INTRODUCING COORDINATES

OBJECTIVE: To introduce finding coordinates on a graph.

MATERIALS: A large supply of stickers of various kinds. On the bulletin board, construct a large 5 × 5 square coordinate graph. The grids can be made using black tape. Place stickers at the intersections of various coordinates (Figure 31–4).

ACTIVITIES: THIS IS THE CITY. DRIVING INTO THE CITY THE CORNER IS HERE AT 0, 0. I WANT TO GO TO (name one of the stickers). TELL ME HOW MANY BLOCKS OVER AND HOW MANY BLOCKS UP I WILL HAVE TO GO. Suppose that the sticker is on 2, 3. YES, I HAVE TO GO OVER TWO BLOCKS AND UP THREE. THIS POINT IS CALLED 2, 3. Point out how the numbers on the bottom and the sides correspond to the point. Go back to 0, 0 and have the children direct you to other points on the graph. Let the children take turns telling you the coordinates of a sticker they would like to have. When they are able to give the correct coordinates, they get a matching sticker to keep.

FOLLOW-UP: During center time, encourage children to explore the coordinate map on their own or with a friend. Suggest they trace trips to different "corners" with their fingers. The children who understand the concept of coordinates can use coordinate paper to complete symmetrical shapes (Figure 31–5) and name the coordinates.

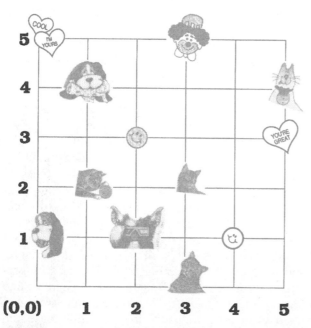

FIGURE 31–4 Coordinate graphing can be introduced using a grid with stickers placed at points to be identified.

point where the two meet, mark the point, and connect it to the previous point and the next point with a line. If two or more types of information are included on the same graph, then geometric symbols are frequently used to indicate which line goes with which set of data (Figure 31–5). In her 1987 article "Coordinate Graphing: Shaping Up a Sticky Situation," Jeanne M. Vissa suggests some creative ways to introduce the use of coordinate (or line) graphing to young children.

Charts and Tables

Charts and **tables** are constructed to organize data before they are graphed. A simple chart consists of tick marks such as depicted in the chart on floating and sinking objects in Unit 10 (see Figure 10–4). This information could be translated into a single variable graph showing frequency of floating or sinking for each object or into a double variable graph showing both (that is, a double-bar or a double-line graph). Simple tables were represented in Figure 31–1. These tables were used to organize the temperature data prior to constructing the graphs.

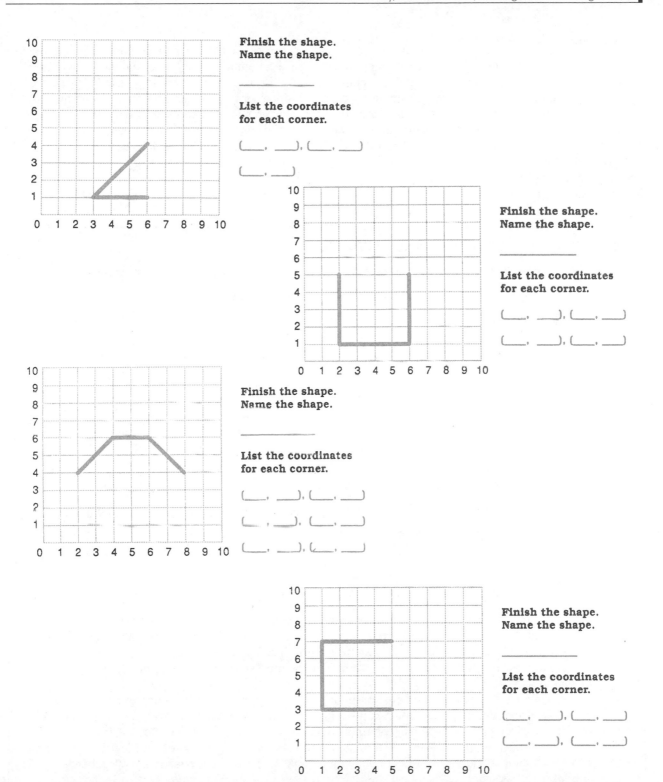

Finish the shape.
Name the shape.

_____

List the coordinates
for each corner.

(__, __), (__, __)

(__, __)

Finish the shape.
Name the shape.

_____

List the coordinates
for each corner.

(__, __), (__, __)

(__, __), (__, __)

Finish the shape.
Name the shape.

_____

List the coordinates
for each corner.

(__, __), (__, __)

(__, __), (__, __)

(__, __), (__, __)

Finish the shape.
Name the shape.

_____

List the coordinates
for each corner.

(__, __), (__, __)

(__, __), (__, __)

FIGURE 31–5   Half of a symmetrical shape can be drawn on a grid for the children to complete.

Algebraic Thinking

Michaele F. Chappell (1997) outlines the roots of algebraic thinking in the primary grades. Primary children are not ready for formal algebraic equations such as $x + 5 = 8$, but they can learn patterns using geometric shapes as variables. For example, in the guess "my rule game," $\square + \square$ can indicate 2 $\square$'s. When doing missing addend problems, such as Tonio has 12¢ and needs 25¢ to buy a candy bar, a triangle can be used to represent the missing addend: $12 + \triangle = 25$. Or counters can be used to set up the problem. Set out 12 counters + an empty paper bag or another container = 25. Ask, "How many counters do we need to put in the bag (cup, jar, or other container) in order to have 25?" A balance could also be used to demonstrate the problem. Chappell believes that the gate to algebra can be opened during the elementary years. The following is a sample activity adapted from those in the NCTM special issue. Additional activities are included in Greenes, Cavanagh, Dacey, Findell, & Small, 2001.

ALGEBRAIC THINKING: BUILDING RECTANGLES*

OBJECTIVE: To introduce the patterns that determine the area of a rectangle using nonstandard units.

MATERIALS: Square tiles from sets such as TexTiles® (Creative Publications) or Algebra Tiles® (Cuisinaire)

ACTIVITY: Provide each child with a group of 20 tiles. USE SOME OF YOUR SQUARE TILES TO MAKE A RECTANGLE WITH A BASE OF 2 TILES. Ask the following kinds of questions.
1. DID YOU ALL MAKE THE SAME RECTANGLE?
2. HOW MANY TILES DID YOU USE IN YOUR RECTANGLE?
3. HOW DID YOU FIGURE OUT HOW MANY TILES YOU USED?
4. WHAT IS THE HEIGHT OF YOUR RECTANGLE?
5. HOW WOULD YOU BUILD A RECTANGLE THAT USES 18 TILES?
6. CAN YOU FIGURE OUT HOW HIGH IT WOULD BE WITHOUT ACTUALLY MAKING IT?
7. IF YOU KNOW HOW HIGH YOU WANT A RECTANGLE TO BE, CAN YOU FIGURE OUT HOW MANY TILES YOU WILL NEED?

EVALUATION: Note the different strategies the students use (i.e., counting one by one, counting by twos, or others).

FOLLOW-UP: Try some of the other activities described in the articles suggested at the end of the unit.

*Adapted from Yackel, 1997.

EXAMPLE WORLD WIDE WEB ACTIVITIES

◆ Geometry through Art. Kindergarten through ninth grade activities to help students develop geometric understanding as they create geometric designs on paper. Link from ENC (Eisenhower National Clearinghouse) or through http://mathforum.org/~sarah/shapiro/shapiro.introduction.html
◆ Graphs, stories, and games from Mega Math. Link at http://www.c3.lanl.gov/mega-math/menu or type mega math in search.
   A series of stories that can be acted out on a floor graph, with a student taking a part of each character
◆ About Shape and About Space. About Shape includes Quilts, Taxicab Treasure Hunt (searching through city blocks), and Corner to Corner (diagonal of a square). About Space includes I Took a Trip on a Train (matching a map with snapshots), Pilot Plans and Silhouettes (design a structure), and Shadows (matching figures with their shadows). An Annenberg Project. Link from http://www.learner.org/teacherslab/ or type Annenberg in search.

Estimation

Estimation is an important activity at the primary level. As children enter the concrete operations period, they can begin to make rational estimates as described by Lang (2001; see Unit 25). A jar can be filled with pennies. Students can predict how many they can hold in one hand. Students can compare estimates. Each student can then take a handful, count them, and compare the amounts with their estimates (Olson & Easley, 1996). Finally, using their handfuls as a base, they can estimate how many pennies the jar holds. Show the students a jar filled with interlocking cubes. Have them guess how many there are. Then remove 10 and connect them into a train. Now the students have more information. Have them make a new estimate. Continue making trains of 10 until the jar is empty (Burns, 1997).

Probability

According to NCTM (2000), probability is very informal at the primary level. It is suggested that children be challenged to answer questions about what is *most likely* and what is *least likely*. For example, in Minnesota in January, is it more likely to snow or rain? Children can tally throws of the dice or the results of tossing a small group of two-sided discs (yellow on one side and red on the other). They will note that some numbers or colors come up more often than others although they are not ready to learn to calculate probabilities as yet.

Integration Across the Content Areas

The concepts described in this unit can be applied across the content areas. Many of the articles suggested at the end of the unit provide examples of activities that integrate mathematics with other content areas.

Evaluation

Note whether children can follow directions and maintain involvement in the activities. Observing the process in these activities is critical. When children are not able to do an activity, it is important to note where the process breaks down. Does the child have the basic idea but just needs a little more practice and guidance? Does the activity seem to be beyond the child's capabilities at this time? These activities require advanced cognitive and perceptual motor development, so children should not be pushed beyond their developmental level. If children work in pairs or small groups of varied ability, the more advanced can assist the less advanced.

Summary

Primary experiences with geometry, spatial sense, graphs, tables, charts, algebraic thinking, estimation, and probability build on preprimary experiences with shape, spatial sense, simpler graphs and charts, and patterns. Primary-level geometry is an informal, intuitively acquired concept. Children gain familiarity with concepts such as line, angle, point, curve, symmetry, and congruence. Geoboard activities are basic at this level.

Geometric and number concepts can be applied to graphing. Advanced children can develop more complex bar graphs and move on to line graphs. Charts and tables are used to organize data, which can then be visually depicted in a graph. Lego®/Logo, Lego®Mindstorms, and LEGO Dacta robotics provide opportunities for more complex experiences combining mathematics, science, and technology. All these activities promote algebraic thinking.

KEY TERMS

symmetry	lines	axes
LOGO	turtle	charts
points	Lego®Logo	tables
curves	line graphs	

SUGGESTED ACTIVITIES

1. Assess some primary children's readiness for the types of geometry and graphing activities described in this unit. Describe the results and your evaluation of their degree of readiness.

2. Plan some activities that would be appropriate for the children you assessed. If possible, use these activities with the children. Evaluate the results. Did the children respond as you expected? Was your assessment accurate? What modifications, if any, would you make the next time? Why?

3. Provide the students in this course with some data. Have them develop some charts or tables using the data. Then have them make some line graphs. Do they have any problems in developing graphs?

4. Add geometry, data collection, computer, and algebraic thinking activities to your Activity File.

5. Using the guidelines from Activity 7, Unit 9, evaluate one or more of the following computer programs.

   ◆ Coco's Math Project 1. Singapore, SG: Times Learning Systems Pte Ltd. (Ages 4 to 10). Involves number, grouping, shapes, weight, matching, and more.

   ◆ Combining Shapes. (Grades 1–2). Pleasantville, NY: Sunburst. Learn about plane figures through a variety of games. (Available in Spanish version)

   ◆ Creating Patterns from Shapes. Pleasantville, NY: Sunburst. Building patterns with shapes and symbols. (Available in Spanish version)

   ◆ The Graph Club. (K–4). Watertown, MA: Tom Snyder. Provides for creating a variety of types of graphs from simple to complex.

   ◆ Graph Power. Newbury Park, CA: Ventura Educational Systems. (K–8)

   ◆ Graphers. (K–4). Pleasantville, NY: Sunburst.

   ◆ Lemonade for Sale. (Grades 2 and 3). Pleasantville, NY: Sunburst. Opportunities to build graphs and practice simple addition, subtraction, and multiplication. (Available in Spanish version)

   ◆ Math Quest with *Aladdin*. Disney interactive. Involves a variety of problem-solving activities.

   ◆ Math Team. (K–3). (1993). Toronto, Ontario, Canada: Philsoft.

   ◆ Math Workshop. (Grades 1–6). Novato, CA: Broderbund Software.

   ◆ Mirror Symmetry. (Grades 2–5). Designed by Tenth Planet. Pleasantville, NY: Sunburst. Exploring lines of symmetry advancing their understanding of geometry and spatial relations. (Available in Spanish version)

   ◆ Shape Up! (PreK–6). Pleasantville, NY: Sunburst. Supports creativity in two- and three-dimensional shape worlds. Shapes can be put together, change size, change orientation in space, change colors, and so on. This program can write labels, stories, or descriptions and print out pages.

   ◆ Tabletop Jr. (1995). Novato, CA: Broderbund Software.

   ◆ Zap! Around Town. (K–3). Pleasantville, NY: Sunburst. For development of mapping and direction skills.

REVIEW

A. List the concepts and experiences that are prerequisite to the geometry and graphing concepts and activities described in this unit.

B. Make three diagrams that illustrate how fractions are visually depicted using geometric shapes.

C. Show on a number line how $4 + 5 = 3 + 6$.

D. Match the terms in Column I with the definitions in Column II.

Column I	Column II
1. Point	a. Correspondence of parts of a figure on opposite sides of a point, line, or plane
2. Curve	
3. Line	
4. Angle	b. The space made by the meeting of two straight lines
5. Congruency	
6. Symmetry	c. An idea that is represented on paper by a dot
	d. Sameness of size and shape
	e. Represented on paper by using a straightedge ruler and pencil
	f. A smooth but not straight line

E. Make a sketch of a geoboard and explain its purpose.

F. Find the following points on the graph: $(0, 0)$, $(3, 2)$, $(3, 4)$, $(0, 3)$, $(4, 1)$, $(1, 2)$.

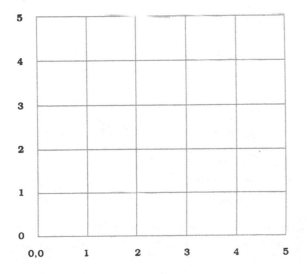

G. Make a line graph using the following data.

Cities	High Temperatures, May 15–20					
	Sat.	Sun.	Mon.	Tues.	Wed.	Thurs.
New York City	73	72	74	64	61	60
Cairo, Egypt	102	111	107	95	93	102

What conclusions can you make from an examination of the graph?

H. Explain how algebraic thinking can be included in the elementary grades curriculum.

I. At what level does probability fit into the kindergarten through grade three curriculum?

REFERENCES

Burns, M. (1997, April). Number sense. *Instructor*, 49–54.

Chappell, M. E. (1997). Preparing students to enter the gate. *Teaching Children Mathematics, 3,* 266–267.

Greenes, C., Cavanagh, M., Dacey, L., Findell, C., & Small, M. (2001). Navigating through algebra in prekindergarten–grade 2. Reston, VA: National Council of Teachers of Mathematics.

Lang, F. K. (2001). What is a "good guess" anyway? Estimation in early childhood. *Teaching Children Mathematics, 7*(8), 462–466.

Moses, B. (1997). Algebra for a new century. *Teaching Children Mathematics, 3,* 264–265.

National Council of Teachers of Mathematics. (2000). *Principles and standards for school mathematics.* Reston, VA: Author. (http://www.nctm.org)

Olson, M., & Easley, B. (1996). Plentiful penny projects to ponder. *Teaching Children Mathematics, 3,* 184–185.

Vissa, J. (1987). Coordinate graphing: Shaping up a sticky situation. *Arithmetic Teacher, 35*(3), 6–10.

Yackel, E. (1997). A foundation for algebraic reasoning in the early grades. *Teaching Children Mathematics, 3,* 276–280.

FURTHER READING AND RESOURCES

General Resources

AIMS Educational Products, AIMS Education Foundation, P.O. Box 8120, Fresno, CA 93747-8120.

Box it or bag it mathematics (K–2). Portland, OR: The Math Learning Center. (800-575-8130) (http://www.mlc.pdx.edu)

Bridges in mathematics (K–2). Portland, OR: The Math Learning Center. (800-575-8130) (http://www.mlc.pdx.edu)

Copley, J. V. (2000). *The young child and mathematics.* Washington, DC: National Association for the Education of Young Children.

Copley, J. V. (Ed.). (1999). *Mathematics in the early years.* Washington, DC: National Association for the Education of Young Children.

Richardson, K. (1999). *Developing number concepts: Planning guide.* Parsippany, NJ: Dale Seymour.

Geometry/Spatial Sense

Ajose, S. A. (1993). Calendar mathematics: Stick math geometry. *Arithmetic Teacher, 41*(2), 100–105.

Brewer, E. J. (1999). Geometry and art. *Teaching Children Mathematics, 6*(4), 220–224, 236.

Dunn, S., & Larson, R. (1990). *Design technology.* London: Falmer Press.

Evered, L. J. (1992). Folded fashions: Symmetry in clothing design. *Arithmetic Teacher, 40*(4), 204–206.

Flores, A. (1995). Bilingual lessons in early-grades geometry. *Teaching Children Mathematics, 1,* 420–424.

Gable, W. (1995). Try an integrated unit on symmetry. *Teaching K–8,* January, 46–47.

Geometry and geometric thinking. (1999). *Teaching Children Mathematics, 5*(6), [Focus issue].

Huse, V. E., Blumel, N. L., & Taylor, R. H. (1994). Making connections: From paper to pop-up books. *Teaching Children Mathematics, 1,* 14–17.

Johnson, P. (1992). *Pop-up paper engineering.* London: Falmer Press.

Lamphere, P. (1995). Geoboard patterns and figures. *Teaching Children Mathematics, 1,* 282–285.

Lehrer, R., & Curtis, C. L. (2000). Why are some solids perfect? *Teaching Children Mathematics, 6*(5), 324–329.

Liedtke, W. W. (1995). Developing spatial abilities in the early grades. *Teaching Children Mathematics, 2,* 12–18.

Linquist, M. M., & Clements, D. H. (2001). Geometry must be vital. *Teaching Children Mathematics, 7*(7), 409–415.

Margerm, P. (1999). An old tale with a new turn—and flip and slide. *Teaching Children Mathematics, 6*(2), 86–90.

Ortiz, E. (1994). Geometry game. *Teaching Children Mathematics, 1,* 231–233.

Penner, E., & Lehrer, R. (2000). The shape of fairness. *Teaching Children Mathematics, 7*(4), 210–214.

Senger, E. S., Platte, S. B., & Van Zandt, J. (1997). Mathematical meaning in context. *Teaching Children Mathematics, 3,* 362–366.

Smith, J. (1995). Links to literature: A different angle for integrating mathematics. *Teaching Children Mathematics, 1,* 288–293.

Wallace, J., & Pearson, J. (1998). What makes a corner a corner? *Teaching Children Mathematics, 5*(1), 6–9.

Collecting and Organizing Data

Baker, A., & Baker, J. (1991). *Counting on a small planet: Activities for environmental mathematics.* Portsmouth, NH: Heinemann.

Barman, C. R., Barman, N. S., Berglund, K., & Goldston, M.J. (1999). Assessing students' ideas about animals. *Science and Children, 37*(1), 44–45.

Berglund, K. (1999). Thought for food. *Science and Children, 36*(4), 38–42.

Bloom, S. J. (1994). Data buddies: Primary-grade mathematicians explore data. *Teaching Children Mathematics, 1,* 80–86.

Bonsangue, M. V., & Pagni, D. L. (1996). Gummy Bears® in the White House. *Teaching Children Mathematics, 2,* 379–381.

Bresser, R., & Sheffield, S. (1996, August). Using kids' names to teach about graphing data. *Instructor,* 88–89.

Helm, J. H. (1997, January). On the path to math. *Early Childhood Today,* 9.

Holden, J. C. (1998). Corn dehydration lab. *Science and Children, 36*(1), 26–29.

Hutchison, L., Ironsmith, M., Snow, C. W., & Poteat, G. M. (2000). Third-grade students investigate and represent data. *Early Childhood Education Journal, 27*(4), 213–218.

Isaacs, A. C., & Kelso, C. R. (1996). Pictures, tables, graphs, and questions: Statistical processes. *Teaching Children Mathematics, 2,* 340–345.

Jorgensen, B. (1996). Hamster math: Authentic experiences in data collection. *Teaching Children Mathematics, 2,* 336–339.

Karp, K. (1994). Telling tales: Creating graphs using multicultural literature. *Teaching Children Mathematics, 1,* 87–91.

Keller, J. D., & Brickman, B. (1998). The ball olympics: Up and down, all around. *Science and Children, 36*(2), 26–31, 56.

Lamphere, P. (1994). Classroom data. *Teaching Children Mathematics, 1,* 28–34.

Larsen, N. J. (1996). Making cents. *Teaching Children Mathematics, 2,* 520–522.

Litton, N. (1995). Graphing from A to Z. *Teaching Children Mathematics, 2,* 220–223.

McGregor, J. (1996). How do you measure up? *Teaching Children Mathematics, 3,* 84–85.

Metheny, D. (1996). Learning to "Ad". *Teaching Children Mathematics, 2,* 284–288.

Pearlman, S., & Pericak-Spector, K. (1995). Graph that data! *Science and Children, 32*(4), 35–37.

Russell, S. J., & Corwin, R. B. (1990). *Used numbers, sorting: Groups and graphs.* Palo Alto, CA: Dale Seymour.

Scribner-MacLean, M., & Greenwood, A. (1998). Invertebrate inquiry. *Science and Children, 35*(8). 18–21.

Seidel, J. D. (1996). *Teaching Children Mathematics, 2,* 192–199.

Stone, A., & Russell, S. J. (1990). *Used numbers, counting: Ourselves and our families.* Palo Alto, CA: Dale Seymour.

Estimation

Guess, graphs, and numbers. (1997, January). *Teaching K–8,* 35.

Computer Resources

Clements, D. H., & Meredith, J. S. (1993). One point of view: A talk with LOGO turtle. *Arithmetic Teacher, 41*(4), 189–191.

Clements, D. H., & Sarama, J. (1997). Computers support algebraic thinking. *Teaching Children Mathematics, 3,* 320–325.

Clements, D. H., & Sarama, J. (2000). Young children's ideas about geometric shapes. *Teaching Children Mathematics, 6*(8), 482–488.

Clements, D. H., & Sarama, J. (2000). Predicting pattern blocks on and off the computer. *Teaching Children Mathematics, 6*(7), 458-461.

Learning and teaching mathematics with technology. (2002). *Teaching Children Mathematics, 8*(6) [Focus issue, forthcoming].

Parker, J., & Widmer, C. C. (1992). Teaching mathematics with technology: Statistics and graphing. *Arithmetic Teacher, 39*(8), 48–52.

Algebraic Thinking

Falkner, K. P., Levi, L., & Carpenter, T. P. (1999). Children's understanding of equality: A foundation for algebra. *Teaching Children Mathematics, 6*(4), 232–237.

Ferrini-Mundy, J., Lappan, G., & Phillips, E. (1997). Experiences with patterning. *Teaching Children Mathematics, 3*, 282–288.

Holly, K. A. (1997). Patterns and functions. *Teaching Children Mathematics, 3*, 312–313.

Lubinski, C. A., & Otto, A. D. (1997). Literature and algebraic reasoning. *Teaching Children Mathematics, 3*, 290–295.

Smith, J. (1995). Threading mathematics into social studies. *Teaching Children Mathematics, 1*, 438–444. (Quilts)

Tierney, C. C., & Nemirovsky, R. (1997). Mathematics of change: Ins and outs or ups and downs. *Teaching Children Mathematics, 3*, 336–339, 345.

Vsiskin, A. (1997). Doing algebra in grades K–4. *Teaching Children Mathematics, 3*, 346–356.

Willoughby, S. S. (1997). Functions: From kindergarten through sixth grade. *Teaching Children Mathematics, 3*, 314–318.

UNIT 32
Measurement with Standard Units

OBJECTIVES

After reading this unit, you should be able to:

◆ List the reasons that measurement is an essential part of the primary mathematics program.

◆ Know when to introduce standard units of measurement for length, time, volume, area, temperature, and money.

◆ Name the two types of standard units of measurement that we use in the United States.

◆ Plan and carry out developmentally appropriate primary-level measurement instruction.

Measurement is an extremely important aspect of mathematics. It is a practical activity that is used in everyday life during experiences such as cooking, shopping, building, and constructing. In the primary curriculum, it is essential to data gathering in science and can also be applied in other areas. Measurement is a major vehicle for integrating mathematics with other content areas. Measuring is also a vehicle for reinforcing other math skills and concepts: The number line is based on length, a popular multiplication model is much like area, and measurement is an area that lends itself naturally to problem-solving activities. Counting, whole number operations, and fractions are used to arrive at measurements and report the results. This unit will build on the basic concepts of measurement described in Units 18, 19, and 22. The focus of this unit is instruction and activities for introducing the concept of standard units and applying the concept to length, volume, area, weight, temperature, time, and money measurement.

NCTM (2000) lists several expectations for primary grade children's accomplishments in measurement. Primary grade children are expected to select an appropriate unit and tool for the attribute being measured, be able to measure objects that require a repeated use of the same tool (e.g., three cups of flour with a cup measure, three-foot table with a foot ruler), use a variety of tools for measuring, and be able to make comparisons and estimates of standard unit measurements.

In Unit 18 (see Figure 18–1), five stages in the development of the concept of measurement were described. During the sensorimotor and preoperational periods, children's measurement activities center on play and imitation and making comparisons (e.g., long-short, heavy-light, full-empty, hot-cold, early-late, rich-poor). During the transition period from ages five to seven, children enjoy working with arbitrary units. During concrete operations (which an individual usually enters at age six or older), they can begin to see the need for standard units (stage four) and begin to develop skills in using them (stage five). Standard units are not introduced for each concept at the same time. In general, the following guidelines can be observed:

◆ Length (linear measure): The units inch/foot and centimeter/meter are introduced in the beginning of primary and for measurement during second grade.

◆ Area: Area is introduced informally with non-standard units in grade one and ties in with multiplication in grade three.

◆ Time: Time measurement devices and vocabulary were introduced prior to primary, but it is generally the end of primary before conventional time is clearly understood and a nondigital clock can be read with accuracy.

◆ Volume (capacity): Volume is learned informally during pouring activities, and accuracy is stressed during preprimary cooking. The concept of units of volume is usually introduced in grade two.

◆ Weight: The standard measurement for weight is usually introduced in third grade.

◆ Temperature: Temperature units are identified, and children may begin to read thermometers in the second grade, but it is usually beyond primary when children really measure temperature with accuracy and understanding.

◆ Money: Coins and bills are identified prior to primary, symbols are associated in early primary, but value does not begin to be understood until the end of primary.

The goal in the primary grades is to introduce the meaning of measurement, needed terminology, important units, and most common measurement tools.

Both **English units** (customary in the United States) and **metric units** are introduced during the primary years. Although the metric system is much easier to use because it is based on 10s and is used as the principal system in most countries, it has not been adopted as the official measure in the United States. In the 1970s there was a movement toward adoption of the system in this country, but it died out, and the U.S. Metric Commission was abolished in 1984. However, children must learn the metric system because it is so widely used around the world as well as in industry and science.

Assessment

Concrete operational thinking is essential for an understanding of the need for and the use of standard units. Conservation tasks for length (see Figure 18–3), weight (see Figure 18–3), and volume were illustrated earlier in the text. In Unit 18, observational assessment guidelines are suggested for finding out what children at the early stages of understanding of measurement know about volume, weight, length, and temperature. Interview tasks for time can be found in Unit 19. Be sure that children can apply nonstandard measure before moving on to standard measure.

Instruction

The concept of measurement develops through measurement experiences. Lecture and demonstration are not adequate for supporting the development of this concept. Also, it is important to take a sequenced approach to the introduction of standard units. Adhere to the following steps.

1. Do comparisons that do not require numbers (see Unit 11).
2. Use nonstandard arbitrary units (see Unit 18).
   a. Find the number of units by counting.
   b. Report the number of units.
3. Compare the thing measured to the units used (e.g., a table's width is measured with paper clips and drinking straws).
4. Introduce standard units appropriate for the same type of measurement.
   a. Find the number of units using standardized measuring instruments (i.e., ruler, scale, cup, liter, thermometer).
   b. Report the number of units.

Introduction of new standard measurement techniques and instruments should always be preceded by comparisons and nonstandard measurement with arbitrary units. Naturalistic and informal measurement experiences should be encouraged at all levels.

The Concept of Unit

Children's ability to measure rests on their understanding of the concept of **unit**. Many children have difficulty perceiving that units can be other than one. That is, one-half foot could be a unit, three centimeters could be a unit, two standard measuring cups could be a unit, one mark on a thermometer equals two degrees, and so on.

By using nonstandard units of measure first, the concept of unit can be developed. Children learn that measurement can be made with an arbitrary unit, but the arbitrary units must be equal to each other when making a specific measurement. For example, when measuring with paper clips, each one must be the same length. Paper clip is not the unit. A paper clip of specific length is the unit. Through the use of arbitrary but equal units used to measure objects, children construct the concept of a unit. The concept is reinforced by using different arbitrary units (one kind at a time) and then comparing the results in terms of the number of units. For example, the children measure Lai's height using Unifix Cubes,® identical drinking straws, and the class math textbook. Soon they realize that measurement with smaller units requires more units than with larger units. When the students move on to standard units, they can compare the number of units needed to measure using teaspoons versus a standard cup measure, inches versus a yardstick, and so on.

Children should be aware that when they use units (arbitrary or standard) they must be accurate. For example, there cannot be gaps or spaces between units when measuring length. That is why it is a good idea to start with Unifix Cubes,® Lots-A-Links,® or some other units that can be stuck together and easily lined up. Once children are able to measure using as many units as needed to measure the whole length, capacity, and so on, then they can advance to using one or more units that must be moved to make a complete measurement. For example, they could make a 10 Unifix Cube® length measure, place it on the item to be measured, mark where it ends, move the measure to that point, keep going until finished, and then add the 10s and the remaining cubes to arrive at the length in cubes. For capacity, individual measuring cups could be filled and then the number of empties counted after a larger container is filled, or one cup could be used and a record kept of how many cupfuls filled the larger container. As children discover these shortcuts to measurement, they will be able to transfer this knowledge over to standard unit measure and understand the rationale behind foot rulers, meter and yardsticks, and quart and liter measures.

Measuring Instruments

With the introduction of standard units comes the introduction of measuring instruments. Rulers, scaled instruments (scales, graduated cylinders, thermometers), and clocks are the tools of standard measurement. Children have problems with these instruments unless they understand what they are measuring and what it means to measure. It is wise to begin with simple versions of the instruments, which are marked only with the unit being used. For example, if the unit is the centimeter, use a ruler that is marked only with centimeters (no millimeters). If the unit is an inch, use a ruler marked only with inches (no one-half, one fourth, and/or one-eighth inches). Be sure the children understand how units are marked. For example, on a ruler, the numbers come after the unit, not before. Even most nine-year-olds will say that the ruler illustrated is five inches, rather than six inches long. You must be sure children understand each number tells how many units have been used. Children need many experiences measuring objects shorter than their ruler

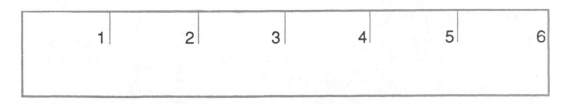

before they move on to longer objects with which they will have to measure, mark, and move the ruler. They also will need to be able to apply their addition skills. For example, if they are using a 12-inch ruler, and they measure something that is 12 inches plus eight inches, can they add 12 + 8? To measure to the nearest one-quarter, one-eighth, or one-sixteenth of an inch, they must understand fractions.

Scaled instruments present a problem because every individual unit is not marked. For example, thermometers are marked every two degrees. A good way to help children understand this concept is to have them make their own instruments. They can make graphs using different scales or make their own graduated cylinders. The latter can be done by taking a large glass and putting a piece of masking tape down the side as shown in the following illustration.

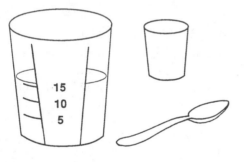

Take a smaller container, fill it with spoonfuls, count how many it holds, and empty it into the glass. Mark the level of the water and the number of spoonfuls. Fill the small container, empty into the glass, and mark again. In the example, the small container holds five teaspoons of water. This measure can be used to find out how much other containers will hold.

Clocks are one of the most difficult instruments for children to understand. Although there are only three measures (hours, minutes, and seconds), the circular movement of the hands makes reading the face difficult. Children vary greatly as to when they are finally able to read a clock face accurately. There is no set age for being able to tell time. Skills needed to tell time must be learned over many years and through practice with clock faces with movable hands. Digital clocks are easier to read but do not provide the child with the visual picture of the relationship between time units.

Money also offers difficulties because the sizes of the coins do not coincide with their value. That is, the dime is smaller than the penny and the nickel. Bills provide no size cues but do have numerical designations that relate one bill to the other. Relating the coins to the bills is a difficult task for young children.

Measurement Activities

This section includes activities that will help children construct the concepts of linear, volume (capacity), area, weight (mass), temperature, time, and money measurement using standard units. Always refer to earlier units for the comparison and arbitrary (nonstandard) unit experiences that need to be done prior to introducing the standard units. Also, remember to work on the concepts of the units used for each type of measurement as well as actual measurement.

ACTIVITIES

STANDARD MEASUREMENT: LINEAR

OBJECTIVE: To be able to use standard units of measure to compare lengths of objects; to discover that the smaller the units, the more will be needed to measure a distance; and to learn to use a ruler to measure objects.

MATERIALS: Rulers (inch/foot, yardstick, centimeter, meter stick); tape measures; paper; pencils; crayons; markers; poster board; and book, *How Big Is a Foot?*

ACTIVITIES: These activities are introduced following many exploratory experiences with comparing visually and with arbitrary units. The same objects can be measured using both methods to emphasize the need for standard units. The first activity is designed to develop an understanding of this need.

1. YOU HAVE MEASURED MANY THINGS AROUND THE ROOM, INCLUDING YOURSELVES, AND MADE COMPARISONS. WHAT YOU COMPARE AGAINST IS CALLED YOUR *UNIT OF MEASUREMENT*. WHAT ARE SOME UNITS OF MEASUREMENT YOU HAVE USED? (Children should name items used such as paper clips, Unifix Cubes®, books, etc.) WHEN YOU TELL HOW LONG OR HOW TALL SOMETHING IS, YOU HAVE TO TELL WHICH UNIT OF MEASURE YOU USED. WHY? WHAT PROBLEM COULD OCCUR IF YOU ARE TELLING THIS INFORMATION TO SOMEONE WHO CANNOT SEE YOUR UNIT OF MEASURE? Encourage discussion. For example, they might suggest that if measuring with Unifix Cubes® you send the person a cube, or if measuring with a piece of string you send the person a piece of string of the same length. Next, read the book *How Big Is a Foot?* Discuss the problem encountered by the king. For ideas on how to use this book, see the article "Exploring Measurement through Literature" by C. A. Lubinski and D. Thiessen in *Teaching Children Mathematics, 2,* 260–263 (1996).

   Now the students should be beginning to understand why standard units of measurement are necessary. Clarify this point by summing up, IF EVERYONE IN THE WORLD KNOWS EXACTLY WHAT THE UNITS OF MEASUREMENT ARE, IT IS MUCH EASIER TO EXPLAIN HOW LONG, WIDE, TALL, ETC. THAT IS WHY WE HAVE *STANDARD* UNITS OF MEASURE. WE USE INCHES, FEET, AND YARDS. (Pass around foot rulers and yardsticks for children to examine and compare.) IN MOST PLACES IN THE WORLD, IN SCIENCE LABORATORIES, AND IN FACTORIES, CENTIMETERS, DECIMETERS, AND METERS ARE USED. Pass around meter sticks. Point out that the base 10 blocks they have been using are marked off in centimeters (1s units) and in decimeters (10s units), and that ten 10s placed end to end is a meter. Have them test this with the meter sticks and the base 10 blocks. THESE UNITS ARE THE SAME EVERYWHERE AND DO NOT CHANGE. GET INTO PAIRS AND MEASURE EACH OTHER'S BODY PARTS USING YOUR RULERS AND TAPE MEASURES. BEFORE YOU START, MAKE A LIST OF THE PARTS YOU PLAN TO MEASURE. Have the students call out the names of the parts they plan to measure. When they finish have them compare their results.

2. Have the children use their foot rulers and two other units (such as a shoe and a pencil) to measure the same objects. Have them record the results in a table.

Object	Length			
	Foot ruler		**Shoe**	**Pencil**
	Feet	*Inches*		
Table				
Windowsill				
Bookshelf				

   Discuss the results and what they mean.

3. Have the children make their own inch and centimeter rulers. Provide them with strips of cardboard 6 inches long, and have them mark them off as indicated on the next page.

   Have them make comparative measures around the classroom. Then send the rulers home along with a note to the parents.

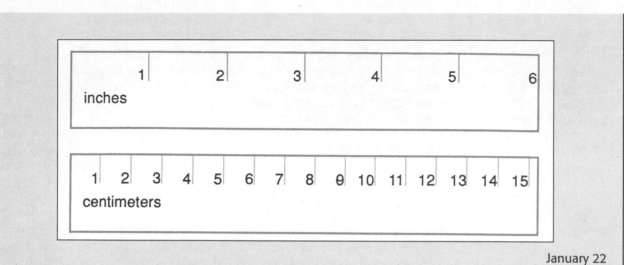

January 22

Dear Parents,

We are working with different ways of measuring length. Your child is bringing home an inch ruler and a centimeter ruler and is supposed to measure six things at home with each ruler and record the results. Please help your child if necessary. Have your child share the results with you and explain the differences in the number of inches versus the number of centimeters of length found for each object. Thanks for your help with this project.

Sincerely,

Jon Wang, Second Grade Teacher

Object	Length	
	Inch ruler	*Centimeter ruler*
1.		
2.		
3.		
4.		
5.		
6.		

FOLLOW-UP: Do many more linear measurement activities using standard units as suggested in the resources at the end of the unit.

STANDARD MEASUREMENT: VOLUME

OBJECTIVE: To be able to use standard units of measure to compare volumes of materials; to learn that the smaller the units, the more will be needed to measure the volume; to learn how to use standard measures of volume such as teaspoons, tablespoons, cups, pints, quarts, and liters.

MATERIALS: Containers of many different sizes (boxes, baskets, buckets, jars, cups, bowls, pans, bottles, plastic bags, and so on) and standard measures of volume (set of customary and set of metric measuring cups, liter and quart measures, customary and metric measuring spoons).

ACTIVITIES: These activities are introduced following many exploratory experiences with comparing visually and with arbitrary units. The same container's capacities can be measured with arbitrary and with standard units to emphasize the need for standard units. The first activity is designed to develop an understanding of this need.

1. Discuss volume following the same format as was used for linear measurement. YOU HAVE EXPLORED THE VOLUME OR SPACE INSIDE OF MANY CONTAINERS BY FILLING AND EMPTYING CONTAINERS OF MANY SIZES AND SHAPES. WHAT KINDS OF UNITS HAVE YOU USED? Encourage them to name some of the smaller units they have used to fill larger containers. See if they can generalize from the length discussion that there are problems in communication when standard units are not used. Pass around the standard measurement materials. Encourage the children to talk about the characteristics of these materials. Do they recognize that they have used these types of things many times to measure ingredients for cooking? Do they notice the numbers and scales marked on the materials?

2. Using the standard units, have the children find out the capacities of the containers previously used for exploration. Have them use materials such as water, rice, beans, and/or sand for these explorations. They should record their findings in a table such as the one below:

NUMBER OF UNITS TO FILL

Container	Measure Used	
	Customary standard cup measure	Small plastic juice glass
1.		
2.		
3.		
4.		
5.		
6.		

FOLLOW-UP: Continue to do exploratory measurement of capacity. Also, continue with cooking activities, giving the children more responsibility for selecting the needed measurement materials.

STANDARD MEASUREMENT: AREA

OBJECTIVE: To explore area in a concrete manner and its relationship to linear measurement.

MATERIALS: Inch and centimeter cubes and two-dimensional patterns with squares and without squares, paper grids, and paper squares (or purchase Learning Measurement Inch by Inch from Lakeshore).

ACTIVITIES: Area can be explored with squared paper and cubes long before formal instruction. Remember that area-type activities are frequently used as the visual representations of multiplication.

1. On poster board, make some shapes such as those shown that are in inch or centimeter units. Have the children find out how many inch or centimeter cubes will cover the whole shape.

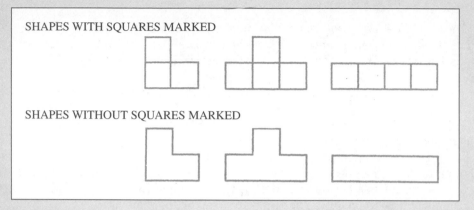

SHAPES WITH SQUARES MARKED

SHAPES WITHOUT SQUARES MARKED

2. Make a supply of paper grids (inch or centimeter squares, about 5 × 4 squares). Make a supply of construction paper squares. Have the children make up their own areas by pasting individual squares on the grid. Have them record on the grid how many squares are in their area. (Or use Learning Measurement Inch by Inch.)

FOLLOW-UP: If rulers have been introduced, have the children measure the lines on the grids and patterns with their rulers. Discuss how they might figure out how many square inches or centimeters are on a plane surface using their rulers.

STANDARD MEASUREMENT: WEIGHT

OBJECTIVE: To be able to use standard units of measure to compare the weights of various materials and to use balance and platform scales.

MATERIALS: Balance scales with English and metric weights, a set of platform scales, a metric/and or customary kitchen balance scale, paper and pencil for recording observations, and many objects and materials that can be weighed.

ACTIVITIES: The children should have already explored weight using comparisons.

1. WHEN YOU LOOK AT TWO OBJECTS, YOU CAN GUESS IF THEY ARE HEAVY OR LIGHT, BUT YOU DON'T REALLY KNOW UNTIL YOU LIFT THEM BECAUSE SIZE CAN FOOL YOU. YOU COULD EASILY LIFT A LARGE BALLOON, BUT A ROCK OF THE SAME SIZE WOULD BE TOO HEAVY TO LIFT (have a balloon and a rock available for them to lift, if possible). A MARSHMALLOW WOULD BE EASIER TO LIFT THAN A LUMP OF LEAD OF THE SAME SIZE. THE LEAD AND THE ROCK HAVE MORE STUFF IN THEM THAN THE BALLOON AND THE MARSHMALLOW. THE MORE STUFF THERE IS IN SOMETHING, THE HARDER A FORCE IN THE EARTH CALLED GRAVITY PULLS ON IT. WHEN SOMETHING IS WEIGHED, WE ARE MEASURING HOW HARD GRAVITY IS PULLING ON IT. YOU HAVE COMPARED MANY KINDS OF THINGS BY PUTTING ONE KIND OF THING ON ONE SIDE OF A BALANCE SCALE AND ANOTHER ON THE OTHER SIDE. NOW YOU WILL WORK WITH CUSTOMARY AND METRIC WEIGHTS IN YOUR PAN BALANCE ON ONE SIDE AND THINGS YOU WANT TO WEIGH ON THE OTHER SIDE. Discuss the sets of pan balance weights and have them available for the children to examine. Explain that they are all made of the same material so that

size is relative to weight. Have the children weigh various objects and materials (water, rice, beans, and so on). Compare the weights of 1 cup of water versus 1 cup of rice or 1 cup of beans. Which weighs more? How much more? Remind the children they will have to add the amounts for each weight to get a total. Suggest that they work in pairs so they can check each other's results.

2. Show the children how to read the dial on the kitchen balance. Provide a variety of things to weigh.
3. If a platform scale for people is available, have everyone in the class weighed, record the results, and have the children make a graph that depicts the results.
4. Have the children go through newspaper grocery store advertisements and cut out pictures of items that are sold by weight and have to be weighed at the store to find out the cost.
5. Have the children weigh two objects at the same time. Remove one and weigh the remaining object. Subtract the weight of the single object from the weight of the two. Now weigh the other object. Is the weight the same as when you subtracted the first weight from the total for both objects?

FOLLOW-UP: Continue putting out interesting things to weigh. Make something with a European recipe that specifies amounts by weight rather than volume.

STANDARD MEASUREMENT: TEMPERATURE

OBJECTIVE: To be able to use standard units of measure to compare temperatures and to learn how to use a thermometer to measure temperature.

MATERIALS: Large demonstration thermometer, small thermometers for student use, outdoor thermometer.

ACTIVITIES: These activities assume that children have talked about and have had experiences with hot, warm, and cold things and hot, comfortable, and cold weather.
1. Have the children examine the demonstration thermometer. Have them decide why there are two scales (Fahrenheit and Celsius) and how each is read. Discuss their experiences with thermometers (when they are ill or go to the doctor for a checkup, for measuring the outdoor and indoor air temperature, for controlling the thermostat on their furnaces and air conditioners).
2. Provide some hot water and ice cubes. Have the children measure the temperature of the water and record the result. Have them add an ice cube, let it melt, measure again, and record the result. Keep adding ice cubes and recording the results. Have the children make a line graph to illustrate how the ice affects the temperature. Is any other factor affecting the water temperature? (Answer: the air temperature) Compare the results with the temperature of tap water.
3. If possible, post an outdoor thermometer outside the classroom window, and have the children record the temperature each day in the morning, at noon, and at the end of the day. After a week, have them make some graphs depicting what they found out. Have interested students write daily weather reports to post on the bulletin board.

FOLLOW-UP: Have interested children record the daily weather forecasts from the radio, TV, or newspaper. Compare the forecast temperatures with those recorded at school.

STANDARD MEASUREMENT: TIME

OBJECTIVE: To be able to use standard units to measure time and to read time accurately from a conventional clock.

MATERIALS: Large clock model with movable hands (such as the well-known Judy Clock), miniature model clocks that can be used individually during small group activities, a 60-minute timer that can be used to help develop a sense of time duration, a class monthly calendar (teacher made or purchased).

ACTIVITIES:
1. Children should have some sense of time sequence and duration by the time they reach the primary level. A timer is still useful to time events such as "Five minutes to finish up" or "Let's see if anyone can finish before the 10-minute timer rings." The major task for the primary child is understanding the clock and what it tells us and eventually learning how to work with time in terms of the amount of time from one clock reading to another. Children can work together with the Judy Clock or with their smaller models, moving the hands and identifying the time. Much of clock knowledge comes from everyday activities through naturalistic and informal experiences. You can support these experiences by having a large wall clock in your classroom and having visual models of important times during the day that the children can match to the real clock. For example, the daily schedule might be put on the wall chart with both a conventional clock face and the digital time indicated for each major time block, such as

2. Clock skills may be broken down as follows:
   a. Identify the hour and the minute hands and the direction in which they move.
   b. Be able to say the time on the clock at the hour, and be able to place the hands of the clock for the hour. Know that the short hand is on the hour, and the long hand is on 12.
   c. Identify that it is after a particular hour.
   d. Count by 5s.
   e. Tell the time to the nearest multiple of 5.
   f. Count on from multiples of 5 (10, 11, 12, . . .).
   g. Write time in digital notation (3:15).
   h. Tell time to the nearest minute, and write it in digital notation.
   i. Match the time on a digital clock to a conventional clock's time.
   j. Identify time before a particular hour and count by 5s to tell how many minutes it is before that hour.
3. Each child can make a clock to take home. Use a poster board circle or paper plate. Provide each child with a paper fastener and a long and short hand. Have them mark the short hand with an *H* and the long hand with an *M*. Send a note home to the parents suggesting some clock activities they can do with their child.
4. Provide the children with blank calendars each month that they can fill in with important dates (holidays, birthdays, etc.).

FOLLOW-UP: Continue to read children stories that include time concepts and time sequence. Have more advanced students who understand how to read clocks and keep track of time keep a diary for a week recording how much time they spend on activities at home (eating, sleeping, doing homework, reading, watching TV, playing outdoors, attending soccer practice, going to dancing lessons, and so on). Have them add up the times at the end of the week and rank the activities from the one with the most time spent to the least time spent. They might even go on to figure out how much time per month and year they spend on each activity if they are consistent from week to week.

STANDARD MEASUREMENT: MONEY

OBJECTIVE: To be able to tell the value of money of different denominations, associate the symbol ¢ with coins and $ with dollars, find the value of a particular set of coins, be able to write the value of particular sets of coins and bills.

MATERIALS: Paper money and coin sets, pictures of coins, "Money Bingo®" game (Trend Enterprises, Inc.).

ACTIVITIES: Money is always a fascinating area for young children. Money activities can be used not only to learn about money but also to provide application for whole number and later for decimal skills.

1. Dramatic play continues to be an important vehicle of learning for primary children. First graders enjoy dramatic play centers such as those described in Unit 22. Second and third graders begin to be more organized and can design their own dramatic play activities using available props. They enjoy writing plays and acting them out. Play money should always be available in the prop box.
2. Make some price tags (first with amounts less than $1, later with more). Have the children pick tags out of a box one at a time and count out the correct amount of play money.
3. Have the children go through catalogs and select items they would like. Have them list the items and the prices and add up their purchases. Younger children can write just the dollar part of the prices.

FOLLOW-UP: Play "Money Bingo®." The bingo cards have groups of coins in each section. Cards with different amounts of cents are picked, and the children have to add up their coins to find out if they have a match.

EXAMPLE WORLD WIDE WEB ACTIVITIES

◆ Time—What Time is it? Link at http://wwwlessonplanspage.com (second and third grade)
◆ Money—Race to a Quarter at Explorer, http://explorer.scrtec.org/, or search type in explorer for link.
◆ Length—Measurement Inch by Inch. Link at http://mathforum.org/
◆ Money—see http://www.lessonplanspage.com/math23.htm

Evaluation

Evaluation of children's progress with measurement should be done with concrete tasks. The following are some examples: Give the children a list of three items in the classroom to measure. Arrange a set of measuring cups, material to measure, and a container to measure into, and have each child turn in his answer. Set up a scale with three items of known weight, have each child weigh each item individually, and record the amount. Put out three model thermometers with different temperatures and have each child in turn tell you the readings and whether they indicate hot, comfortable, or cold. Show the child the time on a model clock and ask him to tell you the time and explain how he knows. Have each child identify coins and then put them together to make various amounts, making the amounts appropriate to the child's level at the time.

Summary

Measurement skills are essential for successful everyday living. People need to know how to measure length, volume, area, weight, temperature, time, and money. These concepts develop gradually through many concrete experiences from gross comparisons (i.e., long-short, a lot-a little bit, heavy-light, hot-cold, early-late, rich-poor) to measurement with arbitrary units, to measurement with standard English (customary) and/or metric units. Measurement activities are valuable opportunities for applying whole number skills, fraction knowledge (and later decimals), and obtaining data that can be graphed for visual interpretation. Measurement concepts are acquired through practice with real measuring tools and real things to measure. Lecture and demonstration alone are not adequate methods of instruction.

KEY TERMS

English units	metric units	unit

SUGGESTED ACTIVITIES

1. On your Activity File cards for this unit, make note of the prerequisite activities in Units 18, 19, and 22.
2. Locate the article by Gretchen L. Johnson on helping preservice teachers understand metrics. Prepare the materials for one or more of the suggested activities and try them out with the other members of your class. Have the students in your class evaluate whether the experience was helpful in providing a better understanding of the metric system and for suggesting some appropriate instructional ideas.
3. Assess one first-grade, one second-grade, and one third-grade student on readiness for using standard units of measure. Write a report describing what you did, recording the children's responses and comparing the three children's readiness.
4. Prepare materials for the suggested evaluation tasks. Evaluate one first-grade, one second-grade, and one third-grade student on their understanding of standard units of measure. Write a report describing what you did, recording the children's responses and comparing the three children's levels of understanding.
5. Plan instructional activities based on the results of your interviews with the primary children. If possible, use the activities with the children.
6. Develop a plan for a measurement center for a first-, second-, or third-grade classroom. Include one station for each type of measurement discussed or five stations for one type of measurement. If possible, procure the materials and set up the center in a classroom for a week. Keep a record of what the children do in the center. At the end of the week, evaluate the center. Was it appropriate? Were the materials set up in such a way that the children could work independently? Did children return again? Did they try the activities at each station? Would you do it the same way next time? Why? What changes would you make?

Using the guidelines from Activity 7, Unit 9, evaluate one or more of the following software programs:

◆ Awesome Animated Monster Maker Math. (Grades 1–6). Houghton Mifflin Interactive. Includes problems solved by measuring and weighing. Links at http://www.terc.edu.

◆ Get Up and Go! (Grades 2 and 3). Pleasantville, NY: Sunburst. Children construct their own timelines.

◆ Infinity City. (Ages 4–8). Headbone Interactive. Areas include money and time.

◆ Learn about Physical Science: Matter, Measurement and Mixtures. (K–2). Pleasantville, NY: Sunburst. Study of matter and how matter can be measured and mixed.

◆ M*A*T*H Circus. (K–8). Greygum Educational software. Reasoning and problem solving, including measurement problems. Link at http://www.terc.edu.

◆ Numbers Undercover. (K–3). Pleasantville, NY: Sunburst. Time, measuring, and money mysteries.
◆ The Penny Pot. (Grades 2–3). Pleasantville, NY: Sunburst. Practice in counting coins.

◆ Trudy's Time and Place House. (Grades K–3). Pleasantville, NY: Sunburst. (Developed by Edmark.) Explores geography and time.

REVIEW

A. List two reasons that measurement is an essential part of the primary mathematics curriculum.
B. There are five stages children pass through on their way to understanding and using standard units of measure. Put the steps in the correct developmental order.
   1. Understands the need for standard units
   2. Works with arbitrary units
   3. Applies standard units of measure
   4. Makes gross comparisons (i.e., heavy-light, hot-cold)
   5. Plays and imitates
C. Children are not ready to understand all the different units of standard measure at the same time. Match the measurement concepts on the left with the usual time of readiness on the right.

Measurement Concept	Time When Ready for Standard Units
1. Length	a. In grade two.
2. Time	b. Introduced in grade two but well beyond primary when accuracy is achieved.
3. Volume	
4. Area	c. Introduced gradually, starting in preprimary, but not done accurately until the end of primary and even later. Instrument is difficult to understand.
5. Weight	
6. Temperature	
7. Money	
	d. Value is not really understood until the end of primary.
	e. Units introduced in grade one; measurement in second grade.
	f. Introduced in grade three.
	g. Mainly informal during primary but important for visual representation of multiplication.

D. Name the two types of units used in the United States. Which is the conventional standard?
E. Why do we need to learn metric if it is not the standard in our country?
F. Which cognitive developmental stage do children need to be in to be able to understand and apply standard units of measure?
G. List the most important factors in the comprehension of the concept of *unit*.
H. Provide two or more examples of the difficulties associated with using measuring instruments. Explain how these difficulties can be eased.
I. Select one measurement area, and describe how you would introduce measurement in that area following the sequence of instruction described in this unit.

REFERENCE

National Council of Teachers of Mathematics. (2000). *Principles and standards for school mathematics.* Reston, VA: Author. (http://ww.nctm.org)

FURTHER READING AND RESOURCES

General References

AIMS Educational Products. AIMS Education Foundation, P.O. Box 8120, Fresno, CA 93747-8120.

Box it or bag it mathematics, (K–2). Portland, OR: The Math Learning Center. (800-575-8130) (http://www.mlc.pdx.edu)

Bridges in mathematics, (K–2). Portland, OR: The Math Learning Center. (800-575-8130) (http://www.mlc.pdx.edu)

Copley, J. V. (2000). *The young child and mathematics.* Washington, DC: National Association for the Education of Young Children.

Copley, J. V. (Ed.). (1999). *Mathematics in the early years.* Washington, DC: National Association for the Education of Young Children.

Dyche, S. E. (1992). In step with the metric system. *Science and Children*, 29(8), 22–23.

Liedtke, W. W. (1990). Measurement. In J. N. Payne (Ed.), *Mathematics for the young child.* Reston, VA: National Council of Teachers of Mathematics.

Richardson, K. (1999). *Developing number concepts: Planning guide.* Parsippany, NJ: Dale Seymour.

Wilson, P. S., & Rowland, R. E. (1993). Teaching measurement. In R. J. Jensen (Ed.), *Research ideas for the classroom: Early childhood mathematics.* New York: Macmillan.

Linear Measurement

Baker, A., & Baker, J. (1991). *Counting on a small planet.* Portsmouth, NH: Heinemann. (See "Design a House.")

Hendrix-Martin, E. (1997). Students use their bodies to measure animals. *Teaching Children Mathematics, 3,* 426–430.

Johns, F. A., & Liske, K. A. (1992). Schoolyard adventuring. *Science and Children, 30*(3), 19–21.

Kelly, B. (1997). Problem solvers: Animals and fences at a zoo. *Teaching Children Mathematics, 3,* 438.

Raulerson, T., & Bentley, L. (1995). Baseball. *Teaching Children Mathematics, 1,* 498–499.

Richardson, K. (1997). Too easy for kindergarten and just right for first grade. *Teaching Children Mathematics, 3,* 432–437.

Ruggles, J., & Slenger, B .S. (1998). The "measure me" doll. *Teaching Children Mathematics, 5*(1), 40–44.

Schwartz, S. L. (1995). Developing power in linear measurement. *Teaching Children Mathematics, 1,* 412–416.

Shipley, L. M. (1994). Long distance. *Teaching Children Mathematics, 1,* 162–163.

Volume

Baker, A., & Baker, J. (1991). *Counting on a small planet.* Portsmouth, NH: Heinemann. (See "Water Use and Abuse.")

Burghardt, B., & Heilman, G. (1994). Water matters. *Teaching Children Mathematics, 1,* 24–25.

Fitzsimmons, P. F., & Goldhaber, J. (1997). Siphons, pumps, and missile launchers: Inquiry at the water tables. *Science and Children, 34*(4), 16–19, 42.

Richardson, K. (1997). See previous section.

Time

Barton, K. C., & Levstik, L. S. (1996). "Back when God was around and everything": Elementary children's understanding of historical time. *American Educational Research Journal, 33,* 419–454.

Lemme, B. (2000). Integrating measurement projects: Sand timers. *Teaching Children Mathematics, 4*(5), 132–135.

Lemme, B. (1998). Putting mathematics into routine classroom tasks. *Teaching Children Mathematics, 4*(5), 250–253.

Martin, H. (1999). Days of the month: The calendar of mathematics. *Teaching Children Mathematics, 5*(9), 530–531.

Shimabukuro, M. A., & Fearing, V. (1993). How does your garlic grow? *Science and Children, 30*(8), 8–11.

Young, T. (1992). It's time for science. *Science and Children, 29*, 32–33.

Area

Nitabach, E., & Lehrer, R. (1996). Developing spatial sense through area measurement. *Teaching Children Mathematics, 2*, 473–477.

Outhred, L. N., & Mitchelmore, M. C. (2000). Young children's intuitive understanding of rectangular area measurement. *Journal for Research in Mathematics Education, 31*(2), 144–167.

Money

Baker, A., & Baker, J. (1991). *Counting on a small planet*. Portsmouth, NH: Heinemann. (See "Green Shopping.")

Clark, D. (1997, January). Grocery store math. *Teaching K–8*, 42–43.

Kulas, L. L. (1997). May I take your order? *Teaching Children Mathematics, 3*, 230–234.

Lemme, B. (1998). Putting mathematics into routine classroom tasks. *Teaching Children Mathematics, 4*(5), 250–253.

Weight

Lennox, J. (1996). "Weighing" dinosaurs. *Science and Children, 34*(3), 16–19.

McGregor, J. (1996). Do you measure up? *Teaching Children Mathematics, 3*, 84–85.

Temperature

Baker, A., & Baker, J. (1991). *Counting on a small planet*. Portsmouth, NH: Heinemann. (See "Baby, It's Cold Outside.")

Chia, D. T. (1998). Weather mathematics: Integrated science and math. *Teaching Children Mathematics, 5*(1), 19–22.

Moore, D. A. (1999). Some like it hot: Promoting measurement and graphical thinking by using temperature. *Teaching Children Mathematics, 5*(9), 538–543.

Emergent Readers' Books

Young, S. L. (1998). *The garage sale*. Columbus, OH: Zaner-Blozer. (Money)

Young, S. L. (1998). *One o'clock is time for one nap*. Columbus, OH: Zaner-Blozer. (Time)

Young, S. L. (1998). *The treasure map*. Columbus, OH: Zaner-Blozer. (Measure distance)

Using Skills, Concepts, and Attitudes for Scientific Investigations in the Primary Grades

UNIT 33
Overview of Primary Science

OBJECTIVES

After reading this unit, you should be able to:

◆ Develop appropriate science learning experiences for the primary age child.

◆ Design lessons that guide students in primary science investigations.

◆ Incorporate process skills into science investigation lessons.

◆ Guide students in collecting, observing, sorting, and classifying objects.

The *National Science Education Standards* (1996) state that science teaching must reflect science as it is practiced and that one goal of science education is to prepare students who understand the modes of reasoning of scientific inquiry and can use them. Specifically, students need to have many and varied opportunities for investigating, collecting, sorting and cataloging, observing, note taking and sketching, interviewing, and polling.

This unit relates the skills needed for primary science investigations and the fundamental process skills to science lessons. Children in the primary grades continue to be avid explorers. Even though they are beginning to refine their inquiry skills, to identify changes in observed events, and to understand relationships among objects and events, they still require time to interact and manipulate concrete objects.

As children leave kindergarten and enter the primary level, they are also leaving the preoperational level and entering concrete operations. They begin to be able to use abstract symbols such as numbers and written words with understanding if they are tied to concrete experiences such as science investigations. They are also entering a period of industriousness in which they enjoy long-term projects, building things, making collections, and playing games that require taking turns, learning systems of rules, and making predictions. Peers are becoming increasingly important; thus, working in small groups becomes a basic instructional strategy.

Primary age children may find it difficult to classify by more than one characteristic, transfer abstract ideas to objects and events outside of their direct experience, and draw inferences from data and identify complex patterns in data taken over a very long time. Additionally, primary age children have difficulty with experimentation as a process of testing ideas and the logic of using evidence to formulate explanations. However, they can design investigations to try things to see what happens—they tend to focus on concrete results of tests and will entertain the ideas of a "fair" test in which only one variable at a time is changed.

The units in this section contain lesson examples, strategies, and classroom vignettes of how some of the science topics suggested by the *National Science Education Standards* (1996) might be taught in the primary grades. The Unifying Concepts and Processes Standard, which highlights the connections between scientific ideas and was discussed in Unit 5, is a natural part of any investigation. Children will not fully understand these powerful ideas that characterize science until they are much older, but aspects of the ideas will be integrated in developmentally appropriate ways in this section.

This unit begins with examples of how the love of collecting and the ability to play games can be applied in the science curriculum. Next, planning for investigations is described, followed by suggestions on how to manage the classroom. Finally, examples of how instructional technology can be used to enhance science investigations are described.

Collecting

Primary children love to collect. They are increasingly aware of details, and their ability to compare and categorize objects is developing. They are apt to begin collecting pocketfuls of small and portable objects that they see around them. Use this natural inclination to encourage children to observe, compare, sort, and classify. Collections can consist of many things such as plants, animals, feathers, fur, rocks, sand, seashells, soils, and anything else that interests children.

However, whatever the composition of the collection, it should be viewed as a means of encouraging inquiry, not as an end in itself. In this way, simple identification of objects does not become the focal point of collecting. Instead, children will learn the basic steps in scientific inquiry.

Getting Started by Using Magnifiers

A **magnifier** is useful for both collecting and classifying. Handheld plastic magnifiers are perfect for all ages, are inexpensive, and have the advantage of being mobile for outdoor explorations. Magnifying boxes are hollow plastic boxes with a removable magnifier at the top. They are ideal for observing small treasures and animals such as live insects. When using magnifiers, carefully catch the insects, observe them, then return them to their environment without injury. In this way, you will encourage humaneness as well as observation.

Children can also use the jumbo-sized magnifier mounted on a three-legged stand. There is no need to hold objects with this type of magnifier, and objects of different sizes can be examined at the same time. Although some dexterity is required for adjusting most magnifiers, the effort is important because the magnifiers are a bridge to using microscopes. In the following scenario, second graders are introduced to magnifiers before collecting (Figure 33–1).

Mrs. Han introduces magnifiers by letting the children explore for a period of time on their own. She does not tell them what to look at; rather, she gives them time to "mess around" with the magnifiers. "Wow!" observes Trang Fung. "Look how big the hair on my arm looks." As she continues to look around at objects close to her, Dean motions her over to his table. "Look, Trang. Look at the sleeve of my shirt." "It looks different. Something is in my shirt." "Mrs. Han," asks Sara, "Do things always look bigger with magnifiers? Can we always see

FIGURE 33–1 Introduce children to magnifiers.

more?" "Let's look through them and see," suggests the teacher.

Mrs. Han plans several opportunities to view objects in different ways. She asks the children to describe the object before viewing with a magnifier, to describe what they see while they are viewing, to compare how objects look under different powers, and to compare and contrast appearances of objects after viewing is completed. She asks, "How does the object appear under the magnifier? Why do you think it looks different?"

The teacher groups the children and has them examine different areas of the room, their clothes, lunch, and a spiderweb. She explains that the magnifying glass itself is called a **lens** and confirms that things look different under a magnifier. She explains that this is because of the way the magnifier is constructed but does not suggest technical explanations. Primary children will enjoy noticing details not seen with the naked eye.

Focusing the Collecting

Practice collecting on the school grounds or in the neighborhood. Help children focus on their collections by giving them suggestions. After collecting, suggest classification systems, let children come up with their own, or try sorting objects in different ways. The primary purpose of collecting is not identification at this age. Rather, collecting should be viewed as an opportunity to encourage inquiry and become aware of the variety of similarities and differences in nature. As children collect, they observe, compare, classify, and begin to think as a scientist might think. The following collecting ideas will get the class started.

1. *Leaves.* Collect and sort leaves by color, shape, vein patterns, edges, and so on. Ask, "How many red leaves can you find? Can you find leaves that are smooth? Do some of the leaves feel different? Try putting all of the leaves that smell the same in a pile." Children will want to associate the leaf with its name on a label (Figure 33–2). Suggestions for displaying collections are found in Unit 40.

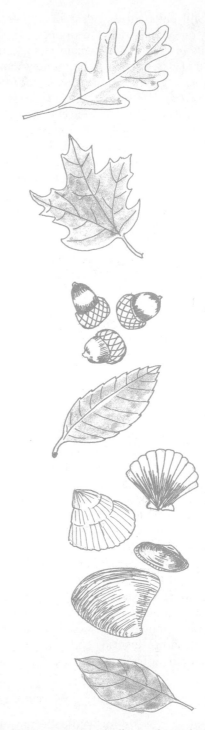

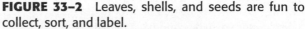

FIGURE 33–2 Leaves, shells, and seeds are fun to collect, sort, and label.

2. *Shells.* Collect different types of empty shells, for example, nutshells, eggshells, snail shells, seashells. Ask, "What kind of objects have a shell? How do you think they use their shell?"

3. *Litter.* Collect litter around the school ground. Ask, "What type of litter did you find most often? Where did you find it?"

4. *Seeds.* Seeds can be found on the ground or flying in the air. Walk through a field, and examine the seeds clinging to your trouser legs and socks. Sort the seeds by size, color, and the way they were dispersed. Ask, "What type of seed did you find most often?" Suggestions for setting up a center on seeds are found in Unit 39.

5. *Spiderwebs.* Spiderwebs are all around us, but children will need practice and patience to collect them. Spray powder on the web, then put a piece of dark paper on one side of it. Hold the web in place with hairspray. Ask, "How are the spiderwebs the same? How are they different?" Children might enjoy pulling twine through white craft glue to duplicate the way a spider forms its web. Let dry and hang.

6. *Feathers.* Feathers can be found at home, at school, and on the way to school. Children will enjoy examining the feathers with magnifiers. Point out the zipperlike barbs that open and close the feathers. Ask, "How are the feathers alike? How do they differ?" If children are studying birds, identify the function of the different types of feathers (Figure 33–3).

7. *Rocks.* Collect rocks and sort them by color, size, shape, texture, and hardness. Ask, "What size rocks do you have? What color rocks do you have? What shapes are your rocks? How do they feel? How are the rocks alike? How are the rocks different? Do the rocks have the same hardness when you scratch them?"

8. *Rubbings.* Another way to collect is to collect impressions of objects. Rubbings of bark and fossils are made by holding one side of a piece of paper against an object and rubbing the other side with a dark crayon. Mount the resulting patterns on colored construction paper, and display. Have the children compare and classify the patterns.

FIGURE 33–3 Zipperlike barbs can be seen with the help of a magnifier.

9. *Modeling clay.* Modeling clay can be used to create an impression of fossils, bark, leaves, and seeds. Simply press the clay against the object, remove, and compare impressions.

10. *Plaster molds.* Footprints can be preserved by forming a plaster mold. Mix plaster, build a small cardboard rim around the footprint, and pour plaster into the impression that you have found. Carefully remove the plaster when dry, and return the cast to the room for comparison (Figure 33–4).

Collecting Small Animals without Backbones

Mr. Wang asks his students, "What is your favorite animal?" "That's easy," Derrick says. "I like lions, seals, and cats." "Me, too," Theresa says. "But I really like horses the best." Brent chimes in that his favorite pet is a gerbil, and Liu Pei insists that dogs are the best animals because they guard your house.

A few students mention reptiles as a favorite animal, but most of the children name mammals. To introduce **invertebrates** as animals and clear up a

FIGURE 33–4 Making a plaster mold of raccoon tracks. "What animal made these tracks?"

common misconception, the teacher has the children run their hands down their back. He asks, "What do you feel?" "Bones," says Theresa. "I feel my backbone." Mr. Wang asks the children if their favorite animals have backbones. "Yes, of course they do," Brent answers.

Mr. Wang explains that not all animals have backbones; these animals are called *invertebrates*. He mentions a few such as worms, sponges, mollusks, starfish, crayfish, spiders, and insects and is surprised at the children's interest.

The teacher decided to plan a collecting trip to a nearby pond and field. Each student was to wear old clothes, including long pants, and bring a washed peanut butter-sized jar. Mr. Wang had prepared insect sweepers and a few catch jars (Figure 33–5).

Before leaving on the trip, Mr. Wang gave instructions. "We will need to be quiet and to look high and low." Derrick cut in, "And under rocks, bushes, and fallen branches." "Yes," the teacher said. "Look carefully where you walk."

The class worked in teams during the hunt, and each team tried to capture only one kind of animal. "Remember where you captured your animal," Mr. Wang reminded the children. "We will turn the insects loose in the same habitat that we found them."

After returning to the room, the teams used nature books to find out how to keep their captives alive. Each animal was displayed with an index card giving its name, habitat where it was found, and the collector's name. The animal was on display for two days and then released to its original habitat. Many questions were raised. "Does my worm like to eat raisins?" Derrick wanted to know. Brent was interested in knowing if his worm was able to see, and Liu Pei won-

INSECT NET

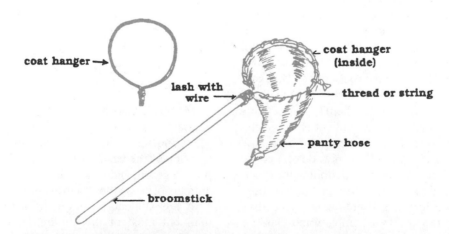

FIGURE 33–5 Making an insect sweeper from discarded nylons and a hanger.

dered if her sow bugs would dig in the dirt of their container.

Mr. Wang encouraged close observation and investigation with such questions as, "Does the animal like rough or smooth surfaces? Does it spend most of its time in the light or in the dark?"

The next day, Liu Pei brought in animals she had found on her way to school. The display was growing. Children classified the animals by color, number of legs, and where they were found. "Let's group the animals into those found on land and those found on water," Theresa said. "Don't forget the air," Brent suggested. "Some were found in the air."

The invertebrate display was an excellent way to observe animals and their habitats. The students had an opportunity to classify, investigate characteristics, study life cycles, and expand their definition of animals. Some students developed a skit involving metamorphosis, others worked on a wall chart, and all gained an appreciation of the little creatures and their world.

Games

Primary age children enjoy games. "Put the Lobster in the Chest" is a game that offers an opportunity for spatial awareness exploration and verbal communication, while reinforcing science content. Refer to Unit 16 for preliminary strategies for using this science board game.

Put the Lobster into the Chest

To play this game, which is similar to "Battleship," you must first create two identical game boards and sets of playing pieces. Correlate the activity to a science topic of your choice. For instance, if you are doing a unit on farm animals, a pasture or a farmyard would be the obvious choice. For example, imagine that you are off the coast of Maine. For the game pieces, select animals commonly found in this setting. In this case, you might include lobsters, crabs, eels, clams, whales, dolphins, and seals. You will need two of each animal. Or, use three-dimensional game pieces.

FIGURE 33–6 "Put the lobster under the plant."

It is best to play this game as a class before having the students break into pairs or small groups. When you give the instruction, "Put the lobster into the chest," students can consult with each other and ask you questions to make sure they know which is the lobster. Separate the players with a box or similar barrier so they cannot see each other's board (Figure 33–6). A typical beginning interchange might go like this:

INITIATOR: Take the long thing with claws and put it beneath the floating green stuff.
FOLLOWER: Just on the sand?
INITIATOR: No. Put it on the sand under the plant.
FOLLOWER: Under the floating stuff near the brown fish?
INITIATOR: That's right.

The follow-up discussion is crucial to this game. After playing, always have the players compare their boards and talk about any differences between them.

Defining Investigations

Hands-on manipulative activities promote literacy skills and the learning of science concepts. Yet, many teachers shy away from including children in the active participation needed to develop these skills and concepts. Messy science investigations are avoided for several common reasons. One reason is that some teachers do not feel comfortable teaching science. Other teachers find managing children and materials an overwhelming task, and still others believe that investigations should be reserved for older children.

These fears should be put to rest. You do not need an extensive science background to guide children in science investigations. What you do need is instruction in how to do it and some background information to enable you to answer some simple questions. What is most essential for teaching science is a teacher's ability and sense of security to say, "I don't know. How do you think we can find the answer to your question?" Explore strategies for teaching investigations to primary age children, and try the suggested strategies for managing children and materials. Early science experiences provide the necessary background for future, more sophisticated skill and concept development.

Teaching Science Investigations

Science investigations usually begin with a question. For example, ask, "How long can you keep an ice cube from melting?" Children can initiate investigations by asking their own questions, such as, "How long will this ice cube last if I leave it on my plate?"

After the initial question or questions, you usually predict what you think is going to happen. In the ice cube example, a child might predict, "I think the ice cube will last until lunch."

Determining variables simply means taking all the factors into account that might affect the outcome of the investigation. Although most third-grade students can handle the term variable, it is not advisable to introduce this term to kindergarten through second-grade children. This component of investigation is usually too difficult for primary age children to understand. Instead, ask questions that help children consider variables in the investigation. For example, ask, "What are we trying to find out? What shall we change?" The idea of keeping something constant can be understood by talking about the idea of fairness. It just would not be fair for everything not to be the same.

Keep records of observations, results, procedures, information obtained, and any measurements collected during the investigation. Conclusions, of course, are statements that tell if the original prediction, hypothesis, was rejected. Ask, "What happened? Is this what you thought would happen? Did anything surprise you?"

This procedure resembles the scientific method for a reason. This is because children are unconsciously using the scientific method as they observe, predict, and reach conclusions. Encouraging them to investigate capitalizes on their natural interest.

In fact, we could call investigations student research. Basically, children are trying to find the answers to questions for which they do not know the answers. As they investigate, they find answers to their questions in the same way a scientist does. They are thinking like a scientist.

Hands-on science means just that—learning from materials and processes of the natural world through direct observation and experimentation. Direct experience, experimentation, and observation are sources of students' learning about science and are essential to learning. This hands-on learning begins in infancy with sensory stimulation that hones infants' observation and discrimination skills and readies them for the more detailed explorations of toddlerhood. However, hands-on instruction alone does not constitute inquiry teaching. There is a substantial difference between an open-ended, inquiry approach to an activity and an approach that is hands-on but does not encourage problem solving and inquiry. For example, one approach to teaching the concept that water expands when it freezes might be as follows:

1. Fill a plastic container with water.
2. Place the container in the freezer and have the children observe the condition of the water after a period of time.
3. Ask the children, "What happened? How would you explain this?"

Compare this lesson to another way to approach the same concept. Assemble materials and present the following challenge: "Can you prove at least three things that happen or don't happen to water when it freezes? Be prepared to share what you have discovered with others."

Both lessons provide children with a teacher-selected topic and a hands-on experience. The first, however, offers only one strategy (a procedure) that can be used to demonstrate an already given solution (water expands). While this is a useful strategy, the second approach promotes inquiry because it requires children to first figure out what they observe happening or not happening to water when it freezes and then plan a way to convince someone else of their discovery.

Although both activities are hands on, use process skills, and require physical manipulation of objects to gain an understanding of a science concept, only the second activity involves problem solving from which inquiry is most likely to spring. By listening to students who are actively engaged in conceptual problem solving and investigations, the teacher will uncover many scientific misconceptions, which will provide instructional materials for years to come (refer to Unit 6 for additional problem-solving suggestions).

Managing the Class

Distributing Materials and Working Together

A lack of classroom management can wreck your best plans. In addition to planning your lesson, give a few moments to consider how you will organize your children and the materials they will work with. The following suggestions will start you thinking.

Organize Children for Learning

Organize the class into teams of no more than four children. It is essential that each child have responsibilities on the team. Designate a team leader, who is responsible for seeing that all materials are correctly obtained, used, and put away. The recorder is responsible for obtaining and putting away, recording, writing books, and reporting results to the class. Appoint a judge, who has the final word in any science activity-related disputes, and an investigator, who is responsible for seeing that the team follows the directions when conducting the science activity. Make sure the children understand their responsibilities. These job roles are easily adaptable for use with most cooperative learning experiences.

Organize Materials for Learning

Materials can be organized several ways. One possibility is to distribute materials from four distribution centers in your room. Each center should be labeled one, two, three, four and contain all the equipment needed for an exploration. Then, number the children in the team one, two, three, four. The ones are responsible for acquiring the materials at distribution center one, the twos at center number two, and so on. Locate the distribution sites in separate areas of the room to reduce confusion, give a time limit for collection of materials, and provide a materials list so the team leaders can check to see that everything needed is on their table.

If you are teaching a structured lesson, you may want to make a list that indicates what each individual will do during the exploration. For example, if you want the children to explore concepts of surface tension with soap and pepper, have the ones pour the water into the cup, the twos tap the pepper in the cup, the threes coat the toothpick with liquid detergent, and the fours plunge the toothpick into the pepper.

Science explorations are fun. To maintain discipline while conducting complex activities with the whole class, an organization system for children and materials is needed. Establish simple and clear rules for classroom operation. Once the children are comfortable with the rules and organization system, you need only periodically review what is expected to keep them on task.

Pocket Management Strategy

Primary teacher Maureen Awbrey prepares for managing children in learning areas by making a personalized library card pocket for each child in her class. Each pocket has the child's picture on it and a distinguishing symbol such as an orange triangle or a green square. Children learn their classroom jobs and become familiar with symbols as they review their job list each morning.

After the children are comfortable with their personal symbols and pockets, Mrs. Awbrey introduces them to the learning areas of the room. Each area is designated by a pocket and symbols that tell the children how many individuals may work in an area. For example, four circles mean that four children are permitted in the area. If Mrs. Awbrey does not want the children to use certain equipment, she places a "closed" sign in the area.

Colored strips of laminated paper containing the child's name and that of an available learning area are kept in the child's pocket. These strips are called *tickets*. When Scott wants to construct a zoo in the block center, he takes his block ticket to the block area and puts it in the pocket. When he is finished working in the block area, he removes his ticket and puts it in a basket. In this way, children rotate through the room and are exposed to a variety of learning experiences.

Sample Investigations

The following investigations allow children to develop science processes as they conduct scientific investigations.

ACTIVITIES

HOW LONG DOES IT TAKE FOR A PAPER TOWEL TO DRY?

CONCEPT: Water disappears into the air during evaporation.

OBJECTIVE: To investigate the length of time it takes for paper towels to dry.

MATERIALS: Bowl of water, paper towels, cardboard, pie plates, variety of fabric swatches..

NATURALISTIC AND INFORMAL ACTIVITIES: Encourage children to experiment with wetting the different swatches of fabric and hanging them on the clothesline. Say, ARE ALL OF YOUR CLOTHES DRY? ARE SOME DRIER THAN OTHERS? WHY DO YOU THINK THAT HAPPENED?

STRUCTURED ACTIVITY: Ask children how their clothes get dry after they are washed. Are they put in a dryer? Are they hung on a line? Say, LET'S PRETEND THESE PAPER TOWELS ARE CLOTHES AND SEE HOW LONG THEY WILL TAKE TO DRY.
1. Soak a paper towel under water.
2. Squeeze out all the water that you can.
3. Open the towel and lay it on a pie plate.
4. Leave the plate on a table. Have children check and record the time.
5. Feel the towel at 30-minute intervals to see if it is dry. When it is dry, record the time.
6. How long did the towel take to dry? Have the groups share their findings on a class chart.

EXTENSIONS: Do you think it will make a difference if you put the towels in the sun or in the shade? Which wet towel do you think will dry first? Do you think wind will make a difference in how fast a paper towel dries? Set up a fan, and create wind. Measure the difference in drying time.

CAN GOLDFISH BE TRAINED?

CONCEPT: Animals can be trained to respond to light and other signals.

OBJECTIVE: Children should be able to train a goldfish to respond to light.

MATERIALS: Goldfish (at least two), tank, flashlight, fish food.

PROCEDURE: Ask, HAVE YOU EVER TRAINED A PET TO DO SOMETHING? Children usually have a dog that sits or stays. DO YOU THINK THAT GOLDFISH KNOW WHEN IT IS TIME TO EAT? HOW COULD WE TRAIN THE GOLDFISH TO GO TO A CORNER OF THEIR TANK TO EAT? Discuss possibilities.

Shine the flashlight into a corner of the tank. Ask, DO THE GOLDFISH SWIM TOWARD THE LIGHT? (No.) Each day sprinkle a little food in the water as you shine the flashlight in the corner (Figure 33–7). Ask, WHAT ARE THE FISH DOING? (Swimming toward the light.)

Do this for several days in a row. Then, shine the light without adding food. Ask, WHAT HAPPENS WHEN YOU ONLY SHINE THE LIGHT? (Fish come to the light, but only for a couple of days if food is not offered.)

EXTENSIONS: Ask, WILL THE FISH RESPOND TO DIFFERENT SIGNALS? DO BOTH FISH RESPOND IN THE SAME WAY? WILL DIFFERENT TYPES OF FISH RESPOND IN THE SAME WAY? Have children record their attempts and successes. They may want to write stories about their fish, tell others, and invite other classes to see their trained fish.

FIGURE 33–7 "Can a goldfish be trained to respond to light?"

FIGURE 33–8 Use a chalkboard for investigating the drying time of wet spots.

Examples of Topics to Investigate

1. Can we design a container to keep an ice cube from melting?
2. Will mold grow on bread?
3. Can we get a mealworm to change direction?
4. What objects in our classroom will a magnet attract?
5. Can a seed grow without dirt?
6. Which part of a wet spot dries faster: the top, middle, or bottom? Or does it all dry at the same time (Figure 33–8)?

Computer Activities That Enhance Logical Thinking

Children like to have fun when they learn. Why not make precomputer activities fun while developing early problem-solving skills? Have students look for patterns, guess the rules that might govern those patterns, and apply the rules to a situation.

The Floor Turtle

In the following scenario, Mrs. Red Fox is aware that young children learn best by becoming physically involved in activities. The teacher selects Valiant Turtle by Harvard Associates, Inc. to spark interaction among her students. Commands typed into Terrapin LOGO move the cordless computerized floor turtle forward or backward and turn as far to the right or left as the child desires.

Sara types TFD 10 (turtle forward 10 steps). "Oh, look, the turtle went forward," she says. Sara then types TBK (turtle backward), TRT, and TLT (turtle right or left turn, respectively), and a number of steps. The class is delighted with the floor turtle's response and everyone wants a turn.

Trang Fung gets ready to make a prediction. She asks, "What commands are you going to give the turtle, Sara? Okay, I think the floor turtle will stop right here." Trang Fung places a piece of masking tape with her name on it on the predicted spot. She waits as Sara gives commands. "Wow, I was really close. Let's try it again, Sara."

As the children play with the floor turtle, they observe unit amounts and estimate distances. Steps and direction are predicted. The following are suggested floor turtle activities.

1. Put a sticker on the floor where the floor turtle will start and another where it stops. Measure the distance.
2. Have a child stand with feet apart in the path of the turtle. Ask, "How many steps will the turtle need to take to pass under Dean's legs?"
3. Have the turtle pass over two different types of floor surfaces. Have students investigate: "Will the turtle travel the same distance over carpet as it will over tile?" This activity will also help children begin to understand friction.
4. Send the floor turtle over a certain path. Have students list the way it will have to move. Ask, "Which way will involve the fewest number of steps?" Children can interact with each other, form and test hypotheses, list a sequence of steps that the floor turtle will follow, and become aware that they control the turtle.

Recognizing Rules for Patterns and Shapes

Elements of a pattern can be recognized and rules developed that apply to those patterns. Gertrude's Secrets by The Learning Company gives children a chance to keep patterns going by offering attribute games. Gertrude's Secrets is an older game but still a favorite with children. Electronic Builder by KidWare also allows children to make their own patterns. Before introducing the pattern games, show the children the space bar and the up, down, left, and right keys on the computer. Mrs. Red Fox designs an off-computer activity that prepares the students for the software.

Mrs. Red Fox makes squares, diamonds, and hexagons with three different colors of construction paper. She shows the children three pieces together that would fit a certain rule; for example, all shapes held up are red. She asks, "Can you tell me a rule for this group?" "Yes," says Dean. "Those shapes are all red." "Good," answers Mrs. Red Fox.

She continues to play games with a secret rule. For example, she holds up cutouts that are all diamonds or all yellow, and the children guess what the rule is. Then she asks, "If all of these pieces are yellow, what other pieces will also fit in this group?" When the children master this game, they are ready to play the game "Loop" on Gertrude's Secrets.

The cutout shapes can also be used to make an attribute train. A piece is selected at random to make the train's "engine." "Cars" are made by attaching a shape that is different in only one way, either shape or color, to the previous one. The game continues until all the shapes have joined the train. Play a game called "Trains" on Gertrude's Secrets when children fully understand the off-computer train game.

Instructional Technology Enhances Unifying Concept and Processes

Instructional technology, such as word processors and digital cameras, provides yet another way for children to document and enhance their science investigations. The focus in the following scenario is on the *National Science Education Standard* of Unifying Concepts and Processes of *change*, *constancy*, and *measurement*.

How My Tree Changes and Stays the Same

Mr. Brown takes the opportunity to encourage his primary students' interest in learning more about the plants and trees that they have observed in the school yard and focus on the unifying concepts of change, constancy, and measurement. At the beginning of the year, he takes his students outside to "adopt" a plant for the year. He takes along a digital camera and lets each team of two or three students take a digital picture of a plant or tree they are interested in observing. He encourages the students to choose a plant that is no taller than they are and to make observations about their plant.

George's team chooses a young sugar maple tree. Mr. Brown asks the team to describe its tree. "It has funny-shaped leaves with pointy tips—and they're green," says Jim. Diana points, "The leaves look almost like my hand, with five 'fingers.'" Mr. Brown asks about the bark of the tree. "Well, it's kind of smooth compared to that tree over there," says George, "and it's kind of gray." Mr. Brown asks the children whether they think their tree will change during the year. Diana says, "It will get bigger." George wonders if trees have flowers like other plants do. Mr. Brown lets the children take pictures of their tree or plant with the digital camera.

Mr. Brown asks, "How can you measure how tall your plant is?" George suggests string, and the children use lengths to measure their plant. Diana takes a picture of George and Jim using a string to measure the height of the small tree. The children also decide to use the string to wrap around the trunk of the tree near the bottom. George suggests that one of them stand by the tree so that they can see how it changes.

The children record their observations, and back in the classroom Mr. Brown downloads the digital images and puts them onto disks for the students to use in their observations. Mr. Brown uses Claris's ClarisWorks, an integrated software package with word processing and drawing capabilities, in his classroom. Mr. Brown has already created a "stationary" file, which cannot be changed by students. When students open the file, it becomes an "untitled" document that is saved by the students when it is time to save. Mr. Brown's stationary file contains a text box that is already set up with very large text and a simple font at the bottom and room at the top for the digital images. Students open the file, insert the digital image, and type their observations in the text box.

The children took their adopted trees very seriously, and often came running into the room with observations about the changes in their plant. About three weeks after the students made their original observations, Diana came into class very excited about the leaves on her tree: "Our tree is changing color." Mr. Brown took advantage of the excitement and took the students, and the digital camera, outside so everyone could make the next set of observations. "Our leaves are turning orange," exclaimed Jim. George noticed that some of the leaves were starting to fall onto the ground. "Look at this," said George, "the last time it had more leaves on this branch, didn't it?" The team wasn't sure about George's observation. Mr. Brown encouraged the students to take another picture so that they could compare the tree to their last picture.

The observations and measurements continued throughout the year. The students took digital images and made a new page for their tree's "change over time" document. In the spring, some of the plants had flowers. Mr. Brown asked, "How have your plants changed during the year?" He used the ClarisWorks documents that the students had done over the year to create a "slideshow" of each team's plant changes over time. The slideshow feature of ClarisWorks turns any word processing, drawing, painting, or even spreadsheet document into a slideshow that can run by itself and continue looping around throughout the day or be shown one slide at a time. PowerPoint 2000 by Microsoft is another software program that can be used to accomplish the above activities.

As students viewed the slideshows, they made comments about how their trees and other plants had changed or stayed the same. "Look at how much bigger our tree got," said Jim. "Yeah, and it changed color during the year. How come Michael's team tree didn't change color?" asked Diane. Michael's team had chosen a young pine tree. Mr. Brown encouraged the students to continue to examine the changes that had occurred during the year as they watched the slideshows and to explore the similarities and differences in how the plants change. Jim wondered what the tree would look like when it was older, so he went out to find a more mature tree to observe.

The activities that have been described on the preceding page are especially useful for children living in areas where seasons are not as pronounced as in other areas. For example, using a digital camera to capture the changes in a tree throughout the year in Florida would help children see the subtle changes that they might otherwise miss.

Instructional technology provided a wonderful means by which student observation could be displayed and evaluated. Digital images made comparison of trees over time much easier, and the slideshow provided additional opportunities to see the changes flash by in minutes. Additionally, the children's documents could be printed out for inclusion in student portfolios or display on bulletin boards.

Summary

When children investigate, they develop science processes and science concepts. Science concepts are the "big ideas" in science; they explain the way the world is viewed.

Primary age children continue to be avid investigators. At this age, they refine their inquiry skills and begin to understand abstract symbols that are tied to concrete experiences. This unit suggests science learning experiences that enhance the primary child's special fondness for collecting and playing games. Ideas for classroom management and use of simple classroom investigations are also suggested.

KEY TERMS

magnifier	determining variables	hypothesis
lens	variable	
invertebrates	conclusions	

SUGGESTED ACTIVITIES

1. Observe differences in the ability to classify. Design lessons that take advantage of children's abilities to observe detail.
2. Begin a collection of 20 objects from nature. How could you use this collection in your teaching? Use the collection in this way and share children's responses with others.
3. Select a collecting topic such as leaves. Describe naturalistic, directed, and structured collecting activities that might take place with leaves. Observe children as they collect and identify each of these three types of learning.
4. Identify the process skills and science concepts emphasized in the investigation activities in this unit. Design an investigation and introduce it to primary age children. Record children's responses. What type of questions did children ask? How did they go about conducting the investigation?
5. Children can use word processors and reference programs to write about science topics. Evaluate one or more of the following computer programs.
6. Use one of the software packages below with children. Ask what they like about the programs and what they would like to see changed.

Word Processing and Integrated Packages

ClarisWorks. Santa Clara, CA: K-12 Micromedia, Inc.

EasyBook. Pleasantville, NY: Sunburst Communications.

Electronic Builder. KidWare Redmond, WA: Edmark.

Gertrude's Secrets. Fremont, CA: The Learning Company.

KidWorks Deluxe or KidWorks 2. Torrance, CA: Davidson & Associates.

Storybook Weaver Deluxe. Minneapolis, MN: MECC.

The Children's Writing and Publishing Center. Fremont, CA: The Learning Company.

Valiant Turtle. Harvard Associates, Inc.

Reference Packages

There are a number of reference programs available. Many of them will also read the text for children. Most include text, pictures, sounds, and video clips.

Compton's Interactive Encyclopedia. Carlsbad, CA: Compton's New Media.

First Connections: The Golden Book Encyclopedia. Lansing, MI: Hartley.

Random House Kids Encyclopedia. Glendale, CA: Knowledge Adventure.

Ultimate Children's Encyclopedia. Fremont, CA: The Learning Company.

REVIEW

A. Give two differences in the way that primary age children learn and the way that kindergarten age children learn.

B. How are primary grade science experiences similar to kindergarten lessons?

C. Why encourage children to collect? When collecting, what preparations and procedures will you follow before, during, and after collecting?

D. What are invertebrates and why should they be mentioned in the early grades?

FURTHER READING AND RESOURCES

Campbell, S. (1987). A playful introduction to computers. *Science and Children, 24*(8), 38–40.

Green, B., & Schlichting, S. (1985). *Explorations and investigations.* Riverview, FL: The Idea Factory, Inc.

Haughland, S. W., & Wright, J. L. (1997). *Young children and technology: A world of discovery.* Boston, MA: Allyn & Bacon.

Kneidel, S. S. (1993). *Creepy crawlies and the scientific method.* Golden, CO: Fulcrum.

Lind, K. K. (1993). Collector's choice. *Science and Children, 31*(3), 34–35.

Lind, K. K. (1997). Science in the developmentally appropriate integrated curriculum. In C. H. Hart, D. C. Burts, & R. Charlesworth (Eds.), *Integrated curriculum and developmentally appropriate practice: Birth to age eight.* Albany, NY: SUNY Press.

Lowery, L. F. (1997). *NSTA pathways to the science standards.* Arlington, VA: National Science Teachers Association.

McClurg, P. (1984). Don't squash it! Collect it! *Science and Children, 21*(8), 8–10.

McIntyre, M. (1984). *Early childhood and science.* Washington, DC: National Science Teachers Association.

National Research Council. (1996). *National science education standards.* Washington, DC: National Academy Press.

National Research Council. (1999). *Selecting instructional materials: a guide for K–12*. Washington, DC: National Academy Press.

Smith, E., Blackmer, M., & Schlichting, S. (1987). *Super science sourcebook*. Riverview, FL: The Idea Factory, Inc.

VanDeman, B. (1984). The fall collection. *Science and Children*, 27(1), 20–21.

Zeitler, W. R., & Barufaldi, J. P. (1988). *Elementary school science instruction—a perspective for teachers*. White Plains, NY: Longman.

UNIT 34
Life Science

OBJECTIVES

After reading this unit, you should be able to:

◆ Develop an understanding of life science concepts that are appropriate for primary grade children.

◆ Develop structured and unstructured science learning activities with primary age children.

◆ Describe appropriate conditions for the care of animals in the classroom.

◆ Apply unit webbing strategies to life science content.

Whether they live in large cities or small towns, children display an eagerness to learn about the living things around them. The countless opportunities that exist to acquire firsthand knowledge of plants and animals make learning fun for both children and teacher. The *National Science Education Standards* (NSES) emphasize that during the primary grades, children begin to develop an understanding of biological concepts through direct experience with living things, their life cycles, and their habitats. Questions such as "Why did that animal eat the other animal?" and "Do all animals eat plants?" are the first of many such questions that begin all investigations. Primary experiences lay the groundwork for the progressive development in the later grades of the major biological concepts.

This unit begins with life science concepts that are basic to primary grade learning; it then presents an example of a seed unit planned with the webbing strategy discussed in Unit 7. Next, guidelines for animal care and a variety of investigations and learning experiences with animals are described. Finally, sources for teaching about plants, animals, and the environment are suggested.

Life Science

The *National Science Education Standards* recommend that as a result of activities in the primary grades, all students should develop an understanding of the characteristics of organisms, the life cycles of organisms, and organisms and environments.

The Characteristics of Organisms

Young children's ideas about the characteristics of organisms develop from basic concepts of living and nonliving things. Piaget noted that many children associate "life" with any objects that are active in any way. Thus, movement becomes the defining characteristic of life, and anthropomorphic explanations are given to organisms. Eventually children's conception of the characteristics of life include other activities such as eating, breathing, and reproduction, but students must have a variety of experiences with organisms to develop this knowledge base.

The science standards point out that primary age children can understand that organisms have basic needs. For example, animals need air, water, and food; plants require air, water, nutrients, and light. Organisms can survive only in environments in which their needs can be met. There are many different environments that support the life of different types of organisms.

Children can begin to understand that each plant or animal has different structures that serve different functions in growth, survival, and reproduction. The behavior of individual organisms is influenced by internal cues (such as hunger) and by external cues (such as a change in the environment). Humans and other organisms have senses that help them detect internal and external cues.

Life Cycles of Organisms

The NSES emphasize that children should begin to understand that plants and animals have life cycles that include being born, developing into adults, reproducing, and eventually dying and that plants and animals closely resemble their parents.

Organisms and Their Environments

Upper primary students will begin to develop the understanding that all animals depend on plants. Some animals eat plants for food and other animals eat the animals that eat plants. A plant or animal's behavior patterns are related to the nature of their environment, including the availability of food and resources and the physical characteristics of the environment.

Children will begin to note that all organisms cause changes in the environment in which they live. Some of these changes are detrimental to the organisms and some are beneficial. Humans depend on their natural

and construct environments and also change the environments in beneficial and harmful ways.

Planning for Life Science

A knowledge of life science concepts is basic to planning and teaching life science to primary age children. The fundamental life science concepts are the major ideas that we want students to understand. Thus, learning experiences are planned around them. For example, Figure 34–1 shows a unit planning web, as described in Unit 7, that focuses learning activities around three basic concepts involving the topic of seeds. The following concepts can be used in lesson planning and are basic to understanding plants, animals, and all living things.

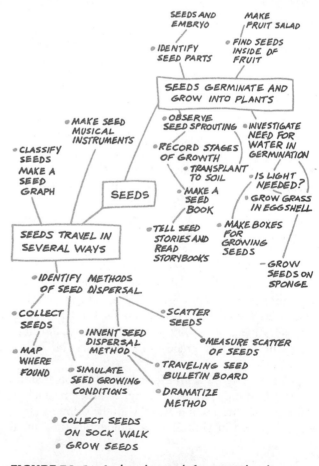

FIGURE 34–1 A planning web for a seed unit.

Living Things

1. Living things can be distinguished from nonliving things.
2. Plants and animals are living things.
3. Animals and plants affect one another.
4. Living things have unique features that help them live in different kinds of places.
5. Most living things need water, food, and air.

Seeds and Plants

1. Seeds differ in size, shape, color, and texture.
2. Seeds **germinate** and grow into a specific type of plant.
3. Some seeds grow inside fruits.
4. Some seeds grow into flowers, shrubs, and trees.
5. Some seeds grow into food that we eat.
6. Seeds are dispersed in several ways.
7. Seeds need water, light, and warmth to grow.
8. Seeds and plants grow and change.
9. Leaves tend to grow toward light, and roots tend to grow into the soil.
10. Plants grow from seeds, roots, and stems.
11. Some plant forms do not have seeds, roots, or stems.
12. Some plants grow in the light, and some plants grow in the dark.
13. Some plants change in different seasons.

Animals

1. Animals need food, water, shelter, and a unique temperature.
2. Animals have individual characteristics.
3. Animals have unique adaptations. They move, eat, live, and behave in ways that help them survive.
4. Animals go through a life cycle.
5. Pets are animals that depend on us for special care. We love and take care of our pets.
6. There are many kinds of pets.
7. Different kinds of pets need different types of care to grow and be healthy.
8. Aquariums are places for fish and other living things to grow.

Planning and Teaching a Seed Unit

The learning experiences suggested in this unit follow the format described in Unit 7 and are designed to meet the needs, interests, and developmental levels of primary age children described in Unit 33. Each lesson states a concept, a teaching objective based on what the child should be able to do, materials needed, and suggestions for teaching the concept. Extensions, integrations, and possible evaluation procedures are indicated in the body of the lesson when appropriate and at the end of the unit.

ACTIVITIES

SEEDS

CONCEPT: Seeds germinate and grow into plants; seeds contain a baby plant.

OBJECTIVE: Discover that a seed has three parts. Identify the **embryo** inside of the seed.

MATERIALS: Lima beans that have been soaked overnight (if you soak them longer, they may rot), paper towels, a variety of seeds.

PROCEDURE: Show children a lima bean seed. Ask, WHAT DO YOU THINK MIGHT BE INSIDE OF THIS SEED? CAN YOU DRAW A PICTURE OF HOW YOU THINK THE INSIDE OF THE SEED LOOKS?

Have children open the lima bean seed with their thumbnails. Ask, WHAT DO YOU NOTICE ABOUT YOUR SEED? HOW DOES THE SEED FEEL? IS THERE A SMELL? DOES THE INSIDE OF THE SEED LOOK LIKE THE PICTURE YOU HAVE DRAWN? Discuss similarities and differences. Have students draw a picture of the bean after it is opened.

Point out that there are three basic parts in all seeds: the seed cover (for protection), food for the baby plant (*cotyledon*), and the baby plant itself (*embryo*). Introduce the term *germinate*. (This is when the seed grows—it sprouts.) Have students paint a picture of the plant as they think it will look when it has grown.

NATURALISTIC AND INFORMAL ACTIVITIES: Have a variety of seeds in the science center so the children can soak them and then see if they have the same parts as the lima beans. When you observe children opening the beans ask, "How are the seeds like the lima beans? How are they different?" This could be done in an unstructured way as part of a seed center. In beans and peas, there are two seed halves. In seeds such as corn and rice, there is only one seed half or cotyledon (Figure 34–2).

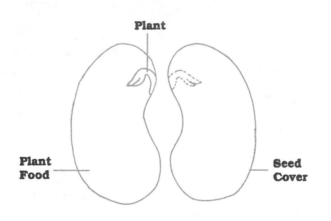

FIGURE 34–2 All seeds have three basic parts.

BABY PLANTS

CONCEPT: Seeds germinate and grow into plants.

OBJECTIVE: Observe and describe how seeds grow into plants. Describe how the embryo grows into a plant.

MATERIALS: Lima beans, paper towels, water, cotton, clear containers or glass tumblers.

PROCEDURE: Say, YESTERDAY WE SAW A BABY PLANT INSIDE OF A SEED. DO YOU THINK IT WILL GROW INTO A BIG PLANT? LET'S FIND OUT.

Soak lima beans overnight. Have children line the inside of a drinking glass with a wet, folded paper towel. Then, stuff cotton into the glass. This holds the paper towel in place.

Put soaked seeds between the paper towel and glass. Then, pour water to the edge of the bottom seed in the glass (the paper towel and cotton will absorb most of the liquid). The sprouting seeds will be easy for the children to see through the clear container. Have the children draw the sprouting lima bean and write a story about the investigation.

Ask, WHAT DO YOU SEE HAPPENING? WHAT COLORS DO YOU SEE? WHICH WAY ARE THE ROOTS GROWING? WHERE IS THE EMBRYO GETTING ITS FOOD? (From the cotyledon.) As the plant gets larger, the seed becomes smaller. In fact, the plant will begin to die when the cotyledon is used up.

When the food provided by the seed is used up, ask, WHAT OTHER TYPE OF FOOD CAN WE GIVE THE PLANT? Discuss the possibility of transplanting the young plants to soil as a continuation of the project.

EXTENSION: This concept can be extended throughout the year. It is a good science activity with the advantage of going from simple observation to experimentation. The concept lends itself to a short study of seeds or an extended study of how light, moisture, heat, color, soil, air, and sound affect the growth of plants.

GLASS GARDEN

CONCEPT: Moisture is needed for seeds to sprout.

OBJECTIVE: Observe the growth of seeds.

MATERIALS: Mung beans, cheesecloth, jar.

PROCEDURE: Soak a handful of mung beans in a jar, and cover the jar tightly with cheesecloth. Protect the jar from light by wrapping it in a towel. Then, have children simulate rain by rinsing and draining the seeds three times a day. Have children predict what will happen to the seeds. Ask, DID THE SEEDS SPROUT EVEN THOUGH THEY WERE IN THE DARK? (Yes.) DO YOU THINK THE SEEDS WILL SPROUT IF WE KEEP THEM IN THE DARK BUT DO NOT WATER THEM? (No.) Repeat the activity, and investigate what will happen if the seeds are kept in the dark and not watered.

NATURALISTIC AND INFORMAL ACTIVITIES: Have a variety of seeds in the science center so the children can experiment with them to see if they all react in the same way as the mung beans.

EXTENSION: You may want to make a salad and top it off with the mung sprouts. Several variables can be tried, one at a time of course, so that children can investigate variables in sprouting seeds and growing plants.

TEACHING NOTE: Lima beans usually work well, but mung beans show the speedy growth that impatient young children may demand. Mung beans will not grow as tall as others, but they will show growth. Corn, on the other hand, takes longer than lima beans to germinate.

WHAT'S INSIDE?

CONCEPT: Seeds come from the fruit of plants.

OBJECTIVE: Discover that seeds develop inside of fruit.

MATERIALS: A variety of fruits, pinecones, flowers, plastic knives, paper towels.

PROCEDURE: Select several fruits, and place them on a table with plastic knives and paper towels. Have children examine the fruits and ask, WHAT DO YOU THINK IS INSIDE OF THE FRUIT?

Invite children to cut the fruits open. Ask, WHAT DID YOU FIND? HOW MANY SEEDS DID YOU FIND? ARE ALL OF THE SEEDS THE SAME COLOR? WHAT DO YOU THINK THE SEEDS ARE DOING INSIDE OF THE FRUIT?

Explain that a fruit is the part of a flowering plant that holds the seeds. Ask, CAN YOU NAME ANY FLOW-ERS IN YOUR BACKYARD THAT HAVE SEEDS? (Sunflowers, dandelions.) ARE THEY FRUITS? (Yes.) Point out that not all fruits are edible.

EXTENSION: Show a picture of a pine tree. Ask, DOES THIS TREE HAVE FLOWERS? (No.) DOES IT HAVE SEEDS? (Yes.) WHERE ARE THE SEEDS? (Cones.) Have children examine pinecones to find out how the seeds are attached. Compare the seeds enclosed in fruits to those attached to cones. Point out that seeds can grow inside of a flower, surrounded by fruit, or in a cone.

TRAVELING SEEDS

CONCEPT: Seeds need to travel to grow.

OBJECTIVE: Investigate why seeds travel by simulating growing conditions.

MATERIALS: Two containers, soil, seeds.

PROCEDURE: Have children bring in seeds from the school grounds or their neighborhood. Examine the seeds, and discuss where they were found. Hold up a seed and ask, DO WE HAVE THIS KIND OF PLANT ON OUR SCHOOL GROUNDS? (No.) HOW DID THE SEED GET HERE? (Wind.) I WONDER WHY IT BLEW AWAY?

After discussing, ask, DO YOU THINK THAT SEEDS WILL GET A CHANCE TO GROW IF THEY ALL FALL AT THE BOTTOM OF THE PARENT PLANT? LET'S SEE WHAT HAPPENS WHEN SEEDS FALL IN ONE PLACE.

Fill two containers with seeds. Have children help plant seeds close together in one container and far apart in the other. Ask, WHICH CONTAINER DO YOU THINK WILL GROW THE MOST PLANTS? Discuss and list suggested reasons. Have children take turns giving all of the seeds water, light, warmth. Watch them for many days. Have children measure the growth of the plants and record what they see. Then ask, IN WHICH CONTAINER DO SEEDS GROW BETTER? (Spaced apart.) In this way, children will see a reason for a seed to travel.

SCATTERING SEEDS

CONCEPT: Seeds are adapted to disperse in several ways.

OBJECTIVE: Identify several ways of dispersing seeds.

MATERIALS: Seeds, magnifying glasses, mittens.

PROCEDURE: Arrange seeds from weeds, grasses, and trees in a science center. Have a magnifying glass and mitten available for students to examine seeds. Give basic directions, and let children "mess around" and explore the seeds. Ask, WHICH SEEDS SEEM TO CATCH IN THE MITTEN? (Hairy ones or ones with burrs.) Have children predict and draw what they think they will see when they observe a burr through a magnifying glass. Say, LET'S LOOK THROUGH THE MAGNIFYING GLASS AND DRAW WHAT WE SEE. Discuss the before and after pictures and describe the tiny hooks and how they are used. Introduce the term *disperse* and use it in sentences and stories about the burr with tiny hooks. Refer to Unit 33 for suggestions for the use of magnifiers.

EXTENSION: Take children outside to explore how different seeds are dispersed by shaking seeds from pods, beating grass seed spikes to release grains, brushing hairy seeds against clothes, and releasing winged seeds. Compare what happens to each seed.

INVENT A SEED

CONCEPT: Seeds are modified to travel in a specific way.

OBJECTIVE: Modify a seed for travel.

MATERIALS: Dried bean or pea seeds, a junk box (colored paper, glue, rubber bands, tape, cotton, ice cream bar sticks, balloons, pipe cleaners, paper clips, string), scissors.

PROCEDURE: Show children a coconut (the largest seed) and ask, HOW DO YOU THINK THIS COCONUT TRAVELS? (Water.) Display pods such as milkweed to demonstrate a pod that bursts and casts its seeds to the wind. HOW WILL THE BURR TRAVEL? (Catch on things.) Birds and other animals eat fruit such as berries. Then, they digest the fruit and leave the seeds somewhere else. WHY DID THE BIRD WANT TO EAT BERRIES? (They were good to eat.) Children will conclude that seeds have specific modifications to travel in specific ways. To reinforce the term *modify*, have students modify their clothes for different weather or activities.

Ask, IF YOU WERE A SEED, HOW WOULD YOU LIKE TO TRAVEL? Discuss preferences, and then assign one of the following means of travel to each small group of children: attract animal, catch on fur, pops or is shot out, floats on water, or carried by wind. Give each group seeds and junk box materials, and ask them to invent a way for their seed to travel. When the children have completed their creations, have them demonstrate how their seed travels (Figure 34–3).

EXTENSION: Make a bulletin board that displays the modified seeds traveling in the way the students intended. Have children examine seeds and think of other objects that work in the same way. (For example, the burr is the inspiration for the development of Velcro®.)

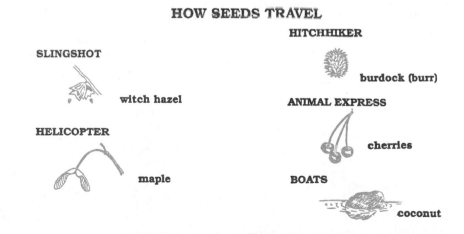

HOW SEEDS TRAVEL

FIGURE 34–3 Seed dispersal methods.

FIGURE 34–4 "Can you grow healthy grass hair for your eggshell people?"

1. **Sock walk.** Drag a sock through a field. Then cover with soil and water, and wait for a variety of plants to grow from the seeds caught on the sock. Or put the sock in a plastic bag, shake the seeds out of the sock, and examine them. Ask, "What types of seeds did the sock attract?"
2. **Egghead hair.** Draw a face on half of an eggshell. Place the egg in an egg carton, and fill the eggshell with moist soil. Sprinkle grass seed on top, then water. Grass will grow in five days. Attach construction paper feet with clay to display (plastic eggs also work well). To show the benefit of light on leaves, first grow the grass hair in the dark. Discuss the resulting pale, thin grass and ask, "How can we make the grass green and healthy?" Place the egg person in the light, and be prepared to trim the healthy green hair (Figure 34–4).
3. **Collections.** Seeds make an easy and fun collection. Collect from your kitchen, playground, or neighborhood.

Investigation Questions for Growing Seeds

1. How deep can you plant a seed and still have it grow?
2. If you crush a seed, will it still grow?
3. In what direction will the sprouts in the glass garden grow if the glass is turned upside down?

Subject Integrations

Science and Math

1. *Seed walk.* Take a seed walk around the school. Ask, "Where shall we look for seeds? What do you think we might see?" Gather seeds, and use as materials to sort, match, count, and weigh in the science center.
2. *How many ways.* Provide a box of seeds for students to classify. Compare size, shape, color, and texture of the seeds. Construct a seed graph.
3. *Greenhouse.* Simulate a greenhouse by placing a plastic bag over a container of germinating seeds. Place seeds in a jar on a moist paper towel. Put the jar inside of a plastic bag, and record the amount of time needed for sprouting. Compare sprouting time with seeds that are not placed in a plastic bag (Figure 34–5).
4. *Cooking.* Create a fruit salad with the fruits gathered for seed activities. Or measure ingredi-

FIGURE 34–5 Make your own greenhouse.

ents, and follow a recipe to make apple pie or other tasty dishes. Nut butter can be made by passing the seeds or nuts through a nut grinder. Store in the refrigerator, and use as spreads.

5. *Seed count.* Have the children add to find out how many seeds were planted or count the number of seeds planted by each child and multiply to see how many seeds there are in all. Next, give problems using different numbers of seeds and children.

Science and Social Studies

1. *Seeds swell.* Years ago, seeds were used to stretch tight leather shoes. To simulate this, fill a small bottle with beans, cover beans with water, close the bottle with plastic wrap, and secure with rubber bands. Beans will swell and lift the plastic.

2. *Neighborhood map.* Have children bring in seeds that they have found. Make a map of where the seeds might be found.

3. *Seeds can be edible.* Try to bridge the gap between the processed food that the children eat and its raw form. Show pictures of wheat, fruit trees, and vegetables growing. Discuss edible seeds such as pumpkin, sunflower, peanuts, and those that are not eaten such as watermelon and apple seeds.

4. *Careers.* Discuss different jobs associated with growing plants. Make hats, and act out these jobs.

5. *Woodworking.* Create boxes and planters for growing seeds.

Science and Language Arts

1. Have students remove the *s* from *seed* and make new words (weed, feed, need, bleed).

2. Pretend you are a seed. Draw a picture, and write a story about how you will look and where you might travel.

3. Dramatize the growth of an embryo into a plant.

4. Make a seed book (in the shape of a lima bean), and fill it with bean stories and drawings.

5. Read, tell, and dramatize stories about seeds such as "Jack and the Beanstalk," "The Story of

Johnny Appleseed," or "The Popcorn Book" by Tomie dePaola.

6. Share the following books aloud, *Growing Vegetable Soup*, *The Carrot Seed*, and *From Seed to Pear*. Have the children make books using a similar theme and share with younger children.

Science and Music

1. Sing songs about seeds and plants from your music book.

2. Use seeds to create musical instruments such as maracas and other types of "shaking" instruments in tubes with plastic lids.

3. Some children can make whistles from acorn caps. Hold thumbs in a V shape, with the top of the thumbs forming the V, under the hollow side of the cap. Blow gently at the base of the V to make a sound.

Science and Art

1. Create landscapes that would be favorable for seed growth.

2. Make faces on moist sponges with birdseed. Trim the green growth into different patterns.

3. Design seed mosaics. Glue seeds to paper or cardboard to make pictures.

4. Jewelry can be made by stringing seeds with thread and needle. You may need to boil seeds and wait for them to soften. Some children might want to paint the seeds and use them to decorate costumes.

5. Stick burrs together to make a basket. What else can you make from burrs? Pinecones and walnut shells can become birds and other creatures by adding glue and construction paper.

Additional Plant Activities Based on Science Concepts

When your unit on seeds is completed, you might want to develop additional concepts about plants. Here are a few suggestions.

Concept: Plants Grow from Roots and Stems

Growing plants from cuttings can be an exciting experience for primary age children. They will enjoy observing familiar products from a grocery bag doing unfamiliar things. Investigations with cuttings are long term and provide opportunities for record keeping, process skill development, and subject integration. You will need water, light, and common vegetables to reinforce that seeds are not the only way that plants reproduce.

1. *Dish garden.* To make a dish garden, cut off the top inch of carrots, beets, or white turnips. Keep the tops in dishes of water while the children observe the roots growing. Shoots will usually appear in a week to 10 days. Ask, "Can you tell what this plant is by the leaves?"
2. *Hanging around.* Suspend a yam or a fresh sweet potato, tapered end down, in a jar filled with water. Insert toothpicks so that only one-third of the sweet potato is in the water (Figure 34–6). Put the jar in a warm, dark place until buds and roots grow. Then put it in a sunny place, and prepare a string trellis for the upcoming foliage to climb. Children can chart the number of days for root and foliage growth and observe and record changes. Ask, "What happens to the sweet potato as the vine grows?"
3. *Pineapple tops.* Cut a 2½ inch section of pineapple fruit below the leaves. Put the pineapple top in a dish with water. When the roots develop, put the plant in potting soil and make a greenhouse by covering it with a plastic bag. Keep the pineapple greenhouse warm but not in direct sunlight. In about three weeks, take the new plant out of the greenhouse, add water, and place it in the sun. Eventually, tiny pineapples may form (six to 12 months).

Concept: Molds Grow in Dark, Moist Conditions

Children have probably seen mold in their own refrigerators or bread baskets but do not realize that mold is an organism called fungi. Observing a mold garden gives children an opportunity to focus on

FIGURE 34–6 "Will a sweet potato grow in a glass of water?"

recording observations, keeping records, and writing predictions as they investigate the world of mold.

1. To begin the lesson, show the children a molding orange and ask, "What is on the orange? Is the orange good to eat? Where have you seen mold?" Make a list of the conditions of the places where mold has been found. There should be replies of "moist," "dark," and types of materials such as fruit and bread.
2. To make the mold garden, fill a glass jar about one-third full of sand. Sprinkle water on the sand, and place items that the children bring in on top of the sand. Screw the lid on the jar and begin observations, discussion, and predictions. "Which objects do you think mold will grow on first? Will any objects not grow mold?" Place the mold garden in a dark place and prepare the children to observe. Changing colors, shapes, and sizes should prove interesting.
3. You might want to mention the important role that fungus plays in breaking down materials and in returning the components to the soil.

Teaching Notes

1. Most mold of this type is harmless, but do not take any chances. Keep the lid on the jar. In addition, have children wash their hands if any moldy items are touched; do not sniff molds (check for mold allergies among students); and when the activity is completed, throw away all mold gardens without opening them and in a tightly sealed bag.

2. Growing mold in soil is speedy because it is rich in organic materials and for that reason is recommended by some science educators. However, a teacher does not know what else might be in the soil sample, ready to grow. Thus, play it safe and slow—stick to sand.

3. Mold is a type of fungus that lacks chlorophyll. Although warmth, darkness, and moisture are ideal conditions for mold growth, neither warmth nor darkness is necessary for growth. Further investigations of conditions for mold growth may be appropriate in your classroom.

Animals in the Classroom

Caring for and studying living things in the classroom and outdoors can be an excellent way to develop a respect for and knowledge of the daily requirements of all forms of life. As children care for a living thing, they seem to develop a sensitivity and sense of responsibility for the life around them. As they maintain the living organism, they become aware of the conditions under which that animal (or plant) survives as well as the conditions under which it will perish. You hope that these understandings and attitudes will carry over into the child's life and the human condition in general.

Before you think about caring for any living organisms, take the precautions listed in this unit. It is vital that living things do not suffer from too much care, such as overfeeding and handling, and too little care, such as improper diet, water, temperature, and shelter. In other words, before allowing an animal in your classroom, be sure you know how to take care of it.

Care of the animal should begin before the animal arrives. It is recommended that the entire class has an opportunity to help prepare the cage or environment. As preparations are made, discuss why you are doing so to develop the children's understanding of the specific needs of a species.

When the animal arrives in class, give the new visitor time to become acclimated to its new surroundings. The expected enthusiasm and interest that an animal visitor is likely to generate may overwhelm the newcomer. Instruct children to quietly observe the animal in pairs for brief periods of time. Then, small groups can watch, always quietly, as everyone (animal and children) adjusts to the environment.

When planning for an animal guest, ask yourself and your students the following questions.

1. What type of cage or environment does this animal require?
2. What temperature must be maintained?
3. What type of food is needed, and how should that food be presented?
4. Will the animal be able to live in the room over weekends? What will happen to the animal during vacations?
5. Is this an endangered animal? Has this animal been illegally captured or imported? For example, for each parrot of many species that a child encounters, about 10 parrots have perished in capture or transport. Or as in the case of a species such as the ball python, some animals will never eat in captivity. Limit animal use to those bred in captivity.
6. Does the animal need special lights? Many reptiles must have ultraviolet light, a warm and cool area of their cage, and live food.
7. Will this animal make a good classroom visitor? Should it be handled? Avoid impulse purchases that will lead to future problems.

Tips for Keeping Animals in the Classroom

When animals are in the classroom, care should be taken to ensure that neither the children nor the animals are harmed. Mammals protect themselves and their young by biting, scratching, and kicking. Pets such as cats, dogs, rabbits, and guinea pigs should be handled properly and should not be disturbed when eating. For example, rats, rabbits, hamsters, and mice are best picked up by the scruff of the neck, with a hand placed under the body for support. In addition:

1. Check school district procedures to determine if there are any local regulations to be observed. Personnel at the local humane society or zoo are often very cooperative in assisting teachers to create a wholesome animal environment in the classroom. However, zoos receive numerous requests for adoption and usually do not want classroom animals for their collection or "feeder stock."
2. Caution students never to tease animals or to insert their fingers or objects through wire mesh cages. Report animal bites and scratches immediately to the school's medical authority. Provide basic first aid. Usually children follow the example set by the teacher. If you treat the animals with respect, the children will, too.
3. Purchase fish from tanks in which all fish appear healthy.
4. Discourage students from bringing personal pets to school. If they are brought into the room, they should be handled only by their owners, provided a place for fresh water and a place to rest, and then sent home.
5. Guidelines for collecting invertebrates and caring for them in the classroom are provided in Unit 33.

Teaching with Animals

Entire teaching units can be designed around observing animals in the classroom. Science concepts and subject integrations occur naturally as children observe, categorize, and communicate their experiences with animals. The benefits of observing animals far outweigh the cautions and are well worth your time and energy. Here are guiding questions and integrations that lead to investigations.

1. Describe how the animal moves. Do you move that way? See if you can figure out why the animal moves in the way that it does. Does anything make it move faster or slower? Add your observations to the observation list (Figure 34–7).

Michael Parker	Gerbils

They play.
The gerbils drink water.
They are hiding in their house.
He's lookin, playin.
He jumped back down in the house.

FIGURE 34–7 Michael observes and records some of the daily activities of gerbils.

2. How does the animal eat its food? Does it use its feet or any other part of its body to help it eat? Does it prefer a specific type of food? Make a chart or graph showing preferences.
3. What do the animals do all day? Keep a record of the animal's activities, or pinpoint several specific behaviors such as recording the type of food eaten. Are there times when the animal is more or less active? Take black-and-white Polaroid® pictures of the animal at the same time of the day. Chart the results.
4. What do the animals do at night? Children have many questions about what the classroom animals do at night. One instructional technology tool for finding an answer to the question, "What does Harry the Hamster do when we leave the room?" is to set up a digital camera, such as the Quickcam, that will take video and time-lapse pictures. For example, the camera can be set to take a picture every 15 minutes or take a five-minute video every 20 minutes. The digital images can provide a way for children to collect data to answer their questions.
5. How do animals react to different objects in their environment? Offer gerbils paper towel tubes, and watch them play. Write a story that sequences the actions of the gerbils.
6. What type of sounds do the animals make? Identify different taped animal sounds, and decide if you can tell the size of an animal by its sound. Have children tape record different sounds made by the animal such as sleeping, eating, playing, drinking. Play the tape and have children make up stories about what they think is happening.

7. How can we keep earthworms in the classroom? Have children research what is required for keeping earthworms healthy. Earthworms make good pets because they can be handled with less stress to the animal than mammals, birds, reptiles, and amphibians.

8. Describe the animal's body covering. Why do you think it has this type of covering? Compare the body coverings of different animals. Design a center that allows children to feel objects that simulate animal coverings (refer to Unit 39). Observe these coverings on a trip to the zoo.

9. How does the animal drink? Can you think of other animals that drink in the same way? Categorize ways that animals drink (a cat laps water, a snake sucks water).

10. Seven- and eight-year-olds are not ready for formal outlining yet, but building a web is a good way to organize what they are learning about animals. This type of organization refreshes memory for what children have seen or studied and relates any information they are collecting. Figure 34–8 presents their ideas in a loosely structured way. The teacher selects the main divisions and writes them on the chalkboard. Then, the children give the main points. If the children are working in committees to research different aspects, this strategy illustrates the relatedness of the entire project.

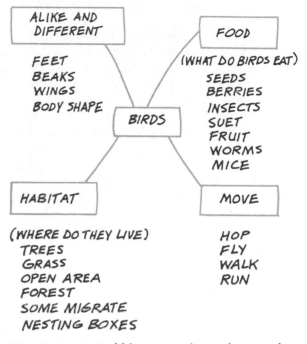

FIGURE 34–8 Webbing to review what we have learned.

A Trip to the Zoo

A trip to the zoo is a terrific way to offer children opportunities to explore the world of animals. Observing animals in a zoo setting is a high interest activity that helps children learn about animals and their needs. The following suggestions are designed to help maximize the unique setting of a zoo.

Before, During, and After

To make the most of your zoo visit, plan learning experiences that will be taught before going to the zoo, during the zoo visit, and after returning to the classroom. For example, you might want to focus your plans on the similarities and differences between reptiles and amphibians. In the following scenario, Mrs. Red Fox decides to relate class discussions and observations to turtles.

Before going to the zoo, Mrs. Red Fox prepares learning stations for her class. The stations will prepare the children for their zoo visit.

Station 1. Mrs. Red Fox prepares items that simulate body covering for the children to feel. To represent the dry, scaly skin of most reptiles, she rolls shelled sunflower seeds in clay. Oiled cellophane represents the moist, glandular skin of most amphibians. As children visit this station, they are invited to touch the simulated coverings and match picture cards of animals that might feel dry or slimy.

Station 2. To emphasize the role of camouflage in both reptiles and amphibians, the teacher prepares two pieces of black construction paper. A yellow pipe cleaner is taped to one piece of paper and a black pipe cleaner is taped to another. Ask, "Which is harder to see? How do you think this helps the animal survive? Design camouflage for a green pipe cleaner that lives in a desert."

Station 3. Some reptiles and amphibians rely on sensing vibrations to "hear" because they do not have outer ears. Mrs. Red Fox has the children tap a tuning fork on a surface and hold it near their ear. She says, "Describe what happens. Tap the fork again and press it against your cheek. What happens this time?" The class discusses how vibrations tell the animal what is happening. Some of the children begin comparing how birds and mammals hear and sense vibrations.

Station 4. Mrs. Red Fox has the children draw what they think a turtle will look like and what kind of home it will have.

At the Zoo

Mrs. Red Fox divides her class into small groups and assigns a chaperone to each small group. Each group has a turtle task card. When the groups come to the turtle exhibit, the chaperone helps the children complete the questions. The children are asked to observe and answer the following questions.

- How many turtles do you see?
- What are they doing?
- Are turtle toes like your toes?
- What are the turtles eating?
- Try walking around the areas as slowly as the turtle is moving. How does it feel?
- How are you and the turtle alike?
- How are you different?
- What other animals are living with the turtle?
- Is it easy to find the turtles in the exhibit?

As the children move to an amphibian exhibit such as frogs, toads, and salamanders, they make comparisons between the turtles and the amphibians. Mrs. Red Fox makes sure that the exhibit signs are read and questions are asked to gather additional information.

After the Zoo Visit

Mrs. Red Fox reinforces what the children have learned with a variety of learning experiences. The class makes turtle candy from caramels, nuts, and chocolate bits, and the children create a play about turtles and how they live.

Each child creates a shoe-box diorama of the turtle habitat. The teacher asks, "Did the turtle live in the same way that you thought it would? What was different? What was the same?" She has the children compare what they knew about turtles before the visit to the diorama that they have created. Mrs. Red Fox has storybooks and reference books available for children to find out more about reptiles and amphibians.

Additional Animal Activities

The following questions and activities can be used before, during, or after a trip to the zoo.

1. "How many toes does a giraffe have? What color is a giraffe's tongue? Can you touch your nose with your tongue?" Explain that giraffes use their tongues the way we use forks and spoons.
2. A snake is covered with scales. Ask, "Are the scales on a snake's stomach the same shape and size as those on its back? Does a snake have feathers? Does a snake have fur?"
3. People have several different types of teeth in their mouth. After looking in a few mouths, have the children look at a crocodile's teeth. "Are the teeth all the same type? Why do you think so?"
4. "What do we use to protect our feet? How are the feet of the sheep and deer adapted to where they live?" When in front of the hoofed animal display, have students stretch out their arms and then slowly move their arms together while looking directly ahead. "When can you see your hands?" Direct the children's attention to the hoofed animals. "Where are the deer's eyes located?" Discuss the location of the eyes, and name some advantages of having eyes that can see behind you.
5. In front of the aquarium ask, "How do you think fish breathe? Do fish have noses?" And, "Find a fish that feeds from the top of the tank. Find one that feeds from the bottom of the tank. Do any of the fish feed in the middle of the tank?"
6. "Do any of the animals have babies?" Refer to these questions when observing animal babies.

"Do the babies look like the adult? How are they different?" And, "Does the baby move around on its own? Is one of the adults taking care of the baby? What is the adult doing for the baby?"

7. Other books that can be read aloud or put in the classroom library are *The Puffins Are Back*; *The Salamander House*; *Frogs, Toads, and Lizards*; *Tigress*; and *Look Out for Turtles*.

Learning at the zoo can be an exciting experience. For a successful trip, plan activities for before, during, and after a zoo visit. If this is your first trip to the zoo, concentrate on familiar body parts and activities. For example, how does the animal move, eat, hear, see, or protect itself? Use these questions to encourage discussion of the special abilities and adaptations of animals.

Summary

Teaching life science concepts on a firsthand basis is essential to planning and teaching science to primary age children. Children display an eagerness in learning about the living things around them. This unit provides activities about seeds, plants, and molds and contains suggestions for caring for and studying living things, both in the classroom and outdoors, and keeping animals in the classroom.

Animal observations capitalize on the interest of children. The benefits of these observations far outweigh any cautions. A trip to the zoo can be a meaningful experience if specific plans are made for the visit. Prepare activities to do before, during, and after the trip. An early morning nature walk can also be used to look for local wildlife.

KEY TERMS

organisms
anthropomorphic

germinate
embryo

amphibians
camouflage

SUGGESTED ACTIVITIES

1. Use a web to plan a unit centered around two concepts important in teaching about animals to primary age children. Groups could brainstorm different concepts and put a web of the results on a large sheet of paper. Teach this unit to primary age children.

2. Would you web the example seed unit in the same way? There are countless ways to web a seed unit. Select different seed or plant concepts around which to focus your planning, and share them with the class. State your rationale.

3. Develop questions and evaluation strategies for the seed unit.

4. Design an activity for teaching with a classroom animal. How many subject integrations will you use in your animal activity?

5. Identify the teaching strategies that were discussed in Units 5, 6, and 7. Compare lists. Which strategies did you use in designing your activity?

6. Visit your school's computer lab. Identify all software that teaches or reinforces life science concepts. Preview several pieces of software that you believe will be helpful in teaching a unit on plants or animals. Choose one piece of software to use as part of a lesson or unit. Develop a lesson and teach it to a small group of children. Write down children's comments and behaviors as they interact with the software. Based on these comments and behaviors, evaluate the effectiveness of the software in helping the students better understand the concept(s) being taught. The following are suggested computer programs.

◆ Adventures with Oslo: World of Water. Lewisville, NC: Science for Kids. (Grades K–6)
◆ "Cell" ebration. Lewisville, NC: Science for Kids. (Grades K–3)
◆ EcoAdventures in the Rainforest. San Diego, CA: Chariot. (Grades 3-up)
◆ Explorapedia: The World of Nature. Redmond, WA: Microsoft. (Grades 2–6)
◆ Get Up Close. Charlotte, VT: Schoolhouse Interactive. (Ages 6+)
◆ Junior Nature Guides. New York: ICE. (Ages 7–12)
◆ Magic Schoolbus: Ocean. Redmond, WA: Microsoft. (Ages 6–10)
◆ Microscope Nature Explorer. Pound Ridge, NY: Orange Cherry. (Ages 8+)
◆ National Geographic CDs for Educators: A World of Animals, A World of Plants, Animals and How They Grow. Washington, DC: National Geographic. (Grades PreK–3)
◆ One Small Square: Backyard. Los Angeles: Virgin Sound and Vision. (Ages 8+)
◆ Sammy's Science House. Redmond, WA: Edmark. (PreK–2)
◆ The Animals 2.0. Novato, CA: Mindscape. (Grades 2–12)
◆ The Backyard. Novato, CA: Broderbund Software. (PreK–2)
◆ The World of Nature. Fairfield, CT: Queque.
◆ Zoboomafoo Animal Alphabet. The Learning Company.
◆ Zookeeper. Torrance, CA: Davidson & Associates. (Grades 1–5)
◆ Zootopia. Galesburg, MI: Lawrence Productions. (Ages 8+)
◆ Zurk's Alaskan Trek. Palo Alto, CA: Soleil Software. (Ages 6–10)
◆ Zurk's Rainforest Lab. Palo Alto, CA: Soleil Software. (PreK–3)

7. Visit two of the Web sites below. Identify the life science concepts being reinforced. How user friendly are the Web sites?

http://www.seaworld.org/infobook.html
http://www.cgee.hamline.edu/frogs/
http://www.exploratorium.edu/frogs/
http://www.kiddyhouse.com/Themes/frogs/frogs. html#lifecyclenationalgeographic.com/ngs/mags /world/world1.htl
http://www.smm.org/sin/monarchs/top.html
http://www.turtles.org

REVIEW

A. List six life science concepts that are appropriate for primary age children.
B. What planning strategy can you use to develop a life science teaching unit?
C. Answer *True* or *False*:
    _____ a. Animals can suffer from overfeeding and too much care.
    _____ b. Wait until the animal arrives before preparing a home.
    _____ c. Children should be encouraged to bring personal pets to the classroom.
    _____ d. Most school systems do not have rules about animals in the classroom.
D. What are questions you should ask yourself as you prepare for an animal in your classroom?
E. What are some appropriate technological resources that can be used with a life science unit? How would they be incorporated?

REFERENCES

Berger, M. (1992). *Look out for turtles!* New York: Harper Collins.

Cowcher, H. (1991). *Tigress*. New York: Farrar, Straus, & Giroux.

Ehlert, L. (1987). *Growing vegetable soup*. San Diego, CA: Harcourt, Brace, Jovanovich.

Gibbons, G. (1991). *The puffins are back*. New York: Harper Collins.

Krauss, R. (1945). *The carrot seed*. New York: Harper & Row.

Mazer, A. (1991). *The salamander house*. New York: Alfred A. Knopf.

Mitgutsch, A. (1971). *From seed to pear*. Minneapolis, MN: Carolrhoda Books.

The National Research Council. (1996). *National science education standards*. Washington, DC: National Academy Press.

Parker, N. W., & Wright, J. R. (1990). *Frogs, toads, and lizards*. New York: Greenwillow.

FURTHER READING AND RESOURCES

Althouse, R. (1988). *Investigating science experiences for young children*. New York: Teachers College Press.

Brainard, A. H., & Wrubel, D. H. (Ed.). (1995). *Through the rainbow: Children, science and literature*. Washington, DC: Council for Elementary Science International.

Brummet, D. C., Lind, K. K., Barman, C. R., DiSpezio, M. A., & Ostlund, L. K. (1995). *Destinations in science*. Menlo Park, CA: Addison-Wesley.

Cobb, V. (1984). *Science experiments you can eat*. New York: J. P. Lippincott Company.

Council for Elementary Science International. (1984). *Outdoor learning experiences*. Columbus, OH: SMEAC Information Reference Center.

Dean, R. A., Dean, M. M., & Motz, L. (1987). *Safety in the elementary classroom*. Washington, DC: National Science Teachers Association.

DeVito, A., & Krockover, G. H. (1980). *Creative sciencing: Ideas and activities for teachers and children*. Boston: Little, Brown.

Gega, P. (1993). *Science in elementary education*. New York: Prentice Hall.

Gega, P., & Peters, J. (1997). *Science in elementary education*. Englewood Cliffs, NJ: Prentice Hall.

Kepler, L. (1996). *Windowsill science centers*. New York: Scholastic.

Lind, K. K. (1995). A trip to the zoo. *Science and Children, 32*(8), 37–38.

Lind, K. K. (1997). Science in the developmentally appropriate integrated curriculum. In C. H. Hart, D. C. Burts, & R. Charlesworth (Eds.), *Integrated curriculum and developmentally appropriate practice: Birth to age eight*. Albany, NY: SUNY Press.

McIntyre, M. (1984). *Early childhood and science*. Washington, DC: National Science Teachers Association.

Raines, S. C., & Canady, R. J. (1992). *Story s-t-r-e-t-c-h-e-r-s for the primary grades*. Mt. Rainier, MD: Gryphon House.

Raines, S. C. (1994). *450 more story s-t-r-e-t-c-h-e-r-s for the primary grades*. Mt. Rainier, MD: Gryphon House.

Sheehan, K., & Waidner, M. (2000). *Earth child 2000*. Tulsa, OK: Council Oak Books.

Tolman, M. N., & Morton, J. O. (1987). *Life science activities for grades 2–8*. West Nyack, NY: Parker Publishing.

UNIT 35
Physical Science

OBJECTIVES

After reading this unit, you should be able to:

◆ Design physical science investigations appropriate for primary age children.

◆ Develop an understanding of physical topics that are appropriate for primary grade children.

◆ Develop structured and unstructured physical science learning activities with primary grade children.

◆ Apply unit webbing strategies to physical science content.

◆ Integrate science with other subject areas.

Physical science experiences are fun and exciting for primary age children. Even though these experiences can be dramatic and astounding for children, teaching the concepts is more foolproof than you might think. This is true for several reasons.

First, the physical sciences abound with opportunities for using discrepant events (discussed in Unit 6) that put students in disequilibrium and ready them for learning. Thus, they are eager and ready to explore. Second, most experiences are instantly repeatable. In this way, the child can continue exploring without elaborate preparation. And finally, the hands-on nature of physical science explorations make them ideal for use with primary age children.

The *National Science Education Standards* (NSES) state that as a result of the activities in the primary grades, all students should develop an understanding of properties of objects and materials; position and motion of objects; and light, heat, electricity, and magnetism. At the primary level, the NSES Content Standards focus on the properties and motion of objects

and on energy. Children can best understand these topics by acting on objects and observing what happens to them.

This unit begins with the physical science concepts that are basic to primary grade learning and presents an example of ways that the topic of air can be integrated with science concepts of movement and changes in matter, gravity, light, and color. The subject integrations and lessons are part of the webbing scheme depicted in Figure 7–4 of Unit 7. Suggestions for the teaching of sound are also included.

Physical Science Concepts

The following concepts are basic to understanding the physical sciences. Use this list to identify concepts around which you can develop a planning web such as those described in Units 7 and 34.

◆ Air takes up space.
◆ Air has weight.
◆ Air is all around us.
◆ Things that make sound vibrate.
◆ Moving air pushes things.
◆ Air slows moving objects.
◆ Things near the earth fall to the ground unless something holds them up.
◆ Everything is made from material called *matter*.
◆ All matter takes up space.
◆ Matter can change into a solid, liquid, or gas.
◆ Matter can be classified according to observable characteristics.
◆ **Physical changes** and **chemical changes** are two basic ways of changing things.
◆ In a physical change, appearances change, and the substance remains the same (tearing paper, chopping wood).
◆ In a chemical change, the characteristics change so that a new substance is formed (burning, rusting).
◆ A mixture consists of two or more substances that retain their separate identities when mixed together.
◆ Temperature tells how hot or cold an object is.
◆ There are many types of energy—light, heat, sound, electricity, motion, magnetic.
◆ Magnets can be used to make some things move without being touched.
◆ Static electricity is produced when two different materials are rubbed together.
◆ There are three parts to a simple electric circuit: a source of electricity, a path for electricity to travel, and something that uses the electricity (a light bulb or bell).
◆ Some materials allow electricity to pass through them.
◆ To see color, light is needed.
◆ The way to change how something is moving is to give it a push or a pull.
◆ Machines make it easier to move things.
◆ Things move in many ways, such as straight, zigzag, around and around, back and forth, and fast and slow.

Planning and Teaching a Unit about Air

The learning experiences suggested in this unit follow the format described in Unit 7 and used in the seed unit (refer to Unit 34). Each lesson states a concept, an objective, materials, and suggestions for teaching the concept. Extensions, integrations, and possible evaluation procedures are indicated in the body of the lesson, when appropriate, and at the end of the unit. The topic of air is explored with bubble and sound lessons.

Exploring Bubbles

Children love to play with bubbles. They love to create bubbles, chase bubbles, and pop bubbles. Why not take advantage of this interest to teach science concepts with a subject children already know something about?

ACTIVITIES

THE BUBBLE MACHINE

CONCEPT: Bubbles have air inside of them.

OBJECTIVE: Construct a bubble machine by manipulating materials to produce bubbles.

MATERIALS: Mix a bubble solution of eight teaspoons (½ cup) liquid Ivory Snow and 1 quart water. Punch holes about halfway down the side of enough paper cups for each child. A box of drinking straws will also be needed. Write each child's name over the hole.

PROCEDURE: Assemble a bubble machine by inserting a straw through a hole in a paper cup and filling with detergent solution to just below the hole. Have the children observe the machine as you blow bubbles. Ask, WHAT DO YOU THINK IS HAPPENING? Have the children assemble bubble machines. Each child should insert a straw into the hole in the side of the paper cup and then pour some detergent solution into the cup just below the hole. Give children time to try bubble blowing and ask, WHAT DO YOUR BUBBLES LOOK LIKE? DESCRIBE YOUR BUBBLES. HOW MANY BUBBLES CAN YOU BLOW? WHAT IS INSIDE OF THE BUBBLE?

EXTENSIONS: Make bubble books with drawings that depict the bubble machine experiences. Encourage children to write about their pictures. Read the books to the class; then put them in the library center for perusal.

INVENTING BUBBLE MACHINES

CONCEPT: Many different shapes will create bubbles.

OBJECTIVE: Make a shape that will create a bubble. Observe air entering bubbles and taking up space.

MATERIALS: Mixed bubble solution; soft, bendable wire; pans for bubble solution.

PROCEDURE: YOUR BUBBLE MACHINE WORKS WELL. CAN YOU BEND WIRE INTO SHAPES THAT WILL MAKE BUBBLES? Have children "mess around" with wire to create a variety of shapes for making bubbles. Have them test the shapes by blowing air into the bubble film or moving the wire shape through the air. Ask, DID YOU MAKE A BUBBLE? WAS YOUR BUBBLE THE SAME SHAPE AS THE WIRE? (Figure 35–1).

NATURALISTIC AND INFORMAL ACTIVITIES: In the science center have other materials available for bubble machine making such as a pierced spatula, turkey baster, berry basket bottom, sieve, and other kitchen items. Ask, WHAT SHAPE DO YOU THINK THESE BUBBLES WILL BE? WHAT DO YOU NOTICE ABOUT THE SIZE OF THE BUBBLES? (Different sizes.) Have children record predictions and results for the different bubble blowers (Figure 35–2).

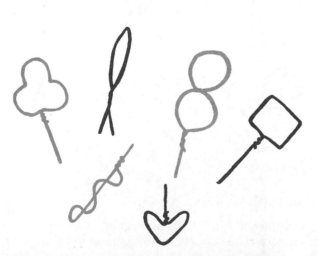

FIGURE 35–1 Wire shapes for blowing bubbles.

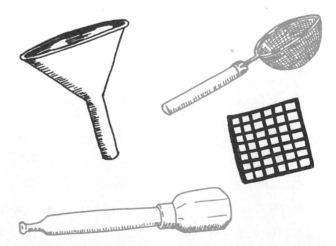

FIGURE 35–2 Kitchen shapes make interesting bubbles.

TABLETOP BUBBLES

CONCEPT: Air takes up space.

OBJECTIVE: Use air to create bubble sculpture. Predict how the bubbles will act on top of tables.

MATERIALS: Bubble solution, straws, cups, flat trays.

PROCEDURE: Have children dip out a small amount of bubble solution on a tray and spread it around. Ask, WHAT DO YOU THINK WILL HAPPEN IF YOU BLOW AIR INTO THE BUBBLE SOLUTION? (Bubbles will form.) Instruct children to dip a straw into the soap on the tray and blow gently. Give them time to "mess around" with tray top bubble blowing. Present challenges. CAN YOU BLOW A BUBBLE THE SIZE OF A BOWL? Have several children work together to make a community bubble. One child begins blowing the bubble and others join in by adding air to the inside of the bubble. (The straws must be wet to avoid breaking the bubble.) Bubble cities of the future can be made by adding more solution to the tray and blowing several bubble domes next to one another.

EXTENSION: Bubbles inside of bubbles. CAN YOU FIT A BUBBLE INSIDE OF A BUBBLE? Have children blow a bubble. Then insert a wet straw inside of the bubble and start a new bubble. WHAT HAPPENS IF THE SIDES TOUCH? (Figure 35–3). Make bubble chains. Have children blow a bubble with a straw. Then, wiggle the straw and blow another one. Soon, a chain of bubbles will form. Ask, HOW MANY BUBBLES CAN YOU MAKE?

Investigation Questions for Exploring Air and Bubbles

1. Will other liquids create bubbles?
2. Will adding a liquid called **glycerin** to the bubble solution make the bubbles stronger? (Yes.)

Can you think of other things to add to the bubble solution to make the bubbles last longer? Test your formulas.

3. Are bubbles always round? (Yes, unless some of them stick together. Forces acting inside and outside of the soap film are the same all over it.)

FIGURE 35–3 "Can you fit a bubble inside of a bubble?"

Subject Integrations

Bubbles and Science

1. *Observe bubbles.* Describe color, movement, size, shape. How many different colors do you see in the soap bubble? How do the colors move and change? Look at the bubbles through different colors of cellophane or polarized sunglasses. Do the bubbles change?
2. *Classify bubbles.* Classify by color, size, shape (bubble machine bubbles will stick together and take different shapes), location, how the bubble was made.

3. *Changes in matter.* Ask children to describe some changes that they notice in bubbles. Ask, "Did anything change?" (Yes.) "Did you see a physical change in the bubble solution?" (Yes, matter changes form only in a physical change.)

Bubbles and Art

1. *Bubble painting.* Mix bubble solution with liquid poster paint. Put the mixture in a bowl. As the child blows into the paint with a straw, a paint bubble dome forms. Lay construction paper over the bubble. As the paint bubble bursts, it splatters paint on the paper.
2. *Bulletin board.* Make a background of large construction paper bubbles. Display children's writing and art activities in this way.

Bubbles and Math

1. *How high?* Measure the height of the bubbles on a tray top. Measure how long a bubble lasts, predict and measure how many bubbles can be blown, and how far they can float. Graph the results.
2. *Lung capacity.* Make a graph of who has the largest lung capacity. Have children discover a way of determining lung capacity by blowing bubbles.

Bubbles and Language Arts

Science experiences can provide inspiration for important first steps in writing.

1. *Bubble books.* Provide paper for children to record their bubble explorations. These can be bubble shaped and illustrated.

2. *Books about bubbles.* Read storybooks about bubbles (Appendix B).
3. *Chart story.* Have children write or dictate stories about what they observed when they examined air inside of bubbles (Figure 35–4).

Bubbles and Food Experiences

Children can observe the tiny air bubbles that go into various whipped mixtures. For example, whipped milk topping can be made for cookies. You will need one-half cup of instant dry skim milk and one-half cup cold water.

Beat with an electric mixer at high speed for four minutes. Have children watch the mixture change. Then, add two tablespoons of sugar and one-half teaspoon vanilla and beat at high speed until the mixture stands in peaks. You may want to add the ingredient "air bubbles" to your recipe. Remind children that air went into what they are eating.

Concept: Air Can Move Things and Slow Things Down

The following suggestions extend science concepts.

1. *Moving bubbles.* Have children move bubbles in the direction they want them to go by fanning them with paper (Figure 35–5).
2. *Paper fans.* Make paper fans to move air. These can be accordion-pleated sheets of paper or small paper plates stapled to ice cream bar sticks.
3. *Glider designs.* Make gliders, and find out how far they can fly.
4. *Straw painting.* Blow paint with plastic straws. Pick up the paint with air pressure (as with the

```
Matthew

To day we were sintest again  it was a lot of fun.  We were seeing
if air took up space.  Some people thoght that it did and some
thoght it didn't.  I blew a very very very very big bubble but it
popped in my face.  There were different colors and shapes.  But
they didn't taste good.
```

FIGURE 35–4 Matthew has made many observations about bubbles.

FIGURE 35–5   "Can you make bubbles move?"

bubble solution), drop it on paper, and blow the puddles of paint into a design.

5. *Make pinwheels.* Have children fold squares of paper and hold them in front of a fan or in the wind. Ask, "What happens to the paper?" (It moves.) Help children make pinwheels from typing paper or wallpaper. A pushpin will hold the pinwheel to a pencil eraser and allow it to turn freely. Ask, "How did we produce motion?"

6. *Air walk.* Take children on a walk to find things that are moved by air. Discuss and write about what you have seen. Local windmills are ideal, but weather socks, flags, trees, seeds, clothes on a clothesline, and other moving things work well.

7. *Exploring parachutes.* Have children make parachutes out of squares of cloth. Tie each corner with string, then thread the four strings through a wooden bead or washer. Drop the parachute from various heights, and predict what will happen. Cut a hole in the top of the parachute, and observe any differences. Make parachutes out of different materials, such as plastic or cupcake liners, and compare their flight.

8. *Baby seeds.* Open milkweed pods in the wind and watch the wind disperse the seeds. Refer to the seed lessons in Unit 34 for further investigations.

9. *Air movers.* Have children experiment with different objects found in the room to see which is most effective in moving bubbles.

Exploring Sound

Children love to make music, but they probably do not know anything about the nature of sound. Help them understand that sound is caused when something vibrates by using the following lessons to teach children to see, hear, and feel the sound vibrations around them. Then, make musical instruments that reinforce the concepts.

GOOD VIBRATIONS

CONCEPT: Sound is caused when something vibrates.

OBJECTIVE: Observe objects vibrating and making sounds. Construct musical instruments based on concepts of sound.

MATERIALS: Paper plates, rubber bands, bottle tops, hole punch, paper cups, waxed paper, coffee cans, flexible tubing.

PROCEDURE:
1. Have children begin vibration observations by gently resting their fingers over their vocal cords and saying "Ahhhh" and "Eeee." Ask, WHAT DO YOU FEEL? (Something moving.) Explain that they are feeling vibrations occurring in their vocal cords, where all sounds they make with their voices come from.
2. Then have them place their fingertips against their lips while they simultaneously blow and hum. Reinforce the connection between vibration and sound by touring your classroom. Ask children to identify things that vibrate—the aquarium pump, kitchen timer, air vent, overhead lights. If possible, let them feel the vibrations in these objects and listen to the sounds each makes.

3. *Drum.* Make a simple drum out of a coffee can that has a plastic top. Place grains of rice on the can lid and tap lightly, while your students watch and listen. Ask, WHAT HAPPENS TO THE RICE WHEN YOU DO THIS? (It bounces up and down to the sound of the drum.)

4. *Drumsticks.* Make drumsticks from tennis balls and dowels. Punch a hole in the ball, apply glue to the end and edges of the dowel or stick, and push it into the center of the ball. Or use a butter brush, wadded up rubber bands, or a plastic lemon (Figure 35–6).

5. *Humming cup.* Make a humming cup by cutting the bottom out of a small paper cup. Then have the children cover the newly opened ends with waxed paper and secure with rubber bands. Say, PLACE YOUR LIPS LIGHTLY AGAINST THE WAXED PAPER END OF THE CUP AND HUM. They will get another feel for sound. Paper towel tubes can be used in a similar way to make horns (Figure 35–7).

6. *More horns.* A yard of flexible tubing will provide a chance to whisper back and forth and feel sound traveling to their ears through a talking tube. Then, tape a funnel to one end and make a buglelike horn.

7. *Tambourines.* You can construct this favorite instrument by decorating and shellacking paper plates in which you have already punched holes. Distribute bottle caps that also have holes punched in them, and have children tie two or three caps to each hole in their plates. This is a noisy but fun way to show the relationship between vibrations and sound.

NATURALISTIC AND INFORMAL ACTIVITIES: Put a variety of musical instruments in a sound center. Give the children time to explore the instruments and record their observations in their science journals.

EXTENSIONS: *Build a Band.* Making musical instruments will give children an opportunity to observe vibrations in other ways. Make a variety of instruments and decorate for a special occasion.

Wind Instruments

Wind instruments such as flutes, whistles, and panpipes depend on vibrating columns of air for their sound. The longer the column of air, the lower the pitch. (The highness or lowness of a sound is its *pitch.* The more vibrations per second, the higher the tone that is produced; the fewer vibrations, the lower the tone.) The following lesson demonstrates the relationship between the length of an air column and musical pitch.

Properties of Matter

The *National Science Education Standards* suggest that young children need to understand that matter can be classified according to observable characteristics

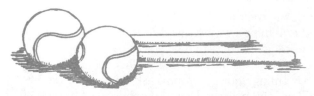

FIGURE 35–6 George makes drumsticks from tennis balls.

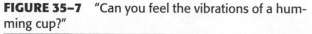

FIGURE 35–7 "Can you feel the vibrations of a humming cup?"

BOTTLES, WATER, AND AIR

CONCEPT: Pitch is the highness or lowness of a sound.

OBJECTIVE: Recognize differences in sound. Construct wind instruments.

MATERIALS: Ten bottles of the same height, water.

PROCEDURE: Prepare by filling glass soda bottles to varying levels with water. (Plastic bottles are too easily knocked over.) Hold up an empty bottle and ask, WHAT DO YOU THINK IS IN THE BOTTLE? WHAT DO YOU THINK WILL HAPPEN IF THE AIR IN THE BOTTLE VIBRATES? Demonstrate by blowing across the top of the empty bottle. Teach children to direct air across the mouth of a bottle. This is worth taking the time to do. Instruct children to press the mouth of the bottle lightly against their lower lip and direct air straight across the mouth of the bottle. (Do not blow into the bottle. The secret is blowing straight across.) Give them time to "mess around" with their new skill. Then ask, WHAT DO YOU THINK WILL HAPPEN IF YOU BLOW ACROSS A BOTTLE WITH WATER IN IT? Pour water into bottles, and have children find out what will happen. Children will discover that the bottles make sounds that vary in pitch. They might even play a tune (Figure 35–8).

NATURALISTIC AND INFORMAL ACTIVITIES: Invite musicians to the classroom to share their instruments and answer questions.

EXTENSION: Emphasize the meaning of pitch by reading a familiar tale in which high- and low-pitched sounds figure. For example, ask children to imitate the three billy goats gruff. Dramatize differences in pitch with voice and body activities.

---

such as size, shape, color, weight, temperature, and the ability to react with other substances. Children's experience observing, manipulating, and classifying common objects provides the foundation for much of their later learning.

Children build concepts related to the properties of objects and materials by engaging in a variety of experiences requiring them to observe and describe the properties of objects, comparing objects for their observable similarities and differences and sorting or grouping objects based on their similarities. The following activities provide early experiences with ordering and classifying according to observable characteristics using the senses.

Shape and Size. Make a "feely sock" for each child that has two objects in it. One object should be the same in all socks, such as a Unifix Cube® or other item that is very familiar to the children. The second object should be distributed in pairs so that there are two socks that match. Ask, "Describe the objects that are in your feely sock." After each child has described the objects in the socks, invite the children to find the sock that matches their sock. When a child believes that he has the match, ask the children to pull out their objects

---

BOTTLES AND WATER

Collect eight bottles to make a scale—your job will be easier if they are all the same kind and size. To tune the bottles, you'll need to fill them to varying heights with water.

Start by dividing the volume of water that one of the bottles could accommodate by the number of notes you wish to produce. For example, if you want a one-octave scale, divide the volume by eight. Then, leaving bottle one empty, put $1/8$ of the volume into bottle two, $1/4$ into bottle three, $3/8$ into bottle four, and so on until bottle eight contains $7/8$ of its volume of water. Adjust the amount of water up and down in the bottles until the scale intervals sound (more or less) true. Use masking tape to mark the correct level on each bottle.

FIGURE 35–8 Formula for bottle music.

and to compare the objects to see if their descriptions of the size, shape, and textures of their object provided accurate details.

Smell. Make "scent jars" from film canisters, pieces of sponge, and food flavorings such as cinnamon oil, peppermint, clove oil, and so on. For each scent, make three canisters. Label the canisters on the bottom with letters or colors so that children can check to make sure they have found the correct matches to their scents. Distribute the canisters and ask the children to smell their canister and describe the scent and anything that smells like the scent. Ask the children to find their matching canisters and discuss the descriptions that helped them find each other.

Temperature. Laminate six different colors of construction paper and lay them side by side to create a classification mat. Place cups of water of differing temperatures on the mats. Ask the children to use their sense of touch to order the cups from hottest to coolest. Children should place the hottest cup at one end and the coolest at the other end, and then try to figure out which ones go in between. When they have arranged the cups, ask them to check their work by using a thermometer or temperature probe. The activity will need to be completed quickly before the temperatures even out. Children can generate their own ways of comparing, and a table or graph can be produced.

Weight. Gather a large selection of balls, including some that are very similar in weight. The collection might include tennis balls, Styrofoam balls, Ping-Pong balls, marbles, ball bearings, softballs, golf balls, and so on. Use the colored mat system described in the Temperature section to provide students with a system for organizing the balls. Ask students to order the balls from heaviest to lightest. Once students have made their determinations, have them use a balance to see if their predictions were correct. Children will have to work to determine the best way to use the balance. Placing the heaviest object in one bucket on the balance and then testing all other objects to see if any are heavier will work well. Once the heaviest has been confirmed, children can continue with the next objects, comparing them all to each other until the order is established. This ordering activity can become a classification activity when objects are combined and weight is used to determine when sets of objects are to be grouped together.

CHANGE

Concept: Chemical changes.

Objective: Explore chemical changes.

Materials: three oz. plastic cups, plastic bowls, four to eight oz. bottles of glue (do not use washable glue), distilled water, borax.

Procedure:
1. Mix equal parts of glue and distilled water into a large container.
2. In a second container, mix one liter of distilled water and one tablespoon of borax.
3. Divide the children into pairs and have one member of each pair measure two oz. of the glue solution into a plastic cup.
4. Have the second child measure two oz. of the borax solution into a second cup.
5. Pour the solutions into the bowl and stir, being careful to keep it in the bowl.
6. Ask, "What happened when you mixed the two solutions? Does the result look like either of the solutions before they were mixed? Is this a new substance?"

Concept: Physical change.

Objective: Explore physical changes.

Materials: water, sand, bowls, paper

Procedure:
1. Have each child pour water and sand in small bowls.
2. Put the bowls in the sun.
3. Before leaving school check the bowls.
4. Ask, "What happened to the sand and water? Has a new substance been formed? Is this a physical or chemical change?"

Exploring Light

Children need many concrete experiences with light to provide the conceptual background necessary for later understanding. Help children understand the *National Science Education Standard* for light— light travels in a straight line until it strikes an object, and light can be reflected by a mirror, refracted by a lens, or absorbed by objects—with the following learning experiences.

Light Beam Tag

To encourage children to discover that light travels in a straight line, play light beam tag with mirror tiles that are at least five-by-five inches (rough edges should be covered with duct tape). Focus the beam on one student's mirror. The student must use the mirror to reflect the beam to another student's mirror. The light intensity should be enough to reflect to two or three children at one time. When two or three children are successfully reflecting each other's beams, clap the chalkboard eraser in the areas where the light is traveling. The class will be able to observe the light beams traveling in straight lines between the children with the mirrors. This activity could also be used to reinforce the concept that light can be reflected by a mirror.

Instructional Technology: The Light Sensor

Young children come up with numerous questions regarding light when they are introduced to instruc-tional technology that measures light levels. The following scenario demonstrates how a light sensor can be introduced to young children.

Early in the year, Mr. Wang had introduced his students to Sensing Science, an elementary-level sensor and probeware package by Data Harvest. Sensing Science is composed of software; probes and sensors that measure temperature, light, sound, motion, and other variables; and the hardware that interfaces the computer and the probes and sensors. The focus of Sensing Science is to teach young children simple data collection and graphing in a developmentally appropriate manner. For instance, the first activity with the light probe involves pointing the sensor toward a bright light. The computer screen turns completely white. When the probe is covered, thus allowing no light, the computer screen turns completely black. When pointed toward varying levels of light, the computer screen turns shades of gray. Mr. Wang asked, "What do you think the sensor was sensing?" After several suggestions and trials, the children quickly realized that the amount of light striking the sensor made the changes.

Mr. Wang showed the children other ways the amount of light could be indicated and features in Sensing Science that recorded the highest and lowest reading like an odometer on a car. There were many opportunities to take measurements and ask questions and a lot of interest in the "snapshots" of light levels that the program can display on a simple table. In this way, the children could compare two or more light levels by comparing the numbers.

The children decided to use the technology to help them solve a problem. The children had been working on constructing a classroom planetarium out of cardboard boxes and glowing star stickers. They had reached the point where they needed a curtain that would cover the entrance and block out all light during their "star shows" yet would be easy to move aside the rest of the time to allow light to enter and be absorbed by the glowing stickers so they would glow brightly during the star shows. Several children brought in materials from home to use for the curtain, including old sheets, blankets, and an old tarp. The children cut the cloth into equal pieces to determine which would block the most light. One piece of cloth was a light color and a medium weave. Another was a gray color and a tight weave. The last one was black and of a loose weave. Most of the children predicted that the black cloth would block the most light. Mr. Wang asked, "How could you use the light sensor to help you solve the problem?" Some of the children decided to find out by putting the cloth over a flashlight and then holding the sensor up to it. Another group decided to cover the light sensor with the cloth and hold it up to the light. Mr. Wang allowed the groups of children to try their investigations. When they were finished, several tables were produced.

The children were amazed that the gray cloth blocked out the most light. Mr. Wang asked, "Why do you think the gray cloth worked the best?" Liu Pei said maybe it had something to do with the color. Maybe all gray cloths worked better than white or black. Derrick thought it had to do with how close together the threads were. He held up each piece of cloth and looked through it, pointing out how much more space was between the threads on the white and black cloths. The other children also observed this and started gathering their materials and setting up additional investi-

gations. Liu Pei wanted to test some cloths that were the same except for their color to see if the gray really worked best. Derrick thought it would be a great idea to do the same thing with some pieces of cloth that were the same color but had different amounts of space between the threads.

Mr. Wang was pleased that the children wanted to do investigations regarding light. He knew that the children would carry out many more investigations throughout the year about concepts regarding how different colors absorb and reflect light. Perhaps the children would want to set up investigations testing the reflective qualities of sheets of construction paper or the amount of light allowed to pass through pieces of colored transparencies. The Sensing Science probes were going to be a great tool to facilitate inquiry in his classroom.

Assessment Strategies

Because many primary children are beginning readers, simple performance assessments designed around process skills and anecdotal records can be used to determine understanding. When recording children's oral explanations of what is happening, it is better to place the emphasis on the child's ability to communicate ideas, rather than the use of terminology. When children are completing a task, write down snippets of informal conversation relating to the task.

Another assessment strategy might include having the children sort objects into categories, setting out an object that does not fit in either category. Observe how the children either incorporate the object or change the categories, and relate these observations to progress.

KEY TERMS

physical changes   chemical changes   glycerin

SUGGESTED ACTIVITIES

1. Which process skills are used in the bubble unit? Identify each skill and how it is incorporated into the study of air inside of bubbles. Teach the unit to children. Which integrations and activities did you use?

2. Interview teachers of primary age children to find out what types of physical science activities they introduce to children. Do any of these activities include the exploration of materials? Record your observations for discussion.

3. Brainstorm strategies to prepare children to understand physical science topics such as magnets, light, and electricity. Pick a topic, and prepare a learning experience that will aid in future concept development.

4. Select a physical science concept, and prepare a learning cycle to teach that concept. Teach it to children. Record your observations for discussion.

5. Present a lesson about sound for primary age children. What types of learning experiences will you design for your students? Explain how you will apply Piaget's theory of development to this topic.

6. Go to a bookstore or library, and identify books to enhance the teaching of physical science. Present an evaluation of these materials and how you might use them to reinforce science concepts.

7. Go to a school system computer support unit and ask for software that complements physical science concepts for young children. If there are any sensors and probes available for use with young children, try them for yourself. Determine which concepts and processes are taught or reinforced by the software. Plan a lesson that uses the software, teach it to a small group of students, and evaluate the lesson's effectiveness. Did the software provide instruction that would be difficult to do in other ways? What are the benefits of using the software or probeware? Share the results with your class. Suggested programs include the following.

◆ Adventures with Oslo: Tools and Gadgets. Lewisville, NC: Science for Kids. (Grades K-up)

◆ Bumptz Science Carnival. Emeryville, CA: Theatrix Interactive. (Grades 1–5)

◆ Gizmos and Gadgets. Fremont, CA: The Learning Company. (Ages 7–12)

◆ Graph Club. Watertown, MA: Tom Snyder Productions. (Grades K–4)

◆ Gryphon Bricks. San Diego, CA: Gryphon Software. (Ages 5+)

◆ Invention Studio. Bethesda, MD: Discovery Communications Inc. (Ages 9+)

◆ Mystery Objects. Minneapolis, MN. MECC (Grades 2–4)

◆ Sammy's Science House. Redmond, WA: Edmark. (PreK-2)

◆ Sensing Science [Sensor and probeware program]. Grand Island, NY: Data Harvest Educational.

◆ Widget Workshop. Walnut Creek, CA: Maxis. (Ages 8–12)

REVIEW

A. Explain why primary age children should explore physical science activities (give at least two reasons).

B. List the major concept areas in physical science that are appropriate for primary age children. Pick four concepts that are about the same topic, such as states of matter, and develop a planning web for teaching those topics.

C. Identify a lesson that you plan to use in teaching a physical science concept in a primary classroom. Using your understanding of age-appropriate science teaching and learning, explain your rationale for selecting the content and teaching strategies in the lesson.

REFERENCE

National Research Council. (1996). *National science education standards*. Washington, DC: National Academy Press.

FURTHER READING AND RESOURCES

Abruscoto, J. (1995). *Teaching children science: A discovery approach* (4th ed.). Needham Heights, MA: Allyn & Bacon.

Allison, L., and Katz, D. 1983. *Gee, wiz!* Boston: Little, Brown and Company.

Althouse, R. (1988). *Investigating science experiences for young children*. New York: Teachers College Press.

Froschauer, L. (1993). *Teaching elementary science with toys: CESI sourcebook VII*. Columbus, OH: ERIC Clearinghouse for Science, Mathematics, and Environmental Science.

Harlan, J. (1995). *Science experiences for early childhood years*. New York: Macmillan.

Hawkinson, J., & Faulhaber, M. (1969). *Music and instruments for children to make*. Chicago: Whitman.

Hillen, J., Mercier, S., & Hoover, E. (1994). *Primarily physics*. Fresno, CA: AIMS Education Foundation.

Lind, K. K. (1985). The beat of the band. *Science and Children, 23*(3): 32–33.

Lind, K. K. (1986). The beat goes on. *Science and Children, 23*(7), 39–41.

Malone, M. (Ed.). (1996). *Physical science activities for elementary and middle school. CESI sourcebook V*. Columbus, OH: ERIC Clearinghouse for Science, Mathematics, and Environmental Science.

Orii, E., & Orii, M. (1989). *Simple science experiments with light*. Milwaulkee, WI: Gareth Stevens Books.

Perez, J. (1988). *Explore and experiment*. Bridgeport, CT: First Teacher Press.

Zubrowski, B. (1979). *Bubbles*. Boston: Little, Brown and Company.

UNIT 36
Earth and Space Science

OBJECTIVES

After reading this unit, you should be able to:

◆ Design earth and space science investigations for primary age children.

◆ Develop an understanding of earth and space science concepts appropriate for primary age children.

◆ Develop structured and unstructured earth and space science learning experiences for primary age children.

The *National Science Education Standards* (NSES) emphasize the observational nature of earth and space science. In primary grades, children learn about Earth and space by making observations as they explore, collect, describe, and record information. Children investigate and gain an understanding of the properties of earth materials such as water, soil, rocks, and **minerals**.

A major role of the teacher in primary earth and space science lessons is to guide children in observing natural changes of all kinds, including cyclical changes, such as the movement of the sun and moon, and variable changes, such as the weather.

Most children in the primary years are able to order and group objects by a single characteristic and to communicate and make comparisons about their observations.

This unit begins with lessons about various earth materials that are used by us in different ways. For example, soil, rocks, and other earth materials are used for building, fuels, and growing plants. Suggestions for introducing children to earth materials, space, and weather. Lessons about rocks that can be developed into a unit and integrated into the classroom are suggested.

Earth and Space Science and the Environment

◆ Earth's materials are rocks, soils, fossil fuels, water, and the gases in Earth's atmosphere.

◆ Earth's materials are nonliving.

◆ Earth's materials have properties that make them useful to us in different ways.

◆ Soils have properties of color and texture.

◆ Soils have the capacity to retain water and help plants survive.

◆ Rocks are formed in different ways.

◆ Rocks are nonliving things.

◆ Sand is made up of tiny pieces of rock.

◆ Water and wind change the surface of the earth.

◆ Mountains and land are made of rocks and soil.

◆ **Evaporation** means a liquid changes into a gas (vapor) in the air.

◆ **Condensation** means a gas changes to a liquid. Water vapor is an example of condensation.

◆ The **atmosphere** is the air around us. It has conditions such as wind, moisture, and temperature. **Weather** is what we call the conditions of the atmosphere.

◆ There are four seasons, and each has unique weather.

◆ Temperature is how hot or cold something is.

◆ Clouds and fog are made of droplets of water.

◆ The earth has a layer of air and water around it.

◆ Water is a liquid and is called *ice* when it is solid.

◆ The sun gives off light and heats and warms the land, air, and water.

◆ A light source at a great distance looks small.

◆ The sun, moon, stars, and clouds have properties, locations, and movements that can be observed and described.

◆ The sun, moon, and stars all appear to move slowly across the sky. The moon appears to change in size and shape. Sometimes the moon can be seen at night, and sometimes it can be seen during the day.

◆ There are many stars in the sky. They do not look the same in brightness and color and are not scattered evenly.

◆ The patterns of stars stay the same and appear to move across the sky.

◆ The quality of air, water, and soil is affected by human activity.

Planning and Teaching a Unit on Rocks

Children need a variety of concrete experiences that enable them to learn the properties of earth materials. For example, as children begin to observe rocks, they will see that some are made up of a single substance but that most are made up of several substances (minerals). Assessment of children's skills and understanding of concepts takes place as children group a variety of rocks according to one of their properties, such as color, pattern, buoyancy, or layering.

The learning experiences suggested in this unit follow the format described in Unit 7 and used in Units 34 and 35. Each lesson states a concept, an objective, materials, and suggestions for teaching the concepts. Extensions, integrations, and possible evaluation procedures are indicated in the body of the lesson, when appropriate, and at the end of the unit.

The following basic geology lessons introduce fundamental concepts and stimulate children's curiosity about rocks, minerals, and earth processes. The strategies will acquaint primary age children with the nature of rocks in a way that is immediate, exciting, and fun.

ACTIVITIES

A CARTON OF ROCKS

NATURALISTIC ACTIVITY: In the science center have a variety of rocks, magnifiers, and books about rocks available for the children to explore and make observations. The books can be used to identify rocks.

INFORMAL ACTIVITY: When the children begin to examine the rocks, ask, "What color, shape, size rocks do you have? Are any of the rocks the same? How are the rocks alike? How are they different?"

STRUCTURED ACTIVITY:

CONCEPT: There are many kinds of rocks.

OBJECTIVES: Observe different types of rocks. Classify rocks in different ways.

MATERIALS: An egg carton for each child or group, small labels that can be glued on the box, pencils or pens, a handful of rocks.

PROCEDURE: Show the children the rocks in your hand. Ask the children, WHAT ARE THESE, AND WHERE ARE THEY FOUND? Give each small group of children a few rocks, and encourage them to develop classification schemes for them, such as flat, speckled, animal-shaped. Younger children will notice size and color first, then shape and the way the rock feels. Have the children develop labels for the categories.

Take the children to any place where there are rocks. Set a generous time limit, and have them search for different types of rocks to fill their egg cartons. Then, have the children share and classify what they have found. Use labels to identify rocks in the egg carton collections (speckled, round, and so on).

EXTENSION:
1. Older children are able to compare rock characteristics with pictures in rock identification handbooks.
2. Use various rocks to create a rock collage.
3. Read *Sylvester and the Magic Pebble* by William Steig. A round red pebble makes a nice prop.

THINKING LIKE A GEOLOGIST

CONCEPT: Some rocks are harder than other rocks.

OBJECTIVE: Examine rocks and minerals to determine how hard they are. Classify rocks by characteristics.

MATERIALS: An assortment of rocks (a rock and mineral set, if possible), roofing nails, pennies.

PROCEDURE: Give groups of children an assortment of rocks to observe. After they have had time to observe the rocks, ask, CAN YOU SCRATCH ANY OF THE ROCKS WITH YOUR FINGERNAIL? As they notice a difference in rocks, ask, CAN SOME ROCKS BE SCRATCHED IN THIS WAY? (Yes.) WHAT ELSE COULD YOU USE TO SCRATCH ROCKS?

After children try to scratch rocks with different objects such as the penny and fingernail, explain that finding out if a rock crumbles easily is one of the things a geologist does. (Even though children may not remember the term, the labeling is important.)

Tell the children that they are going to think like a geologist and determine how hard a rock is. Make a list of ways that the children will test the rocks. For example
   ◆ can be rubbed off on fingers
   ◆ can be scratched with fingernail
   ◆ can be scratched with a penny
   ◆ hard to scratch

Have the children test the rocks and place them with the statement that best describes the rock. Ask, WHICH ROCKS DO YOU THINK ARE THE HARDEST? (Those that are hard to scratch; Figure 36–1).

Then, take the children outside to see which rocks can be used to draw streaks or lines on the sidewalk. Children might even see distinctive colors. Ask, WHAT COLORS ARE THE STREAKS? Have children compare the colors in the rocks with the colors of the streaks. Ask, CAN WE CLASSIFY ROCKS IN THIS WAY? (Yes.) You may want to review some of the ways that geologists classify rocks (appearance, texture, hardness, color). Graph the findings.

EXTENSION: As children wash their hands, compare wet and dry rocks. What differences do they notice? Geologists use hardness and streak tests to identify minerals. Introduce the term *minerals* when children notice bits of color in the rocks. Explain that rocks are made up of many different ingredients (minerals).

EXPLORING COOKIES

CONCEPT: Rocks are formed in different ways.

OBJECTIVE: Identify similarities between rocks and cookies. Stimulate curiosity about earth processes.

MATERIALS: Oatmeal chocolate chip cookie recipe on chart and on index cards, ingredients for making cookies (two cookies for each child).

PROCEDURE: Pass out recipe cards to the small groups. Show the children what the various ingredients look like as you discuss those used in making oatmeal chocolate chip cookies. Give each small group of children samples of the cookie ingredients. Bake the cookies. Then, give each child two cookies (one to examine and one to eat).

Have the children explore the cookie and compare the ingredients and the information on the recipe card with the final product. Ask, CAN YOU SEE THE INGREDIENTS? (Some of them.) WHICH INGREDIENTS DO YOU SEE? CAN YOU TASTE ANY OF THE INGREDIENTS? (Figure 36–2) DO THE INGREDIENTS LOOK THE SAME? (No, some have changed.) Once the children recognize that some ingredients are still recognizable after baking and some are no longer in the same state, ask, IN WHAT WAY HAVE THEY CHANGED? (Melted, dissolved, and so on.) WHAT CHANGED THE INGREDIENTS? (Mixing, pressing, heat.) Discuss heat and chemical changes, if appropriate.

Give children an assortment of rocks, and tell them that rocks have ingredients, too. The earth acts like a baker and turns ingredients into rocks. (Rock ingredients, *minerals*, are turned into rock by pressure, heat, and moving around.) Let children handle mineral samples and try to find evidence of these samples in the rocks.

EXTENSION: Take a rock field trip. Have each child find an egg-sized rock. Wrap the rock in cloth and have an adult hit it with a hammer. Use hand lenses to examine the pieces of broken rock. Ask, HOW MANY PIECES OF ROCK ARE THERE NOW? Have the children explore the shape, size, and color of the fragments and describe the inside and outside appearance of the rock. The inside of a dull-looking rock is usually filled with pattern, texture, and color. Use a small light to help compare the shine and luster of various rocks. Have the children draw or color what they see through the hand lens.

FIGURE 36–1   Labeling rocks by hardness.

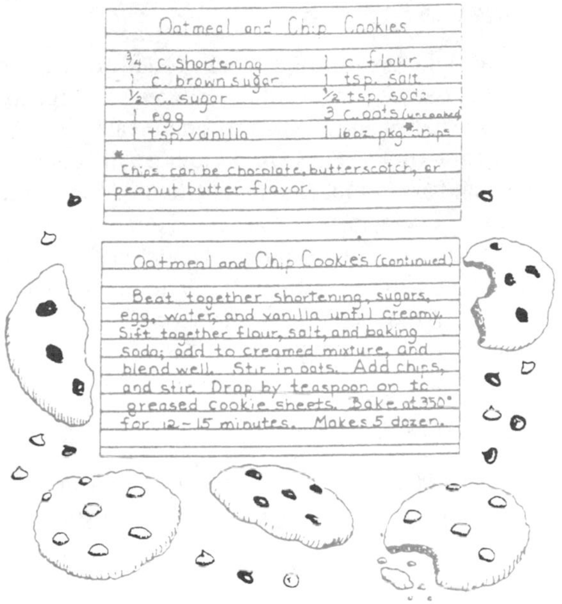

FIGURE 36–2   "Compare the ingredients for making cookies with the cookies."

EXAMPLE WORLD WIDE WEB ACTIVITIES

◆ Earth site that provides information and interactive games. Link at http://www.msha.gov/KIDS/KIDSHP.HTM

◆ NASA kids site with games and information. Link at http://www.nasa.gov/kids.html

---

How Rocks Are Formed

Primary students commonly believe that the ground is composed mostly of soil and that rocks are only what they can hold and carry in their hands. Through pictures and discussion of mountains, cliffs, and deserts, help students understand the great variety, size, and distribution of rocks on and in the earth. Most of the earth's crust is solid rock, a nonliving material made of different kinds of minerals. The forces that make the major types of rock are too complex for lower-level primary grades to understand. However, you may want to introduce upper-level children to a few examples that simulate the basic ways that rocks are formed.

You can make the study of rocks more meaningful for your students if you know the basic way rocks are formed and a few common examples of each.

Igneous Rocks

Igneous rocks are formed through the cooling of magma or lava. Examples of igneous rocks formed by the rapid cooling of surface lava are pumice, obsidian, and basalt. Granite is the most common example of slow, below-surface cooling of molten rock. Refer to the igneous rock fudge cooking experience integration.

Sedimentary Rocks

These rocks are formed from eroded rocks, sand, clay, silt, pebbles, and other stones. Compressed skeletons, shells, and dissolved chemicals also form sedimentary rocks. These rocks are usually deposited in layers and are compacted and cemented by the pressure of the overlying sediments. Examples of sedimentary rocks are conglomerate, sandstone, shale, and limestone. Fossils are frequently found in sedimentary rock. Refer to the "pudding stone" cooking experience integration.

Metamorphic Rocks

The term *metamorphic* means "changed in form." Metamorphic rock is formed when sedimentary and igneous rocks are completely changed in form through pressure and heat. For example, limestone becomes marble, shale becomes slate, and sandstone may become quartzite. These rocks are harder than most rocks.

Show the effect of pressure by pressing a bag of marshmallows or several spongy rubber balls under books on a flat surface. Have the children describe the change in the physical appearance of the objects, and relate the change to the metamorphic process.

To simulate the effect of heat on the rocks, melt several different colored marshmallows together into one interlocking marshmallow. Have children observe and describe the changes.

Subject Integrations

Rocks and Science

1. *Smooth rocks.* Additional ideas about rocks and their formation can be introduced by walking along a beach or stream and observing the smooth stones at the bottom of the stream or on the shore. Children can collect rocks and begin to draw comparisons about what makes the rocks smooth. Have them watch the action of the waves or stream. Ask, "What is happening?" Compare using sandpaper with the action of sand against the rocks.

2. Many children may not make the connection between rocks and sand as broken pieces of rock (sand also contains bits of broken and worn-down sea shells). Have students use hand lenses to examine and compare grains of sand and rocks.

3. *Sand from rocks.* Have children rub two rocks together to simulate wear on them. Discuss how this wear might take place in nature (water current, waterfalls, wind, and so on).

Rocks and Art

1. *Rock gardens.* Construct small rock gardens. Use pictures of Japanese gardens as inspiration.
2. *Rock necklaces.* Glue yarn to the back of flat, round rocks to make necklaces.
3. *Vegetable fossils.* Make mold fossils of vegetables.

Rocks and Language Arts and Reading

1. *Storybooks.* Read *Stone Soup*, and make vegetable soup. See Unit 26 for suggestions.
2. *Rock-shaped book.* Make rock-shaped covers for this bookmaking activity from brown construction paper. Inside pages should also be in the shape of the rock cover. Punch two holes in the top of the book, and fasten with metal rings or yarn. You may want to start the book with phrases like "A rock is a _____" (Figure 36–3).
3. *My rock.* Have each child select a rock and describe it. The children can record or dictate descriptions. Encourage them by asking, "What does your rock feel like? Does your rock have a smell?" Stimulate thinking with, "My rock is as sparkly as a _____." Then have children write a biography of their rock.

Rocks and Math

1. *Ordering rocks.* Put rocks in order of size, shape, weight, and color, then from smoothest to roughest. Try doing this activity blindfolded.
2. *Weighing rocks.* Use a small balance to weigh rocks. Predict which rocks are the heaviest.
3. *Flannelboard rocks.* Make flannelboard rock shapes for math problem solving. Different

FIGURE 36–3 "Record observations in your rock-shaped book."

FIGURE 36–4 Making a conglomerate rock.

sizes, colors, and shapes can be put in order, organized into patterns, sorted, counted, added, and subtracted.

4. *Rock jar.* Fill a jar with rocks, and have the children estimate how many rocks are in the jar. Verify the number of rocks in the jar by counting by groups of 10.

5. *Dinosaur rocks.* Have children predict the number of rocks needed to build a dinosaur cave. Children can determine the needs of a dinosaur, such as enough rocks to shelter it and keep larger dinosaurs out of the cave.

Rocks and Cooking Experiences

1. *Igneous rock fudge.* After showing children pictures of volcanoes, find out what children know about them. Have pumice available for the children to examine. Some children might notice that the stone is light and has air bubble spaces. Explain that igneous means fire and that the pumice stone is an igneous rock that was once hot, liquid iron in a volcano that hardened as it cooled.

To illustrate how lava cools, make fudge in a medium-sized pan. Mix one-third cup water, one cup sugar, a pinch of salt, three tablespoons of cocoa, and one teaspoon of vanilla. Boil the mixture for three minutes, and cool in one of two ways. To cool the fudge fast and produce a shiny, smooth surface (black glassy obsidian is a good example), pour some of the mixture into a pie plate that is resting in a bowl of ice. For rough and lumpy granitelike fudge, cool at room temperature in another pie pan. Ask, "Which way do you think the piece of granite was cooled?"

2. *Pudding stones.* To illustrate conglomerate rock called pudding stone, have the children mix papier-mâché and add various types of gravel and weathered stones to the mixture. Or, make pudding and add raisins and other food bits for a tasty pudding stone snack (Figure 36–4).

Rocks and Social Studies

1. *Geologist.* Have a geologist visit the class and discuss his or her job and the tools he or she uses.

2. *Mapping.* Group the children into pairs and allow them to hunt for rocks on the playground. After returning to the classroom have each pair draw a map of where their rocks were found. Discuss each map, focusing on prominent land features in each area.

Fossils

Children will not be able to grasp the enormous time spans represented in the lessons about fossils

FIGURE 36–5 Making a mold fossil.

and dinosaurs. It is most important that they understand that the dinosaurs existed long before humans; cartoon depictions of cave dwellers and dinosaurs are inaccurate.

Fossils can be shells and bones, prints of leaves, shells, footprints, trees that have turned to stone, or insects that were trapped in tree sap. Discuss how the fossils might have been formed and whether they came from a plant or an animal. Ask, "What living things from the past can be identified by fossils?"

One way to illustrate this is to have students wear old shoes and go outside to make footprints in mud or damp sand. Have various students walk, jump, and so on and ask other students to figure out from the prints how each person was moving.

Fossils are most likely to be found in sedimentary rock. One way children can recognize this kind of rock is that it crumbles or scratches fairly easily and may have a smell when it gets wet. To make a fossil, give the children a few leaves and have them press them into clay. Remove the leaf and observe the imprint (Figure 36–5). Encourage the children to match the various leaves with the imprint that was made.

Soil Samples

Visiting an outdoor study site on a regular basis will encourage children to observe the properties and changes in earth materials and vegetation. As children collect rocks and observe the vegetation, they will become aware that soil varies in texture, color, and fertility from place to place. The study site is also a good place to observe erosion and the effect of seasonal changes on the ground.

If the weather permits, take children outside to the study site to gather soil samples from different areas of the study site. Using a garden trowel, place the soil samples in separate plastic containers and label the containers. Of course, you want to be sure there is no broken glass or other dangerous materials in the ground.

After initial observations at the study site, cover several of the classroom tables with newspapers and distribute hand lenses for children to gain a close-up look at the small rocks, soils, and grains of sand that may be in the soil. After the children have had time to explore, ask them to describe the soil. Encourage them to smell the soil and look for color and other properties. As the children describe the soil, record their responses on a chart. Encourage further observations by asking, "Is your sample wet or dry? Do you see any plants or bugs?" Children will begin to compare areas of the study sites and generate more questions.

After the students have had time to explore the study plot soil, continue the observations with a lesson on soil composition. Ask, "What do you think is in soil?" Children begin to understand that soil is made of broken and pulverized bits of rock and organic matter, such as decayed leaves and plants and the remains of animals, which provide the nutrients necessary for plant growth.

Half fill a jar with water, then spoon in soil that has a good mixture of humus, clay, sand, and gravel (you may need to add some of these ingredients). Shake the jar well, then set it on a table for children to observe the layers of materials as they settle. As the soil settles, examine the layers with a hand lens. Discuss the color and what might be in each layer, such as bits of gravel, some sand, fine pieces of rock that form, mud and clay, and plant and insect parts. Children will enjoy exploring the soil samples used in the demonstration. Return to the question, "What do you think is in soil?"

Take a second trip to the study plot site. Spread the children out around the site. Use plastic hoops (sorting or hula) to create defined observation areas. Give each child a magnifier. Have the children observe the area and draw and/or describe the soil, vegetation, and insects within the space. After returning to the classroom compare and then graph the results.

Revisit the study site before and after a shower. Notice how the soil types change when wet. As the children walk along, ask, "How does the hard-packed soil feel as you walk on it? How does the loose soil on the baseball field feel? How do you think the loose soil will feel after a rain?"

All living things depend in some part on soil for their food. People use soil for many purposes, including growing food and building homes. Encourage children to continue their soil explorations and begin to generate a list and picture collage of the uses of soil. As a culminating experience, either visit your local cooperative extension office or invite a staff member to visit the class and discuss soil testing.

Weather

Lessons on weather and seasons are especially appropriate for primary age children. In addition to discussing and studying the daily weather, take the children on a field trip to observe weather equipment in action. Local trip opportunities might include airports, television and radio stations, or high school or college weather stations. Visiting a weather station familiarizes children with the instruments and information they will study as they follow and record changes in weather and differences in seasons. Include constructing weather instruments, graphing, storybooks, subject integrations, and hands-on experiences as you teach children about weather.

Temperature, rain, and snow tend to be high, medium, and low in the same months every year. Have children plot patterns of the freezing of water, melting of ice, and disappearance of water on cold surfaces. The following lessons in temperature and sunlight provide an opportunity for children to begin to correlate changes in daily temperature with seasons.

A Lesson on Temperature

Begin a discussion of temperature by asking children to explain how they know if it is hot or cold outside. After discussing observations, introduce the idea of using a thermometer as a way of measuring temperature. Distribute thermometers to pairs or small groups to examine, and have the children record their observations. Ask, "What happens when you hold the ther-

mometer between your hands for a minute? Is the temperature different when you hold the thermometer at the base of the bulb?" And, "What do you think will happen if you put the thermometer in a glass of cold water? What will happen if you put the thermometer in a glass of hot water?"

Provide the groups with cups of hot and cold water, and let them investigate what will happen when the thermometers are placed in the cups of water. Have the children keep a record of their investigations and share results with other groups. Keeping records helps children to articulate their observations about how the thermometer works.

Pairs or groups of children will enjoy checking and recording temperature readings at different times of the day in a chosen location in the classroom or on the school grounds. Over a period of days, they can compare the pattern that emerges and make predictions. Because the goal of this lesson is for children to be aware that the temperature varies at different times of the day and thermometers can be difficult to read, temperature need not be measured precisely. Challenge children to find the hottest and coldest location in the room and on the playground.

Keep a class temperature chart so that the patterns seen over weeks and months can be related to the changing seasons. Identify clothing, activities, and food that are associated with each season. Include them on the temperature chart. A large paper body figure, such as those described in Unit 38, could be clothed to reflect seasonal changes.

Children may enjoy brainstorming words associated with each season and creating a "Hot and Cold" book following a pattern such as "as hot as _____" or "as cold as _____." Encourage the sensory aspect of the seasons by discussing seasonal smells, sounds, and tastes. One way to do this is to collect pictures from magazines that represent the sights, sounds, tastes, and activities of the season and display them as posters. A touch board made from objects found in the seasons provides an interesting class display. Refer to the temperature activity in Unit 35.

Extending the Concept

To extend the concept ask, "Do you think shadows affect temperature? How could you test your idea?

Record what happens." To continue the investigation of factors that can affect an object's temperature, such as color, ask, "Do you think there will be a difference between a thermometer placed in a dark-colored envelope and one placed in a light-colored envelope? Why do you think so?" Challenge children to find the hottest and coldest location in the classroom or on the playground, and ask them to give reasons for the varying temperatures. Encourage children to design ways to test different ideas.

In the same way, the length of sunlight at the same time of day each month can be recorded. Children can observe and record the daylight or dark when they come to school, eat supper, or go to bed. Discuss how the length of days affects our lives. As the year progresses, children will begin to correlate the changes in daily temperature and sunlight with the seasons.

To extend the concept of seasons, choose a tree from either the playground or an adjacent area and conduct observations periodically throughout the year. Have the children work in pairs using a digital video camera or a camera that utilizes still shots. The observations should include size of the tree, colors of the bark and the leaves, amount of leaves (lots, few, and so on), smell of leaves, and feel of leaves. Play back the video or show the series of still shots and have the children discuss the changes in the tree over the year and the seasons associated with the video.

A Thermometer Table

Construct a thermometer table by having the children collect a variety of thermometers to compare and explore, such as oven thermometers, indoor-outdoor thermometers, and the many kinds of thermometers used to measure the body temperature.

A Party for All Seasons

At the beginning or the end of each season, children may want to have a season party. Planning groups will enjoy designing and creating the many aspects of the season party. The party could include single-portion recipes and samples of seasonal food, aromatic jars, touch boxes, and music and pantomime games of the indoor and outdoor activities typically done in each season. Children will enjoy painting murals and pictures of seasonal activities and constructing props for the activities.

Water

Evaporation and *condensation* mean *disappear* and *reappear*. Years before children begin to understand that evaporating water that appears to disappear is still present in the form of small molecules (water vapor), they can observe the process and should be provided many opportunities to explore the phenomena. The following lesson, "Wet Spots," is an example that allows children to see the effect of the science concept.

The process of evaporating water spots will reinforce the NSES content standard of inquiry as well as the content of changes in matter. Mr. Wang makes a large wet spot on the chalkboard and draws a circle around it every minute. As the water disappears slowly, a series of chalk circles are left on the board. Mr. Wang asks the child, "How could you evaporate the water more quickly?" George says, "Blow on it." Sarah wants to use a blow dryer. Some children want to shine a light on it. Mr. Wang encourages the children to try all of their suggestions, one variable at a time.

The wet spots lesson continues the next day with more questions. Children want to know if the time of day makes a difference and whether cold or hot water would evaporate faster. Some even began to invent ways to evaporate the water spot without touching it. Mr. Wang challenges the children to find a way to preserve a wet spot for a long time. Refer to Unit 33 for more ideas for more investigations.

Puddle Pictures

Ask, "What happens to puddles on warm sunny days?" Have children use a paintbrush to make a picture on the sidewalk. Carefully trace around the puddle with sidewalk chalk to create a picture. Ask, "How did the water in your puddle picture change? Where do you think the water goes when it dries?" And, "What does it change into?" Have the children record the progress of the evaporating puddle on paper and with different colored chalk to mark the progress of the disappearing puddle. Ask, "What caused the water to change into water vapor?"

Relate this experience to observations of the drying process in the home. Have the children predict the fastest way to dry a shirt: lay it flat, hang it on a clothesline, or crumple it up in a bundle? Ask, "How can you be sure the water goes into the air?" Help children design an investigation that does not expose the camp shirt (or paper towel) to the air. Develop the idea that when water dries, it *evaporates*, or changes into a gas called *water vapor*.

Ask children to look for examples of water changing from water vapor back into a liquid such as dew on the grass, frost on the window, and fog or steam on the mirror.

Once children have observed examples of evaporation and they have begun to understand the role of heat, then it is time to focus on examples of condensation. Begin the experience by asking the children to predict what they think happens when cold air and hot air collide. After predictions are made, pour very hot water into a large-mouth glass jar. Make a pocket out of tin foil and insert it into the mouth of the jar. Put ice cubes into the pocket. Have the children observe and explain what they think happened.

Space Science

Space travel, the moon, sun, and stars intrigue young children. They will not be able to comprehend the vastness of space or the enormity of the sun, moon, and earth, yet there are aspects of space science that they can readily observe.

The sun is the most observable object in the sky. (CAUTION: Children should never look directly into the sun.) Ask, "On what side of the building does the sun shine in the morning?" Then, "On what side of the building does the sun shine when we leave for the day?" Take the children for a walk around the building, and note where the sun's rays are shining at different times of the day. Draw these changes on a chart. Ask, "Why do you think that the sun's rays shine in different places?"

Take the children outside of the building in the morning, and have them draw the school building and the location of the sun. Begin a bulletin board mural. Make the school building and surrounding features, and have the children place a construction paper sun where it belongs in the morning sky. Then make paper sun rays shining on the school building.

Shadow play is a natural for young children as they learn about the sun. Draw chalk outlines of the shadows cast, and then try casting shadows on a cloudy day. Ask, "Do you have a shadow today? Why not?" Discuss the color of the sun and the moon. Ask, "Is the moon the same color every night? Can you see the moon during the day?" (Yes.) Many children think that the moon goes to bed at night. Help them speculate on why the moon does not look as bright during the day.

If children think that the stars are held up with tape, do not discourage them. They are in good intellectual company. Aristotle, for example, thought that stars were embedded in concentric crystalline spheres. A primary age child cannot understand such concepts. Help the child notice that things in the sky look different at various times of the day and night.

Moon Patterns

The child's concept and grasp of the universe grows slowly over time. Ideas about light and sight are prerequisites to understanding the night sky. The priority in space-related lessons for young children is on describing what the sky looks like and identifying changes in shape and movement. The moon looks different every day and makes an ideal subject for observing and comparing.

Children can easily observe the pattern that the moon makes as it goes from one full moon to the next. Since moon phases appear at regular intervals, they can serve as a natural clock. It is not important that children remember the names of the phases of the moon, but that they see the pattern of change in the sky. As children record the differences that they see, they should describe and compare the various shapes the moon seems to have (Figure 36–6). The observations can be recorded in special moon watch books made of construction paper and writing paper in the shape of the moon.

The Dos and Don'ts of Using Binoculars

This is an ideal time to introduce the children to binoculars and telescopes. By third grade, children should know that binoculars and telescopes magnify the appearance of objects in the sky. The craters, mountains, and other features on the moon's surface will provide a source of much discussion and imagination. Binoculars work especially well with young children.

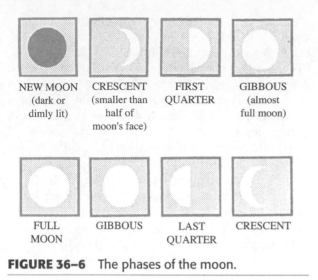

NEW MOON (dark or dimly lit) CRESCENT (smaller than half of moon's face) FIRST QUARTER GIBBOUS (almost full moon)

FULL MOON GIBBOUS LAST QUARTER CRESCENT

FIGURE 36–6 The phases of the moon.

The following are some binocular dos and don'ts: Do *not* try to find an object with the binoculars held up to your eyes. *Do* look at the object you want to look at, and *then* bring the binoculars up to your eyes. This will work better if you focus the binoculars first. To do this, look at an object, bring the binoculars up to your eyes, and then focus until the object is clear. Caution children to *never* look at the sun with a pair of binoculars or a telescope. Possible blindness could be the result.

Craters of the Moon

As children look at the moon more closely and more often, they will begin to notice the many interesting features that can be seen by the naked eye or with binoculars. Take advantage of children's natural interest in the night sky, and let them record and draw their observations in greater detail.

Children will enjoy creating a lunar landscape. This can be done in the sand table by dropping different size balls into very wet sand. If a sand table is not available, a box of sand makes a good substitute. The children can compare the splatter marks extending from the impression made from the ball as it hits the sand to similar marks seen on the moon. Have the children compare the drawing that they have made of their moon observations with the sand craters they have made.

Features of the moon are ideal for simulation with clay and other sculpting materials. Murals, paintings, and other art forms provide reinforcement for the children's observations. If the child does not remember how a feature looks or her drawing is not as clear as she wants it to be, she can easily look at the moon the next night.

Observing the moon cycle will stimulate children's natural curiosity. They will want to know more about the night sky. There are a variety of things in the sky that can be seen at night. Planets, comets, meteors, stars, satellites, and airplanes fill the sky. The familiar patterns of stars called **constellations** will provide much excitement. Keep in mind that it is not important for children to know the names of the constellations. They need to be aware that the pattern of stars stays the same as it appears to move across the sky. This movement is another pattern of movement in the sky that is readily observed.

Summary

Rocks and minerals are not simply objects lying on the ground. They are part of the continually changing process of the earth. As children study earth science topics such as rocks, minerals, weather, and space, they study the conditions and forces that affect their planet. An early introduction to these difficult concepts exposes children to their world and helps ready them for future understanding.

KEY TERMS

minerals	atmosphere	igneous rocks	metamorphic rocks
evaporation	weather	sedimentary rocks	constellations
condensation	geologist	fossils	

SUGGESTED ACTIVITIES

1. Recall your rock collecting experiences in elementary school. Where did you find your rocks? Did you display your rocks? Did you know what your rocks were or how they were formed? What did you learn when you did a collection? What educational value do you attribute to doing collections?

2. Make your own teaching web. Select lessons from the rock unit, and design a unit that is appropriate for a group of children you are teaching. You should add ideas to the ones presented. Teach the lesson to children, and record your observations for class discussion.

3. Which process skills are used in the rock unit? Give an example of each skill and when it was used. Can you think of additional ways to integrate process skills into the unit on rocks?

4. Present a lesson on weather to primary age children. What types of learning experiences will you design for your students? How do you plan to apply what you know about Piaget's theory of development to the teaching of weather?

5. Examine a teacher's edition of an elementary school science textbook. Identify a lesson on rocks and one on weather. Do you agree with the way the lesson is presented? Explain why or why not. How would you teach the lesson?

6. Select an earth science topic and concept and prepare a learning cycle lesson to teach that idea. Teach it to children.

7. Imagine that your class has just returned from collecting rocks. What types of questions will you ask to help students generate a list of characteristics that can be used to classify rocks into different groups? Your questions could take a variety of forms. Use your question list with children, and note the interactions for class discussion.

8. Locate software that is available at your school or in your school system that teaches or reinforces earth or space science concepts. Try the software yourself and select a program to present to the class.

Web Sites and Software

http://www.bom.gov.au/climate/current/. This site shows graphs of different types of weather.

http://www.earthwatch.com. Provides current weather information with satellite and radar images.

http://www.nasaexplores.com/cig-bin/index.pl. NASA Explores: Lesson plans that focus on different types of weather.

http://www.reeusda.gov . U.S. Department of Agriculture program that provides research and information for a variety of earth science topics. Also provides links to individual sites in each state.

EcoAdventures in the Rainforest. San Diego, CA: Chariot. (Grades 3–up)

Eyewitness References: Encyclopedia of Space and the Universe. London: Dorling Kindersley. (Ages 8+)

Magic School Bus: Earth. Redmond, WA: Microsoft. (Ages 6–10)

Magic School Bus: Solar System. Redmond, WA: Microsoft. (Ages 6–10)

National Geographic CDs for Educators: Earth. Washington, DC: National Geographic. (PreK–3)

National Geographic CDs for Educators: Exploring the Solar System and Beyond. Washington, DC: National Geographic. (PreK–3)

National Geographic CDs for Educators: Seasons. Washington, DC: National Geographic. (PreK–3)

Night Sky Interactive. Escondido, CA: Beachware. (Ages 8+)

Sammy's Science House. Redmond, WA: Edmark. (PreK–2)

REVIEW

A. What is the purpose of introducing young children to earth science concepts?
B. List three earth and space science concepts appro-

priate for primary age children and create a planning web for teaching at least one of these concepts.

REFERENCES

The National Research Council. (1996). *National science education standards.* Washington, DC: National Academy Press.

Steig, W. (1973). *Sylvester and the magic pebble.* New York: Simon & Schuster.

FURTHER READING AND RESOURCES

Brainard, A. H., & Wrubel, D. H. (1995). *Through the rainbow: Children, science, and literature.* Washington, DC: The Council for Elementary Science International.

Brummet, D. C., Lind, K. K., Barman, C. R., DiSpezio, M. A., & Ostlund, K. L. (1995). *Destinations in science.* Menlo Park, CA: Addison-Wesley.

Dighe, J. (1993). Children and the earth. *Young Children, 48*(3), 58–63.

Gega, P. (1993). *Science in elementary education.* New York: Macmillan.

Herman, M. L., Passineau, J. F., Schimpf, A. L., & Treuer, P. (1991). *Teaching kids to love the earth.* Duluth, MN: Pfeifer-Hamilton.

Kepler, L. (1996). *Windowsill science centers.* New York: Scholastic.

Lind, K. K. (1991). *Water, stones, and fossil bones.* Washington, DC: National Science Teachers Association.

Lowery, L. (1997) (Ed.). *Pathways to the science standards.* Arlington, VA: National Teachers Association.

McBiles, J. L. (1985). *Mining, minerals, and me.* Nashua, NH: Delta Education.

McCormack, A. (1979). *Outdoor areas as learning laboratories.* Council for Elementary Science International Sourcebook. Columbus, OH: SMEAC Information Reference Center.

Perez, J. (1988). *Explore and experiment.* Bridgeport, CT: First Teacher Press.

Raines, S. C. (1994). *450 More story s-t-r-e-t-c-h-e-r-s for the primary grades.* Mt. Rainier, MD: Gryphon House.

Raines, S. C., & Canady, R. J. (1992). *Story s-t-r-e-t-c-h-e-r-s for the primary grades.* Mt. Rainier, MD: Gryphon House.

Renner, J. W., & Marek, E. A. (1988). *The learning cycle and elementary school science teaching.* Portsmouth, NH: Heinemann.

Sheehan, K., & Waidner, M. (2000). *Earth child 2000.* Tulsa, OK: Council Oak Books.

Spizman, R. F., & Garber, M. (1991). *What on earth you can do with kids?* Carthage, IL: Good Apple.

Williams, R. A., Rockwell, R. E., & Sherwood, E. A. (1987). *Mudpies to magnets.* Mt. Rainier, MD: Gryphon House.

UNIT 37
Environmental Awareness

OBJECTIVES

After reading this unit, you should be able to:

◆ Design environmental awareness investigations for primary age children.

◆ Develop an understanding of environmental concepts appropriate for primary age children.

◆ Develop structured and unstructured environmental learning experiences for primary age children.

In the past, environmental science topics have been included with other earth and space science topics. In 1996 the *National Science Education Standards* (NSES) identified these topics with the *Science in Personal and Social Perspectives* standard. Under this standard children are expected to develop an understanding of the characteristics and changes in populations, types of resources, changes in the environment, and science and technology in local challenges. A major role of the teacher in the primary grades is to guide children in investigating and gaining an understanding of the characteristics and changes within their local and regional population, resources available in our world, and how our decisions make an impact on the availability of those resources.

Environmental Awareness

Environmental investigations are a natural way for children to enjoy and explore the world around them. When children explore the environment, they will engage in active participation and cooperation as they begin developing their own understanding. Experiences are often free or inexpensive and readily accessible to a variety of audiences and learning styles.

The suggestions and lessons in this section are based on one or more of the three common approaches to environmental education outlined by Dighe (1993).

1. *The Awareness Approach* focuses on children's feelings and appreciation of the world around them.

2. *The Environmental Concept Approach* introduces ideas that will lead to learning about environmental concerns.
3. *The Conservation Approach* provides opportunities for children to take action and see a result of that action.

The results of these lessons need to be observable and should not be too dramatic or controversial. To be effective, children need to see a direct result of their actions. For example, children can see a direct result of picking up trash or monitoring use of lights in the room.

To introduce the word *environment*, use a brainstorming approach: Write the word on the chalkboard and ask, "What do you think the word *environment* means?" List the ideas named by the children, and keep that list posted. Children may want to modify the list as their awareness of the environment progresses. Periodically, have the children return to modify the list as meaning develops.

Water Changes the Earth

Water is everywhere. It flows in rivers and streams and makes up the oceans that cover the earth's surface. Draw children's attention to the bodies of water around them—rivers, lakes, oceans, and the like. Show pictures of different bodies of water, and discuss experiences.

Water is the single most important force that shapes the surface of the earth. Water from melting glaciers, rain, and snow forms streams and rivers and moves sand, which gradually wears away mountains and carves hills and valleys. To explore the concept of **erosion**, complete the following activity.

ACTIVITIES

WATER CHANGES

CONCEPT: Water changes the face of the earth.

OBJECTIVES: Observe and record changes in the soil as a result of moving water.

MATERIALS: rocks, soil, liter soda bottles filled with water, ½ gallon paper milk cartons, trays, scissors or knives.

PROCEDURE: Divide children into pairs. Give each pair a milk carton, some soil and rocks, a liter soda bottle, tray, and a pair of scissors. Have the children cut the panel of the milk carton under the spout (Figure 37–1). Fill the carton ¾ full with soil and rocks. Put the carton in the tray and place a rock under one end of the carton. Make a small channel for a stream to flow. Ask the children, WHAT WILL HAPPEN WHEN YOU POUR WATER IN THE CHANNEL? One of the pair should slowly pour the water in the higher end of the tray. The other partner should observe and record what happens through writing or drawing. Ask the children, WHAT HAPPENED WHEN YOU POURED WATER INTO THE CHANNEL? After the children have discussed their observations ask, WHAT DO YOU THINK WILL HAPPEN IF WE ADD A SMALL AMOUNT OF ROCKS AND GRAVEL TO THE CHANNEL?

EXTENSION:
1. Find a river or stream and have the children take samples of muddy water so they can observe the sediment when it settles.

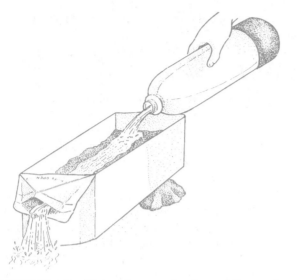

FIGURE 37–1 Water changes the face of the earth.

Take a class walk, and look for evidence of water changing the surface of the earth. Discuss how these changes can be beneficial or harmful (Figure 37–1).

Using Water

Living things—people, plants, and animals—consist mainly of water and must have it to live. In fact, water is more important for survival than food. Ask children to name some of the ways they use water. Encourage responses by asking, "What are some other ways people use water? Why is water important to business? To people who fish or raise farm animals?" Begin a chart to record children's responses to the ways living things use water. Add to the chart throughout the lesson as other uses of water are discussed.

After completing the following activity, it will emerge that the school depends on water in many ways. Children may appreciate its availability and how difficult life would be without such access to water. Encourage children to draw or cut out pictures of water uses in their home or school.

Ask children to keep a personal "Water Use Log." They should record their use of water for one day. Begin by recording activities from the time they get up until the time they fall asleep.

HOW OUR SCHOOL USES WATER

CONCEPT: People are dependent on water. Water is used in many ways.

OBJECTIVES: Investigate and record how water is used.

MATERIALS: Investigation journals, pens, pencils, cameras (optional).

PROCEDURE: Ask the children, HOW DO YOU THINK WATER IS USED AT OUR SCHOOL? Assign groups of children locations such as the kitchen, bathroom, art room, cleaning closets, and water fountains. Brainstorm with the children a list of questions to be asked to find out where the water comes from, how it is used, and how the water used could be measured. Have each group observe in its designated area and interview people who use or work in the area. After completing their research, groups should return to the classroom and a summary of the collected information should be made and discussed. Discuss questions such as: HOW MANY WATER SOURCES WERE FOUND? HOW MUCH WATER DOES THE SCHOOL USE? IS WATER WASTED? and WHAT WOULD WE DO IF WE DIDN'T HAVE WATER?

EXTENSION:
1. Have children record how their family uses water during one evening.
2. Visit a local aquarium and see how it uses water. How is its water use similar or different from that of the school?

Be a Water Saver

Discuss ways that people waste water, and begin a list of suggestions for how we can save water. To further the awareness of water that is sometimes wasted, suggest that children become water inspectors. Each child or team should list everything in the classroom and at home that requires water and investigate possible ways that water is wasted.

When children have completed their survey ask, "Where did you find leaky faucets? Does the toilet tank leak?" To find out if a toilet tank leaks, put food coloring in the tank, and wait 15 minutes. If the water in the bowl turns the color you put in the tank, you have a leak. Ask, "How many leaky toilets can you find? How many leaky toilets are in our school? Whom do you need to tell about your findings?"

Water wasted from leaky faucets can be measured by placing a cup under the faucet and collecting the drips (Figure 37–2). Ask, "How much water drips from the faucet in one hour?" Collect the water, and have the children think of a way to use the water instead of pouring it down the drain.

After investigating and studying water waste, children may then want to explain how they personally plan to conserve water. Children can illustrate one way they use water wisely. Have students pantomime a

FIGURE 37–2 "How much water is wasted?"

scene to show a way to conserve water at home or at school.

Water for a Day

Provide each student with a paper cup and a one-liter bottle of water. Tell them that this is their day's water supply for drinking, washing their hands, and so on. However, tell students they can flush the toilet. Tape faucets shut, and put a tub in the sink to collect water that would have gone down the drain. Have the children predict how much water they will use and record this information on a chart. At the end of the day, have them use a large graduated cylinder to measure any water that remains in their bottles and the water in the tub. Record the data on charts, and water the plants with the remaining water. Ask, "Did you use as much water as you thought you would use?"

Is This Water Clean?

As more people use water, there has been an increase in water **pollution**. In some areas, raw sewage is pumped into rivers and streams, pesticides and fertilizers are washed from lawns and farmland into the water system, and pollutants such as metals and petroleum products may enter a river or an ocean. It is important to point out that not all pollutants are visible. Some children think that because water looks clear, it is safe to drink. Emphasize to children they should never drink water unless they know it is safe.

Is It Safe to Drink?

Every day, wastes are being pumped into the world's water supply, but they are not always easy to detect. To develop the idea that you cannot always see pollution in water, cut off the bottom of a piece of celery, and divide the celery in half lengthwise. Fill two glasses halfway with apple juice, and add three drops of red food coloring to one and three drops of blue food coloring to the other. Place one-half of the celery in each glass, and let it stand for several hours. Take the celery out, and cut it into slices. Ask, "What color is the celery at the top of the stalk? Taste the celery. Can you taste the apple juice?" Try this investigation with food coloring and water.

After completing this activity, read the children's book *Magic School Bus: Through the Waterworks*. Take a trip to the local water treatment facility or have a representative visit your classroom. If you have the opportunity to visit a local facility, make a class book upon returning to record the children's observations. The children's software, Magic School Bus: Through the Waterworks can be used as a center activity. Once the children have had an opportunity to explore the software, discuss how the children's trip in the software is alike or different from that your class experienced.

How Much Trash?

It is an understatement to say that humans throw away a lot of garbage and trash in a lifetime. To provide children with an opportunity to see how much garbage they use in one day, suggest that they place the garbage they normally toss out in a day or a week in a large **biodegradable** trash bag. They may be able to take this trash bag with them for a day. That night, sort the garbage from the trash bag into labeled categories of use such as organic, paper, plastics, metal, glass, clothes, and mysterious items that do not seem to fit the other categories. This is an especially appropriate classroom or family experience. The bags can be weighed. Most people create at least four pounds of garbage each day. Ways to **recycle** trash can be explored. Ask, "Which bag weighs the most? Which weighs the least?" And, "Which bag has the most trash in it? Who created most of this trash? Can any of the items be used again?"

A mathematics connection would be to have the children problem solve how much garbage a family of four produces in a day, week, or month. Have children measure the area that four pounds of trash covers. Next, have the children problem solve the area needed to store trash for a family of four for a day, week, or month.

Recycling

One of the best ways to recycle is to reuse materials instead of discarding them. Many of the items that are thrown away can be used again in the everyday classroom environment. Look around the classroom, and list the items being reused such as boxes, Styrofoam

FIGURE 37–3 Packaged in recycled materials.

chips, sheets of paper, larger pieces of cloth, rope, yarn, string, plastic jugs, wood scraps, old magazines, rug scraps, and many more.

The symbol in Figure 37–3 means *packaged in recycled materials*. How many items in your home come in recycled packaging? How many items can you find in the classroom or in the school?

Recycling Survey

Have children brainstorm a list of suggestions for a recycling survey. Ask them what they want to know about the recycling habits of their families. Items might include, Do you recycle? If so, do you recycle aluminum cans? Additional suggestions might be grocery bags, newspapers, magazines, plastic bottles, plastic containers, and glass bottles and jars. Ask, "Do you think recycling is important? Why or why not?" After developing the survey, have the children give their survey to their family and friends. Compile the results of the survey on a bulletin board made of a huge brown paper bag and discuss the results with the children. Ask, "Does anything about the results on our chart surprise you?"

Keeping the Earth Clean

Make a class book of all of the things you can do to help keep the earth clean. Then take the class on a scavenger hunt. Put the children in pairs, and give each pair a short list of items to locate (newspaper, soda can, candy wrapper, and so on). Children can draw or plot on a map where they found each item (Figure 37–4). Have the children compare findings and discuss how the items might have ended up where they did.

FIGURE 37–4 "Let's keep the earth clean."

Litter Collage

Gather people's litter and nature's litter (fallen leaves, twigs, seed pods, and so on), and make a collage from each. Have the children write descriptions under the human litter and nature's litter. Bury some of the litter made by people and some of the litter made by nature. After a month, dig it up, and see what happened to the litter.

Save a Tree

Making paper is a fun and inexpensive way to emphasize the recycling process. Have the children save old newspapers instead of throwing them away. You will also need the following items: a large plastic pan or wading pool filled with warm water, an eggbeater, wire mesh screens, sponges, cotton cloth, and a rolling pin.

Shred paper into strips, and place them into water. Use the eggbeater, a whip, or an old blender to mash the paper into the consistency of oatmeal. For fancy paper, children can sprinkle bits of thread or flower petals into the pulp. To make the sheets of paper, spread and press the pulp onto a wire mesh screen, first dipping the screen under the pulp in the pan of water. Remove excess water from the sheet and underside of the screen.

Place the sheets of paper onto a cotton cloth, cover it with fabric, and squeeze out remaining moisture with a rolling pin. Let the sheets dry, trim them to a desirable size, and the children will be ready to write.

Paper Logs

Paper logs can be made for holiday treats by putting 20 or 30 sheets of newspaper together and adding a cup of crushed pine cones or cedar shavings between every few pages. These sections are tightly rolled and tied loosely at the end. Fill the pool with water and enough cones and chips to cover half of the water's surface. Add three cups of salt to the mixture (for extra pretty flames), and put the logs in to soak for a week. Turn them once a day. Dry the logs, and give them as presents (Figure 37–5).

Another activity that can be used to explore biodegradable and nonbiodegradable materials is creating a class **landfill**. This should be done outside in a secure area. Have the children collect a variety of paper, Styrofoam, food products (these can be obtained from the school cafeteria), soil, and water. Divide the children into small groups and give each group a large, black trash bag. They are to choose the materials they feel are most likely to break down. Have the children layer the materials in the trash bag and cover with soil. Add

FIGURE 37–5 Paper logs.

DISAPPEARING PEANUTS

CONCEPT: Biodegradable materials can be used to complete tasks previously completed with non-biodegradable materials.

OBJECTIVES: To explore how biodegradable packing peanuts change form when water is applied.

MATERIALS: Biodegradable peanuts in a bag marked 1, non-biodegradable packing peanuts in a bag marked 2, water, trays.

PROCEDURE: Have the children take a small amount of packing peanuts from bag 1 and bag 2 and put each in a bowl. Observe the peanuts carefully in each bowl. Ask, HOW ARE THEY ALIKE AND HOW ARE THEY DIFFERENT? WHAT DO YOU THINK WILL HAPPEN WHEN YOU ADD WATER TO EACH OF THE BOWLS? Add water and observe. Ask, WHAT HAPPENED WHEN YOU ADDED WATER? ONCE YOU FINISHED USING THE PACKING PEANUTS, WHICH WOULD TAKE UP LESS SPACE IN A LANDFILL?

EXTENSION:
1. Experiment with other packing materials to see if they are biodegradable.
2. Call local moving companies and suppliers of moving materials to see if they use biodegradable materials? How does the information you collect your local landfill?

EXAMPLE WORLD WIDE WEB ACTIVITIES

◆ http://www.epa.gov/students/recycle_city.htm. Children can tour various sections of the city to see how various organizations and citizens reduce, reuse, and recycle. The children can also take on the role of the city manager who has been hired to help the city reduce its waste.

◆ http://www.epa.gov/epaoswer/osw/kids.htm. More online activities for children.

water so that the materials are moist but not flooded. Tape each bag shut, label the bag with the group name, and leave it for two weeks. At the end of the two weeks, open the bags and look to see what degraded and what did not. Were the children's predictions correct? This could be followed by a visit to a local landfill.

Summary

Environmental awareness is a growing topic in education. Helping children gain an understanding that there is only a finite amount of natural resources and that they must be conserved is important. Children will find it empowering to know that their efforts make a difference.

KEY TERMS

resources	erosion	recycle
environment	pollution	landfill
conservation	biodegradable	

SUGGESTED ACTIVITIES

1. Choose one of the activities discussed in the unit and use it with children. Record your observations for class discussion.
2. Examine a teacher's edition of an elementary science textbook. Make a list of environmental awareness topics discussed in the text. What types of hands-on activities are suggested?
3. Select an environmental topic and concept and prepare a learning cycle lesson to teach that idea. Use the lesson with children.
4. Locate software that is available at your school that reinforces environmental science concepts. Try the software. Record your observations for class discussion.

Web Sites and Software

http://www.rice.edu/armadillo/Projrcys/Star/Facilitators/Mledwith/environ.html—Recycling unit and resource links.

http://www.a-horizon.com/compost/compost_menu.html—Composting information, activities, and resources.

http://www.epa.gov/—U.S. Environmental Protection Agency with activities for children, lesson plans for teachers, links to resources.

http://www.kid-at-art.com/—art projects using "trash."

http://www.dep.state.pa.us/dep/deputate/enved/Rec_Lessons/contnets.htm—Recycling lesson plans for kindergarten through grade 12 students from the Pennsylvania Department of Environmental Protection.

SimTown. Walnut Creek, CA: Maxis. (Ages eight through 12)

Zurk's Alaskan Trek. Palo Alto, CA: Soleil Software. (Ages six through 10)

Zurk's Rainforest Lab. Palo Alto, CA: Soleil Software. (Pre-K through grade three)

REVIEW

A. What are the three types of basic approaches used to teach environmental education? Identify one activity in this unit for each of these approaches.
B. What are typical topics and concepts included in environmental awareness programs? Why should this be included?
C. How would you include technology in your environmental education program?

REFERENCES

Cole, J. (1986). *Magic school bus: Through the water-works.* New York: Scholastic.

Dighe, J. (1993). Children and the earth. *Young Children, 48*(3), 58–63.

Lind, K. K. (1991). *Water, stones, and fossils bones.* Washington, DC: National Science Teachers Association.

National Research Council. (1996). *National science education standards.* Washington, DC: National Academy Press.

FURTHER READING AND RESOURCES

Basile, C., & White, C. (2000). Respecting living things: Environmental literacy for young children. *Early Childhood Education Journal, 28*(1), 57–61.

Basile, C., & White, C. (2000). A walk in the park is just the beginning. *Dimensions, 28*(3), 3–7.

Hurwitz, S. (1999, May–June). The adventure outside your classroom door. *Child Care Information Exchange* (127), 45–60.

Hyers, K. (1999, May–June). Nurturing environmental awareness in children. *Child Care Information Exchange* (127), 45–60.

Kelly, A. (1999, May–June). Environmental education as a teaching tool. *Child Care Information Exchange* (127), 45–60.

Kupetz, B. N., & Twiest, M. M. (2000). Nature, literature, and young children. *Young Children, 55*(1), 59–63.

Levine, S., & Grafton, A. (1992). *Projects for a healthy planet.* New York: John Wiley & Sons.

McMahon, M. M., O'Hara, S. P., Holliday, W. G., McCormack, B. B., & Gibson, E. M. (2000). Curriculum with a common thread. *Science and Children, 37*(7), 30–35, 57.

Shantal, R. (1998). Age-appropriate ecology: Are you practicing it? *Young Children, 53*(1), 70–71.

Snyder, S. L. (1999, May–June). Summertime science for school-agers. *Child Care Information Exchange* (127), 45–60.

Stephens, K. (1999, May–June). Sharing nature with children. *Child Care Information Exchange* (127), 45–60.

UNIT 38
Health and Nutrition

OBJECTIVES

After reading this unit, you should be able to:

◆ Design health and nutrition investigations for primary age children.

◆ Develop an understanding of health and nutrition topics that are appropriate for primary age children.

◆ Develop structured and unstructured learning experiences in health, nutrition, and the human body.

◆ Integrate science in the primary grades with other subjects.

Optimum growth and development depend on good nutrition, adequate experience, plenty of rest, and proper cleanliness. Concepts in health and nutrition need to be introduced to young children so they learn how to take care of their bodies and develop beneficial lifelong habits at an early age. This unit suggests experiences that help children learn about themselves through exploring the human diet, major food groups, and the human body. Lesson ideas for promoting good health habits are also presented.

The *National Science Education Standards* suggest that children should learn to apply science to personal and social perspectives, learn critical thinking, and develop the ability to produce useful ideas. The problems that are dealt with in this standard (personal

health, populations, environments, resources, and technology) are extremely complex. Reality is not simple, and it is hard for young children to see the underlying ideas. We can begin by building a base for extending children's perceptions in later years. Appropriate concepts for the early primary years focus on children developing an understanding that cleanliness, nutrition, exercise, and rest are necessary for good health. From an early age, children need to follow rules and make logical decisions such as looking both ways before crossing the street for their own safety and health.

Keep in mind that primary grade children tend to think that all microbes are "germs" and connect eating certain foods with being healthy. They understand hazards such as pollution only to the extent that they themselves might be affected in a direct way. Primary age children tend to expect adults to remove all dangers and risk in their environment and they understand cause and effect only to the extent of understanding the consequences. For example, children understand the connection between not wearing a coat on a cold day and the outcome of catching a cold, but they will not consider intervening variables such as lowered resistance.

Primary age children are beginning to develop an interest in how their bodies work. Upper primary grade children can learn about personal health by studying the structures of the human body, the functions of these structures, and nutrition as the source of energy.

The following health, nutrition, and human body concepts are basic to primary grade learning.

◆ Eating a variety of healthful foods and getting enough exercise and rest help people to stay healthy.

◆ Some things people take into their bodies from the environment can hurt them.

◆ A balanced diet consists of **carbohydrates, fats, proteins, vitamins, minerals,** and water.

◆ A diet that is a balance of food groups plus water makes up a healthful regimen for normal people.

◆ You can help yourself stay healthy.

◆ The human body can be affected by a variety of diseases.

◆ Some diseases are caused by germs; some are not. Washing one's hands with soap and water reduces the number of germs that can get into the body or be passed on to other people.

◆ The human body carries on life processes.

◆ Food is the fuel and the building material of the body.

◆ The human body must take in and digest food.

◆ Humans have a distinct body structure for walking, holding, seeing, and talking.

◆ The human body consists of a number of groups of organs that work together to perform a particular function.

◆ Movement of the human body is made possible by the skeleton and muscles.

◆ The human body takes in oxygen and gives off **carbon dioxide**.

◆ The **circulatory system** is the transportation system of the body.

◆ Humans reproduce and give off waste products.

◆ The brain enables human beings to think; it sends messages to other body parts to help them to work properly.

◆ Senses can warn individuals about danger; muscles help them fight, hide, or get out of danger.

◆ Humans observe and learn by seeing, hearing, feeling, tasting, and smelling.

◆ Men and women have made a variety of contributions to science and technology.

Explorations in Health and Nutrition

The learning experiences suggested in this unit introduce fundamental concepts that acquaint children with their bodies and how to stay healthy. Topics include good health habits; treatment of cuts and scrapes; how the body gains energy; the food pyramid and food activities; and bones, teeth, vitamins, and minerals.

Health Habits

Good health habits begin early in a child's life. Encourage children to begin an understanding of what healthy living really means by providing a variety of instructional techniques and subject integrations that relate to the child's life. Here are a few to get you started.

ACTIVITIES

ARE YOUR HANDS DIRTY?

CONCEPT: Hands that look clean can still be dirty.

OBJECTIVE: Observe the growth of mold on potatoes. Compare the effect of mold growth resulting from handling potatoes with washed and unwashed hands.

MATERIALS: Two small potatoes, potato peeler, two clean jars with lids that seal, labels, marker.

PROCEDURE: Have children examine their hands. Ask, ARE YOUR HANDS CLEAN? DO YOU SEE ANY DIRT ON THEM? Discuss how hands look when they are dirty. WHAT IS THE DIRTIEST YOUR HANDS HAVE EVER BEEN? THE CLEANEST?

Peel two potatoes, ask a child to handle one of them, and put it in a jar. (Select a child who has not washed his or her hands for several hours.) Point out that the child's hands appear to be clean.

Label the jar with the name of the child and the words *unwashed hands*. Instruct a child to wash his or her hands, handle the second potato, and put it in the remaining jar. Label the jar with the child's name and the words *washed hands*. Discuss the relative cleanliness of the washed hands potato.

Place the two jars in a warm place where the children can observe and record what happens. Compare what is happening to the potatoes after a day or two. (Mold is likely to form on the potato handled by unwashed hands.) Compare the potatoes, and discuss how the mold got on the potato (Figure 38–1). (Refer to Unit 34 for additional mold lessons.)

EXTENSION: Have children describe and draw what the unwashed and washed hands looked like. Ask, DID THE UNWASHED HANDS LOOK DIRTY? (No.) This would be a good time to discuss germs and the importance of washing hands before handling food. Have children design posters to encourage hand washing before meals.

Good health habits chart. Keep a record of your health habits. Answer questions about yourself for a week. (For example: I brushed my teeth after every meal. I took a bath or shower. I washed my hands before meals today. I exercised today.) At the end of the week, look at all of your answers. What can you do to improve your health habits?

Washed Hands

Unwashed Hands

FIGURE 38–1 "What is happening in the unwashed hands jar?"

APPLES AND ME

CONCEPT: Microorganisms (germs) can enter our body through cuts and scrapes in the skin.

OBJECTIVE: Compare the healing of injuries on an apple with injuries on our skin. Describe how antiseptic keeps germs out of our body.

MATERIALS: Three apples, soil or other type of dirt, antiseptic, two sewing needles.

PROCEDURE: Lead the children in a discussion of current injuries that they have received. Such incidents are a common happening in the primary grades. Encourage children to tell how the injury occurred and how it was treated.

Then hold an apple in your hand. Ask, HOW IS THE COVERING OF AN APPLE SIMILAR TO YOUR SKIN? HOW IS IT DIFFERENT? LET'S SEE WHAT HAPPENS WHEN THE SURFACE OF AN APPLE IS INJURED.

Label one apple the *control apple*. You will not injure this apple. Label the second apple *no antiseptic*, and the third apple *antiseptic*. Then, stir one of the needles in dirt, and puncture the second apple three times. Stir the other needle in dirt, sterilize the needle with antiseptic, and puncture the third apple (Figure 38–2). Place the three apples in a sunny place, and have the children keep a record of changes in the apples. Ask, WHAT DO YOU THINK THEY WILL LOOK LIKE IN ONE DAY? As children record the progress, discuss possible reasons for differences in the appearance of the apples. (The apple punctured by the unsterilized needle will rot fairly quickly.)

After several days, cut all of the apples in half, including the control apple. Ask, WHAT CHANGES DO YOU SEE IN THE APPLES? WHICH APPLE LOOKS THE WORST? DID STERILIZING THE NEEDLE MAKE ANY DIFFERENCE? WHAT DO YOU THINK WOULD HAPPEN IF THE SURFACE OF YOUR BODY WERE PUNCTURED? Discuss the best possible action to take in case of an injury. (Refer to the mold activities in Unit 34.)

EXTENSION: Sterilize the needles in different ways, such as using a candle flame to simulate heat sterilization or applying various commercial antiseptics to compare products.

Children will be interested in trying out this experiment with different types of foods and different types of injuries (scraping, cutting, slicing, and so on). Ask, IS THERE ANY SPECIAL WOUND THAT WILL LET THE MOST MICROORGANISMS FIND THEIR WAY THROUGH YOUR SKIN AND INTO YOUR BODY? (Puncture wounds.)

Test types of dirt. Fingernail dirt, shoe dirt, desk dirt. Find out if some dirt is "dirtier" than others.

Germ story. Write a story about the invading germs and what can be done to stop them. Children will enjoy acting out the invasions of germs into the body and their subsequent destruction by antiseptic.

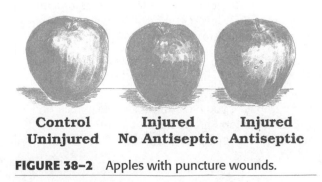

Control   **Injured**   **Injured**
Uninjured   **No Antiseptic**   **Antiseptic**

FIGURE 38–2   Apples with puncture wounds.

Foods We Eat

PLANT POWER

CONCEPT: We get energy from plants.

OBJECTIVE: Identify the parts of plants that store food and the parts we eat.

MATERIALS: A variety of foods, toothpicks.

PROCEDURE: When teaching about foods, it is important to stress that they are necessary for growth and development. One way to do this is to compare children's bodies to the bean seeds in Unit 34. Ask, WHERE DID THE BEANS GET THE ENERGY TO SPROUT? (From the food stored in them.) Remind children that young plants use the food stored in the seed to grow. Ask, CAN YOU GET ENERGY FROM SEEDS? (Yes, when you eat them.)

Show the children different plants, and ask, WHERE DO YOU THINK GREEN PLANTS STORE THEIR FOOD? (Leaves.) Hold up carrots and turnip plants and ask, WHERE DO THESE PLANTS STORE THEIR FOOD? (Roots.) Show a picture of sugarcane plants (or a piece, if available) and ask, WHERE DO YOU THINK THE SUGARCANE STORES ITS FOOD? (Stem, which is between the root and the leaves.) Remember that the white potato is really a stem plant and the sweet potato is a root plant.

After you assess student progress, you may want to continue the lesson by introducing them to fruits, which store food; food for plants; and flowers that store food such as broccoli and cauliflower. Ask, WHERE DO YOU THINK THESE PLANTS STORE FOOD? (Flowers.)

EXTENSION: Reinforce the idea that energy comes from plants and their stored food with a plant-tasting party. You will need enough food samples for the entire class to taste. (You could ask each child to bring a sample.) Before the tasting party, have the children group plants by the parts that store food, wash the plants, cut them into bite-size parts, and put a toothpick in each piece. Ask, DO WE USE ALL OF THESE PLANT PARTS FOR FOOD? (Yes, taste seeds, leaves, roots, stems, fruits, and flowers and discuss favorite plant parts.)

FOOD PYRAMID

CONCEPT: Foods from the basic groups provide the nutrients necessary for good health.

OBJECTIVE: Identify the food groups and the number of servings per day that are suggested (Figure 38–3).

MATERIALS: Magazine pictures of food.

PROCEDURE: Have children cut out magazine pictures from each food group. Mount the pictures on construction paper, add identifying food group labels, and pin to a bulletin board. Let the children decide if the pictures are labeled correctly. Move misplaced pictures to the correct categories and create a food pyramid.

EXTENSION: *Bag it.* Label lunch bags for each food group. Then, cut out and laminate pictures of food. Have children sort the cutouts into the correct bags. You can use this idea in a center or as an interactive bulletin board.

Food group biography. Choose a group, and write your biography. If you were a food group, which one would you be? What would it be like to be this food group? Does your food group have a future?

Sell your food group. Make a television or radio commercial that will persuade the class that your food group is worthy of being eaten every day.

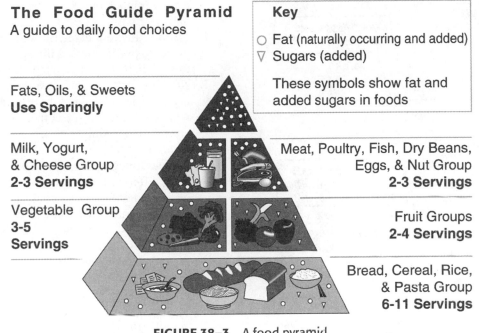

The Food Guide Pyramid
A guide to daily food choices

Key

○ Fat (naturally occurring and added)
▽ Sugars (added)

These symbols show fat and
added sugars in foods

Fats, Oils, & Sweets
Use Sparingly

Milk, Yogurt,
& Cheese Group
2-3 Servings

Meat, Poultry, Fish, Dry Beans,
Eggs, & Nut Group
2-3 Servings

Vegetable Group
**3-5
Servings**

Fruit Groups
2-4 Servings

Bread, Cereal, Rice,
& Pasta Group
6-11 Servings

FIGURE 38–3   A food pyramid.

Additional Food Activities

1. *Fatty foods.* Ask, "How can you find out if food has fat in it?" Place a drop of liquid fat on a piece of brown paper. Hold the paper up to the light and ask, "Does the light come through where the fat is?" After a few hours ask, "Is the spot dry or does it stay the same?" (Stays the same.) Test the fat in foods such as peanut butter, nuts, olives, and milk by leaving the food on brown paper for a few hours. Then ask, "Is the spot dry, or does it stay the same?" After testing several foods ask, "How do you know there is fat in these foods?" (Fatty oils stay on the paper.)

2. *Sugar time.* Show the children a variety of food containers (jars, boxes, and so on). Have them predict which foods contain sugar. After they write their predictions on a prediction sheet, have them read the ingredients on the food containers to check their predictions. Explain that the ingredients are listed in sequence from greatest amount to smallest. Also note information on vitamin, mineral, and calorie content. Compare results. Then, write the word *sugar* on the chalkboard. Ask, "Does the list on the label say sugar?" (Not always.) Introduce the children to some of the ways sugars are listed: corn syrup, maltose, sucrose, fructose, corn sweetener, syrup, dextrose, glucose, lactose, molasses. Discuss the amount of sugar in foods, and decide if eating a lot of sugar is a good idea.

3. *Classify foods.* Give children practice in identifying which foods belong in which food group by making charts and food group books. This can be done by using pictures; classifying individual children's diets; and analyzing school lunch menus, the contents of bag lunches, and the evening meal.

4. *Finding out.* Divide the class into small groups, and give each questions to explore about different food groups. Make a web of their findings as they share with the class (Figure 38–4).

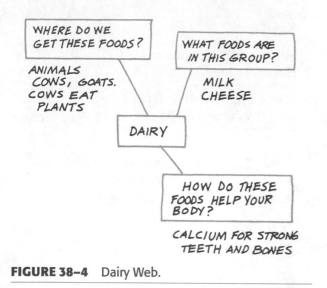

FIGURE 38–4 Dairy Web.

5. *Foods I like chart.* Have children write the names of the foods they would like to eat for breakfast, lunch, and dinner on a chart. Then, make a chart, and list the foods that they actually eat at these meals. Compare the charts and identify foods that are high in fats, carbohydrates, and sugar (potato chips, and so on). Discuss the nutritional value of the foods. Children might want to keep a log of foods that they eat for breakfast over a week's time (or food eaten for lunch or dinner). Compare class eating habits.

6. *Visitors.* Invite a cafeteria worker or restaurant owner to talk about cleanliness and a nutritionist to explain how the lunch menus are created.

7. *Tasting party.* One effective method of evaluating food learning is to have a tasting party in which the children select their meal from a variety of foods. Simply observe which foods the children select to make up the meal.

8. *Recipes.* Integrate social studies by tasting foods from different countries or from different areas of town. Families also cook in different ways. Discuss similarities and differences, and make recipe books of favorite recipes. Have parents or other guests from a variety of ethnic backgrounds make one of their special dishes or share some special food with the class (refer to the many food activities in previous units). This activity is more effective if families share favorite foods throughout the year instead of just at one time. This will help avoid using a tourist approach to diversity.

We Are What We Eat

Study vitamins and minerals as far as the developmental level of your students permits. Here are a few ideas to get you started.

KEEPING BONES AND TEETH STRONG

CONCEPT: Food supplies the body with important minerals. Calcium is a mineral that is used to make bones and teeth strong.

OBJECTIVE: Test rocks for the presence of calcium. Observe evidence of calcium.

MATERIALS: Pieces of limestone, chalk, marble, vinegar, hand lenses, medicine droppers.

CAUTION: Hydrochloric acid is usually used for this test. However, when working with young children, use vinegar.

PROCEDURE: Show children the rocks, and ask, WHAT ARE ROCKS MADE OF? (Many answers; one will probably be minerals.) Tell the children that they can test for the presence of a mineral called calcium by dropping acid or vinegar on a rock.

Give children samples of limestone. Ask, WHAT DO YOU THINK WILL HAPPEN IF WE DROP VINEGAR ON A ROCK? Instruct the children to fill the medicine dropper and carefully drop the vinegar on the rocks. Have the children observe and record what happens to the rocks. (Bubbles form.) Generate a list of words that describe children's observations. (Fizz, bubble, smell, and so on.) Explain that the bubbles indicate calcium is present.

EXTENSION: Children enjoy comparing the hard parts of their bodies to rocks. Ask, HOW ARE BONES AND TEETH LIKE ROCKS? (They both contain minerals.) Explain that two minerals, calcium and phosphorus, combine to make bones and teeth hard. Good sources include milk and other dairy foods, fruits, and vegetables. Other foods, such as eggs, leafy green vegetables, meats, grains, and nuts, have some calcium. Bring an end to the lesson by asking, WHERE DO WE GET THE CALCIUM TO MAKE OUR BONES AND TEETH STRONG? (From our foods.)

Chicken bones. Testing the brittleness of chicken bones can help children understand that bones are more likely to break if they do not have the necessary minerals. To conduct this test, scrub two large chicken bones thoroughly. Soak one in water and one in vinegar for several days. Have the children compare the bones with handheld lenses and note any differences. Then, predict which of the two bones will break more easily. (Vinegar dissolves calcium and phosphorus.) Compare the chicken bones to human bones.

Tear or crush? Have the children examine their teeth with mirrors and identify different sizes and shapes of teeth. How are the front teeth shaped? Ask, WHEN DO YOU USE YOUR FRONT TEETH? HOW DO YOUR FRONT TEETH HELP YOU EAT? WHAT TYPES OF FOOD DO YOU NEED TO CRUSH TO EAT? WHICH TEETH HELP YOU CRUSH FOOD?

This would be a good time to discuss carnivorous and herbivorous animals. Show pictures of animals eating. Ask, WHAT TYPE OF TEETH DO THESE ANIMALS HAVE? After categorizing animals (and dinosaurs) by what they eat and discussing the shape and use of teeth, ask WHICH CATEGORY DO WE BELONG IN? (Both.) WHY? (We have several types of teeth. We eat both plants and animals.)

How do nutrients get into food? To show how the roots of vegetables take in minerals from the soil, mix red food coloring and water. Have children observe the small rootlets that grow from the core of a carrot. Then, submerge the carrot in dyed water for 24 hours. Ask, WHAT HAPPENED TO THE RED COLOR? (Passes to the core of the carrot.) HOW DID IT GET THERE? (Through the rootlets.)

You may want to set up this observation with several different vegetables. Children will discover that dissolved minerals come into plants through plant roots. Let them decide that as we eat the plants, we take in the same minerals.

Then ask, IF PLANTS GET MINERALS FROM SOIL WATER, CAN WE GET MINERALS FROM WATER, TOO? (Yes.) Minerals in water are sulfur, chlorine, sodium, calcium, magnesium, potassium, fluorine. Discuss how we get minerals from water. (Drink, eat, plants, animals.)

Additional Mineral Activities

Iron. Iron is a mineral that you need in your blood. The iron combines with protein to form a compound that makes blood red. This compound also carries oxygen to all parts of your body. Meats, beans, peas, grains, and leafy vegetables are good sources of iron. Children will enjoy acting out the oxygen processing function of iron. Ask, "How do we get iron into our bodies?"

Children can "become" blood platelets, oxygen, and food by wearing appropriate labels and drawings.

Make a vein path with red yarn for the children to follow as they trace the journey of a blood platelet. Have children create a script about how iron enters the body and what it does to help them stay healthy.

Anemia. You can get sick if you do not get enough iron. Ask, "Do you eat foods that give your body iron?" Discuss foods that contain iron. Explain that when you have had a good night's sleep but still are tired all the time, you may be anemic. People with anemia get tired easily because their blood does not carry enough oxygen. Ask, "What can you do to avoid getting anemia?" (Eat foods that contain iron.)

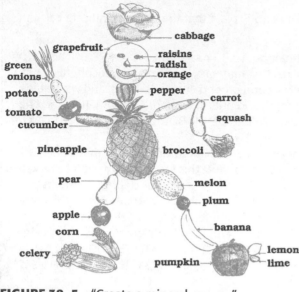

FIGURE 38–5 "Create a mineral person."

Plan a meal. Have children plan a meal for someone with anemia. If you are studying vitamins, children could plan a meal for someone with beriberi. (People with beriberi lack essential vitamins and minerals and are too weak to use their muscles to do work.)

Mineral people. Study the labels of common foods. Categorize cans and boxes of food by the minerals they contain. Then make mineral people such as an Iron Person or a Calcium Person. These figures can be made from the actual foods or boxes or pictures of these foods (Figure 38–5). Then, decide what foods are needed to create Vitamin People.

Strategies for Teaching the Human Body

The internal anatomy of the human body is a difficult concept for young children to understand. Concrete experiences on which to base understandings can be difficult to provide. Refer to Unit 26 to review the garbage bag strategy for introducing children to the inside of the human body. In addition to the suggestions in Unit 26, the following suggestions will help you provide the children with concrete learning strategies.

Inside of Me

Although it is difficult to observe the inside of the human body, children can infer that muscles, bones, and organs are inside of them. For example, bones give the body shape, help the body move, and protect the organs. Preliminary activities should include body awareness activities in which children explore, feel, and identify some of the major bones. Observation of X-ray films can further enhance the children's concept of bones. Then, trace a Halloween skeleton, cut out the bones, and assemble the skeleton using paper fasteners as joints. Try some of the following strategies for teaching about bones with children.

Our Skeleton Has Joints

Have the children move their arms and legs in a way that explores the way joints work: marching, saluting, swinging arms and legs, and acting like a windmill. Ask, "Do your legs bend when you march? Can you march without bending your legs? Is it easy to do?" Point out and explore the joints that help your body move. Discover the difference between hinge joints, which bend one way, and ball and socket joints, which can bend, twist, and rotate (Figure 38–6).

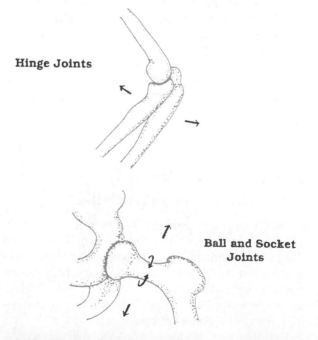

FIGURE 38–6 A ball and socket joint and a hinge joint.

Find the Joints

Have children work in pairs to make a paper body and locate joints. Have one child lie on a piece of butcher paper and the other child draw the outline of the body. Then, have the children locate joints on the paper body. Discuss why the type of joint used in the body is the most appropriate. Ask, "What would happen if we had a ball and socket joint in our knees?"

Writing about Bones

Explore the advantages and disadvantages of different types of joints by having children write stories about children with joints in different places. For example, if a child had a hinge joint where a shoulder joint is needed, how would the child move? What would a day in the life of that child be like?

Do Chickens Have Joints?

Find out if the children think that a chicken has joints. Then, make chicken bones available to demonstrate how joints work. After children have had time to explore the chicken bones, ask, "How is your skeleton like a chicken skeleton?" (Both have joints and other similarities.)

Finger Bones

Have children place their fingers over the light of a flashlight. Ask, "What do you see? How can you tell that you have bones inside of your fingers?" Have a doctor visit your class and discuss the use of X-rays. The children will enjoy seeing X-ray pictures of bones, especially broken bones. This would be a good time to discuss first aid for broken bones.

Bone Music and Art

Sing "Dry Bones." ("The toe bone's connected to the foot bone, the foot bone's connected to the ankle bone," and so on.) Children can compare skeleton poster bones as they sing, or a model of the backbone can be made with yarn and pieces of macaroni.

Make a Muscle

Young children enjoy flexing their arm muscles and feeling the muscles they can make, but they might think that arm muscles are the only ones they have. Encourage them to discover other muscles by raising their heels off the ground in a tiptoe position. Ask, "Can you feel your muscles move as they do this?" Have the children lie on mats, stretch out like a cat, then curl up into a ball. Ask, "Which muscles can you feel now?"

Explore facial muscles by wiggling noses and raising eyebrows. Ask, "Does your tongue have muscles?" (Yes.) Give children time to find unexpected muscles in their bodies. Then, apply some of the bone and joint learning experiences to teaching about muscles.

All about Me

Children like to know that they are the same as others and that they are different, too. Discuss the similarities and differences in people that make them who they are. Give children opportunities to explore their bodies and what makes them an individual.

Exploring the Body: Using Hands and Feet to Help Us Move

Ask children to find out how many things they can do with their hands such as wave, rub, scratch, or make a fist. Then, find out how many things can be done with their feet: skip, hop, walk, tiptoe. Have children write or dictate a list of their findings. Ask, "Can you think of something that you cannot do with your hands or cannot do with your feet? How important it your thumb?" Have the children do an activity without using their thumbs.

Paper Bodies

Full-sized paper outlines of a child's body can be used as a starting point for many learning experiences. Partners take turns tracing around each other on butcher paper with a crayon (Figure 38–7). Then, each child cuts out his or her body by following along the lines. Examples include:

◆ *Story character body.* After the paper body is made, have the children study their faces in a mirror and draw their features on one side of the paper body. Children will enjoy creating a

FIGURE 38–7 "Make a paper body."

fantasy body or storybook character on their own body shape.

◆ *Math body.* The cutout paper body can be an easy way for children to measure parts of their character's body. They can measure length of body, arms, and so on, and add weight and physical characteristics on a chart.

◆ *Action body.* After children are familiar with body tracing, let them trace each other in action poses and guess who is doing what and with what. Have magazines available for references of how a dancer uses muscles, how joints bend as an athlete runs, and how joints are used to sit in a chair.

◆ *I am curious.* Have children fill the paper body with magazine pictures depicting things they like to do, are curious about, or want to learn about. Ask, "What would you like to learn more about? Find things that you are curious about." Make "I Am Curious" bodies and the like.

◆ *Body mobile.* Separate this body at the joints and attach the body parts with yarn. These body mobiles can hang from the ceiling.

◆ *Body parts.* Cut-up paper bodies can be added to a bulletin board or center. The body part bulletin board features an envelope of body parts that are assembled with thumbtacks. Labels may be added to name the parts, bones, joints, or organs that are being emphasized (Figure 38–8).

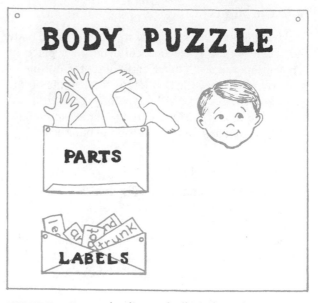

FIGURE 38–8 A body part bulletin board.

Senses

Studying the senses and how they can be used to gather information is a natural exploration for young children. Refer to Units 16, 24, 26, and 36 for exploration ideas and to the senses learning center in Unit 39 for suggestions. The following sense walk experience is a useful beginning or extension for an ongoing study of the senses:

Sense Walk

Ask the children to be absolutely silent as they take a walk around school. Plan to pass the lunchroom; office; custodian's area; gymnasium; other classrooms; and special area rooms, such as art and music. Instruct children to use their senses to notice as many things as they can. When you return to class, make a class chart or web of all the things noticed on the walk, such as different types of noises, smells, textures, sounds, and activity. Ask questions to encourage thinking, such as, "Did the floor of the office feel like the floor of the classroom?" On a different day, take the class on an outside walk and brainstorm an experience web with the children to reinforce observations (Figure 38–9).

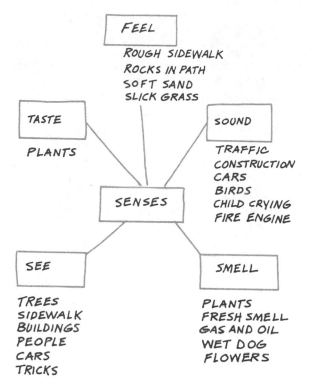

FEEL
ROUGH SIDEWALK
ROCKS IN PATH
SOFT SAND
SLICK GRASS

TASTE
PLANTS

SOUND
TRAFFIC
CONSTRUCTION
CARS
BIRDS
CHILD CRYING
FIRE ENGINE

SENSES

SEE
TREES
SIDEWALK
BUILDINGS
PEOPLE
CARS
TRICKS

SMELL
PLANTS
FRESH SMELL
GAS AND OIL
WET DOG
FLOWERS

FIGURE 38–9   Brainstorm with an experience web.

Summary

Good health and nutrition habits begin early in a child's life. For children to begin to understand what it means to be healthy, they need to be exposed to a variety of learning experiences. These experiences need to be integrated into the child's life to have meaning and be as concrete as possible for better understanding.

Although children are curious about their bodies and how they work, their knowledge of internal anatomy is limited, and children find the subject especially difficult to understand. Concrete experiences on which to base learning about bones, muscles, and organs must be provided to ensure understanding.

EXAMPLE WORLD WIDE WEB ACTIVITIES

◆ http://www.nutritionexplorations.org. Games, recipes, and information about nutrition from the National Dairy Council.

◆ http://www.exhibits.pacsci.org/nutrition/. Games and information for children about nutrition and physical activity from the Pacific Science Center.

KEY TERMS

nutrition	fats	minerals
germs	proteins	carbon dioxide
carbohydrates	vitamins	circulatory system

SUGGESTED ACTIVITIES

1. Assemble materials for one of the suggested learning activities. Try out the lesson with a small group of primary age children. Report to the class on what you did and how the children responded. How did you evaluate the children's responses? Would you change the activity if you were to teach it again?

2. Design a nutrition learning strategy for your Activity File. Which process skills will you emphasize? How many areas of the curriculum can you integrate into this lesson?

3. Develop your own teaching web. Select lessons from this unit, and design a teaching unit that is appropriate for a group of children you are teaching.

4. Prepare a learning cycle lesson to teach a health, nutrition, or human body concept. Teach it to a group of children, and report to the class. What was the advantage of using the learning cycle? Would another teaching strategy have worked better with this concept or group of children?

5. Locate software in your school's library that teaches or reinforces health and nutrition concepts. Preview the software. Select one piece of software to introduce to a small group of children. As the children interact with the software, record their comments and behaviors. Use this to evaluate the software's instructional effectiveness. Write an evaluation in which you address (1) the concept(s) upon which the software focuses, (2) how developmentally appropriate the software's instructional activities are, and (3) how well the students appeared to learn the concepts being taught or reinforced. Present these findings to your class.

REVIEW

A. List two reasons health and nutrition education should be an essential part of the science curriculum in the primary grades.

B. Develop a rationale for including health and nutrition concepts in the study of science in the school.

C. Discuss how you would adapt health and nutrition activities for preoperational children and then concrete operational children.

REFERENCE

National Research Council (1996). *National science education standards*. Washington, DC: National Academy Press.

FURTHER READING AND RESOURCES

Abruscoto, J. (1995). *Teaching children science: A discovery approach* (4th ed.). Needham Heights, MA: Allyn & Bacon.

Abruscato, J. (2000). *Whizbangers and wonderments*. Boston: Allyn & Bacon.

Allison, L. (1976). *Blood and guts*. Boston: Little, Brown.

Bershad, C., & Bernick, D. (1979). *Bodyworks: The kids' guide to food and physical fitness*. New York: Random House.

Brummet, D. C., Lind, K. K., Barman, C. R., DiSpezio, M. A., & Ostlund, K. L. (1995). *Destinations in science.* Menlo Park, CA: Addison-Wesley.

Carter, C. D., & Phillips, F. K. (1979). *Activities that teach health.* New York: Instructor Publications, Inc.

Harlan, J. (1995). *Science experiences for the early childhood years.* New York: Macmillan.

Hendry, L. (1987). *Foodworks.* Menlo Park, CA: Addison-Wesley.

Herbert, D. (1980). *Mr. Wizard's supermarket science.* New York: Random House.

Katz, L. G. (1988). *Early childhood education: What research tells us.* Bloomington, IN: Phi Delta Kappa Educational Foundation.

Kepler, L. (1996). *Windowsill science centers.* New York: Scholastic.

King, M. D., (2000). Rev up your veggies! *Science and children, 38*(1), 20–25.

Lind, K. K. (1983). Apples, oranges, baseballs and me. In D. Stroak (Ed.), *Understanding the healthy body* (pp. 123–125). Columbus, OH: SMEAC Information Reference Center.

Lind, K. K. (1985). The inside story. *Science and children, 22*(4), 122–123.

Lowery, L. F. (1997). *NSTA pathways to the science standards.* Arlington, VA: National Science Teachers Association.

The National Research Council. (1996). *National science education standards.* Washington, DC: National Academy Press.

Science and Children. (1982), Skeleton Poster. Washington, DC: National Science Teachers Association.

Sherwood, E. A., Williams, R. A., & Rockwell, R. E. (1990). *Mudpies to magnets.* Mt. Rainier, MD: Gryphon House.

Stronck, D. (1983). *Understanding the human body.* Columbus, OH: SMEAC Information Reference Center.

Web Sites and Software

http://www.bbc.co.uk/health/kids. Take a tour of how different systems in the body work.

http://www.brainpop.com/health/seeall.html. Cartoons and activities for children about how the body works.

http://www.exhibits.pacsci.org/nutrition/. Games and information for children about nutrition and physical activity from the Pacific Science Center.

http://www.nutritionexplorations.org. Games, recipes, and information about nutrition from the National Dairy Council.

http://www.soyunica.gov. Information and games about health, nutrition, body image, and self-esteem. Available in English and Spanish.

http://www.Yourchildshealth.echn.ca/hsc/echn.nsf/Pages/agechoice. Games and stories about your child's health. Organized by age groups.

Betty Crocker Cooking with Kids. Fairfield, NJ: Allegro New Media. (Ages 6+)

Body Park. Needham, MA: Virtual Entertainment. (PreK–6)

"Cell"ebration. Lewisville, NC: Science for Kids. (K–3)

Dr. Health'nstein's Body Fun. San Francisco: Star-Press Multimedia. (Ages 7–14)

Incredible Lab. Pleasantville, NY: Sunburst Communications.

Mayo Clinic Family Health Book. Rochester, MN: IVI Publishing. (All grades)

Mc, Myself, and I. Chicago: Jostens Learning. (K–3)

National Geographic CDs for Educators: The Human Body. Washington, DC: National Geographic. (Pre-K–3)

Science #5, House a Fire! Fire Prevention. San Ramon, CA: The Ellen Nelson Learning Library, Decision Development Corporation. (3–5 grades)

The Magic Schoolbus: Human Body. Redmond, WA: Microsoft. (Ages 6–10)

The Ultimate 3-D Skeleton. London: Dorling Kindersley. (Ages 8+)

The Ultimate Human Body. London: Dorling Kindersley. (Ages 8+)

Welcome to Bodyland. Rochester, MN: IVI Publishing. (Pre-K–2)

What Is a Belly Button. Rochester, MN: IVI Publishing. (Pre-K–3)

The Math and Science Environment

UNIT 39

Materials and Resources for Math and Science

OBJECTIVES

After reading this unit, you should be able to:

◆ Set up learning centers for math and science.

◆ Select appropriate materials for teaching math and science.

◆ List examples of basic materials that can be used to support specific math and science concept development.

Whether learning experiences are presented in an informal, unstructured, or structured approach (a learning cycle, discrepant event, or demonstration) or are used in learning centers or manipulated by an entire class at one time, manipulative science and mathematics require materials for children to explore. Hands-on mathematics and science require that materials be handled, stored, distributed, and replaced whenever they are used. Do not be discouraged. In the long run, once the materials are accumulated and organized, less time is needed for teacher preparation because much of the classroom instruction will be carried out by the interaction of the child and the materials.

There are categories of math and science materials that can be used to guide selections. In Unit 3, six categories of math materials were discussed: real objects, real objects used with pictorial representations, two-dimensional cutouts, pictures, wipe-off folders, and paper and pencil. These categories follow a developmental sequence from the concrete manipulative to the abstract representational. Preoperational children work with only the first four types of materials. During the transition to concrete operations, the last two categories may be available for those children who can deal with them. All through the concrete operations period, new concepts and skills should be introduced with concrete manipulative and pictorial materials before moving on to the abstract representational.

Many kinds of concrete manipulative materials have been introduced throughout the preceding units. Some are very versatile, and others serve specific functions. Pictorial manipulatives and other picture materials have also been suggested. Children's picture books are an especially rich source of pictorial and language information, as was suggested in Unit 15. Stories, poems, and pictures enrich the math curriculum. These materials help teach math vocabulary, illustrate the use of math in a variety of settings, and expand children's ideas of how math can be used. Books should be carefully selected. Be sure the illustrations accurately portray the concepts the book purports to help teach. As noted in Unit 24, special care must be taken when selecting counting books because the illustrations are frequently inaccurate in their depiction of the set/symbol relationships. The teacher should ask, Which concept or concepts are illustrated in this book? How will reading this story or poem help Richard, Liu Pei, or Mary to better understand this concept? Books should have good artwork and be colorful and well written. NCTM, the National Council of Teachers of Mathematics, publishes a resource catalog (see address in Figure 39–3).

There are several general categories of science materials. The most complete listing of available materials appears each January in *Science and Children*, a journal of the National Science Teachers Association, available through NSTA Publications. This useful supplement answers the question, "Where do I go for help?" The publication is organized into four main sections: equipment/supplies, media producers, computers/software, and publishers. This unit offers suggestions for the selection of basic science materials and resources and preparing science learning centers. The guidelines for selecting math materials for young children can also be applied to selecting science materials.

Basic Math and Science Materials

There are two basic types of math and science materials: those you purchase, and those you "scrounge." Purchased materials include textbook publishers' kits, general kits, and items purchased at supply houses or local retailers. Materials that are scrounged or contributed by parents and other benevolent individuals are known by many teachers as "good junk." Regardless of how the materials are acquired, they must be organized and managed in a way that promotes learning. (Refer to Unit 33 for additional suggestions for classroom management.)

The Good Junk Box: Things to Scrounge

Many teachers rely on boxes of miscellaneous materials that have been gathered from many sources. Such a junk box comes in handy. Invite children, friends, businesspeople, and others to add to your junk box. Once people know you collect odds and ends, they will remember you when they are ready to throw something away; for example

- Glass containers and two-liter bottles make good aquariums, terrariums, and places to display animals.
- Aluminum foil, pie plates, and freezer food containers are useful for numerous activities.
- Film cans make smell and sound containers.
- Hardware supplies are always welcome for the tool center; plastic tubing, garden hoses, and funnels are ideal for water play and making musical instruments.
- Candles, thumbtacks, paper clips, and sink and float items come in handy.
- Refrigerator magnets are useful for magnet experiences; old, leaky aquariums make good housing for small mammals or reptiles.
- Oatmeal containers make drums; shoe boxes are great for dioramas and general organization and storage.
- Toys, clocks, and kitchen tools can be added to the machine center.
- Flashlights, batteries, and wire from telephone lines can be used for electricity experiments.
- Pipe cleaners are always useful for art; buttons and other small objects are needed for classifying and comparing.
- Straws, balloons, paper cups, pieces of fabric, and wallpaper are objects for the touch box.
- Some stores invite teachers to collect their old carpet and wallpaper sample books.
- Always keep an eye out for feathers, unusual rocks, shells, seed-growing containers, plastic eggs—the list is endless.
- Items that can be counted, sorted, graphed, and so on, such as plastic lids from bottles, jars, and other containers; thread spools; pinecones; seashells; buttons; and seeds are useful.
- Egg cartons and frozen food containers can be used for sorting.
- String, ribbon, sticks, and so on can be used for comparing lengths and for informal measuring.
- Small boxes (i.e., frozen foods, and so on) can be used for construction projects.

See Unit 41 for additional suggestions.

Some teachers send home a list of "junk" items at the beginning of the year. Parents are asked to bring or send available items to school. Such a list will be easy to complete when you become familiar with "good junk" and have an idea of some of the items that you will use during the year. In addition, parents are usually responsive to special requests such as vegetables for the vegetable activities like those in Unit 26 or ingredients for the cooking activities in Unit 36.

Commercial Materials for Science

Your school district might decide to purchase a kit from a publisher when selecting a textbook for teaching science. Publisher kits are available from most major companies and contain materials specifically designed to implement the activities suggested in the textbook. These kits can be helpful in providing the hands-on component of a textbook-based science program.

General kits are available from many sources and range in size from small boxes to large pieces of furniture with built-in equipment such as sinks and cabinets. General kits contain basic materials but may not be directed to your specific needs. An advantage of the boxes or rolling tables is that they are easy to circulate among teachers.

Specific topic kits such as "Mining, Minerals, and Me" from Delta Education (suggested in Unit 36) are boxed by topic and grade level. The idea is to provide the teacher with the materials necessary to teach a specific science topic. Teachers' manuals and materials allow teachers to use the kit as a supplement to a textbook or as the major means of teaching a science concept.

Advantages and Disadvantages of Kits

Most kits contain a limited amount of consumable supplies, usually just enough for a class to do all of the activities covered in the teacher manual. Reordering must be continuous for the kit to be used again. However, the kits also contain permanent supplies such as magnifiers, clay, small plastic aquariums, petri dishes, balances, and the like.

The major drawbacks to commercial kits of any type are maintaining the consumables in the kits and finding the money to purchase the kits. Kits are self-contained, complete, and ready for use; consequently, they are also expensive.

Purchased Equipment

There are some items that you might have to purchase to be an effective science teacher. This list includes magnifiers, eyedroppers, plastic tubing, mirrors, a rock and mineral set, magnets, batteries, and bulbs. If you select just one of these items, do not hesitate to choose magnifiers as the most useful piece of science equipment for the early childhood classroom. (Refer to Unit 33 for suggestions on using magnifiers.)

Although they are not interactive in the same way as rollers, ramps, and constructions, magnifiers provide children with their first look at fascinating magnified objects. Piaget was a biologist and probably would have wholeheartedly approved. It is hard to believe that he did not eagerly explore his environment up close at an early age.

There are a multitude of commercially available materials for mathematics. Some materials are very versatile and can be used in the development of more than one concept. Basic materials include unit blocks with miniature animals, people, and vehicles; construction materials (Figure 39–1); Unifix Cubes®; Lego®; Multilinks®; pegboards and pegs; picture lotto games; beads and strings; attribute blocks; geoboards; balance scales; a thermometer; a flannelboard and a magnet board with felt and magnet pieces for concept activities; Montessori Cylinder Blocks® (Figure 39–2); a manipulative clock; base 10 blocks; and fraction pies. Hand calculators and computers should also be available. The list is endless. Search through the major catalogs (Figure 39–3), and decide what you can afford. Also consider assembling and making materials (see the resource lists at the end of each unit).

Organizing and Storing Materials

As you collect and develop materials for teaching science and math, storage might become a problem. Most commercial kits have neat, ready-made labeled boxes, but the "junk box" system will need some organizing.

One way to manage a variety of materials is to place them in shoe boxes. The shoe boxes contain the

Blockbusters	Crystal Climbers	Wonderforms	Block Head
Lego®	Rig-A-Jig	Geo-D-Stix	Snap-N-Play Blocks
Free Form Posts	Color Cone	Connector	Channel Blocks
Sprocketeers	Tectonic	Wood'n Molds	Wee Waffle Blocks
Tinkertoys	Structo-Brics	Poki Blocks	Struts
Toy Makers	Giant Structo-Cubes	Multi-fit	Duplo®
Cloth Cubes	Floresco	Disco Shapes	Gear Circus
Snap Wall	Ring-A-Majigs	Snap Blocks	Create It
Lock & Stack Blocks	Crystal Octons	Bristle Blocks	LASY Construction Kits
Giant Interlockers	Ji-gan-tiks	Bristle Bears	Giant Double Towers
Unifix Cubes®	Mobilo	Brio Builder	Gears! Gears!
Unit Blocks	Locktagons	Flexo	Frontier Logs 'N Blocks
Flexibricks	Connect-A-Cube	Klondikers	Marble Run
Play Shapes	Tuff Tuff Blocks	Beam and Boards	Construction Rug
Stackobats	Polydron	Hex-A-Links	Sturdiblocks
Magnetic Blocks	Play Squares	Pipe Construction	Giant Edu-Blocks
Form-A-Tions	3D Geoshapes	Bendits	Soft Big-Blocks
Poly-M	Learning Links	K'Nex	Galaxy Builder
Omnifix	Tower-ifics	Habitat	Building Clowns
Multilinks	Edu-Builder	Busy Blocks	Building Shapes
Jumbo Cuisinaire Rods	Groovy Parts	Space Wheels	Bolt Builder
Mega Blocks	Octagons	Magnastiks	Light Table and Accessories
Lincoln Logs	Girders	Keeptacks	Beads
Baufix	Play-Panels	Balancing H Blocks	Cuisinaire® Rods

FIGURE 39–1 Construction materials for math.

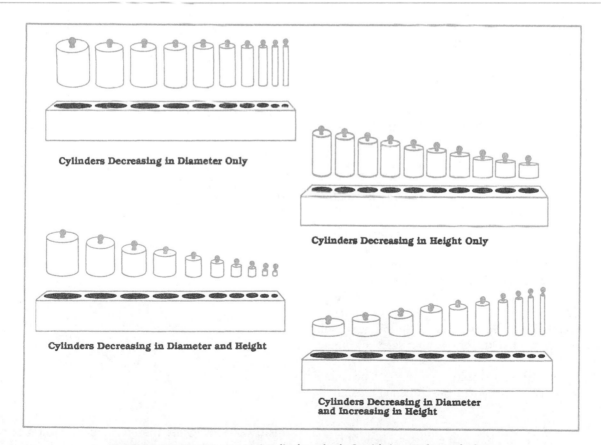

Cylinders Decreasing in Diameter Only

Cylinders Decreasing in Height Only

Cylinders Decreasing in Diameter and Height

Cylinders Decreasing in Diameter
and Increasing in Height

FIGURE 39–2 Montessori Cylinder Blocks® with insets for ordering.

- AIMS Educational Foundation, P.O. Box 8120, Fresno, CA 93747-8120. Phone: 888-733-2467; Fax: 559-255-6396; E-mail: AIMSed@AIMSed.org.
- AGS - American Guidance Service, 4201 Woodland Rd., Circle Pines, MN 55014-1796. Phone: 1-800-328-2560; Fax: 800-471-8457; E-mail: customerservice@agsnet.com; http://www.agsnet.com.
- Annenberg/CPB, 401 9th St., NW, Washington, DC 20004. Phones: 202-879-9654 and 800-LEARNER; Fax: 802-846-1850; E-mail: acpbreso@resolut.com.
- Community Playthings, P.O. Box 901, Route 213, Rifton, NY 12471. Phone: 800-777-4244; Fax: 800-336-5948.
- Constructive Playthings, 13201 Arrington Rd., Grandview, MO 64030-2886. Phone: 800-448-4115; Kansas City area, 800-448-1412; http://www.cptoys.com.
- Creative Educational Surplus, 1000 Apollo Road, Eagan, MN 55121-2240. Phone: 800-886-6428; http://www.creativesurplus.com.
- Creative Publications (Wright Group/McGraw Hill), 1221 Avenue of the Americas, New York, NY 10020. Phone: 800-624-0822; http://www.mimosausa.com.
- Cuisinaire, P.O. Box 5040, White Plains, NY 10602-5040. Phone 877-411-2761; Fax: 877-368-9033 or 877-368-9034; http://www.cuisinaire.com.
- Dale Seymour Publications® at Pearson Learning, P.O. Box 2649, Columbus, OH 43216-2649. Phone: 800-321-3106; Fax: 800-393-3156; http://www.pearsonlearning.com.
- Delta Education, P.O. Box 3000, Nashua, NH 03061-3000. Phone: 800-442-5444; Fax: 800-282-9560; http://www.delta-ed.com.
- Didax Educational Resources, 395 Main Street, Rowley, MA 01969-0907. Phone: 800-458-0024; Fax: 800-350-2345; http://www.didaxinc.com.
- Early Childhood Direct, P.O. Box 369, Landisville, PA 17538. Phone: 800-784-5717; Fax: 800-219-5253; http://www.123ecd.com and http://www.chimetime.com.
- Insect Lore, P.O. Box 1535, Shafter, CA 93263. Phone: 800-LIVE BUG (800-548-3284); Fax: 661-746-0334; http://www.insectlore.com.
- Kaplan, P.O. Box 609, 1310 Lewisville-Clemmons Rd., Lewisville, NC 27023-0609. Phone: 800-334-2014; Fax: 800-452-7526; http://www.kaplanco.com.
- Lakeshore Learning Materials Company, 2695 E. Dominguez Street, P.O. Box 6261, Carson, CA 90749. Phone: 800-421-5354; local: 310-537-8600; Fax: 310-537-5403; http://www.lakeshore-learning.org.
- Nasco, 901 Janesville Avenue, Fort Atchinson, WI 53538; Nasco West, 1524 Princeton Avenue, Modesto, CA 95352. Phone: 800-558-9595 and 209-545-1600; Fax 209-545-1669; E-mail: info@nascofa.com; http://www.nascofa.com.
- National Council of Teachers of Mathematics, 1906 Association Drive, Reston, VA 22091-1593. Phone: 800-235-7566; Fax: 703-476-2970: Fax on demand: 800-220-8483; E-mail: nctm@nctm.org; http://www.nctm.org.
- National Science Teachers Association, P.O. Box 90214, Washington, DC 20090-0214. Phone: 800-277-5300. Fax: 301-843-0159; http://www.nsta.org/store/.
- Nienhuis Montessori U.S.A., 320 Pioneer Way, Mountain View, CA 94041. Phone: 800-942-8697; Fax: 650-964-8162; E-mail: catalog@nienhauis.com; http://www.nienhauis.com.
- PCI Educational Publishing, P.O. Box 34270, San Antonio, TX 78265-4270. Phone: 800-594-4263; Fax: 888-259-8284.
- Reading Rainbow (literature videos). Phone: 800-228-4630; E-mail: gpn@unl.edu; http://www.gpn.unl.edu/rainbow/teachers/mainmenu.htm.
- Rigby Education, 1000 Hart Rd., Barrington, IL 60010 and P.O. Box 797, Crystal Lake, IL 60039-0797. Phone: 800-822-8661; Fax: 800-427-4429; http://www.rigby.com.
- The Wright Group/McGraw-Hill, 19201 120th Ave. NE, Suite 100, Bothell, WA 98011. Phone: 800-648-2970; Fax: 800-543-7323; E-mail: wg-support@mcgraw-hill.com; http://www.wrightgroup.com.
- Zaner-Bloser, P.O. Box 16764, Columbus, OH 43216-6764. Phone: 800-421-3018; Fax: 800-992-6087; http://www.zaner-bloser.com.

FIGURE 39–3 Math and science materials catalogs.

equipment needed to teach a specific concept. If the boxes are clearly marked, they can be very convenient. The trick is to keep everything you need in the box such as homemade equipment materials, task cards, materials to duplicate, and bulletin board ideas. To be effective, the box, envelope, or grocery bag should display a materials list on the outside. In this way, you have a self-contained kit for teaching science (Figure 39–4).

Materials relating to a learning center can be stored in boxes under or near the science center. Materials will be handy, and older children will be able to get their own materials. Primary age children can be very effective organizers. They will enjoy and benefit from the job of inventorying science materials.

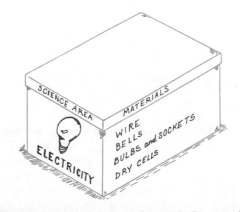

FIGURE 39–4 Store materials needed to teach concepts in a labeled shoe box.

The Math Learning Center

Materials in the math center should be neatly organized and displayed. Place the materials in containers on low shelves where they are readily accessible to the students. Be sure the procedures for removing, using, and replacing materials are clearly understood by the children. Sometimes a specialized center (i.e., for measurement or classification) can add to the excitement of learning.

Materials can be rotated according to the children's needs and interests and to keep their interest engaged. When new materials are introduced, the teacher should allow opportunities for exploration before the materials are used for structured activities.

Math centers can also focus on specific concepts when these concepts are being introduced. Focused centers can be set up for any of the skills and concepts in the text. Math centers can be set up relative to available space and furnishings. A center might be a set of shelves with an adjacent table and chairs or carpeted area, a small table with a few different materials each day, or a space on the floor where math materials are placed. In one primary classroom in Guilderland, New York, a math bed was installed. A blackboard was at one end and shelves for books and materials at the other end: a comfortable and inviting math center.

The math center should be available to every child, every day. Too frequently, the math center is open only to those children who finish their workbook and other reproducible paper assignments. Unfortunately, it is probably the children who do not finish their paper and pencil work who are most in need of experiences with concrete manipulative materials. If workbooks are required, after they have been introduced, put them on a special shelf in the math center and let the children who are ready select them from among the other materials available.

Many teachers, especially in the primary grades, feel pressured to follow the textbook and teach whole group math lessons without the use of manipulatives to introduce concepts as described throughout this text. It is possible to find a compromise that is beneficial for both students and teacher. For example, one first-grade teacher, feeling discouraged with the progress her students were making in mathematics, decided to try a new approach: She took the objectives for the text assigned to her class and found developmentally appropriate activities that correlated with each one. She selected the activities from *Developing Number Concepts Using Unifix Cubes*® (Richardson, 1984), *Mathematics Their Way* (Baratta-Lorton, 1989), *Workjobs* (Baratta-Lorton, 1972), and *Workjobs II* (Baratta-Lorton, 1978). She then assembled the necessary materials. She introduced each concept to the whole class and then divided the class into small groups to work with the concrete materials. The children felt more satisfied, performed their tasks with enthusiasm, and even commented on how much fun it was not to have to write! The teacher had time to circulate and help individual children. A positive side effect emerged from the opportunity to "talk" math: The children's language was extended, and unclear points were clarified. Peer tutoring developed naturally, to the advantage of both the tutors and those who needed help. The games and manipulatives were available for further use during the children's free choice time. The teacher's enthusiasm and the enthusiasm of the students were picked up by the other first-grade teachers and the principal. The teacher was asked to in-service the other first-grade teachers so that they could adopt the same system.

The Science Learning Center

You know that the interests of children stem from the kinds of learning materials and experiences available to them. One way to provide stimulating explorations is by setting up learning centers appropriate for an individual child or for a small group of children. As children work in centers, they learn to learn on their own in a planned environment. In this way, instruction is individualized, and children have time to explore science materials.

There are several different types of science learning centers, characterized by different purposes and modes of operation. The basic centers can be labeled Discovery Center, Open Learning Center, Inquiry Learning Center, and Science Interest Center.

Discovery Center

The word *discovery* implies that some action will be taken on materials and that questions and comments about what is happening take place. All is not quiet in a discovery center. Thus, it should be located away from listening and literacy centers. Discovery centers can be located on large tables, desks against a wall, or any spot that has room. Mobile discovery centers made of trays, shoe boxes, or baskets can simply be picked up and taken to a designated spot on the floor. An area rug makes a good place to work without taking up too much space.

In Figure 39–5, activity trays are used to explore concepts about air. As with any learning center, the size of your center area and ages of the children must be taken into account. For the five activity trays described in Figure 39–5, it is recommended that the teacher use two trays with five-year-olds and initially, one tray with younger children.

Open Learning Center

The science center in an open classroom is very creative and contains an abundance of manipulative materials, the majority of which are homemade. Using minimum directions, the child might be asked to "invent something" with these materials. Guidance is provided in the way of helpful suggestions or questions as the children pursue and tinker with their invention.

An example of an open center is a sink and float center. In this center, reinforcing the concept of sink and float is the central objective. The center contains a plastic tub half full of water and a box of familiar materials. On the blackboard are the questions, "What will float?" and "What will sink?" With no further direction, the children explore the questions with the materials.

Teacher evaluation is not formal; rather, the teacher visits the center and satisfies any concerns about children's progress. The teacher might find children making piles of things that do and do not float or trying to sink something that they thought would float. Some teachers suggest that the children communicate what happened at the center by drawing or writing a few sentences.

MATERIALS	PROCEDURE	PROPERTIES TO OBSERVE	EXTENSIONS
Several varying sizes of paper or plastic bags	Hold the bags open and describe what you see inside. Hold the bag closed and squeeze it. Do you feel anything? Try it again with a different bag.	Air can be felt even when it cannot be seen.	Try this activity with balloons. Ask children what happens to the air when the balloon is flat.
Balloons	Blow up a balloon. Hold the mouth of the balloon shut with your fingers. Open your fingers slightly and let some air out. What do you hear? Do your fingers feel anything?	Air can make noise and be felt.	Use flutes, recorders, or whistles to demonstrate how air can make different types of noise.
Paper and a stapler	Fold the paper accordion style and staple the end to make a fan. What do you feel when you wave the fan near your face?	Air can be moved and felt.	Use a fan or look outside on a windy day to observe how air moves and how air can move other things.

FIGURE 39–5 Using Activity trays to observe properties of air.

Inquiry Learning Center

A more directed discovery approach focuses on a science concept or topic and contains materials to be manipulated by the children, directions for the investigation, and open-ended questions to be asked at the end of the inquiry. The objective is not to reinforce a concept but to engage the child in problem solving beyond what is known to gain new insights.

At an inquiry center, the child might find directions that say, "Using the materials in this box, find a way to light the bulb," or, "What kinds of materials are attracted to magnets?" Science concepts are turned into questions that are placed on activity cards. There might be a single task or a series of tasks that a primary age child can complete in 15 or 30 minutes.

It would be foolish to send children to an inquiry center without adequate preparation. Discuss directions, procedures, and task cards with the children before beginning center work. The children are expected to achieve a desired learning outcome. So, if things do not go smoothly, ask yourself the following questions: Were the directions clear? Did the children know where to begin and end? Did they know what to do when they were finished? Is the center appropriate for the age group? Did the first group using the center know how to restore the materials for the next group?

Science Interest Center

Science interest corners, tables, and centers are popular in many schools. This interest center reinforces, enriches, and supplements ongoing programs with materials that stimulate children's interest. The primary goal of the center is to motivate children to want to learn more about the subject at the center.

As general rules, children are not required to visit this center, and no formal evaluation of their activities is recorded. Many times the center repeats a lesson exploration. For example, if the class has done the "Thinking Like a Geologist" lesson described in Unit 36, some children might want to try scratching minerals to test hardness or classifying the available rocks. Filmstrips, storybooks, and resource books on rocks and minerals should be available for the children to

explore. Children could practice their measuring skills by using string to measure an assortment of objects or become acquainted with a balance scale by comparing the weight of different rocks.

Plan Your Center

State learning center objectives in such a way that you know what you want the child to learn. Know your children's developmental level. You can avoid inadvertently creating busywork for students by taking steps to carefully plan the concepts to be developed at the center. Start by writing a sentence that communicates what the child is expected to learn at the center. Children must be able to participate in the activities and methods independently. Evaluate the center by asking yourself: Is the center effective in achieving my objectives? How can the center be improved? Figure 39–6 suggests a guide to planning a learning center.

Selecting Math Materials

In each classroom, each child has her individual and age-appropriate needs in mathematics. Every school and classroom includes children who are at various levels of concept development. It is important to provide a wide array of math materials and time to explore them freely.

In Unit 3, three considerations regarding selection of math and science materials were discussed.

- The materials should be sturdy and versatile.
- The materials should fit the outcome objectives selected.
- The materials should fit the developmental levels of the children.

In addition, the following should be considered.

- The materials should be safe.
- The materials should be easily supervised.
- The materials should be free of gender, ethnic, age, and socioeconomic bias.

What is the purpose or objective?

Who will be using this learning center?

What are the concepts children should learn?

What are the skills children should learn?

What activities will take place?

What materials need to be available?

What are the learning objectives?

How will childrens' progress be evaluated?

FIGURE 39–6 Questions to ask when planning a learning center.

◆ Book illustrations and content and drawings, photos, and other materials should include depictions of members of diverse cultures in nonstereotyped dress and engaged in authentic activities.

When selecting materials, versatility is important; that is, can the materials be used on a regular basis for teaching a variety of concepts? For example, unit blocks, Unifix Cubes,® and Multilinks® would fit this criteria. No material should be a health hazard. Avoid anything made from a toxic material and anything with sharp edges or small parts or pieces that can lodge in noses or ears or be swallowed.

When taking over a new classroom or at the end of each year in a current classroom, take an inventory of materials. Note the condition of materials: Are parts missing? Do materials need mending or replacement? Are there materials for all concepts in the program? Are there materials for naturalistic, informal, and structured experiences? Are both indoor and outdoor materials and equipment in good condition? With this information in hand, decisions can be made as to what is on hand and what needs to be purchased. In preprimary, when children have shorter attention spans, it is recommended that a variety of small sets of materials (enough for two or three children to share at one

time) be purchased. In the primary grades, start with a classroom set of Unifix® materials. These materials are among the most versatile because they can be used for teaching almost every primary mathematics concept. Many accessories are available and there are numerous resources, already mentioned in this text, from which to select activities. Gradually add base 10 blocks, fraction materials, and other manipulatives.

Another source of materials are those that can be made by teachers and/or volunteer parents. Waste materials may also be donated. Parents can be asked to save egg cartons, buttons, boxes and other containers, bottle caps, yarn, ribbon, and other materials that can be used in the math program (see the list in Unit 41). Parents might also donate inexpensive items such as toothpicks, golf tees, playing cards, funnels, measuring cups, and so on. Lumber companies might donate scrap lumber. Restaurant supply companies will often sell teachers trays, various sized containers, and the like at low prices. Try to convince your principal to let you spend your share of supply money on concrete manipulative materials and supplies for making two-dimensional manipulatives, rather than investing in workbooks and copy paper. Some resources for ideas for teacher-made materials are listed at the end of each unit and some frequently used catalogs are shown in Figure 39–3.

Selecting Science Materials

Providing materials that encourage children to "mess around" and explore is the responsibility of the teacher. At the center, children use the process skills to observe, investigate, classify, and maybe hypothesize. Because this learning is not accidental, planning must go into setting up centers and selecting materials. After completing the planning guide suggested in Figure 39–6, consider the following criteria in selecting and arranging materials.

1. *Are the materials open-ended?* Can they be used in more than one way? For example, water play provides the opportunity to explore measuring or floating.

2. *Are the materials designed for action?* In science, children do something to materials to make something else happen. If substances are to be dissolved, which will offer the best comparison: salt, sugar, or pudding mix?

3. *Are the materials arranged to encourage communication among children?* If appropriate, place materials to create cooperation and conversation. Arrange materials in categories such as pitchers of water in one section of the center, substances to be tested in another, and spoons and dishes for mixing in another. Children quickly learn to cooperate and communicate to complete the activity.

4. *Is there a variety of materials?* If the center is to be used over an extended period, some children will visit it many times. A variety of materials will prevent overexposure to the exploration.

5. *Do the materials encourage "What if _____" statements?* The sink and float activity described in the open classroom learning center invites children to predict what will happen if they try to float a marble, toothpick, or sponge.

6. *Are the materials appropriate for the maturity of the children?* Consider the maturity level of the class. Select materials that the children can handle safely and effectively.

7. *Do the materials allow for individual differences such as ability, interest, working space, and style?* After considering floating and sinking, some children will begin to consider size and other characteristics of the available objects. Have objects with a variety of textures and features available.

8. *How much direction do the materials require?* In giving directions, consider the age of the children. Four- and five-year-olds might receive directions from a cassette recording, but three-year-olds and young fours respond best to personal directions. Rebus-type directions are also appropriate.

9. *Do the materials stress process skills?* Process skills are the fundamental skills that are emphasized in science explorations with young children. These skills will come naturally from manipulating materials. However, a variety of appropriate materials is required for this to happen.

10. *Are the materials nonbiased?* Where appropriate, materials should illustrate authentic nonbiased dress and activities.

Sensory Learning Center

Children have a "sense-able" approach to the world around them. The approach that they use is as basic to science as it is natural to young children. Use the type of center you prefer to give children an opportunity to taste, smell, touch, observe, and hear their environment.

Thinking Like a Criminologist

Skin prints are a way to take a closer look at the skin children live in. They enjoy examining their fingertips, taking their own fingerprints, and thinking like a criminologist at this center. Because a criminologist investigates crimes by analyzing clues in a systematic way, studying fingerprints is an important part of this job.

You will need one No. 2 pencil, white scratch paper, plain paper, a handheld lens, and a damp paper towel at this station. Show children how to rub soft pencil lead onto a sheet of paper and pick up a good smudge with one finger. Then, they carefully pick up the smudge with a piece of clear tape, pull it away, and press the fingerprint onto a clean paper.

Begin by having students make a set of their own fingerprints on a sheet of clean paper. If someone makes a mistake, simply peel off the tape and start over. Then create a classroom mystery for your students to solve. Ask, "Who was the last person to use the pencil sharpener?" Each group that visits the center can be a group of "suspects." Prepare prints in advance, then show prints that were "found" on the pencil sharpener. Have the children use the handheld lens to compare their prints to the set belonging to the "criminal."

Integrate fingerprinting into art by letting the children use ink pads to make prints from their hands or fingers. Children can bring the prints to life by adding legs, arms, and other features. Fingerprint stories can be developed, and you may even want to include toe prints as a homework assignment. You could go further and classify fingerprints into three basic patterns: whorl, arch, and loop. Refer to the further readings list for resources.

Do You Hear What I Hear?

Walk in the hallway with a tape recorder and record five interesting sounds. Bring the tape back to the classroom, provide earphones, and have the children draw a picture of the sounds that they hear. Children enjoy using a tape recorder. Let them take turns tape recording sounds during recess, assemblies, or the lunch period. Challenge them to record unusual sounds and infer what is making the sounds. Add further interest to this center by sending the tape recorder home with a child to tape "home sounds." As children identify the home sounds at the center, have them compare and contrast the sounds in their own home and write a story about the sounds and how they are created.

The tape recorder also makes a good listening center for a variety of tapes and records. Many of the recordings should be stories. Children will enjoy illustrating the stories. Some will enjoy taping a story of their own for use in the center or as background for plays, puppet shows, and radio programs.

Red, Yellow, and Blue

The object of this center is to mix the primary colors and observe and record the results. Have the children record the color that results from dropping the correct amounts of color into the correct container.

Smells, Smells, Smells

Gather small amounts of familiar substances with distinctive odors, such as coffee, popcorn, orange extract, hot chocolate, onions, apples, and peanut butter. Put the items in jars, shoe boxes, plastic sandwich bags, or loosely tied brown paper bags—whichever seems appropriate—and leave small holes in the containers so that the odors can escape. As children take turns smelling the containers, ask them to describe the various odors and guess what might be producing these distinctive smells. Make a duplicate set of containers, and ask the children to match the ones that smell alike.

Be sure to show children the safe way to smell an unknown substance: They should gently fan the air between their noses and the container with one hand and breathe normally. The scent will come to them.

Apple or Potato?

Spread vegetable pieces on a plate for children to taste. They will have to work in pairs. One puts on a blindfold, holds his nose, and tries to guess what he is tasting. The other child keeps a record by writing down what the vegetable piece really is and what his partner thinks it is. Then, the children trade places, redo the test, and compare their scores.

The children will be surprised that they made a lot of wrong guesses. This is because it is hard to tell one food from another of similar texture. The secret lies inside the nose. Tongues tell only if something is sweet, sour, salty, or bitter; the rest of the information comes from the odor of the food. Lead children to the conclusion that they would have a hard time tasting without their sense of smell.

Tasting liquids that children drink frequently is fun. Pour some milk, orange juice, water, soda, or other popular drinks into paper cups or clean milk cartons and provide clean straws for tasting. Have the children describe the taste and guess what it might be. Some children will enjoy drawing a picture of their favorite flavor. A sip of water or bite of bread in between items helps clear their palates.

Technology

Computer software suggestions have been inserted throughout the text. Ideally, each classroom should have two or three computers where children can take turns exploring a variety of software. There should also be time for searching the Web for information and using e-mail to communicate with others regarding problems to solve and information to share. Many early childhood and science and mathematics journals have software reviews in every issue and frequent reports from teachers describing how their students use technology. Further suggestions are included in Unit 40.

Summary

Stimulating science and math lessons do not happen by accident. The materials selected to teach science and math and the format that they are presented in are essential for successful explorations. Whether materials are purchased or scrounged, they must be flexible and appropriate to the developmental age of the child and the type of science and math learning that is required. Learning centers are designed and used to meet specific teaching objectives and must be evaluated for their effectiveness.

Lists of resource books for teachers and further reading lists are included in this unit. Lists of children's book are in Appendix B.

SUGGESTED ACTIVITIES

1. Obtain a copy of the current NSTA Supplement of Science Education Suppliers. Select a science concept and list materials that could be used in teaching that concept.
2. Reflect on the nature of science materials. Then, make a list of materials needed for teaching a science unit that you have developed. Where will you get these materials? How will you organize them for hands-on teaching?
3. Construct a learning center. Use the center with a group of children, and share the effectiveness of the materials with the class.
4. Compile a list of free and inexpensive science teaching materials. Send for some of these materials, and evaluate if they are appropriate for young children. Share this information with the class.
5. Visit a preschool, kindergarten, and primary class. Compare the science teaching materials used in these classes. What are the similarities and differences?
6. Visit a local educational materials store. Make a list of available math materials and their prices. Bring the list to class.
7. Participate in a small group in class, and compare math materials lists. Make cooperative decisions as to what math materials should be purchased if a new prekindergarten, kindergarten, and/or primary classroom is to be furnished. Each group should consider cost as well as purpose.
8. Go to the library. Find and read at least 10 children's picture books that contain math concepts (see Appendix B for suggestions). Write a description of each one. Tell how each book could be used with children.
9. Make two different "homemade" math resources that could be used with young children. Select from books, journals, and/or the Internet. Share the materials with the class. Be prepared to show the class how the resources can be made.
10. Visit two preschool, kindergarten, and/or primary classes. Ask to look at the math materials used. Diagram the math learning center or math shelves. Share the information with your class. Tell the strong and weak points of the math setup. List any changes that would make it better.
11. Add a math and science materials list to each of the units in your Activity File/Notebook.
12. Send for free commercial catalogs. Make a list of math materials that are new in each. Write down the descriptions presented in the catalogs. Share this information with your class.

REVIEW

A. Why are learning centers essential for science and math learning?

B. What are the two main types of science equipment?

C. List some useful items for a science junk box.

D. What are some of the advantages of science kits? What are some of the disadvantages?

E. Match the description with the center.

_____ Discovery Center

_____ Open Learning Center

_____ Inquiry Learning Center

_____ Science Interest Center

1. Children explore a concept with as little direction as possible. A leading question.
2. Little direction is given. Children "mess around" with materials at small tables or trays.
3. A directed discovery approach focuses on a concept. This center includes directions and is used to encourage children to go beyond what they know about a concept.
4. This center motivates children to want to learn about its materials.

F. Describe each of the following materials.

1. Concrete manipulative math materials
2. Abstract representational math materials

G. Respond to each of the following situations.

1. Mrs. Anderson has four lotto games with some of the cards missing, two geoboards with five rubber bands, and a few unit blocks in her preschool classroom. Mr. Brown has three complete lotto games, a set of Unifix Cubes,® a set of unit blocks, a big tub of a variety of jar lids, and three shape puzzles. Give your opinion of the quality of math materials in each classroom. Why do you believe as you do?
2. Miss Collins says she does not believe it is appropriate to teach math to young children. When you observe in her kindergarten, you see children playing at a water table with various containers. Others are weighing toy cars on a balance scale. Is Miss Collins teaching math? If so, explain how.
3. Mr. Dominic teaches first grade. He is going to set up a math center. He has been given $300 to purchase basic materials. He asks for your help. What would you suggest?
4. Mrs. Edwards teaches second grade. She has just read this book. She is trying hard to provide a developmentally appropriate math environment. However, she cannot decide how to begin. What suggestions would you give her?

REFERENCES

Baratta-Lorton, M. (1972). *Workjobs.* Menlo Park, CA: Addison-Wesley.

Baratta-Lorton, M. (1978). *Workjobs II.* Menlo Park, CA: Addison-Wesley.

Baratta-Lorton, M. (1989). *Mathematics their way.* Menlo Park, CA: Addison-Wesley.

National Council of Teachers of Mathematics. (2000). *Principles and standards for school mathematics.* Reston, VA: Author. (http://www.nctm.org)

Richardson, K. (1984). *Developing number concepts using Unifix Cubes.*® Menlo Park, CA: Addison-Wesley.

FURTHER READING AND RESOURCES

Bloomer, A. M., & Carlson, P. A. T. (1993). *Activity math: Using manipulatives in the classroom.* Menlo Park, CA: Addison-Wesley.

Burns, M. (1996). What I learned from teaching second grade. *Teaching Children Mathematics, 3*, 124–127.

Carin, A. A., & Sund, R. B. (1992). *Teaching science through discovery.* New York: Macmillan.

Cook, H., & Matthew, C. E. (1998). Lessons from a "Living Fossil." *Science and Children, 36*(3), 16–19.

Cooper, C. H. (1997). *Counting your way through 1, 2, 3, school library media series No. 8.* Lanham, MD: Scarecrow Press.

Copley, J. V. (2000). *The young child and mathematics.* Washington, DC: National Association for the Education of Young Children.

Copley, J. V. (Ed.). (1999). *Mathematics in the early years.* Washington, DC: National Association for the Education of Young Children.

Esler, W., & Esler, M. (2001). *Teaching elementary science* (8th ed.). Belmont, CA: Wadsworth.

Gilmore, V. (1979). Helpful hints—Coca-Cola bottle terrarium. *Science and Children, 16*(7).

Green, M. D. (1996). *474 science activities for young children.* Clifton Park, NY: Delmar Learning.

Hoffman, A. C., & Glannon, A. M. (1993). *Kits, games and manipulatives for the elementary school classroom: A source book.* New York: Garland.

Hopkins, T. (2000). *1001 best websites for educators.* Westminster, CA: Teacher Created Materials.

Houle, G. B. (1987). *Learning centers for young children* (3rd ed.). West Greenwich, RI: Tot-lot Child Care Products.

Isbell, R., & Exelby, B. (2001). *Early learning environments that work.* Beltsville, MD: Gryphon House.

Jacobs, V. R., Bennett, T. R., & Bullock, C. (2000). Selecting books in Spanish to teach mathematics. *Teaching Children Mathematics*, 6(9), 582–587.

Jasmine, G. (2000). *Early childhood activities with internet connections.* Westminster, CA: Teacher Created Materials.

Kerr, S. (1993). *Science centers A to Z.* Wheeling, IL: Look At Me Productions, Inc.

Kopp, J. (1992). *Frog math: Predict, ponder, play, Gr. K–3.* From Lawrence Hall of Science, distributed by ETA.

MacDonald, S. (2001). *Block book: The complete guide to learning and playing with blocks.* Beltsville, MD: Gryphon House.

Madrazo, G. M., Jr. (1997). Using trade books to teach and learn science. *Science and Children, 34*(6), 20–21.

Math Power. Monthly student activities math magazine published by Scholastic, 555 Broadway, Room 336, New York, NY 10012-3999.

McIntyre, M. (1984). *Early childhood and science.* Washington, DC: National Science Teachers Association.

National Council of Teachers of Mathematics. (Forthcoming series). *Navigations, pre-K–2.* Reston, VA: Author.

Oppenheim, C. (1993). *Science is fun! For families and classroom groups.* St. Louis, MO: Cracom Co.

Poppe, C. A., & Van Matre, N. (1985). *Science learning centers for the primary grades.* West Nyack, NY: Center for Applied Research in Education.

Rackow, S. J. (Ed.). (1999). K–8 Science and mathematics education [Special issue]. *The ERIC Review, 6*(2).

Radeloff, D. J. (2001). Science discovery centers: Stimulating young children's minds. *Focus on Pre-K and K, 13*(3), 1–3. (ACEI publication)

Richardson, K. (1999). *Developing number concepts. Planning guide.* Parsippany, NJ: Dale Seymour.

Rule, A. C., & Barrera, M. T., III. (1999). Science object boxes. *Science and Children, 37*(2) 30–35, 63.

Schwartz, S. (1995). Planting mathematics in the classroom. *Teaching Children Mathematics, 2*, 42–46.

Sharp, J. M. (1996). Manipulatives for the metal chalkboard. *Teaching Children Mathematics, 2*, 280–281.

Sheffield, S. (1995). *Math and literature (K–3): Book two.* Sausalito, CA: Math Solutions.

Sherfey, G. R., & Huff, P. (1976). Designing the science learning center. *Science and Children, 14*(3), 12.

Straker, A. (1993). *Talking points in mathematics.* New York: Cambridge University Press.

Wakefield, A. P. (1998). *Early childhood number games.* Boston: Allyn & Bacon.

West, S., & Cox, A. (2001). *Sand and water play.* Beltsville, MD: Gryphon House.

Note: Resource reviews appear in each issue of *Science and Children* and *Teaching Children Mathematics* as well as other early childhood periodicals.

UNIT 40
Math and Science in Action

OBJECTIVES

After reading this unit, you should be able to:

◆ Understand the value of children working together cooperatively.

◆ Plan and use blocks for math and science experiences.

◆ Describe the benefits of using blocks with primary age children.

◆ Plan and use woodworking for math and science experiences.

◆ Plan and use math and science games and activities with young children.

◆ Plan and use outdoor activities with young children.

◆ Understand how technology can contribute to active mathematics and science learning.

◆ Explain the value of culturally relevant mathematics activities.

As reviewed in Units 1 and 3, action in mathematics and science involves hands-on problem solving and inquiry. NCTM (2000) describes five process standards of which problem solving is first, followed by reasoning, communicating, connections, and representations. This unit provides an overview of the kinds of activities that should be observed in action in early childhood classrooms.

Math and science go on all the time in the developmentally appropriate classroom for young children.

The block builder, like any engineer, builds her building so it will stand up and serve a planned function. The young carpenter measures wood and swings his hammer to get the most power when he hits the nail. Children do finger plays and action songs and explore the outdoors while they apply math and science concepts. As children move into concrete operations, math and science in action include more complex group games and activities and the introduction of team sports and preplanned building and science projects.

Children continue to be active learners in the primary grades. This is a fact from research based on Piagetian theory. Unfortunately, the active opportunities provided by blocks and outdoor explorations are not always considered in curriculum plans for primary age children. This is a mistake. Remember, primary age children are still concrete operation thinkers who learn to understand the world around them through actively engaging in explorations.

Block play and outdoor explorations give children many opportunities to investigate, test, and change objects. It is from these interactions that children build their own model of the world. (Refer to concept development in Units 1 through 6 to refresh your memory.)

This unit focuses on the relationship of blocks, woodworking, songs, action games, problem solving, outdoor activities, technology, and culturally relevant activities that meet the affective, cognitive, and psychomotor learning needs of the young child. The emphasis is on active learning both indoors and outdoors.

A math lesson that meets the NCTM standards should include the following factors (Burrill, 1997): manipulatives, cooperative groups, a teacher who is a facilitator, the use of technology, opportunities to write, and strong connections to the children's world. Activities that meet these criteria can provide a program that will avoid the *Math Curse* (Scieszka and Smith, 1995). As described in Unit 2, math and science in action includes hands-on projects for both individual and group work. Both individuals and groups of two or more can organize their work using the K-W-D-L model (Shaw, Chambless, Chessin, Price, & Beardain, 1997). *K* involves recording what is known from studying the problem to be solved. *W* stands for what (we) I want to find out, that is, identify the question. The *L* step involves recording what the student or group of students has learned. The answer is stated and defended and the process of problem solving is described. This defense is the *D* step—what we (I) did. An important aspect of a problem-solving approach to math and science is allowing plenty of time for students to think through and discuss their solution processes. Even in the midst of lively discussion, a long pause in the conversation may be needed for students to reflect on the problems so that they can create their own unique solutions.

Blocks

Blocks are probably the play material most used by young children. Unfortunately, blocks are seldom seen in classrooms beyond the kindergarten level, while they have the potential to function as valuable concept-building materials for primary children. Research reported by Wolfgang, Stannard, & Jones (2001) indicates that young children's block play performance during preschool is a predictor of mathematics achievement in middle school and high school.

Children apply basic concepts as they explore the relationships among the various sizes and shapes in a set of unit blocks. They note that two of one size may equal one of another, some are longer and some shorter, some are square, some are rectangular, others are triangular, and still others are curved. They are working with fractions and parts and wholes (Figure 40–1). MacDonald (2001) lists 29 mathematics and 20 science concepts and skills that children can construct and apply when building with unit blocks. Further, according to MacDonald block play enhances concepts and skills in art, literacy, physical development, social studies, and socioemotional development.

The block area needs plenty of space. The blocks and the small vehicles, people dolls, and animals that enhance the accompanying dramatic play activities

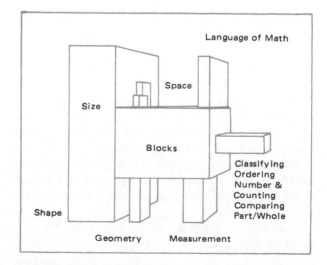

FIGURE 40–1 Children can construct many concepts as they work with blocks.

should be neatly organized on low shelves where they can be easily reached by the children. Shelves should be marked with outlines of each block shape so that the children can return the blocks to the proper place (and practice some one-to-one correspondence). Start the year with a small, easy-to-handle set. As time goes by, more blocks and more shapes can be introduced. The teacher can facilitate exploration by asking questions and making comments. For example, Mrs. Red Fox notes that Trang Fung has used all square blocks in her structure, whereas Sara has developed her structure with larger units. "It looks like each of you have your favorite-sized blocks."

Blocks can be purchased in sets of various sizes. There are a variety of shapes and sizes in each set. The basic unit is a brick-shaped rectangle that is $1\frac{3}{8}'' \times 2\frac{3}{4}'' \times 5\frac{1}{2}''$. The variety of shapes and sizes is listed in Figure 40–2. Unit blocks should be made of good, strong, hard wood with beveled edges so that they will not wear down or splinter. They should be smoothly sanded. The sizes must be precise so that building can be done effectively.

Unit block sets are very expensive, but with good care, they last for many years. Keep them dry and free of dust. Occasionally they should be oiled or waxed.

At the beginning stage, the child may just handle the blocks and carry them from place to place. At the second stage, the children make rows and lines of blocks. At the third stage, children build bridges. At the fourth stage, children make simple enclosures. At the fifth stage, the children make patterns. These patterns may be balanced and symmetric. At the sixth stage, the children name the structures and use them for dramatic play. At the last stage, the children make structures that represent familiar buildings, such as their own home or even their whole city.

Children enjoy using other types of building materials besides unit blocks. Many preschools have large, hollow, wood blocks. At a lower cost, there are cardboard blocks. Cardboard boxes can enhance the imaginative activity of young children. Large boxes can be the focus of walking *around*, climbing *in*, and climbing *over*. Boxes can be moved about and combined in many different ways, providing experiences with weight, size, shape, and volume. Sheets and blankets can add to the variety of structures. Blocks and boxes provide a rich opportunity for math in action.

	Name	Nursery	Kgn. & Primary
	Square	40	80
	Unit	96	192
	Double Unit	48	96
	Quadruple Unit	16	32
	Pillar	24	48
	Half Pillar	24	48
	Small Triangle	24	48
	Large Triangle	24	48
	Small Column	16	32
	Large Column	8	16
	Ramp	16	32
	Ellipse		8
	Curve	8	16
	¼ Circle		8
	Large Switch & Gothic Door		4
	Small Switch		4
	Large Buttress		4
	½ Arch & Small Buttress		4
	Arch & ½ Circle		4
	Roofboard		24
	Number of Shapes	12	23
	Number of Pieces	344	760

FIGURE 40–2 Childcraft block sets.

Blocks, Science, and Children

Block building and play are not isolated from science. The very nature of building a structure requires that children deal with the processes of science as discussed in Unit 5. As children build, they compare, classify, predict, and interpret problems. Scientific thinking is stimulated as children discover and invent new forms; expand experiences; explore major conceptual ideas in science; measure; and work with space, change, and pattern.

Blocks Encourage Thinking

Blocks force children to distinguish, classify, and sort. This can be seen as a group of second graders learns the different properties of blocks by re-creating a field trip to the zoo. As they plan and build, they deal with the fact that each block has different qualities. Size, shape, weight, thickness, width, and length are considered. As construction progresses, the blocks become fulcrums and levers. Guiding questions such as, "Can you make a ramp for unloading the rhinoceros?" and, "Where will you put the access road for delivering food to the animals?" will help children focus on an aspect of construction. Some children create zoo animals, workers, and visitors to dramatize a day at the zoo.

Allow time for children to verbalize why they are arranging the zoo in a particular way. This will encourage children to share their problem-solving strategy and will help them to clarify thinking. By observing the children at play, you will also gain insight into their thinking.

Balance, Predictions, Interactions, and Movement

One emphasis in science is interactions within systems. In block building, the blocks form a system that is kept in equilibrium through balance. As children build, they work with a cause-and-effect approach to predict stress and to keep the forces of gravity from tumbling their structure. The idea that each part added to the structure contributes to the whole is constantly reinforced as children maintain the stability of their structure.

Balancing blocks is an effective way to explore cause and effect. By seeing the reaction of what they do, children begin to learn cause and effect. The following ideas emphasize action and cause and effect.

1. *Dominoes.* Children develop spatial relationships as they predict what will happen to an arrangement of dominoes (Figure 40–3). Ask, "Can you arrange the dominoes in such a way that they will all be knocked down?"
2. *Construct and roll.* Arrange plastic bottles or blocks in a variety of ways, and have the children try to knock them over with a ball. This bowlinglike game encourages children to keep score and establish a correspondence between the way blocks are arranged and how the ball is rolled. Ask, "What action caused the blocks to fall down? What action started the ball moving? Did the ball knock down every bottle that fell? If not, what made them fall?"
3. *Pendulum release.* In a pendulum game, a ball moves without being pushed; it is released. Children structure space as they place blocks in a position to be knocked down by the pendulum bob. Have children predict, "If the ball pendulum is pulled back and released, will it knock over the block?"

Pendulums can be made life-sized by securing one end of a length of cotton string to the ceiling and attaching a weighted bob to the other end. Weighted bobs for the pendulum can be made by tying a plastic pill vial filled with sand to the cotton string. However, a smaller model may be more practical. Try this first and then tell

FIGURE 40–3 "Arrange the dominoes so that they all will be knocked down."

FIGURE 40–4 "Can you control the speed of the ball?"

the children how to expand to a life-sized model. One end of a length of cotton string or fish line must be attached to a stable support that allows for a swinging motion. A simple effective pendulum can be constructed by placing an eye screw into a board, suspending the board between the backs of two chairs, and attaching the string with the pendulum bob. Children can sit on the floor and explore the action of the pendulum.

4. *Inclines.* In incline activities, the ball moves when released. Exactly where the ball goes is determined by manipulating the incline and the ball. Have children change the incline in different ways to control what happens to the ball. Children will enjoy creating games such as catching the ball with a cup, racing different-sized balls down the incline, and measuring how far the ball travels (Figure 40–4).

5. *Buttons and bobby pins.* The object of this tilt game is to jiggle a button from start to finish without letting it fall off of the board or through a hole. The button or ball is guided by tilting and wiggling the board. To make the game, cut several holes in cardboard, and rub the board with a piece of waxed paper. Position bobby pins with the raised side up on the board, mark a start and finish, and begin the game.

Pinball Wizards

Children can create pinball machines from scraps of plywood, strips of wood, glue, nails, plastic caps,

and marbles. The challenge is for children to invent ways to make a marble fall down a series of ramps and make the trip as long as possible. Have the children glue wooden strips to a backboard at different angles. Then have them adjust their obstacles of nails and blocks as they try out the marble. Ask, "Can you think of a way to slow down the marble?" (You might want to introduce the concept of friction.)

Blocks and Marbles

Balance and action can be seen as children assemble plastic ramps and chutes with commercial toys such as Marbleworks® from Discovery Toys. Children gain a familiarity with concepts such as gravity, acceleration, and momentum when they design and create a maze of movement by fitting pieces together. To further introduce children to the principle of cause and effect, ask, "What action starts the marble moving?" Then have children predict the way in which the marble will move. Creating different pathways and exploring how the marble moves on them can be exciting.

Complex block and marble sets seem to fascinate primary age children. In these sets children arrange attractive wooden sections to allow marbles to travel through holes and grooved blocks of different lengths. Children enjoy controlling the movement of the marble down the construction and creating changes that determine direction and speed of the marble. Children can make their own marble runs from decorative molding that is available in paneling supply stores. The track can be nailed onto boards, taped down, or held for observing the movement of marbles (some will move at breakneck speeds). Have your students add a tunnel, try different types of balls, and find ways to use friction to slow down the marbles.

Another Type of Construction

Constructions introduce children to the conditions and limitations of space. They learn to bridge space with appropriate-sized blocks and objects and enclose space in different ways. The following ideas involve creating your own construction set with straws.

Use large straws for straw construction, and connect them with string, pipe cleaners, or paper clips. String is the most difficult to use but makes the most permanent construction. Simply stick the string in one end of the straw, and suck on the other end. The string will come through.

You will have to form a triangle with three straws. A triangle is the only shape made with straws that is rigid enough for building. If you are using string as a connector, tie the ends together to form a triangle, or thread three straws on one string to form the triangle.

Pipe cleaners as connectors are another method of building with straws. Push a pipe cleaner halfway into the end of one straw, then slip another straw over the other end of the pipe cleaner. Double up the pipe cleaners for a tighter fit. Children can twist and turn this construction in many ways.

Many teachers recommend paper clips as ideal connectors in straw building. Open a paper clip, bend out the two ends, and slip each end into a straw. Paper clips are rigid and allow for complex building. You might have to add as many as three paper clips to give the structure strength. Paper clips may also be chained for a flexible joint between two straws. Challenge children to think and construct. Ask, "How tall a structure can you make? Why did your structure collapse? Can you make a bridge?"

When the straw frame stands by itself, test it. Ask, "Can you think of a way to test the strength of your structure?" Place a paper clip through a paper cup and hang it somewhere on the straw structure. Ask, "How many paper cups can your structure support? How many paper clips will make the frame work?"

Block City

Blocks in the classroom provide many opportunities to integrate basic reading and writing, science, math skills and concepts, and social studies into the construction process. Opportunities for integration abound as children explore the busy life of a block city.

Mr. Wang's second grade created a city of blocks. Buildings had to be accurate in the city, and each child builder represented herself in the daily acting out of city life. The block building sessions were preceded by class discussion as the children planned the daily block activities. Accessories (labeled boxes of food, clothing, computers, typewriters, and the like) were constructed from a variety of materials. Children played

the roles of shopkeepers, bankers, and other workers. They made decisions such as where the people in the block city would get their money.

When the children had to put out an imaginary fire, they immediately saw a problem. How would they get water to the blaze? This discovery led to an investigation of how water gets into hydrants, utility covers, and water pipes. The children responded to the emergency by adding plastic tubing to the city as well as wire for electricity and telephones.

Not only was the city becoming more realistic, it was becoming less magical. Children no longer thought that water magically appeared when the water faucet was turned on. They knew that a system of pipes carried the water. In fact, the workings of a city in general became less magical. Many common misconceptions were dispelled, and an understanding of how a city functions began to develop.

The Edible Village

Mrs. Moore's first-grade class integrated the study of their neighborhood with block building. After determining the different sections of the neighborhood and buildings they needed to create, each child was assigned a building. The class created their neighborhood with blocks made of graham crackers. They used flattened caramels for roadways and lollipops for streetlights. Coconut spread over white icing gave the illusion of snow.

The students mixed yellow and green food coloring into icing to create differently colored buildings. Recipes for icing provided opportunities to use measurements and follow directions in sequence. Writing about the creation of the village and what might be happening within graham cracker walls became a springboard for discussion.

Children made decisions about what should and should not be included in the village. They determined the authenticity of buildings and building size. This activity is especially appropriate for primary age children. Children in this age group are able to incorporate more detail and can be exposed to another's viewpoint. For example, the teacher asked, "How will the people know that school is open?" Children began asking each other, "Do we need a hospital? What about a gas station?"

If your city or town is located near a river or lake, be sure to include it in construction. Paper straw bridges could be added and the geography of your area explored. You will find that as the children develop questions, they are motivated to find the answers because they need to know something for construction of the city. Thus, the block experience also becomes a first research experience.

Woodworking

Most young children enjoy working with wood. Woodworking provides hands-on experience with measurement, balance, power, and spatial and size relationships. They use informal measurement as they check to see if they have a piece of wood that is the one they need and if they have a nail that is the correct length. As children move into the primary level, they can apply standard measurement: "I will need 12 pieces of 12- by 8-inch plywood for my birdhouse." The more advanced primary children can follow simple instructions and use patterns to make projects.

For effective woodworking, the classroom should have a sturdy workbench, good-quality real tools, and assorted pieces of soft wood. The workbench should be large enough for at least two children to work at the same time. Woodworking must always be closely supervised. Workbenches designed for children can be purchased from the major school supply companies, or a large, old tree stump can be used.

The basic components of a high-quality tool set for four- and five-year-olds are illustrated in Figure 40–5. Older children can use a greater variety of tools. The tools should be easily accessible when in use but kept in a locked closet or on a high shelf when not in use. Beginners do best with short nails with large heads.

Soft wood such as pine is easy to work with. When sawing is introduced, the wood should be put in a vise so it will hold steady and so the child's hands will not be in the line of the saw.

Experienced woodworkers enjoy creating projects using odds and ends with their wood. Wheels can be made from bottle caps and windows from plastic lids. Scraps of cloth or ribbon can be glued on to the wood. Children can apply their math vocabulary as they explain their finished projects.

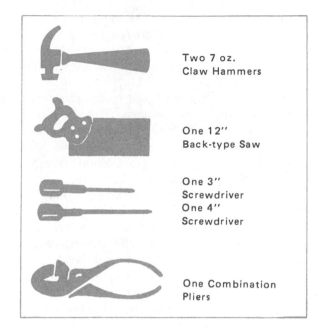

Two 7 oz. Claw Hammers

One 12'' Back-type Saw

One 3'' Screwdriver
One 4'' Screwdriver

One Combination Pliers

FIGURE 40–5 Basic woodworking tools for four- and five-year-olds: Start with these and add more as children become proficient.

Math Games

As described in Unit 24, board games provide opportunities for counting and one-to-one correspondence. They also provide opportunities for developing social skills such as cooperation and following rules.

Young children enjoy playing games. Some four-year-olds and most five-year-olds enjoy playing board games. For the preschooler, games should be simple with a minimum of rules.

Board games provide an excellent way to teach math. *Candyland,® Numberland Counting Game,® Chutes and Ladders,® Fraction Brothers Circus,® Memory,® Picture Dominoes,® Picture Nines®* (a domino game), *Candyland Bingo,® Triominos,® Connect Four,® Count-a-Color,® Farm Lotto,®* and other bingo and lotto boxed games can be purchased. Board game patterns can be obtained from early childhood publications and **Internet** sites. For more advanced children, basic concepts can be practiced using board games such as *Multiplication/Division Quizmo,® Addition/*

Subtraction Mathfacts Game,® *Multiplication/Division Mathfacts Game,®* *UNO,®* *UNO Dominoes,®* *Yahtzee,®* and *IMMA Whiz Math Games.®* *Pay the Cashier®* and *Count your Change®* are games that help children learn money concepts.

Lakeshore has wooden board games that provide materials for the youngest game players. *Number Bingo* can be purchased from Constructive Playthings. Early Childhood Direct carries *Color and Shape Bingo* and *Bingo Bears.™* Early Childhood Direct has an set of readiness math games and some more advanced games (*Number Start, Number Detective,* and *Playcount*).

Other basic board games were described in Unit 24. Card games enjoyed by primary children include those suggested by Kamii (see Unit 27) and those that are perennial favorites such as "Go Fish," "Concentration," "Crazy Eights," "Old Maid," "Flinch," "Solitaire," and "Fantan." Look through catalogs, and examine games at exhibitors' displays when you attend professional meetings. There is a vast selection available.

Young children enjoy bowling games and games that involve aiming. Dropping clothespins into a container or throwing beanbags through a hole or into a container are appropriate for young children. Once they learn the game, they can keep track of their successes using Unifix Cubes® or making tick marks to keep score.

Outdoors or in the gym, children can have races. They can estimate how far they can throw a ball, a beanbag, or a paper plate. Primary children can measure with a yardstick and compare their estimates with their actual throwing distances.

Primary children enjoy jumping rope. A popular jingle that requires counting is

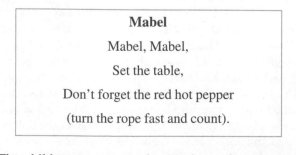

Mabel

Mabel, Mabel,

Set the table,

Don't forget the red hot pepper

(turn the rope fast and count).

The children try to see who can jump the most red hot peppers. During the primary years, children are in the stage of industry versus inferiority. The struggle between these forces leads them into a natural interest in competitive activities, such as the games listed, and into team sports and races. Adults have to take care to find ways for each of the children to achieve so that they do not experience inferiority feelings. Primary children enjoy races that give them practice in time and distance relationships. Hurdle jumping can begin with high and low jumps then move into standard measures of height. Balls, beanbags, or Frisbees can be thrown and the distances compared and measured. Team sports require scorekeeping and an understanding of *more, less,* and *ordinal relations* (that is, who is up first, second, third, and so on).

Primary children also enjoy math puzzlers and brainteasers that give them practice in problem solving. Some of these types of problems were introduced in Unit 3. The following are additional examples.

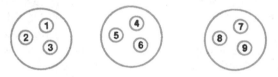

Move one so each set has a sum of 15.

Magic Triangles

Write the numbers 1 through 6 in the circles of the triangle below in such a way as to have a total of nine (or 10 or 11 or 12) on each side.

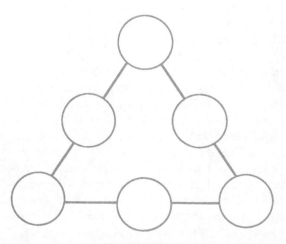

Totals of Nine

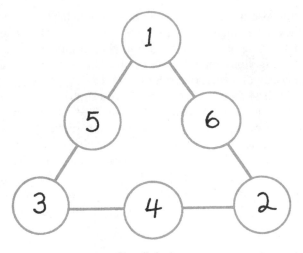

One Solution

The Lady and the Tiger

How many different squares can you count?

How many different triangles can you count?

Answers: 11 squares   19 triangles

Your Number

Ask someone to think of a number, but keep it secret. Now tell him to double the number, add eight to the result, divide by two, and subtract the original number. Then have him write down the answer but tell him not to show it to you until you predict the answer. The answer will always be four.

Young children enjoy games. Board, target, and action games offer them opportunities to apply math concepts. Through observation of children playing games, adults can obtain information regarding a child's development of math skills and concepts. Each issue of *Teaching Children Mathematics* includes a thematic section called Math by the Month that poses problems for elementary students beginning with kindergarten through grade two. For example, in May 2001 the theme was Summer Fun. Four problems were presented for kindergarten through grade two: one involved addition and subtraction, another was a geometry walk based in a shape book, a third focused on graphing favorite ice cream flavors, and the fourth used nonstandard and standard foot measurement.

Finger Plays and Action Songs

Many finger plays and action songs include the application of math concepts. Children may have to hear the song or finger play several times before they join in. If the teacher keeps repeating it, the students will gradually learn and participate. Favorite finger plays are "Five Little Monkeys Jumping on the Bed" and "Five Little Ducks Swimming in a Pond." A longtime favorite song is "Johnny Works with One Hammer." Counting rhymes are particularly enjoyed (Arenson, 1998). Two examples are

---

One potato,

Two potato,

Three potato,

Four;

Five potato,

Six potato,

Seven potato,

More.

Here is the beehive (fist closed),

Where are the bees?

Hidden away where nobody sees.

Soon they come creeping out of the hive,

(open fingers one at a time)

One! Two! Three! Four! Five!

See the resources listed at the end of the unit. Finger plays and action songs help children learn math concepts through body actions.

Math in the Environment

The outdoors provides many opportunities for mathematics applications. Children can count the number of windows they can see from the playground. They can do informal measurements of playground equipment and distances across the playground. Shadows can be measured at different times of the day.

Baker and Baker (1991) suggest many outdoor activities in their book *Counting on a Small Planet*. For example, in the activity "All That Rubbish," children examine the rubbish left in their lunch boxes after they have eaten. They chart the results over time and develop conclusions regarding their rubbish. Other investigations include noise pollution, water use and abuse, wind, and other outdoor topics.

A first-grade unit on the rain forest provided many mathematics applications (Thornton, Dee, Damkoehler, Gehrenbeck, & Jones, 1995). The study of the rain forest provided opportunities to advance the students' number sense as they created a sense of the space occupied by the rain forest, built a classroom rain forest, and used related problem-solving experiences. The students kept journals, made graphs, and did estimating.

Science in Action: The Playground

Virtually all outdoors is science. This is where children can become a part of the natural world. Whether you use the outdoor environment around you to extend and enhance indoor science lessons or design lessons that focus on available outdoor resources, your students will benefit from the experience.

Children will be enthusiastic about exploring the "real" world. After all, "The real thing is worth a thousand pictures." Although this old saying and many of the suggestions for implementing outdoor learning overlap with field trip experiences, many of the learning strategies suggested can also be done in an urban setting. School yards, sidewalks, vacant lots, any strip of ground can be an area for outdoor learning. The important thing is to get your students outdoors and engage them in challenging learning.

Specific plans for outdoor learning will help ensure a successful experience. The following suggestions include teaching strategies that focus on specific science learnings. Refer to Units 33, 34, 36, and 41 for more outdoor and environmental education ideas.

Animal Study Activities

Animal homes, habits, and behaviors fascinate children. To begin a successful outdoor experience, assess the previous experiences, skills, and attention spans of your students. Then, review the teacher preparation and control suggestions at the end of this unit, and begin.

Animal Homes

Involve children in the study of animal homes. First discuss, "Where might an animal live?" Then plan a field trip to look for animal homes. When planning a trip, keep in mind that most animals make their homes on southern slopes (sunny and warm). When you find a home, examine the area for tracks. Make a cast of the tracks and determine if the home is in use. Ask, "How can we tell if an animal lives here?" (One way is to look for signs such as food scraps and activity around the entrance.) Discuss possible reasons for the selection of this particular location for an animal home, and speculate on the possible enemies and living habits of the occupant (Figure 40–6).

Finding Insects

Insects can be hard to find, but signs of their presence are common. The paper nest of a hornet or mud nest of a wasp can be found on buildings, rocks, or some tree branches. Be careful—if the nests are occupied, the owners may sting.

The presence of bark beetles can be seen by the "tunnel" left when they strip bark from logs. Most children are familiar with ant nests and know how to

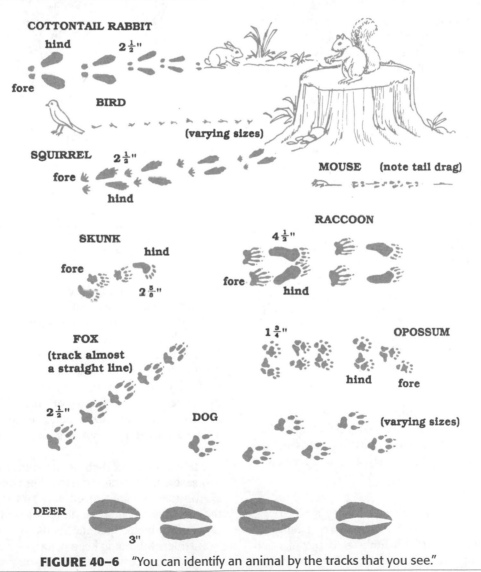

FIGURE 40–6   "You can identify an animal by the tracks that you see."

find them. Fallen logs are good locations for observing insects in the winter. The insects are usually sluggish, and the stinging types can be more easily observed.

Follow animal home observations with discussion. Ask questions such as, "What have we learned about the kinds of animals that live around our school? What are their needs?" Pick one animal to focus on. Have children write about what one of the animals is thinking as it prepares a home.

A Different Type of Home

The next time you see a swollen, tumorlike bulge on the stem, flower head, stalk, or root of some plants, you might be looking at a unique insect home called a *gall*. The purpose of a gall is to provide an animal home. This happens when some species of insects cause specific kinds of plants to form galls around them. The gall has a hard outer wall and contains a food supply from the plant tissue. Have your students search for galls growing on flowers, bushes, or trees. Lead the children to discover that certain types of galls are found on specific plants. For example, a gall found on a Canada goldenrod (*Solidago canadensis*) is caused by a small, brown-winged fly. This fly (*Eurosta solidaginis*) forms a gall only on the Canada goldenrod (Figure 40–7).

Children will enjoy dramatizing the life of a gall insect. Say, "Pretend you are tiny and helpless. Find a place where you can be safe." Have the children pull jackets over their heads to simulate how protected the insect feels. Make a large papier-mâché gall for children to crawl into. Furnish it with a battery-powered light, and children will enjoy crawling in to read, write poems, or turn the light off and simply speculate about what it would be like to be a gall insect inside its home.

Interview a Spider

Children enjoy becoming reporters and interviewing various wildlife. After discussing what a reporter does and the techniques of interviewing, teams of children can decide on an animal they want to interview.

Birds, Birds, Birds

A bird feeder is a good place to begin observing birds. If you do not have a suitable tree near your school, make your own with limbs or cornstalks tied together and propped up to provide perches and shelter.

FIGURE 40–7 A gall is a different type of insect home.

You will be providing birds with much-needed food, and as the birds come to eat, children will have a chance to observe them and their activities at close range.

Children will enjoy making seasonal ornaments and garlands for a holiday tree. Also, use ground feeders or seed dispensers as added attractions for the birds. To decorate a tree, have students string foods that appeal to a wide range of birds. Give them cubes of cheese, popcorn, raisins, and peanuts (in shells). To attract fruit-eating songbirds, add dried fruits to the strings.

Plain peanuts in their shells appeal to both insect- and seed-eating birds, so hang them on fishing line or skewer them on galvanized wire and attach the line to the tree. Then watch the antics of birds such as blue jays as they break open the shells.

Instruct children to keep a notebook of which foods various birds most like to eat. If you prefer, feed birds in aluminum TV dinner trays. Mount the trays on a board and puncture them so that excess moisture can drain out. Fill the different compartments in the trays with cracked corn, sunflower seeds, commercial bird-seed, and fruit. Then watch as the birds come to feed, and ask questions that help students focus on the differences in the birds' feeding habits. "Which birds prefer to eat on the ground? Do all of the birds eat seeds? Which like fruit the best?"

Have children begin a class (and personal) list of the birds that visit your feeder. With a little practice, children might be beginning a lifelong hobby and interest. You need to be familiar with the birds in your area that will most likely appear at the feeder. Each bird has its own specific habits, food preferences, and actions. Take the children on a field trip and compare birds seen with the birds that visit the school yard feeder. (Refer to Unit 41 for additional bird activities.)

Outdoor Plants

My Wild Plant

Observing a wild plant and learning as much as possible through observation makes a good long-term activity for spring. Visit a vacant lot or school parking lot with the children, and try to find a spot not likely to be mowed, paved, or interfered with during spring months. Or contact your school maintenance personnel, and ask them to leave a small section of the school yard untouched for a month.

Have each child select one wild plant as her own for close study. A label with a child's name on it can be taped around the stems of the plant she selects. Encourage children to begin a plant notebook to make entries about their plant (Figure 40–8); for example

1. Describe the plant as it appears today.
2. Measure everything you can with a tape measure.
3. Count all plant parts. Does the plant have an odor?
4. What textures did you find on the plant? (You might be able to record these with crayon rubbings.)
5. Does your plant make any sounds?
6. What other plants are the nearest neighbors of yours?

FIGURE 40–8 "Describe your plant as it appears today."

7. Do any animals live on or visit your plant?

During subsequent visits, determine how the plant has grown and changed. Decide what effect the plant has on other plants and animals living nearby, and determine what is good or bad about this plant. Encourage children to make drawings and take photographs so that they will be able to share the story of their plant with others. Then, predict what the plant and growing site will be like in one year.

Hugging a Tree

A variation of selecting a special plant is to have children work in pairs to explore a tree. Blindfold one of the partners. Have the other partner lead the blindfolded one to a tree. Give the children time to touch, smell, and hug the tree. Then, bring the children back to a starting point, take the blindfold off, and ask, "Can you find the tree that you hugged?" Children will enjoy finding a special tree to hug; some might even want to whisper a secret to the tree.

Adopt a Rock

Have children select a favorite rock for their collection and examine it closely. Then, put the rock in a bowl with other rocks. Ask, "Can you find your rock?" Blindfold students and pass the rocks around the group. Ask, "Which rock feels like your rock?" Then, help children trace the rock to the meal eaten last night. For example, rocks break down into soil, plants grow in soil, and animals live in plants.

What's for Dinner?

After adopting a rock, say to the children, "Go home tonight, and list everything you have for dinner." The next day, have children work in groups to discuss the dinner menu and analyze where their food comes from. Help children trace every food back to a plant; for example, milk to cow to grass. Have reference books available for children to consult. Encourage the children to reach the conclusion that all animals and people need food, and that we all depend upon plants for food. Ask, "Do the plants need people and animals?" After a lively discussion, point out the decay of animal life that nourishes plants. Then, create a food chain for your bulletin board by using yarn to connect pictures of animals, plants, soil, and rocks. Add the sun, and have children create their own food chains to hang from a hanger (Figure 40–9).

Scavenger Hunts and Other 10-Minute Activities

Scavenger hunts are an excellent way to challenge children while focusing their attention on the task at hand. Make up a set of file cards they can take out with them. Each card should have a challenge on it; for example

- Find a seed.
- Find three pieces of litter.
- Find something a bird uses for nesting material.
- Find something red.
- Find something a squirrel would eat.
- Find something that makes its own food.
- Find something that shows signs of erosion.
- Find something that shows change.
- Find a bird's feather.

Caution the children to collect only small quantities of the item on their card, or not to collect at all if they will damage something. In this case, write a description of the situation. Pass out the cards, and tell the individuals or teams that they have 10 minutes to meet the challenge. Discuss the findings back in the classroom.

Circle Game

If the ground is dry, sit in a circle, and pass an object such as a rock, leaf, or twig around the circle. As each child touches the object, he or she must say something that is observed about the object. Say, "You will need to listen and not repeat an observation made by anyone else." Remember, observations are made with the senses. Do not accept inferences or predictions.

While you are still in the circle, move the children apart so that they do not touch each other, and ask them to close their eyes and explore the area around them with just their hands (and bare feet, if the weather is nice). Then ask them to describe or write the textures that they felt.

Outdoor Learning and Writing Experiences

Writing, drawing, and dictating can be integrated with outdoor learning experiences. Here are a few suggestions.

- Write poems about something that was observed during an outdoor experience.
- Write a story about a living thing in the outdoors that has the power to speak to the humans

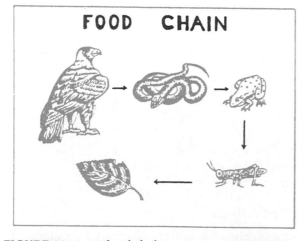

FIGURE 40–9 A food chain.

that come to visit its outdoor area. What might the living thing say? What questions might it ask you?

♦ Write and draw posters that describe outdoor experiences.
♦ Keep a written log of outdoor activities.
♦ Write a short play about the outdoor trip.
♦ Write letters to someone about one aspect of the outdoor experience.
♦ Dictate stories about an incident or observation made during the outdoor experience.
♦ Write how you would feel if you were a plant and it didn't rain for a long time.

Planning for Outdoor Learning

Taking children outdoors can be a challenge if you are not prepared. To ensure the greatest value from the experience, teachers of all age groups should consider the following.

1. Think about your purpose for including outdoor experiences. How will children benefit? What type of preparation do the children need before they go outdoors?
2. What are the logistics? Will you walk, drive, or ride in cars? What type of clothing is needed? Should you take snacks? Are there people to contact? What are the water and toilet facilities? How much help do you need?
3. Which science concepts will be developed? What do you hope to accomplish?
4. Have you planned what you will be teaching before the experience, during the activity, and after the experience?
5. How much talking do you really need to do?
6. How will you evaluate the experience?
7. What types of follow-up learning will be provided? What subjects can you integrate into the experience?

Attention Grabbers

Devices for grabbing the attention of a group can be physical, such as pulling out a huge beef thigh bone from your bag when you want to discuss animal bones. The bone will be heavy, but this action is guaranteed to grab the attention of your group.

More subtle attention grabbers include:

1. Look intently at an object to focus group attention on the same object.
2. Have children remind you of tasks, carry various items, assist with the activity, and lead in other tasks. This participation helps keep their attention.
3. Lowering your voice when you want to make a point works well in the classroom and outdoors.
4. Change your position. Sit down with the children when they begin to wander, and regroup them.
5. Give the children specific items to look for or match, notes to take, or specific jobs. Children tend to lose interest if they do not have a task.

Additional Control Strategies

Although you might be proficient at controlling children indoors, the outdoors can be quite a different matter. Here are a few tips.

1. Before the outdoor experience, set up a firm set of rules (as you do indoors). As you know, it is far easier to relax rules than the other way around. However, hurting and frightening animals, crushing plants, and littering should not be tolerated.
2. When children become too active, try an attention grabber, or initiate an activity designed to give children a chance to run. For example, "Run to the big pine tree and back to me." Relays with rocks as batons will also expend excess energy.
3. Have a prearranged attention signal for activities that require wandering. A whistle, bell, or hand signals work well.
4. When one child is talking and others desperately want your attention, place your hand on their hand to let them know that you recognize them.
5. Let different children enjoy leading the adventure. Occasionally, remove yourself from the line, take a different place in line, and go in a different direction. In this way, you lead the group in a new direction with different children directly behind you.

6. Play follow the leader with you as the leader as you guide the line where you want it to go. If there is snow on the ground, have the children walk like wolves: Wolves walk along a trail in single file, putting their feet in the footprints of the wolf ahead of them. If you are at the zoo, try walking to the next exhibit like the animal you have just been observing would walk.

7. Be flexible. If something is not working, just change the activity. Later you can analyze why something was not working the way you had planned.

Exciting outdoor activities do not happen by chance. Begin by planning carefully what you want the children to learn. Then teach the lesson, and evaluate the children's learning and your preparation. You will be off to a good start as an outdoor science educator.

Technology

Throughout this text relevant technology has been suggested. More software is being put on CD-ROM. For example, Microsoft has produced The Magic School Bus Explores the Ocean. Children ages six to 10 will enjoy accompanying Ms. Frizzle and her class on a field trip to the sandy beaches and to the ocean's depths. The program also includes games, experiments, and a treasure hunt. Microsoft has also produced Dinosaurs for children in grades two to 12. This program takes children on a trip to explore the time of the dinosaurs. (See a review of both CD-ROMs in the January 1997 issue of *Science and Children*.)

Exciting adventures await students as they use the Internet. The **World Wide Web** provides opportunities for teachers to share ideas while students can expand their knowledge. For example, a science teacher in Virginia whose students were interested in comparing Atlantic coast shells with shells found in other parts of the world assisted them in connecting with schools in other countries through the Internet (Holden, 1996). The students made contact through e-mail and initiated an exchange of beach materials. Another teacher focused on mathematical thinking by having her students investigate pet ownership around the world through the Internet (Lynes, 1997). The students applied several standards areas: problem solv-

ing, communication, reasoning, and connections. The Global Schoolhouse at http://www.Lightspan.com provides access to collaborative projects and communication tools (classroom conferencing, mailing list, and discussion boards).

Instructional Technology in Action

Instruction technology offers many opportunities for children to learn more about the world around them than would be possible in the confines of the classroom or school yard. There are numerous pieces of software available for young children that encourage critical thinking and problem solving. For example, young children can plan towns, roads, parks, and more by using Stickybear Town Builder by Optimum Resource for grades kindergarten to three, or SimTown by Maxis for ages eight to 12. The popular children's magazine, *Highlights*, offers interactive computer software that includes a science corner, hidden pictures, and rebus stories. Edmark offers Thinkin' Things 1 and Thinkin' Things 2 in which children build higher-level thinking skills as they determine secret rules, make logical comparisons, and determine patterns. Sammy's Science House by Edmark offers pre-K to grade two children a gadget builder and opportunities to sort and classify plants and animals, to sequence events in a filmlike fashion, and to explore different weather conditions.

The Internet and the World Wide Web (WWW) offer opportunities for students to interact with other students—and even scientists—from across the world, to see images otherwise inaccessible, and to play educational games. Most Web **browsers**, such as *Webcrawler*, *Yahoo*, *Lycos*, and *Excite*, offer some sort of "Just for Kids" option on their home page. You can also find great Web sites by doing a search on a Web browser. For example, you might enter the words "kids and science" in a text box on your Web browser and see what links show up. Once you locate sites that you want your children to use, be sure to make a **bookmark** of that site. Bookmarks are used in the popular search engine *Netscape Navigator*. A bookmark allows you to "mark" the site you are at and then call it back up without having to do a search or type an Internet address, or **URL**. Other search engines have similar features, although they may not be referred to as bookmarks.

There are many resources available to find out more about using the World Wide Web in your classroom. Wentworth Worldwide Media offers a number of products that can be useful. First, a guide titled Educator's Internet Companion has information on how to find Web sites with lesson plans and how to share ideas with others via the Web and provides many WWW addresses so that you can start "surfing the WWW" right away. Second, a special newsletter titled *Classroom Connect* is available and offers nine monthly issues jam-packed with ideas, WWW addresses, and lesson plan ideas.

If your school does not have access to the World Wide Web, there are options for you to explore that use WWW sites. For example, WebWhacker is a piece of software that allows the user to **download** entire sites for later use on a computer that is not connected to the WWW. However, not all sites will download and the download process can be rather lengthy. Nonetheless, for those that can download, it is wonderful to be able to **surf** the WWW without even having a WWW connection! Additionally, Classroom Connect offers software (the Educator's Internet CD Club) that includes entire Web sites and lesson plans without the need for WWW access.

Culturally Relevant Mathematics and Science

Remember that the first NCTM (2000) principle is the equity principle. "Excellence in mathematics education requires equity—high expectations and strong support of all students" (p.12). Respect for and accommodation to differences is essential to instruction in both mathematics and science. As a follow-up to support and elaborate on the equity principle, a special issue of *Teaching Children Mathematics* (Barta, 2001, February) consists of articles that looks at various aspects of mathematics and culture.

In Unit 2, ethnomathematics, the natural mathematics that children learn in their culture, was described. Information regarding ethnomathematics can be obtained from the International Study Group on Ethnomathematics Web site at http://www.rpi.edu/~eglash/isgem.htm (Eglash, 2001). It is essential to discover and build on the mathematics that children bring to

school. It is also necessary to use culturally relevant materials and activities. For example, many of the books suggested throughout the text reflect cultural diversity (see especially Unit 15 and Appendix B). Some books are written in English but focus on other cultures. For example, in the book *Round Is a Mooncake* (Thong, 2000), a young girl seeks out shapes in a Chinese American setting. In *Feast for Ten* (Falwell, 1993) an African American family is followed through shopping to cooking to serving and eating a meal. Other books are written in other languages as translations of English language classics or as stories written originally in other languages. Books in Spanish are increasing in number and are reviewed yearly in *Science and Children* and frequently in *Young Children*. Advice on selecting mathematics-related books in Spanish is the subject of an article by Jacobs, Bennett, and Bullock (2000).

Culturally relevant mathematics and science can be integrated with social studies. Internet activities such as those just described can provide opportunities to learn about other geographic areas and their cultures while obtaining science knowledge and applying mathematics knowledge. Upper grade or younger advanced students can study and compare the mathematical systems of other cultures such as Native American, Roman, and Egyptian. Calendars of various cultures can be compared, such as Chinese, Jewish, and Muslim (Zaslavsky, 2001). White (2001) describes how geometry was explored by first graders through comparing fabrics from different cultures.

Summary

Math and science in action mean children exploring the environment. This is done through woodworking, block constructing, game playing, and exploring the outdoor areas in their environment. Math and science in action mean children saying, singing, and acting out math and science language and concepts.

When children make block-building decisions, they are thinking like scientists. They focus on a problem and use the thinking skills of math and science to arrive at a solution or conclusions. Block building and other indoor and outdoor explorations give children an opportunity to learn by manipulating and acting on their environment as they build their own model of the world.

The outdoor environment can be used to extend and enhance indoor lessons or as a specific place for engaging children in challenging learning. Suggestions have been given about how to work directly with outdoor learning as well as strategies for focusing children's attention on outdoor learning and encouraging higher-level math and science thinking. Once children learn how to learn outdoors, they will enjoy the fascinating world around them. Technology provides increasing opportunities for learning about science and applying mathematical skills and concepts through software applications and through the broad domain opened up through the Internet. Equity is an essential principle of mathematics and science instruction. Focusing on children's cultural mathematics and science and comparisons with the mathematics and science of other cultures shows respect for diversity.

KEY TERMS

Internet
World Wide Web
browsers

bookmark
URL
download

surf

SUGGESTED ACTIVITIES

1. Visit a school supply or a toy store, and examine the types of blocks available for purchase. How do they compare with the blocks described in this unit?

2. Look through some educational supply catalogs (see list in Unit 39), and note the prices of various sets and types of blocks. Which would you select? How much would they cost?

3. Observe some preschool, kindergarten, and/or primary students playing with blocks. See if you can categorize the developmental stages of their block building. Report on your observations in class.

4. Visit a local hardware store or a local discount store hardware department. Record the types of tools available and the prices. Compare your findings with the prices of similar toys in educational catalogs.

5. Find five math finger plays, songs, and or rhymes. Teach them to the other members of the class.

6. Try out a math board game or a math action game with a small group of children. Share your experience with the class.

7. Design an outdoor activity, and teach it to a group of primary age children. Share your experience with the class.

8. Secure samples of outdoor education resources. Modify them for primary grades, and include them in your file.

9. Locate a classroom that is hooked into the Internet. Find out if the students are using the Internet in any math- and/or science-related activities.

10. Prepare a list of positive reinforcement statements that you will use when implementing outdoor education. How do the strategies compare with those used in an indoor setting? Discuss reasons for any differences.

11. Evaluate a computer program for young children that emphasizes one of the concepts or skills discussed in this unit. Please refer to other recommended computer resources in other units. The software mentioned in this chapter includes:
    ◆ Highlights Interactive. Portland, OR: Creative Multimedia. (Ages 5–8)
    ◆ Sammy's Science House. Redmond, WA: Edmark. (Pre-K–2)
    ◆ SimTown. Walnut Creek, CA: Maxis. (Ages 8–12)
    ◆ Stickybear Town Builder. Norfolk, CT: Optimum Resource. (K–3)
    ◆ Thinkin' Things 1 and Thinkin' Things 2. Redmond, WA: Edmark. (Ages 4–13)

Other software selections you might explore:

◆ Learn about Series. (Grades K–2). Pleasantville, NY: Sunburst. A variety of selections such as senses, astronomy, matter, measurement and mixtures, and more.

◆ Memory Fun! (Grades K–3). Pleasantville, NY: Sunburst. Designed like the memory game Concentration. Provides experience in categorizing and memory.

◆ Pajama Sam® 2: Thunder and Lightning Aren't So Frightening. (Ages 3 to 8). Woodinville, WA: Humongous. Exploration of weather with puzzles, games, and fantastic friends.

◆ Thinkin' Things Fripple Town. (Grades K–3). Redmond, WA: Edmark. Promotes thinking skills through art, geography, language arts, mathematics, and science.

◆ WebWhacker [Computer utility program]. Houston, TX: Forefront Direct. (Utility for adult use)

The Educator's Internet Companion, Classroom Connect, and the Educators' Internet CD Club are available from Wentworth Worldwide Media (address in Appendix B).

There are several "search engines" on the World Wide Web. Most of them are accessible by typing the Internet address in the URL text box of your browser (i.e., Netscape Navigator or Microsoft Explorer). For example

Webcrawler: http://www.webcrawler.com
Yahoo: http://www.yahoo.com
Excite: http://www.excite.com
Lycos: http://www.lycos.com

REVIEW

A. Explain the benefits of block play for young children.

B. List several types of block accessory toys.

C. Describe how to set up a woodworking area.

D. At which stage of block building is each of the following examples?
1. Putting blocks in rows
2. Carrying blocks around
3. Building structures for dramatic play
4. Building simple enclosures

E. List some popular early childhood board games.

F. Explain how finger plays and action songs can support math concept development.

G. Explain the value of the World Wide Web to math and science instruction.

H. What are the benefits of including outdoor activities with primary age children?

I. Describe at least two factors that support cultural equity.

REFERENCES

Arenson, R. (Illustrator). (1998). *One, two, skip a few! First number rhymes.* New York: Barefoot Books.

Baker, A., & Baker, J. (1991). *Counting on a small planet: Activities for environmental mathematics.* Portsmouth, NH: Heinemann.

Barta, J. (Ed.). (2001). Mathematics and culture [Special issue]. *Teaching Children Mathematics, 7*(6).

Burrill, G. (1997, April). Show me the math! *NCTM News Bulletin, 3.*

Eglash, R. (2001). News from the net: The international study group on ethnomathematics. *Teaching Children Mathematics, 7*(6), 336.

Fallwell, C. (1993). *Feast for 10.* New York: Clarion.

Holden, J. C. (1996). The science exchange program. *Science and Children, 34*(3), 20–21.

Jacobs, V. R., Bennett, T. R., & Bullock, C. (2000). Selecting books in Spanish to teach mathematics. *Teaching Children Mathematics, 6*(9), 582–587.

Lynes, K. (1997). Tech time: Mining mathematics through the Internet! *Teaching Children Mathematics, 3*(7), 394–396.

MacDonald, S. (2001). *Block play: The complete guide to learning and playing with blocks.* Beltsville, MD: Gryphon House.

National Council of Teachers of Mathematics. (2000). *Principles and standards for school mathematics.* Reston, VA: Author. (http://www.nctm.org)

Scieszka, J., & Smith, L. (1995). *Math curse.* New York: Viking.

Shaw, G. M., Chambless, M. S., Chessin, D. R., Price, V., & Beardain, G. (1997). Cooperative problem solving: Using K-W-D-L as an organizational technique. *Teaching Children Mathematics, 3,* 482–486.

Thong, R. (2000). *Round is a mooncake.* San Francisco: Chronicle Books.

Thornton, C. A., Dee, D., Damkoehler, D. D., Gehrenbeck, H., & Jones, G. A. (1995). The children's rain forest. *Teaching Children Mathematics, 2*(3), 144–148.

White, D. Y. (2001). Kenta, kilts, and kimonos: Exploring cultures and mathematics through fabrics. *Teaching Children Mathematics, 7*(6), 354–359.

Wolfgang, C. H., Stannard, L. L., & Jones, I. (2001). Block play performance among preschoolers as a predictor of later school achievement in mathematics. *Journal of Research in Childhood Education, 15*(2), 173–180.

Zaslavsky, C. (2001). Developing number sense: What can other cultures tell us? *Teaching Children Mathematics, 7*(6), 312–319.

FURTHER READING AND RESOURCES

Planning the Environment and the Curriculum

Copley, J. V. (2000). *The young child and mathematics.* Washington, DC: National Association for the Education of Young Children.

Copley, J. V. (Ed.). (1999). *Mathematics in the early years.* Washington, DC: National Association for the Education of Young Children.

Richardson, K. (1999). *Developing number concepts: Planning guide.* Parsippany, NJ: Dale Seymour.

Learning Together

Artzt, A. F., & Newman, C. M. (1990). *How to use cooperative learning in the mathematics class.* Reston, VA: National Council of Teachers of Mathematics.

Barone, M. M., & Taylor, L. (1996). Peer tutoring with mathematics manipulatives: A practical guide. *Teaching Children Mathematics, 3*(1), 8–15.

Gondree, L. L., & Doran, A. (1998). Teach me some science: An elementary/middle school partnership. *Science and Children, 36*(3), 44–48.

Russell, S. J., & Corwin, R. B. (1993). Talking mathematics: "Going slow" and "Letting go". *Phi Delta Kappan, 74*(7), 555–558.

Schulte, P. L. (1999). Lessons in cooperative learning. *Science and Children, 36*(7), 44–47.

Woodworking

Skeen, P., Garner, A. P., & Cartwright, S. (1984). *Woodworking for young children.* Washington, DC: National Association for the Education of Young Children.

Blocks and Construction

Dunn, S., & Larson, R. (1990). *Design technology.* London: Falmer Press.

Hirsch, E. (Ed.). (1984). *The block book.* Washington, DC: National Association for the Education of Young Children.

Johnson, P. (1992). *Pop-up engineering.* London: Falmer Press.

Kamii, S., & DeVries, R. (1993). *Physical knowledge in preschool education: Implications of Piaget's theory* (Rev. ed.). Englewood Cliffs, NJ: Prentice Hall.

Lind, K. K., & Milburn, M. J. (1988). The mechanized child. *Elementary School Notes, 3*(5), 32–33.

Lind, K. K., & Milburn, M. J. (1988). More for the mechanized child. *Science and Children, 25*(6), 39–40.

Wolfgang, C. H., Stannard, L. L., & Jones, I. (2001). Block play performance among preschoolers as a predictor of later school achievement in mathematics. *Journal of Research in Childhood Education*, *15*(2), 173–180.

Wellhousen, K., & Kieff, J. (2001). *A constructivist approach to block play in early childhood.* Clifton Park, NY: Delmar Learning.

Zubrowski, B. (1981). *Messing around with drinking straw construction.* Boston: Little, Brown.

Games

Feldman, J. R. (1994). *Complete handbook of indoor and outdoor games for young children.* Englewood Cliffs, NJ: Prentice Hall.

Kamii, C. (1985). *Young children reinvent arithmetic.* New York: Teachers College Press.

Kamii, C. (1989). *Young children continue to reinvent arithmetic, 2nd Grade.* New York: Teachers College Press.

Kamii, C. (1994). *Young children continue to reinvent arithmetic: 3rd grade.* New York: Teachers College Press.

Kamii, C., & DeVries, R. (1980). *Group games in early education.* Washington, DC: National Association for the Education of Young Children.

Worstell, E. V. (1961). *Jump the rope jingles.* New York: Collier Books.

Finger Plays, Songs and Rhymes

Aruego, J., & Dewey, A. (Illustrators). (1989). *Five little ducks.* New York: Crown.

Christelow, E. (1991). *Five little monkeys sitting in a tree.* New York: Clarion.

Croll, C. (2001). *Fingerplays and songs for the very young.* New York: Random House.

Cromwell, L., & Hibner, D. (1976). *Finger frolics.* Livonia, MI: Partner Press.

Haines, B. J. E., & Gerber, L. L. (2000). *Leading young children to music* (6th ed.). Columbus, OH: Merrill/Prentice Hall.

Kitson, J. (2000). *Fabulous holiday and seasonal fingerplays.* Clifton Park, NY: Delmar Learning.

Pica, R. (1999). *Moving & learning across the curriculum.* Clifton Park, NY: Delmar Learning.

Schiller, P., & Moore, T. (1993). *Where is thumbkin?* Beltsville, MD: Gryphon House.

Umansky, K., & Fisher, C. (1999). *Nonsense counting rhymes.* Oxford: Oxford University Press.

Weimer, T. E. (1993). *Space songs for children.* Greenville, SC: Pearce-Evetts Publishing.

Technology

Ashby, N. (2001, May). Just a click away: Technology connects a rural Louisiana school district to the rest of the world. *Community Update*, *87*, 4–5.

Clements, D. H. (1999). Young children and technology. In *Dialogue on early childhood science, mathematics and technology education* (pp. 92–105). Washington, DC: American Association for the Advancement of Science.

Computer technology tool kit. (1997). White Plains, NY: Addison-Wesley Longman Supplementary Division.

Coulter, B. (2000). What's it like where you live? *Science and Children*, *37*(4), 46–50.

Craig, D. R. (1999). Science and technology: A great combination. *Science and Children*, *36*(4), 28–32.

The educator's guide to the Internet. (1997). White Plains, NY: Addison-Wesley Longman Supplementary Division.

Haugland, S. W., & Wright, J. L. (1997). *Young children and technology: A world of discovery.* Boston: Allyn & Bacon.

Haury, D. L., & Milbourne, L. A. (1999). Internet resources. In S. J. Rakow, Ed., *ERIC Review: K–8 Science and Math Education*, 6(2), 66-67.

Integrating computers into your classroom: Elementary education, math, and science. (1997). White Plains, NY: Addison-Wesley Longman Supplementary Division.

O'Brien, G. E., & Lewis, S. P. (1999). Connecting to resources on the Internet. *Science and Children*, *36*(8), 42–45. (Includes list of Internet sites.)

Patti, C. A., & Dziubek, P. (1998). MCS sets sail on the Internet. *Science and Children*, *36*(2), 32–36.

Perry, L. (2000). Multimedia rocks. *Science and Children*, *37*(8), 24–27.

Smith, S. W. (2000). Get connected to science. *Science and Children*, *37*(7), 22–25. (Includes resource lists.)

Steffe, L. P. (Ed.). (1994). Mathematical learning in computer microworlds. *Journal of Research in Childhood Education* [Special issue], *8*(2).

Unifix Software Basic Version, Version 1. (1996). Rowley, MA: Didax.

Usiskin, Z. (Ed.). (1999, May/June). Groping and hoping for a consensus on calculator use. *Mathematics Education Dialogues.*

Other Resources in Technology

- PBS TeacherSource provides a variety of math activitis that relate to public television programs such as *Arthur*, *Mr. Rogers' Neighborhood*, and others. Link at http://www.pbs.org/teachersource/math/preschool.shtm.
- Stormie provides many ideas for math and integration. Link at http://www.preschoolbystormie.com.
- Ask Dr. Math provides a problem of the week for elementary level students: Link from http://www.forum.swarthmore.edu/elempow/calendar.html.
- For information on assessment, check at http://www.enc.org/topics/assessment/.
- Scilinks. Connects textbooks to Internet resources. Link from http://www.scilinks.org/about.html.

Action Books, Articles, and Videos

Althouse, R. (1997, January). Everyday math. *Early Childhood Today*, 37–46.

Bloomer, A. M., & Carlson, P. A. T. (1993). *Activity math: Using manipulatives in the classroom.* Menlo Park, CA: Addison-Wesley.

Brown, S. (1997). First graders write to discover mathematics' relevancy. *Young Children, 52*(4), 51–53.

Burton, G., and others. (1991). *Addenda series: First grade book.* Reston, VA: National Council of Teachers of Mathematics.

Clancy, L. (1993). *Hands-on discovery center activities.* Englewood Cliffs, NJ: Prentice-Hall.

Desouza, J. M. S., & Jereb, J. (2000). Gravitating toward Reggio. *Science and Children*, *37*(7), 26–29.

Hagerott, S. G. (1997). Physics for first graders. *Phi Delta Kappan, 78*(9), 717–720.

Heuser, D. (2000). Mathematics workshops: Mathematics class becomes learner centered. *Teaching Children Mathematics*, *6*(5), 288–295.

Hildebrand, C., Ludeman, C. J., & Mullin, J. (1999). Integrating mathematics with problem solving using the mathematician's chair. *Teaching Children Mathematics*, *5*(7), 434–441.

Jones, I. (1999). A workshop approach. *Science and Children*, *37*(3), 26–30, 55. (Designs for science learning centers.)

Kellogh, R. D. (1996). *Integrating mathematics and science for kindergarten and primary children* (Vol. I). New York: Prentice Hall.

Kroll, L., & Halaby, M. (1997). Writing to learn mathematics in the primary school. *Young Children, 52*(4), 54–60.

Leitze, A. R. (1997). Connecting process problem solving to children's literature. *Teaching Children Mathematics, 3*(7), 398–405.

Lewis, C., & Lewis, T. (1995). I can hear the math in this book! *Teaching Children Mathematics, 2*(3), 166–167.

Martens, M. L. (1999). Productive questions: Tools for supporting constructivist learning. *Science and Children, 36*, 24–27, 53.

Overholt, J. L., Dickson, S., & White-Holtz, J. (1999). *Big math activities for young children.* Clifton Park, NY: Delmar Learning

Reading Rainbow (literature videos). Phone: 800-228-4630; E-mail: gpn@unl.edu; http://www.gpn.unl.edu/rainbow/teachers/mainmenu.htm.

Shaw, D. G., Cook, C., & Rebelin, T. (2000). Science fairs for all. *Science and Children*, *38*(2), 14–19.

Smith, N. L., Babione, C., & Vick, B. J. (1999). Dumpling soup: Exploring kitchens, cultures, and mathematics. *Teaching Children Mathematics*, *6*(3), 148–152.

Starkey, M. A. (1995). Their world. *Teaching Children Mathematics, 2*(3), 192–195.

Stein, M., McNair, S., & Butcher, J. (2001). Drawing on student understanding. *Science and Children, 38*(4), 22.

Swindal, D. N. (2000). Learning geometry and a new language. *Teaching Children Mathematics, 7*(4), 246–250.

Warfield, J. (2001). Teaching kindergarten children to solve word problems. *Early Childhood Education Journal*, *28*(3), 161–168.

Wethered, P. A. (1997). An intergalactic voyage: Families, teachers, and students enjoy a week of space projects and activities. *Science and Children, 34*(8), 14–17.

Wickett, M. S. (1997). Links to literature. Serving up number sense and problem solving: *Dinner at the panda palace. Teaching Children Mathematics,* 3(9), 476–480.

Studying the Environment

Aram, R. J., Whitson, S., & Dieckhoff, R. (2001). Habitat sweet habitat. *Science and Children*, *38*(4), 23–27.

Cohen, S. (Ed.). (1992). Promoting ecological awareness in children [Special issue]. *Childhood Education*, *68*(5).

LeBeau, S. (1997). Mathematics and the environment. *Teaching Children Mathematics, 3*(8), 440–441.

Lingelback, J. (1986). *Hands-on nature.* Woodstock, VT: Vermont Institute of Natural Science.

McCormack, A. J. (1979). *Outdoor areas as learning laboratories: Council for Elementary Science International sourcebook I.* Columbus, OH: SMEAC Information Reference Center.

Melber, L. W. (2000). Nature in the city. *Science and Children*, *37*(7), 18–21, 57.

Millward, R. E. (2000). Photographing wildlife. *Science and Children*, *37*(5), 28–31, 53.

Sisson, E. A. (1981). *Nature with children of all ages.* New York: Prentice Hall.

UNIT 41
Math and Science in the Home

OBJECTIVES

After reading this unit, you should be able to:

◆ Explain the importance of the home as an educational setting.

◆ Be knowledgeable about strategies for family involvement in math and science.

◆ Provide families with strategies and activities for teaching children at home.

◆ Describe a variety of math and science activities that relate math and science to a child's everyday life.

The home is the first educational setting. Learning happens on a daily basis in the home: Children learn as they cook, set the table, sort laundry, observe ants, watch birds, or take a walk in the backyard, neighborhood, or the park. Teachers of young children are in a unique position to help families make good use of these home learning opportunities. This unit provides guidelines for parents and other family members as teachers. It focuses on specific suggestions for emphasizing science and math as vehicles for family learning.

Parents and other family members need to understand that children are eager to learn and can learn if the experiences are developmentally appropriate. As teachers of young children, you can assist parents in recognizing that they do not need to go overboard purchasing expensive materials when there are a multitude of learning opportunities that center on everyday activities using resources naturally present in the environment.

Approaches to Family Involvement in Math and Science

Encourage family members to find the math and science in their homes. A large part of a child's time is spent in school, but the majority of time is still spent outside of the classroom. Every day at home is filled with opportunities to explore and ask questions that encourage thinking. It should be stressed that family entertainment does not have to be passive, such as watching TV. Activities that incorporate daily routines such as cooking, playing games, doing simple projects, finding materials to bring to school, and exploring the lives of living creatures and plants are suggested as opportunities for discovery, science and math, and family fun.

Getting the Family Involved

Changes in our economy and lifestyles have resulted in a multitude of family configurations that were rare or nonexistent in the past. A large percentage of mothers of young children work either to boost the family income or because they are the major breadwinner, so they are not as available as their counterparts were in the past. Fathers work longer hours, sometimes holding down two jobs, and are also less able than in the past to participate in school-based activities. Family involvement in education has changed from the view that only parents could be active participants by coming to school and assisting with classroom activities and attending parent meetings and conferences. These are still important activities, but involvement has been expanded to include all family members and caregivers and to focus on opening lines of communication. Families are now provided with home learning tasks that can be performed as part of everyday living. Further, the use of home visits as a means for developing a good relationship with families is moving up from prekindergarten into the elementary school. The following are suggestions for getting families involved and engaging them in their roles as teachers.

A first step could be the publication of a newsletter that could be sent home each month telling about the past month's events and including information about upcoming activities. Future activities could be described and/or sent in the form of a monthly calendar. Children can contribute to the newsletter. They can draw pictures and dictate and/or write news stories describing their experiences at school. Two or three children might be asked to contribute to each newsletter. Suggested home activities may be included in the newsletter and/or sent home as a separate booklet. See the NAEYC publication *Family-friendly Communication for Early Childhood Programs* (Diffily & Morrison, 1996).

Getting parents or other family members to school for a meeting can be difficult. However, it is important

---

KINDERGARTEN NEWS

Published by Mr. Jones's Class *Carver School*
October 1, 2001

School Gets Off to a Good Start

The day after Labor Day, the children started kindergarten. Eight children came each day to get acquainted with the room and find out what we do in kindergarten. Several children have contributed descriptions of what they liked best about coming to kindergarten.

José: I like being bigger than the 4-year-old classes.

Mimi: I like painting and playing house.

Ronny: My favorite was drawing and writing with markers on big paper and playing with trucks and blocks.

Nina: I liked finding my new friend Marcus.

Buddy the Bunny Joins Us

Last week, we had a late arrival in our class. Mr. Ortiz, who manages a pet store at the mall, brought us a black-and-white rabbit with a cage and a supply of food. The class discussed a number of names. The majority voted for the name Buddy ("'cause he will be our best friend"). Buddy is very friendly and enjoys fresh vegetables. If your child asks to bring a carrot or a little piece of lettuce, please send it, if possible. The children are taking turns bringing treats for Buddy.

The Month Ahead

We are looking forward to fall. We are reading the outdoor temperature every morning and recording the data on a graph. We watch each day for the leaves to change. Our observations are written and drawn in our daily class journal. We are planning a walk around the block to collect samples of the leaves that fall from the trees. We will report next month on what we see and what we find.

---

that they become acquainted with the activities, the environment, their child's teacher, and families of other students. Meetings should provide important information and involve active experiences that will give families an understanding of appropriate educational experiences that can be followed up in the home.

The students should be actively involved in the planning so that their excitement and enthusiasm for the event will spill over to their parents. A program that has shown a great deal of success is *Family Math* (Stenmark, Thompson, & Cossey, 1986). Parents come to school and do math activities with their children. They are then provided with instructions for follow-up activities they can do at home. The same procedure could be followed with science (or better yet, math and science could be combined). Another procedure is to hold a Science and/or Math Fun Day (Carey, 1990). For a Fun Day, several activities are set up in a large area, such as a gym or cafeteria. Families can be invited to take part as volunteer helpers and as active participants with their children. By having the Fun Day extend over several hours, busy people can more likely find a time when they can join in. See other resources listed at the end of the unit.

Families can also be asked to send waste materials to school as needed. The items listed in Figure 41–2 as aids to learning math at home are also useful at school. If the children each bring a pack of small brown paper lunch bags to school at the beginning of the year, when an item is needed the children can draw and/or write the name of the item on the bag, take it home, and ask their parents to put the item in the bag to take to school. Do not be concerned if the younger children write symbols that are not conventional pictures or words—they will know what it is and can read the symbol to adults.

Family members who have the time may volunteer to assist in the classroom. Those who are not free during the day or prefer not to be involved in the classroom are often delighted to make games and other materials at home. There should always be an open invitation for family members to visit school.

Parents or other major caregivers need to meet with their child's teacher in one-to-one conferences to exchange information about children's activities and progress. At these times, teacher and parent or other family member (and even the child) can review the student's portfolio of work and discuss goals for the future. At the same time, family members can describe what they have been doing at home with the child and relate any home events that may be affecting the child's behavior.

Homework becomes an important type of activity in the primary grades. Children can work their way into the more formal homework activities by bringing things requested from home as a part of their prekindergarten and kindergarten experiences. These activities help them to develop responsibility and accustom parents to supporting classroom instruction. Homework should always be an extension of what has been taught at school. It may involve bringing some material to school; doing a simple project; or obtaining some information from a newspaper, magazine, or reference book. Be sure that all the information needed to guide the child to the completion of the assignment is included in the instructions. Assignments for young children should be something that can be easily completed in 10 to 15 minutes. Even kindergarten teachers are being pressured to provide homework assignments. These assignments should be interactive, requiring a parent or sibling to assist. Figure 41-1 is an example of an activity that works very well with kindergartners. Articles by Kliman (1999) and by Kline (1999) provide ideas for home math support and activities. The February 1998 issue of *Teaching Children Mathematics* focuses on parent and community involvement (Edge, 1998).

An increasingly popular method for promoting developmentally appropriate home learning activities involves putting together small kits of materials that can be checked out and taken home for two or three days (Franklin & Krebill, 1993; Orman, 1993; Czerniak, 1994; Merenda, 1995). Each kit includes materials and instruction for a home activity and some means for parents and children to return a report on the outcome along with the kit. Many of the activities suggested later in the unit could be made into take-home kits.

Resources are available on the Internet that teachers can download to share with families or that families with Internet connections can download themselves. Family packs and resource information are available from TERC at http://www.terc.edu/TEMPLATE/project/. A government publication, *Early Childhood: Where Learning Begins. Mathematics*, provides mathematical activities for parents and their two- to five-year-old children. The Web address is http://www.ed.gov/pubs/earlymath. To link into family Web sites, try http://www.internet4kids. Teachers may also recommend some of the software described and listed in this text.

Take Home Activity

Hello Family!

We have been working with groups of the amounts 0 to 10. *Ten Black Dots* is one of the books we are using to relate literature and math.

What can you do with ten black dots? This is a question we have worked on. In the book, rhymes suggest answers such as:

1. One dot can make a sun or a moon when day is done.
2. Two dots can make the eyes of a fox or the eyes of keys that open locks.

We have been working with black dots in class. Now it's time to do a job at home.

Home Job

1. Talk to your child about how dots can be used to make a picture. Make a list of ideas. Ten black dots are included below.
2. Have your child draw a picture including one or more black dots. Have the child write or dictate for you one or two sentences about the picture. A page can be attached for writing and drawing.

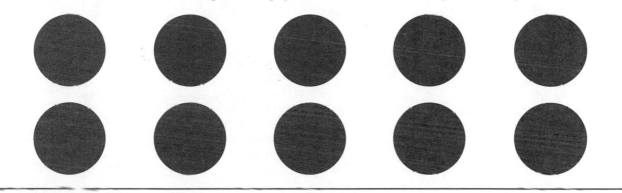

FIGURE 41-1   *Ten Black Dots* Take Home Activity. Based on *Ten Black Dots* by D. Crews, 1986, New York: Mulberry. Created by Rosalind Charlesworth. Note: A page can be attached for writing and drawing at home.

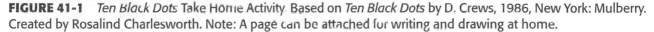

Guidelines for Families as Teachers at Home

Many families have questions about how they can provide learning experiences at home. They need to be reassured that naturalistic and informal experiences are at the heart of home learning. All during early childhood, play is the major vehicle for learning, both at school and at home. Exploration and discovery through play allow children to construct concepts. Adults need to be encouraged to be positive models for their children. If adults are enthusiastic learners, their children are more likely to be enthusiastic learners, too.

Families can provide a close relationship where exploration is encouraged and where one-to-one conversation can enrich the young child's math and science language development. Adults and older children must be cautioned to be patient and allow children the opportunity to explore, reflect, and construct concepts. They need to understand that children learn through repetition. Children do the same activities over and over before they assimilate what the experience has to offer and feel confident in their understandings. Families also need to understand that children learn through concrete experiences. They need to learn how to use simple household items and waste materials (Figure 41–2) as the focus for learning.

From the Kitchen

egg cartons
cereal boxes and other empty food boxes
margarine tubs
milk cartons
milk jugs
plastic lids
pumpkin seeds
nuts
nutshells
straws
dry peas, beans, rice
coffee can and lids
other food and juice cans
baby food jars
potato chip cans
frozen food cartons
yogurt, cottage cheese,
    sour cream, or dip containers
milk bottle lids
individual small cereal boxes
soft drink bottle caps
plastic holder (soft drink six-pack carrier)
paper plates
coffee grounds
plastic bottles or jugs (soap, bleach, etc.)
plastic or metal tops or lids
Styrofoam meat plates (trays)
plastic bag twists
cardboard rolls (paper towels, foil, etc.)
kitchen scales
plastic forks, spoons
cleaned and dried bones

From Outside

pebbles   bird feathers
rocks and stones   acorns
twigs, sticks, bark   animal teeth
leaves and weeds   insects
pinecones and nuts   mosses
seeds   abandoned nests
corn kernels and husks nonpoisonous plants
soybeans
flowers
clay, mud, dirt, sand
seashells

From All Around the House

sponges
magazines with pictures
catalogs (general, seed, etc.)
old crayons
shoe boxes and other small boxes (i.e., bar soap,
    toothpaste, aspirin, tape, etc.)
other cardboard boxes
    (not corrugated)
corrugated cardboard
cardboard tablet backs
scraps of wallpaper, carpeting
Contac paper®
toothbrushes (for spattering paint)
lumber scraps
gift wrap (used or scraps)
gift wrap ribbon and bows
old greeting cards (pictures)
newspapers
jewelry
wire
clothesline
clocks
watches
small appliances
rubber or plastic hose
plastic tubing
plastic tubs
nails and screws
wood scraps
tools

From Sewing Scraps

buttons
snaps
fabric
felt
thread
yarn
lace
ribbon
trim
rickrack
spools

FIGURE 41–2 Math and science materials found at home.

Provide examples of naturalistic, informal, and structured home learning experiences. *Naturalistic experiences* are those in which a concept is applied in an everyday activity, such as sorting laundry, counting out tableware, following an ant trail in the backyard, or watching the clock to get to an appointment on time. *Informal experiences* take place when the alert adult finds a way to involve the child in an activity such as asking the child to set the table, measure out cooking ingredients, learn his telephone number, and count the money in his piggy bank. The adult can also sing a song or chant a rhyme on the spur of the moment and provide materials the child can use on his own (such as blocks, sets of dishes, construction materials, and the like). *Structured activities* usually are not appropriate before age three. Adults need to take care that, when they introduce structured activities, they do not pressure the child if he seems uninterested or not ready. Suggest that adults pull back and try again in two or three weeks. Emphasize that children need time to explore materials before adults present structured questions or problems to them.

Math and Science in the Home, Yard, Neighborhood, and Park

There are many math and science activities that can be done in the home, backyard, neighborhood, park, or even on a vacation trip. Any of the following activities could be included in a home newsletter and/or activity booklet or monthly calendar. Activities begin with daily home routines and then move into other areas.

Daily Routines

Families should be encouraged to emphasize the skills of science as they go about their daily routines; for example.

1. As laundry is sorted and socks are matched, talk about the differences and similarities in the articles. Then fold the clothes, and put them in the correct places. Ask, "Where do the pants go? Where shall we put the t-shirts?" Even small children will begin the process of classification as they note the differences in characteristics.

2. Children can examine their bodies and compare themselves to animals in a concrete way. They have five toes on each foot, but a horse does not. When a family takes a trip to a farm or a duck pond, the differences and similarities in animal feet can be noted. Ask, "How many toes do you have? How are your toes different from a duck's? Why do you think a duck has a web between its toes?" Activities like this help children be aware of differences in animals and offer opportunities to discuss why an animal is structured in a certain way.

3. When kitchen utensils are returned to drawers after washing or food is put away after a shopping trip, discuss why they go where they do. Say, "Where shall we put the spoons? Should the crackers go in the cupboard or the refrigerator?" Some parents might want to lay items such as spoons, spatulas, or cups on the table and see how many ways children can devise to group items: for example, things you eat with, things you cook with, things you stir with, and so on.

4. Begin a bottle cap collection for classifying, counting, and crafts. Have children sort caps by size, color, and function. Trace around the caps to make designs. Then paste the caps on cardboard, and paint it.

5. Collect scraps of wood, and make things with the wood. Give children a hammer and some nails and say, "Let's make something with this wood." When the wood sculpture is completed, name it, and propose a function.

6. As children work with tools such as a hammer; screwdriver; tape measure; and various types of screws, bolts, and nails, ask "What do we do with this? How is this tool used?" If something needs to be fixed, let the children help fix the item. Children enjoy practicing tightening and loosening screws in a board. Simply begin the screws in a board, and let children practice the type of motion needed to operate a screwdriver.

Cooking with Children

Cooking provides many opportunities for parents to provide children with practical applications of science and math. When someone is cooking, the child can measure the ingredients, observe them as they change form during cooking (or mixing), and taste the final product.

Children should be given as much responsibility for the food preparation as possible. This might include shopping for the food; washing; possibly cutting (carefully supervised, of course); reading and following the recipe; baking, cooking, or freezing; setting the food on the table; and cleaning up. The more the parent does, the less the child learns.

Try making an easy pizza. You will need muffins, tomato sauce, oregano, meat, and mozzarella cheese slices. Spread one-half of the muffin with a tablespoon of tomato sauce. Add a pinch of oregano. Sprinkle meat on the sauce, and add a layer of cheese. Place the little pizza on a cookie sheet, and bake for 10 minutes at 425°.

Children enjoy getting creative with food. Create Bugs on a Log by spreading peanut butter in pieces of celery. Top off the "log" with raisin "bugs."

Make Summer Slush. Freeze a favorite fruit juice in ice cube trays. After the cubes are hard, place them in the blender, and blend. Add extra juice if needed for a slushy consistency.

The seeds from a jack-o'-lantern or a Thanksgiving pumpkin pie can be saved. They should be thoroughly cleaned and then dipped in a solution of salt water (one tablespoon salt in one and one-half cups of water). Drain off the water, and spread the seeds on an ungreased cookie sheet. Bake at 350°. Stir every five minutes to be sure that they dry out and toast lightly on all sides. When lightly toasted, remove from oven, cool, crack, and eat.

Curious George's favorite is to spread a banana with peanut butter and roll it in ground nuts or wheat germ. Also fun to make with peanut butter are Kid Feeders. Bird feeders made with peanut butter on pinecones can be made the same day children make Kid Feeders. Quarter an apple, and spread peanut butter on the cut sides. Roll the apple slices in one or more of the following: wheat germ, raisins, coconut, ground nuts, or sesame seeds.

Math and Science Activities Here and There

The following are a selection of home math and science activities. For more ideas, see the resources listed at the end of the unit.

Find the Numerals

Using a newspaper page of grocery advertisements, find and mark numbers that are alike, that is, "Find all the fours." The child with well-developed motor skills can cut out the numerals and glue those that are alike on separate sheets of paper to make a number book.

A Monthly Caterpillar

Cut out and number one circle for each day of the month. Make a caterpillar head from one additional circle. Tape the head to the refrigerator or cabinet door. Each day, add the appropriately numbered circle. Point to and count the numbers.

Traveling Numerals

When driving or walking along highways and streets, have the child watch for numerals to identify.

Snack Shapes

Cut sandwiches into circles, squares, rectangles, and/or triangles. Buy crackers in a variety of shapes.

Fraction Food

When the parent or the child is cutting foods (especially bananas or carrots), suggest that the foods be cut in two pieces (halves), three pieces (thirds), and so on. Introduce fraction vocabulary.

How Many?

Play counting games, such as "How many doorknobs in this room?," "How many legs on the kitchen chairs?," "How many numbers on the microwave?," and so on.

Measure Things

Encourage the child to describe the size of things using comparison words: *big*(*-ger*, *-est*), *small*(*-er*, *-est*), *tall* (*-er*, *-est*), *short* (*-er*, *-est*), *wide* (*-r*, *-st*), *narrow* (*-er*, *-est*), and the like. Keep a record of the child's height and weight with a wall measurement poster so the numbers can be checked at any time. Compare the child's measurements with her siblings, friends, and adults. Have the younger child do informal measurements of things in the house and outdoors using paper clips, toothpicks, body parts (such as hands or feet), string, and so on. Have the older (primary level) child use a clearly labeled ruler.

Learn about Money

Play simple games. For example, play store using objects such as empty food containers or the child's toys. Mark each item with a price tag in an amount understandable at the child's developmental level: in pennies for younger children and in larger amounts for older children. Work with pennies at first, having the child count out the number of pennies needed to buy an item. When the child is successful with pennies, introduce the nickel as equal to five pennies. Price some items above 5¢, and have the child work with pennies and nickels. Go on to dimes and then quarters when the child is ready.

Growing Things

Children enjoy caring for and observing their own plants as they grow. Bean seeds usually grow fast and do well under any circumstances. Place three bean seeds in a plastic bag with airholes or in a plastic cup along with a wet paper towel. This way the roots and the stems can be observed. Keep a record of the plants' growth. Point out the roots, stems, and leaves. Keep the paper towel wet.

Bathtub Fun

Keep a supply of safe plastic containers and plastic boats in the bathroom. Let the child explore these materials during bath time.

Freezing and Melting

Put ice or snow in a bowl, and place it in a warm place. Watch it melt. Then take the water in the bowl, and freeze it outside or in the refrigerator. Have the child describe what he observes.

Eye Spy

Encourage both observational and questioning skills. Take turns describing objects in the room and have the other person(s) guess what it is by asking up to 20 questions.

Math and Science in Nature

The outdoors affords many opportunities for family activities that center on nature. Whether in urban, suburban, or small town settings, the outdoors affords rich opportunities for observation and interaction.

Who Invited the Ants?

Encourage families to use their backyard as a resource for teaching science. Many of the activities found in previous units are appropriate for use in the home. Select topics that are relevant to family life, and suggest them to parents. For example, the following suggestions turn uninvited picnic visitors into a family science exploration.

You will need a spoonful of tuna, a spoonful of honey, and a piece of fruit for this activity. Ask, "What would ants eat if you invited them to a family picnic? Let's have a picnic for the ants in our backyard." Then let the fun begin. However, a few cautions should be noted. Ants belong to the same family as bees and wasps (some ants sting). They have strong jaws and their bites can hurt a lot, so be very careful when dealing with ants.

To begin explorations, go on an anthill hunt, usually a small pile of dirt with a hole in the middle of it. Or, if you spot any ants, follow them back to their home. If this does not work, any bare patch of ground will be fine for observing ants.

Arrange the food on the ground (one foot apart). Put the honey on a leaf and place the leaf, tuna, and fruit directly on the ground. Observe closely. Ask, "Which kind of food do the ants go to first? Do you think the ants go to their favorite food or to the food closest to them? Do all of the ants choose the same food?"

Observe ant behavior by asking, "Do the ants carry the food back to the anthill, or eat it on the spot?" Sometimes ants act like messenger ants. When they find food, they go back to the nest and tell the others. Then everybody comes to your picnic.

This activity extends to the sense of smell. Ask, "How do you think that the ants know where to find the food? Can they see the food? Can they hear the food?" Explain that as the ant runs to tell about the picnic, it leaves a scent trail for the other ants to follow.

Scent Trails

Which member of the ant family can smell the best? Make a scent trail on your lawn by placing drops of extract on pieces of cut-up sponge. Use several distinctive scents, such as peppermint, cinnamon, or lemon, and create trails. See if family members can find and follow the trail. Mixing extract with water and spraying it with a spray bottle in a trail pattern on the ground also works well.

Families will enjoy learning more about their picnic visitors. Most of the ants that we see are worker ants. Their job is to build and maintain the nest and find food for the colony. Soldier ants live up to their name by defending the anthill against invaders. There is only one queen ant. She rules the nest and lays the eggs that populate the colony. Some queen ants can live 15 years.

There are a variety of ants with interesting habits and lifestyles to discover. For example, some ants even keep tiny insects called aphids to produce a sweet juice for them. The ants "milk" them for the sweet juice in much the same way that cows are milked. Another kind of ant farmer chews up leaves and spreads them out so that an edible fungus will grow. Some worker honey pot ants use their second stomach to store honeydew. They get so fat with honeydew that they hang in their nest like honey pots. Other ants take the honeydew from them when they are hungry.

Feed the Birds in the Backyard or Park

To help the children recognize different kinds of birds and to find differences in birds' sizes, shapes, feeding styles, and food preferences, create your own bird feeding program. In addition to the suggestions for learning about birds found in Unit 40, make beef suet—hard fat from about the kidneys and loins—to help keep up the birds' energy. The suet helps birds maintain their high body temperature. Ask a butcher for suet that is short and not stringy (stringy suet is hard for the birds to eat and does not melt down smoothly).

You can offer the suet to the birds in many ways. Try putting it in a soap dish attached to a tree limb with chicken wire, or hang it in an onion bag or lobster bait bag. Or make suet ornaments with grapefruit rinds or coconut shells. To do so, chop the suet, or put it through a meat grinder, and then melt it in a double boiler. Pour the liquid suet into the rinds or shells to which you have already attached wire or string hangers, and set the containers aside in a cool place until the suet hardens. Then hang them on your tree.

How about a bottle cap suet log? Simply nail bottle caps to one side of a dead bough. Pour melted suet into the caps and set the bough aside until the suet hardens. Woodpeckers and other medium-sized birds will gather around to eat from the suet log.

Or make attractive suet pinecones. Melt the suet, and spoon it over the pinecones (to which you have already attached string or wire). Sprinkle the cones with millet, push sunflower seeds down into the cone's scales, and spoon more warm suet over the cones to secure the seeds. Place the cones on waxed paper and refrigerate until firm. Later, hang the cones from the tree as a snack for small birds such as chickadees.

Peanut butter mixture makes great food for birds, too, because peanuts have high nutritional content and mixtures made with them can be spread on tree bark, placed in the holes of a log or a bottle cap feeder, or hung from pinecones. But before giving the peanut butter to birds, be sure to mix cornmeal into it (one cup of peanut butter to five cups cornmeal). This will make the peanut butter mixture easier for the birds to swallow. It is possible for birds to choke on peanut butter when it is not mixed with anything.

Try mounting a whole ear of dried corn in a conspicuous place, perhaps by nailing it to a post. Then have the children predict which birds will be able to eat the corn (Figure 41–3). (Only birds with large beaks will be able to crack the whole kernels of corn.)

A Family Bird Walk

A bird walk will heighten the observational skills of everyone involved. Here are some things to look for. Families can look for birds that do the following.

- hop when they move on the ground
- peck at the ground
- hold their heads to one side and appear to be listening to something in the ground
- flap their wings a lot when they fly
- glide and hardly move their wings
- climb on the side of trees
- fly alone
- fly with many other birds

FIGURE 41–3 "What kind of food do you think birds feed their young?"

- make a lot of noise
- eat alone
- blend in well with the grass, trees, or sky

Select a favorite bird, and find out as much as you can about it. This can be a family project. Use birdcall audio tapes or videotapes to identify the birds that have been seen and heard on the bird walk. Children will enjoy creating bird stories, art projects, puzzles, and reading more about the birds they have observed.

The following books are helpful in identifying birds and creating a backyard habitat.

Burke, K. (1983). *How to attract birds*. San Francisco: Ortho Books. A well-illustrated book with an informative text about providing food, water, and nest sites for both eastern and western birds.

Cook, B. C. (1978). *Invite a bird to dinner*. New York: Lathrop. A children's book about feeding birds with good ideas for making feeders out of everyday materials.

Cosgrove, I. (1976). *My recipes are for the birds*. New York: Doubleday. A book full of recipes, featuring treats such as Cardinal Casserole, Finch Fries, and Dove Delight.

Kress, S. W. (1985). *The Audubon Society guide to attracting birds*. New York: Scribner's.

Rocks, Seashells, Trees, and Seeds

The following are a selection of activities from a group assembled by teachers Lisa Kirk and Carla Schild for a workshop, "Nature's Math Connection."

Rocks

Rocks always hold a fascination for children. The colors, shapes, and textures afford opportunities for observation and exploration. Rocks can be categorized by size, shape, and color and from smoothest to roughest. With a pan balance, they can be weighed and predictions can be made about which will be heaviest and lightest. Rocks can be washed, and the children can discover that the colors change.

Seashells

Seashells, sand dollars, and starfish can be compared for similarities and differences. Shells can be sorted, counted, and graphed. They can be sorted by size, shape, color, pattern, or other common features.

Trees and Seeds

In the backyard, the neighborhood, or the park, children can find leaves, seeds, and cones. A tree walk can prove very interesting. Carry a paper or plastic bag for collecting treasures. First talk about what you might collect, and then begin your hunt. Children can use some of their collection to make a collage; they can glue items onto cardboard. They can sort the items and count and graph the groups. Visit a tree and discuss the parts: trunk, bark, branches, leaves or needles, pods or cones, and roots. Observe the tree in different seasons of the year. Draw pictures of the tree and describe it in each season.

Summary

Science and mathematics can provide many opportunities for informal family sharing. Family members can encourage children to explore, ask questions, and think about the world around them. A single guiding question from an adult can turn a daily routine into a learning experience. As children cook, observe, sort, investigate, and construct, they are using the skills needed to learn science and mathematics. Birds, ants, rocks, trees, shells, and other outdoor inhabitants make ideal subjects for observation and exploration.

SUGGESTED ACTIVITIES

1. Observe a parent-teacher conference. Note how the teacher reports on the child's science and math concepts development and how the parents respond.
2. Write a family newsletter that focuses on science and math in the home. Share the newsletter with the class.
3. Reflect on your own science and math in the home experiences, either as a child or as a parent. What kinds of opportunities were available to you? Which do you provide?
4. Make a list of guidelines for families to follow when teaching science to their young children at home.
5. Add 15 home science and 15 home math activities to your Activity File/Notebook: five prekindergarten, five kindergarten, and five primary.
6. Plan a science and math in the home workshop for families. Present the workshop to the class.
7. Interview at least three parents. Ask them what types of science and math activities they do with their children. Find out what problems, concerns, or needs they might have in doing science with their children.

REVIEW

A. Why is the home a good place to emphasize science and math?
B. List three opportunities for learning science and math in the home.
C. How does cooking relate to science and math?
D. Describe two family nature activities involving math and science.

REFERENCES

Carey, J. H. (1990). Science fun: Have a field day in the gym. *Science and Children*, *28*(2), 16–19.

Czerniak, C. M. (1994). Backpack science. *Science and Children*, *32*(1), 46–47.

Diffily, D., & Morrison, K. (Eds.). (1996). *Family-friendly communication for early childhood programs.* Washington, DC: National Association for the Education of Young Children.

Edge, D. (Ed.). (1998). Beyond the classroom: Linking mathematics learning with parents, communities, and business and industry [Special issue]. *Teaching Children Mathematics*, *4*(6).

Franklin, J., & Krebill, J. (1993). Take-home kits. *Arithmetic Teacher*, *40*(8), 442–448.

Kliman, M. (1999). Parents and children doing mathematics at home. *Teaching Children Mathematics*, *6*(3), 140–146.

Kline, K. (1999). Helping at home. *Teaching Children Mathematics*, *5*(8), 456–460.

Merenda, R. C. (1995). A book, a bed, a bag: Interactive homework for "10." *Teaching Children Mathematics*, *1*(5), 262–266.

Orman, S. A. (1993). Mathematics backpacks: Making the home-school connection. *Arithmetic Teacher*, *40*(6), 306–308.

Stenmark, D. D., Thompson, V., & Cossey, R. (1986). *Family math.* Berkeley, CA. University of California Press.

FURTHER READING AND RESOURCES

Teacher Resources

Brandou, B. (1997). Observing moon phases. *Science and Children, 34*(8), 19–21, 48.

Copley, J. V. (2000). *The young child and mathematics.* Washington, DC: National Association for the Education of Young Children.

Copley, J. V. (Ed.). (1999). *Mathematics in the early years.* Washington, DC: National Association for the Education of Young Children.

Families involved in real science together. (1996). *Science and Children* [Special issue], *34*(2).

Hall, J. B., & Acri, R. P. (1995). A fourth-grade family math night. *Teaching Children Mathematics, 2*(1), 8–10.

Lazerick, B., & Seidel, J. D. (1996). Tech times news from the net. Helping your child learn math. *Teaching Children Mathematics, 3*(3), 141.

Lind, K. K. (1986). The bird's Christmas. *Science and Children*, *24*(3), 34–35.

MCCPTA-EPI Hands-on Science (1987). *Putting together a family science festival.* Washington, DC: National Science Teachers Association.

National Council of Teachers of Mathematics. (2000). *Principles and standards for school mathematics.* Reston, VA: Author. (http://www.nctm.org)

O'Connell, S. R. (1992). Math pairs —Parents as partners. *Arithmetic Teacher, 40*(1), 10–12.

Pearlman, S., & Pericak-Spector, K. (1992). Helping hands from home. *Science and Children, 29*(7), 12–14.

Richardson, K. (1999). *Developing number concepts: Planning guide.* Parsippany, NJ: Dale Seymour.

Roberts, D. (1999). The sky's the limit. *Science and Children*, 37(1), 33–37.

Saarimaki, P. (1995). Math by the month. Math in your world. *Teaching Children Mathematics, 1*(9), 565–573.

Smith, L. K., & Tolman, M. N. (1997). Parents share their attitudes and expectations. *Science and Children, 34*(8), 40–43.

Szemcsak, D. D., & West, O. J. (1996). The whole town is talking about it . . . "Math Month," that is. *Teaching Children Mathematics, 3*(4), 170–173.

Washington, V., Johnson, V., & McCracken, J. B. (1995). *Grassroots success! Preparing families and schools for each other.* Washington, DC: National Association for the Education of Young Children.

Weiss, H. B. (1999). Partnerships among families, early childhood educators, and communities to promote early learning in science, mathematics and technology. In *Dialogue on early childhood science, mathematics, and technology education.* Washington, DC: American Association for the Advancement of Science.

Family Resources

Albyn, C. L., & Webb, L. S. (1993). *The multicultural cookbook for students.* Phoenix, AZ: Oryx.

Allison, L., & Weston, M. (1993). *Eenie meenie miney MATH.* Boston: Little, Brown and Company.

Allison, L., & Weston, M. (1994). *Pint-size SCIENCE.* Boston: Little, Brown and Company.

Bell, J. L. (1993). *Soap science.* Reading, MA: Addison-Wesley.

Baratta-Lorton, M. (1975). *Workjobs for parents.* Menlo Park, CA: Addison-Wesley.

Bennett, S., & Bennett, R. (1993). *The official playroom activity book.* New York: Random House.

Carson, M. S. (1989). *The scientific kid.* New York: Harper and Row.

Gordon, M. (1995). *Simple science: Float and sink.* New York: Thomson Learning.

Hart, A., & Mantell, P. (1992). *Kids and weekends: Creative ways to make special days.* Charlotte, VT. Williamson.

Kenschaft, P. C. (1997). *Math power: How to help your child love math, even if you don't.* Reading, MA: Addison-Wesley Longman.

Lewis, J. (1989). *Rub-a-dub-dub science in the tub.* New York: Meadowbrook.

McCracken, J. B. *More than 1, 2, 3: The real basics of mathematics.* Washington, DC: National Association for the Education of Young Children.

Polonsky, L. (1995). *Math for the very young: A handbook of activities for parents and teachers.* New York: Wiley.

Slavin, S. (1995). *Math for your first- and second-grader.* New York: Wiley.

Smithsonian Family Learning Project. (1987). *Science activity book*. New York: Galison Books.

Wanamaker, N., Hearn, K., & Richard, S. (1979). *More than graham crackers*. Washington, DC: National Association for the Education of Young Children.

Wellnitz, W. R. (1992). *Science in your backyard*. Blue Ridge Summit, PA: TAB Books.

Wyler, R. (1986). *Science fun with mud and dirt*. New York: Simon & Schuster.

Appendices

APPENDIX A
Developmental Assessment Tasks*

CONTENTS

Sensorimotor Levels

Preoperational Levels

Math Language

Concrete Operations

References

*Tasks that have been used as samples in the text

Sensorimotor: Level 1

1A

General Development

METHOD: Interview.

SKILLS: Perceptual/motor.

MATERIALS: Familiar object/toy such as a rattle.

PROCEDURES/EVALUATION:
1. Talk to the infant. Notice if he seems to attend and respond (by looking at you, making sounds, and/or changing facial expression).
2. Hold a familiar object within the infant's reach. Note if he reaches out for it.
3. Move the object through the air across the infant's line of vision. He should follow it with his eyes.
4. Hand the small toy to the infant. He should hold it for two to three seconds.

1B

General Development

METHOD: Observation.

SKILLS: Perceptual/motor.

MATERIALS: Assortment of appropriate infant toys.

PROCEDURES/EVALUATION:
1. Note each time you offer the infant a toy. Does she usually grab hold of it?
2. Place the infant where it is possible for her to observe the surroundings (such as in an infant seat) in a situation where there is a lot of activity. Note if her eyes follow the activity and if she seems to be interested and curious.

1C

General Development

METHOD: Interview and observation.

SKILLS: Perceptual/motor.

MATERIALS: Several nontoxic objects/toys including infant's favorite toy.

PROCEDURES/EVALUATION:
1. One by one, hand the infant a series of nontoxic objects. Note how many of his senses he uses for exploring the objects. He should be using eyes, mouth, and hands.

2. Place yourself out of the infant's line of vision. Call out to him. Note if he turns his head toward your voice.
3. When the infant drops an object, note whether he picks it up again.
4. When the infant is eating, notice if he can hold his bottle in both hands by himself.
5. Show the infant his favorite toy. Slowly move the toy to a hiding place. Note if the infant follows with his eyes as the toy is hidden.

1D   **Sensorimotor**
                                                                                        Age 12 months

General Development

METHOD: Interview and observation.

SKILLS: Perceptual/motor and receptive language.

MATERIALS: Two bells or rattles; two blocks or other small objects; two clear plastic cups; pillow or empty box; a cookie, if desired.

PROCEDURES/EVALUATIONS:
1. Note if the infant will imitate you when you do the following activities (for each task provide the infant with a duplicate set of materials).
    a. Shake a bell (or a rattle).
    b. Play peek-a-boo by placing your open palms in front of your eyes.
    c. Put a block (or other small object) into a cup; take it out of the cup, and place it next to the cup.
2. Partially hide a familiar toy or a cookie under a pillow or a box as the child watches. Note whether the infant searches for it.
3. Note whether the infant is creeping, crawling, pulling up to her feet, trying to walk, or is actually walking.
4. Note whether the infant responds to the following verbal commands:
    a. NO, NO.
    b. GIVE ME THE (name of object).

Sensorimotor: Level 2

2A   **Sensorimotor**
                                                                                        Ages 12–18 months

General Development

METHOD: Interview and observation.

SKILLS: Perceptual/motor and receptive language.

MATERIALS: Several safe containers (i.e., plastic is good) and a supply of safe, nontoxic objects.

PROCEDURES/EVALUATION:
1. Give the child several containers and the supply of small objects. Note if he fills the containers with objects and dumps them out repeatedly.
2. Tell the child, POINT TO YOUR NOSE, HEAD, EYES, FOOT, STOMACH.
3. Hide a familiar object completely. Note whether the child searches for it.

2B
Sensorimotor
Ages 18–24 months

General Development

METHOD: Interview and observation.

SKILLS: Perceptual/motor and receptive and expressive language.

MATERIALS: Child's own toys (or other assortment provided by you, such as a ball, toy dog, toy car, blocks, baby bottle, doll, and the like).

PROCEDURES/EVALUATIONS:
1. During playtime observations, note if the child is beginning to organize objects in rows and put similar objects together in groups.
2. Ask the child to point to familiar objects. POINT TO THE BALL (CHAIR, DOLL, CAR).
3. Note whether the child begins to name the parts of her body (usually two parts at 18 months).

Preoperational: Level 3

3A*
Preoperational
Ages 2–3

One-to-One Correspondence: see Unit 8 for task

3B
Preoperational
Ages 2–3

Number Sense and Counting: Unit 9

METHOD: Interview.

SKILL: Child understands the concept of "twoness" and can rational count at least two objects.

MATERIALS: Ten counters (cube blocks, Unifix Cubes®, or other objects).

PROCEDURES:
1. Ask, HOW OLD ARE YOU?
2. Give the child two objects. HOW MANY (name of objects) ARE THERE? If the child succeeds, try three objects. Go on as far as the child can go.

EVALUATION:
1. May hold up appropriate number of fingers or answer "two" or "three."
2. Should be able to rational count two objects (or possibly recognize two without counting).

3C   **Preoperational**
                                                                          Ages 2–3

Logic and Classifying, Informal Sorting: Unit 10

METHOD: Observation and informal interviewing.

SKILL: While playing, the child groups toys by various criteria such as color, shape, size, class name, and so on.

MATERIALS: Assortment of normal toys for 2- to 3-year-olds.

PROCEDURE: As the child plays, note whether toys are grouped by classification criteria (see Unit 10). Ask, SHOW ME THE RED BLOCKS. WHICH CAR IS THE BIGGEST? FIND SOME SQUARE BLOCKS.

EVALUATION: The child should naturally group by similarities, should be able to group objects by at least one or two colors, and should be able to find objects from the same class.

3D   **Preoperational**
                                                                          Ages 2–3

Comparing, Informal Measurement: Unit 11

METHOD: Interview.

SKILL: Child can respond to comparison terms applied to familiar objects.

MATERIALS: Pairs of objects that vary on comparative criteria, such as
                 large-small   heavy-light
                 long-short   cold-hot
                 fat-skinny   higher-lower

PROCEDURE: Show the child the pairs of objects one pair at a time. Ask, POINT TO THE BIG (BALL). POINT TO THE SMALL or LITTLE (BALL). Continue with other pairs of objects and object concept words.

EVALUATION: Note how many of the objects the child can identify correctly.

3E   **Preoperational**
                                                                          Ages 2–3

Comparing, Number: Unit 11

METHOD: Interview.

SKILL: Shown a set of one and six or more, the child can identify which set has more.

MATERIALS: Twenty counters (i.e., pennies, Unifix Cubes®, cube blocks).

PROCEDURE: Place two groups of objects in front of the child: one group with a set of one object and one group with a set of six or more. Ask, WHICH HAS MORE (object name)? POINT TO THE ONE WITH MORE.

EVALUATION: Note if the child identifies the group that contains more.

3F   **Preoperational**
                                                                         Ages 2–3

Shape, Matching: Unit 12

METHOD: Interview.

SKILL: Child can match an object or cutout shape to another of the same size and shape.

MATERIALS: Attribute blocks or shape cutouts; one red circle, square, and triangle; one green circle, square, and triangle. All should be the same relative size.

PROCEDURE: Place the three green shapes in front of the child. One at a time, show the child each of the red shapes and tell the child, FIND A GREEN SHAPE THAT IS THE SAME AS THIS RED ONE.

EVALUATION: The child should be able to make all three matches.

3G*   **Preoperational**
                                                                         Ages 2–3

Space, Position: see Unit 13 for task

3H*   **Preoperational**
                                                                         Ages 2–3

Parts and Wholes, Missing Parts: see Unit 14 for task

3I   **Preoperational**
                                                                         Ages 2–3

Ordering, Size: Unit 17

METHOD: Interview.

SKILL: Child can order three objects that vary in one size dimension.

MATERIALS: Three objects of the same shape that vary in one size dimension, such as diameter:

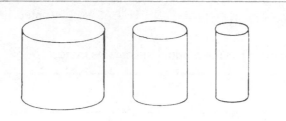

Paper towel rolls can be cut into proportional lengths (heights) for this task. More objects can be available in reserve to be used for more difficult seriation tasks.

PROCEDURE: WATCH WHAT I DO. Line up the objects in order from fattest to thinnest (longest to shortest, tallest to shortest). NOW I'LL MIX THEM UP. (Do so.) PUT THEM IN A ROW LIKE I DID. If the child does the task with three objects, try it with five.

EVALUATION: Note whether the objects are placed in a correct sequence.

3J   **Preoperational**
                                                                        Ages 2–3

Measuring, Volume: Unit 18

METHOD: Observation.

SKILL: Child evidences an understanding that different containers hold different amounts.

MATERIALS: A large container filled with small objects such as small blocks, paper clips, table tennis balls, or teddy bear counters or with a substance such as water, rice, or legumes; several different-sized small containers for pouring.

PROCEDURE: Let the children experiment with filling and pouring. Note any behavior that indicates they recognize that different containers hold different amounts.

EVALUATION: Children should experiment, filling containers and pouring back into the large container, pouring into larger small containers, and into smaller containers. Note behaviors such as whether they line up smaller containers and fill each from a larger container or fill a larger container using a smaller one.

Preoperational: Level 4

4A   **Preoperational**
                                                                        Ages 2–3

One-to-One Correspondence, Same Things/Related Things: Unit 8

METHOD: Interview.

SKILLS:
1. Child can match, in one-to-one correspondence, pairs of objects that are alike.
2. Child can match, in one-to-one correspondence, pairs of objects that are related but not alike.

MATERIALS:
1. Four different pairs of matching objects (such as two toy cars, two small plastic animals, two coins, two blocks).
2. Two groups of four related objects such as four cups and four saucers, four cowboys and four horses, four flowers and four flowerpots, four hats and four heads.

PROCEDURES:
1. Matching like pairs. Place the objects in front of the child in a random array. FIND THE THINGS THAT BELONG TOGETHER. If there is no response, pick up one. FIND ONE LIKE THIS. When the match is made, FIND SOME OTHER THINGS THAT BELONG TOGETHER. If there is no spontaneous response, continue to select objects, and ask the child to find the one like each.
2. Matching related pairs. Place two related groups of four in front of the child in a random array. FIND A CUP FOR EACH SAUCER (or COWBOY FOR EACH HORSE).

EVALUATION:
1. Note if the child matches spontaneously, and if he makes an organized pattern (such as placing the pairs side by side or in a row).
2. Note if the child is organized and uses a pattern for placing the objects (such as placing the objects in two matching rows).

4B

**Preoperational
Ages 3–4**

Number Sense and Counting, Rote and Rational: Unit 9

METHOD: Interview.

SKILL: Child can rote and rational count.

MATERIALS: Twenty counters (i.e., cube blocks, pennies, Unifix Cubes®).

PROCEDURE: First have the child rote count. COUNT FOR ME. START WITH ONE AND COUNT. If the child hesitates, ONE, TWO, _____ . WHAT COMES NEXT? Next ask, HOW OLD ARE YOU? Finally, place four counters in front of the child. COUNT THE (objects). HOW MANY (_____) ARE THERE? If the child cannot count four items, try two or three. If she counts four easily, put out more counters, and ask her to count as many as she can.

EVALUATION: Note if she can rote count more than five and rational count at least five items. When she rational counts more than four, she should keep track of each item by touching each methodically or moving those counted to the side.

4C

**Preoperational
Ages 3–4**

Logic and Classifying, Object Sorting: Unit 10

METHOD: Interview.

SKILL: Child can sort objects into groups using logical criteria.

MATERIALS: Twelve objects: 2 red, 2 blue, 2 green, 2 yellow, 2 orange, 2 purple. There should be at least 5 kinds of objects; for example:

Color	Object 1	Object 2
red	block	car
blue	ball	cup
green	comb	car
yellow	block	bead
orange	comb	cup
purple	bead	ribbon

In addition, you will need 6 to 10 small containers (bowls or boxes).

PROCEDURE: Place the 12 objects in random array in front of the child. Provide him with the containers. PUT THE TOYS THAT BELONG TOGETHER IN A BOWL (BOX). USE AS MANY BOWLS (BOXES) AS YOU NEED.

EVALUATION: Note whether the child uses any specific criteria as he makes his groups.

4D*

**Preoperational
Ages 3–4**

Comparing, Number: see Unit 11 for task

4E*

**Preoperational
Ages 3–4**

Shape, Identification: see Unit 12 for task

4F*

**Preoperational
Ages 3–4**

Space, Position: see Unit 13 for task

4G*

**Preoperational
Ages 3–6**

Rote Counting: see Unit 9 for task

4H*   **Preoperational**
                                                                            Ages 3–6

Rational Counting: see Unit 9 for task

4I*   **Preoperational**
                                                                            Ages 3–6

Time, Identify Clock or Watch: see Unit 19 for task

4J*   **Preoperational**
                                                                            Ages 3–6

Symbols, Recognition: see Unit 23 for task

Preoperational: Level 5

5A   **Preoperational**
                                                                            Ages 4–5

One-to-One Correspondence, Same Things/Related Things: Unit 8
Do tasks in 4A (1 and 2) using more pairs of objects.

5B   **Preoperational**
                                                                            Ages 4–5

Number Sense and Counting, Rote and Rational: Unit 9
See 4B, 4G, and 4H.

5C   **Preoperational**
                                                                            Ages 4–5

Comparing, Number: Unit 11

METHOD: Interview.

SKILL: The child can compare the amounts in groups up to five and label the ones that are more,
                 less, and fewer.

MATERIALS: Ten counters (i.e., chips, inch cubes, Unifix Cubes®).

PROCEDURE: Present the following groups for comparison in sequence:

> 1 versus 5
> 4 versus 1
> 2 versus 5
> 3 versus 2
> 5 versus 4

Each time a pair of groups is presented, ask, DOES ONE GROUP HAVE MORE? If the answer is yes, POINT TO THE GROUP THAT HAS MORE. Ask, HOW DO YOU KNOW THAT GROUP HAS MORE? If the child responds correctly to *more*, present the pairs again using LESS and FEWER.

EVALUATION: Note for which comparisons the child responds correctly. Can she give a logical reason for her choices (such as "Four is more than one" or "I counted them"), or does she place them in one-to-one correspondence?

5D* Preoperational Ages 4–5

Comparing, Informal Measurement: see Unit 11 for task

5E* Preoperational Ages 4–5

Shape, Geometric Shape Recognition: see Unit 12 for task

5F* Preoperational Ages 4–5

Parts and Wholes, Parts of a Whole: see Unit 14 for task

5G* Preoperational Ages 4–5

Ordering, Sequential/Ordinal Number: see Unit 17 for task

5H* Preoperational Ages 4–5

Time, Labeling, and Sequence: see Unit 19 for task

5I   **Preoperational**
                                                                              Ages 4–5

Practical Activities, Money: Unit 22

METHOD: Observation and interview.

SKILL: Child understands that money is exchanged for goods and services and can identify nickel, dime, penny, and dollar bill.

MATERIALS:
1. Play money and store props for dramatic play.
2. Nickel, dime, penny, and dollar bill.

PROCEDURE:
1. Set up play money and props for dramatic play as described in Unit 22. Observe the child, and note if he demonstrates some concept of exchanging money for goods and services and of giving and receiving change.
2. Show the child a nickel, dime, penny, and dollar bill. TELL ME THE NAME OF EACH OF THESE.

EVALUATION: Note the child's knowledge of money during dramatic play and note which, if any, of the pieces of money he recognizes.

The following tasks can be presented first between ages four and five and then repeated as the child's concepts and skills grow and expand.

5J*   **Preoperational**
                                                                              Ages 4–6

Logic and Classifying, Free Sort: see Unit 10 for task

5K*   **Preoperational**
                                                                              Ages 4–6

Logic and Classifying, Clue Sort: see Unit 10 for task

5L*   **Preoperational**
                                                                              Ages 4–6

Symbols, Sequencing: see Unit 23 for task

5M	Preoperational Ages 4–5

Naturalistic and Informal Activities

METHOD: Observation.

SKILL: Child can demonstrate a knowledge of math concepts and skills during naturalistic and informal activities.

MATERIALS: Math center (three-dimensional and two-dimensional materials), sand/water/legume pouring table, dramatic play props, unit blocks and accessories, cooking center, math concept books.

PROCEDURE: Develop a recording system and keep a record of behaviors such as the following.
◆ Chooses to work in the math center.
◆ Selects math concept books to look at.
◆ Chooses to work in the cooking center.
◆ Selects working with sand, water, or legumes.
◆ Can give each person one napkin, one glass of juice, and so on.
◆ Spontaneously counts objects or people.
◆ While playing, spontaneously separates objects or pictures into logical groups.
◆ Spontaneously uses comparison words (e.g., This one is *bigger*).
◆ Chooses to build with blocks.
◆ Knows the parts of people and objects.
◆ Demonstrates a knowledge of *first, biggest, heaviest,* and other order concepts.
◆ Does informal measurement such as identifying hot and cold, a bigger container and a smaller container, and so on.
◆ Evidences a concept of time (What do we do next? Is it time for lunch?).
◆ Points out number symbols in the environment.
◆ Uses the language of math (whether he or she understands the concepts or not).

EVALUATION: Child should show an increase in frequency of these behaviors as the year progresses.

Preoperational: Level 6

6A*	Preoperational Ages 5–6

One-to-One Correspondence: see Unit 8 for task

6B

Number Sense and Counting, Rote and Rational: Unit 9

METHOD: Interview.

SKILL: Child can rote and rational count.

MATERIALS: Fifty counters (i.e., chips, cube blocks, Unifix Cubes®).

PROCEDURES:
1. **Rote counting.** COUNT FOR ME AS FAR AS YOU CAN. If the child hesitates, say ONE, TWO, _____ . WHAT'S NEXT?
2. **Rational counting.** Present the child with 20 objects. HOW MANY _____ ARE THERE? COUNT THEM FOR ME.

EVALUATION:
1. **Rote.** By age 5, the child should be able to count to 10 or more; by age 6, to 20 or more. Note if any number names are missed or repeated.
2. **Rational.** Note the degree of accuracy and organization. Does she place the objects to ensure that no object is counted more than once or that any object is missed? Note how far she goes without making a mistake. Does she repeat any number names? Skip any? By age 6, she should be able to go beyond 10 objects with accuracy.

6C

Shape, Recognition and Reproduction: Unit 12

METHOD: Interview.

SKILL #1:   Identify shapes, Task 4E.

SKILL #2:   Child can identify shapes in the environment.

MATERIALS: Natural environment.

PROCEDURE: LOOK AROUND THE ROOM. FIND AS MANY SHAPES AS YOU CAN. WHICH THINGS ARE SQUARE SHAPES? CIRCLES? RECTANGLES? TRIANGLES?

EVALUATION: Note how observant the child is. Does she note the obvious shapes, such as windows, doors, and tables? Does she look beyond the obvious? How many shapes and which shapes is she able to find?

SKILL #3:   Child will reproduce shapes by copying.

MATERIALS: Shape cards (4E); plain white paper; a choice of pencils, crayons, and markers.

PROCEDURE:
1. COPY THE CIRCLE.
2. COPY THE SQUARE.
3. COPY THE TRIANGLE.

EVALUATION: Note how closely each reproduction resembles its model. Is the circle complete and round? Does the square have four sides and square corners? Does the triangle have three straight sides and pointed corners?

6D*   **Preoperational**
                                                                                          Ages 5–6

Parts and Wholes, Parts of Sets: see Unit 14 for task

6E   **Preoperational**
                                                                                          Ages 5–6

Ordering, Size and Amount: Unit 17

METHOD: Interview.

SKILLS: Child can order 10 objects that vary in one criteria and five sets with amounts from one to five.

MATERIALS:
1. **Size.** Ten objects or cutouts that vary in size, length, height, or width. An example for length is shown below:

2. **Amount.** Five sets of objects consisting of one, two, three, four, and five objects each.

PROCEDURE:
1. **Size.** Place the 10 objects or cutouts in front of the child in a random arrangement. FIND THE (BIGGEST, LONGEST, TALLEST, OR WIDEST). PUT THEM ALL IN A ROW FROM _____ TO _____.
2. **Amount.** Place the five sets in front of the child in a random arrangement. PUT THESE IN ORDER FROM THE SMALLEST BUNCH (GROUP) TO THE LARGEST BUNCH (GROUP).

EVALUATION:
1. **Size.** Preoperational children will usually get the two extremes but may mix up the in-between sizes. Putting 10 in the correct order would be an indication that the child is entering concrete operations.
2. **Amount.** Most 5s can order the five sets. If they order them easily, try some larger amounts.

6F   **Preoperational**
                                                                                          Ages 5–6

Measurement; Length, Weight, and Time: Units 18 and 19

METHOD: Interview.

SKILLS: Child can explain the function of a ruler, discriminate larger from heavier, and identify and explain the function of a clock.

MATERIALS:
1. **Length.** A foot ruler.
2. **Weight.** A plastic golf ball and a marble or other pair of objects where the larger is the lighter.
3. **Time.** A clock (with a conventional face).

PROCEDURES:
1. Show the child the rules. WHAT IS THIS? WHAT DO WE DO WITH IT? SHOW ME HOW IT IS USED.
2. Give the child the two objects, one in each hand. Ask, WHICH IS BIGGER? WHICH IS HEAVIER? WHY IS THE SMALL _____ HEAVIER?
3. Show the child the clock. WHAT IS THIS? WHY DO WE HAVE IT? TELL ME HOW IT WORKS.

EVALUATION: Note how many details the child can give about each of the measuring instruments. Is she accurate? Can she tell which of the objects is heavier? Can she provide a reason for the lighter being larger and the smaller heavier?

6G   **Preoperational**
                                                                          Ages 5–6

Practical Activities, Money: Unit 22

METHOD: Interview.

SKILL: Child can recognize money and tell which pieces of money will buy more.

MATERIALS:
1. Pictures of coins, bills, and other similar looking items.
2. Selection of pennies, nickels, dimes, and quarters.

PROCEDURE:
1. Show the child the pictures. FIND THE PICTURES OF MONEY. After he has found the pictures of money, ask, WHAT IS THE NAME OF THIS? as you point to each picture of money.
2. Put the coins in front of the child. Ask, WHICH WILL BUY THE MOST? IF YOU HAVE THESE FIVE PENNIES (put five pennies in one pile) AND I WANT TWO CENTS FOR A PIECE OF CANDY, HOW MANY PENNIES WILL YOU HAVE TO GIVE ME FOR THE CANDY?

EVALUATION: Note which picture of money the child can identify. Note if he knows which coins are worth the most. Many young children equate worth and size and thus think a nickel will buy more than a dime.

Check back to 5J, 5K, and 5L, then go on to the next tasks. The following tasks can be presented first between ages five and six and then repeated as the child's concepts and skills grow and expand.

6H*   **Transitional Period**
                                                                          Ages 5–7

Ordering, Double Seriation: see Unit 17 for task

6I*

**Transitional Period
Ages 5–7**

Ordering, Patterning: see Unit 17 for task

6J*

**Preoperational
Ages 5 and older**

Symbols, One More Than: see Unit 23 for task

6K*

**Preoperational/Concrete
Ages 5–7**

Sets and Symbols, Write/Reproduce Numerals: see Unit 24 for task

---

6L*

**Preoperational/Concrete
Ages 5–7**

Sets and Symbols, Match Sets to Symbols: see Unit 24 for task

---

6M*

**Preoperational/Concrete
Ages 5–7**

Sets and Symbols, Match Symbols to Sets: see Unit 24 for task

---

6N

**Preoperational/Concrete
Ages 5–6**

Naturalistic and Informal Activities: Units 1–25

METHOD: Observation.

SKILL: Child demonstrates a knowledge of math concepts and skills during naturalistic and informal activities.

MATERIALS: See task 5M.

PROCEDURE: See task 5M. Add the following behaviors to your list:

◆ Demonstrates an understanding of *more than, the same amount,* and *less than* by responding appropriately to questions such as, "Do we have the same number of children as we have chairs?"

◆ Can match a set to a symbol and a symbol to a set (for example, if the daily attendance total says 22, he can get 22 napkins for snack).

◆ Can do applied concrete whole number operations (for example, if four children plan to draw and two more children join them, he knows that there are now six children, or if he has three friends and eight cars to play with he figures out that each friend can use two cars).

EVALUATION: Child should show an increase in frequency of these behaviors as the year progresses.

Math Language: Level 7

By the time the child is between five and one-half and six and one-half years of age, she should be using most of the words listed in Unit 15. The following tasks can be used to find out which words the child uses in an open-ended situation. Show each picture individually. Say, "I have some pictures to show you. Here is the first one. Tell me about it." For each picture, tape record or write down the child's responses. Later list all the math words. Compare this with the list of math words she uses in class.

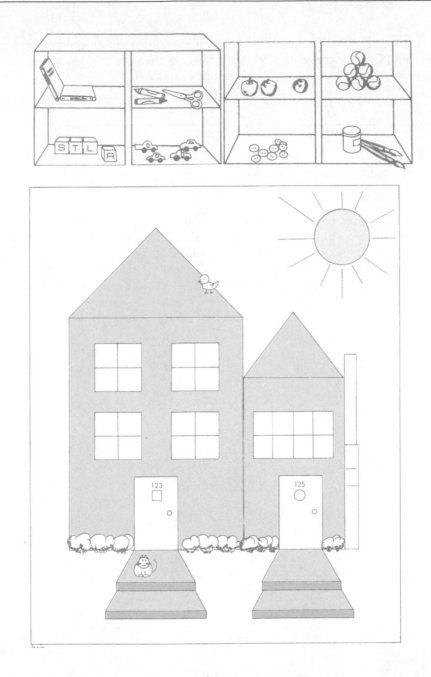

Concrete Operations: Level 8

The following tasks are all indicators of the child's cognitive developmental level. The child who can accomplish all these tasks should be ready for the primary-level instruction described in Section 5.

8A

Concrete Operations
Ages 6–7

Conservation of Number: Unit 1

METHOD: Interview.

SKILL: Child can solve the number conservation problem.

MATERIALS: Twenty chips, blocks, or coins, all the same size, shape, and color.

PROCEDURE: Set up a row of nine objects. Then proceed through the following four tasks.

1. MAKE A ROW JUST LIKE THIS ONE (point to yours).

   Child ☐ ☐ ☐ ☐ ☐ ☐ ☐ ☐ ☐

   Adult ☐ ☐ ☐ ☐ ☐ ☐ ☐ ☐ ☐

   DOES ONE ROW HAVE MORE BLOCKS (CHIPS, COINS), OR DO THEY BOTH HAVE THE SAME AMOUNT? HOW DO YOU KNOW? If child agrees to equality, go on to the next tasks.

2. Task 2

   NOW WATCH WHAT I DO. (Push yours together.)

   Child ☐ ☐ ☐ ☐ ☐ ☐ ☐ ☐ ☐

   Adult   ☐☐☐☐☐☐☐☐☐

   DOES ONE ROW HAVE MORE BLOCKS, OR DO THEY BOTH HAVE THE SAME AMOUNT? WHY? (If the child says one row has more, MAKE THEM HAVE THE SAME AMOUNT AGAIN.) (If the child says they have the same amount, tell him, LINE THEM UP LIKE THEY WERE BEFORE I MOVED THEM.) Go on to task 3 and task 4 following the same steps as above.

3. Task 3

   Child   ☐☐☐☐☐☐☐☐☐

   Adult ☐☐☐☐   ☐☐☐☐☐

4. Task 4

   Child ☐☐☐☐☐☐☐☐☐

   Adult   ☐☐☐☐☐☐☐☐☐

EVALUATION: If the child is unable to do Task 1 (one-to-one correspondence), do not proceed any further. He needs to work further on this concept and needs time for development. If he succeeds with Task 1, go on to 2, 3, and 4. Note which of the following categories fit his responses:

Nonconserver 1. Indicates longer rows have more but cannot give a logical reason (for example, the child may say, "I don't know," "My mother says so," or gives no answer).

Nonconserver 2. Indicates longer rows have more and gives logical reasons, such as "It's longer," "The long row has more," and the like.

Transitional. Says both rows still have the same amount but has to check by counting or placing in one-to-one correspondence.

Conserver. Completely sure that both rows still have the same amount. May say, "You just moved them."

8B

**Concrete Operations
Ages 6–7**

Symbols and Sets, Matching and Writing: Units 23, 24

METHOD: Interview.

SKILL: Child can match sets to symbols and write symbols.

MATERIALS: Cards with numerals 0 to 20, a supply of counters, paper, and writing implements.

PROCEDURE:
1. Present the child with sets of counters. Start with amounts under 10. If the child can do these, go on to the teens. MATCH THE NUMBERS TO THE SETS.
2. Put the numeral cards and counters away. Give the child a piece of paper and a choice of writing instruments. WRITE AS MANY NUMBERS AS YOU CAN. START WITH ZERO.

EVALUATION: Note how high the child can go in matching sets and symbols and in writing numerals.

8C

**Concrete Operations
Ages 6–7**

Multiple Classification: Unit 25

METHOD: Interview.

SKILL: Child can group shapes by more than one criterion.

MATERIALS: Make 36 cardboard shapes.
1. Four squares (one each red, yellow, blue, and green).
2. Four triangles (one each red, yellow, blue, and green).
3. Four circles (one each red, yellow, blue, and green).
4. Make three sets of each in three sizes.

PROCEDURE: Place all the shapes in a random array in front of the child. DIVIDE (SORT, PILE) THESE SHAPES INTO GROUPS, ANY WAY YOU WANT TO. After the child has sorted on one attribute (shape, color, or size) say, NOW DIVIDE (SORT, PILE) THEM ANOTHER WAY. The preoperational child will normally refuse to conceptualize another way of grouping.

EVALUATION: The preoperational child will center on the first sort and will not try another criterion. The concrete operations child will sort by color, shape, and size.

8D

**Concrete Operations
Ages 6–7**

Class Inclusion: Unit 25

METHOD: Interview.

SKILL: Child can perceive that there are classes within classes.

MATERIALS: Make a set of materials using objects, cutouts, or pictures of objects such as the following.
1. Twelve wooden beads of the same size and shape differing only in color (e.g., 4 red and 8 blue).
2. Twelve pictures of flowers: eight tulips and four daisies.
3. Twelve pictures of animals: eight dogs and four cats.

PROCEDURE: Place the objects (pictures) in front of the child in random order. PUT THE (object name) TOGETHER THAT ARE THE SAME. Then after they have grouped into two subcategories ask, ARE THERE MORE (WOODEN BEADS, FLOWERS, OR ANIMALS) OR MORE (BLUE BEADS, TULIPS, OR DOGS)? Have them compare the overall class or category with the larger sub-class.

EVALUATION: The preoperational child will have difficulty conceptualizing parts and wholes of sets at the same time.

Concrete Operations: Level 9

9A*   **Concrete Operations**
Ages 6–8

Addition, Combining Sets up to 10: see Unit 27 for task

9B*   **Concrete Operations**
Ages 6–8

Subtraction, Sets of 10 and Less: see Unit 27 for task

9C   **Concrete Operations**
Ages 6–8

Addition and Subtraction, Understanding Notation: Unit 27

METHOD: Interview or small group.

SKILL: Child understands the connection between notation and concrete problems.

MATERIALS: Counters (i.e., chips, Unifix Cubes®, cube blocks), pencil, and paper.

PROCEDURE: Each child should have a supply of counters, pencils, and paper. TAKE THREE RED (name of counter). NOW PUT TWO GREEN (name of counter) WITH THE THREE RED. WRITE A NUMBER SENTENCE THAT TELLS WHAT YOU DID. When finished, PUT THE RED AND GREEN (counters) BACK. TAKE OUT SIX YELLOW (counters). SEPARATE THREE OF THE YELLOW (counters) FROM THE SIX. WRITE A NUMBER SENTENCE THAT TELLS WHAT YOU DID. Continue with more addition and subtraction problems. Written story problems could be given to the children who know how to read.

EVALUATION: Note if the children are able to use the correct notation, that is, $3 + 2 = 5$ and $6 - 3 = 3$.

9D   **Concrete Operations**
                                                                          Ages 6–8

Addition and Subtraction, Create Problems: Unit 27

METHOD: Interview or small group.

SKILL: Given a number sentence, the child can create a problem.

MATERIALS: Counters (i.e., chips, Unifix Cubes®, cube blocks), pencil, and paper.

PROCEDURE: Give the children the number sentences below. Tell them to make up a story to go with each one using their counters to represent the characters in the story. Nonreaders/nonwriters can dictate their stories; reader/writers can write the stories themselves. Number sentences
1. $3 + 5 = 8$ 2. $6 - 4 = 2$

EVALUATION: Note if the dictated or written problem relates correctly to the number sentence.

9E   **Concrete Operations**
                                                                          Ages 6–8

Addition and Subtraction, Translating Symbols into Concrete Actions: Unit 27

METHOD: Interview or small group.

SKILL: The child can translate written problems into concrete actions.

MATERIALS: Counters (i.e., chips, Unifix Cubes®, cube blocks), pencil, paper, and several addition and subtraction problems.

PROBLEMS

1. $9 - 4$	2. $4 + 5$
3. $3 + 2$	4. $8 - 6$
5. $1 + 7$	6. $6 - 3$
7. $4 - 1$	8. $2 + 6$
9. $5 + 3$	10. $7 - 2$

PROCEDURE: Give each child a supply of counters, a pencil, and paper with one or more written problems like those above. It is best to give the problems one at a time the first time. Then give more as the children become more proficient. Point to the first problem, if there is more than one. LOOK AT THIS PROBLEM. SHOW ME THE PROBLEM WITH (counters). NOW WRITE THE ANSWER. READ THE PROBLEM AND THE ANSWER TO ME. If they do this one correctly, have them continue on their own. Ask them to show you if there are any problems they can do without the cubes.

EVALUATION: Note whether the children do the problems correctly and especially whether they are accurate in translating the signs. For example, for problem 1, a child might take nine counters and then take four, ignoring the − sign. It is not uncommon for children to omit the = sign. That is, they might write 4 + 5 9. Some children might be able to tell you that 2 + 6 = 8, and the like, but not be able to show you with the counters. This behavior indicates the children have learned to use the symbols in a rote fashion but do not understand the concepts that the symbols stand for.

9F*   **Concrete Operations**
                                                                          Ages 7–8

Multiplication, Readiness: see Unit 27 for task

9G   **Concrete Operations**
                                                                          Ages 7–8

Multiplication, The Process: Unit 27

METHOD: Interview.

SKILL: Child understands the process of multiplication.

MATERIALS: Counters (i.e., chips, Unifix Cubes®, cube blocks), pencil, and paper.
1. Show the child patterns of counters such as

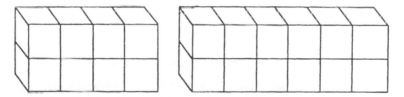

   For each pattern, WRITE AN EQUATION (or NUMBER SENTENCE) THAT TELLS ABOUT THIS PATTERN.
2. WITH YOUR (counters), SHOW ME TWO TIMES TWO. (Try 3 × 4, 5 × 2, and so on).

EVALUATION:
1. Note if the child writes (a) 2 × 4 = 8 or 4 × 2 = 8 (b) 2 × 6 = 12 or 6 × 2 = 12. It is not uncommon for a child to write 3 × 4 = 12 for the second equation. This response would indicate she has memorized 3 times 4 equals 12 without a basic understanding of the multiplication concept.
2. For 2 × 2, the child should make two groups of two; for 3 × 4, three groups of four; for 5 × 2, five groups of two. Some children will reverse the numbers, such as two groups of five for the last problem. Other children may just make two groups, such as a group of five and a group of two for 5 × 2.

9H

**Concrete Operations
Ages 7–8**

Multiplication, Using Symbols: Unit 27

METHOD: Interview.

SKILL: Child can solve written multiplication problems.

MATERIALS: Counters (i.e., chips, Unifix Cubes,® cube blocks), pencil, and paper.

PROCEDURE: One at a time, give the child written multiplication problems. Tell her, WORK OUT THE PROBLEM WITH COUNTERS AND WRITE DOWN THE ANSWER.

EVALUATION: Note whether the child makes the appropriate number of sets of the right amount. Note whether the child does the correct operation. Sometimes children will forget and add instead of multiply. That is, a child might write $3 \times 2 = 5$.

9I*

**Concrete Operations
Ages 7–8**

Division, Basic Concept: see Unit 27 for task

9J

**Concrete Operations
Ages 7–8**

Division, Symbols: Unit 27

METHOD: Interview.

SKILL: Child understands the use of symbols in division problems.

MATERIALS: Counters (i.e., chips, Unifix Cubes,® cube blocks), pencil, and paper.

PROCEDURE: Give the child a division story problem such as Chan has eight bean seeds. He wants to plant two in each small pot. How many pots will he need? READ THE PROBLEM, AND SOLVE IT. WRITE THE NUMBER SENTENCE FOR THE PROBLEM ON YOUR PAPER.

EVALUATION: Note if the child can write the correct number sentence. If she can't do the problem from memory, does she figure out that she can use her counters or draw a picture to assist in finding the answer?

9K*

**Concrete Operations
Ages 6–8**

Patterns, Extension in Three Dimensions: see Unit 28 for task

---

9L **Concrete Operations**
Ages 7–8

Patterns, Creation: Unit 28

METHOD: Interview.

SKILL: Child can create patterns using discrete objects.

MATERIALS: Concrete objects such as chips, Unifix Cubes®, or cube blocks.

PROCEDURE: USING YOUR (counters), MAKE YOUR OWN PATTERN AS YOU HAVE DONE WITH PATTERN STARTERS I HAVE GIVEN YOU. When the child is finished, TELL ME ABOUT YOUR PATTERN.

EVALUATION: Note if the child has actually developed a repeated pattern and if she is able to tell you the pattern in words.

9M* **Concrete Operations**
Ages 7–9

Patterns, Number Multiples: see Unit 28 for task

9N* **Concrete Operations**
Ages 6–8

Fractions, Equivalent Parts: see Unit 29 for task

9O* **Concrete Operations**
Ages 6–8

Fractions, One-Half of a Group: see Unit 29 for task

9P* **Concrete Operations**
Ages 7–8

Place Value, Groups of 10: see Unit 30 for task

9Q* **Concrete Operations**
Ages 7–8

Place Value, Grouping to Identify an Amount: see Unit 30 for task

9R Concrete Operations
Ages 7–8

Place Value, Symbols to Concrete Representations: Unit 30

METHOD: Interview or small group.

SKILL: Child can translate from written numerals to concrete representations.

MATERIALS: Base 10 blocks or similar material (i.e., Unifix Cubes®, sticks, or straws and rubber bands for bundling); 8 or 10 cards, each with a double-digit number written on it (for example, 38, 72, 45, 83, 27, 96, 51, 50).

PROCEDURE: USING YOUR BASE 10 BLOCKS, MAKE GROUPS FOR EACH NUMERAL. After each group has been constructed, TELL ME HOW YOU KNOW THAT YOU HAVE (number).

EVALUATION: Note if the child constructs the correct amount of 10s and units and can explain accurately how the construction is represented by the numeral.

9S Concrete Operations

Geometry, Graphs, Charts, and Tables: Unit 31
See the prerequisite concepts and skills in Units 12, 13, 20, and 25 and assessment tasks 3F, 3G, 4E, 5E, and 6C.

9T Concrete Operations

Measurement with Standard Units: Unit 32
See prerequisite concepts in Units 18 and 19, and assessment tasks 3J, 4I, 5H, 5I, levels 7(2), 8A, and 8B.

9U Concrete Operations
Writing Problems: Unit 15

METHOD: Observation, interview, review of children's written products.

SKILL: Children can write and/or draw their own problems and solutions to problems presented to them in their math journals. They can also record their general feelings about mathematics and their descriptions of what they have learned.

MATERIALS: Notebook and writing tools (pencils, pens, crayons, felt-tip pens).

PROCEDURE: Students should have regular daily opportunities to record their mathematics experiences in their math journals. The journals might contain solutions to problems they have identified and problems derived from class work such as from literature selections. They can also be encouraged to record how they are feeling about mathematics and explain what they are learning.

EVALUATIONS: Have the students read their entries to you and you review what they have produced. Look for evidence of their mathematical thinking and their approach to problem solving. Also look for their feelings about math and their view of what they know. Note growth in written expression and organization of illustrated problem solutions. Discuss with the children entries they choose to select for inclusion in their portfolio.

REFERENCES AND RESOURCES

General Resources

Baroody, A. J. (1988). *Children's mathematical thinking.* New York: Teachers College Press. This book includes many examples of children's common mistakes and misconceptions.

Bredekamp, S., & Rosegrant, T. (Eds.). (1995). *Reaching potentials: Transforming early childhood curriculum and assessment* (Vol. 2). Washington, DC: National Association for the Education of Young Children. Defines appropriate assessment strategies for young children.

Copley, J. V. (1999). Assessing mathematical understanding of the young child. In *Mathematics in the early years* (pp. 182–188). Reston, VA: National Council of Teachers of Mathematics and Washington, DC: National Association for the Education of Young Children. Provides an overview of early childhood mathematics assessment.

Labinowicz, E. (1985). *Learning from children: New beginnings for teaching numerical thinking.* Menlo Park, CA: Addison-Wesley. Chapter 2 describes the basics of the interview method, Appendix B gives interview hints, and Appendix F provides some starting points for interviews.

National Council of Teachers of Mathematics. (2000). *Principles and standards for school mathematics.* Reston, VA: Author. (http://www.nctm.org)

Richardson, K. (1984). *Developing number concepts using Unifix Cubes.*® Menlo Park, CA: Addison-Wesley. At the end of each chapter, there is a section on analyzing and assessing children's needs.

Webb, N. L. (1993). (Ed.). *Assessment in the mathematics classroom: 1993 yearbook.* Reston, VA: National Council of Teachers of Mathematics. This book contains a series of chapters relevant to assessment in general and relative to grade level and specific skill areas.

Kathy Richardson Materials

Kathy Richardson's materials always take an assessment approach.

Richardson, K. (1990). *A look at children's thinking: Videos for K–2 mathematics.* Norman, OK: Educational Enrichment.

Richardson, K. (1999). *Developing number concepts: Addition and subtraction.* White Plains, NY: Dale Seymour.

Richardson, K. (1999). *Developing number concepts: Counting, comparing and pattern.* White Plains, NY: Dale Seymour.

Richardson, K. (1999). *Developing number concepts: Place value, multiplication and division.* White Plains, NY: Dale Seymour.

Richardson, K. (1999). *Developing number concepts: Planning guide.* White Plains, NY: Dale Seymour

Internet Connections

Eisenhower National Clearinghouse. Link at http://www.enc.org/topics/assessment/. Articles on math and science assessment in general, classroom assessment, and standardized assessment.

ERIC Clearinghouse on Elementary and Early Childhood Education. Link at http://www.ericps.ed.uiuc.edu/eece/pubs/digests/. ERIC digests include articles on early childhood assessment.

See Unit 4 for additional resources.

Children's Books, Software, and Web Sites with Math and Science Concepts

CONTENTS*

*Bold numbers indicating relevant units follow each book entry

Bibliography for Adult Reference

Burns, M. (1992). *Mathematics and literature (K–3)*. White Plains, NY: Cuisinaire Co.

Ducolon, C. K. (2000). Quality literature as a springboard to problem solving. *Teaching Children Mathematics, 6*(7), 442–446.

Fleege, P. O., & Thompson, D. R. (2000). From habits to legs: Using science-themed counting books to foster connections. *Teaching Children Mathematics, 7*(2), 74–78.

Hellwig, S. J., Monroe, E. E., & Jacobs, J. S. (2000). Making informed choices: Selecting children's trade books for mathematics instruction. *Teaching Children Mathematics, 7*(3), 138–143.

Jacobs, V. R., Bennet, T. R., & Bullock, C. (2000). Selecting books in Spanish to teach mathematics. *Teaching Children Mathematics, 6*(9), 582–587.

Outstanding science trade books for children for 2000. (2000). *Science and Children, 37*(6), 19–25.

Outstanding science trade books for children—2001. (2001). *Science and Children, 38*(6), 27–34.

Rice, D. C., Dudley, A. P., & Williams, C. S. (2001). How do you choose science trade books? *Science and Children, 38*(6), 18–22.

Roberts, P. L. (1990). *Counting books are more than numbers*. Hamden, CT: Shoe String Press.

Schon, I. (2001). Libros de ciencias en Español. *Science and Children, 38*(6),05 23–26.

Schon, I. (2000). Libros de ciencias en Español. *Science and Children, 37*(6), 26–29.

Sheffield, S. (1995). *Math and literature (K–3): Book 2*. Sausalito, CA: Math Solutions.

Thiessen, D., Matthias, M., & Smith, J. (1998). *The wonderful world of mathematics: A critically annotated list of children's books in mathematics* (2nd ed.). Reston, VA: National Council of Teachers of Mathematics.

Welchman-Tischler, R. (1993). *How to use children's literature to teach mathematics*. Reston, VA: National Council of Teachers of Mathematics.

Whitin, D. J., & Wilde, S. (1992). *Read any good math lately? Children's books for mathematical learning, K–6*. Portsmouth, NH: Heinemann.

Whitin, D. J., & Wilde, S. (1995). *It's the story that counts: More children's books for mathematical learning, K–6*. Portsmouth, NH: Heinemann.

See Zaner-Bloser's *Science for Emergent Readers* and *Reading and Math* series.

Also see end-of-unit references and monthly reviews in *Teaching Children Mathematics* and *Science and Children*.

Fundamental Concepts

One-to-One Correspondence

Jocelyn, M. (1999). *Hannah and the seven dresses*. East Rutherford, NJ: Penguin Putnam; **8, 19**.

Marzollo, J. (1994). *Ten cats have hats*. Jefferson City, MO: Scholastic Professional; **8, 9**.

Slobodkina, E. (1968). *Se venden gorras*. New York: Harper; **8, 32**.

Slobodkina, E. (1976). *Caps for sale*. New York: Scholastic. Ages 3–6; **8, 15**.

The three bears. (1973). New York: Golden Press. Ages 2–5; **8, 9, 17**.

The Three Billy Goats Gruff. (1968). New York: Grosset & Dunlap. Ages 2–5; **8, 9**.

Wade, L. (1998). *The Cheerios® play book*. New York: Simon & Schuster; **8**.

Number Sense and Counting

Many of the books listed in this section include ordinal numbers. Most also include number symbols.

Aker, S. (1990). *What comes in 2's, 3's, and 4's?* New York: Simon & Schuster. Ages 4–6; **9**.

Anno, M. (1982). *Anno's counting house*. New York: Philomel. Ages 4–7; **9**.

Anno, M. (1986). *Anno's counting book*. New York: HarperCollins. Ages 4–6; **9**.

Aurego, J., & Dewey, A. (1989). *Five little ducks*. New York: Crown; **9**.

Ballart, E. (1992). *Let's count*. Charlottsville, VA: Thomasson-Grant. **9, 30**.

Bang, M. (1983). *Ten, nine, eight*. New York: Greenwillow. Ages 3–5; **9**.

Blumenthal, N. (1989). *Count-a-saurus*, New York: Four Winds Press. Ages 3–6; **9**.

Boynton, S. (1978). *Hippos go berserk*. Chicago: Recycled Paper Press. Ages 3–6; **9, 11, 25, 27**.

Brusca, M. C., & Wilson, T. (1995). *Tres amigos: Un cuento para cantar* [Three friends: A counting book]. New York: Holt, Rinehart, & Winston; **9**.

Carle, E. (1969). *The very hungry caterpillar*. Mountain View, CA: Collins and World. Ages 3–5; **9, 17, 19, 21, 26**.

Carter, D. A. (1988). *How many bugs in a box?* New York: Simon & Schuster. Ages 3–6; **9**.

Christelow, E. (1989). *Five little monkeys jumping on the bed*. New York: Clarion; **9**.

Christelow, E. (1991). *Five little monkeys sitting in a tree*. New York: Clarion; **9**.

Crews, D. (1985). *Ten black dots, revised*. New York: Greenwillow. Ages 4–6; **9**.

Cutler, D. S. (1991). *One hundred monkeys*. New York: Simon & Schuster. Ages 3–6; **9**.

Dunbar, J. (1990). *Ten little mice*. San Diego, CA: HBJ. Ages 3–6; **9**.

Elkin, B., & Kratky, L. J. (Trans.). (1986). *Seis pescadores disparatados* [Six foolish fishermen]. Chicago: Children's Press; **9**

Elkin, B. (1968, 1971). *Six foolish fishermen*. New York: Scholastic. Ages 3–6; **9, 33**.

Falwell, C. (1993). *Feast for 10*. New York: Clarion; **9**.

Feelings, M. (1976). *Moja means one: Swahili counting book*. New York: Dial. Ages 3–6; **9**.

Flemming, D. (1992). *Count*. New York: Holt; **9**.

Friskey, M. (1946). *Chicken little count to ten*. New York: Harcourt, Brace. Ages 3–8; **9, 23, 24**.

Frith, M. (1973). *I'll teach my dog 100 words*. New York: Random House. Ages 3–6; **9**.

Gag, W. (1928, 1956, 1977). *Millions of cats*. New York: Coward-McCann. Ages 3–5; **9, 15, 11**.

Getty Museum. (n.d.). *1 to 10 and back again: A Getty Museum counting book*. Los Angeles: Author; **9, 23, 24**.

Gibson, R. (1998). *I can count*. London: Usborne Playtime; **9, 23, 24**.

Grindley, S. (1996). *Four black puppies*. Cambridge, MA: Candlewick; **9**.

Grossman, V. (1991). *Ten little rabbits*. San Francisco: Chronicle Books. Ages 3–6; **9**.

Hamm, D. J. (1991). *How many feet in the bed?* New York: Simon & Schuster. Ages 3–6; **9**.

Heller, N. (1994). *Ten old pails*. New York: Greenwillow; **9**.

Hewavisenti, L. (1991). *Fun with math: Counting*. Chicago: Franklin Watts; **9**.

Hoban, T. (1999). *Let's count*. New York: Greenwillow/William Morrow; **9**.

Howe, C. (1983). *Counting penguins*. New York: Harper. Ages 3–5; **9, 21, 26**.

Hudson, C. W. (1987). *Afro-bets 1, 2, 3 book*. Orange, NJ: Just Us Productions; **9, 23, 24**.

Hulme, J. N. (1991). *Sea squares*. Waltham, MA: Little, Brown. Ages 4–6; **9**.

Jonas, A. (1995). *Splash!* New York: Greenwillow; **9**.

Keats, E. J. (1972). *Over in the meadow*. New York: Scholastic. Ages 3–5; **9**.

Kitamura, S. (1986). *When sheep cannot sleep? The counting book*. New York: Farrar, Straus, & Giroux. Ages 2–5; **9**.

Leedy, L. (1985). *A number of dragons*. New York: Holiday House. Ages 1–3; **9**.

Lowell, S. (1992). *The three little javelinas*. New York: Scholastic; **9**.

Mayer, M., & McDermott, G. (1987). *The Brambleberrys animal book of counting*. Honesdale, PA: Boyds Mill Press. Ages 3–6; **9**.

McGrath, B. B. (1994). *The m&m's counting book*. Watertown, MA: Charlesbridge; **9, 20, 27**.

Micklethwait, L. (1993). *I spy two eyes: Numbers in art*. Fairfield, NJ: Greenwillow Books; **9**.

Moerbeek, K., & Dijs, C. (1988). *Six brave explorers*. Los Angeles: Price Stern Sloan. Ages 4–6; **9**.

Moss, L. (1995). *Zin! Zin! Zin! A violin*. New York: Scholastic; **9, 15**.

Pomerantz, C. (1984). *One duck, another duck*. New York: Greenwillow. Ages 3–7; **9**.

Roth, C. (1999). *Ten clean pigs, ten dirty pigs*. New York: North-South Books; **9**.

Ryan, P. M., & Pallotta, J. (1996). *The crayon counting book*. Watertown, MA: Charlesbridge; **9**.

Samton, S. W. (1991). *Moon to sun*. Honesdale, PA: Boyds Mill Press; **9**.

Samton, S. W. (1991). *On the river*. Honesdale, PA: Boyds Mill Press. Ages 4–6; **9**.

Samton, S. W. (1991). *The world from my window*. Honesdale, PA: Boyds Mill Press; **9**.

Scarry, R. (1975). *Best counting book ever*. New York: Random House. Ages 2–8; **9, 19**.

Sendak, M. (1975). *Seven little monsters*. New York: Scholastic; **9**.

Seuss, Dr. (1938). *The 500 hats of Bartholomew Cubbins*. Eau Claire, WI: Hale and Co. Ages 3–7; **9**.

Seuss, Dr. (1960). *One fish, two fish, red fish, blue fish*. New York: Random House. Ages 3–7; **9, 11, 15, 18**.

Sheppard, J. (1990). *The right number of elephants*. New York: Harper-Collins. Ages 4–6; **9**.

Slobodkina, E. (1940, 1947, 1968). *Caps for sale*. New York: Young Scott; **9, 32**.

Slobodkina, E. (1940, 1947, 1968, translation 1995). *Se venden gorras*. New York: Harper Arco Iris; **9, 32**.

Steiner, C. (1960). *Ten in a family*. New York: Alfred A. Knopf. Ages 3–5; **9**.

Stoddart, G., & Baker, M. (1982). *One, two number zoo*. London: Hodder & Stoughton. Ages 5–7; **9, 21, 36, 35**.

Storms, R. (1986). *1, 2, 3: A teaching train book*. Miami, FL: Ottenheimer.

Tafuri, N. (1986). *Who's counting?* New York: Greenwillow. Ages 2–5; **9**.

Thorne-Thomsen, K., & Rocheleau, P. (1999). *A Shaker's dozen counting book*. San Francisco: Chronicle Books; **9, 32**.

Thornhill, J. (1989). *The wildlife 1-2-3: A nature counting book*. New York: Simon & Schuster. Ages 3–6; **9**.

Ungerer, T. (1962). *The three robbers*. New York: Antheum. Ages 3–5; **9**.

Von Noorden, D. (1994). *The lifesize animal counting book*. New York: Dorling Kindersley; **9, 16**.

Walton, R. (1993). *How many How many How many*. Cambridge, MA: Candlewick Press; **9**.

Wildsmith, B. (1965). *Brian Wildsmith's 1, 2, 3's*. New York: Franklin Watts. Ages 3–5; **9**.

Classification

Cabrera, J. (1997). *Cat's colors*. New York: Puffin; **10**.

Fiammenghi, G. (1999). *A collection for Kate*. New York: Kane; **9, 10, 11**.

Gordon, M. (1986). *Colors*. Morristown, NJ: Silver-Burdett. Ages 2–6; **10**.

Hill, E. (1982). *What does what?* Los Angeles: Price/Stern/ Sloan. Ages 2–4; **10**.

Hoban, T. (1978). *Is it red? Is it yellow? Is it blue?* New York: Greenwillow. Ages 2–5; **10**.

Hughes, S. (1986). *Colors*. New York: Lothrop. Ages 2–4; **10**.

Johnson, J. (1985). *Firefighters A–Z*. New York: Walker. Ages 5–8; **10, 22**.

Wildsmith B. (1967). *Brian Wildsmith's wild animals*. New York: Franklin Watts. Ages 3–8; **10, 21, 26, 35**.

Wildsmith, B. (1968). *Brian Wildsmith's fishes*. New York: Franklin Watts. Ages 3–8; **10, 21, 26, 35**.

Winthrop, E. (1986). *Shoes*. New York: Harper & Row. Ages 3–7; **10, 22**.

Comparing

Bourgeois, P., & Clark, B. (1987). *Big Sarah's little boots*. New York: Scholastic. Ages 3–5; **11**.

Brenner, B. (1966). *Mr. Tall and Mr. Small*. Menlo Park, CA: Addison-Wesley Ages 4–7; **11, 21, 26, 35**.

Broger, A., & Kalow, G. (1977). *Good morning whale*. New York: Macmillan. Ages 3–6; **11, 21, 26, 35**.

Carle, E. (1977). *The grouchy ladybug*. New York: Crowell. Ages 3–5; **11, 21, 26**.

Eastman, P. D. (1973). *Big dog, little dog*. New York: Random House. Ages 3–4; **11, 21, 26**.

Gordon, M. (1986). *Opposites*. Morristown, NJ: Silver-Burdett. Ages 3–5; **11**.

Graham, A., & Wood, W. (1991). *Angus thought he was big*. Hicksville, NY: Macmillan Whole-Language Big Book Program. Ages 3–5; **11**.

Grender, I. (1975). *Playing with shapes and sizes*. New York: Knopf/Pinwheel Books. Ages 3–6; **11, 12**.

Hoban, T. (1972). *Push pull, empty full*. New York: Macmillan. Ages 3–5; **11**.

Horn, A. (1974). *You can be taller*. Boston: Little, Brown. Ages 3–5; **11**.

Hughes, S. (1985). *Bathwater's hot*. New York: Lothrop. Ages 1–2; **11, 21, 26**.

Hughes, S. (1985). *Noises*. New York: Lothrop. Ages 1–2; **11, 21, 26**.

Lewis, J. (1963). *The tortoise and the hare*. Chicago: Whitman. Ages 4–8; **11, 18**.

Lionni, L. (1968). *The biggest house in the world*. New York: Pantheon. Ages 2–6; **11, 21, 26**.

McMillan, B. (1986). *Becca backward, Becca forward*. New York: Lothrop. Ages 3–6; **11**.

Miller, N. (1990). *Emmett's snowball*. New York: Henry Holt. K–3 and above; **11, 21, 26, 32**.

Most, B. (1989). *The littlest dinosaurs*. New York: Harcourt Brace; **11**.

Presland, J. (1975). *Same and different*. Purton Wilts, England: Child's Play (International), Ltd. Ages 4–7; **11**.

Scarry, R. (1976). *Short and tall*. New York: Golden Press. Ages 2–7; **11**.

Scarry, R. (1986). *Big and little: A book of opposites*. Racine, WI: Western. Ages 3–7; **11**.

Shapiro, L. (1978). *Pop-up opposites*. Los Angeles: Price/Stern/ Sloan. Ages 3–5; **11**.

Early Geometry: Shape

Anno, M. (1991). *Anno's math games III*. New York: Philomel. K–6; **12, 25, 31**.

Budney, B. (1954). *A kiss is round*. New York: Lothrop, Lee, & Shepard. Ages 2–6; **12**.

Carle, E. (1974). *My very first book of shapes*. New York: Crowell. Ages 3–6; **12**.

Dodds, D. A. (1994). *The shape of things*. Cambridge, MA: Candlewick Press; **12**

Ehlert, L. (1990). *Color farm*. New York: Harper-Collins; **12, 22, 25**.

Emberley, E. (1961). *A wing on a flea: A book about shapes*. Boston: Little, Brown. Ages 5–8; **12**.

Emberley, E. (1970). *Ed Emberley's drawing book of animals*. Boston: Little, Brown. Ages 6–8; **12**.

Emberley, E. (1972). *Ed Emberley's drawing book: Make a world*. Boston: Little, Brown. Ages 6–8; **12**.

Emberley, E. (1995). *El ala de la polilla: Un libro de figuras* [The wing on a flea: A book about shapes]. New York: Scholastic; **12**.

Hefter, R. (1976). *The strawberry book of shapes*. New York: Weekly Reader Books. Ages 3–7; **12**.

Hewavisenti, L. (1991). *Shapes and solids*. Chicago: Franklin Watts; **12, 31**.

Hoban, T. (1974). *Circles, triangles, and squares*. New York: Macmillan. Ages 5–8.

Hoban, T. (1983). *Round and round and round*. New York: Greenwillow. Ages 3–6; **12**.

Hoban, T. (1986). *Shapes, shapes, shapes*. New York: Greenwillow. Ages 3–7; **12**.

Hoban, T. (1997). *Look book*. New York: Morrow Junior Books; **12**.

MacKinnon, D. (1992). *What shape?* New York: Dial; **12**.

Shapes: Circle/Square/Triangle (3 books). (1992). New York: Books for Young Readers. Ages 3–6; **12**.

Sullivan, J. (1963). *Round is a pancake*. New York: Holt, Rinehart, & Winston. Ages 3–5; **12**.

Supraner, R. (1975). *Draw me a square, draw me a triangle, & draw me a circle*. New York: Simon & Schuster/Nutmeg. Ages 3–6; **12**.

Thong, R. (2000). *Round is a mooncake: A book of shapes*. San Francisco: Chronicle Books; **12**.

Early Geometry: Space

Barton, B. (1981). *Building a house*. New York: Greenwillow. Ages 4–7; **13, 14, 19**.

Berenstain, S., & Berenstain, J. (1968). *Inside, outside, upside down*. New York: Random House. Ages 3–7; **13**.

Brown, M. (1949). *Two little trains*. New York: Scott, Foresman. Ages 2–4; **13, 15**.

Carle, E. (1972). *The secret birthday message*. New York: Crowell. Ages 3–7; **13**.

Dunrea, O. (1985). *Fergus and the bridey*. New York: Holiday. Ages 4–7; **13**.

Hill, E. (1980). *Where's Spot?* New York: Putnam's Sons. Ages 2–4; **13**.

Lionni, L. (1983). *Where?* New York: Pantheon. Ages 2–3; **13**.

Maestro, B., & Maestro, G. (1976). *Where is my friend?* New York: Crown. Ages 2–4; **13**.

Martin, B., Jr. (1971). *Going up, going down*. New York: Holt, Rinehart, & Winston. Ages 6–8; **13, 9**.

Russo, M. (1986). *The line up book*. New York: Greenwillow. Ages 3–5; **13**.

Teulade, P. (1999). *El más bonito de todos regalos del mundo* [The most beautiful gift in the world]. Barcelona, Spain: Editorial Corimbo; **13**.

Weimer, T. E. (1993). *Space songs for children*. Greenville, SC: Pearce-Evetts. Ages 5–7; **13**.

Parts and Wholes

Axworthy, A. (Illustrator). (1998). *Guess what I am*. Cambridge, MA: Candlewick; **14**.

Burton, M. R. (1988). *Tail Toes Eyes Ears Nose*. New York: Harper Trophy; **14, 21, 26**.

Carle, E. (1987). *Do you want to be my friend?* New York: Harper Trophy; **14**.

Dubov, C. S. (1986). *Alexsandra, where are your toes?* New York: St. Martin's Press. Ages 1½–3; **14, 21, 26**.

Dubov, C. S. (1986). *Alexsandra, where is your nose?* New York: St. Martin's Press. Ages 1½–3; **14, 21, 26**.

Hutchins, P., & Marcuse, A. (Trans.) (1994). *Llaman a la puerta* [The doorbell rang]. New York: Mulberry; **14, 27**.

Le Tord, B. (1985). *Good wood bear*. New York: Bradbury. Ages 4–7; **14, 32**.

Mathews, L. (1979). *Gator pie*. New York: Scholastic. Ages 4–7; **14, 25**.

Language

Arenson, R. (Illustrator). (1989). *One, two, skip a few: First number rhymes*. Brooklyn, NY: Barefoot Poetry Collections; **15**.

Bemelmans, L. (1969). *Madeline*. New York: Viking. Ages 4–7; **15, 8, 9, 19**.

Duvoisin, R. (1974). *Petunia takes a trip*. New York: Knopf/Pinwheel. Ages 4–7; **11, 15, 18, 21, 26, 35**.

Hoff, S. (1959). *Julius*. New York: Harper & Row. Ages 4–7; **15, 21, 26, 35**.

Mathematics in the kitchen, Mathematics at the farm, Mathematics in buildings, Mathematics on the playground, Mathematics in the circus ring. (1978). Milwaukee: MacDonald–Raintree. Ages 3–7; **15**.

McKellar, S. (1993). *Counting rhymes*. New York: Dorling Kindersley; **15, 27**.

Shelby, A. (1990). *We keep a store*. New York: Orchard Books. All ages; **15, 22**.

Umansky, K., & Fisher, C. (1999). *Nonsense counting rhymes*. Oxford: Oxford University Press; **15**.

Application of Fundamental Concepts

Ordering, Seriation, and Patterning

Aker, S. (1990). *What comes in 2's, 3's, & 4's?* New York: Aladdin; **17, 23, 24**.

Asbjörsen, P. C., & Moe, J. E. (1957). *The three billy goats gruff*. New York: Harcourt, Brace, Jovanovich. Ages 2–5; **9, 11, 15, 17**.

Brett, J. (1987). *Goldilocks and the three bears*. New York: Dodd, Mead. Ages 3–5; **17, 21, 26**.

Clements, A. (1992). *Mother Earth's counting book*. New York: Simon & Schuster. Ages 5 and up; **17, 25, 28**.

Hoban, T. (1992). *Look up, look down*. New York: Greenwillow. Ages 5–8; **17**.

Ipcar, C. (1972). *The biggest fish in the sea*. New York: Viking. Ages 3–6; **17, 21, 26, 35**.

Macauly, D. (1987). *Why the chicken crossed the road*. Boston: Houghton-Mifflin. Ages 4–8; **17**.

Maestro, B., & Maestro, G. (1977). *Harriet goes to the circus*. New York: Crown. Ages 5–8; **17, 21, 26, 35**.

Mahy, M. (1987). *17 kings and 42 elephants*. New York: Dial. Ages 2–6; **9, 17, 21, 26, 35**.

Martin, B., Jr. (1963). *One, two, three, four*. New York: Holt, Rinehart, & Winston. Ages 5–7; **9, 17**.

Martin, B., Jr. (1970). *Monday, Monday, I like Monday*. New York: Holt, Rinehart, & Winston. Ages 5–8; **17, 19**.

Measurement: Volume, Weight, and Length

Allen, P. (1983). *Who sank the boat?* New York: Coward. Ages 3–5; **18**.

Anderson, L. C. (1983). *The wonderful shrinking shirt*. Niles, IL: Whitman. Ages 3–5; **18**.

Bennett, V. (1975). *My measure it book*. New York: Grosset & Dunlap. Ages 3–5; **18**.

Demi. (1997). *One grain of rice*. New York: Scholastic; **18**.

Henkes, K. (1995). *The biggest boy*. New York: Greenwillow; **18**.

Lionni, L. (1960). *Inch by inch*. New York: Astor-Honor. Ages 3–5; **17, 21, 26**.

McMillan, B. (1987). *Step by step*. New York: Lothrop. Ages 3–6; **18, 19**.

Myller, R. (1972). *How big is a foot?* New York: Atheneum. Ages 6–8; **18, 32**.

Parkinson, K. (1986). *The enormous turnip*. Niles, IL: Whitman. Ages 4–7; **18, 32, 35**.

Russo, M. (1986). *The lineup book*. New York: Greenwillow. Ages 2–4; **18**.

Schlein, M. (1954). *Heavy is a hippopotamus*. New York: Scott. Ages 3–6; **18, 21, 26**.

Shapp, M., & Shapp, C. (1975). *Let's find out about what's light and what's heavy*. New York: Franklin Watts. Ages 6–8; **18, 32**.

Ward, L. (1952). *The biggest bear*. Boston: Houghton-Mifflin. Ages 3–5; **18, 19**.

Zion, G. (1959). *The plant sitter*. New York: Harper & Row. Ages 3–6; **18, 19**.

Measurement: Time

Bancroft, H., & Van Gelde, R. G. (1963). *Animals in winter*. New York: Scholastic. Ages 3–6; **19, 32**.

Barrett, J. (1976). *Benjamin's 365 birthdays*. New York: Atheneum. Ages 3–6; **19**.

Berenstain, S., & Berenstain, J. (1973). *The bear's almanac*. New York: Random House. Ages 3–6; **19, 32**.

Bonne, R. (1961). *I know an old lady*. New York: Scholastic. Ages 3–5; **19**.

Brown, M. W. (1947). *Goodnight moon*. New York: Harper & Row. Ages 3–6; **19**.

Brown, M. (1984). *Arthur's Christmas*. Boston: Little, Brown. Ages 6–8; **32**.

Carle, E. (1977). *The very hungry caterpillar*. New York: Collins & World. Ages 3–5; **19, 21, 26**.

Carle, E. (1993). *Today is Monday*. New York: Scholastic; **19**.

Carle, E., & Marcuse, A. E. (trans.). (1994). *La oruga muy hambrienta* [The hungry caterpillar]. New York: Philomel; **19, 21, 26**.

Carle, E., & Mlawer, T. (Trans.). (1996). *La mariquita malhumorada* [The grouchy ladybug]. New York: HarperCollins; **19, 21, 26**.

Castle, C. (1985). *The hare and the tortoise*. New York: Dial. Ages 5–8; **19, 32**.

Chalmers, M. (1988). *Easter parade*. New York: Harper. Ages 3–6; **19, 32**.

DePaola, T. (1986). *Merry Christmas, Strega Nona*. San Diego, CA: Harcourt, Brace. Ages 3–6; **19, 32**.

Duvoisin, R. (1956). *The house of four seasons*. New York: Lothrop, Lee, & Shepard. Ages 3–6; **19, 32**.

Flournoy, V. (1985). *Patchwork quilt*. New York: Dial. Ages 4–8; **19, 32**.

Hall, B. (1973). *What ever happens to baby animals?* New York: Golden Press. Ages 2–5; **17, 19**.

Hauge, C., & Hauge, M. (1974). *Gingerbread man*. New York: Golden Press. Ages 2–5; **17, 19**.

Hayes, S. (1986). *Happy Christmas Gemma*. New York: Lothrop. Ages 2–5; **19**.

Hooper, M. (1985). *Seven eggs*. New York: Harper & Row. Ages 3–5; **8, 17, 19**.

Kelleritti, H. (1985). *Henry's Fourth of July*. New York: Greenwillow. Ages 3–6; **19**.

Kraus, R. (1972). *Milton the early riser*. New York: Prentice Hall. Ages 2–5; **19**.

Krementz, J. (1986). *Zachary goes to the zoo*. New York: Random House. Ages 2–8; **19, 21, 26, 32, 35**.

Leslie, S. (1977). *Seasons*. New York: Platt & Munk. Ages 2–5; **19**.

McCully, E. A. (1985). *First snow*. New York: Warner. Ages 3–5; **19, 21, 26**.

Miles, B. (1973). *A day of autumn*. New York: Random House. Ages 3–5; **19**.

Ormerodi, J. (1981). *Sunshine*. New York: Lothrop, Lee, & Shepard. Ages 2–6; **19**.

Pearson, S. (1988). *My favorite time of year*. New York: Harper & Row. Ages 3–7; **19, 32, 35**.

Porter Productions. (1975). *My tell time book*. New York: Grosset & Dunlap. Ages 5–7; **19, 32**.

Prelutsky, J. (1984). *It's snowing! It's snowing!* New York: Greenwillow. Ages 4–7; **19, 21, 26, 32, 37**.

Provensen, A., & Provensen, M. (1976). *A book of seasons*. New York: Random House. Ages 3–5; **19**.

Richards, K. (2000). *It's about time, Max!* New York: Kane Press; **19**.

Robison, A. (1973). *Pamela Jane's week*. Racine, WI: Whitman Books, Western Publishing. Ages 2–5; **19**.

Rockwell, A. (1985). *First comes spring*. New York: Crowell. Ages 2–6; **19, 21, 26, 32, 37**.

Rutland, J. (1976). *Time*. New York: Grosset & Dunlap. Ages 2–7; **19, 32**.

Scarry, R. (1976). *All day long*. New York: Golden Press. Ages 3–6; **19, 32**.

Schlein, M. (1955). *It's about time*. New York: Young Scott. Ages 3–7; **19, 32**.

Schwerin, D. (1984). *The tomorrow book*. New York: Pantheon. Ages 3–6; **19**.

Todd, K. (1982). *Snow*. Reading, MA: Addison-Wesley. Ages 3–8; **19, 21, 26, 32, 37**.

Tudor, T. (1957). *Around the year*. New York: Henry Z. Walck. Ages 3–5; **19**.

Tudor, T. (1977). *A time to keep: The Tasha Tudor book of holidays*. New York: Rand McNally. Ages 3–6; **19**.

Vincent, G. (1984). *Merry Christmas, Ernest & Celestine*. New York: Greenwillow. Ages 4–8; **19, 32**.

Wolff, A. (1984). *A year of birds*. New York: Dodd, Mead. Ages 3–6; **19, 21, 26**.

Zolotow, C. (1984). *I know an old lady*. New York: Greenwillow. Ages 4–8; **19, 21, 26, 32**.

Practical Activities/Integration

Cohn, J. M., & Elliott, D. L. (1992). *Recycling for math*. Berkeley, CA: Educational Materials Associates. For teachers of kindergarten and up; **22**.

Shelby, A. (1990). *We keep a store*. New York: Orchard Books. All ages; **15, 22**.

Money

Asch, F. (1976). *Good lemonade*. Ontario, Canada: Nelson, Foster, & Scott. Ages 6–8; **32**.

Brenner, B. (1963). *The five pennies*. New York: Random House. Ages 6–7; **22, 32**.

Brisson, P. (1993). *Benny's pennys*. New York: Bantam Doubleday; **22, 25, 32**.

Credle, E. (1969). *Little pest Pico*. Ontario, Canada: Nelson, Foster, & Scott. Ages 6–8; **32**.

deRubertis, B. (1999). *Deena's lucky penny*. New York: Kane Press; **22, 32**.

Gill, S., & Tobola, D. (2000). *The big buck adventure*. Watertown, MA: Charlesbridge; **22, 32**.

Hoban, L. (1981). *Arthur's funny money*. New York: Harper & Row. Ages 4–7; **22, 32**.

Kirn, A. (1969). *Two pesos for Catalina*. New York: Scholastic. Ages 6–8; **22, 32**.

Martin, B., Jr. (1963). *Ten pennies for candy*. New York: Holt, Rinehart, and Winston. Ages 5–7; **22, 32**.

Rockwell, A. (1984). *Our garage sale*. New York: Greenwillow. Ages 3–5; **22**.

Slobodkina, E. (1940, 1947, 1968). *Caps for sale*. New York: Young Scott; **9, 22, 32**.

Slobokina, E. (1940, 1947, 1968, translation 1995). *Se venden gorras*. New York: Harper Arco Iris; **9, 22, 32**.

Thornburgh, R. (1999). *Count on Pablo*. New York: Kane; **22, 25, 32**.

Food (also see Unit 22)

Brown, M. (1947). *Stone soup*. New York: Charles Scribner's. Ages 3–5; **22, 32, 38**.

Carle, E. (1970). *Pancakes, pancakes*. New York: Knopf. Ages 3–5; **22**.

Ehlert, L. (1987). *Growing vegetable soup*. San Diego, CA: Harcourt, Brace, Jovanovich. Ages 3–6; **22, 32, 38**.

Hoban, R. (1964). *Bread and jam for Frances*. New York: Scholastic. Ages 3–7; **22, 38**.

McCloskey, R. (1948). *Blueberries for Sal*. New York: Viking. Ages 3–6; **22, 38**.

Norquist, S. (1985). *Pancake pie*. New York: Morrow. Ages 4–8; **22, 32, 38**.

Sendak, M. (1962). *Chicken soup with rice*. New York: Harper & Row. Ages 3–5; **22**.

Sendak, M. (1970). *In the night kitchen*. New York: Harper & Row. Ages 4–6; **22, 32, 38**.

Seymour, P. (1981). *Food*. Los Angeles: Intervisual Communications. Ages 2–5; **22**.

Thayer, J. (1961). *The blueberry pie elf*. Edinburgh, Scotland: Oliver & Boyd. Ages 4–7; **22, 32, 38**.

Cookbooks (also see Unit 22)

Can be adapted to all ages

Ault, R. (1974). *Kids are natural cooks*. Boston: Houghton-Mifflin; **22, 32, 38**.

Better Homes and Gardens new junior cookbook. (1979). Des Moines, IA: Meredith; **22, 32, 38**.

Kementz, J. (1985). *The fun of cooking*. New York: Knopf; **22, 32, 38**.

Pratt, D. (1998). *Hey kids, you're cookin' now: A global awareness cooking adventure*. [On-line] Available: http://www.Amazon.com

Rothstein, G. L. (1994). *From soup to nuts: Multicultural cooking activities and recipes*. New York: Scholastic; **22, 32, 38**.

Sesame Street cookbook. (1978). New York: Platt & Munk. **22, 32, 38**.

Shepard, E. H. (1993). *Winnie-the-Pooh's teatime cookbook*. [On-line] Available: http://www.Amazon.com

Walker, B., & Williams, G. (1995). *Little house cookbook*. [On-line] Available: http://www.Amazon.com

Walt Disney's Mickey Mouse cookbook. (1975). New York: Golden Press; **22, 32, 38**.

Warner, P. (1999). *Healthy snacks for kids (Nitty Gritty Cookbooks)*. [On-line] Available: http://www.Amazon.com

Williamson, S., & Williamson, Z. (1992). *Kids cook! Fabulous food for the whole family*. Charlotte, VT: Williamson Publishing Co; **22, 32, 38**.

Science

Helman, A. (1996). *1 2 3 Moose:A Pacific Northwest counting book*. Seattle, WA: Sasquatch Books; **9, 16, 21, 22, 26**.

Kusugak, M. A. (1996). *My Arctic 1, 2, 3*. Toronto: Annick, Ltd; **9, 16, 21, 22, 26**.

Pallotta, J. (1992). *The icky bug counting book*. Watertown, MA: Charlesbridge; **9, 16, 21, 22, 26**.

Stevens, J., & Crummel, S. S. (1999). *Cook-a-doodle-do*. New York: Harcourt Brace. (See TCM, May 2001 for activity); **22**.

Thornhill, J. (1989). *The wildlife 1-2-3: A nature counting book*. New York: Simon & Schuster; **9, 16, 21, 22, 26**.

Toft, K. M., & Sheather, A. (1998). *One less fish*. Watertown, MA: Charlesgate; **9**.

Wadsworth, G. (1997). *One on a web*. Watertown, MA: Charlesbridge; **9, 16, 21, 22, 26**.

Wadsworth, G. (1999). *One tiger growls*. Watertown, MA: Charlesbridge; **9, 16, 21, 22, 26**.

Wood, J. *One tortoise, ten wallabies: A wildlife counting book*; **9, 16, 21, 22, 26**.

Symbols and Higher-Level Activities

Groups and Symbols

Aker, S. (1990). *What comes in 2's, 3's, & 4's?* New York: Aladdin; **17, 23, 24, 25**.

Alain (Bruslein, A.). (1964). *One, two, three going to sea*. New York: Scholastic. Ages 5–7; **23, 24, 25, 27**.

Anno, M. (1977). *Anno's counting book*. New York: Crowell. Ages 5–7; **23, 24, 25**.

Balet, J. B. (1959). *The five Rollatinis*. Philadelphia: Lippincott. Ages 4–7; **23, 24, 25**.

Duvoisin, R. (1955). *Two lonely ducks*. New York: Knopf. Ages 4–7; **21, 23, 24, 25, 26, 35**.

Duvoisin, R. (1955). *1000 Christmas beards*. New York: Knopf. Ages 3–7; **23, 24, 25**.

Federico, H. (1963). *The golden happy book of numbers*. New York: Golden Press. Ages 3–7; **23, 24, 25**.

Franco, B. (1999). *The tortoise who bragged: A Chinese tale with trigrams*. Sunnyvale, CA: Stokes Publishing; **25**.

Françoise (Seignobosc, F.) (1951). *Jean-Marie counts her sheep*. New York: Charles Scribner's Sons. Ages 3–6; **23, 24, 25**.

Friskey, M. (1940). *Seven diving ducks*. New York: McKay. Ages 4–6; **23, 24, 25**.

Garne, S. T. (1992). *One white sail*. New York: Green Tiger Press. Ages 5–8; **25, 26, 27**.

Getty Museum. (n.d.). *1 to 10 and back again: A Getty Museum counting book*. Los Angeles: Author; **9, 23, 24, 25**.

Gibson, R. (1998). *I can count*. London: Usborne Playtime; **9, 23, 24, 25**.

Guettier, B. (1999). *The father who had ten children*. East Rutherford, NJ: Dial/Penguin; **23, 24, 25**.

Hoban, T. (1987). *Letters & 99 cents*. New York: Greenwillow. Ages 4–8; **23, 24, 25, 32**.

Hudson, C. W. (1987). *Afro-bets 1, 2, 3 book*. Orange, NJ: Just Us Productions; **9, 23, 24**.

Hulme, J. N. (1993). *Sea squares*. New York: Hyperion; **9, 23, 24, 25**.

Johnson, S. T. (1998). *City by numbers*. New York: Viking/Penguin; **23**.

Keats, E. J. (1971). *Over in the meadow*. New York: Scholastic. Ages 3–5; **23, 24**.

Kherdian, D., & Hogrogian, N. (1990). *The cat's midsummer jamboree*. New York: Philomel. Ages 5–8; **25, 26, 27**.

LeSeig, T. (1974). *Whacky Wednesday*. New York: Random House. Ages 5–8; **25**.

McNutt, D. (1979). *There was an old lady who lived in a 1*. Palo Alto, CA: Creative Publications. Ages 4–6; **9, 23, 24**.

Merriam, E. (1993). *12 ways to get to 11*. New York: Aladdin; **24, 25, 27**.

Numbers: Match-up flip book. (1984). St. Paul, MN: Trend. Ages 4–8; **23, 24**.

Thaler, M. (1991). *Seven little hippos*. Old Tappan, NJ: Simon & Schuster. Ages 5–8; **25, 26, 27**.

Zaslavsky, C. (1999). *Count on your fingers African style*. New York: Writers and Readers Publishing; **25**.

Mathematics Concepts and Activities for the Primary Grades

As already noted, many of the books listed are appropriate for preprimary and primary children. Many books that are read-along books for the younger children become books for individual reading for older children. A few additional titles are included here.

Anderson, L. (1971). *Two hundred rabbits*. New York: Penguin Books. Ages 7–9; **27**.

Barry, D. (1994). *The Rajah's rice: A mathematical folktale from India*. New York: Freeman; **32**.

Belov, R. (1971). *Money, money, money*. New York: Scholastic. Ages 6–8; **32**.

Boynton, S. (1987). *Hippos go berserk*. Chicago: Recycled Paper Press: **30**.

Bruchac, J., & London, J. (1992). *Thirteen moons on turtle's back: A Native American year of moons*. New York: Philomel; **32**.

Calmenson, S., & Cole, J. (1998). *Get well gators!* New York: Morrow Junior Books; **27**.

Cave, K., & Riddel, C. (1992). *Out for the count: A counting adventure*. New York: Simon & Schuster. Ages 6–8; **27, 30**.

Cobb, A. (2000). *The long wait*. New York: Kane Press; **30**.

Dahl, R. (1990). *Esio trot*. New York: Viking. Ages 7–8; **32**.

Darwin, S., Grout, B., & McCoy, D. (Eds.). (1992). *How do octopi eat pizza pie?* Alexandria, VA: Time-Life for Children. Ages 6–9; **27, 31, 32**.

Darwin, S., Grout, B., & McCoy, D. (Eds.). (1992). *Look both ways*. Alexandria, VA: Time-Life for Children. Ages 6–9; **27, 31, 32**.

Dennis, J. R. (1971). *Fractions are parts of things*. New York: Crowell. Ages 7–8; **29**.

Friedman, A. (1994). *A cloak for the dreamer*. Jefferson City, MO: Scholastic Professional; **31**.

Friskey, M. (1963). *Mystery of the farmer's three fives*. Chicago: Children's Press. Ages 6–8; **27**.

Gibson, R. (1998). *I can count*. London: Usborne Playtime; **30**.

Gordon, J. R. (1991). *Six sleepy sheep*. Honesdale, PA: Boyds Mill Press. Ages 6–8; **27, 28**.

Harper, D. (1998). *Telling time with big mama cat*. San Diego: Harcourt Brace; **32**.

Hawkins, C. (1984). *Take away monsters*. New York: Putnam's Sons. Ages 3–5; **25, 27**.

Heide, F. P. (1994). *The bigness contest*. Boston: Little, Brown; **32**.

Hewavisenti, L. (1991). *Measuring*. Chicago: Franklin Watts; **32**.

Hindley, J. (1994). *The wheeling and whirling-around book*. Cambridge, MA: Candlewick Press; **31**.

Hoban, T. (1998). *More, fewer, less*. New York: Greenwillow; **30**.

Hulme, J. N. (1995). *Counting by kangaroos: A multiplication concept book*. New York: Scientific American Books; **27, 28**.

Johnson, J. (1995). *How big is a whale?* Skokie, IL: Rand McNally; **32, 34**.

Johnson, J. (1995). *How fast is a cheetah?* Skokie, IL: Rand McNally; **32, 34**.

Krudwig, V. L. (1998). *Cucumber soup* [Sopa de pepino]. Golden, CO: Fulcrum Publishing; **18, 32**.

Leedy, L. (1994). *Fraction action*. New York: Holiday House; **29**.

Llewellyn, C. (1992). *My first book of time*. New York: Dorling Kindersley; **32**.

Maestro, B. (1993). *The story of money*. New York: Clarion Books. Ages 6–9; **32**.

Martin, B., Jr. (1963). *Five is five*. New York: Holt, Rinehart, & Winston. Ages 6–8; **25, 27**.

Martin, B., Jr. (1964). *Delight in number*. New York: Holt, Rinehart, & Winston. Ages 6–8; **9, 27, 32**.

Martin, B., Jr. (1964). *Four threes are twelve*. New York: Holt, Rinehart, & Winston. Ages 6–8; **25, 27**.

Martin, B., Jr. (1964). *If you can count to ten*. New York: Holt, Rinehart, & Winston. Ages 6–8; **25, 27**.

Martin, B., Jr. (1971). *Number patterns make sense*. New York: Holt, Rinehart, & Winston. Ages 8–9; **28, 33**.

McMillan, B. (1991). *Eating fractions*. Jefferson City, MO: Scholastic Book Services. Ages 6–9; **29**.

Merriam. E. (1993). *12 ways to get to 11*. New York: Aladdin; **24, 25, 27**.

Morgan, S. (1994). *The world of shapes, squares, and cubes*. New York: Thomson Learning; **31**.

Morgan, R. (1997). *In the next three seconds*. New York: Lodestar; **32**.

Morris, A. (1995). *Shoes, shoes, shoes*. New York: Lothrop, Lee & Shepard; **32**.

Nesbit, E. (1989). *Melisande*. San Diego, CA: Harcourt, Brace, Jovanovich. Ages 6–8; **32**.

Neuschwander, C. (1998). *Amanda Bean's amazing dream—a mathematical story*. New York: Scholastic; **27**.

O'Donnell, E. L., & Schmidt, K. L. (1991). *The twelve days of summer*. New York: William Morrow. Ages 6–8; **27**.

Older, J. (2000). *Telling time*. Watertown, MA: Charlesbridge; **32**.

Pinczes, E. J. (1993). *One hundred hungry ants*. New York: Scholastic; **30**.

Schertle, A. (1987). *Jeremy Bean's St. Patrick's Day*. New York: Morrow. Ages 5–8; **19, 32**.

Schleim, M. (1972). *Moon months and sun days*. Reading, MA: Young Scott. Ages 6–8; **19, 32**.

Schwartz, D. M. (1985). *How much is a million*. New York: Scholastic; **30**.

Schwartz, D. M. (1989). *If you made a million*. New York: Scholastic; **30**.

Scienszka, J., & Smith, L. (1995). *Math curse*. New York: Viking; **27**.

Sharman, L. (1994). *The amazing book of shapes*. New York: Dorling Kindersley; **31**.

Tompert, A. (1990). *Grandfather Tang's story*. New York: Crown; **31**.

Viorst, J. (1978). *Alexander who used to be rich last Sunday*. New York: Alladin; **27, 32**.

Viorst, J. (1992). *Sunday morning*. New York: Atheneum. Ages 6–8; **32**.

Weston, M. (1992). *Bea's four bears*. New York: Clarion Books. Ages 6–8; **27**.

Ye, T. (1998). *Weighing the elephant*. Buffalo, NY: Annick Press; **32**.

Books That Support Science Investigations

See the reviews and articles in each issue of *Teaching Children Mathematics* and *Science and Children*. Each year in the March issue of *Science and Children*, there is a section on the year's outstanding trade books in both English and Spanish.

Series

Cole, J. (1997). *El autobus magico* [The magic school bus]. New York: Scholastic. Grades 2–4; **34, 35, 36, 37**.

Delafosse, C., & Jeunesse, G. (1998). *Yo observo: Los animales marinos; Los animales bajo tierra; Las casas de los insectos; Los dinosaurios* [I see: Marine animals; Animals underground; Insects' houses; Dinosaurs]. Ages 5–8; **21, 26, 34**.

Falk, J. H., & Rosenberg, K. S. (1999). *Bite-sized science.* Chicago: Chicago Review. Grades K–3. Recommended for family activities.

Glesecke, E. (1999). *Outside my window: Birds, trees, flowers, and mammals.* Portsmouth, NH: Heinemann Library. Ages 4–8; **21, 26, 34**.

Willis, S. (1999). *How, why and what series in Spanish on floating, weight, moon phases, rain, flight, time, distance, speed for grades 2–4.* New York: Franklin Watts; **34, 35, 36**.

Life Science

Animals

Aranega, S., & Portell, J. (1999). *El elefante* [Elephant]. Barcelona: La Galera. Grades 1–3; **34**.

Arnold, C. (1987). *Kangaroo/Koala.* New York: Morrow. Ages 7–10; **34**.

Arnold, C. (1996). *Bats.* New York: William Morrow. Grades 1–3; **26, 34**.

Arnold, C. (1996). *Fox.* New York: Morrow Junior Books. (Grades 2-5). 34

Arnosky, J. (1986). *Deer at the brook.* New York: Lothrop. Ages 1–6; **21, 26, 34**.

Arnosky, J. (1987). *Raccoons and ripe corn.* New York: Lothrop. Ages 3–6; **21, 26, 34**.

Arnosky, J. (1994). *All about alligators.* New York: Scholastic. Grades K–3; **16, 21, 26, 34**.

Arnosky, J. (1995). *All about owls.* New York: Scholastic. Grades K–3; **16, 21, 26, 34**.

Banks, M. (1990). *Animals of the night.* New York: Scribner. Ages 4–6; **21, 26, 34**.

Bond, F. (1987). *Wake up, Vladimir.* New York: Harper & Row. Ages 3–5; **21, 26**.

Bussolati, E. (2000). *Los animales y sus crias* [Animals and their young]. Madrid, Editorial Edaf. Grades pre-K–1; **16, 21, 26, 34**.

Bussolati, E. (1999). *Busca y encuentra* [Search and find]. Madrid, Editorial Edaf. Grades pre-K–1); **16, 21, 26, 34**.

Campbell, R. (2000). *Oscar en la granja* [Oh dear!]. Barcelona: Ediciones Elfos. Grades pre-K–1; **16, 21, 26, 34**.

Carle, E. (1987). *Have you seen my cat?* New York: Scholastic. **16, 21, 34**.

Cole, S. (1985). *When the tide is low.* New York: Lothrop. Ages 3–9; **21, 26, 34**.

Cowcher, H. (1991). *Tigress.* New York: Garrar. Ages 4–8; **21, 26, 34, 36**.

Crow, S. L. (1985). *Penguins and polar bears.* Washington, DC: National Geographic. All ages; **21, 26, 34**.

Davis, K. (1999). *Quien salta?* [Who hops?]. Barcelona: Editorial Juventud. Grades pre-K–3; **16, 21, 26, 34**.

Diehl, J., & Plumb, D. (2000). *What's the difference? 10 animal look-alikes.* New York: Kingfisher. Grades K–4; **26, 34**.

Ehlert, L. (1990). *Feathers for lunch.* San Diego, CA: Harcourt Brace and Company. Ages 4–7; **16, 21, 26, 34**.

Fischer-Nagel, H., & Fischer-Nagel, A. (1986). *Inside the burrow: The life of the golden hamster.* Minneapolis, MN: Carolrhoda. Ages 7–10; **34**.

Flack, M. (1930). *Angus and the ducks.* New York: Doubleday. Ages 3–6; **21, 26, 34**.

Fleming, D. (1993). *In the small, small pond.* New York: Henry Holt. Ages 4–8; **21, 26, 34**.

Fowler, A. (1992). *It's best to leave a snake alone.* Chicago: Children's Press; **21, 26, 34**.

Fredericks, A. D. (2000). *Slugs.* Minneapolis, MN: Lerner. Grades K–6; **26, 34**.

Freeman, D. (1968). *Corduroy.* New York: Viking. [(1976). Penguin]. Ages 3–6; **21, 26, 34**.

Gallagher, K. E. (2001). *The cottontail rabbits.* Minneapolis, MN: Lerner. Grades K–4; **26, 34**.

George, T. C. (2000). *Jellies: The life of jellyfish.* Brookfield, CT: Millbrook Press. Grades K–3; **26, 34**.

Gibbons, G. (1993). *Frogs.* New York: Holiday House. Grades pre-K–3; **16, 21, 26, 34**.

Gill, P. (1990). *Birds.* New York: Eagle Books. Ages 4–8; **21, 26, 34**.

Hickman, P. (1999). *My first look at: A new duck.* Niagara Falls, NY: Kids Can Press. Grades K–3; **26, 34**.

Hirschi, R. (1991). *Loon lake.* New York: Cobblehill. Ages 4–8; **21, 26, 34**.

Horenstein, H. (1999). *A is for...? A photographer's alphabet of animals.* New York: Harcourt Brace. Grades K–3; **26, 34**.

Horowitz, R. (2000). *Crab moon.* Cambridge, MA: Candlewick. Grades K–6; **34**.

James, S. (1991). *Dear Mr. Blueberry.* New York: McElderry. Ages 3–8; **16, 21, 26, 34, 36**.

Jango-Cohen, J. (2000). *Clinging sea horses.* Minneapolis, MN: Lerner. Grades K–4; **26, 34**.

Jenkins, M. (1999). *The emperor's egg.* Cambridge, MA: Candlewick. Grades K–6; **26, 34**.

Johnson, R. L. (2001). *A walk in the desert; A walk in the prairie; A walk in the rain forest.* Minneapolis, MN: Lerner. Grades K–8; **34**.

Johnson, S. A. (1982). *Inside an egg.* Minneapolis, MN: Lerner Publications; **21, 26, 34**.

Johnston, G., & Cutchins, J. (1991). *Slippery babies: Young frogs, toads, and salamanders.* New York: Morrow. Ages 5–8; **21, 26, 34**.

Koelling, C. (1978). *Whose house is this?* Los Angeles: Price/Stern/Sloan. Ages 3–5; **21, 26**.

Krementz, J. (1986). *Holly's farm animals.* New York: Random House. Ages 3–8; **21, 26, 34**.

Lewin, T., & Lewin, B. (1999). *Gorilla walk*. New York: Lothrop/ HarperCollins. Grades K–6; **26, 34**.

Ling, M., & Atkinson, M. (1997). *The snake book*. New York: Dorling Kindersley. Grades 1 and up; **34**.

Lionni, L. (1963). *Swimmy*. New York: Pantheon. Ages 3–6; **21, 26, 34**.

London, J. (1999). *Baby whale's journey*. San Francisco: Chronicle. Grades K–3; **26, 34**.

Mason, A. (2000). *Starting with science series: Living things*. Toronto, ON: Kids Can Press. Grades K–4; **26, 34**.

McCloskey, R. (1941). *Make way for ducklings*. New York: Viking. [(1976). Penguin]. Ages 4–6; **21, 26, 34**.

McFarland, C. (1990). *Cows in the parlor: A visit to a dairy farm*. New York: Atheneum. Ages 5–8; **21, 26, 34**.

Mitsuko and Kamiko (A. Coll-Vinent, trans.). (1999). *El elefante* [Elephant]. Madrid: El Editorial Carimbo. Grades pre-K–1; **16, 21, 26, 34**.

Mitsuko and Kamiko (A. Coll-Vinent, trans.). (1999). *El gato* [Cat]. Madrid: El Editorial Carimbo. Grades pre-K–1; **16, 21, 26, 34**.

Murphy, J. (1993). *Backyard bear*. New York: Scholastic. Grades 2–4; **34**.

National Geographic Society (Ed.). (1985). *Books for young explorers—Set XII*. Washington, DC: Editor. Ages 3–8; **21, 26, 34**.

Netherton, J. (2000). *Red-eyed tree frogs*. Minneapolis, MN: Lerner. Grades K–4; **26, 34**.

Nicholson, D. (1987). *Wild boars*. Minneapolis, MN: Carolrhoda. Ages 6–10; **34**.

Paladino, C. (1991). *Pomona: The birth of a penguin*. New York: Watts. Ages 5–8; **21, 26, 34**.

Pallotta, J. (1986). *The BIRD alphabet book*. Watertown, MA: Charlesbridge; **16, 21, 34**.

Pallotta, J. (1989). *The yucky reptile alphabet book*. Watertown, MA: Charlesbridge; **16, 21, 34**.

Patent, D. H. (1987). *All about whales*. New York: Holiday House. Ages 6–9; **34**.

Patent, D. H. (1993). *Looking at penguins*. New York: Holiday House. Grades 1–3; **34**.

Patent, D. H. (1994). *Looking at bears*. New York: Holiday House. Grades 1–3; **34**.

Potter, B. (1902). *The tale of Peter Rabbit*. New York: Warne. Ages 4–6; **21, 26, 34**.

Powzyk, J. (1985). *Wallaby Creek*. New York: Lothrop. Ages 6–9; **34**.

Robinson, C. (1999). *In the wild: Whales*. Portsmouth, NH: Heinemann. Grades 1–2; **34**.

Roy, R. (1982). *What has ten legs and eats cornflakes? A pet book*. New York: Clarion/ Houghton. Ages 5–8; **34**.

Savage, S. (1992). *Making tracks*. New York: Lodestar. Ages 4–8; **21, 26, 34, 36**.

Savage, S. (2000). *What's the difference?: Birds*. Sydney, NSW, Australia: Steck Vaughn. Grades K–4; **26, 34**.

Sheldon, D. (1991). *The whales' song*. New York: Dial. Ages 4–8; **21, 26, 34**.

Simon, S. (1999). *Crocodiles & alligators*. New York: HarperCollins. Grades K–6; **26, 34**.

Souza, A. (1992). *Slinky snakes*. Minneapolis, MN: Carolrhoda; **34**.

Stanley, C. (1991). *Busy, busy squirrels*. New York: Cobblehill. Ages 4–8; **21, 26, 34, 36**.

Stuart, D. (1994). *Bats: Mysterious flyers of the night*. Minneapolis, MN: Carolrhoda. Grades 2–5; **34**.

Sussman, S., & Sussman, R. J. (1987). *Lies (people believe) about animals*. Niles, IL: Whitman. Ages 7–12; **34**.

Tagholm, S. (2000). *Animal lives: The rabbit*. New York: Kingfisher. Grades K–3; **26, 34**.

Weller, F. (1991). *I wonder if I'll see a whale*. New York: Philomel. Ages 4–8; **21, 26, 34**.

Wildsmith, B. (1983). *The owl and the woodpecker*. New York: Oxford University Press. Ages 4–7; **21, 26, 34**.

Yamashita, K. (1993). *Paws, wings, and hooves*. Minneapolis, MN: Lerner. Ages 6–8; **26, 34**.

Yolen, J. (1988). *Owl moon*. New York: Philomel. Grades pre-K–1; **16, 21, 26, 34**.

Bugs, Spiders, Bees, and Butterflies

Allen, J., & Humphries, T. (2000). *Are you a ladybug?* New York: Kingfisher Books. Grades K–4; **26, 34**.

Arnosky, J. (1996). *Crinkleroot's guide to knowing butterflies and moths*. New York: Simon & Schuster Books for Young Readers. Primary grades; **34**.

Berenstain, S., & Berenstain, J. (1962). *The big honey hunt*. New York: Random House. Ages 3–8; **21, 26, 34**.

Carle, E. (1969). *The very hungry caterpillar*. New York: Philomel. Ages 3–6; **21, 26, 34**.

Carle, E. (1977). *The grouchy ladybug*. New York: Crowell. Ages 3–6; **21, 26, 34**.

Carle, E. (1981). *The honeybee and the robber*. New York: Philomel. Ages 3–6; **21, 26, 34**.

Carle, E. (1984). *The very busy spider*. New York: Philomel. Ages 3–6; **21, 26, 34**.

Clay, P., & Clay, H. (1984). *Ants*. London: A & C Black; **21, 26, 34**.

Dallinger, J. (1981). *Spiders*. Minneapolis, MN: Lerner Publications; **21, 26, 34**.

Facklam, M. (1996). *Creepy, crawly caterpillars*. Boston: Little, Brown. Grades 2–4; **34**.

Fischer-Nagel, H., & Fischer-Nagel, A. (1986). *Life of the ladybug*. Minneapolis, MN: Carolrhoda. Ages 7–10; **34**.

Fleming, D. (1991). *In the tall, tall grass*. New York: Henry Holt. Ages 4–8; **21, 26, 33, 34**.

Guiberson, B. (1991). *Cactus hotel*. New York: Holt. Ages 4–8; **21, 26, 34, 36**.

Hartley, K., Macro, C., & Taylor, P. (1999). *Bug books: Ant, bee, caterpillar, centipede, cockroach, grasshopper, ladybug, mosquito, snail, spider, termite, and worm*. Portsmouth, NH: Heinemann Library (Rigby). Grades 2–3; **34**.

Jeunesse, G., & de Hugo, P. (1998). *Los bichos de la casa* [House bugs]. Madrid: Ediciones SM. Grades 2–4; **34**.

Kneidel, S. S. (1993). *Creepy crawlies and the scientific method.* Washington, DC: National Science Teachers Association. Grades K–6; **26, 34**.

McNulty, F. (1986). *The lady and the spider.* New York: Harper & Row. Ages 5–8; **34**.

Overbeck, C. (1982). *Ants.* Minneapolis, MN: Lerner; **21, 26, 34**.

Pallotta, J. (1986). *The icky bug alphabet book.* Watertown, MA: Charlesbridge; **16, 21, 34**.

Palotta, J. (1992). *The icky bug counting book.* Watertown, MA: Charlesbridge. Ages 4–8; **16, 21, 26, 33, 34**.

Parker, N. W. (1987). *Bugs.* New York: Greenwillow. Ages 8–10; **34**.

Pinczes, E. J. (1993). *One hundred hungry ants.* New York: Scholastic; **16, 21, 34**.

Plants

Adler, D. A. (1999). *A picture book of George Washington Carver.* New York: Holiday House. Grades K–6; **26, 34**.

Bash, B. (1990). *Desert giant: The world of the saguaro cactus.* Boston: Little, Brown. Ages 5–8; **21, 26, 34, 36**.

Burns, D. L., & Burns, J. A. (1998). *Plant a garden in your sneaker.* Washington, DC: National Science Teachers Association. Grades 2–6; **34**.

Ehlert, L. (1991). *Red leaf, yellow leaf.* San Diego, CA: Harcourt Brace and Company. Ages 4–8; **21, 26, 34, 36**.

Florian, D. (1991). *Vegetable garden.* New York: Harcourt Brace. Ages 3–5; **16, 21, 26, 34, 37**.

Gibbons, G. (1984). *The seasons of Arnold's apple tree.* San Diego, CA: Harcourt Brace. Ages 3–9; **21, 26, 34**.

Gibbons, G. (1991). *From seed to plant.* New York: Holiday House. Ages 5–8; **21, 26, 34**.

Gibbons, G. (1999). *The pumpkin book.* New York: Holiday House. Grades K–6; **26, 34**.

Hall, Z. (1994). *It's pumpkin time!* New York: Scholastic; **16, 21, 34**.

Hindley, J. (1990). *The tree.* New York: Clarkson Potter. Ages 6–12; **26, 34, 36**.

Hirschi, R. (1991). *Fall.* New York: Cobblehill. Ages 4–8; **21, 26, 34, 36**.

Hiscock, B. (1991). *The big tree.* New York: Atheneum. Ages 5–12; **21, 26, 34, 36**.

Johnson, R. L. (2001). *A walk in the desert; A walk in the prairie; A walk in the rain forest.* Minneapolis, MN: Lerner. Grades K–8; **34**.

Krauss, R. (1945). *The carrot seed.* New York: Harper & Row. Ages 3–5; **21, 22, 26, 28**.

Lauber, P. (1988). *Seeds: Pop, stick, glide.* New York: Crown. Ages 6–8; **26, 34**.

Mitgutsch, A. (1986). *From wood to paper.* Minneapolis, MN: Carolrhoda. Ages 4–7; **21, 26, 34**.

Oechsli, H., & Oechsli, K. (1985). *In my garden: A child's gardening book.* New York: Macmillan. Ages 5–9; **21, 26, 34**.

Ontario Science Centre. *Starting with science series: Plants.* Niagara Falls, NY: Kids Can Press. Grades K–4; **26, 34**.

Posada, M. (2000). *Dandelions: Stars in the grass.* Minneapolis, MN: Carolrhoda/Lerner. Grades K–3; **26, 34**.

Romanova, N. (1985). *Once there was a tree.* New York: Dial. Ages 3–9; **21, 26, 34**.

Schnieper, C. (1987). *An apple tree through the year.* Minneapolis, MN: Carolrhoda. Ages 7–10; **34**.

Silverstein, S. (1964). *The giving tree.* New York: Harper & Row. Ages 3–8; **21, 26, 34**.

Watts, B. (1990). *Tomato.* Morristown, NJ: Silver Burdett & Ginn. Ages 5–8; **21, 26, 34**.

Physical Science

Adler, D. A. (1999). *How tall, how short, how far away.* New York: Houghton Mifflin. Grades K–3; **26, 35**.

Ardley, N. (1991). *The science book of air.* New York: Harcourt Brace and Company. Ages 6–8; **21, 26, 35**.

Brandt, K. (1985). *Sound.* Mahwah, NJ: Troll Associates. Ages 3–5; **21, 26**.

Branley, F. (1996). *What makes a magnet?* New York: HarperCollins. Grades K–6; **26, 35**.

Brown, R. (1991). *The world that Jack built.* New York: Dutton. Ages 4–6; **21, 26, 35**.

Burton, V. L. (1939). *Mike Mulligan and his steam shovel.* Boston: Houghton Mifflin. Ages 3–5; **21, 26**.

Carle, E. (1990). *Pancakes, pancakes!* New York: Scholastic; **16, 21, 35**.

Cobb, V. (1983). *Gobs of goo.* Philadelphia: Lippincott. Ages 6–8; **35**.

Crampton, G. (1986). *Scuffy the tugboat.* New York: Western. Ages 3–5; **21, 26**.

DePaola, T. (1978). *The popcorn book.* New York: Scholastic; **16, 21, 35**.

Fowler, R. (1986). *Mr. Little's noisy boat.* New York: Grosset & Dunlap. Ages 0–9; **21, 26, 35**.

Graham, J. B. (1999). *Flicker flash.* New York: Houghton Mifflin. All ages; **16, 21, 26, 35**.

Hickman, P., & Stephens, P. (2000). *Animals in motion: How animals swim, jump, slither, and glide.* Niagara Falls, NY: Kids Can Press. Grades K–8; **26, 35**.

Hulme, J. (1991). *Sea squares.* New York: Hyperion. Ages 4–8; **21, 26, 34, 35**.

Isadora, R. (1985). *I touch.* New York: Greenwillow Books. Ages 0–2; **21, 38**.

Kimiko (A. Coll-Vinent, trans.). (1999). *El avion* [Airplane]. Madrid: Editorial Corimbo. Grades pre-K–1; **16, 21, 26, 35**.

Koningsburg, E. I. (1991). *Samuel Todd's book of great inventions.* New York: Atheneum. Ages 4–7; **21, 26, 35**.

Murata, Michinori. (1993). *Science is all around you: Water and light.* Minneapolis, MN: Lerner. Ages 6–8; **26, 35, 36**.

Ontario Science Centre. (2000). *Starting with science: Solids, liquids, and gases.* Niagara Falls, NY: Kids Can Press. Grades K–4; **26, 35**.

Piper, W. (1984). *The little engine that could.* New York: Putnam. Ages 3–5; **21, 26**.

Pluckrose, H. (1986). *Think about hearing.* New York: Franklin Watts. Ages 4–8; **21, 26, 35, 38**.

Robbins, K. (1991). *Bridges.* New York: Dial. Ages 5–12; **21, 26, 35**.

Rockwell, A. (1986). *Things that go.* New York: Dutton. Ages 3–5; **21, 26**.

Scarry, R. (1986). *Splish-Splash sounds.* Racine, WI: Western Publishing, Inc. Ages 3–7; **21, 26, 35**.

Simon, S. (1985). *Soap bubble magic.* New York: Lothrop. Ages 6–9; **35**.

Taylor, K. (1992). *Flying start science series: Water; light; action; structure.* New York: John Wiley & Sons. Ages 3–9; **16, 21, 35, 36**.

Wyler, R. (1986). *Science fun with toy boats and planes.* New York: Julian Messner. Ages 5–9; **35**.

Earth and Space Science

Aliki. (1990). *Fossils tell of long ago.* New York: Harper-Collins. Ages 5–8; **21, 26, 36**.

Arnold, C. (1987). *Trapped in tar: Fossils from the Ice Age.* New York: Clarion. Ages 7–10; **36**.

Baird, A. (1996). *The U.S. Space Camp book of astronauts.* New York: Morrow; **36**.

Barrett, J. (1978). *Cloudy with a chance of meatballs.* New York: Macmillan; **16, 21, 36**.

Barton, B. (1990). *Bones, bones, dinosaur bones.* New York: Harper-Collins. Ages 5–7; **21, 26, 36**.

Bauer, C. F. (1987). *Midnight snowman.* New York: Atheneum. Ages 4–7; **19, 21, 26, 36**.

Branley, F. M. (2000). *The international space station.* New York: Harper Trophy; **36**.

Branley, F. M. (1982). *Water for the world.* New York: Crowell. Ages 7–11; **36**.

Branley, F. M. (1983). *Rain and hail.* New York: Crowell. Ages 5–7; **36**.

Branley, F. M. (1985). *Flash, crash, rumble, and roll.* New York: Crowell. Ages 5–7; **36**.

Branley, F. M. (1985). *Volcanoes.* New York: Crowell. Ages 6–8; **36**.

Branley, F. M. (1986). *Air is all around us.* New York: Crowell. Ages 3–6; **21, 26, 36**.

Branley, F. M. (1986). *Journey into a black hole.* New York: Crowell. Ages 8–10; **36**.

Branley, F. M. (1987). *The moon seems to change/The planets in our solar system/Rockets and satellites.* New York: Crowell. Ages 5–8; **36**.

Carrick, C. (1983). *Patrick's dinosaurs.* New York: Clarion. Ages 4–8; **21, 34, 35, 36**.

Caveney, S., & Giesen, R. (1977). *Where am I?* (Rev. ed.). Minneapolis, MN: Lerner Publications. Ages 5–8; **36**.

Cole, J. (1987). *Evolution.* New York: Crowell. Ages 5–8; **34, 36**.

Cole, J. (1987). *The magic school bus inside the earth.* New York: Scholastic; **21, 26, 36**.

Cole, J. (1992). *The magic school bus on the ocean floor.* New York: Scholastic; **36**.

Dunphy, M. (1999). *Here is the African savanna.* New York: Hyperion. Grades K–6; **26, 36**.

Earle, S. A. (1999). *Hello, fish! Visiting the coral reef.* Washington, DC: National Geographic. Grades K–3; **26, 36**.

Hoban, T. (1990). *Shadows and reflections.* New York: Greenwillow. Ages 4–8; **26, 36**.

Kandoian, E. (1990). *Under the sun.* New York: Putnam. Ages 4–6; **21, 26, 36**.

Keats, E. J. (1981). *Regards to the man in the moon.* New York: Four Winds. Ages 3–6; **21, 26, 36**.

Krupp, E. C. (2000). *The rainbow and you.* New York: HarperCollins. Grades K–4; **26, 36**.

Langley, A. (2001). *The Oxford first book of space.* New York: Oxford University Press. Grades K–4; **36**.

Lewison, W. (1990). *Mud.* New York: Random House. Ages 5–8; **21, 26, 36**.

Lindbergh, R. (1998). *Que es el sol?* [What is the sun?] New York: Lectorum. Ages 5–7; **16, 21, 26, 36**.

Livingston, M. (1992). *Light and shadow.* New York: Holiday House. Ages 4–7; **21, 26, 35, 36**.

Lye, K. (1987). *Deserts.* Morristown, NJ: Silver Burdett. Ages 8–14; **36**.

Maki, C. (1993). *Snowflakes, sugar, and salt.* New York: Lerner. Ages 6–8; **21, 26, 35, 36**.

Malnig, A. (1985). *Where the waves break: Life at the edge of the sea.* Minneapolis, MN: Carolrhoda. Ages 7–10; **36**.

Markle, S. (1987). *Digging deeper.* New York: Lothrop. Ages 8–12; **36**.

McMillan, B. (1990). *One sun: A book of terse verse.* New York: Holiday House. Ages 5–8; **21, 26, 36**.

Most, B. (1991). *A dinosaur named after me.* San Diego, CA: Harcourt Brace and Company. Ages 4–8; **21, 26, 36**.

Otto, C. (1992). *That sky, that rain.* New York: Harper. Ages 4–7; **21, 26, 36**.

Pallotta, J. (1986). *The ocean alphabet book.* Watertown, MA: Charlesbridge; **16, 21, 36**.

Parmall, P. (1991). *The rock.* New York: Macmillan. Ages 5–8; **21, 26, 36**.

Ressmeyer, R. (1992). *Astronaut to zodiac.* New York: Crown. Ages 5–12; **26, 36**.

Rocks and minerals. (1988). London: Natural History Museum. Ages 7–12; **36**.

Schlein, M. (1991). *Discovering dinosaur babies.* New York: Four Winds. Ages 6–9; **26, 36**.

Schmid, E. (1990). *The water's journey*. New York: North-South Books. Ages 6–8; **26, 36**.

Seymour, S. (1999). *Tornadoes*. New York: Morrow/Harper-Collins. Grades K–6; **26, 36**.

Souza, D. (1992). *Powerful waves*. Minneapolis, MN: Carolrhoda. Ages 6–12; **26, 36**.

Szilagyi, M. (1985). *Thunderstorms*. New York: Bradbury. Ages 3–9; **21, 26, 36**.

Wade, H. (1977). *Sand*. Milwaukee, WI: Raintree. Ages 4–8; **21, 26, 36**.

Weimer, T. E. (1993). *Space songs for children*. Pittsburgh, PA: Pearce-Evetts. Ages 5–8; **21, 26**.

Environmental Science: Ecology, Nature, and Conservation

Allen, M. (1991). *Changes*. New York: Macmillan. Ages 4–7; **21, 26, 34, 36**.

Arnosky, A. (1991). *The empty lot*. Boston: Little, Brown. Ages 4–8; **21, 26, 34, 36, 39**.

Bash, B. (1990). *Urban roosts: Where birds nest in the city*. Boston: Little, Brown. Ages 6–12; **26, 34, 36**.

Bruchac, J. (1992). *Native American animal stories*. Golden, CO: Fulcrum Publishing. Ages 5–8; **21, 26, 36**.

Cherry, L. (1990). *The great kapok tree: A tale of the Amazon rain forest*. New York: Gulliver. Ages 6–12; **26, 34, 36**.

Fernandes, K. (1991). *Zebo and the dirty planet*. Ontario, Canada: Firefly Books; **16, 21, 36**.

George, W. (1991). *Fishing at Long Pond*. New York: Greenwillow. Ages 4–8; **21, 26, 34, 36**.

Glaser, L. (2000). *Our big home: An earth poem*. Brookfield, CT: Millbrook Press. Grades K–3; **26, 37**.

Greene, C. (1991). *The old ladies who liked cats*. New York: Harper-Collins. Ages 5–8; **21, 26, 34, 36**.

Hines, A. (1991). *Remember the butterflies*. New York: Dutton. Ages 4–7; **16, 21, 26, 34, 36**.

Kaner, E. (1999). *Animal defenses: How animals protect themselves*. Niagara Falls, NY: Kids Can Press. Grades K–3; **26, 37**.

Kuhn, D. (1990). *More than just a vegetable garden*. New York: Silver Press. Ages 6–8; **26, 34, 36, 37**.

Leslie, C. (1991). *Nature all year long*. New York: Greenwillow. Ages 6–8; **26, 34, 36, 39**.

Levine, S., & Grafton, A. (1992). *Projects for a healthy planet*. New York: Wiley. Ages 6–12; **26, 34, 36, 39**.

Locker, T. (1991). *The land of the gray wolf*. New York: Dial. Ages 4–8; **21, 26, 34, 36**.

Miller, D. S. (2000). *River of life*. New York: Clarion. Grades K–3; **26, 37**.

Moss, M. (2000). *This is the tree*. La Jolla, CA: Kane/Miller. Grades K–3; **26, 37**.

Norsgaard, E. J. (1990). *Nature's great balancing act: In our own backyard*. New York: Cobblehill. Ages 7–12; **26, 34, 36**.

Parnall, P. (1990). *Woodpile*. New York: Macmillan. Ages 5–8; **21, 26, 34, 36, 39**.

Russell, H. R. (1998). *Ten-minute field trips*. Washington, DC: National Science Teachers Association. Grades K–8; **26, 34**.

Sackett, E. (1991). *Danger on the African grassland*. Boston: Little, Brown. Ages 5–8; **21, 26, 34, 36**.

Sanders, S. R. (1999). *Crawdad creek*. Washington, DC: National Geographic. Grades K–6; **26, 37**.

Shetterly, S. H. (1999). *Shelterwood*. Gardiner, ME: Tilbury House. Grades K–6; **26, 37**.

Siebert, D. (1991). *Sierra*. New York: Harper-Collins. Ages 5–8; **21, 26, 34, 36**.

Stock, C. (1991). *When the woods hum*. New York: Morrow. Ages 4–8; **16, 21, 34, 36, 39**.

Taylor, K., & Burton, J. (1993). *Forest life*. New York: Dorling Kindersley. Ages 7–12; **34, 35, 36**.

Tresselt, A. (1992). *The gift of the tree*. New York: Lothrop, Lee & Shepard. Ages 5–8; **21, 26, 34, 36**.

Health Science

Aliki. (1989). *Mis cinco sentidos* [My five senses]. New York: Harper Arco Iris; **16, 21, 36**.

Aliki. (1990). *My feet*. New York: Harper-Collins. Ages 4–6; **21, 26, 37**.

Brandenburg, A. (1976). *Corn is maize: The gift of the Indians*. New York: Crowell. Ages 3–5; **21, 22, 26, 37**.

Brown, M. (1947). *Stone soup*. New York: Charles Scribner's Sons. Ages 3–6; **21, 26, 37**.

Carle, E. (1970). *Pancakes, pancakes*. New York: Knopf. Ages 3–5; **21, 22, 26, 37**.

Cole, J. (1989). *The magic school bus: Inside the human body*. New York: Scholastic. Ages 6–8; **21, 26, 37**.

de Bourgoing, P., & Hahn, N. (1998) *Visita al medico* [Visit to the doctor]. Madrid: La Galera. Ages 3–6; **16, 21, 26**.

Farmer, J. (1999). *Bananas!* Watertown, MA: Charlesbridge. Grades K–6; **26, 38**.

Manning, M., & Granstrom, B. (1999). *Mi cuerpo, tu cuerpo* [My body, your body]. Madrid: Ediciones SM. Grades 1–3; **34**.

Manning, M., & Granstrom, B. (1999). *El mundo está lleno de bebés!* [The world is full of babies!]. Madrid: Ediciones SM. Grades 1–3; **34**.

McMillan, B. (1994). *Sense suspense: A guessing game for the five senses*. New York: Scholastic; **16, 21, 36**.

Ontario Science Center. (1987). *Foodworks*. Reading, PA: Addison-Wesley. Ages 8–12; **37**.

Pomerantz, C. (1984). *Whiff, whiff, nibble, and chew*. New York: Greenwillow. Ages 4–8; **21, 26, 35**.

Rice, J. (1989). *Those mean nasty downright disgusting but . . . Invisible germs*. Minneapolis, MN: Toys 'n Things Press; **21, 26, 37**.

Roca, N. (2000). *Tu cuerpo, de la cabeza, a los pies* [Your body, from head to toe]. Barcelona: Editorial Molino. Grades 2–4; **34**.

Sekido, I. (1993). *Science all around you: Fruits, roots, and fungi*. Minneapolis, MN: Ages 6–8; **26, 34, 36, 37**.

Sendak, M. (1962). *Chicken soup with rice*. New York: Harper & Row. Ages 3–5; **21, 22, 26, 28**.

Sendak, M. (1970). *In the night kitchen*. New York: Harper & Row. Ages 3–5; **21, 26, 28**.

Shaw, D. (1983). *Germs!* New York: Holiday House. Ages 8–12; **37**.

Skeleton. (1988). London: Natural History Museum. Ages 7–12; **37**.

Suhr, M. (1992). *I'm alive series: How I breathe; I am growing; I can move; When I eat*. Minneapolis, MN: Carolrhoda. Ages 4–6; **21, 26, 37**.

Children's Periodicals That Emphasize Math and Science Concepts

Barney Magazine and *Barney Family: Ideas for Parents* (magazine). P.O. Box 7402, Red Oak, IA 51591. Phone: 515-243-4543.

Beyond Counting. A quarterly newsletter. P.O. Box 218, Barrington, RI 02806.

Chickadee: The Canadian Magazine for Children. Young Naturalist Foundation, 56 the Esplanade, Suite 304, Toronto, Ontario, Canada M5E 1A7. Ages 3–9.

Child Life. P.O. Box 10681, Des Moines, IA 50381. Ages 7–9.

Children's Playmate Magazine. Children's Better Health Institute, 1100 Waterway Blvd., P.O. Box 567, Indianapolis, IN 46206. Ages 4–8.

Koala Club News. Zoological Society of San Diego, Inc., P.O. Box 551, San Diego, CA 92212. Ages 6–15.

Living Planet. World Wildlife Fund, 1250 24th St., NW, Washington, DC 20037. Web site: http://www.worldwildlife.org

Math Power. Monthly magazine (eight issues) with activities for elementary grades. Scholastic, 2931 East McCarty Street, P.O. Box 3710, Jefferson City, MO 65102-3710. Phone: 800-631-1586; E-mail: mathpower@scholastic.com

National Geographic News. P.O. Box 2330, Washington, DC 20009. Ages 5–12.

Ranger Rick's Nature Magazine. National Wildlife Federation, Box 2038, Harlan, IA. Web site: http://www.nwf.org™. Phone: 800-611-1599. Ages 5–11.

Scienceland, Inc. 501 5th Avenue, Suite 2102, New York, NY 10017. Ages 3–12.

Science Weekly. P.O. Box 70154, Washington, DC 20088. Ages 4–12.

Scholastic Let's Find Out. Scholastic Magazines, 1290 Wall Street West, Lyndhurst, NJ 07071. Age 5.

Sesame Street. Children's Television Workshop, P.O. Box 2896, Boulder, CO 80322. Ages 3–8.

3 2 1 Contact. P.O. Box 2933, Boulder, CO 80322. Ages 6–14.

Wild Animal Baby. (10 issues). National Wildlife Federation, Box 2038, Harlan, IA. (12 months to 3 years).

Your Big Back Yard. National Wildlife Federation, Box 2038, Harlan, IA. Web site http://www.nwf.org™. Phone: 800-611-1599. Ages 3–5.

Instructional Technology Publishers Used in This Text

Advanced Ideas
2902 San Pablo Avenue
Berkeley, CA 94702

Allegro New Media
16 Passaic Avenue
Building 6
Fairfield, NJ 07004
800-424-1992
http://www.allegronm.com

American Guidance Service
Publishers' Building
P.O. Box 99
Circle Pines, MN 55014

Apple Computer, Inc.
1 Infinite Loop
Cupertino, CA 95014
800-767-2775
www.apple.com

Beachware
9419 Mt. Israel Road
Escondido, CA 92029
619-735-8945

Broderbund Software, Inc.
500 Redwood Boulevard
Novato, CA 94947
800-521-6263
www.broderbund.com

CBS Software, CBS, Inc.
One Fawcett Place
Greenwich, CT 06836

Chariot
3659 India Street
Suite 100HE
San Diego, CA 92103
800-242-7468

Claris
P.O. Box 58268
5210 Patrick Henry Drive
Santa Clara, CA 95052
800-325-2748
www.claris.com

Compton's New Media
2320 Camino Vida Roble
Carlsbad, CA 92009
800-862-2206

Connectix
2655 Campus Drive
San Mateo, CA 94403
800-950-5880
www.connectix.com

Counterpoint Software, Inc.
4005 West 65th Street
Minneapolis, MN 55435

Creative Multimedia
225 SW Broadway, #600
Portland, OR 97205
800-331-1369
www.creativemm.com

Davidson & Associates, Inc. (Cendant Software)
19840 Pioneer Avenue
Torrance, CA 90503-1660
800-545-7677

D.C. Heath and Company
125 Spring Street
Lexington, MA 02173

Data Harvest Educational
363 Lang Boulevard
Grand Island, NY 14072-3123
800-436-3062
www/dhe@interlog.com

Decision Development Company
2680 Bishop Drive
Suite 122
San Ramon, CA 94583
800-835-4332
www.DDC2000@AOL.COM

DIDAX Educational Resources
395 Main Street
Rowley, MA 01969-0907

Discovery Channel Multimedia
7770 Wisconsin Avenue
Bethesda, MD 20814
800-762-2189
www.discovery.com

DK Multimedia (Dorling Kinderlsey)
95 Madison Avenue
New York, NY 10016
800-356-6575
www.dk.com

DLM
SRA/McGraw-Hill
www.sra4kids/dlm/

EDC
Educational Development Center
Boca Raton, FL
(IBM Company)

Edmark
P.O. Box 97021
Redmond, WA 98073-9721
800-362-2890
www.edmark.com

Edu-Ware Services, Inc.
P.O. Box 22222
Agoura, CA 91301

EduQuest
P.O. Box 2150
Atlanta, GA 30055
800-IBM-3327

Edutek Corporation
P.O. Box 2560
Palo Alto, CA 94702

Energy Center
Sonoma State University
Rohnert Park, CA 94928

Flix Productions
Animated Educational Software
601 Ranch Road
Delvalle, TX 78617
512-247-3974

ForeFront
1330 Post Oak Boulevard
Suite 1300
Houston, TX 77056
800-653-4933
www.ffg.com

Gryphon Software
7220 Trade Street, #120
San Diego, CA 92121
619-454-6836

Harper & Row
Keystone Industrial Park
Scranton, PA 18512

Hartley
3451 Dunckel Road
Suite 200
Lansing, MI 48911
800-247-1380

Harvard Associates Inc.
101 Holworthy Street
Cambridge, MA 02138
617-492-0660
www.info@terrapinlogo.com

Hayden Software Company
600 Suffolk Street
Lowell, MA 01853

Headbone Interactive
www.headbone.com/abouthb/

Humongous Entertainment
13110 N.E. 177th Place
Woodinville, WA 98072
206-485-1212

ICE
575 Lexington Avenue, Suite 410
New York, NY 10022
212-572-8331

IVI Publishing
155 First Avenue, SW
#930
Rochester, MN 55902
507-282-2076

Jostens Learning Corp.
224 N. Desplaines Street, #400
Chicago, IL 60661
312-441-4700

Knowledge Avenue
1311 Grand Central Avenue
Glendale, CA 91201
800-542-4240
www.adventure.com

LCSI®
P.O. Box 162
Highgate Springs, VT 05460
800-321-5646
Fax: 514-331-1380
www.microworlds.com/info/

Lawrence Hall of Science
University of California
Berkeley, CA 94720

Lawrence Productions
1800 S. 35th Street
Galesburg, MI 49053
616-665-7075

The Learning Company
6493 Kaiser Drive
Fremont, CA 94555
800-852-2255
www.learningco.com

Learning in Motion
500 Seabright Ave., Ste. 105
Santa Cruz, CA 95062
800-560-5670
helpdesk@learn.motion.com

Learning Well
200 South Service Road
Roslyn Heights, NY 11577

LEGO®MINDSTORMS™
Pearson Educational Publishing
Kamico Instructional Media
5917 Maury's Trail
Austin, TX 78730-2767
512-343-0801
Mindstorms.Lego.com/products/

Maxis
2121 N. California Blvd., #600
Walnut Creek, CA 94596
800-336-2947
www.maxis.com

MECC
6160 Summit Drive, North
Minneapolis, MN 55430
800-685-6322
www.mecc.com

Microsoft
1 Microsoft Way
Redmond, WA 98052
800-426-9400
www.microsoft.com

Midwest Software
Box 214
Farmington, MI 48024

Milliken Publishing Company
1100 Research Boulevard
St. Louis, MO 63132-0579

Mindscape
88 Roland Way
Novato, CA 94945
800-283-8499
www.mindscape.com

National Geographic
1145 17th Street, NW
Washington, DC 20036
800-368-2728

OL-Opportunities for Learning
20417 Nordhoff Street
Department KSP
Chatsworth, CA 91311

Optical Data Corporation
30 Technology Drive
Warren, NJ 07060

Optimum Resource, Inc.
18 Hunter Read
Hilton Head Island, SC 29926
888-784-2592

Orange Cherry
P.O. Box 390
Westchester Avenue
Market Plaza Building
Pound Ridge, NY 10576
800-672-6002

Panda/Learning Technologies
4255 LBJ Freeway, #131
Dallas, TX 75244

Pearson Educational Publishing
Kamico Industrial Media
5917 Maury's Trail
Austin, TX 78730-2767
512-343-0801

Pelican Software
768 Farmington Avenue
Farmington, CT 06032

Philsoft
World Trade Centre
10 Yonge Street, Suite 2808
Toronto, ON M5E 1R4
416-603-9251

Polarware
1055 Paramount Parkway, Suite A
Batavia, IL 60510

Queque
338 Commerce Drive
Fairfield, CT 06432
800-232-2224

Random House, Inc.
201 East 50th Street
New York, NY 10022
800-733-3000
www.randomhouse.com

Reader's Digest Software
Microcomputer Software Division
Pleasantville, NY 10570

ROBOLAB
National Instruments
LEGO®Dacta
www.ni.com/robolab/

Robotics Network
www.lego.com/robotics/
Tenth Planet
Pleasantville, NY
www.tenthplanet.com

Scholastic, Inc.
555 Broadway
New York, NY 10012

Schoolhouse Interactive
2635 Lake Road
Charlotte, VT 05445
www.sara-jordan.com/
    edu-mart/getupcls/getupcls.htm

Science for Kids
6251 Shallowford Road
Lewisville, NC 27023
910-945-9000

Scott, Foresman, & Company
1900 East Lake Avenue
Glenview, IL 60025

Sierra On-Line, Inc.
Sierra On-Line Building
Coarsegold, CA 93614

Soleil Software
3853 Grove Court
Palo Alto, CA 94303
800-501-0110
www.soleil.com

Spinnaker
1 Kendall Square
Cambridge, MA 02139

Springboard Software, Inc.
7807 Creekbridge Circle
Minneapolis, MN 55435

StarPress Multimedia
303 Sacramento Street 2/F
San Francisco, CA 94111
800-500-8682

Stone and Associates
7910 Ivanhoe Avenue, STE139
La Jolla, CA 92037

Sunburst Communications
101 Castleton Street
Pleasantville, NY 10570
www.nysunburst.com

Tenth Planet
Pleasantville, NY
www. Tenthplanet.com

Theatrix Interactive
1250 45th Street
Suite 150
Emeryville, CA 94608
800-955-8749

Times Learning Systems, Pte., Ltd.
Times Centre
1 New Industrial Rd.
Singapore 536196
SINGAPORE
Marketing 380-7447
Customer Support 380-7443
tls@tp1.com.sg
Fax: 380-7445
www.timesmm.com.sg/timeseol/

Tom Snyder Productions
80 Coolidge Hill Road
Watertown, MA 02172-2817
800-342-0236

Troll Associates
100 Corporate Drive
Mahwah, NJ 07430

Ventura Educational Systems
3440 Brokenhill Street
Newbury Park, CA 91320

Virgin Sound and Vision
122 S. Robertson Boulevard
Los Angeles, CA 90048
800-814-3530

Virtual Entertainment
200 Highland Avenue
Needham, MA 02194
800-303-9545
www.virtent.com

Waterford Institute
1480 East 9400 South
Sandy, UT 84092

Weekly Reader Family Software
Xerox Education Publications
Middletown, CT 06457

Wentworth Worldwide Media, Inc.
P.O. Box 10488
Lancaster, PA 17605
800-638-1639
www.wentworth.com

Wings for Learning
1600 Green Hills Road
P.O. Box 660002
Scotts Valley, CA 95067-0002

Websites for Math and Science Information and Activities

Reviewed in *Teaching Children Mathematics*

- www.dcmrats.org. Aunty Math problems. Primary level. Aunt Mathilda poses problems.
- www.terc.edu/mathequity/gw/. TERC has many resources in math and science, including family resources and software reviews.
- www.gsn.org. The Global Schoolhouse at http://www.lightspan.com connects students and teachers with the world. You and your students can communicate with colleagues around the world. Lighthouse provides math and science lesson plans. This site also provides lists of sites for professional development.
- www.education-world.com. Vast resources and many links, including to preschool sites.
  - www.by.net/~stormie/ Preschool Teacher
  - www.perpetualpreschool.com
- www.learner.org. Annenberg math and science project—teachers' lab provides math and science guides for K–12 teachers.
- www.nctm.org. National Council of Teachers of Mathematics site includes information about the organization and its publications, the principles and standards, current issues, and links to mathematics resources.
- naeyc.org. National Association for the Education of Young Children provides information on the organization, its activities and publications.

- www.enc.org. Eisenhower National Clearinghouse. Includes links to many sites.
- http://mathforum.org/. Swarthmore's math forum has links to many resources. Has prekindergarten and kindergarten to grade two sections, which focus on many sites.
- www.ed.gov/pubs/parents/math. The U.S. Department of Education has published a booklet for parents, *Early Childhood Where Learning Begins: Mathematics*, which can also be printed from the site. Excellent resource.
- nsta.org. National Science Teachers Association—provides information on activities and publications.

Recommended in 1001 Best Web Sites for Educators, Teacher Created Materials, Inc. (2000).

- Faldo.atmos.uiuc.edu/CLA. Collaborative lesson archive for teacher resources.
- school.discovery.com. Discovery Channel School has lesson plans and resources organized by grade.
- www.seaworld.org/teacher guides/. Sea World Educational Resources provides lesson plans and resource guides for undersea study.
- Explorer.scrtec.org/explorer. Explorer is a search engine that searches for math and science instructional software, lesson plans, student-created materials, and so on.
- www.theideabox.com. The Idea Box—Early Childhood Education and Activity Resources provides a link of the week and a free newsletter.

APPENDIX C
Code of Practice on Use of Animals in Schools

This code of practice is recommended by the National Science Teachers Association for use throughout the United States by elementary, middle/junior high, and high school teachers and students. It applies to educational projects conducted and lessons taught involving live organisms in schools or in school-related activities such as science fairs, science clubs, and science competitions.

The purpose of these guidelines is to enrich education by encouraging students to observe living organisms and to learn proper respect for life. The study of living organisms is essential for an understanding of living processes. This study must be coupled with the observance of humane animal care and treatment.

I. Care and Responsibility for Animals in the Classroom

A. A teacher must have a clear understanding of and a strong commitment to the responsible care of living animals before making any decision to use live animals for educational study. Preparation for the use of live animals should include acquisition of knowledge on care appropriate to the species being used, including housing, food, exercise, and the appropriate placement of the animals at the conclusion of the study.

B. Teachers should try to ensure that living animals entering the classroom are healthy and free of transmissible disease or other problems that may endanger human health. Not all species are appropriate. Wild animals are not appropriate because they may carry parasites or serious diseases.

C. Maintaining good health and providing optimal care based on an understanding of the life habits of each species used is of primary importance. Animal quarters shall be spacious, shall avoid overcrowding, and shall be sanitary. Handling shall be gentle. Food shall be appropriate to the animal's normal diet and of sufficient quantity and balance to maintain a good standard of nutrition at all times. No animal shall be allowed less than the optimum maintenance level of nutrition. Clean drinking water shall always be available. Adequate provision for care shall be made at all times including vacation times.

D. All aspects of animal care and treatment shall be supervised by a qualified ADULT WHO IS KNOWLEDGEABLE ABOUT RESEARCH METHODS, BIOLOGY, CARE, AND HUSBANDRY OF THE SPECIES BEING STUDIED.

E. Supervisors and students should be familiar with *literature on care and handling* of living organisms. Practical training in these techniques is encouraged.

F. Adequate plans should be made to *control possible unwanted breedings* of the species during the project period.

G. Appropriate plans should be made for future care of animals at the conclusion of the study.

H. As a general rule, laboratory-bred animals should not be released into the wild as they may disturb the natural ecology of the environment.

I. On rare occasions it may be necessary to sacrifice an animal for educational purposes. This shall be done only in a manner accepted and approved by the American Veterinary Association, by a person experienced in these techniques, and at the discretion of the teacher. It should not be done in the presence of immature or young students who may be upset by witnessing such a procedure. Maximum efforts should be made to study as many biological principles as possible from a single animal.

J. The procurement, care, and use of animals must comply with existing local, state, and federal regulations.

II. Experimental Studies of Animals in the Classroom

A. When biological procedures involving living organisms are called for, every effort should be made to use plants or invertebrate animals when possible.

B. No experimental procedure shall be attempted on mammals, birds, reptiles, amphibians, or fish that causes the animal unnecessary pain or discomfort.

C. It is recommended that preserved vertebrate specimens be used for dissections.

D. Students shall not perform dissection surgery on vertebrate animals except under direct supervision of a qualified biomedical scientist or trained adult supervisor.

E. *Experimental procedures* including the use of pathogens, ionizing radiation, toxic chemicals, and chemicals producing birth defects must be under the supervision of a biomedical scientist or an adult trained in the specific techniques. Such procedures should be done in appropriate laboratory facilities that adhere to safety guidelines.

F. *Behavior studies should use only reward* (such as providing food) and not punishment in training programs. When food is used as a reward, it should not be withheld for more than 12 hours.

G. If embryos are subjected to invasive or potentially damaging manipulation, the embryo must be destroyed prior to hatching. If normal embryos are hatched, provisions must be made for their care and maintenance.

III. Research Investigations Involving Vertebrate Animals

The National Science Teachers Association recognizes that an exceptionally talented student may wish to conduct research in the biological or medical sciences and endorses procedures for student research as follows:

A. Protocols of extracurricular projects involving animals should be reviewed in advance of the start of the work by a qualified adult supervisor.

B. Preferably, extracurricular projects should be carried out in an approved area of the school or research facility.

C. The project should be carried out with the utmost regard for the humane care and treatment of the animals involved in the project.

—*Adopted by the NSTA Board of Directors in July 1985.*

Hampton, C.H., Hampton, C.D., & Kammer, D.C. (1988) *Classroom creature culture.* Washington, D.C.: National Science Association.
1. NSTA Care of Animals Position Statement
2. Guidelines for Proper Care of Living Organisms
3. Sources for Teaching About Plants, Animals, and the Environment

Glossary

A

abstract symbolic activities—activities that involve the manipulation of groups using number symbols.

accommodation—when new information that does not fit into an existing scheme is modified or a new one is made.

action symbols—symbols that tell what action to take such as + (add) or × (multiply).

add—to join groups.

algebra—at the preoperational level algebraic thinking involves discovering and creating patterns.

algorithms—step-by-step procedures for solving problems.

almost whole—when a small part of something is removed, young children will view it as almost whole.

amphibians—animals that live both on land and in water.

anthropomorphic—giving human shapes or characteristics to animals.

arbitrary units—the third stage of measurement where anything can be used as a unit of measure. Extends through the latter part of the preoperational period.

assess—the first step in instruction; where are the children now in their development?

assimilation—fitting information into an existing scheme.

association—one of the criteria that can be used as a common feature to form a group (i.e., things that do a job together, come from the same place, or belong to a special person).

atmosphere—gaseous mass surrounding a star, planet, and so on. All of Earth's air.

autonomy—the aim of education is to achieve independent thinking.

awareness—the first stage in the learning cycle as adapted to early childhood education: a broad recognition of objects, people, events, and concepts that develops from experience.

axes—the names for the left side and bottom of a line graph.

B

basic facts—number combinations that add up to one through 10.

bilateral symmetry—a line can be drawn through the middle of the shape or object and divided. Each side or part would be exactly like the other half.

biodegradable—capable of being readily decomposed by biological means.

bookmark—allows one to mark a Web site that one may want to visit again without having to conduct another search.

browser—enables searches on the World Wide Web.

C

camouflage—the appearance of an animal, insect, or others that allows it to blend with its environment for protection.

carbohydrates—organic compound comprised of carbon, hydrogen, and oxygen found in foods such as sugars and starches.

carbon dioxide—odorless gas that passes out of the lungs.

cardinal meaning—the last number counted is the amount in the group.

cardinality—an understanding that the last number named is the amount in a group.

centration—the characteristic of preoperational children that causes them to focus on the most obvious aspects of what they perceive.

charts and tables—ways of visually depicting data.

checklist—a list of skills that can be dated as children accomplish them.

chemical change—a change where substances mix and form something new.

choose objectives—after assessment, decide what the child should learn next.

chrysalis—an insect in the developmental stage, between the larval stage and adult stage, when the insect is in a case or cocoon.

circle—a continuous curved line.

circulatory system—body system relating to the circulation of the blood.

class inclusion—one class may be included in another (beagles and poodles are included in the class of dogs).

class name—one of the criteria that can be used as a common feature to form a group (i.e., animals, furniture, people).

classification—putting things into logical groups.

classifying—grouping or sorting according to properties such as size, shape, color, use, and so on.

cognitive structure—the grouping of closely related facts and phenomena related to a concept.

color—one criterion that can be used to place things in a logical group.

common features—one of the criteria that can be used to form a group (i.e., all have doors, handles, points).

communicating—recording ideas, directions, and descriptions orally or in written form such as pictures, maps, graphs, or journals so others can understand what you mean. One of the science process skills.

communication—oral, written, and pictorial language are used to explain problem-solving and reasoning processes.

comparing—finding a relationship between two items or groups of items based on a specific characteristic or attribute. One of the science process skills.

comparison stage—the second stage of measurement that extends through the preoperational period. Comparisons such as weight, length, and temperature are made.

compost—a mixture of decomposing vegetable refuse, manure, and the like for fertilizing soil.

computational fluency—computing with efficiency, accuracy, and flexibility.

concept application phase—after completing investigations and problem-solving experiences, taking the knowledge and applying it to a new situation. This phase expands the concept.

concept introduction phase—initial investigation and problem-solving experiences designed by the teacher and/or children to acquire knowledge of a topic. This phase provides opportunities to accommodate information.

concepts—the building blocks of knowledge; they allow for organizing and categorizing information.

conceptual subitizing—seeing number patterns within a group such as a large number of dots (usually more than five).

conclusions—statements that tell if the original prediction or hypothesis was rejected.

concrete operations—the third period identified by Piaget during which children attain conservation.

concrete whole number operations—solving simple addition, subtraction, division, and multiplication problems using concrete materials.

concreteness—the degree to which materials approach reality.

condensation—to pass into a denser form, as vapor into a liquid.

connections—the bridge between the informal mathematics learned out of school with the formalities of school mathematics. Concrete materials can serve this function.

conservation—the ability to retain the original picture in the mind when material has been changed in its arrangement in space. The care and protection of natural resources.

constellations—a number of fixed stars arbitrarily considered a group, usually referred to by a name or number.

construction—making a space for some particular items to fit into.

contrived problems—problems devised by the teacher for which the teacher models a problem-solving procedure.

convergent questions and directions—having only one possible answer or activity.

cube—a three-dimensional figure with sides that are six equal-sized squares.

cultural time—the time that is fixed by clocks and calendars.

curiosity—a desire to learn or know.

curves—curved but not straight paths that connect two points.

cylinder—a three-dimensional figure with circular parallel bases.

D

data collection—recording information collected during observations.

defining and controlling variables—determining which variables in an investigation should be studied or should be controlled to conduct a controlled experiment. One of the science process skills.

descriptive lessons—lessons in which children mainly observe, interact, and describe their observations.

determining variables—taking all the factors into account that might affect the outcome of the investigation.

development—changes that take place due to growth and experience.

direction—in spatial relations, indicates "which way" (i.e., up, down, across).

discrepant event—an event that has an unexpected conclusion.

disequilibrium—when children realize that they do not understand something they previously thought they understood.

distance—in spatial relations, indicates relative distance (e.g., near or far).

divergent questions and directions—provide opportunities for guessing and experimenting.

divide—to separate a whole into parts.

dividend—the amount to be broken into equal parts in the division operation.

divisor—the number of parts that a group is divided into in the division operation.

download—loading information into a personal computer from the Internet.

dramatic role-play—taking on roles in pretend play.

duration—has to do with how long an event takes (e.g., minutes, days, etc.).

E

embryo—rudimentary plant contained in a seed.

English units—units of measure customarily used in the United States (such as inches, feet, and yards).

environment—all the conditions, circumstances, and influences surrounding and affecting the development of an organism or group of organisms.

equal—when groups have the same amount.

equality—a condition indicated by the (=) action sign.

equals—an action term represented by the sign (=).

equilibrium—when children have enough information to satisfy their curiosity and to create a new cognitive structure.

erosion—the moving away of soil by water or wind.

estimation—making a sensible and reasonable guess regarding how many or how much without counting or measuring.

ethnomathematics—mathematics learned outside of school.

evaluate—to find out if an objective has been reached through observation or questioning.

evaporation—changing into vapor or the removal of moisture from milk, fruit, and so on.

exploration—the second stage in the learning cycle as adapted to early childhood education: the construction of personal meaning.

F

factors—the numbers operated on in multiplication.

fats—an oily, yellow or white substance found in plant and animal matter.

formal operations—Piaget's final period that extends from about age 11 through adulthood.

fossils—hardened remains of animal or plant life from a previous geological period.

fourths—the parts of a substance or a group when the substance or group is separated or divided into four equal parts.

fractions—an area of formal mathematics that grows out of an informal understanding of parts and wholes. During the primary grades children learn about halves, fourths, and thirds. They also use terms such as *pieces*, *whole*, and *almost whole*.

function—one of the criteria that can be used as a common feature to form a group (i.e., all used for the same thing such as eating, playing music).

G

general time words—words such as time and age.

geoboard—a square board with headed screws or pegs sticking up at equal intervals. Rubber bands are stretched between pegs to make a variety of shapes.

geologist—specialist in geology.

germinate—to start developing or growing; to begin sprouting.

germs—microscopic organisms that cause disease.

glycerin—a thick, odorless, colorless liquid prepared from hydrolysis of fats and oils.

goals—broad statements that indicate what you want children to know and be able to do on completion of a certain unit of curriculum.

graphs—visual representations of two or more comparisons.

graphs, object graphs—the first stage in graphing using real objects such as cube blocks. Usually two items are compared.

graphs, picture graphs—the second stage of graphing where more than two categories may be compared and a more permanent record kept such as drawing pictures.

graphs, square paper graphs—the third stage of graphing where more than two categories may be compared and a more permanent record kept such as using paper squares.

graphs, squared paper—the fourth stage of graphing where data are recorded by shading in squares on squared paper.

grouping—the process of placing two or more smaller groups into a larger group.

H

half—a fraction term that can be used informally with young children. It indicates the division of a whole into two parts that are the same.

halves—the parts of a substance or a group when the substance or group is separated or divided into two equal parts.

heuristics—Questions that children generate when solving problems.

hierarchical classification—there are classes within classes with a series developing larger and larger classes.

holistic evaluations—evaluation in which a rubric is used to place portfolios in groups such as strong, average, and weak.

hypotheses—devising a statement, based on observations, that can be tested by experiment. One of the science process skills.

I

igneous rocks—rocks formed through cooling of magma or lava.

inferring—based on observations but suggests more meaning about a situation than can be directly observed. One of the science process skills.

informal learning—learning experiences initiated by the adult as children engage in their everyday natural activities.

informal measurement—measurement done by comparison or using nonstandard units (i.e., a shoe, a paper clip, a block).

inquiry—the third stage in the learning cycle. As adapted to early childhood education: learners compare their findings and is a major focus of science process skill.

integrated curriculum—curriculum that integrates math, science, social studies, language arts, music and movement, and visual arts, usually through projects and/or thematic units.

Internet—the worldwide computer connection.

invertebrate—having no backbone or spinal column.

L

landfill—an area of land where garbage is stored, mainly items that cannot be recycled.

larva—insect in the earliest stage of development.

learning cycle—phases of learning used for curriculum development and as teaching strategies: exploration, concept development, concept application.

Lego®/logo—a combination of Lego® bricks and Logo programming that children can use to explore physics, technology, and mathematics.

length—in measurement denotes how long, wide, or deep.

lens—a piece of glass with two curved surfaces, which is used in a magnifier to enlarge images.

less than (<)—a group or quantity comparison term and symbol.

lesson plan—a planned, sequenced series of steps to be implemented in order to accomplish a goal or objective. An educational activity plan.

line graphs—graphs made on squared paper grids connecting data points.

lines—connections between two points.

logical grouping—groups whose members have a logical connection (such as number, color, shape, or class).

logico-mathematical knowledge—knowledge that enables us to organize and make sense out of the world, such as classification and number concepts.

LOGO—a computer language that can be applied to many geometric experiences.

M

machine—a device that transmits or changes the application of energy, as in pulley, lever, or screw.

magnifier—lenses that enlarge the apparent size of an object.

mammals—a group of vertebrates the females of which have milk-secreting glands for feeding their young.

manipulative materials—materials that have parts and pieces that can be picked up and moved by the child in the process of problem solving.

material—one criterion that can be used to place items in a logical group (i.e., wood, plastic, glass).

measurement—assigning a number to things so they can be compared on the same attributes.

measuring—quantitative descriptions made by an observer either directly through observation or indirectly with a unit of measure. One of the science process skills.

metamorphic rocks—rocks formed when sedimentary and igneous rocks are completely changed in form through pressure and heat.

metric units—measurement units based on groups of 10.

minerals—inorganic substances that occur naturally in the earth and have a consistent and distinctive set of physical properties.

more than (>)—a group or quantity comparison term and symbol.

multiple classification—requires classifying according to more than one criterion.

multiple intelligences—areas of strength identified by Howard Gardner.

N

National Science Education Standards—national expectations for what children will know and be able to do in the area of science.

naturalistic learning—learning that occurs as children go about their daily activities.

nonroutine problems—problems that involve more than one step and do not follow a predictable pattern.

notation—number and operations symbols.

number—one of the criteria that can be used to form a group (i.e., pairs or other groups of the same amount).

number sense—the concept or understanding of number.

number sentences—sentences that symbolize an operation such $3 + 4 = 7$ or $8 > 6$.

numerals—number symbols (i.e., 1, 2, 3, etc.)

nutrition—a process by which an organism takes food to promote growth.

O

object permanence—the realization that objects exist even when they are out of sight.

object recognition—the ability to identify objects using previously acquired information such as color, shape, and size.

objectives—state how you plan to achieve your goals.

observing—using the senses to gather information about objects and events. One of the science process skills.

one-to-one correspondence—the understanding that one group has as many members as another.

one more than—a concept basic to sequencing or ordering groups of amounts each one more than the other.

ordering—putting items in a logical sequence.

organisms—any living thing.

organization/pattern—arrangement of parts in a space so that they all fit.

P

parts—things have parts (e.g., legs, doors, handles) and groups have parts (e.g., each child gets two cookies).

pattern—one criterion that can be used to place items in a logical group (i.e., stripes, dots, plaid).

patterning—making or discovering auditory, visual, and motor regularities.

perceptual subitizing—being able to state how many are in a group without counting or grouping.

performance-based assessment—giving one or more students a task to do, which will indicate the student level of understanding of science concepts and thinking skills.

personal experience—the view of time held by young children (e.g., "When I was a baby.").

physical change—when the physical appearance of a substance changes but is not chemically altered.

physical knowledge—knowledge of things in their environment and their characteristics.

place value—pertains to an understanding that the same numeral represents different amounts, depending on its position.

plan experiences—decide which strategies should be used to enable the child to accomplish instructional objectives.

play—the major medium through which children learn.

play stage—the first stage of measurement during which children imitate adults and/or older children using measurement tools such as rulers or measuring cups. This stage extends into the preoperational period.

points—introduced as small dots and later applied to making line graphs.

pollution—to make unclean or impure as in water, air, soil, and the like.

portfolio—a purposeful collection of student work.

position—in spatial relations, an indication of "where" (i.e., on, off, under, over).

preconcepts—incomplete concepts that develop before true concepts.

predicting—making reasonable guesses or estimations based on observations and prior knowledge and experiences. One of the science process skills.

preoperational period—the second Piagetian developmental period that extends from about age two to age seven.

preprimary—the period before children enter first grade.

primary—grades one through three.

principles—basic rules that guide high-quality mathematics education.

problem solving—a major mathematics process standard.

process skills—label for fundamental mathematics concepts such as classifying, comparing, and measuring when applied to science.

product—the result of a multiplication operation.

proteins—nitrogenous substances consisting of amino acids, carbon, hydrogen, oxygen, nitrogen, and sometimes sulfur, occurring in all animal and plant matter.

pupa—an insect in the stage of development between the larval and adult forms.

Q

quantities above ten—when children understand the base quantity of ten they can move on to working with larger quantities.

quantity comparison—considering two groups of objects and deciding if they have the same amount or if one group has more.

quotient—the result of the division operation.

R

rational counting—attaching a number name to each object counted.

reasoning—the ability that enables children to draw logical conclusions, apply logical classification skills, justify problem solutions, and make sense out of mathematics and science.

record folder—a collection of anecdotal records and checklists.

rectangular prism—a three-dimensional figure with identical rectangular bases and four rectangular sides.

recycle—reusing existing materials.

regrouping—moving groups from one column of numbers to another.

relational symbols—indicate that quantities are related, such as = (equal), > (greater than), and < (less than).

relational time words—words such as soon, yesterday, early, etc..

remainder—in division the result may not come out with equal groups; there may be a remainder.

renaming—after a group has been moved using regrouping, the new number is renamed.

representation—demonstrating thought and understanding through oral and written language, physical gestures, drawings, and invented and conventional symbols.

representative thought—the ability to think through the solution to a problem before acting.

reptiles—a group of cold-blooded vertebrates that crawl on their bellies or creep on short, stubby legs.

resources—anything that can be used to fill a need. Natural resources include coal, water, and so on.

reversibility—when the arrangement of material is changed, the mind can reverse the process of change and visualize the original arrangement.

rote counting—reciting the names of the numerals in order from memory.

routine problems—problems that follow a predictable pattern.

rubrics—evaluation guides that show students' criteria for self-assessment.

S

scaffolding—assistance in learning from someone who is more mature.

sedimentary rocks—rocks formed from eroded rocks, sand, clay, silt, pebbles, and other stones.

select materials—decide which materials should be used in order to carry out an instructional plan.

self-correcting materials—materials that the child can use independently by trial and error to solve a problem with little or no adult assistance.

self-regulation—active mental process of forming concepts.

senses—sight, touch, smell, hearing, and taste.

sensorimotor period—first cognitive developmental period identified by Piaget. Extends from birth to about age two.

sequence—time as related to the order of events.

seriation—putting items in a logical sequence.

shape—one criterion that can be used to place items in a logical group (i.e., square, circular, triangular) and can be reproduced with geoboards or stencils.

signs—the tools of the mind, such as language, that we use for thinking.

size—a measurement term referring to volume, height, weight, and/or length.

skepticism—attitude that does not allow a person to accept things easily on face value.

skip counting—counting using quantities and number symbols other than ones such as "2-4-6-8 . . . " or "5-10-15 . . . "

social activity—time as viewed from the sequence of routine daily activities.

social knowledge—the knowledge created by people, such as rules of conduct.

sorting—the process of separating a larger group into two or more smaller groups.

spatial relations—a critical element in geometry.

special days time words—time as indicated by holidays and other special days.

specific duration time words—clock (minutes, hours) and calendar (days, weeks) words.

specific time words—words which refer to a specific time such as morning and night.

sphere—a three-dimensional circular figure.

square—a shape with four equal sides and four points or corners.

standard units—units of measurement that are standardized such as inches, centimeters, pounds, liters, and miles that everyone agrees on. Children begin to understand the need for standard units during the concrete operational period.

standards—provide guidance as to what children should know and be able to do at different ages and stages.

structured learning—learning in which the adult chooses the experience for the child and provides some direction to the child's actions.

subitizing—knowing instantly how many is in a group without counting.

subset—a smaller group within a larger group.

subtract—separate a group into two smaller groups.

sum—when groups are combined the result is referred to as the sum.

surf—a term referring to exploring the Internet.

symbolic behaviors—behaviors that appear during representational play when children use materials to represent something else, such as sand for food.

symbolic level—the stage at which children have connected sets and symbols and can record the solutions to concrete problems using number symbols.

symmetry—correspondence of two sides of a figure on each side of a line.

T

teach—do planned experiences with children.

teachable moment—a time when adults recognize that a child has selected to do an activity that provides a time to insert instruction.

temperature—in measurement, denotes how hot or cold.

terrapins—North American freshwater or tidewater turtles.

texture—one of the criteria that can be used as a common feature to form a group (i.e., rough, smooth, hard, soft).

thematic units and projects—instructional methods that provide for the integration of math, science, and other content areas.

thirds—the parts of a substance or a group when the substance or group is separated or divided into three equal parts.

time as cultural time—the time that is fixed by clocks and calendars.

time as personal experience—young children have their own past, present, and future, such as "When I was a baby . . ."

time as social activity—the importance of daily routines in sequence is critical for young children.

time duration—how long an event takes.

time sequence—the order of events, such as daily routines.

time words—time-related vocabulary that is acquired gradually.

time words, general—words such as time and age.

time words, relational—words such as soon, tomorrow, now, etc.

time words, special days—Christmas, Kwanza, Ramadan, Passover, holiday, birthday, etc.

time words, specific—words such as parts of the day like morning and afternoon.

time words, specific duration—clock, watch, calendar words.

times—the action term for multiplication.

tortoise—a turtle that lives on land.

total—the resulting group amount when groups are combined.

trading—what happens when numbers are regrouped.

triangle—a shape with three straight sides and three points.

triangular prism—a three-dimensional figure with identical triangular bases and three rectangular sides.

turtle—the name for the cursor when using LOGO language to solve geometry problems.

U

understanding—the basic premise of the NCTM principles and standards that stands in opposition to just memorizing.

unit—measurements must be made with the same unit to be accurate and comparable.

URL—an Internet address.

utilization—the fourth stage in the learning cycle as adapted to early childhood education: learners can apply and use their understandings in new settings and situations.

V

variables—anything changeable.

vertebrate—having a spine or backbone.

vertebrates—having a backbone or spinal column.

vitamins—complex organic substances found in most foods and needed for a normal functioning body.

volume—in measurement, denotes how much.

W

weather—the general condition of the atmosphere at a given time in regard to temperature, moisture, cloudiness, and so on.

webbing—strategy used to depict a variety of possible concepts and curricular experiences.

weight—in measurement, denotes how heavy.

whole language philosophy—an approach to reading and the language arts that integrates written and spoken language in meaningful contexts.

whole number operations—addition, subtraction, multiplication, and division.

wholes—all of some object or a group of objects.

World Wide Web (WWW)—contains Internet sites that enable students and teachers to connect with others around the world and to seek out a multitude of information.

Z

zone of proximal development (ZPD)—the area between where the child is now operating independently and where the child might be able to operate mentally with the assistance of an adult or a more mature peer.

Index